ARS EROTICA

The term *ars erotica* refers to the styles and techniques of lovemaking with the honorific title of art. But in what sense are these practices artistic, and how do they contribute to the aesthetics and ethics of self-cultivation in the art of living? In this book, Richard Shusterman offers a critical, comparative analysis of the erotic theories proposed by the most influential premodern cultural traditions that shaped our contemporary world. Beginning with ancient Greece, whose god of desiring love gave eroticism its name, Shusterman examines the Judeo-Christian biblical tradition and the classical erotic theories of Chinese, Indian, Islamic, and Japanese cultures, before concluding with medieval and Renaissance Europe. His exploration of their errors and insights shows how we could improve the quality of life and love today. By using the engine of eros to cultivate qualities of sensitivity, grace, skill, and self-mastery, we can reimagine a richer, more positive vision of sex education.

RICHARD SHUSTERMAN is the Dorothy F. Schmidt Eminent Scholar in the Humanities at Florida Atlantic University. His books include *Pragmatist Aesthetics* (published in fifteen languages), *Body Consciousness*, and *Thinking through the Body*. For his pioneering work in philosophy and somaesthetics, he was awarded the title of Chevalier de l'Ordre des Palmes Académiques by the French Republic.

Ars Erotica

Sex and Somaesthetics in the Classical Arts of Love

RICHARD SHUSTERMAN
Florida Atlantic University

CAMBRIDGE
UNIVERSITY PRESS

University Printing House, Cambridge CB2 8BS, United Kingdom

One Liberty Plaza, 20th Floor, New York, NY 10006, USA

477 Williamstown Road, Port Melbourne, VIC 3207, Australia

314–321, 3rd Floor, Plot 3, Splendor Forum, Jasola District Centre, New Delhi – 110025, India

79 Anson Road, #06–04/06, Singapore 079906

Cambridge University Press is part of the University of Cambridge.

It furthers the University's mission by disseminating knowledge in the pursuit of education, learning, and research at the highest international levels of excellence.

www.cambridge.org
Information on this title: www.cambridge.org/9781107004764
DOI: 10.1017/9780511791888

First published 2021

Printed in the United Kingdom by TJ Books Limited, Padstow Cornwall

A catalogue record for this publication is available from the British Library.

Library of Congress Cataloging-in-Publication Data
NAMES: Shusterman, Richard, author.
TITLE: Ars erotica : sex and somaesthetics in the classical arts of love / Richard Shusterman, Florida Atlantic University.
DESCRIPTION: Cambridge, United Kingdom ; New York, NY : Cambridge University Press, 2021. | Includes bibliographical references and index.
IDENTIFIERS: LCCN 2020020963 (print) | LCCN 2020020964 (ebook) | ISBN 9781107004764 (hardback) | ISBN 9780521181204 (paperback) | ISBN 9780511791888 (epub)
SUBJECTS: LCSH: Erotica–Philosophy–History. | Love–Philosophy–History. | Sex–Philosophy–History.
CLASSIFICATION: LCC HQ458 .S58 2021 (print) | LCC HQ458 (ebook) | DDC 128/.46–dc23
LC record available at https://lccn.loc.gov/2020020963
LC ebook record available at https://lccn.loc.gov/2020020964

ISBN 978-1-107-00476-4 Hardback
ISBN 978-0-521-18120-4 Paperback

For A.G.

Contents

Preface

I greet the publication of this book with a strange blend of relief and anxiety. The reason for these mixed emotions is the book's untimely character. It is untimely in two senses. First, it took far much longer to complete than I originally promised my publisher and myself, so I am relieved that it is finally finished though embarrassed that it was not on time. More troubling, however, is the untimeliness of the book's interest in erotic desire and lovemaking, an interest decidedly not in tune with the current cultural atmosphere, particularly in the academic world to which I belong. In recent years, increasing revelations of persistent patterns of deplorable sexual predatory behavior have cast a dark cloud of suspicion around the very idea of erotic love and sexual pursuits. Such despicable behavior reflects long established and deeply rooted cultural attitudes that are not sufficiently respectful to women and that both presume and serve patriarchy's essential stance of male dominance. Sex is an arena where men have traditionally felt the need to assert their dominance (in theory and in practice) by objectifying and using women for pleasure and progeny, probably because they implicitly have felt or feared their own inadequacy when compared with the erotic and generative powers of women. This need to assert male dominance also contributed to the sexual abuse of boys.

Whatever its reasons (and even if it sometimes extends to the love of boys), erotic theory of the major philosophical traditions has contributed to the objectification and subjugation of women through ideas that foster exploitative misogynistic attitudes. With today's attempts to eradicate sexist prejudice, there is understandably great sensitivity to examining these erotic theories in a thoughtful, careful, even if critical, way. One worries that even merely making them a subject of serious study risks condoning the troubling attitudes they express, and that it might be best to simply eschew such study, as I was often tempted (and advised) to do. These feelings of internal resistance, compounded by worries of how this research would be received, contributed to the delays in the book's completion. So too did the not surprising unwillingness of grant-awarding bodies to fund such research. However, the topic of erotic love and the aesthetics of lovemaking seemed too important to ignore, not simply for my particular research project of somaesthetics but also for more effectively treating the traditional issues of predatory sexism that continue to shape erotic mindsets today. Besides objectifying and subjugating women, traditional theories of *ars erotica* sometimes offend through their dominant heteronormativity. There are, however, important exceptions. The influential Platonic theories of love are firmly grounded in Greek homosexual erotic theory and practice, while Asian erotic theory likewise examines same-sex love. Today's trends of sexual and gender diversity that break with the simple binary model of male and female could find interesting roots in some classical theories the book examines, even if most of its discussions reflect the traditional privileging of heterosexual lovemaking.

In any case, we can better handle the problems of sexism and heteronormativity by understanding their foundations in the history of erotic theory in the world's most influential premodern cultures, whose fundamental concepts and views still pervade contemporary sexual attitudes. Critical study of these classic erotic theories provides genealogical tools to analyze and neutralize the complex and multiple roots of sexist thinking, while allowing us to recover whatever positive, redeeming elements these theories may contain. It seems unwise to assume that they contain nothing at all worthwhile, given their wide-ranging diversity, scope, and influence. Condemning them all in their entirety risks losing useful ideas. This book explores the aesthetic dimension of traditional *ars erotica* where I believe we might find some fruitful insights. The aesthetic, as I understand it, includes not only matters of beauty and art, but also countless other attractive qualities (grace, elegance, harmony, refinement, sensitivity, intelligence, charm, style, care, expressive meanings) that pertain to one's person, character, and conduct of life. Moreover, building on its etymology (from the Greek word for sensory perception, *aisthesis*) and its founding formulation by Alexander Baumgarten, I see aesthetics as very much concerned with the cultivation of sensory perception and the improvement in performance that enhanced perception can bring. Such enhanced performance includes conduct that expresses the beauties of virtue. Classical theories of *ars erotica* propose many techniques for improving one's personal form (in appearance and conduct) and one's perceptual and performative skills that enable a more sensitive awareness of the feelings of others (even if one could, in principle, use this greater sensitivity to exploit rather than help those others).

The book's concern for *ars erotica* derives from my research in somaesthetics, the critical study and meliorative cultivation of the body as a site of sensory appreciation or perception (aesthesis) and of creative self-fashioning in which one uses one's bodily appearance and conduct to express one's values and shape oneself. This focus on somaesthetic cultivation derived in turn from my long-standing interest in the practice of philosophy as an art of living, a conception of philosophy that was very prominent in the ancient world but that lost its centrality with the professionalization of philosophy as a university subject in modern times. If philosophy is a way of life, then the soma (the sentient, purposive, lived body) is the necessary medium through which one practices philosophy as an art of living. Pierre Hadot and Michel Foucault pioneered the late twentieth-century resurgence of this vision of philosophy, with Foucault emphasizing and thematizing its aesthetic dimension through his notion of an "aesthetics of existence" that extends into ethics and politics.

Foucault, moreover, insisted that this lived aesthetics had a crucial somatic dimension in which one's sexuality (one's erotic desires and the way one expressed and managed them) played an important role. He therefore devoted his final years of research to an extensive study of sexuality in Western culture, but died before completing the project. Initially, Foucault planned a six-volume project entitled *The History of Sexuality*, with the first introductory volume published in 1976, together with a list of the five planned subsequent book titles. None of those titles, however, ever appeared, because of the difficulties he faced in pursuing this initial project. The research was incredibly demanding, and it required moving in unanticipated directions. Finally, eight years later, shortly before his death in 1984, Foucault published two other volumes of *The History of Sexuality* (*The Use of Pleasures* and *Care of the Self*), together with a revised and abridged program of only four volumes for the entire work. The final volume, *Les aveux de la chair*, was posthumously published only in 2018, reconstructed from manuscripts.

My book on *ars erotica* owes a deep debt to Foucault's ideas, though I diverge from them in important ways, as the reader will discover. Foucault's extensive delays and difficulties in completing his project, which was limited to Western thinking in ancient Greco-Roman culture and early Christianity, should have warned me against undertaking my study of *ars erotica* in a more global, multicultural way. However, in our age of progressively transcultural globalization, it is important to look beyond Foucault's focus on the West and its ancient thought. This broader focus enormously complicated my research efforts, as I increasingly realized the vast amount of relevant material for my inquiry and the severe limits of my knowledge. Each chapter here treats topics worthy of book-length studies, even if one limits oneself to theoretical texts and neglects (as I have largely done) the fictional literature and visual art concerning *ars erotica*. Foucault always arouses my admiration for his powerful work as an advocate, activist, and theorist of homosexual erotic life. His trailblazing study of eroticism, however inspiringly insightful, understandably reflects his own personal interests and enthusiasms, as it should. Because my erotic experience has been mostly heterosexual, this book presents a somewhat different perspective than Foucault's, but one that hopes to complement rather than replace his impressive work.

The book is a blend of philosophy and cultural history of ideas because I think we cannot properly understand the philosophical meanings and arguments concerning *ars erotica* without setting them in their historical, cultural context, even if our viewpoint on that distant context is inextricably that of our own time. My immense debts to historians of philosophy and culture I register in the book's bibliography. Many colleagues have offered helpful information, commentary, and critical advice with respect to the book's various chapters, even if discussing these matters occasionally caused them some embarrassment. In order to spare these friends further embarrassment, I offer here a general expression of thanks and will refrain from the academic ritual of naming names. However, I must specify my abiding gratitude to the Schmidt Family Foundation, which most generously supports my work at Florida Atlantic University, and to Beatrice Rehl, my editor at Cambridge University Press, for her gracious and patient understanding in waiting for me to deliver this book, at last.

Abbreviations

AC *The Analects of Confucius: A Philosophical Translation.* Trans. Roger Ames and Henry Rosemont.
AE Abelard, Peter. *Abelard: Ethical Writings.* Trans. P. V. Spade.
AR Kalyanamalla. *Ananga Ranga.* Trans. F. F. Arbuthnot and Richard Burton.
ART *Kautilya's Arthashastra.* Trans. Rudrapatna Shamasastry.
BC Castiglione, Baldesar. *The Book of the Courtier.* Trans. George Bull.
BS Brown, Peter. *The Body and Society: Men, Women, and Sexual Renunciation in Early Christianity.*
BW Ibn al-Arabi. Muhammad. *The Bezels of Wisdom.* Trans. R. W. J. Austin.
CG Augustine. *City of God.* Trans. Henry Bettenson.
Char Plato, *Charmides.*
CL *Andreas Capellanus on Love.* Trans. P. G. Walsh.
CM *The Life of Christina of Markyate.* Ed. S. Fanous and H. Leyser. Trans. C. H. Talbot.
CON Cassian, John. *The Conferences.* Trans. Boniface Ramsey.
CWZ *The Complete Works of Chuang Tzu* (Zhuangzi). Trans. Burton Watson.
DGH Dover, K. J. *Greek Homosexuality.*
DIL D'Aragona, Tullia. *Dialogue on the Infinity of Love.* Trans. Rinaldina Russell and Bruce Merry.
DJ *Tao Te Ching (Daodejing).* Trans. D. C. Lau.
DL Ebreo, Leone. *The Philosophy of Love* (*Dialoghi d'amore*). Trans. F. Friedeberg-Seeley and J. H. Barnes.
DL1 Diogenes Laertius. *Lives of Eminent Philosophers*, vol. 1. Trans. R. D. Hicks.
DL2 *Lives of Eminent Philosophers*, vol. 2. Trans. R. D. Hicks.

EI Urabe, Kaneyoshi. *Essays in Idleness: The* Tsurezuregusa *of Kenkō*. Trans. Donald Keene.

EM Ghazali, Abu Hamid al-. *Book on the Etiquette of Marriage*. In *Marriage and Sexuality in Islam*. Trans. Madelain Farah.

EOM Bruno, Giordano. *Cause, Principle and Unity: And Essays on Magic*. Trans. R. J. Blackwell.

EP Katib, Ali ibn Nasr al-. *The Encyclopedia of Pleasure*. Ed. Salah Addin Khawwam. Trans. Adnan Jarkas and Salah Addin Khawwam.

EW Erasmus, Desiderius. *Erasmus on Women*. Ed. Erika Rummel

FC Ficino, Marsilio. *Marsilio Ficino's Commentary on Plato's "Symposium": The Text and a Translation, with an Introduction*. Trans. S. R. Jayne.

GL *The Four Books: Confucian Analects, the Great Learning, the Doctrine of the Mean, and the Works of Mencius*. Trans. James Legge.

GM Augustine. *De bono conjugali* (*On the Good of Marriage*). Trans. C. L. Cornish.

GY *The Gossamer Years: The Diary of a Noblewoman of Heian Japan*. Trans. Edward Seidensticker.

HBW *Hanfeizi: Basic Writings*. Trans. Burton Watson.

HF Bruno, Giordano. *The Heroic Frenzies*. Trans. P. E. Memmo.

HS Foucault, Michel. *The History of Sexuality, vol. 1: An Introduction*. Trans. Robert Hurley.

HS2 Foucault, Michel. *The History of Sexuality, vol. 2: The Use of Pleasure*. Trans. Robert Hurley.

HS3 Foucault, Michel. *The History of Sexuality, vol. 3: The Care of the Self*. Trans. Robert Hurley.

INS Cassian, John. *The Institutes*. Trans. Boniface Ramsey.

JCM *St. John Chrysostom: On Marriage and Family Life*. Trans. C. P. Roth and David Anderson.

KKS Kokkoka. *Koka Shastra*. Trans. Alex Comfort.

KS Vatsyayana, Mallanaga. *Kamasutra*. Trans. Wendy Doniger and Sudhir Kakar.

LAH Bayle, Pierre. *Letters of Abelard and Heloise*.

LLHA *The Lost Love Letters of Heloise and Abelard*. Ed. C. J. Mews.

LM *The Diary of Lady Murasaki*. Trans. Richard Bowring.

LN Lucretius. *On the Nature of the Universe*. Trans. R. E. Latham.

M Montaigne, Michel de. *The Complete Essays of Montaigne*. Trans. Donald Frame.

MB	Donner, Fred M. *Muhammad and the Believers: At the Origins of Islam.*
MC	Augustine. *On Marriage and Concupiscence.* Trans. Peter Holmes and Robert Ernest Wallace.
MCL	*Manu's Code of Law: A Critical Edition and Translation of the Manava-Dharmasastra.* Trans. Patrick Olivelle.
MG	Danielou, Alain. *The Myths and Gods of India.*
MR	Musonius Rufus. *Lectures.* In *Musonius Rufus: "The Roman Socrates."* Trans. Cora Lutz.
N	*The Natyaśastra*, 2 vols. Trans. Manomohan Ghosh.
NE	Aristotle, *Nicomachean Ethics.*
PA2	Aristotle, *Prior Analytics II.*
PB	Sei Shonagon. *The Pillow Book of Sei Shōnagon.* Trans. Arthur Waley.
PDL	Plutarch. *Dialogue on Love.* In *Moralia*, vol. 9. Trans. E. L. Minar, F. H. Sandbach, and W. C. Helmbold.
PG	Nafzawi, Umar ibn Muhammad. *The Perfumed Garden.* Trans. Jim Colville.
Pol.	Aristotle, *Politics.*
Q	*The Quran.*
RD	Ibn Hazm, Ali ibn Aḥmad. *The Ring of the Dove.* Trans. A. J. Arberry.
Rep	Plato, *Republic.*
Rhet.	Aristotle, *Rhetoric.*
RPA	Aretino, Pietro. *The Ragionamenti, or Dialogues of the Divine Pietro Aretino Literally Translated into English.*
SEA	Doniger, Wendy. *Siva: The Erotic Ascetic.*
SI	Bouhdiba, Abdelwahab. *Sexuality in Islam.* Trans. Alan Sheridan.
SL	Van Gulik, Robert. *Sexual Life in Ancient China: A Preliminary Survey of Chinese Sex and Society from ca. 1500 B.C. till 1644 A.D.*
ST	Aquinas, Thomas. *Summa theologica.*
Sym	Plato, *Symposium.*
TG	Murasaki, Shikibu. *The Tale of Genji.* Trans. Edward Seidensticker.
TI	*Tales of Ise: Lyrical Episodes from Tenth-Century Japan.* Trans. Helen Craig McCullough.
Wile	Wile, Douglas. *Art of the Bedchamber: The Chinese Sexual Yoga Classics Including Women's Solo Meditation Texts.*
Xen	Xenophon, *Conversations of Socrates.* Trans. Hugh Tredennick and Robin Waterfield.

1

Ars Erotica and the Question of Aesthetics

I TERMINOLOGY

The Latin term *ars erotica*, while sometimes referring to works of fine art with overtly erotic content, is more notably used to designate skilled methods or styles of lovemaking that are thereby elevated with the honorific term "art." This notion of the art of love – with its various techniques, strategies, and aims – is the principal focus of this study. In what way, however, is such art truly artistic in the aesthetic sense that theorists of art and beauty have traditionally identified with art and have persistently sought to explain? This book, an exploratory essay of philosophical somaesthetics, provides materials for answering this question by examining the most influential ways that *ars erotica* has been theorized in different historical cultures and periods.[1] To what extent those past cultures actually practiced such erotic methods lies beyond our scope of inquiry, which is essentially theoretical. Though historically informed, the book aims at exploring key philosophical ideas and arguments rather than providing a full-blown cultural history of lovemaking. Its study of past theory has the forward-looking goal of helping us to avoid possible blind spots in our current understanding of lovemaking by revisiting some elements of ancient erotic thought.

One of the book's central arguments is that the techniques and disciplines of traditional *ars erotica* were designed not only to enhance sexual satisfaction but also to provide distinctive aesthetic pleasures and to cultivate qualities of understanding, sensibility, grace, skill, and self-mastery that go far beyond the limits of sexual activity. In other words, such art sought to provide an aesthetic education that, by developing character, sensitivity,

[1] For a systematic account of somaesthetics, see Richard Shusterman, *Body Consciousness: A Philosophy of Mindfulness and Somaesthetics* (Cambridge: Cambridge University Press, 2008).

taste, and interpersonal awareness, could contribute to what many consider the highest art of all: the art of living. If eros, in the broad sense of desire and attraction between people, pervades so much of our social life, then the right sort of erotic knowledge could promote better affective relations between persons of all kinds, not just between lovers. A philosophical study of *ars erotica* could therefore yield useful ethical insights for the conduct of life that transcend the sexual realm. In this sense, the book's reorientation of our thinking on eroticism could stimulate broader changes in practice.

As sex belongs to human nature, it is equally fashioned by culture, which determines not only the sexual norms and taboos of a society but also its sense of beauty and range of erotically charged acts, objects, and meanings. If philosophy helps shape a culture, then that culture's philosophical views should shape its *ars erotica.* The differing cosmic, religious, and moral visions of different cultures – with their distinctive ideals of self-realization and social harmony – find expression in differences in their *ars erotica.* As sexual expression provides a powerful medium for shaping one's own subjectivity and interpersonal relations, the practice of *ars erotica* can constitute an important mode of self-cultivation with explicit regard for others. By examining the diverse ways that different cultures have conceived and advocated the art of love, we can see to what extent and in what manner such erotic practices really reflect the categories of aesthetics and art, but also in what ways they reflect key philosophical ideas that shape those cultures. Comparing these different theories of *ars erotica* may reveal important commonalities (such as the objectification of women) but also might provide materials for a superior synthesis or erotic pluralism that could better serve our transcultural world.

These initial paragraphs already announce three of the book's main questions: In what ways can *ars erotica* be appreciated (and practiced) in terms of aesthetics and the fine arts? How can it be used as a means for self-cultivation to enrich both self and other? How does its distinctive shaping of biological functions and somatic energies reflect (and sustain) a culture's background ideologies and social order so that the seemingly universal human sexual drive takes on divergent forms and meanings both across different cultures and within the same culture at different times and places? Before exploring these questions through the historical theories this book covers, we need to articulate them more clearly. But we should begin by clarifying some puzzling aspects of the very term "*ars erotica.*"

Etymologically, it is a strange hybrid of the Latin word for art (*ars*) and the Greek word for love (*eros*). Its sense as "the art of love" goes back to ancient times and is rendered in impeccable Latin in Ovid's *Ars amatoria*, one of the masterworks in erotic theory despite its jocular, versifying style. The actual term "*ars erotica*" is of much more recent vintage. Its wide currency seems to originate with Michel Foucault's use of the term in his influential *History of Sexuality*, whose first volume distinguishes sharply between the modern Western study of sex as *scientia sexualis* and non-Western sexual knowledge in the form of *ars erotica*.[2] Foucault does not explain why he uses this mongrel term, but let me offer one reason it seems a useful hybrid. The Latin *amor*, like our English word "love," is extremely ambiguous. Not only denoting erotic and romantic love ("Amor" being Cupid's other Roman name), it also refers to other, milder forms of affection, friendship, and even mere liking. The Greek language of love was much more precise, discriminating between four important kinds of love. As *eros* (ἔρως) denoted passionate, sensual, desiring love, so *agape* (ἀγάπη) expressed a deep, unconditional, more-than-sensual form of love that was then adopted and transformed into the Christian concept of love. If *philia* (φιλία) connoted the general notion of affectionate commitment to friends, family, or one's community, then *storge* (στοργή) conveyed the special natural affection that parents have for children and that could extend to other family members. The Greek term *eros* is clearly better than the Latin *amor* for conveying the specific notion of physical love and lovemaking while not being confined to it. But the Latin term *ars* (so close to its English

[2] Michel Foucault, *The History of Sexuality*, vol. 1, trans. Robert Hurley (New York: Vintage, 1980), 57–58. Foucault's list of cultures "with an ars erotica" includes "China, Japan, India, Rome, [and] the Arabo-Moslem societies." In his vision of *ars erotica* and even in his choice of this term to designate sexual practice, Foucault may have been particularly influenced by the Chinese account of *ars erotica* presented in Robert van Gulik's work on the subject, for van Gulik chose the terms *ars* or art to translate the Chinese term shu 術, which more precisely means "technique" or "procedure" and which the Chinese used when describing erotic techniques (techniques of the bedroom). This term thus appears in the expression *fangzhong shu* 房中術, which is rendered in van Gulik's English translation as "Art of the Bedchamber." Van Gulik's book was published in French translation by Foucault's Parisian publisher Gallimard in 1971 as *La vie sexuelle dans la Chine ancienne*; its original English version was *Sexual Life in Ancient China: A Preliminary Survey of Chinese Sex and Society from ca. 1500 B.C. till 1644 A.D.* (Leiden: Brill, 1961), see 121 for quotation. Foucault explicitly refers to van Gulik when speaking of Chinese "erotic art" or "arts of conjugal pleasure," in Michel Foucault, *The History of Sexuality*, vol. 2, trans. Robert Hurley (New York: Vintage, 1986), 137, 143. In a later interview he furthermore highlights the Chinese *ars erotica* while claiming that Greek and Roman culture really had nothing comparable (at least in terms of importance). See Michel Foucault, "On the Genealogy of Ethics: An Overview of Work in Progress," in *Essential Works of Michel Foucault*, vol. 1, ed. Paul Rabinow (New York: New Press, 1997), 259. The sinologist Kristofer Schipper, who contests some of van Gulik's account of Chinese sexology, likewise uses the phrase "Art of the Bedroom." See his book *The Taoist Body*, trans. Karen Duval (Berkeley: University of California Press, 1993), 148.

counterpart) is best for evoking our notion of art as rich in creativity, skill, and pleasure, while the ancient Greek word for art – techne (τέχνη) – could suggest the arid narrowness of mechanical technique.

The hybrid "*ars erotica*" combines the advantages of both languages and in so doing also provides a provocative example of creative coupling, thus symbolically expressing its referent. The word *ars* is in the singular nominal case (its plural being *artes*), so *ars erotica*, like "art" or "fine art," is grammatically a mass noun that takes the singular verb and would have no definite article. But like art or fine art, *ars erotica* includes many genres, styles, and forms. To convey that plurality I will often speak of *ars erotica* as the erotic arts and occasionally will use the phrase "the *ars erotica*" in a plural sense as elliptical for "the diverse forms or styles of *ars erotica*," since the Latin plural *artes* seems awkward and foreign, while *ars* has the "s" suggestive of the English plural. In such occasions, the definite article should *not* be understood as assuming there is only one such art.

II AESTHETICS

Over its long history as a cherished and fiercely contested concept, art has acquired a number of meanings. In its oldest and widest sense, deriving from the Greek term *techne*, art denotes any skill, craft, or branch of learning, typically one that involves some organizing principles of practice. In this sense, we speak of the liberal arts, or the martial arts, or even the arts of conversation or of salesmanship. *Ars erotica* is clearly art in this most general sense, providing an attractive counterpart to the martial arts, as the deities Amor and Venus do to the god Mars. Since the eighteenth century, however, art has assumed a narrower, dominant sense that is closely bound up with the notions of fine art and aesthetic experience. Here art requires more than mere mastery of skills, principles, or learning; it essentially involves experienced pleasures of form, feeling, and meaning. Moreover, the requisite feelings and pleasures are defined in terms of aesthetics – a realm devoted to beauty, sublimity, expressive meanings, significant forms, delightful sensory perceptions, imaginative ideas, creative designs, and other important values central to the fine arts.[3] The pleasures, feelings, meanings, and skills

[3] Our notion of the fine arts did not really exist in ancient times, and neither, in a strict sense, did the theoretical field called aesthetics. Alexander Baumgarten initiated this field by coining the concept of aesthetics in the mid-eighteenth century. For the historical formation of our concept of art, see Paul Kristeller, "The Modern System of the Arts: A Study in the History of Aesthetics" (Parts I and II), *Journal of the History of Ideas* 12, no. 4 (1951): 496–527; and *Journal of the History of Ideas* 13, no. 1 (1952): 17–46.

involved in a particular practice should therefore be recognizably aesthetic in character if we are to consider that practice as truly art in the more specific modern sense.

Can *ars erotica* be considered art in this aesthetic sense? What indeed are its aesthetic or artistic features, and how are they best characterized and understood? How do they relate to their counterparts in more paradigmatic artistic domains? What, for example, would be the counterpart of an artwork in *ars erotica*? Could it be an isolated coital coupling; a long session of lovemaking with multiple coital episodes; a whole night of courtship and consummation perhaps starting with drinks and dinner, a concert, and extended foreplay and then finishing with a conjugal bath and breakfast? Could an erotic artwork be construed even in terms of an entire love affair that could extend over weeks or longer? Such questions of work-identity also arise in the fine arts: We speak of James Joyce's *Dubliners* and George Herbert's *The Temple* as particular works of literature, but we also consider the particular stories and poems in these respective works as individual literary works in their own right. Where could *ars erotica* fit in our classification of art forms? If it is essentially a performing art, then how does its performance differ from the mere performance of a sexual act? Can we further identify different genres of *ars erotica* that particular performances could be ascribed to – for example, by classifying them into oral, genital, and anal sex with their different postures, movements, and performative processes? Or should we instead classify them in terms of the gender roles of the partners or in terms of the situational logic of performance: the couple's first kiss or coital episode, the marriage night, or "makeup" sex after a quarrel? What are the general aesthetic principles that govern the erotic arts? Do they form a coherent system or are there conflicting aesthetic principles in different genres, styles, or traditions of *ars erotica*? Properly addressing such questions calls for an exploration of the culturally diverse theories of *ars erotica* undertaken in the following chapters, but I offer here an introductory outline of some key aesthetic features that those theories display.

First is the incorporation of fine arts and other paradigmatically aesthetic activities into the practice of *ars erotica*. Poetry and music, for example, are invoked for courtship and enhancing mood; perfumes may be concocted or blended to create an attractively sensual ambience. Culinary arts provide appealing food and drink that promote desire and can improve sexual performance; arts of design (including flower arrangement) enrich the sensuous attraction of the bedstead, making it an appealing stage to attract and stimulate lovemaking. Finally, arts of fashion and grooming serve to heighten the beauty and sexual allure of the lovers. They also offer lovers a wide range of looks and costumes that evoke different personalities or social identities and thus can add the spice of variety to erotic play by imaginatively enlarging its range of dramatis personae, even if the very same two bodies are involved.

A second key aesthetic feature of *ars erotica* is its emphasis on beauty and pleasure rather than mere utility. While sex obviously has an essential reproductive function, *ars erotica*'s prime focus is typically on enjoying lovemaking for its own sake (in terms of its sensory pleasures and expressive feelings and meanings) rather than for the production of children or some other external end or product. If aesthetic experience is characterized by its immediately experienced value rather than deferred utility, this does not preclude its involving a process that is temporally extended and mediated through stages. Our enjoyment of reading a poem, watching a film, or listening to a sonata cannot occur in an instant; it takes time. But the felt value is still immediate in the sense that we do not have to wait until the final word, image, or note in order to enjoy the work. Rather, we appreciate the work at each stage of its unfolding process, and this developing appreciation is essential to appreciating the work's conclusion and the work as a whole. The aesthetic experience of climbing a mountain is not just enjoying the view from the summit but savoring the different stages of the climb and their directional movement toward its peak. In the same way, *ars erotica*'s aesthetic design seeks to ensure that sexual pleasure is not confined to the moment of orgasmic release but instead delightfully pervades the whole temporally developing process leading up to and then away from the anticipated sexual climax, even if it does not come.

This implies a third key aesthetic feature of *ars erotica*: its highlighting of form. What distinguishes a performance of erotic artistry from mere sexual performance is attention to formal and structural qualities. Just like a successful piece of theater or music, a superior performance of *ars erotica* typically has a sense of developing wholeness, with a beginning, middle, and end whose stages are organically related to enhance the pleasures of dynamic harmony and interest. Theories of *ars erotica* are designed to achieve this intensifying developmental unity through successive, integrated stages of action, even if these stages are sometimes temporally compressed. This formal emphasis expresses a concern for unifying ambience and focus, so that discordant feelings or distracting elements are kept away. Another aspect of *ars erotica*'s formalism is expressed in its staging of the act of love within an attractive mise-en-scène that helps dramatize and intensify the experience by demarcating it from the ordinary humdrum flow of life. What precisely constitutes an attractively erotic mise-en-scène can differ significantly according to cultural tradition and changing context, ranging from the opulent to the humble, from the meticulously prepared to the impulsively improvised through the hurried heat of passion.

Beyond these formalist concerns is a fourth aesthetic feature: the drive for stylization. *Ars erotica* is distinguished from mere sex by the careful attention it gives not simply to which erotic acts are performed – a kiss, caress, cuddle, or love moan – but to *how* one performs them. Besides advice on the proper sequencing and combination of erotic actions or movements (which can give lovemaking an appealingly ritualistic sense of order and measure), we find directions for stylizing the precise manner of action: a light, brushing kiss; a tightly clasping embrace; a playful pinch; a rapid or slow, shallow or deep, hesitantly gentle or boldly forceful penetration of the tongue or other body part into some erogenous zone of one's partner. One general aesthetic dimension of stylization is the attentive, cultivating use of the artistic medium. In *ars erotica* this key medium is the human soma, which the erotic arts seek to cultivate both in terms of beautifying the soma's aesthetic surface (through cosmetics, fragrances, fashion, and regimes of body sculpting) and in terms of sharpening the soma's perceptual acuity, its discriminating sensibility and awareness of its own feelings and those of the lovers with whom it interacts, and its consequent performative skills.

Aesthetics was first established in modern times as a science of sensory perception rather than a theory of beauty. Deriving it from the Greek word *aisthesis* (αἴσθησις) for sensory perception, whose traces are also found in the notion of an anesthetic (something that renders us unconscious, insensible, and incapable of proper perception), Alexander Baumgarten founded aesthetics in the 1750s as a science concerned with perfecting perception, not just explaining it theoretically. He defined it as "the science of sensory cognition" whose aim was "the perfection of sensory cognition as such."[4] Contemporary somaesthetics shares this meliorative practical impulse while conceiving of the body as sentient, purposive soma (unlike Baumgarten's view of the body as mindless flesh).[5] Because *ars erotica* displays the same critical meliorative approach to the soma as both an alluringly expressive

[4] My citations from Baumgarten are from the bilingual (Latin-German) abridged edition of *Aesthetica*, Alexander Baumgarten, *Theoretische Ästhetik: Die grundlengenden Abschnitte aus der "Aesthetica"* (1750/58), trans. H. R. Schweizer (Hamburg: Felix Meiner, 1988), 3, 11; §§1, 14.

[5] For the relationship of somaesthetics to Baumgarten's founding project of aesthetics, see Richard Shusterman, "Somaesthetics: A Disciplinary Proposal," *Journal of Aesthetics and Art Criticism* 57 (1999): 299–313. For the application of somaesthetics to the arts, see my *Thinking through the Body: Essays in Somaesthetics* (Cambridge: Cambridge University Press, 2012), which includes a preliminary application to *ars erotica*.

external appearance and a perceiving, savoring, performative subjectivity, we could consider it a paradigmatically somaesthetic art.

Symbolic richness is a fifth aesthetic feature of *ars erotica*. Although visually identical to real Brillo cartons, Andy Warhol's *Brillo Boxes* is experienced as a richly meaningful artwork by symbolically representing both the real world of commercial objects and the vast intricacies of the art world and its traditions. A line drawing of a mountain and a line graph depicting a stock's changing value may be visually identical, yet the former is experienced as more aesthetic because it is richer in meaning through the fact that the color, thickness, and intensity of its line (and not just its location on the horizontal and vertical axes) function symbolically. Common sentiment may endorse the popular lyric: "You must remember this; a kiss is just a kiss." But in *ars erotica*, we should instead remember that a kiss can mean much more: the sealing of a vow, a mark of acceptance or provocation, or even (as the *Kamasutra* points out) a prefiguring symbol of the sort of coital style desired.

A sixth aesthetic aspect of *ars erotica* concerns its evaluative dimension: a concern with distinctive achievements of beauty, performative virtuousity, or superior taste that finds expression in critical judgments, connoisseurship, rankings, and competitions. In *ars erotica* we see this dimension in the classificatory rankings of different types of women and men in terms of their sexual desirability, but also in rankings of different pairings of men and women. Indian erotic theories, for instance, assess the varying suitability of different male–female pairings in terms of comparative genital size, excitability, and other matters relevant to the pair's compatibility for erotic success. In the Japanese pleasure quarters of Yoshiwara, courtesans had official rankings, determined not simply by their feminine beauty but especially by their skills in the fine arts and arts of love. Male suitors competed for the status of being their most preferred clients, such preferences being measured in part by a courtesan's acts of sacrificial devotion (*shinju*) that themselves were ranked in terms of their level of self-sacrifice that could reach levels of violent self-mutilation.

Consider a final trio of similarities between the fine and erotic arts. If fine art and aesthetic experience arise through natural drives and energies as shaped by culturally constructed forms and attitudes, then *ars erotica* surely shares this hybrid status of nature and culture. Moreover, as art involves the dramatization of experience by presenting and intensifying it within a formal frame, so *ars erotica* dramatizes the vivid experience of sexual desire and fulfillment by staging it through distinctive steps and methods designed to heighten its aesthetic form. Cognitive and ethical ambivalence is yet another shared feature. As art's aesthetic education provides delightfully insightful instruction but is equally famous for purveying misleading fictions that perniciously corrupt rather than positively cultivate, so *ars erotica*'s carnal knowledge includes both penetrating cognition and distracting delusion, revealing the intimate facts of life while conversely feeding fantasies of romantic passion that distort the truth, becloud reason, and even debauch character. Erotic artistry, moreover, can so enchantingly embellish a relation of sexual exploitation with an aura of beauty, pleasure, and refinement that even the lovers themselves fail to see its destructive, immoral unseemliness.

III SELF-CULTIVATION

The notion of aesthetic education highlights our second major theme: *ars erotica* as a means of cultivating one's humanity, a method of meliorative care of the self that likewise essentially implies a regard for others, most minimally for one's erotic partners but also more widely for society with its customs and mores. A discipline of critical and reflective practice, *ars erotica* is also rich in pleasurable sensations, dynamic action, and spontaneous movements and feelings. Advocates claim it distinguishes human lovemaking from mere animal coupling by enveloping the sexual act within a complex network of multilayered meanings and aesthetic qualities. It does so by situating that act not only within an open narrative structure of performance that allows the individual to exercise creative choice and decision making (rather than being dictated by unreflective animal instincts with hardwired responses and fixed goals) but also within an enriching social context and cultural tradition. If the exercise of creative personal choice gives the erotic act the heightened significance of individual intentionality and aesthetic taste, then the sociocultural background further multiplies the possibilities of meaning and the discrimination of aesthetic features through the erotic performance's relation to historical precedents, social norms, cultural values, and artistic genre traditions. By means of such intertextual signifying, for Indian *ars erotica*, a particular sequence of coital postures can symbolize the successive incarnations of Krishna, while a certain pattern of love bites connotes a meaningful mandala. Moreover, in communicating such meanings and values (that are often complex, subtle, and not easily discerned), we exercise and develop our sensorimotor and cognitive faculties. *Ars erotica* can thus serve as an aesthetic discipline to sharpen our perceptual powers and heighten our refinement through the alluringly gratifying experience of love's sensual delights.

By presenting a pleasurable path for self-cultivating refinement that is also essentially social or other-directed, *ars erotica* offers a radically different perspective on sex education than our conventional one but that is nonetheless deeply grounded in ancient traditions of theory and practice. Our standard conception of sex education focuses on physiological mechanics, hygienic prescriptions, and moral proscriptions about sex that are aimed at avoiding problems or pathologies such as unwanted pregnancies, sexually transmitted diseases, sex crimes, and varieties of social stigma and psychological damage due to inappropriate sexual behavior. Rather than this purely negative focus, *ars erotica* provides a positive yet critical vision of sexuality, an educational path for improving our handling of life's inescapable erotic dimension by providing real benefits beyond the evasion of sex-related troubles. These edifying benefits transcend the augmenting of pleasure, skill, and beauty in our sexual performance. They extend into a broad range of perceptual and performative skills and forms of knowledge that enhance our powers more generally in the conduct of life. In this sense, *ars erotica*'s sex education should be understood as not simply an education *about* sex but an education *through* sex. By this I mean an edification of self and other that uses the potent energy of sexual desire and deploys the meliorative exercise of erotic skills, techniques, and forms of knowledge to render the experience of this desire and the performative process of its fulfillment more richly enjoyable, rewarding, and instructive, in cognitive, aesthetic, and ethical terms.[6]

The varieties of erotically fueled edification range from self-knowledge and knowing other persons to a more general knowledge of culture and the world.[7] One way *ars erotica* enhances cognition is by improving our perceptual powers through the sharpening of our attentive focus and acuity of the senses and affect. Attentive discipline in lovemaking promotes

[6] The deep connection of sex and knowledge has ancient roots even in cultures whose *ars erotica* was underdeveloped. The Old Testament, for example, uses the Hebrew verb "to know" (*yada* ידע) in order to indicate sexual intercourse (as in Genesis 4:1: "And Adam knew Eve his wife; and she conceived, and bare Cain"). This biblical usage carried over into nineteenth-century British law, where "carnal knowledge" designated sexual intercourse implying penile penetration of female (or male) erogenous openings. Therefore, "it shall not be necessary in any of those Cases to prove the actual Emission of Seed in order to constitute a carnal Knowledge, but that the carnal Knowledge shall be deemed complete upon Proof of Penetration only." See "The Offences against the Person Act of 1828," in *The Statues of the United Kingdom of Great Britain and Ireland, 1829* (London: His Majesty's Statute and Law Printers, 1829), 198.

[7] Goethe claims more generally that passionate love is the essential engine of knowledge. "One comes to know nothing other than what one loves, and the deeper and more complete the knowledge, the stronger, sturdier, and livelier must the love, indeed the passion, be." From his letter of May 10, 1812, to F. H. Jacobi in Max Jacobi, ed., *Briefwechsel zwischen Goethe und F. H. Jacobi* (Leipzig: Weidmann, 1846), 254; also available at www.zeno.org/Literatur/M/Goethe,+Johann+Wolfgang/Briefe/1812 (my translation).

observational skills in discerning the feelings of others; it teaches, for example, how to read subtle, unintended sensory signals that indicate a potential lover is reciprocally interested or erotically aroused, and also to what level this arousal extends and how to intensify it. Noticing the direction of a rapid glance or a faint quiver of the lips, feeling the precise location of a muffled tremor of the flesh, sensing a slight shifting of the pelvis, or a change of moisture in the mouth can guide the lover to respond with the right sort of touch to the proper place. But such subtle sensory signals can also indicate when a lover is not really in the mood for lovemaking or has become tired with its current performance, even if it may have initially been thoroughly enjoyed. Though deception is always possible, good lovers know best when their partners are faking it. Such somaesthetic skills of reading fine shades of affect and body language extend, of course, beyond sexual encounters to the interpersonal matters of everyday life in which we need to discriminate the interest, approachability, moods, feelings, aspirations, cravings, tastes, and needs of our interlocutors in order to orient and reshape our behavior to achieve our ends. Eros is not limited to the bedroom; attraction is the engine and energy of life. It makes the world go round while animating innumerable interpersonal sub-orbits.

Ars erotica's lessons in perceptual acuity include self-knowledge, enabling lovers to discriminate more rapidly and more precisely the levels of their own erotic interest, energy, or arousal. This in turn allows one to choose more wisely if and when to initiate an erotic encounter and how better to manage one's resources of power and endurance to achieve the desired erotic results. Such improved sensory self-knowledge can further provide, as its practical correlate, a greater mastery of self-control. Realizing that one is overeager in entering an erotic engagement (say, by noticing one's short, erratic breathing) allows for calming down by adjusting one's breathing and relaxing one's pace and body rhythms. In the same way, a clear and early sensing of the approach of sexual climax can help us to slow things down in order to avert this outcome and thus prolong the pleasures of approaching it. Improved proprioceptive awareness through sustained practice can likewise teach individuals which particular techniques of movement, breathing, pauses, and patterns of muscular contraction work best for them in their personal efforts of sexual self-control.

In making the case for *ars erotica*'s perceptual training, we already suggested its providing emotional knowledge by improving perceptual discriminations that can inform lovers of their partners' affective condition (their current mood, intensity of desire, or state of arousal) and of their own. Besides gauging the pitch of passion, the art of lovemaking includes stages of sustained courtship and continuing postcoital courtesies of conduct that offer further opportunities for emotional learning about more lasting affective states: esteem, trust, jealousy, empathy, compassion, and, of course, abiding love. If folk psychology has long realized that sexual experience encourages an emotional closeness between lovers that facilitates a deeper sharing of feelings, then neurologists now claim to know the brain chemistry through which sexual pleasure creates emotional intimacy, which can richly enhance our knowledge of the sentiments.[8] In any case, *ars erotica*'s disciplined attention to erotic experience can improve appraisals of the quality and depth of our feelings, helping to distinguish, for example, between an affection based on the sensual pleasures of good sex and a more complex amatory affection, perhaps for someone whose lovemaking offers less intense sexual delights.

Besides sensory and emotional instruction, *ars erotica* fosters ethical learning in three ways. First, when pursued as a disciplined, reflective practice, it demands careful consideration and navigation of the ethical norms, values, and taboos that govern sexual behavior in a given society. At the simplest level, in initiating an erotic encounter one needs to know, for that culture, what kinds of partners are legally forbidden or ethically wrong (such as children, family members, students, teachers, the wives and husbands of others) and what kinds of acts (sodomy, oral sex, masturbation, intercourse during menstruation) are similarly taboo. Even if one decides on occasion to flout such ethical prohibitions, *ars erotica* insists on learning them sufficiently to recognize the transgressive import of such action, whether one seeks to savor it (if we believe that transgression intensifies erotic pleasure) or simply wants to conceal it from others to avoid unwanted consequences of punishment or moral censure.

Second, mastery in *ars erotica* implies making oneself appealing enough to attract, charm, and satisfy one's lovers. In order for such appeal and satisfaction to be most powerful and enduring, one needs more than good looks and physical prowess but also the allure of a winning personality worthy of esteem and a character endowed with valued virtues that make one a desirable partner. Excellence in the art of lovemaking means creating a character worth loving, which in turn means knowing the ethical values that make one most attractively admirable. Theories of *ars erotica* thus give explicit attention to developing such character traits that make a lover ethically appealing; how, for example, to exercise and demonstrate courtesy,

[8] See Jaak Panksepp, *Affective Neuroscience: The Foundations of Human and Animal Emotions* (Oxford: Oxford University Press, 1998), 240–242.

generosity, understanding, and trustworthiness. Third, *ars erotica* teaches us how to read the character of others to detect moral flaws that pose risks for erotic fulfillment. Those other persons extend beyond one's potential lovers; they include go-betweens, confidants, and friends whose services or complicity may be needed in initiating or sustaining the erotic relationship and in preserving its secrecy, if secrecy is necessary.

Ars erotica further offers a path to scientific knowledge, especially concerning embodiment. Sexuality's reproductive function constitutes a key aspect of life experience that is intimately linked to bodily health, both in positive terms as an expression of vitality and in negative terms of sexually transmitted illness. Empirically based theorizing on ways to improve erotic satisfaction and performance while avoiding sexual ailments has formed a significant part of health literature from antiquity. The ancient Chinese texts on *ars erotica* were grouped with medical books, and these erotic treatises (like those of Indian, Greek, and other cultures) are filled with presumed physiological facts relating to sexual performance and health. This book's ensuing chapters show how such physiological teachings range from classifications of body types to calendars for fertility and arousal; from aphrodisiacs and cosmetic tips for attracting and keeping lovers to remedies for curing sexual complaints and related health ailments; from the biomechanics of foreplay techniques to coital body postures that heighten the pleasures of lovemaking or its reproductive power. In aiming to perfect one's overall appeal as a lover – and recognizing that such appeal is enhanced by wide-ranging scientific erudition (which enriches one's conversational powers), *ars erotica*'s concern with science sometimes transcends its focus on human physiology. Indian theory, for example, highlights the value of knowing astronomy to enchant one's partner by deftly presenting the alluring beauties of the sky and perhaps comparing them to that heavenly body on earth who is listening with rapt attention. In European medieval and Renaissance texts (but also in later works of Denis Diderot and the Marquis de Sade), lovers similarly seek to impress and excite their partners by demonstrating scientific knowledge, including philosophical erudition and skills of argument.

Ars erotica's concern with somatic knowledge goes well beyond the facts of physiology. It seems equally if not even more focused on practical know-how, on perfecting performative somatic skills of lovemaking. Its many proposed methods of foreplay and coital techniques can, of course, be appreciated as propositional knowledge describing possibilities of action, but, for the most part, they are primarily meant to be incorporated in actual praxis as practical somatic savoir-faire. Talking the talk does not entail knowing how to walk the walk; ability to accurately describe a posture in no way ensures knowing how to attain and sustain it in practice. The same goes for methods of foreplay and coital phrasing of movements aimed at deploying different rhythms and techniques to heighten interest and expressive meaning and to maintain proper pacing to ensure endurance and self-control in timing one's climax. As in the fine arts, practical know-how makes all the difference in performance, and there is no discursive substitute for this practical skill.

With respect to such practical know-how, we again should challenge the dogma that "a kiss is just a kiss," not simply because there are a variety of kinds of kissing, but also because each concrete kiss of any genre has its own particular qualities of sense and meaning and can be performed with skillful grace or lamentable clumsiness. Perfecting practical skills generally demands sustained practice, which typically requires considerable time. Perfecting practice in *ars erotica* further requires a cooperative, sensitive, and honestly responsive partner who is also willing to take the time, effort, and risks of practice (that, with sex, can be morally and medically extremely severe). These two factors raise troubling issues of social inequality. Many people lack the leisure and resources for sustained study and training in *ars erotica*, and women are far more vulnerable to risks and exploitation. Although most theorists in the field emphasize the importance of extensive erotic study, others (like Montaigne) privilege natural spontaneity and youthful vigor.

We should recall that *ars erotica*'s practical know-how goes beyond the physical contact of foreplay and coitus. It includes knowing how to dress and groom; how to dance, sing, or play an instrument; how to walk, eat, drink, and gesture in a refined way; how to recite love poetry with compelling expressiveness; and so on. If *ars erotica* emphasizes such strenuous, time-consuming practical somatic training, then this may be one reason why we body-shy, time-stressed, idealist intellectuals tend to avoid its study and instead concentrate on aesthetic practices that are more discursive and less risky and somatically centered. Because of the many cultures (including our own) where a focus on erotic pursuits too often takes the form of sexual predation, ethically concerned thinkers understandably neglect or reject the field of *ars erotica*. That its training includes other forms of know-how that are costly in time, money, or instructional preparation – decorating one's rooms, purchasing fine gifts, preparing delicacies of food and drink, composing well-written love letters or poems, commenting learnedly on the arts – explains why *ars erotica* has traditionally focused on society's privileged class, even though all classes of people are physiologically and emotionally equipped for it. If this gives further reason for shunning eroticism as morally suspect, then one might argue that today's society provides better resources of leisure, education, and gender equality to reconstruct an ethically fairer contemporary *ars erotica* by refashioning some useful elements of the past. However, far more progress in gender justice is necessary to overcome the entrenched evils of predatory male domination in our erotic traditions.

Social knowledge is essential to *ars erotica*'s program of edification. Its ethical teaching already implies this, because the legal prohibitions and moral norms, taboos, and ideals that *ars erotica* maps and navigates are essentially shaped by the social world and thus intrinsically instruct us about it. Historically, that social world involved a hierarchy of classes and genders, so the erotic arts were first designed to serve the interests of men of the dominant class who had the leisure, material means, and authority to pursue refined erotic satisfactions, often in polygynous societies in which a man could supplement his several wives with many concubines. Male privilege, however, was not sufficient for being an expert lover. This required mastery of the proper social etiquette and sophisticated manners to attract desirable partners without offending decorum and good taste; one needed to know the society's topography of classes and social roles not only to choose an appropriate lover but also to select the style of lovemaking to suit that choice of person. In assessing and handling go-betweens, confidants, servants, and other facilitators in arranging erotic trysts, social knowledge was crucial for achieving access to lovers and for protecting one's lovemaking from the censure of public exposure. It is not surprising, then, that the *Kamasutra* includes "knowledge of the rules of society" and "etiquette" among the "subsidiary sciences" or "arts that should be studied" by both men and women who seek to excel as lovers.[9]

Among its cognitive dimensions, *ars erotica* is especially rich in cultural knowledge. Theories often insist that it demands an education in the fine arts and other artistic practices whose charms bring powers of seduction and provide a finer sense of beauty and meaning that can enhance the quality of erotic performance, making it not only a sensual but an aesthetic delight. They advocate such training for both men and women, even when those same theories sharply contrast the gender roles in courtship and lovemaking.

[9] See chapter 3 of Vatsyayana's *Kamasutra*. The first quotation is taken from the original translation by Richard Burton and F. F. Arbuthnot, *The Kama Sutra of Vatsyayana* (London: Unwin, 1988), 111. The other quotations are from a newer translation, *Kamasutra*, by Wendy Doniger and Sudhir Kakar (Oxford: Oxford University Press, 2009), 13–15.

Beyond the fine arts of music, painting, poetry, and dance, such theories highlight aesthetic artistry in flower arrangement, interior design (especially of the bedroom), fashion (including jewelry), culinary arts, cosmetics, and the creation and blending of perfumes as important for stylizing and embellishing the erotic performance. The *Kamasutra*, the *Art of Courtly Love*, and Ovid's *Art of Love*, for example, urge the lover to cultivate the arts, including the art of rhetoric that heightens one's powers of persuasion while burnishing one's image as attractively brilliant. Hence Ovid insists that one should "learn to speak not only perfect Latin but good Greek."[10]

Ars erotica includes instruction in its own distinctive traditions. Besides their rich diversity of sexual techniques, such traditions provide lovers with knowledge of established erotic conventions, including symbolic tokens of loving commitment that enhance the meaning of erotic engagement and heighten the drama of romance. In Japan's seventeenth-century courtesan culture, these tokens of the mistress's love were sometimes exceedingly violent. Carefully codified and ranked in terms of sacrificial, self-mutilating devotion, they ranged from sending the lover a nail from her finger or sending him love oaths written in her blood to radical acts of cutting off all her hair or tattooing the lover's name on her body, or even cutting off an entire finger to present him with an extravagant testimony of her passionate love.[11] The *ars erotica* regarding such acts involved not only techniques of how to perform them correctly and safely, but also methods of how best to fake them to preserve the courtesan's somatic condition intact while still convincing her lover of her self-sacrificing fervor.

Beyond the fine, liberal, and useful arts, *ars erotica*'s range of knowledge extends into the deepest principles that shape a culture, namely, the fundamental philosophical and religious views or values that structure and guide its way of life. Our now dominantly secular perspective may make us forget culture's profound and powerful religious connection. But culture, in the broad anthropological sense, is "a system of shared beliefs, values, customs, behaviors, and artifacts that the members of society use to cope with their world and with one another, and that are transmitted from generation to generation through learning."[12] In this sense, as T. S. Eliot remarks, it seems

[10] Ovid, *The Art of Love*, trans. James Michie (New York: Modern Library, 2002), 65.

[11] See Lawrence Rogers, "She Loves Me, She Loves Me Not: *Shinju* and *Shikido Okagami*," *Monumenta Nipponica* 49, no. 1 (1994): 31–60.

[12] D. G. Bates and F. Plog, *Cultural Anthropology* (New York: McGraw-Hill, 1990), 7.

that "no culture has appeared or developed except together with a religion."[13] Today's secular culture is no exception, as its ideological roots are firmly grounded in the Western Christian tradition from which it developed through certain movements of reform in Christianity.[14] In any case, cultures of the past have been so indissolubly linked to religion that their forms of *ars erotica* always somehow involve religious knowledge, even when they forgo affirming religious faith or even express vehemently antireligious attitudes. The atheist Sade, for example, amply displays such knowledge in making religious sacrilege a key ingredient of erotic performance.

Religion finds expression in the very name and notion of *ars erotica*, which is etymologically defined by the Greek god Eros. The various forms and traits of this god, as described by Greek religious myth, along with those of the goddess Aphrodite, essentially shaped Greek and then Roman erotic theory. Chinese *ars erotica*, whose practice was especially central to certain strains of Daoism, is rich in religious meaning. Copulation between male and female embodies the basic mingling of essential complementarities that create and sustain the universe: "The union of man and woman is the *dao* of 'one *yin* and one *yang*' . . . *Yin* and *yang*, man and woman, this is the *dao* of heaven and earth."[15] Such cosmic understanding of sex endows Chinese *ars erotica* with a sacred, ritualistic dimension that guides its performative practice. Because sexual union exemplifies the union of heaven and earth, the man (as representing heaven's higher standing) should take the active, initiating, superior position in intercourse, since "what is above acts and what is below follows."[16]

Religion is no less central to Indian *ars erotica*. Its sensory pleasure (*kama*) is explicitly designed – along with material prosperity (*artha*) and the performance of duty (*dharma*) – to fulfill a complete life that leads to religious salvation or liberation (*moksha*). India's founding text of *ars erotica*, the *Kamasutra*, was allegedly composed by a religious scholar who based his work on more ancient erotic texts that go back to the god Śiva, who is said to have discovered sexual intercourse (with his own female emanation) and then passionately praised its pleasures in thousands of books. India's later erotic masterwork, *The Ananga Ranga*, opens by invoking the divine and insisting that the wonderful pleasures of sex remain "second" and

[13] T. S. Eliot, *Notes on the Definition of Culture* (London: Faber, 1965), 15.

[14] See Charles Taylor, *A Secular Age* (Cambridge, MA: Harvard University Press, 2007).

[15] See *The Wondrous Discourse of Su Nū*, in *Art of the Bedchamber: The Chinese Sexual Yoga Classics*, ed. Douglas Wile (Albany: SUNY Press, 1992), 123–124.

[16] *Tung Hsüan Tzu*, in ibid., 108.

"subordinate" to the joy of knowing God but eventually lead to such "divine knowledge." It further claims that "every Shloka (stanza) of this work has a double signification [of religious and erotic meaning] ... and may be interpreted as either mystical or amatory."[17] Similarly, Islam's classic of erotic theory, *The Perfumed Garden*, begins by praising God for having created the natural pleasures of sex and then invokes divine authority for the heterosexual genital acts its religion privileges as the only natural ones (much as the other Abrahamic religions do). "God ... has placed man's greatest pleasure in the natural parts of woman, and has destined the natural parts of man to afford the greatest enjoyment to woman."[18]

I emphasize the cultural and religious dimensions of *ars erotica* partly to underline one of its most fundamental principles: that erotic artistry essentially distinguishes the lovemaking of humans from the sexual play of animals, even if their respective sexual activities share a defining reproductive function as well as many features of physiology and brain chemistry. *Ars erotica* theory sometimes starts by defending its entire project against the charge that sex is a mindless, instinctive activity of our brute animal nature and that it therefore neither requires nor deserves educational training, thoughtfully disciplined practice, or reflective theory. If theorists appeal to the distinctive nature of human sexual practice as a ground for justifying the very notion of *ars erotica*, then the latter's complex practices – rich in aesthetic qualities of refinement, meaning, and cultural import – reciprocally serve to justify human sexuality's claim to distinction, at least when it is properly practiced as erotic art.

Highlighting *ars erotica*'s religious aspect is especially important for two reasons. First, it strengthens human lovemaking's distinction from other mammalian mating in terms of the species specificity of religion. Scholars increasingly make claims for animal culture as characterized by social learning and the transmission of new behavior (both among peers in a group of animals and between generations of the group). Some even think of animals practicing forms of language or art such as varieties of birdsong. But no one speaks of animals practicing a religion. Religion remains something whose possession distinctively elevates humans over brutes, just as it aims, at least in principle, to render our behavior less brutish. The same could be said for *ars erotica*'s transfiguration of animal desire into humanized beauty of sensitive, meaningful, aesthetic performance. Second, religion

[17] Kalyanamalla, *Ananga Ranga*, trans. F. F. Arbuthnot and Richard Burton (New York: Medical Press, 1964), xxi–xxii.

[18] Shayk Nafzawi, *The Perfumed Garden*, trans. Richard Burton (New York: Castle Books, 1964), 7.

may be the factor that most pervasively defines a particular culture's *ars erotica*. If the art of lovemaking is an expression of humans' cultural difference from mere animality, then this art, despite its roots in our shared human biology, is shaped differently by the different historical cultures in which it has developed; and such differences loom especially large across different religious traditions. Some religious cultures cultivate *ars erotica* more elaborately than others. Some indeed discourage it, at least in its more sensual forms, but they cannot thrive by permanently and totally negating sexual expression because its reproductive function is essential to its long-term demographic flourishing.

These two points help explain the fascinating forms of religious *ars erotica* that essentially reject or transcend the carnal, genital, procreative dimension of lovemaking for the spiritual love for God. Most familiar to us through Christian forms of monastic celibacy, such erotic desire is aimed at increasing closeness to God, and its ultimate culmination would be union with God and an elevation to a higher, beatific, quasi-divine existence. Although spiritual and chaste, it is not without ardent somaesthetic expression, for example, in adoring acts of worship and ascetic self-sacrifice or in the somatically felt emotions of longing and passionate pleasures of divine grace and inspiration. Such desiring love of God also finds expression in a chaste but powerfully binding love for fellow humans who join with the fervent religious suitor in the loving service of God. In such spiritual erotics, desiring lovers may long to share each other's company and even share chaste kisses and embraces to demonstrate their solidarity of loving passion for the divine. If Christian doctrine praised the chaste communal love of God as particularly elevating, it equally feared the dangers of such love degenerating into carnal lust or serving to conceal it. This is partly because secular and religious eroticism often display similar linguistic forms, images, and attitudes. If secular *ars erotica* sometimes borrows elements from the divine love of God, then conversely religion's desire for union with God seems modeled on the secular notion of amorous physical union, where God is the dominant and often male-gendered partner while the human soul is pictured as weaker or dependently feminine.

IV CHAPTER OUTLINES

To explore the variety of *ars erotica*'s forms while assessing their aesthetic import and their role in self-cultivation and ethical development, Chapters 2–8 examine the most influential erotic theories of both Western and Asian traditions, from ancient times through the Renaissance. Although these theories and traditions are historically related and consequently somewhat intertwined in the book's narrative, the chapters can also be read separately and out of order, particularly those dealing with Asian erotics. Briefly sketching the chapters' contents here could help orient the reader.

Chapter 2 examines the erotic philosophies of ancient Greece and their development in Roman times. In contrast to Judeo-Christian monotheism, Greek polytheistic mythology was rich in male and female deities prone to diverse sexual desires and adventures, and this generated a lushly polymorphic eroticism whose aims included far more than procreation. The different sociopolitical institutions, socioeconomic conditions, and reigning ideologies of Greece's independent city-states further multiplied the range of sexual forms and styles. Plurality and contestation pervade the erotic field. Homosexuality, lesbianism, bisexuality, and sex with courtesans, slaves, and adolescent children all find their proponents, as does conventional marriage, which was often defended by strict adultery laws and virulent condemnations of pederasty. If some philosophers advocated wife sharing, others instead opposed marriage altogether and recommended sexual abstinence.

Pervading the wide variety of its erotic forms was Greek culture's heroic machismo and its intense love of beauty. This not only inspired its wondrous arts but also promoted a distinctively aesthetic approach to erotic experience whose satisfactions were more than merely sexual and sensate. Pleasures of form and meaning were crucial. The visual pleasures of beautiful bodily form were heightened through athletics and artistic rendering. Rituals of courtship and sexual initiation as well as sexually steeped entertainment forms (such as the drinking party, or *symposium*) provided enjoyable richness of erotic meaning, while competitive rivalry in wooing along with imaginative role-playing and coital position-taking added further creative spice to the Greek aesthetics of lovemaking. The chapter explores these multiple aesthetic dimensions in Greek and Roman *ars erotica*. It also examines how the aesthetic shaping of erotic experience formed an integral part of their vision of life as a project of self-cultivation and self-stylization aimed at living in an admirably beautiful way, typically characterized by the beauty of harmony and order. Such disciplined self-fashioning required virtue, but also cultivated it.

As there are different forms of harmonious living, so we find different models of virtue and different strategies for harmonizing erotic desire with one's vision of what constitutes a beautiful life, including those that advocate sexual abstinence to ensure one's psychic equilibrium and rational control. Chapter 2 examines these different harmonizing strategies in Greek and

Roman theory from Plato, Xenophon, and Aristotle through to the Cynics, Cyrenaics, Stoics, Epicureans, Neoplatonists, and, finally, the hedonistic irony of Ovid's *The Art of Love*. The conflicting strategies of these authors reveal a deep division in Greco-Roman erotic thought. On the one hand, we find a profound appreciation of bodily beauty and the sensory delights of lovemaking (which included aesthetic and emotional as well as physical intensities) but, on the other, the rejection of bodily passion as antithetical to reason, harmony, and lasting pleasure. Among those who took the latter view, Platonistic theorists advocated a transcendental idealism that directed passionate desire away from material bodies toward higher spiritual beauties, while Epicureans conversely denied the very idea of immaterial spiritual things and rejected passionate desire altogether. Recognizing, however, that physical lovemaking is pleasurable and necessary for procreation, Epicureans cautioned against converting a basic physical instinct into an emotionally overwhelming erotic passion that distorts our thinking and upsets our equilibrium.

This variety of contesting views on erotic love and sexual desire discouraged the development of a comprehensive, systematic Greco-Roman *ars erotica* of the kind we find in India (the topic of Chapter 5). One recurrent Greco-Roman debate concerned the philosophical vision of homosexual love as somehow superior to the love of women (because of its greater freedom from nature and from the conventional social constraints of marriage), despite the fact that it remained on the margins of social legitimacy and was often explicitly outlawed. Another controversy concerned whether erotic love and marriage were compatible with a philosophical life. Some of these ancient tensions return to haunt medieval and Renaissance erotic theory, which borrowed heavily from classical sources along with Christian ones that were themselves heavily influenced by Greco-Roman thought. However, before turning to these later periods of Western erotic theorizing, the book's next chapters explore the erotic cultures of ancient Asia, starting with the Hebrew culture that eventually generated Christianity, whose attitudes to sex exercised an enormous albeit constraining influence on Western *ars erotica*.

Chapter 3's treatment of the Judeo-Christian views on lovemaking begins with the Old Testament's first book of Genesis. If God's injunction that humankind be fruitful and multiply should encourage attention to lovemaking, then this erotic direction is thwarted in multiple ways that involve some doctrinal puzzles. Although humans (with their sexed bodies) are claimed to be in God's image, God's bodily image remains obscure and strictly prohibited to represent. Whether God has sexual organs remains a mystery;

and what would a monotheistic God do with them, with whom would he engage in sexual activity? Unlike pagan religions with their fertility cults, Hebrew culture lacked a divine model for *ars erotica* and therefore focused its erotic theorizing narrowly on the pragmatics of reproduction. This focus on progeny rather than pleasure sheds light on some enigmatic features of Mosaic law. The duty of circumcision, for example, by depriving the penis of its most sensitive, pleasure-providing foreskin, symbolizes the subordination of man's instrument of erotic desire to God's will rather than human satisfactions. But semen, despite being the substance necessary for fulfilling God's procreative commandment, is condemned as an unclean, contaminating issue unless it is deposited where it can impregnate. The same focus on Hebrew progeny explains the various prohibitions of homosexuality, bestiality, masturbation, coitus interruptus, and intercourse during menstruation. A similar logic accounts for other Hebrew sexual doctrines: polygyny, levirate marriage, exclusion of the genitally damaged, and the divine condemnations of adultery, incest, and marrying outside the faith. After contrasting these condemnations not only with their surprisingly fruitful violations in Old Testament narratives but also with the mysteriously vibrant eroticism of the Song of Songs, the chapter turns to the Christian New Testament and Church doctrines on sex.

St. Paul's celebration of celibacy and permanent virginity differs sharply from the Hebrew insistence on progeny but even more drastically discourages the development of erotic arts. Conceding it is better to marry than to burn through sins of fornication, Paul confines legitimate sex to marriage while limiting marriage to a single partner of the opposite sex. He nonetheless contends that it is still better to abjure all forms of carnal love and devote one's desire wholly to God. With Paul we see how the carnality of erotic desire takes on a more than physical meaning, as even the soul becomes carnal when one's mind is infected with sexual lust, even if the person does not physically seek to satisfy it. If Paul (allegedly a Roman citizen and educated in Hellenistic thought) found inspiration in Christ's exemplary life to privilege celibate chastity, he could also find confirmation from certain Greek philosophical views that celibate life was preferable to marriage. Examining Christianity's most influential theories of marital sex and sin, the chapter also elaborates the loftier visions of divinely spiritual erotics developed by Church theologians (from Clement, Tertullian, and Origen through Jerome, Chrysostom, Cassian, Augustine, and finally to Aquinas), who drew not only on scripture but also heavily on the Greek philosophical tradition. Augustine receives particular attention because his influential theory of original sin introduced a distinctively rich psychological dimension to the analysis of sexual desire, including an intriguing explanation of impotence and a fascinating vision of how couples might have enjoyed the pleasures of sex without sin or discomfort in an unfallen world.

Chapter 4 examines the ancient Chinese tradition of *ars erotica*, arguably the oldest in the world and remarkable in its wide-ranging, transdisciplinary import. Although Foucault defined the Chinese *ars erotica* as an aesthetic pursuit of pure pleasure and thus in stark opposition to the medicalized discourse of sex in Western culture, we show how Chinese theories of lovemaking instead deploy sexual pleasure to serve overarching health and medical aims. Far from unrestrained hedonism, China's *ars erotica* is deeply concerned with matters of religion, ritual, government and household management, and ethical self-cultivation through disciplined self-regulation. Lovemaking, moreover, has ontological import. It not only furthers life through procreation, but its creative union of opposite sexes symbolizes (as it enacts) the fruitful cosmic unity of complementary opposites (like heaven and earth) that produces the rich manifold of things. Its practical functions, however, do not preclude lovemaking's expression of aesthetic values and the development of artistically styled techniques in Chinese sexual practice. This is partly because in Chinese philosophies (unlike our dominant modern Western tradition) there is no opposition between the practical and the aesthetic.

After noting the different textual genres of Chinese erotic theory, the chapter sketches the background of medical, cosmological, and religious beliefs and changing sociohistorical contexts that shaped such theory over its long history. Patriarchy and polygyny were abiding, formative social institutions. We then analyze the powerful blend of aesthetic, functional, and ethical features of classical Chinese sexual theories, showing how their *ars erotica* deploys the fine arts and the aesthetic principles of harmony, timing, rhythm, unity in variety, and meditative monitoring in the conduct of lovemaking, while also adopting different ideals of physical beauty at different times. Foot-binding, for example, came in and out of fashion as an aesthetically beautiful form with strong erotic connotations. The chapter concludes by examining how China's *ars erotica* contributes to the crucial ethical project of self-cultivation not only by heightening physical vitality (for excellence of virtuous action) but also by enhancing mental power and balance through transformative sublimation of the abundant somatic energy of sex. Self-cultivation through sex took different forms in Confucian and Daoist thought and practice.

Indian sexology, the focus of Chapter 5, might be as old as China's, and it is equally rich, even though its surviving texts are not as numerous. It is especially outstanding in combining systematic comprehensiveness with intricate detail while carefully integrating practical methods with general philosophical principles. India, moreover, provides the most richly aesthetic vision of *ars erotica* and intriguingly combines erotic desire with ascetic spirituality. The divine Śiva, god of ascetic meditation and sexual potency, aptly serves as the mythological source of Indian sexology, and the chapter begins by sketching key mythological, religious, social, and artistic contexts that shaped Indian *ars erotica*. Its founding text, the *Kamasutra*, emerged (probably in the third century) around the time of India's inaugural work of dramatic and aesthetic theory (the *Natyaśastra*), and it displays deep connections with the aesthetics of classical Indian drama, dance, poetry, and visual art.

Aesthetics pervades Indian erotic theory, shaping its concepts, language, techniques, and criteria for good lovemaking. The aesthetic aims that govern Indian *ars erotica* extend, however, beyond mere sensory beauty and pleasure to embrace important cognitive, psychological, ethical, and spiritual objectives. These include training for greater mastery of perception and control of one's emotions, but also greater understanding of the character, feelings, moods, and needs of other persons, especially those with whom we need to partner in lovemaking. The *Kamasutra*, allegedly written in the spirit of "chastity and in the highest meditation" (KS 171) in fact defines the purpose of its *ars erotica* precisely in such terms of enhanced knowledge, mastery of the senses, and self-control for general success in the art of living rather than the pursuit of passionate pleasures.[19] A later classic of Indian erotic theory, the sixteenth-century *Ananga Ranga*, even suggests that the *ars erotica* prepares us for spiritual life and religious enlightenment by promoting marital pleasure and harmony, and thus ensuring that we reach a stage where we no longer lust for sensual delights. The chapter's study of Indian sexology also draws on the twelfth-century *Koka Shastra*. Together these three canonical texts reveal an enduringly stable common core of erotic doctrines while differing on some specifics that reflect changes in Indian society, most notably a continuous trend toward emphasizing marital sex with increasing prohibitions of conduct that is harmful to marriage.

Chapters 6 and 7 turn to the *ars erotica* of Islamic and Japanese culture, respectively. Both derive in significant ways from older, richer cultural traditions of erotic theory, and both display a distinctively keen appreciation of the seductive aesthetics of perfume and an intriguing combination of great

[19] Vatsyayana Mallanaga, *Kamasutra*, trans. Doniger and Kakar, 171.

delicacy and extreme violence. Exploring the ways the Islamic and Japanese *ars erotica* derive and diverge from their formative sources provides further insight into how matters of sexual artistry and taste are transformed when transplanted into different ideological and cultural frameworks. Although Muslim erotic theory drew heavily from Indian and Greco-Roman thought, it had to adapt its borrowings from these polytheistic cultures to the monotheistic framework of Islam. If the Japanese conception of *ars erotica* developed in a cultural framework steeped in Chinese traditional arts and religions, it was also shaped by local Japanese mythological, cultural, and political factors.

Chapter 6 begins by explaining how Islam's religious laws and doctrines (as expressed in the Quran, *hadith*, and *fiqh*) shaped sexual practices both within its polygyny institution of marriage (including the distinctive Islamic notion of provisional marriage, *nika mut'ah*) and outside it (sex with slaves, concubines, and women of conquered foes). As Islam rapidly spread through the fiercely conquering power of its male warriors, it is not surprising that its erotic theory often highlights the pleasurable expression of passionate, even violent, male force. However, like Greco-Roman and Indian cultures, Islam includes erotic traditions that harness the powerful energy of sexual desire for ethical and spiritual self-cultivation that raises us to higher levels of love and perfection. Explaining how the Prophet Mohammed's polygynous love of women is exemplary for affirming the compatibility of lovemaking with the highest virtue, we then show how Sufi thinkers like al-Ghazali and al-Arabi defend sex as a path of spiritualization that combines asceticism with pleasure and transforms the carnal love of women into the holy love of God.

After noting the role of sex in Japanese culture's founding mythology, Chapter 7 explores three key traditions of classical Japanese eroticism. The courtly love tradition of the Heian Dynasty (794–1185), largely formulated by noblewomen writers, was extremely romantic and aesthetically refined, and its strong aesthetic impulse (backed by courtly pedigree) deeply colored later erotic traditions. Emphasizing accomplishments in the arts, tenderness of feeling, elegance of manners, sensitivity, and discretion, it also advocated controlled desire, detached enjoyment, and concealment and understatement that called for the powers and pleasures of imaginative fulfillment. The second important erotic tradition was that of male love, which developed among the Buddhist monks and samurai warriors, encouraged by the special intimacy of living together while being largely isolated from conventional life and society. If the monks' and samurais' versions of male love embodied some of the distinctive pedagogical and ethical features of Greek pederasty, these worthier features were harder to maintain when this tradition of the love of boys later spread to city life, with attractive young men (particularly, Kabuki actors) as the erotic targets. The chapter closes by examining the erotic connoisseurship of high-class courtesan culture in Edo society that in 1617 established the famous walled-in pleasure district of Yoshiwara in what is now Tokyo. Aiming to emulate the aesthetic elegance and refinement of Heian eroticism, the courtesan's *ars erotica* emphasized mastery of the fine arts and fashion and her display of chic and graceful manners far more than her sexual skills. It also privileged a man's winning her heart more than his enjoying her body. However, beneath its veneer of elegant refinement, Japan's elite courtesan culture carried the ugly evils of commercialism, commodification of women, deceit, distrust, and even bloody violence.

Chapter 8, the book's final chapter, turns back to the West by examining key issues and texts in the secular erotic theory of medieval and Renaissance Europe. Although dominantly Christian, that culture drew strongly on other traditions. Since Roman times, Christianity borrowed many ideas from classical pagan Greco-Roman thought, but medieval monastic learning generated an increasing interest in classical culture that later fully flowered in the Renaissance. Medieval Europe also learned from its encounters with Islamic culture, through the Crusades and the Arab conquests of large parts of Europe. These different cultural traditions contained a variety of divergent attitudes and practices that pervaded European erotic thinking of the time and that proved very difficult to harmonize. After sketching some of the historical factors that explain this rich mix of erotic perspectives, the chapter examines three central philosophical ideals of love that essentially shaped medieval erotic theory, generating its dilemmas and debates. First is the classical idea of loving friendship in the pure pursuit of virtue that ennobles lovers and that is free from any sort of need, dependence, or appetite for gain, whether financial, political, or hedonic. This ideal effectively limited love to relationships between virtuous men since women lacked the required socioeconomic independence and freedom. But its exclusive male focus raised Christian fears of homosexual sin. The second ideal saw love as the supreme, beneficent force that unifies and sustains the cosmos and whose naturalistic expression was the heterosexual union of procreative love that should be socially structured and sanctified by marriage. The third erotic ideal sought spiritual union with the divine through celibate chastity in directing one's undivided desire to God alone. Disdaining sexual coupling as basely animalistic, it also disparaged marriage as too conventional to be uplifting.

Exploring the difficulties that reconciling these different ideals posed for medieval and Renaissance erotic theory, the chapter examines several key moments of this tradition, two from the Middle Ages and three from the Renaissance. We begin with Heloise and Abelard's debates over the compatibility of passionate love and marriage with high virtue and the consummate love of God. Despite their different views, both lovers agreed that marriage and its duties were too ordinary and unfree to inspire love's ennobling passion and singular virtue. The so-called art of courtly love then developed a program for extramarital heterosexual desire that nonetheless professed to be ennobling and virtuous. It sought to justify this claim through the purity of respectful, devoted service that it directed toward the beloved woman (always deemed superior to her male suitor) and through the noble acts that the male lover undertook to impress the beloved with his virtue. If courtly love reflects a rise in woman's stature from earlier medieval views that were horribly misogynist, our analysis reveals its strong residual sexism as well as its problematic class privilege and its flagrant violation of Christian ethics.

The ideal of eros as an uplifting, instructive power found ardent advocates in Renaissance Neoplatonism, and we examine the views of four such theorists working in Italy, beginning with Marsilio Ficino (Plato's great translator), who sought to synthesize Platonic philosophy and Christian theology. Identifying God as the source of all love and beauty (as well as their desired goal), Ficino had little regard for physical lovemaking, whose extreme passion he claimed was too unruly to have the harmony and reasonableness demanded of true beauty and love. Scornful of material bodies, he instead desired union with God, though he admitted that bodily beauty could serve as a hook to catch people and lead them to God's beauty and love. Giordano Bruno, an adventurous defrocked priest who was burned at the stake for heresy and magic, shared Ficino's and other Renaissance Neoplatonists' identification of God as the source and perfection of beauty, goodness, and love whose binding spirit pervades the universe. Bruno, however, displayed far greater appreciation of sexual love's uplifting potential to lead us closer to God, even when it includes vulgar varieties of carnal connection that Christian doctrine vehemently condemned. In contrast, the nobleman courtier Baldassare Castiglione insisted on integrating refined manners, knowledge of the arts, and a genuine respect for women into an argument for the uplifting power of love that eschews all extramarital love and that ultimately aims to transcend all earthly love for the single-minded pursuit of the purely spiritual love of God. Among these Neoplationists, Leon Ebreo, a Jewish physician of Hispanic origin who fled to Italy to escape the Spanish Inquisition, provided the strongest case for marriage and its use of sexual union to promote the ennobling aims of knowledge, goodness, and even spiritual love. Passionate love, for Leone, thrives in marriage and increases through marital sex. Such marital passion can effectively lead us higher toward cognitive union with God, while offering the worldly benefits of marriage.

From the spiritual heights of divine Neoplatonism we turn to the down-to-earth erotic views of two Renaissance humanist skeptics: Erasmus and Montaigne. An ordained monk and progressive scholar-reformer (and a priest's illegitimate son), Erasmus so strongly praised marriage that fellow clergy condemned him for attacking the Christian celibate ideal. Although insisting that marriage was the only option for sexual expression, Erasmus chose not to marry and painted marital sex in such extremely dull and dour colors that render it incompatible with the passionate pleasures of lovemaking. Marriage was for begetting children, not for erotic delights whose pursuit led husbands to treat their wives as prostitutes. If Montaigne, in contrast, was a wealthy secular nobleman rich in carnal experience (both marital and other), he nonetheless concurred that marriage was not the proper place for erotic passions and pleasures. But this did not mean abstaining from them, because, in proper measure and with proper caution, they are essential to a person's physical and psychological health. Montaigne thus recommends erotic love outside the bonds of marriage (for women as well as men), though with discretion and regard for the reputation of both one's spouse and one's partners in adultery.

Finally, we consider two contrasting forms of erotic theory from Renaissance courtesan culture that dismissed the ideals of marriage and of lofty celibate devotion to God but instead insisted on the pleasures of love outside the frame of religious sacrament. The philosophical *Dialogue on the Infinity of Love* (written by the Italian courtesan Tullia d'Aragona) advocates an ennobling, refined erotic love that is motivated and guided by rational appreciation of the beloved's virtues and seeks a virtuous transformation of the self through spiritual union with the beloved. But it likewise affirms the body's desire for physical union through sexual copulation and the enjoyment of the body's senses. If Tullia privileged spiritual union, reason, and the higher sense of sight over more vulgar love that is driven by bodily appetites and the lower senses of taste and touch, she nonetheless endorses carnal love and all its sensual delights provided that they are enjoyed in moderation as determined by reason. She even recognized that love can develop upward from the vulgar form driven by sexual appetite to a more refined, virtuous, and spiritual (yet also corporeal) love that is governed by reason and that (through its rational character) is free from possessive jealousy. This allows both courtesans and their client-lovers to enjoy the benefits of multiple erotic friendships (with their multiplied bounty of sensuous and spiritual delights), even if both courtesans and their gentlemen can have their special favorites. Next, in the ribald dialogues of Pietro Aretino we explore the ruder, lustier, and mercenary aspects of courtesan culture's *ars erotica*, examining the courtesan's special techniques of seduction and lovemaking to heighten her lovers' pleasure along with her methods of pretense to maintain their affection and financial support.

The chapter closes with a speculative hypothesis. After millennia during which beauty was intimately linked to eros, and indeed conceptually defined by it, as the object that inspired desiring love, the eighteenth century witnessed, in the birth of the field of aesthetics, a new discourse of beauty. An important aspect of this new aesthetic discourse was that beauty should be appreciated through an attitude of disinterested contemplation rather than an erotic desire for union. If the divorce of beauty from eros was a factor that helped generate modern aesthetics, it is possible that currents of materialism and libertinism in the seventeenth and eighteenth centuries helped generate the divorce by making it far more difficult to maintain the vision of erotic love as an uplifting spiritual desire for union of immaterial, virtuous souls. If it was harder to distinguish love from lust, then it was safer, for high-minded or pious thinkers, to separate beauty from eros and its associations with carnal appetites for sensual delights and union. If Europe invented modern aesthetics to displace beauty's earlier discourse of love, then modern aesthetics' neglect of *ars erotica* seems perfectly logical, however unfortunate and misguided.

2

Dialectics of Desire and Virtue

Aesthetics, Power, and Self-Cultivation in Greco-Roman Erotic Theory

I MYTHOLOGY

The Greeks provided Western culture with the foundations for whatever aesthetic richness its erotic theory enjoys. This includes the paradoxical eros of chastity that Christianity developed by drawing on Greek models of philosophical idealism and asceticism, whose influence continued through the Roman Empire when Christianity absorbed them. The richness of Greek erotic thought lies partly in its multiple ambiguities, and part of this ambiguity can be traced to the polysemic polytheism of Greek religion, whose influence on Roman civilization also impacted its erotic theory. Although the Greek god Eros (whom the Romans called Cupid) gave eroticism its name, he was not the only god central to Greek views of lovemaking and sexual desire. Aphrodite, goddess of love and beauty (known as Venus in Rome), also played a defining role. Moreover, within each of these two seemingly singular Greek gods we find a nest of divergent personae or meanings. Greek mythology provides us with at least three different forms of the god Eros. The first Eros to appear, in Hesiod's *Theogony* (116), is not the familiar chubby, child-like, winged son of Aphrodite. Instead, Hesiod portrays Eros as one of the very first or oldest gods, existing before the birth of Aphrodite and the other Olympians. "Verily at the first Chaos [Air] came to be, but next wide-bosomed Earth [Gaia], the ever-sure foundation of all the deathless ones who hold the peaks of snowy Olympus, and dim Tartarus [Hell] in the depth of the wide-pathed Earth, and Eros [Love], fairest among the deathless gods, who unnerves the limbs and overcomes the mind and wise counsels of all gods and all men within them."[1]

[1] Hesiod, *Theogony*, in *Hesiod, the Homeric Hymns, and Homerica*, trans. Hugh G. Evelyn-White (Cambridge, MA: Harvard University Press, 1959), 87. Here and elsewhere in this section, parenthetical citations refer to line numbers from this Hesiod text.

In this earliest introduction to Eros we already find the essential Greek link between erotic desire and beauty, along with the recognition that such beauty-inspired desire has enormous power to capture us both physically and mentally, weakening our limbs with longing and overwhelming the voice of reason and the strength of will. Later sources identify Eros as a younger god, most typically the male child of Aphrodite and Ares (though other parentage is sometimes given). In his essential incarnation as Aphrodite's son, he is sometimes accompanied by other child-like attendants of Aphrodite known as the *erotes*: Himeros (urgent, impetuous desire), Pothos (yearning or longing), and Anteros (reciprocated desire or requited love). Theorists appeal to these contrasting old and young personae in characterizing love. In Plato's *Symposium*, Eros is first praised by one speaker for being "one of the most ancient gods" (178b), but then a rival speaker commends him as "the youngest of the gods," whose youth is part of why "he is the most beautiful and the best" and also "the happiest of them all" (195a).[2] A third, though less familiar, version of Eros derives from Orphic cosmogony. Here Phanes, the primeval god of procreation, is identified with the older Eros, but this Phanes/Eros is conceived as being hatched from the primordial world egg and portrayed as a winged, hermaphroditic deity, suggesting both the soaring force of desire and the complete powers of sexual reproduction.[3]

Aphrodite likewise presents more than one persona. In Hesiod's famous version of her birth, she is the nonsexual product of divine castration. The god Cronos castrates his father Heaven (Uranus) with "a great long sickle" of flint that was fashioned by goddess Earth to be used against Heaven (who was both her son and her consort) because Heaven had been hiding their children within Earth, which greatly discomforted her. Cronos stealthily commits this castration at night when Heaven "longing for love . . . lay about Earth spreading himself full upon her." After brutally cutting off the procreative act and instrument, Cronos cast Heaven's severed genitals "into the surging sea," where "a white foam spread around them from the immortal flesh, and in it there grew a maiden" that "men call Aphrodite . . . the

[2] I refer to Plato here and elsewhere in this chapter by using the Stephanus numbers. I cite from the translations in John M. Cooper, ed., *Plato: Complete Works* (Indianapolis: Hackett, 1997), 463, 477–478. Unless otherwise indicated, subsequent Plato quotations are sourced from the English translations in this edition.

[3] Aristophanes, for example, refers to this version of Eros in his comedy *Birds*. For more detailed discussion, see Claude Calame, *The Poetics of Eros in Ancient Greece*, trans. Janet Lloyd (Princeton: Princeton University Press, 2013), 193–195.

foam-born goddess" (176–198).[4] However, in Homer's *Iliad* and *Odyssey* and other ancient sources, Aphrodite is instead sexually sired by Zeus with the Titan goddess Dione as her mother.

Parallel to these different births, Aphrodite had two contrasting personae whose radical difference is invoked in Plato's *Symposium* to recommend the virtue of homosexual love (Sym 180c–185e). Heavenly Aphrodite (Aphrodite Urania), whose nonsexual ("purely male") birth from Heaven's genitals implies a higher, purer, spiritual love beyond the carnal desire of our animal sexual reproduction, is what inspires the noblest, uplifting forms of homosexual love (Sym 181c). Though this heavenly love can include physical expression, it makes "virtue [the] central concern" (Sym 185c). In contrast, "Common Aphrodite" (Aphrodite Pandemos, literally that "of all the people") is "the vulgar goddess" inspiring "the love felt by the vulgar, who are attached to women no less than to boys, to the body more than to the soul, and to the least intelligent partners, since all they care about is completing the sexual act" (Sym 181b, 185c). Perhaps through this common, carnal god, Greeks came to use *aphrodisia* as their general term to denote sexual intercourse (whether heterosexual or homosexual). If "there is some justification for the generalization that genital activity as a whole is the province of Aphrodite and the obsessive focusing of desire on one person, which we call 'falling in love,' the province of Eros," this distinction is never drawn explicitly, as the relationship between these two gods of love is ambiguous and variously described through their multiple myths and personae.[5]

This polysemic plurality of love gods nourishes a richly polymorphic eroticism: homosexual and heterosexual; marital and extramarital; for procreation and purely for pleasure; deploying genital, anal, and oral modes; between same-aged lovers and partners from different generations. Transcending the boundaries of nations, cultures, and races, erotic love also transgresses the taboos of incest and bestiality, and even the division between mortals and gods. Moreover, in contrast to Judeo-Christian monotheism where God himself has no sexual partner, Greek polytheism provides instructive models of divine lovemaking inspired by beauty and pursued for pleasure rather than procreation. Indeed, Greek mythology often presents progeny not as the erotic goal but as a threatening hindrance to or dangerous by-product of lovemaking. The birth of Aphrodite as a result of Cronos

[4] Hesiod, *Theogony*, in Evelyn-White, trans., *Hesiod*, 91, 93.

[5] K. J. Dover, *Greek Homosexuality* (Cambridge, MA: Harvard University Press, 1978), 63; hereafter DGH.

castrating his offspring-producing father in the midst of the latter's coital efforts is just one of many examples.

The aesthetic richness of Greek eroticism is likewise nourished by identifying its twin gods of desire and love with outstanding beauty. Even Hesiod's "old" Eros is described as "fairest among the deathless gods" (120), while Aphrodite's beauty is uncontestably overwhelming. This essential connection of sexual desire to beauty rather than simply to physical urge or reproductive need promotes an *ars erotica* oriented toward aesthetic values and creative expression. Moreover, as both gods combine beauty with violence (Aphrodite being born of cruel castration and Eros attacking his victims with arrows), they provide a fertile ground for promoting the productive tensions of tenderness and aggression that nourish love's sweet wounds.

If Greek mythology's erotic pluralism and concern for beauty encourage a polymorphic aesthetic approach to sexual love, then its account of woman's creation highlights the artistic dimension of human sexual difference and desire. The Greeks believed that "tribes of men lived on earth" quite happily and "free from ills and hard toil," until they angered Zeus, who then ordered that woman be created to punish them; woman designed as a "beautiful evil" to make men pay the price for Prometheus's theft of fire. Instructing the artisan god Hephaestus (the frequently cuckolded husband of Aphrodite) to "mix earth with water . . . to fashion a sweet, lovely maiden-shape, like to the immortal goddesses in face," Zeus then had all the gods bestow their special gifts on this divinely designed living doll (which he named Pandora because all gifted her).[6] Highlighted among her endowments are the artistic gifts of needlework, weaving, and fine clothes from the goddess Athena, but also aesthetic "grace" from Aphrodite and the arts of "crafty words" and deception from Hermes. The invention of woman as a beautiful sexual "snare" replete with artistic gifts to make men "glad of heart while they embrace their own destruction" is a myth that both reflects as it promotes an eroticism inspired by aesthetic values and artistic principles. Unfortunately, however, it equally reflects and promotes a troubling misogyny that shaped Greek eroticism and still deeply darkens our own. Before examining more closely how Greek erotic theory develops the aesthetic dimensions of its mythological roots, we should note how the sociopolitical pluralities of Greek culture also contribute to the rich complexity of its eroticism.

[6] Hesiod, *Works and Days* (lines 60–105) in Evelyn-White, trans., *Hesiod*, 7–9. See also Andrew Stewart, *Art, Desire, and the Body in Ancient Greece* (Cambridge: Cambridge University Press, 1997), 107.

II SOCIETY AND HISTORY

One readily speaks of ancient Greek culture as a whole, but we should not forget that it changed significantly over the course of its four major historical periods (archaic, classical, Hellenistic, and Roman) extending roughly from 800 BCE to 400 CE, when it disintegrated along with the western half of the Roman Empire. Moreover, during the archaic and classical periods, Greek culture was derived from a constellation of hundreds of sovereign city-states scattered throughout the Mediterranean region. Though "constituting a linguistic and cultural continuum," these independent city-states had their own distinctive institutions and traditions, "admitting of striking differences in political structure and social ideals" (DGH 3). Such differences extend also to sexual matters and erotic practices. Corinth, for example, was known as a center of prostitution famous for high-level courtesans, while Sparta was instead renowned for its martial, male homoeroticism (even though it belonged, like Corinth, to the Dorian group of city-states that considered themselves as sharing a common ancestry and cultural tradition). Athens, in contrast, belonged to Ionian culture, whose strong presence in the Aegean region helped to enrich it with imports from the Middle East and encourage an erotic style more luxurious than Sparta's.

Different political and social institutions promote different erotic ideologies and practices, channeling sexual energy into certain preferred directions while also provoking resistance through transgressive erotic forms. Extremely strict Athenian laws against adultery, which allowed a wronged husband to kill the male adulterer on the spot if caught in the act in the marital house (to which Athenian wives and daughters were normally confined) certainly encouraged Athenian men to direct their erotic interests elsewhere. Moreover, because the Athenian concept of adultery (*moichos*) was widely construed to pertain not only to a man's legally wedded wife but to any female belonging to his home, or *oikos* –including his daughters, sisters, mothers, or even concubines, Athenian males' options for lovemaking were even further limited. Not surprisingly, prostitution prospered in various forms. Solon, celebrated as the founder of Athenian democracy, is also credited for encouraging prostitution through laws allowing the establishment of cheap brothels.[7] Not only could their taxes increase civic revenue, their services enabled even poor men to enjoy sexual satisfaction without the costly trouble of marriage and without the risks of courting

[7] James Davidson, *Courtesans and Fishcakes: The Consuming Passions of Classical Athens* (Chicago: University of Chicago Press, 2011), 75–85.

virtuous women or indeed any woman protected by the broad adultery laws.[8] (Lacking such laws, Spartan erotics took a very different form.) Solon, moreover, shaped Athenian pederasty by introducing laws not only "prohibiting slaves from entering gymnasia" (a standard site for sexual cruising where young men exercised naked and rubbed themselves in oil) but also punishing them for forming "liaisons with freeborn boys," thus giving older Athenian men a less contested field to win young lovers.[9]

Besides explicit laws, other social institutions differently fashioned the erotic in the different Greek city-states. Sparta, whose military virtues were partly inspired by anxieties about uprisings from other communities that "they had conquered and reduced to slavery," devoted its social institutions to producing excellent combat troops, steeled in physical powers, courage, and strong bonds of communal male loyalty. Consider its famously strict education regimen known as the *agoge*. At the age of seven, male children were taken from their families and introduced to its distinctive curriculum. Housed in a special school where they slept in barracks, the boys ate communal meals, were arranged into groups or teams of age mates (called *agelai*, or herds), and rigorously trained in athletics, mock fighting, and harsh disciplines of endurance to make them as tough and as loyal as possible. At twenty, after gaining combat experience, they graduated from the *agoge* and could marry but "were still required to bunk with their mess mates," now organized into communal meal groups called *syssitia*. Their "conjugal visits to the bride's home were infrequent and clandestine." At age thirty, "they could finally leave the barracks and live in their own households, but they continued to dine with their eating group into old age."[10]

Such mandatory living arrangements obviously constrained the possibilities for heterosexual *ars erotica*. How could a Spartan man find the time and place to court an available female and engage her in leisured erotic dalliance, which in Athens was readily provided by its own famous institution of

[8] The laws of Syracuse (another Dorian city) identified erotic targets through sumptuary laws. Forbidding a woman from "wearing gold ornaments or gaily colored dresses ... unless she admitted she was a common prostitute," they also apparently prescribed that "a man might not make himself look beautiful or dress elaborately ... unless he confessed to being an adulterer or a *kinaidos* (a male seducer of men)." Ibid., 73, 165.

[9] Marilyn B. Skinner, *Sexuality in Greek and Roman Culture* (Oxford: Blackwell, 2005), 112. Similarly, the Athenian law Pericles introduced in 451 BCE restricting citizenship to children whose parents were both citizens seems to have rekindled husbands' erotic interest in their legal Athenian wives, because it discouraged them from extended dalliance with attractive foreign concubines. This was a popular custom practiced by aristocratic Athenians and one that Pericles himself indulged in after he made the law.

[10] Skinner, *Sexuality*, 64.

relaxed communal dining and drinking – the *symposium*, which included the female companionship of courtesans, flute girls, and dancers? In contrast, the Spartan system encouraged a rich expression of homoerotic forms, which could include "frequent and casual homosexual relations" with "males of [one's] own unit" but especially "the much more intense *erastes-eromenos* relationship, as elsewhere in the Greek world," in which a mature male lover (the *erastes*) sought to win the love of an attractive adolescent boy or young man (the beloved *eromenos*) by inspiring the lad with his exemplary devotion and virtues, virtues that the young beloved would aim to emulate.[11] In Sparta these love-inspiring manly virtues were largely military-related, while in the cultured Athenian context they were more broadly ethical, philosophical, and aesthetic.

Sparta's social institutions shaped female sexuality as well. Unlike Athenian women, who were largely hidden from the public and confined to the *oikos*, Spartan women showed more of their bodies and exercised outdoors. Wearing short dresses slit at the thigh (unlike the longer gowns of other Greek women), they sometimes shed them to exercise naked like the men and also to sing and dance naked in ritual processionals of young men and women, such as those related to festivals like the Gymnopaedia. In such parades, Spartan men could examine prospective brides, while the parading young women would likewise assess the men, openly praising some and mocking others, thus displaying the distinctive female Spartan boldness. Trained from youth for such assertive independence, Spartan girls were also organized into "herds" where they studied not the typical woman's work of cooking and weaving "but instead practiced dancing, singing, and athletics, including running, wrestling, discus throwing, javelin, and ball games."[12]

As "their physical fitness was legendary," so "their beauty was proverbial," the ideal being "lithe, fast, slim, and tall, with fine ankles, strong thighs, firm breasts, and long auburn hair." Marriage did not kill their independence. With married men essentially confined to their barracks or even further away on the battlefield, women assumed responsibilities for governing households (including the owning and managing of land). "Polyandry became acceptable when the male population began to decline in the fifth century, and many Spartan women managed two households," while Athenian wives and daughters were always treated as statutory minors totally dominated by their male protectors.[13] Partly to insure that brides would not be overly dominated and treated as children, the Spartan marriage had

[11] Dover, *Greek Homosexuality*, 193, 202.
[12] Stewart, *Art, Desire, and the Body*, 113.
[13] Ibid., 113–114.

to wait until the woman was in her late teens, while in Athens and Crete brides married as early as fourteen.[14] Sparta's older age for brides is also justified by the same "eugenic" reason that motivates their rigorous physical training: a child bride was considered unfit for producing superior offspring. To sustain its domination of the far more numerous conquered populations under its control, Sparta designed its institutions and erotic life for breeding the healthiest citizens to generate the strongest progeny and then training them into the most potent force for sustaining its military regime, both at home and on the battlefield.

Besides the naked parades, other distinctive rituals helped style Greek eroticism. One striking case is the ritual abduction of a beloved young male by his older lover. Practiced in Crete, where male education and communal dining traditions were similar to Sparta's, the ritual began by the lover announcing the intended abduction to the boy's family (who would be honored by this attention if the lover was an admirable man). The family would make a token gesture of physical resistance when the actual abduction occurred, symbolically allowing for the lover to show his physical prowess, and then chasing the couple to the door of the lover's communal dining hall. The couple would then escape into the countryside to hunt and feast for two months, together with friends. On their return the boy received ritual gifts (including a military outfit) that marked the elevation of his status and progress to manhood. Scholars believe that these Cretan love relations were also physically consummated as part of the initiation rites of manhood. Relating this ritual to those of more modern Melanesian warrior communities where physical insemination by the mature warrior was thought to insure the boy's acquiring full manhood and overcoming childhood's feminine influences, some experts argue that such homosexual initiation practices were common in preliterate Indo-European cultures.[15] The Spartan marriage rite likewise involved a staged, symbolic abduction by force, expressing the husband's physical prowess and his passionate desire – both presumed to be key ingredients for producing strong offspring. It further included a ritual cutting of the bride's hair and dressing her in men's clothes before sexually consummating the marriage, thus symbolically altering her gender identity to convey male strength and her solidarity with the groom but also to suggest her manly independence.

[14] In Xenophon's dialogue *The Estate-Manager*, the main speaker explains how he educates his fourteen-year-old bride; in Hugh Tredennick and Robin Waterfield, trans., *Conversations of Socrates* (London: Penguin, 1990), 299–300.

[15] For more details on this topic, see Skinner, *Sexuality*, 66–67.

Rather than rough abduction scenarios, Athens reveled in its renowned symposium, an erotically charged social ritual whose etymological roots of "drinking together" convey only a small part of its sensory pleasures and cultural meanings. According to classical Athenian sources, the ritual drinking did not begin until the guests had eaten an adequate dinner (which typically consisted of bread as the staple topped by cheese, oil, vegetables, and sometimes the luxury of fish), and the wine was usually diluted with water in a mixing bowl, resulting in a diminished but still inebriating alcoholic content. Although essentially designed for male camaraderie (like the communal male dining in Sparta and Crete), Athenian symposia included sexually attractive and available females as part of the mix. Describing "the world of the symposium ... [as] the most familiar face of Greek prostitution," one scholar writes: "Getting hold of women was as much a part of preparations for a dinner-party as going shopping for fish, wine and perfume. Some of the girls, the *mousourgoi*, could entertain with instruments, usually the 'flute' or harp, others could dance or sing." These "music-girls ... played an important role at the symposium, entertaining the guests with music at the beginning and with sex at the end of the party," while also "providing the rhythm for the mixing and distributing of the wine as well as the singing." Flute girls were particularly notorious for their erotic functions that extended well beyond the dining hall; their rhythms and sexual antics energized a third stage in unbridled symposia, "the *kamos*, a conga of revellers that took the drinking-party out into the city on expeditions of riot and debauch."[16]

Flute girls and their ilk were not always the only available females present in the symposium; higher-class courtesans (hetaerae) could also be there. Unlike the hired musical staff (male and female), these hetaerae were treated as participant companions rather than employees, and they were valued for their entertaining conversation, aesthetic refinements, and distinctive beauty rather than mere sexual services. Although ultimately dependent economically on their various suitors and lovers, hetaerae had the distinction of bestowing their sexual favors by choice rather than selling them in the manner of prostitutes. As participant companions (the word "hetaera" literally meaning companion), they would share the two-person couch on which symposiasts would lounge in the customary reclining position for such ritual eating and drinking. This close proximity of lying together on a couch

[16] Davidson, *Courtesans and Fishcakes*, 81, 92. This symposiastic ritual explains the drunken intrusions (first of Alcibiades, then of other revelers) that conclude Plato's famous dialogue *Symposium*.

intensified the erotic energy that was already heightened by wine, music, perfumes, and the presence of some beautiful young bodies of both sexes, so that the Athenian symposiast was powerfully primed for sensuous dalliance in this richly aesthetic, indulgent ambiance. The contrast with Spartan sexual culture reflects the disparity between Sparta's intensely military creed and an Athenian ideology that prized the pleasures of philosophy and the arts. Sparta's martial culture of male homoeroticism and greater female independence proved powerful enough to promote a strong current of lesbian eroticism, not only between girls of the "herd" but also between girls and older married women (in relations modeled on the nurturing male *eromenos-erastes* relationship). These lesbian relations "are amply attested and were apparently not discouraged" in Sparta, unlike in other Greek cities.[17] As Plutarch insists in describing the power of Spartan same-sex love, "this sort of love was so approved among them that even the maidens found lovers in good and noble women."[18]

In Greek erotic thinking gender identities and sexual roles go far beyond the simple dichotomies of male and female. Among women, we find virgins, brides, wives, widows, concubines, slave girls, flute girls, prostitutes, and courtesans of various levels of refinement. Athenian men knew how to exploit this variety to satisfy their diverse sexual needs. Attacking a prostitute in a court proceeding, one orator affirms available alternatives: "Hetaeras we keep for pleasure, concubines for attending day-by-day to the body and wives for producing heirs, and for standing trusty guard on our household property."[19] Erotic identities also varied among males. Besides the roles of *eromenos* and *erastes*, there were slave boys and male prostitutes for casual sex, adulterous womanizers, and the *kinaidos*, or effeminate male (whose effeminacy could be expressed either by a willingness to be penetrated in anal intercourse or simply by an excessive indulgence in sex whether heterosexual or homosexual). There were also eunuchs and old men whose disabilities allegedly freed them from the "tyranny" of sexual drives.[20]

Erotic gender roles and erotic expectations reflect underlying ideologies concerning the fundamental features of male and female sexuality, as described by Greek medical theory and commonsense dogma. Ever since

[17] Stewart, *Art, Desire, and the Body*, 113

[18] Plutarch, "Lycurgus," in *Parallel Lives*, trans. Bernadotte Perrin (Cambridge, MA: Harvard University Press, 1998), 265.

[19] The orator is Apollodorus, quoted in Davidson, *Courtesans and Fishcakes*, 73.

[20] For more detailed discussion, see Dover, *Greek Homosexuality*, 19–23, 49–81, 100–109, and Davidson, *Courtesans and Fishcakes*, 80–86. The idea of sex as "a savage and tyrannical master" is attributed to Sophocles in Plato's *Republic*, 329c.

Hippocrates initiated Greek medicine, the male body always served as the superior norm. Plato's *Timaeus* (90e–91d) speculates that a "first generation" of men existed before women came into being. Those first men "who lived cowardly or immoral lives were ... reborn in the second generation as women, and it was therefore at that point of time that the gods produced sexual love" by creating the different male and female genitals. Though fundamentally different (the male organ desiring to penetrate and emit sperm, the female to receive seed and bear children), each genital form constitutes a "living creature itself instinct with life" and with a will of its own. Just as "a man's genitals are naturally disobedient and self-willed, like a creature that will not listen to reason," so the womb of women "is a living creature within them which longs to bear children" and if "left unfertilized" too long "causes extreme unrest, strays about the body, ... and causes ... disorders of all kinds."[21] Women thus have a strong physical need for sex, even simply to stay healthy. This echoes Hippocratic doctrine that intercourse is essential for women's health by keeping the womb adequately moist and the blood sufficiently warm and fluid for easy menstrual flow.

Hippocrates argued that despite their essentially different sexual organs, when a man and a woman engage in intercourse each emits sperm (of both male and female kinds), and the sex of the child is determined by whether the stronger (male) sperm or the weaker (female) sperm predominates. Popular dogma of that time, however, denied the mother an active share in the child's heredity.[22] Aristotle later came to a similar conclusion, arguing that "male and female differ in respect of their *logos*," the former "possessing the principle of movement and generation" thus serving as the active cause, while the female is limited to "possessing that of matter" for the fetus. This is because she does not have sufficient heat to produce real sperm (an intensified condensed "residue derived from useful nourishment ... in its final form," which in humans is blood) but can provide only a weaker counterpart residue – menstrual blood – to nourish the embryo.[23] In defining the female as a defective or "deformed male," Aristotle recognized (unlike Hippocrates) the structural similarity of male and female reproductive organs, a view Galen later affirmed in defining the female sex organs as essentially structured like the male's but simply turned inside out and placed inside the body.

[21] I cite from H. D. P. Lee, trans., *Timaeus* (London: Penguin, 1965), 120.

[22] Skinner, *Sexuality*, 152.

[23] Aristotle, *Generation of Animals* (716a5–23, 726a26–28), trans. A. L. Peck (Cambridge, MA: Harvard University Press, 1943), 11, 89. One reason for seeing the sperm in terms of nourishment is the strong feeling of depleted energy after ejaculation. Here and elsewhere I use Bekker numbers to cite quotations from the works of Aristotle.

Such physiological theories impacted eroticism in different ways. Regarding the womb as a hungry receptacle demanding to be filled and fertilized problematically portrayed women as continually longing for genital penetration. Encouraging men to make advances, it also gave the Athenians a reason for locking up their women to protect family honor and purity of lineage from adulterous female insatiability. Woman's allegedly overwhelming need for intercourse and consequent diminished capacity to resist erotic passion can also explain why men bore far greater blame and punishment for adultery. Moreover, given Greek physiological doctrines concerning female insatiability and the significant depletion of energy and moisture involved in male ejaculation, men (defined as naturally hotter and dryer than women) were cautioned to carefully regulate their erotic encounters in order to preserve their strength and health, particularly in the hot summer months when the extra heat of sexual passion could easily render them far too hot and dry to be healthy. The belief that genitalia "will not listen to reason" further encouraged men to avoid sexual indulgence for the sake of mental health.

Greek medicine also explained the sexual deviations from its erotic gender norms, notably homosexual males who enjoyed being penetrated in anal intercourse. Their deviant taste was the product of both nature and nurture. Like women, they were considered defective or "deformed" males, in whom "the passages" carrying semen to the penis were obstructed, so that the seminal fluid instead "flows into the anus" and "collects there," rendering the anal areas extremely sensitive to erotic stimulation and "desir[ing] friction."[24] Unlike the penis, however, which can fully expel its semen with a powerful ejaculation, the anal area cannot and thus remains always sensitive to erotic arousal. Such men, therefore, become "insatiable like women," as they can never fully release their semen through ejaculation to free themselves from the erotic excitement it arouses. Even physiologically normal men capable of ejaculating through the penis can, however, through the habit of being penetrated anally, acquire this defective physiological tendency. Through repeated erotic stimulation of the anus, semen is habituated to flow in that direction rather than forward to the penis, so that the anal area is increasingly charged with erotic energy, becoming the center of sexual excitement and pleasure but never able to be fully satisfied. This makes the anally penetrated man increasingly a slave of passion and the

[24] The citations in this paragraph are from Aristotle, *Problems*, Book IV, trans. Robert Mayhew (Cambridge, MA: Harvard University Press, 2011), 167–171. Subsequent quotations from *Problems* are also taken from this edition.

effeminate "desire to be passive." Thus "the habit becomes more like a nature." For such reasons, there was considerable concern about males being subjected to anal sex even in societies that affirmed the culture of pederasty. Defenders of pederasty (like Plutarch in his life of Lycurgus) often explicitly denied that such love was physically consummated by penetrating the beloved, because such an act might bring shameful corruption to the youth in question whom the older lover should want to ennoble and protect rather than harm. Such concerns created an ambiguous terrain in which a richly complex *ars erotica* of male–male love could evolve.

Even within the same city-state, eroticism took different forms at different times through changing political institutions and ideologies. Pericles' citizenship law of 451 BCE to sway Athenians from their taste for costly foreign courtesans belongs to a general trend toward democratic ideology away from the extravagance that flourished under the aristocratic rule of the so-called tyrants and oligarchs. Such luxury included elaborate symposia, expensive courtesans and entertainments, fine clothing, and the courtship of the most attractive and noble young men. Athens had established itself as the wealthiest of the city-states through its close trade connections with the many Ionian settlements on the Asia Minor coast from which it imported costly goods of Persia and the East. As Thucydides writes, "the Athenians were among the very first of the Greeks to put aside their weapons and ... change to more luxurious ways."[25] But the series of Greek wars with Persia from 490 to 479 made such imports unpopular, just as it elevated admiration for self-sacrificing solidarity and hardihood in battle rather than self-indulgent refinement in fashionable delicacies.

Although Athens remained a society with very unequal distribution of wealth – so much so that Aristotle could describe democracy as "where the poor rule," the rising democratic ideology that all citizens were equal under law discouraged the highborn rich from flaunting their wealth and delicacy as much as they did during the period of aristocratic rule.[26] It negatively contrasted the notion of *habrosyne* (being delicate-minded or oriented toward luxurious refinement) to manly self-control and moderation (*sophrosyne*). Defeat by Sparta in the Peloponnesian War underlined the need for manly toughness. With its proud status as the Greek capital of art

[25] See Thucydides, trans. Charles Forster Smith, *History of the Peloponnesian War*, Books I and II (Cambridge, MA: Harvard University Press, 1919), 11.

[26] Aristotle, *Politics* 1280a1–4, in Richard McKeon, ed., *The Basic Works of Aristotle* (New York: Random House, 1968), 1187. Unless otherwise noted, further quotations from the works of Aristotle are taken from this edition. Individual works will hereafter be abbreviated as follows: *Nicomachean Ethics* (NE); *Politics* (Pol.); *Prior Analytics II* (PA2); *Rhetoric* (Rhet.).

and learning, Athens nonetheless maintained some of the refined aesthetic tastes and practices of earlier times, supported by its cadre of rich families that continued to enjoy their wealth in Athenian democracy and often used it to sponsor aesthetic goods for the public.

Turning from these diverse social factors to the specific aesthetics of Greek eroticism, we will concentrate on its Athenian expression while occasionally invoking other styles for contrast. Three reasons compel this focus. As Greece's acknowledged cultural capital, Athens provides the most ample, elaborate, and sophisticated collection of texts concerning erotic thought. These include not only poetry and drama, detailed legal discourse of various kinds (ranging from laws to arguments of prosecution and speeches of defense), and detailed philosophical discussions, but also the pictorial texts of painting and sculpture. The city's divine, name-giving patron is, after all, Athena, the goddess of wisdom and the arts.

Second, as a comparatively affluent society shaped by a taste for the pleasures of leisure and beauty, Athens enjoyed a culture with both the material resources and the aesthetic sensibilities for *ars erotica* to flourish, along with philosophy. Good philosophy, like good lovemaking, requires taking one's time, sharpening one's skills, and devoting careful, critical, imaginative attention to what one is doing in order to do it better and derive from it the most satisfaction for oneself and one's fellow participants. Taking the time to develop one's skills and carefully apply them in practice implies having sufficient leisure from other tasks and also a certain measure of material support to sustain such leisure and training.[27] Socrates repeatedly describes himself as a master of erotics, explaining this in terms of his philosophical skills in ways we soon examine.[28] Third, as the renowned hub of the arts, Athens offers the most aesthetically motivated and sophisticated expression of Greek culture, whose taste for beauty and artistry should find erotic expression as well. How then to define its aesthetics of eros?

[27] Dover (*Greek Homosexuality*, 150) notes that "pursuing the object of one's love" even in Athens, was "a luxury" that only the wealthier classes could pursue as "a diversion of time and effort from profitable work to an activity which, even if successful, will do nothing to feed and clothe the lover." He also cites a fragment from the dramatist Akhaios: "There is no eros of the beautiful in an empty stomach; Aphrodite is a curse to the hungry."

[28] See Plato's *Symposium* (198d) and Xenophon's *Symposium* (also translated as *The Dinner-Party*). In the latter Socrates provocatively prides himself on his "skill as a pimp" or erotic "procurer." See Xenophon, *The Dinner-Party* in *Conversations of Socrates*, 238, 249–251.

III AESTHETIC PRINCIPLES

1. We should begin with the Greek devotion to beauty. Eros serves Aphrodite not merely in her role as goddess of sexual love but in her personification of *beauty*, a notion that Athenian aristocracy tended to associate with nobility and virtue (construed as an ethical beauty of character and refinement that implied intelligence and integrity). The term *kalos kai agathos* ("beautiful and good") captured this idea and was used to commend excellent persons and the fine actions they performed. Indeed, to appreciate such virtue along with physical beauty constituted in itself an admirable quality, implying a certain degree of noble refinement.[29] The Greek proverb that "beautiful things are difficult" (*chalepa ta kala*) that Plato repeatedly invokes (in *Greater Hippias*, *Cratylus*, and *Republic*) could surely apply to the demanding ideal of combining superior virtue and beauty, since the desire to possess them both can create troubling tensions.

This proved particularly evident in pederastic love, demanding a delicate, aesthetically sensitive *ars erotica* of courtship and consummation. Sexually attracted to the beloved's youthful beauty but also to his noble character, the older *erastes* sought intimate physical contact with the *eromenos* yet had to pursue it by respecting and even improving his beloved's character and reputation. These could be ruined by the scandal of being anally penetrated (a mark of unmanly submission) or by the shame of desiring genital contact with the *erastes* (regarded as a mark of unbecoming feminine softness and sensuality in a young man). The *erastes*' aim of winning the beloved through attractive virtue, magnanimity, and loving concern would likewise be ruined by a vulgar expression of lust, since the *eromenos*, as a refined person of beauty, would not want to blemish his noble character either by submitting to such lust or by loving someone who violated the refined standard of *kalos kai agathos* by crude demands of genital contact. Negotiating this tricky ethical-aesthetic terrain required considerable sensitivity and good taste from both partners, as well as prudent confidentiality, especially if the *eromenos* chose to submit to intercourse. Other than the high road of sublimating physical desire by nonsexual expression of erotic love (a path urged and exemplified by Socrates) or instead maintaining a shamed secrecy about enjoying anal penetration, the most popular pederastic option was

[29] To capture this sense of refinement, translators in suitable contexts translate *kalon* as "fine" rather than "beautiful" and distinguish it from the merely pleasant or pleasurable. In *Greater Hippias* Plato refuses to see eating, drinking, and lovemaking as beautiful or fine in this sense of refinement, and even describes "making love" as "the foulest thing to be seen," although "it is most pleasant" (299a).

intercrural sex, which the Greeks called *diamerizein*, "doing [it] between the thighs." In pictorial representations of this position, "the *erastes* and *eromenos* stand facing one another; the *erastes* grasps the *eromenos* round the torso, bows his head on to or even below the shoulder of the *eromenos*, bends his knees and thrusts his penis between the *eromenos*'s thighs just below the scrotum," while the *eromenos* often looks away with downcast eyes to demonstrate a noble detachment from lustful desire and a charmingly tactful reluctance to see his admired older lover in its throes.[30]

Even high-minded Greek philosophers loved bodily beauty. Not only appreciating it in others, Socrates sought to improve his own beauty through dance and exercise. Although already old and famously ugly, he insisted that "it is a shame to let yourself grow old through neglect before seeing how you can develop the maximum beauty and strength of body."[31] In the refined circles he frequented, bodily beauty proved most irresistible when displayed by an intelligent young man of noble character, who would attract many *erastai* (as well as admirers of his own age) longing to win him as *eromenos*. Thus young Charmides (whom Socrates meets in the wrestling arena of a gymnasium) is surrounded by desiring devotees and praised for his "splendid face," a "body . . . so perfect," but also a "well-formed soul" (Char 154d). Even before Charmides poses a question, Socrates confesses to being inflamed by the beauty of the youth's bewitching "full gaze" and the sight of his intimate body parts. "I saw inside his cloak and caught on fire and was quite beside myself" (Char 155d).[32]

2. This emphasis on sight and the power of the gaze constitutes a second aesthetic feature of Greek eroticism. Vision was the chief aesthetic sense for appreciating beauty as well as the supreme cognitive sense. It can perceive from afar with greater clarity than other senses, thus allowing critical

[30] Dover, *Greek Homosexuality*, 98.

[31] Xenophon, "Memoirs of Socrates" (3:12), in *Conversations of Socrates*, 172.

[32] A later Hellenistic text describing pederasty notes that love's "ladder of pleasure . . . has for its first step that of sight" but then proceeds to give a recipe for physical seduction through stages of touch, beginning with only "the fingertips [whose] waves of enjoyment run into the whole body." After "achieving this, love attempts the third stage and tries a kiss, not making it a violent one at first, but lightly bringing lips close to lips so that they part before completing full contact, without leaving the slightest cause for suspicion." Then erotic desire "adjusts itself to the success gained and melts into ever more importunate embraces, sometimes gently opening the mouth and leaving neither hand idle . . . [T]he furtive hand wantonly glides down into the bosom and squeezes for a moment the breasts swollen past their normal size and makes a smooth sweep to grasp with the fingers the belly throbbing full spate with passion, and thereafter the early down of adolescence, and . . . makes a start with the thighs and, to quote the comic poet, 'strikes the target.'" See Pseudo-Lucian's *Erotes*, trans. M. D. Macleod, in *The Works of Lucian in Eight Volumes* (Cambridge, MA: Harvard University Press, 1967), vol. 8, 233.

distance and objective precision. Along with their many different words for looking, the ocular-centric Greeks shared "the common belief that the eyes actually emitted light rather than simply reflected it," making "vision a doubly active process."[33] As the emitted light from one's eyes touched the object it illuminated, one's "glance was always tactile . . . and always carried a libidinal supplement," positive or negative, intense or mild, "never neutral." Conversely, seen objects radiated their own visual energy. Beauty was thus an active force that attracted the eyes and could ensnare the person (or god) who perceived it. Inspired by sight, beauty-provoked desire was not simply a feeling in the body but "a force radiating from the object of affection."[34] We see this power in Aphrodite's gift of beauty to Pandora, which "shed grace upon her head and cruel longing and cares that weary the limbs."[35] Aphrodite's bewitching breast-band that Hera borrowed to deceive Zeus (*Iliad* 14.153–351) symbolized this power because its beauty radiated "all kinds of spell[:] . . . lovemaking, and yearning, and bantering persuasion, which steals away the mind of even those who think prudently."[36] For Plato "the eyes are the most beautiful part" of a body (Rep 420c), but also the "natural route to the soul" (*Phaedrus* 255d).

The capacity of the gaze both to capture and to be captured by beauty provides fertile options for artful techniques of exposure and concealment that add aesthetic zest and richness to erotic play. Averting the eyes can serve to protect one from being overwhelmed by the passionate sight of one's lover, but it can also serve as a seductive device of coquettish coyness (or unfeigned shyness that may be equally seductive). The famous love encounter of Aphrodite with the mortal Anchises displays both uses. After winning him with her stunning looks (though disguised in mortal mien so that "he should not be frightened when he took heed of her with his eyes"), "laughter-loving Aphrodite, with face turned away and lovely eyes downcast," seductively "crept to the well-spread couch" of lovemaking. When later awakened by the goddess in her divine form that "shone unearthly beauty," Anchises "saw the neck and lovely eyes of Aphrodite" and was so awed by her sight that "he turned his eyes aside another way, hiding his comely face with his cloak."[37] Sight's erotic power is not limited to attracting lovers; it extends to the consummation of lovemaking. The first three sections of Aristotle's alleged treatise on "Problems Concerning Sexual Intercourse" specifically

[33] Stewart, *Art, Desire, and the Body*, 19. [34] Ibid. [35] Hesiod, *Works and Days*, 7.

[36] Cited in Skinner, *Sexuality*, 24.

[37] The quotations are from Hymn V "To Aphrodite" (lines 53–198), from *The Homeric Hymns* in Evelyn-White, trans., *Hesiod*, 411, 413, 417, 419.

focus on the eyes because they "very noticeably cooperate in the act by contracting around the time of the emission of seed," which is hampered "when the eyes are cast down."[38]

The aesthetic play of sight and concealment to intensify one's erotic power was key to the seductive artistry of the hetaera, but also relevant to other erotic targets. Unlike Athenian wives and daughters, who were essentially confined to their home and thus hidden from view, the hetaera could show herself in public when she wished, and she could also show as much or as little of her body as she wished to the intimates she chose to associate with. This differentiated her clearly from prostitutes and flute girls, whose sexual services could be bought, and from a man's concubines and slaves, who were always available as owned. Such autonomy for the freedom-loving and competitive Athenians made the courtesan's company and sexual favors a hotly desired and contested prize that she would utilize to make her fortune and sustain her relative independence, which along with her beauty and other aesthetic graces was part of her charm. To magnify her appeal, the courtesan artfully strove to strike the right balance of exposure: revealing her beauty enough to render it renowned and widely desired, yet also sufficiently concealing it to make it highly prized and paid for.

Xenophon captures this erotic play of vision in his account of Socrates' encounter with a famous Athenian courtesan, "a beautiful woman called Theodote."[39] Impressed by the claim that "her beauty was beyond description" and aware that she allowed certain artists "to paint her picture," though carefully controlling how much "she let them see," Socrates sought to view her charms. Knowing that a courtesan like Theodote makes her fortune by men paying for the privilege of seeing her up close and being seen as her companion, Socrates employs the dialectics of vision to argue that she gets the better of the deal. The courtesan profits more in being seen (through increased renown and consequent income) than those who see her because they inevitably suffer from lingering desires for more intimate contact that her beauty arouses. Since the high-class hetaera's erotic power and aesthetic appeal derived as much from concealing her body as from judiciously revealing it, she would be loath to unveil her body in public, particularly her more intimate body parts.[40] The dramatic power of such exposure could

[38] Aristotle, *Problems*, Book IV.2, pp. 145–147.

[39] Xenophon, "Memoirs of Socrates," (3:11), in *Conversations of Socrates*, 167–192, quotations from 167–168.

[40] As courtesans grew older and less attractive, they often had to show and give more of themselves to make a living, sometimes stooping to explicit forms of prostitution.

be invoked, however, in cases of dire need, as in the famous trial of Phryne. Perhaps the most renowned of *megalomisthoi* ("high-fee") hetaerae, she posed for celebrated artists yet was very careful of not showing too much of her astounding beauty. Allegedly, she "was even more beautiful in those parts not exposed to view. Because of that it was not easy to see her naked. She always wore a little chiton clinging to her flesh and did not use the public baths." However, when Phryne's trial defense seemed doomed to failure, her lawyer "led Phryne herself into view, tore off her tunic-layers, [and] exposed her breasts," a sight that "filled the jurors with religious awe and stopped them from condemning to death Aphrodite's representative and attendant."[41] The artistry of this rare, dramatic disclosure of hidden beauty combined so much aesthetic and erotic power as to sway the standard all-male Athenian jury.

3. Eros for the Greeks is distinctively aesthetic in that it inspires art and is reciprocally served by artistic fashioning. The delights of lovemaking involve aesthetic pleasures of meaning and form, not just raw sensation. As Euripides claimed, "Eros surely teaches a poet, even the one who was previously uninspired."[42] Sophocles was notorious for the love of boys, which seems to have stirred his creative talents, and Sappho likewise testifies to erotic desire as stimulating poetic creation. It was no less inspiring in the plastic arts. Phryne had two famous artist-lovers whose passion for her was expressed in celebrated works of art. "It was from her," reports Hermippus of Smyrna, "that Apelles [a renowned fourth-century painter] painted his likeness of Aphrodite coming out of the sea."[43] She likewise inspired another lover, the sculptor Praxiteles, to create one of the two most celebrated and influential works of Greek statuary, his *Aphrodite of Knidos*. Allegedly, he not only modeled it on Phryne but also gifted her a statue of Eros to gain and keep her love, attaching the poignant epigram: "Praxiteles portrayed with precision the Love which he suffered, hammering out the archetype from his own heart. To Phryne he gave me [i.e., Eros/Love], in return for me."[44] Art thus serves erotic desire not only by expressing it but by inducing it, through its aesthetic effects, in the beloved. Indeed, according to one story, the Phryne-modeled statue of *Aphrodite of Knidos* proved so erotically enticing that a young man from a decent family fell ardently in love with it and hid himself one night in the temple that housed the sculpture so that he could sexually enjoy it. Engaging the Phryne/Aphrodite figure from behind, his

[41] Cited in Davidson, *Courtesans and Fishcakes*, 134.

[42] Cited in Calame, *The Poetics of Eros*, 199.

[43] Cited in Davidson, *Courtesans and Fishcakes*, 134.

[44] Cited in ibid., 121.

loving left a dark "mark on one thigh [of its otherwise unblemished 'brightness of ... marble'] like a stain on a dress," before he totally vanished in shame, presumably through suicide.[45] The Greek proclivity to associate desirably beautiful bodies with beautiful sculptures of bodies also ran in the other direction, where living beauties were described in terms of statuary, as when Socrates remarks how the many lovers of the beautiful young Charmides "all gazed at him as if he were a statue" (Char 154d).

The practice of symposia exemplifies the crucial role of arts in Athenian *ars erotica.* Music and dance were essential elements for creating an erotic mood. Musicians and dancers, both male and female, functioned not simply to arouse the symposiasts' erotic desire but often also to provide its consummation. Hence the flute girls' reputation for prostitution. Plato's *Symposium* is uniquely chaste in excluding any such sensuality from the outset as its participants "dispense with the flute-girl," "refrain from [the customary] heavy drinking," and instead devote themselves to the entertainment of improvisational oratory and "conversation" about love (Sym 176d–e). Oratory, however, was itself a cherished Athenian art and (like music) prized for its aesthetic powers of persuasion, while Peitho, goddess of persuasion and charming eloquence, was the standard companion of Aphrodite and Eros. For cultured Athenians, beauty of language and thought possessed considerable powers of erotic arousal, as Alcibiades indicates at the end of this dialogue in confessing his passion for Socrates (222b).

Although similarly focused on intellectual conversation rather than heavy drinking and sexual acts, Xenophon's *Symposium* (sometimes translated as *The Dinner-Party*) highlights the role of music and dance for inspiring erotic desire in the typical symposium. Through the artistic efforts of the party's Syracusan dancing master (whose team includes a flute girl, another girl "who was an acrobatic dancer, and a very attractive boy who both played the lyre and danced extremely well" and slept "every night" with the master), the symposiasts avow that, like wine, "this combination of youthful beauty and music ... awakens thoughts of love" (Xen 230, 235, 249). After leading his drinking companions in song, Socrates develops an argument that noble pederastic love (in contrast to vulgar Aphrodite) will "set love of the mind above physical gratification" (Xen 262). Nonetheless, the dialogue ends by dramatically vindicating the compelling beauty of heterosexual lovemaking as presented in an entertainment choreographed by the Syracusan in which the two attractive young dancers play Dionysus and Ariadne in amorous

[45] The story appears in Pseudo-Lucian's *Erotes*, in *The Works of Lucian in Eight Volumes*, vol. 8, 167–177, quotations from 173.

exchange. Seeing that the performing pair were not simply pretending to embrace but "actually kissing with their lips," the symposiasts "were all carried away with excitement as they watched," and when they "eventually saw them in each other's arms and going off as if to bed, the bachelors swore that they would get married, and the married men mounted their horses and rode away to their own wives with the same end in view" (Xen 266). Here the choreographed artistry of erotic dramatization stirs the desire for its real-life enactment.

4. Ever since Kant, the aesthetic has been defined by its contrast with the practical or instrumental. Properly understood, the idea is not that aesthetic practices have no use but that their primary value resides in the pleasures of the experience itself rather than in serving as a means to some external, practical function. Although Greek aesthetic theory is remote from Kant's austere demand for disinterested appreciation devoid of sensual delight, Athenian eroticism is distinctively aesthetic in highlighting pleasure over pure functionality.[46] Recall the remark that while wives function as instruments for "producing heirs" and protecting "household property," "hetaeras we keep for pleasure."[47] This valued pleasure cannot be equated with the mere sensual satisfaction of genital release, which the wives could normally supply. Good-looking wives could further supply pleasures of beauty, though we find condemnations of their using makeup and other accessories to heighten their allure, as that was seen as ignoble deception unbefitting their role.[48] Sex with one's wife was aesthetically hampered in other ways. Dictated by duty (Solon's law requiring it "not less than three times a month"), it was also limited by the wife's defining sexual role of procreation. Because there existed many religion-inspired or medically endorsed restrictions regarding the proper seasons, days, times, conditions, and actions for intercourse that were designed to generate healthy progeny, lovemaking with one's wife was seriously constrained in its aesthetic freedom and variety.[49]

[46] See Immanuel Kant, *The Critique of Judgment*, trans. J. C. Meredith (Oxford: Oxford University Press, 1986), 65. For a critique of Kant's ideal of disinterestedness from an embodied, pragmatist perspective, see my *Pragmatist Aesthetics* (Oxford: Blackwell, 1992).

[47] Davidson, *Courtesans and Fishcakes*, 73.

[48] Xenophon, "The Estate-Manager," section 10, in *Conversations of Socrates*, 325.

[49] Plato gives a sense of such restrictions needed to produce "progeny of the best and finest quality" by requiring that the husband approach his marital lovemaking in terms of "the task of begetting children [and] with a sense of responsibility" and thus avoid "drunken relaxation" and "raging passion," which will "produce absolutely degenerate creatures." See Plato, *Laws* VI, 775b–e; 783e.

Of course, if a wife proved insufficiently attractive or erotically unwilling, a man could always use his concubines or slaves to gratify his sexual urges, as they were responsible for attending to his everyday bodily needs. Prostitutes were also readily available as inexpensive means for sexual satisfaction of all kinds.

The courtesan, in contrast, provided distinctively aesthetic pleasures. Beyond the charms of her physical beauty, conversational skills, and artistic talents, she offered the entertainments of refined courtship and the playful pursuits of seductive persuasion and amorous conquest that the highly cultured and competitive Athenians relished. Because the hetaera's highly prized favors and affection were not for sale but had to be earned through artful pursuit and persuasion, and because she had to be won in agonistic rivalry with other suitors, the conquest (and keeping) of a hetaera provided Athenian gentlemen with an entertaining erotic sport that appealed to their competitive spirit. Not only an attractive challenge in herself, she provided a site where one's own refined excellence and erotic mastery could be tested against other men's. One's victories in such erotic tournaments (besides the sensual, affective, and aesthetic delights of lovemaking) would yield the further joys of proud achievement, heightened reputation, and enhanced self-esteem.

The same exciting drama of competitive struggle for uncertain victory enriched the aesthetic value of pederastic love. Like the hetaera's, the loving favors of the *eromenos* were not for sale but only awarded as a deferred and uncertain recompense for gifts the lover bestowed. The lover's gifts included presents, but more important was the rewarding display of virtue, tactful devotion, and cultured refinement through which he bested other suitors while ennobling his beloved through such exemplary character and conduct. The lover's taste was tested not only in his choice of beloved but also in the refined care with which he pursued his desire: what physical favors he asked for and when. The beloved's taste and artful grace could likewise be displayed not only in his choice of lover but in the degree and timing of his granting of physical favors to the lover he accepted and the elegant way he dealt with devoted admirers he rejected. The complexities of navigating these contested, conflicted, and ethically ambiguous waters offered rich intricacies of meaning and artfulness that refined Athenians found intensely alluring. It is no wonder that their *ars erotica* focused on high-class hetaerae and noble youth. Such love could claim aesthetic superiority in eschewing the natural instrumental function of lovemaking as procreation that humans shared with common beasts and that was identified with the vulgar Aphrodite. But pederasty was also denounced precisely for its "unnatural" acts and artificial pleasures, ultimately resulting in its loss of prestige in Hellenistic and Roman culture.[50]

5. With its concern for beauty and taste and its privileged foci of pederasty and courtesans, what did Athens find erotically most attractive? That which made a youth most aesthetically desirable was a harmonious mixture of natural bodily beauty and culturally acquired skills and virtues. In terms of boys' physical charms, Solon conventionally praises "the sweetness of their thighs and their lips," while Demosthenes lauds his beloved in terms that integrate body and soul: "the hue of your flesh, by virtue of which your limbs and your whole body are rendered resplendent," and the eyes whose beautiful "glance" displays the "fine qualities" of "your character." That character is one in which kindness and dignity, gentleness and courage, and other seemingly conflicting virtues are "all . . . properly harmonized" in a "personality [that] "enhances in your every action the superb comeliness of your body."[51]

Sculpture can give us a sense of the Greek ideal of male beauty, which was distinctively modeled on youthfulness and balance, as aptly exemplified in the famous *Doryphoros* statue by Polykleitos: "The epitome of Measure (*to metron*) or the Mean (*to meson*), it adopted a posture that was intermediate between rest and movement." Presenting "a virile youth . . . on the brink of manhood," its "pose was rigorously worked out so that each weight-bearing limb or muscle was placed in diagonal opposition to a relaxed one; its body was perfectly proportioned" with all the parts properly related "to one another and to the whole."[52] The youth's calmly "neutral expression and slightly lowered and averted head" strikes the golden mean between "macho

[50] Pederasty, argues Plato in Laws 636b–c, has "corrupted the natural pleasures of sex, which are common to man and beast"; both "homosexual intercourse and lesbianism" are condemned as "unnatural crimes" that are "committed because men and women cannot control their desire for pleasure."

[51] For Solon, see Foucault's citation from Plutarch's *Dialogue on Love*, in Michel Foucault, *The History of Sexuality, vol. 3: The Care of the Self* , trans. Robert Hurley (New York: Pantheon, 1986), 201; hereafter HS3; and for Demosthenes, "The Erotic Essay," in N. D. Dewitt and N. J. DeWitt, trans., *Demosthenes: Funeral Speech, Erotic Essay, Exordia and Letters* (Cambridge, MA: Harvard University Press, 1949) 51, 53, online at http://perseus.uchicago.edu/perseus-cgi/citequery3.pl?dbname=GreekFeb2011&getid=1&query=Dem.%2061. Dover suggests that the apparent preference for a tanned hue reflects the manliness of outdoor life of athletics (*Greek Homosexuality*, 69). Beardlessness (as well as lack of torso and pubic hair) was another expression of the youthful ideal of Greek beauty, so even fully adult heroes were typically portrayed as beardless and without body hair (71).

[52] Stewart, *Art, Desire, and the Body*, 88. Greek painters shared the aesthetic ideal of youth, and, as Dover argues, "their adoption of the ideal youthful penis as the standard for men, heroes, and gods" is one item in their general tendency to "youthen" everything (*Greek Homosexuality*, 135).

arrogance" and "meek" compliance to the erotic gaze; his undersized penis (typical and valorized in Greek art for suggesting both youthfulness and sexual self-control) is likewise balanced by his body's "mature muscularity" that demonstrates the youth's power to resist domination and sustain his admirable manly autonomy, which includes the ethical virtue of self-mastery.[53] His muscles symbolize both physical and mental strength because their size and hardness are products not only of nature but of cultural training requiring knowledge and self-discipline, in contrast to the penis whose hardening growth instead symbolizes man's lack of self-control.

Praxiteles' sculpture of the naked Aphrodite (modeled on the beautiful Phryne) suggests the ideal aesthetics of the female form. Tall, with long limbs "gracefully proportioned, her flesh soft and yielding," with ample, "well-delineated" buttocks and a rounded belly, "her lips slightly parted in a smile, and her eyes shining, clear, and melting," she still manages to "maintain her distance and dignity as a goddess" by her confident, yet modest posture in which her hand calmly shields her genital area in which there is neither any pubic hair nor even the sign of a vulva.[54] In contrast to the masculine tan, white skin seems to be the female aesthetic ideal.

Aesthetic pleasures of erotic experience are not limited to perceptions of the desired object but include the inner feelings of the desiring lover. If these pleasures are typically commingled with painful feelings of unease, disappointment, or anxiety from lack of adequate contact with the beloved, then such nuanced blending only enriches their aesthetic quality and meaning through the spice of contrast rather than the cloying monotony of satisfaction. These "mixtures," Plato contends, procure such intense pleasures in "the more profligate and mindless" person that "he calls them supreme" (*Philebus* 47a–c). If Sappho famously described eros as ambivalently "bittersweet," this did not deter a later female poet she inspired from claiming "nothing is sweeter than desire: All other delights are second."[55] Though Plato more negatively characterized erotic desire (along with the appetites of hunger and thirst) as a disturbing, irritating lack (*Gorgias*, *Republic*, *Philebus*), he nonetheless recognized in *Phaedrus* its positive power to warm and delight while growing wings for the soul to rise higher. If Plato's *Republic* (329c) quotes Sophocles as praising old age for freeing him from the tyranny

[53] Stewart, *Art, Desire, and the Body*, 92. [54] Ibid., 99, 100, 101, 107.

[55] This is the first line of Poem 1, by the Hellenistic (ca. third century BCE) poet Nossis, cited in Ellen Greene, ed., *Women Poets in Ancient Greece and Rome* (Norman: University of Oklahoma Press, 2005), 125.

of sexual desire for women (he anyway apparently preferred boys), then Mimnermus poetically presents the more common (and perhaps more honest) view in which old age is "painful" because of its diminished erotic energy and action that makes one sadly "hateful to boys, contemptible to women."[56] Inner feelings of sexual desire as proprioceptively sensed in erection express a virile power associated with youth and vigor that older men seem reluctant to abandon, perhaps because it forms part of their identity. Moreover, for the agonistic Greek male, the greater the felt force of erotic desire, the greater the pleasure one could feel in mastering it. Ancient Greek dogma, however, claimed that women's inner sexual enjoyment far exceeded men's, apparently because their physiological need for it was greater. The mythical prophet Tiresias, who experienced life in both sexes, claimed (when asked to resolve a debate between Zeus and Hera) that women's sexual pleasure was nine times greater than men's – an answer for which Hera struck him blind.[57]

6. Besides the pleasurable aesthetic perceptions from the external senses and inner bodily feelings, Greek eroticism expressed itself aesthetically through its stylization of lovemaking as part of an art of living aimed at a beautiful, memorable life, guided by the aesthetic-ethical idea of *kalos-kai-agathos*. Michel Foucault repeatedly makes this point in contrasting Greek sexual theory to Christianity. Rather than a rigid code of prohibitions, Greek erotic thought pursued "an aesthetics of existence" involving "formal principles in the use of pleasures, in the way one distributed them, in the limits one observed, in the hierarchy one respected."[58] Its aim was to ensure that the "moral value" of one's life "took on the brilliance of a beauty" of admirable, harmonious order achieved through "moderation and restraint" in sexual behavior along with other practices. Rather than being dictated by strict commandments, such "sexual moderation was an exercise of freedom that took form in self-mastery" through one's choice of shaping oneself in the light of different ways of regulating one's erotic behavior, one's particular way of "stylizing" it in terms of different possible "stylizations." This choice included one's selection of the objects of desire, the ways one pursued those desires, and the degree, frequency, or form in which one consummated, sublimated, or restrained them (HS2 89, 90, 93).

[56] Skinner, *Sexuality*, 58.

[57] For this myth, see Apollodorus, *The Library*, Book III.vi, 5–7 (Cambridge, MA: Harvard University Press, 1921), vol. 2, 361–367, where Tiresias claims, "if the pleasures of love be reckoned at ten, men enjoy one and women nine" (367).

[58] Michel Foucault, *The History of Sexuality, vol. 2: The Use of Pleasure*, trans. R. Hurley (Vintage: New York, 1986), 89; hereafter HS2.

Foucault provides detailed descriptions of various erotic choices and the criteria governing them but does not explain what makes these choices specifically aesthetic. The mere use of formal principles or stylization does not entail distinctively aesthetic forms or styles; nor does mere orderly or moderate behavior. We can agree with Foucault that self-mastery served as an "aesthetic value" for the Greeks because it rendered a person "able to give one's conduct the form that would assure one of a name meriting remembrance" (HS2 93). But admirably memorable conduct can express itself in deeds or works that are not distinctively aesthetic, such as acts of military heroism or political leadership. We can, however, adopt Foucault's general notion of formal principles to suggest an aesthetic feature of Greek eroticism related to a classical principle of aesthetic form: unity in variety. If Foucault emphasizes sexual moderation and restraint that points to unity and order, while likewise defining Greek "aesthetics of existence" in terms of a diminution or "rarefaction of sexual activity" (HS2 92), then we should conversely highlight also the rich pluralism of Greek erotic expression. Embracing both heterosexual and homosexual love, marital and nonmarital sex, genital and nongenital lovemaking, the Greeks endorsed a multiplicity of erotic venues (symposium, brothel, home, and street) along with a variety of sexual positions. Even confining ourselves to coital postures – omitting the very popular forms of intercrural and anal sex and the less favored practice of oral sex (considered particularly degrading to the one performing it) – we find a diversity of approved positions (that, when commercially offered, commanded varying prices). Aristophanes, in *Frogs*, already notes a courtesan who seems to have mastered twelve of them.[59] There were apparently numerous Greek sex manuals describing the various sex positions as well as methods of seduction, but they have not survived, apart from a few fragments. The alleged authors of the most famous of these manuals are (perhaps legendary) women: Philaenis of Samos, whose scant surviving fragments concern seduction and kisses but not coital postures, and Elephantis, a courtesan based in Hellenistic Egypt about whom nothing remains but her reputation.[60]

Besides the familiar missionary position, three other coital postures are worth noting. Two of the most popular involve penetration from behind. The *kubda* ("bent forward") position where the woman stands or stoops

[59] Aristophanes speaks metaphorically of her "twelve-stringed music," line 1328. See also Davidson, *Courtesans and Fishcakes*, 118.

[60] For more details on these fragments and on Elephantis, see Dominic Montserrat, *Sex and Society in Graeco-Roman Egypt* (London: Kegan Paul, 1966), 113–114.

bending forward – typically with her head lowered and her hands resting on the ground or on some other stationary object (such as a piece of furniture) to give her stability – seems to be the most common and inexpensive.[61] The *lorda* ("bent backward") position involves her leaning back against the man's chest to stabilize herself while he is thrusting. For the Greeks, these rear-entry positions had the advantage of expressing the man's dominance while presenting a prominent stabilized target for penetration along with an accessible anal alternative that was best for contraception. A third position known as *kelēs*, or "racehorse," in which the woman straddles and rides the recumbent man, was apparently highly desired by men but was also the most expensive. If Greek machismo might discourage men from being on the bottom, their aristocratic ideology that prized leisure over labor could counter that concern. A man could then demonstrate his penetrative power while reclining and letting the woman perform the labor of thrusting. In convincing a woman to do this work (thus overcoming the dictates of her modesty and the female ideology of being passive in sex), the man could highlight his power by showing his domination even when recumbently "ridden" by her.

7. The coital metaphor of riding a racehorse suggests the imaginative play of lovemaking, which includes pretending, staging, and the acting-out of roles. This aspect of play, pretense, artifice, and mise-en-scène is a key dimension of Greek eroticism that further links it to aesthetics and the fine arts. We noted the feigned ritual abduction of the bride in the Spartan marriage ceremony and the similarly staged pederastic abduction in Cretan initiation rites to manhood. But the symposia, courtesans, and pederasty of Athenian culture provided a far broader field for imaginative role-playing and games of courtship that could enrich eroticism with aesthetic qualities of drama, suspense, and creativity. Drawing on Kenneth Dover, Foucault describes Athenian pederastic practice as a "whole social game" involving conventional roles (for both the *erastes* and the young *eromenos*) and general "rules of conduct" but without any rigidly fixed prescriptions of behavior. Being "a game that was 'open'" in many ways with respect to precise strategies and outcomes, pederastic courtship encouraged imaginative strategies and involved "a whole game of delays and obstacles" that added the spice of variety, struggle, and uncertainty with respect to which sexual favors would be granted, when, and even where (HS2 196–197). The courtship of courtesans was likewise an open game of imaginative acting in which

[61] I take the three positions discussed in this paragraph from Davidson, *Courtesans and Fishcakes*, 118.

suitors offered gifts as tokens of true love rather than payment for sex, while the courtesan pretended to grant her sexual favors out of pure affection and friendship. Socrates ironically highlights this notion of "friends" and their "generous" gifts in his dialogue with the courtesan Theodote, while also exploring her artifice of heightening suitors' desire by the play of deferral and of combining modesty with hints of her willingness to grant them sexual satisfaction.[62] Playful stratagems of staged seduction were practiced also in casual encounters, as when Sophocles succeeds in kissing the handsome boy serving him wine by asking the boy to blow away a piece of straw from his wine cup but then bringing the cup close to his own mouth so that their lips would come very close together.[63]

IV TENSIONS BETWEEN EROS AND PHILOSOPHY

The intimate linkage of eros with seductive artistry and deceptive enchantment posed a problem for Greek philosophers, particularly for those who could not eschew erotic beauty despite their paramount commitment to truth and virtue. We find this tension prefigured in the mythological background that helped shape the philosophical tradition, including its key maxim "know thyself" inscribed on Apollo's Temple at Delphi. As the god of truth and knowledge, Apollo inspires philosophy, but Greek myth further depicts him as the enemy of Eros. After insulting the love god's archery ability, Apollo pays the price by being pierced by an arrow of love for Daphne, who (pierced instead by an arrow of loathing) flees and ultimately eludes him by being transformed into a tree. Until he fell victim to Eros's arrows, Apollo had been completely chaste like his twin sister Artemis, who along with two other virginal goddesses are said to be the only individuals (human or divine) able to resist Aphrodite's seductive powers of love and beauty. Athena is one of those chaste defiers of eros, who, as goddess of wisdom and patron deity of Athens, can serve as the goddess of Greek philosophy.

Mythology also links love's beguiling persuasive powers with Aphrodite's divine female attendant Peitho (goddess of persuasion) and with Pandora (the primordial seductress of mankind), while philosophy defines itself by combatting the sophistic wiles of persuasive rhetoric with the contrasting ideal of honestly pursuing truth. Philosophy, then, must struggle either to reject the powers of erotic beauty, desire, and persuasion or to reconcile

[62] Xenophon, *Memoirs of Socrates*, 167–171.

[63] See Davidson, *Courtesans and Fishcakes*, 166–167.

them somehow with the rational, truth-seeking values that it champions. The figure of Socrates is so fascinating because he embodies the tension of holding those opposites together. Portraying himself as philosophy's rationalist champion against sophistry but also as a "master of the art of love" whose skills of compelling argumentation match sophistry's powers of persuasion, Socrates describes even Eros himself as a spirit who in seeking "the beautiful and the good" is "always a philosopher" but also a seductive "enchanter" and "sophist" (Sym 198d, 203d).[64]

If its bewitching power poses such a challenge to philosophy's rational agenda, why not simply reject erotic desire? How could Socrates (and some others) see it as philosophy's ally in the quest for wisdom, albeit an often problematic one? The answer, I believe, lies in recognizing the enormous educational potential of erotic love, not only through its aesthetic pleasures of form, meaning, and quality but also for its intense motivational force that amazingly amplifies our energies to expand our experience and transcend our limits. If biblical Hebrew suggests this cognitive connection by using the verb "know" to indicate coitus, then ancient Greek evokes it through the verb *mnaomai* (μνάομαι), which means not only being mindful or turning one's mind to something or to someone but also "to woo for one's bride" or to court a lover.[65] Like the quest for knowledge, eros implies a self that intently seeks to reach beyond itself to grasp another. Both these desires express a mindful, dynamic yearning for something outside the self that provides (if only implicitly) self-knowledge of its own limits and deficiency as well as its feelings of desire. Both the cognitive and the erotic quest reflect *wanting* in the dual senses of desire and perceived lack.

The convergence of eros and self-knowledge finds picturesque expression in the famous fable of love that Aristophanes recounts in Plato's *Symposium* (189e–193a). Humans originally comprised three sexes (all male, all female, and of both sexes), and each individual was twice of what humans are today in terms of limbs, faces, genitals, ears, and so on. Doubled in this way, they could look forward and backward and cartwheel rapidly in any direction.

[64] The last three quotations in the sentence from 203d are from the well-known translation by Benjamin Jowett, http://classics.mit.edu/Plato/symposium.html. Socrates, a master at holding dualities in productive tension, allegedly had two wives, and some sources report he had them simultaneously. See Diogenes Laertius, "Socrates," trans. R. D. Hicks, in *Diogenes Laertius: Lives of Eminent Philosophers* (Cambridge, MA: Harvard University Press, 1925), vol. 1, 157; hereafter DL1.

[65] Liddell and Scott, *An Intermediate Greek-English Lexicon* (Oxford: Oxford University Press, 1997), 516.

To diminish their threatening power, an anxious Zeus cut each of these primordial humans in half, giving us our now familiar bodily form. Erotic desire, Aristophanes claims, is the craving of each (now halved) human to find and unite with his or her primordial counterpart. The fable further explains the diversity of gender preference. As the originally androgynous humans seek their true counterpart in heterosexual connections, those humans who were primordially all-male yearn to unite with men, while the primordially all-female seek lesbian union. The target of erotic desire thus tells a person what one (primordially) is and how one best completes oneself. "Know thyself" here clearly means know your desire. But desire's unruly passion risks blinding us from other important dimensions of self-knowledge that may require stricter self-mastery, while focusing on the self's primordial past distracts us from efforts to improve its present and future state.

The difficulty of harmonizing eros with philosophy is compounded by at least three oppositional tensions in the very notion of erotic love that are reflected in the variant Greek terminologies and mythologies that shaped it. First is the tension between erotic desire as the lust for simply physical pleasure (something that humans share with animals) and, in contrast, eros as a craving also for the pleasures of form and beauty, including the beauty of virtue. If even beasts enjoy the pleasures of sex (*ta aphrodisia*), then advocates of eros distinguish a higher form of erotic love, one that is more spiritual, meaningful, and discriminating in beauty, though it need not eschew sensuous delights. Frequently invoked to promote pederasty, such love is linked specifically with Eros (a male god) or Heavenly Aphrodite (born directly from male genitals without any female lover) in order to distance it from the base carnality of Aphrodite Pandemos, which aims at the commonplace pleasures of heterosexual reproduction rather than the edifying beauty of virtuous refinement through erotically inspired cultivation of character. If pederasty faced recurrent criticism for being contrary to nature, then its divergence from the ordinary, animal reproductive functions necessary for natural life elevated it with the mark of cultural distinction and creative freedom. This line of reasoning frequently occurs in arguments for same-sex lovemaking from antiquity to today, from Plato to Foucault.[66] The

[66] For a critical somaesthetic account of Foucault's aesthetic advocacy of consensual homosexual S&M, see the first chapter ("Somaesthetics and Care of the Self: The Case of Foucault") in Richard Shusterman, *Body Consciousness: A Philosophy of Mindfulness and Somaesthetics* (Cambridge: Cambridge University Press, 2008), 15–48.

contrast between sensual pleasures biologically generated from reproductive drives versus other erotic pleasures suggests a corollary distinction between sex that serves the practical function of procreation versus eroticism that can be appreciated in itself and for its specific aesthetic values, even if these values can find their own pragmatic justifications.

A second tension concerns whether erotic love is narrowly oriented toward satisfactions of the individual's own desires or whether it is also significantly other-directed in the sense of being guided by an active concern for the welfare of one's object of desire. Recognizing that the desired object is a human subject worthy of respectful care and cultivation, this latter form of loving desire includes the desire to be desired or appreciated in return through the beloved's recognition of the lover's noble expression of care. Such attention and reciprocal affection affords both lover and beloved greater self-knowledge and self-realization as they affectively reach beyond themselves. Of course, even selfish erotic desire is always directed toward some other individual, but this "other" is seen merely as an instrumental commodity for one's sexual satisfaction rather than a human subject worthy of respectful care and whose happiness forms part of the lover's desire. Greek myth suggests divine exemplars of these different attitudes. If Zeus shows his love for the boy Ganymede by granting him eternal youth and divine immortality, then Aphrodite demonstrates a selfish erotic desire in disguising herself as human to seduce young Anchises, then leaving him wasted from the power of her lovemaking and eventually crippling him for mentioning it. Such gender-marked myths clearly encourage the ideal of pederasty along with the blight of misogyny.

A third tension is between erotic love as irrational enchantment and more reasonable, prudent desire. Profoundly aware of love's power to radically disturb the mind and divert the will from the path of virtue, Greek philosophers frequently associated eros with irrationality and even madness. Plato's *Republic* (403a, 329c) describes sex as the maddest of pleasures and a tyrannical master, although his *Phaedrus* (244a) describes erotic love more positively as a divine madness, or *mania*, a heavenly inspiration generated by beauty that his *Symposium* indeed portrays as philosophy's motivating spiritual force. Should one's choices in love be thoroughly guided by reason or instead left to the powers of passion? If philosophers sometimes diverged on this issue, it is partly because they differed on whether erotic mania was intrinsically deceptive and damaging or whether its crazed enthusiasm that overwhelms self-regarding self-control could instead awaken us beneficially to higher values and realities beyond ordinary rational self-interest.

Plato and Aristotle

These tensions find clear expression in the stark contrast between Plato's lyrically positive accounts of pederastic desire as a divinely inspired stimulus toward spiritual development (in such dialogues as the *Symposium* and *Phaedrus*) and his later condemnations of same-sex lovemaking in the *Laws*. The latter portrays pederasty as despicably immoral, crudely physical, unhealthily unnatural, and "unholy," because it diverts sexual energy from realizing the only immortality nature provides human kind: "immortality by procreation" (*Laws* 636b–c, 721c–d, 783a–d). Plato here brands sexual desire as an unruly, sensual, unreasonable passion that selfishly diverts love from more social expression, including genuine care for the beloved. By simply enjoying the beloved's body "like a luscious fruit ... without showing any respect for the beloved's character and disposition," it stands in contrast to true love, which is instead a "desire of soul for soul" in which physical desire counts "for very little" and is thus satisfied with chaste gazing, while regarding genital lust as "outrageous" (*Laws* 837c–d). Plato thus recommends laws confining lovemaking to heterosexual acts aimed at procreation with spouses, forbidding "not only homosexual relations ... but also the sowing of seeds on rocks and stone where it will never take root" or in "any female 'soil' in which we'd be sorry to have the seed develop." Hence, "no one will dare to have relations with any respectable citizen woman except his own wedded wife, or sow illegitimate and bastard seed in courtesans, or sterile seed in males in defiance of nature." Restricting sex to marital lovemaking usefully "tends to check the raging fury of the sexual instinct" while also inspiring men's "affection for their own wives" (*Laws* 838e–839b, 841d).[67]

We can conveniently map other Greek (and Roman) philosophical approaches to eros by their positions regarding these three tensions. Aristotle, for instance, regards love's sensual dimension as inferior, identifying its desire with the natural appetites of hunger and thirst that demand reasonable satisfaction but hold dangers of excess and self-indulgence. Closely linked (like those other appetites) to the more primitive sense of touch, the

[67] Plato's *Laws* thus clearly departs from the radical, eugenic, sexual views of his *Republic*. There in the governing class of guardians, we should have "the women exercising naked in the palestras with the men," since they also share in the duties of the guardian men (452a–b). Moreover, "all these [guardian] women are to belong in common to all the men" (guardians), and "the children too are to be possessed in common, so that no parent will know his own offspring or any child his parent," and "the best men must have sex with the best women as frequently as possible" to ensure the best offspring for the state (457c–d, 459d–e).

physical pleasure of lovemaking is "brutish" because "it attaches to us not as men but as animals" (NE 1118a26, 1118b2). Erotic desire, however, remains a more complicated, sophisticated, cognitive craving because its delights are also intimately related to "the form" and sight of the beloved and imaginative acts of remembering (NE 1167a3–8, 1171b29–33; Rhet. 1370b19–25).

Concerning the second tension, Aristotle highlights the importance of other-directed concern for the beloved, arguing that a true lover would rather have the beloved's loving regard than the physical delights of actual intercourse. "To receive affection then is preferable in love to sexual intercourse.... And if it is most dependent on receiving affection, then this is its end. Intercourse then either is not an end at all or is an end relative to the further end, the receiving of affection" (PA2 68b3–5). An Aristotelian text (now believed to be written by his student), implores the husband to regard his wife "with unstinting care" as "the partner of his life and parenthood," recognizing that a wife "is best honored when she sees that her husband is faithful to her, and has no preference for another woman." A man "of sound mind" will not therefore "have random intercourse with women" and "should approach his wife in honorable wise, full of self-restraint and awe; ... suggesting only such acts as are themselves lawful and honorable" (*Oeconomica* Bk3.1–3).[68] Aristotle apparently practiced such concern, not only for his wife, who predeceased him at an early age (after giving him a daughter), but also for his concubine, who bore him a son. Regarding marriage as essential for the proper generation and rearing of children (and thus for the survival of the household and the political state), Aristotle offers some eugenically instrumental views concerning "who are fit to marry" and at "what age" and "season of the year," and also regarding the forms of "exercise and ... nourishing diet" that are "most advantageous to the offspring" (Pol. 1334b30–1335b19). Recognizing that marriage served more than reproductive functions, he insists that its bonds of friendship were both essential and natural and that "both utility and pleasure seem to be found in this kind of friendship" between decidedly unequal partners (NE 1162a25). Nothing in his advocacy of marriage, however, implies a prohibition of pederasty or of extramarital sex that did not involve the committing of adultery in the specific, asymmetrical Greek sense of sleeping with another man's wife.

[68] *Oeconomica*, in Hugh Tredennick and G. C. Armstrong, trans., *Aristotle Metaphysics, vol. 2: Books 10–14. Oeconomica. Magna Moralia* (Cambridge, MA: Harvard University Press, 1935), 407, 409, 411.

Aristotle's appreciation of marriage's functions and pleasures strikingly neglects the erotic. But this is not entirely surprising, if we recall the third tension in the notion of lovemaking: irrational, enchanting passion versus reasonable, prudent pleasure-taking. Aristotle affirms marital sex on rational grounds but regards erotic desire as a dangerously irrational power that can divert us from the natural, healthy limits of appetite and from reason's moderate mean. Defining erotic desire as "a sort of excess of friendship [*philia*] ... that can only be felt towards one person" (NE 1171a10–13), Aristotle's scientific rationalism pathologizes it as a damaging excess rather than regarding it as a divinely inspiring (albeit troublesome) enchantment. "The bad man is bad by virtue of pursuing the excess, not by virtue of pursuing the necessary pleasures (for *all* men enjoy in some way or other both dainty foods and wines and sexual intercourse, but not all men do so as they ought)" (NE 1154a16–19). Good marriages, good households, and good citizens with good characters cannot rely on disorderly, disproportionate passions that defy the rule of reason and the natural and social norms of pleasure. For Aristotle, reasonably measured sexual pleasures (*ta aphrodisia*), along with affectionate friendship and reciprocal interests, provide the proper foundation for marriage, family, and society.

Cynics, Stoics, and Epicureans

Deriving their name from the Greek word for dog, the Cynics took humankind's animal nature as the guide for proper living. They consequently found nothing wrong with the sensual aspect of our sexual appetites and pleasures, nor with the cruder animal ways of gratification. Diogenes, founder of the school, advocated a crudely simple art of living. Famous for eating raw food, sleeping in a tub, and walking barefoot in the snow, he also masturbated in the marketplace to satisfy his sexual desire, explaining that "he wished it were as easy to relieve hunger by rubbing an empty stomach."[69] Rejecting the legal institution of marriage as a social imposition on our natural desires and freedom, Diogenes advocated a "community of wives, recognizing no other marriage than a union of the man who persuades with the woman who consents" (DL2 75). Apart from such consent, no concern for the woman seems called for. If Diogenes refused to condemn the pleasures of masturbation, polygamy, or pederasty as unnatural, this was not simply

[69] Diogenes Laertius, "Diogenes," in R. D. Hicks, trans., *Diogenes Laertius: Lives of Eminent Philosophers* (Cambridge, MA: Harvard University Press, 1925), vol. 2, 47; hereafter DL2.

because they responded to raw physical urges but also because he regarded human nature as distinctively malleable through training (*askesis*), as habits become one's second nature. Thus "even the despising of pleasure is itself most pleasurable, when we are habituated to it" by choice (DL2 73), an idea that Christian ascetics later embraced in their celebration of austere abstinence as a divinely directed *ars erotica*. Diogenes likewise acknowledged erotic love's masochistic pleasures: "Lovers [*erontas*]," he declared, "derive their pleasures from their misfortune" (DL2 69). His most distinguished Cynic disciple, Crates, who was so "ugly to look at" that people laughed at him "performing his gymnastic exercises," reluctantly married Hipparchia after he tried to dissuade her by taking "off his clothes before her face" and telling her that that was all she would get in marrying him (DL2 95, 101). Love should not rest on the enchantment of erotic mystery. Rumor alleges that they would even "make love in public,"[70] as appropriate to Cynic dog-like virtue and naked honesty, but their deepest bond of desire was philosophical rather than sensual.

Zeno, founder of the Stoic school, began as a student of Crates but then shaped a different philosophy to avoid "Cynic shamelessness" (DL2 113). Early Stoic thought on the erotic is hard to define because most of the relevant texts have not survived, so we must rely on much later doxographers whose reports are not always clear or consistent. In contrast to Plato's dualism of body and soul, Zeno and his early Stoic followers (such as Cleanthes and Chrysippus) were materialists, believing that all existents were corporeal, including the soul and even God (who pervaded the natural world). They defined virtue "as life in accordance with nature" (including "our own human nature as well as that of the universe"), because nature is governed by "the right reason which pervades all things, and is identical with ... Zeus, lord and ruler of all that is" (DL2 195–197). They likewise defined values as "any contribution to harmonious living" or to "life according to nature" (DL2 211). Harmonious living meant calmly accepting whatever nature brings us and avoiding harmfully irrational passions of desire, anger, or grief that arise from not getting all that we wish.

Erotic desire can be either a positive rational inclination in accord with nature's right reason or a negative irrational passion. This difference can explain why the Stoics affirm "the wise man will feel affection [*erasthesesthai*] for the youths who by their countenance show a natural endowment for virtue" while also claiming that "the passion of love is a craving from

70 Donald Dudley, *A History of Cynicism: From Diogenes to the Sixth Century* (London: Methuen, 1937), 5.

which good [*spoudaios*, virtuous, serious] men are free" (DL2 219, 235). Erotic desire is not a mere bodily experience, since it involves sensory "presentations and impulses" in the "ruling part of the soul" that also holds our "rational" powers and "has its seat in the heart" (DL2 263). Such desire is good when it is governed by reason, directed toward friendship (rather than mere physical satisfaction), concerned with the beloved's "regard" and welfare, and thus seeks to develop the beloved's potential for virtue, thereby contributing to the greater welfare and harmony of the community. Zeno thus could assert that "Eros is the divinity who promotes the security of the city."[71] Claiming the Stoic "definition of love is an effort toward friendliness due to visible beauty appearing, its sole end being friendship, not bodily enjoyment," Diogenes Laertius adds that Stoics thus explain why the soldier Thrasonides abstained from sexually taking a woman he held captive and deeply desired. Because he loved her yet realized she hated him, he rationally respected her feelings in the aim of friendship (DL2 235). Conversely, "being worthy of sexual love means the same as being worthy of friendship and not the same as being worthy of being enjoyed."[72] The beautiful appearance that inspires Stoic love is understood as implying goodness, *kalon kai agathon*. If "beauty they describe as the bloom or flower of virtue," then this is partly because the Stoics claim that a "man's character could be known from his looks" (DL2 235, 279). It is also because they define the beauty of virtue in terms of "four species, namely, what is just, courageous, orderly and wise; for it is under these forms that fair deeds are accomplished" (DL2 207). Virtue is a disposition that manifests itself in the blooming of beautiful acts. By Stoic criteria, a person who behaves badly could not truly be beautiful despite having an attractive face and figure. Indeed, even these good-looking features would be rendered unattractive through immoral behavior or gestures.

For Stoicism, the wise person's love is not an irrational passion or enchantment "sent by the gods" but instead a rational regard that appreciates virtue and harmony and seeks to enhance them (DL2 235). Free from frenzy, this rational erotic love may find pleasure in sexual expression, but only within the appropriate forms and contexts that accord with nature's right reason and virtue. This surely includes procreative sex, without which

[71] The statement (cited in Skinner, *Sexuality*, 161) comes from Book 13, section 561c of *Deipnosophistae*, a work by Athenaeus, a Greek rhetorician who straddled the late second century and early third century CE. For an excellent study of Zeno's idea of "the city of love," see Malcolm Schofield, *The Stoic Idea of the City* (Chicago: University of Chicago Press, 1999), chapter 2.

[72] This description of Stoic love comes from the fifth-century CE Greek doxographer Stobaeus, in his *Anthology* (5b9), as cited in B. Inwood and L. P. Gerson, trans., *Hellenistic Philosophy: Introductory Readings* (Indianapolis: Hackett, 1997), 206.

no community can survive. Hence "the wise man . . . will marry . . . and beget children" (DL2 225–227). Indeed, Zeno radically recommends that "amongst the wise there should be a community of wives with free choice of partners" where everyone would "feel paternal affection for all the children alike, and there will be an end of the jealousies arising from adultery" (DL2 235). The Stoics of Roman times (examined later in this chapter) were far more skeptical of erotic rationality and thus opposed the sexual promiscuity of group marriage and pederastic relations.

By privileging virtue as defining the good life, the Stoics opposed the Epicurean view that pleasure is the key to happiness, "our first and kindred good" that provides "the starting-point of every choice" (DL2 655). But in claiming that "pleasure is the end and aim" of life, Epicureans did "not mean . . . the pleasures of sensuality . . . By pleasure [they] mean the absence of pain in the body and of trouble in the soul." Intense sexual pleasures are likely to provoke such somatic and psychological troubles through their problematic side effects. Hence, it is the "sober reasoning" of "prudence" and "not an unbroken succession of drinking-bouts and of revelry, not sexual love [enjoying boys or women], not the enjoyment of the fish and other delicacies of a luxurious table, which produce a pleasant life" (DL2 657).

Epicurus distinguishes between desires that are "(1) natural and necessary, others [that are] (2) natural but not necessary, [and] still others (3) [that are] neither natural nor necessary but generated by senseless whims. All desires that do not lead to physical pain if not satisfied are unnecessary."[73] Like hunger and thirst, sex is a natural desire, but, unlike them, it is not necessary, for we can abstain from satisfying it without physical pain; and, he claims, we are generally much better off by abstaining. "The Epicureans do not suffer the wise man to fall in love," because it violated their view of pleasure as healthy tranquility (DL2 645). First, in its form of physical pleasure, erotic passion endangers bodily health by sapping one's energy, if not also risking disease or injury.[74] Second, even without its physical-sexual expression, erotic desire remains troublesome because it overwhelms prudential reason, disturbs the tranquility of one's own soul, and creates complications with

[73] Epicurus, "Leading Doctrines," in George Strodach, trans., *Epicurus* (New York: Penguin, 2012), 177.

[74] Here Epicurus echoes the warning of Pythagoras against "sexual indulgence": "'Keep to the winter for sexual pleasures (*ta aphrodisia*), in summer abstain; they are less harmful in autumn and spring, but they are always harmful and not conducive to health.' Asked once when a man should consort with a woman, he replied, 'When you want to lose what strength you have.'" Diogenes Laertius "Pythagoras," DL2, 329.

others. To some extent, children (even healthy ones) could be included in these complications, for their care provides further reasons for anxiety and distress. Hence "the wise man [will not] marry and raise a family" (DL2 645). Nor will he seek pleasure in nonmarital sex, which holds greater risks. Epicurus cautions a disciple: "I learn from your letter that carnal disturbances make you excessively inclined to sexual intercourse. Well, so long as you do not break any laws or disturb well-established conventions or annoy any of your neighbors or wear down your body or use up your funds, you may carry out your own plans as you like. However, it is impossible not to be affected by at least one of these things. Sex never benefited any man, and it's a marvel if it hasn't injured him."[75]

Epicurus also offers a practical remedy to break free of desire's enchantment: "If you subtract seeing, social contact, and sexual intercourse, the erotic passion dissolves."[76] Can an Epicurean still enjoy sex by savoring it tranquilly without disruptive passion? Cicero's critical testimony suggests this possibility, since he claims Epicurus includes "the pleasures we get from sex" together with the aesthetic pleasures "from listening to songs, from looking at [beautiful] shapes, from smooth motions, . . . [and] other pleasures which affect any of man's senses" as all contributing to the meaning we have of the pleasurable as good.[77] Epicurus moreover admits that marriage is sometimes prudent, so "occasionally [the wise man] may marry owing to special circumstances in his life" (DL2 645).

V EROTIC EDUCATION

For all their diverging views on eros, Greek philosophers converge in recognizing its importance for educational projects of self-cultivation, notwithstanding its threat to rationality, ethical conduct, and the disciplined self-restraint needed to realize true virtue and happiness. As a dangerous force to be mastered, eros provides valuable material for the pursuit of self-knowledge and self-control. Its teaching of self-mastery need not be an absolute rejection of desire through utter abstinence by savage repression. Instead, erotic desire provides a fruitful field for developing more sensitively nuanced modes of self-awareness, self-regulation, and self-cultivation that successfully distinguish between harmful desires and those worth pursuing. Justifiable desires should be reasonable in their form (in terms of object, act,

[75] Epicurus, "The Vatican Collection of Aphorisms," 51, in *Epicurus*, 182. [76] Ibid., 18, 181.

[77] Cicero, *Tusculan Disputations* 3.41–42, as quoted in B. Inwood and L. P. Gerson, trans., *The Epicurus Reader* (Indianapolis: Hackett, 1994), 58.

and conditions or modes of fulfillment), beneficial in their likely consequences, and sufficiently manageable in their degree rather than uncontrollably frenzied. But even an unreasonable desire could sometimes be useful by providing the subject with an instructive challenge for honing his powers of judgment, self-knowledge, and self-control.

These uses of desire focus on the lover's own edification, but the classic Greek model of love (epitomized in pederasty) highlights its pedagogical value for the beloved. The older, more accomplished lover is committed to caring for the beloved by educating him in the ways of knowledge and virtue, precisely by exemplifying those ways. The Stoics thus describe "virtue in sexual matters" as "knowledge of how to hunt for talented young boys, which encourages them to virtuous knowledge; and in general, knowledge of proper sexual activity."[78] For virtue-oriented philosophers, this pedagogical model of love implies that the lover's erotic passion must not override his sense of proper behavior, and that the beloved should not yield to unseemly desire in performing improper sexual acts. Indeed, a noble youth should not succumb to feelings of erotic passion for the older lover even when accepting the lover's sexual advances (out of affectionate, grateful admiration), since the Greeks regarded erotic desire as irrationally inappropriate when felt by the beloved youth toward an older man, although not inappropriate for the elder to feel toward him. As Xenophon explains, a proper youth "does not even share the man's enjoyment of sexual intercourse as a woman does"; instead, he remains "sober" while his older lover is "drunk with sexual excitement."[79] Though based on pederasty, the erotic model of instruction could extend to heterosexual couples as Xenophon describes in Isomachus' loving lessons to his young wife in *Oeconomicus.*[80] Though wives were expected to enjoy being genitally penetrated (as a natural, biologically necessary need), virtue demanded that they enjoy it chastely – only in appropriate forms with their lawful husband, who would instruct her in those forms. Erotic education from a virtuous older lover

[78] Stobaeus, *Anthology* (5b9), in *Hellenistic Philosophy*, 207. The passage elaborates how "sexual activity just by itself is an indifferent [thing]," because it can be performed with virtue or with vice. The wise man "does everything in accordance with all the virtues," and thus "acts with good sense and dialectically and sympotically [i.e., with proper symposium behavior] and erotically; but the erotic man is so called in two senses, the one who is virtuous and gets his quality from virtue, and the one who is blamed, who gets his quality from vice – a sort of sex-fiend" (206–207).

[79] Xenophon, *The Dinner-Party* (or *Symposium*, 8:15), in *Conversations of Socrates*, 261.

[80] Xenophon, "The Estate-Manager," in *Conversations of Socrates*, 310–327.

could enrich the younger person's lovemaking skills, including those concerned with somatic self-control and with the feelings of one's partner.

Conventional thinking emphasized the older lover's role as desiring pursuer and teacher of the beautiful beloved, but Plato's Socrates ingeniously reverses and mixes these roles to create an erotic model that is richer through its reciprocity of relations. Here the pursuing lover becomes also a beauty pursued by the desiring beloved who in turn promotes the lover's own self-cultivation. In a culture that prized beauty and youth, Socrates was an old and famously ugly man (snub-nosed, with bulging eyes). But through his enchanting virtues as a philosophical lover, the beautiful youths he courted become ardently attracted to him, while he could soberly regard their passion with affectionate understanding but sensual restraint. The handsome Alcibiades drunkenly confesses at the end of the *Symposium* (219b–d) how he unsuccessfully sought to seduce Socrates one night by lying down and embracing him, but that Socrates, while not removing himself rudely from this embrace, chastely abstained from sexual behavior. Socrates thus taught his dissolute beloved a lesson in self-control while also developing his own charismatically virtuous self-mastery by practicing it. Socrates moreover insists, in recounting the prophet Diotima's erotic wisdom, that rather than one-sidedly inseminating the beautiful beloved with ideas "to educate him," the lover is himself impregnated "with ideas and arguments about virtue" by "contact with someone beautiful." The lover thus "conceives and gives birth to [those virtuous things that] he has been carrying inside him" only through contact with the beautiful beloved, and "in common with him, he nurtures the newborn" (Sym 209b–c). If the beloved's beauty is a stimulus of desire that edifies the lover to give birth to virtue, then the desire for beauty likewise affects the beloved, who learns virtue from seeing and loving its beauty in the ways his lover embodies it.

Besides transcending the asymmetrical relationship of lover and beloved, Socrates highlights the instructive mediating role of philosophy in eroticism. Love is not simply a matter of two individuals, but a relationship between them that involves tertiary, facilitating factors – most obviously, the power of beauty, which Socrates sees as acting like a midwife (in giving birth to virtue) and thus identifies with "the goddess who presides at childbirth" (Sym 207d). Socrates typically describes himself in terms of erotic mediating roles, whether as a midwife and matchmaker (*Theatetus* 150a-151b) or (more provocatively) as a go-between, procurer, or pimp who can make his clients "agreeable" or "pleasing" (Xenophon's *Symposium* 3.10; 4.56–64). The courtesan Theodote thus asks his help to "hunt for friends" (her euphemism for pay-giving lovers) with his skill in devising snares of attraction, including "love charms and spells" that Socrates ironically mentions (Xenophon, *Memoirs of Socrates* 3.11). In contrast, philosophy's mediating role in love eschews deceptive persuasions and magic potions, relying instead on the teaching and practice of real virtue that makes both lover and beloved beautifully noble and harmoniously agreeable.

Phaedrus explains this beautifying effect of virtue while also proposing another way that love instructs us beyond its teaching of disciplined self-mastery – the very different lesson of growth through self-abandonment to the divine enchantment of erotic desire. Countering the roguish argument that the beloved should prefer a nonlover to the lover because the lover's passionate desire renders him dangerously out of control, Socrates admits that erotic passion is a form of madness as it implies loss of prudential self-restraint. However, he insists that along with prophecy, ritual incantations, and poetry, erotic passion is "a god-sent madness" that elevates and provides "the best things that we have" (*Phaedrus* 244a, 245b).

Plato's charming explanation of this divine gift involves analogizing the human soul to a "natural union of a team of winged horses and their charioteer" (*Phaedrus* 246a). The team has one noble horse and one basely sensual one, who makes it difficult for the charioteer to guide the soul to fly smoothly and reach the spiritual heights that gods can reach and where the divinely true and beautiful immaterial Forms are clearly visible, a vision that nourishes the soul's wings, its most divine part. Dragged toward earth by the bad horse, human souls lose their wings and become imprisoned in bodies, and thereafter suffer a long series of incarnations lasting thousands of years (*Phaedrus* 246b–249a). Philosophers, as lovers of wisdom and beauty, enjoy the shortest period of suffering because they maintain the clearest memory of those divine Forms. As the most radiant of those realities, beauty is visible even in its inferior earthly manifestations. The divine madness of erotic love is when a person "sees the beauty we have down here [on earth by noticing the personal beauty of the beloved, a boy in this pederastic tale] and is reminded of true beauty" in its divine Form (*Phaedrus* 249d). This causes the lover's soul to grow wings and induces all sorts of irrationally unconventional behavior in which the lover regards the beloved boy like a god and seeks to win his favor.

But underlying the strange behavior of lovers is their aim to educate the beloved boy into being like the gods they truly worship, "convincing the boy they love and training him to follow their god's pattern and way of life." In doing so the lovers "show no envy, no mean-spirited lack of generosity toward the boy but make every effort" to shape him in the god-like virtues they admire and emulate (*Phaedrus* 253b–c). The lover thus gallantly abstains from sexual assaults on his beloved, violently reining in the sensual steed of his soul (that rages for sexual contact) and thereby embodying the beauty of virtue, spurred by the beloved's beauty but ultimately inspired by divine beauty. When the beloved sees this beauty reflected in the lover's noble behavior, he falls in love with the lover. Now filled with erotic desire ("though weaker" than the lover's), the beloved "wants to see, touch, kiss, and lie down" with the person who loves him so nobly; and to some extent he acts on that desire with "hugs and kisses" (*Phaedrus* 255e–256a). At this point, if both lovers resist their sensual steeds and refrain from genital sex, they will enjoy an earthly life of "happiness and harmony" (*Phaedrus* 256b) through self-control of their soul's baser element, while also winning their wings at death.[81] But even if their self-control falters and they sexually consummate their love, the lovers still achieve the joys of firm friendship in life, while their wings in death, though not yet won, "are bursting to sprout" (*Phaedrus* 256a–d).

Despite praising the self-control of total abstinence as a truly "Olympic" victory (*Phaedrus* 256b), Socrates insists that love's rewards are "as great as divine gifts should be" precisely because we lose our self-control in love's beauty-inspired madness, which takes us beyond our ordinary selves and selfishness to raise us closer to the divine. In contrast, a nonlover's friendship "is diluted by human self-control; all it pays are cheap, human dividends," governed by prudential calculations (*Phaedrus* 256e). The lover's desire, even if irrational, is therefore superior to the perfect self-control of the nonlover because it expresses a self that has been enlarged and ennobled beyond self-centeredness toward a greater vision of transcendent truths and a greater capacity for the beauty of virtue. Teaching both self-knowledge and knowledge of others, erotic love trains us in virtue both through self-control and through uplifting self-abandonment. Indeed, love's self-abandonment paradoxically provides a superb opportunity to train higher levels of self-control by testing self-mastery in the very process of losing one's normal self-possession when possessed by erotic desire provoked by beauty emanating from its divine souce.

Plato's *Phaedrus* sympathetically tolerates same-sex lovemaking though recommending full genital abstinence as the high road in pederastic love, but his later views in *Laws* are more harshly restrictive. Condemning all pederasty, *Laws* affirms "the sexual act only for its natural purpose [of]

[81] I here prefer the translation of μακάριον μὲν καὶ ὁμονοητικὸν in the translation of H. N. Fowler, in *Plato: Euthyphro, Apology, Crito, Phaedo, Phaedrus* (Cambridge, MA: Harvard University Press, 1925), 501.

procreation" with one's lawful spouse. Beyond its aim "to check the raging fury of the sexual instinct" and augment men's "affection for their own wives" (as sole providers of sexual delight), this limiting of sex also "discourages excess in food and drink," thus enabling "the conquest of pleasure" with respect to these three powerful instinctive passions by which men "make beasts of themselves ... wallowing in all kinds of food and drink and indulging every kind of sexual pleasure" (*Laws* 831e, 838e–839b, 840c). Pederasty, lesbianism, sodomy, and other "unnatural crimes" are committed because men and women cannot control their desire for pleasure (*Laws* 636c). But laws and other restrictive methods can help us win "this victory" of control in "the conquest of pleasure" by reducing its delightfully experienced presence in our lives. Plato's logic is that "the appetite for pleasures, which is very strong and grows by being fed, can be *starved*," either by the distraction of hard work or by measures that make us "incapable of having sexual intercourse without feeling ashamed; our shame would lead to infrequent indulgence, and infrequent indulgence would make the desire less compulsive" (*Laws* 840c–841b).

Plato's argument that sexual pleasure, as an addictive habit, should be starved does not consider that repressing this natural drive could instead intensify one's appetite. Moreover, his argument for severely restricting sexual pleasure stands in tension with his positive treatment of drinking pleasures earlier in *Laws*, which not only tolerates but even advocates heavy social drinking as a "test" and "training" ground for virtue. Because a drunken man "loses all his inhibitions," if he can learn to maintain proper behavior even when drunkenness robs him of sober self-control, he proves his virtue while further honing it through present practice. Although "inevitably roused by the wine," the well-trained inebriate "would show himself strong enough to escape its other effects: his virtue would prevent him from committing even one serious improper act," and "he would leave off" drinking at the point when he sensed it would overwhelm him. Thus, in contrast to sexual pleasure, Plato commends heavy drinking as a useful practice in reducing our "shamelessness and audacity" and as a nonrisky test of character (*Laws* 637d, 648b–649e). This "wholly innocuous 'examination by recreation'" in inebriation, Plato insists, is far less dangerous than testing a person's virtue with respect to "sexual pleasures ... by putting him in charge of your wife and sons and daughters" (650a).

Such arguments, I submit, do not preclude the educational potential of sexual desire. Even if some sexual pleasures seem more dangerous in their likely consequences than heavy drinking, this does not mean all sexual pleasures (in their abundant variety) are too risky to use in training for virtue. Nor does it oblige exposing trainees to one's wife or children. There surely were other willing alternatives present in Athenian drinking parties, whose inebriated behavior was deemed too threatening for wives and daughters to witness. If Plato argues that drunken pleasure is safe because one could first practice it all "alone and in privacy" before risking exposure to other people, then we should recall that some sexual pleasures likewise allow private and solitary practice without procreative risk. One can explore the feelings, energies, and thresholds of these forms of sexual pleasure, learning to savor and magnify one's delight without being overwhelmed by it. This mastery of pleasure (notably different from repressive self-control) can be imported into our sexual experience with others, where one's heightened erotic expertise (both perceptual and performative) is translated into greater sensitivity to one's partners' needs and feelings and how best to satisfy them to enhance the quality (or virtue) of one's love relationships. The early Stoics apparently grasped this point in affirming the homology of virtues of drink and sex. As Stobaeus describes this attitude in a report already noted: "They understand virtue exercised at a symposium as similar to virtue in sexual matters, the one being knowledge which is concerned with what is appropriate at a symposium, viz. of how one should run symposia and how one should drink at them; and the other is knowledge of how to hunt for talented young boys, which encourages them to virtuous knowledge; and in general, knowledge of proper sexual activity."[82]

Devoted to beauty, love's edifying power also instructs us in harmony, whose achievement is not only an aesthetic grace but also an ethical and psychological virtue that finds expression in a variety of Greek terms and uses, including the ideas of harmony with nature and with social law to ensure "a harmonious disposition" for "harmonious living" (DL2 197, 211).[83] If love can teach social harmony by building on the intimate concord between lover and beloved, then it also proves an excellent training ground for developing the psychological harmony of the self, which is often described in terms of the unity of good order and self-mastery. Thus, the ideal philosophical lovers of Plato's *Phaedrus* live happily in harmony (*homonoetikon*) because they are "self-controlled and orderly" (*enkrateis hautôn kai kosmioi ontes*, 256b).[84]

[82] Stobaeus, *Anthology* (5b9), in *Hellenistic Philosophy*, 206.

[83] Among the relevant Greek terms for harmony, we find *homonoetikon*, *homologos*, *symmetros*, *symphonos*.

[84] The translation I use here is Fowler's.

Harmony implies some sort of unity in variety, but harmonies differ in how much divergent variety they allow. In more restrictive, purist harmonies the different elements are held tightly together by a single overarching principle or by a firm ruling hierarchy that establishes order. Pluralistic harmonies instead emphasize rich variety at the risk of having a looser, more fragile unity. The dominant trend in Greek erotic theory is for restrictive harmonies that seek strong unity by two related methods: divisionary distinction and exclusionary concentration. The first involves separating the biological dimension of sexual desire with its physical pleasures of lovemaking (*ta aphrodisia*) from the psychological, spiritual fervor of erotic love (*eros*). Plato's strategy for harmony in the erotic-affirming dialogues is to celebrate the higher, spiritual desire as the valuable essence of erotic love, while relegating its physical expression in sexual contact to an inferior category. Sexual desire is either an initial, primitive stage that must be transcended in climbing the ladder of elevated love (*Symposium*) or a threatening, demeaning disturbance (identified with the soul's ignoble lust) that one can occasionally tolerate but must hold strictly in check to achieve the highest happiness and harmony with one's beloved (*Phaedrus*).

A similar distinction of the biological from the psychological underlies the Cynics' harmonizing strategy of one-sidedly affirming the physical needs and pleasures of sex as ordained by our animal nature while eschewing the particularist romantic passion of erotic love. The Stoics, in privileging nature's right reason as the key to harmony, likewise reject eros in its passionate form of irrational enchantment but endorse the physical act of human lovemaking as a natural need that is also a rationally grounded activity, when properly pursued with virtue. This is not simply a matter of limiting oneself to appropriate sexual acts and partners; Stoics further distinguish the sage's erotic behavior that is free from psychological passion and guided by virtuous reason from an irrationally passionate erotic craving that is ignoble and detrimental (whether physically or merely psychologically expressed), even if its object is acceptable. Epicureans likewise eschew the psychological passion of eros because it disturbs the harmony of even-tempered tranquility, even if they grudgingly permit the enjoyment of Aphrodite's physical pleasures in the rare circumstances where their many harmful effects are minimized. Nonetheless, Epicurus insists that sexual pleasures (like those of food and drink) are not what create "a life of pleasure," which instead results from "sober reasoning . . . searching out the grounds of every choice and avoidance," while "banishing those beliefs" that cause "tumults . . . of the soul" (DL2 657).

Besides this strategy of harmonizing by distinguishing physical sex from romantic passion, we find attempts to achieve a harmonious combination of physical and psychological desires by concentrating on a limited focus: a single suitable person for a restricted range of erotic acts. If the not-quite-perfect lovers in *Phaedrus* suggest this strategy, physically satisfying their exclusive passion for each other but only "sparingly" (256c), then Plato's *Laws* exemplify it more explicitly. Sexual pleasures are not abjured but confined to enjoyment with one's spouse for purposes of procreation, and this exclusionary channeling of physical delight "inspires men with affection for their own wives" (839b), thus intensifying the psychological bond of love through sensual satisfaction. Aristotle seems to takes a similar line in his positive account of marriage. His claim that "to receive affection … is preferable in love to sexual intercourse" does not imply that these ends cannot be combined, since he indeed asserts that intercourse could be "an end relative to the further end … of receiving affection" (PA2 68b3–5).

Both harmonizing strategies, however, seek unity by restraining the range of eroticism, whether through psychological disinvestment from one's sexual partners, refraining physically from sexual activity (in some cases reaching total abstinence), or radically limiting the people and acts through which one's desire is expressed or satisfied. Foucault characterizes this basic strategy as "the rarefaction of sexual activity," achieving a harmony that is orderly and beautiful by "establishing the individual as a moderate subject leading a life of moderation" (HS2 89–90,92). Such moderation or temperance (*sophrosyne*), he explains, requires an "agonistic relation" to desire and pleasure (HS2 65). One need not eschew them entirely. But since the extremely strong and frenzied pleasures of sex seem especially challenging to enjoy with an attitude of rational, orderly moderation, there is a need to curb them "by adopting a combative attitude" of "self-mastery" through strictly disciplined restraint of these carnal passionate pleasures, by vigilant self-control dictated and enforced by the higher governing rule of reason (HS2 64, 66, 68). As Plato's *Republic* excludes sexual acts from "the right way" of pederastic love because of their mad, immoderate pleasures (403a–b), so Aristotle, wary of wild pleasures, insists that the temperate man does not enjoy "the things that the self-indulgent man enjoys most – but rather dislikes them" and seeks only "the things that … make for health or for good condition … moderately … [as] the right rule prescribes" (NE 1119a10–20).

This harmonizing through self-repressing restriction is surely the dominant approach in Greek erotic theory, but another strategy is vaguely suggested in accounts of Aristippus (435–356 BCE), disciple of Socrates and founder of the Cyrenaic school. Privileging pleasure in a more positive and dynamically intense sense than Epicurus, Aristippus had particular respect for somatic pleasures, especially those carnal delights that philosophy's mainstream fearfully deplored and sought to conquer. Repeatedly criticized for "luxury" and "extravagance" in relishing expensive delicacies of fine food and wine and the company of choice courtesans, Aristippus argued that "there is nothing to hinder a man living extravagantly and well" and that "if it were wrong to be extravagant, it would not be in vogue at the festivals of the gods" (DL1 195, 197, 199). The problem is not in savoring a rich variety of intense pleasures but rather in becoming so addicted to them that their absence would render one miserable. Aristippus "derived pleasure from what was present" but did not toil or yearn for "something not present" (DL1 195).

Psychological and sensual flexibility to accord with changing contexts is the key to harmony in this pluralistic, nonrestrictive model. Being "capable of adapting himself to place, time, and person," Aristippus "could always turn the situation to good account" and perform "his part appropriately under whatever circumstances" (DL1 195). Rather than regimenting harmony through a fixed order defined by a single, ruling, prudentially rational, and pleasure-repressing part of the soul, Aristippus suggests that self-regulation can mean surfing skillfully along with one's energizing desires, allowing oneself to be carried forward by one's pleasures until they lose their appeal or feel wrong or too risky. Happy to carry off all three courtesans when he was offered the choice of one, Aristippus was also happy to let them go without having sex with them (DL1 197). When he entered the house of a courtesan and noticed that "one of the lads with him blushed," he remarked that "it is not going in that is dangerous, but being unable to go out" (DL1 199). Censured for losing himself in sexual pleasures with the famous courtesan Lais, Aristippus replied, "I have Lais, not she me; and it is not abstinence from [using] pleasures that is best, but mastery over them without ever being worsted" (DL1 203, 205).[85] Such mastery, for him, was not a matter of subduing pleasures but of skillfully and sympathetically managing their use. In claiming that "bodily training contributes to the acquisition of virtue," the Cyrenaics could reasonably affirm a somatic education that included sexual pleasures with skilled courtesans (DL1 221). Besides developing our sensorimotor and affective capacities, such training

[85] I insert in brackets the English translation of the verb χρῆσθαι, which appears in the Greek and essentially means "to use."

could hone one's character (conceived as a richly resilient, flexible harmony) by testing it in challenging conditions of indulgence, analogous to Plato's plea for the educational value of heavy drinking.

VI THE ROMAN CONTEXT

As with mythology, Roman sexology drew heavily on Greek culture, though some salient differences emerged through Rome's different societal and political structures. If sexual acts were still essentially regarded in terms of a domination–submission relationship, this relationship took different forms in Rome's Republic and Empire than it did in the Greek city-state, where "the male citizen population was relatively small and homogeneous," so that the key criterion "for dominance over boys, women, and non-citizens [including slaves] was adult manhood."[86] Rome presented a much more complex, nuanced social structure of power relations that extended from elite senators and knights to freeborn citizens, freed slaves, and slaves at various levels of bondage and servitude. As power ultimately rested on social advantage rather than sex, upper-class women could appropriate males of lower birth to enjoy their sexual favors. Likewise, because of Rome's powerful patronage system, "ex-masters might continue to expect sexual services from freed slaves." Moreover, its strict laws against sexually penetrating Roman citizens meant that pederasty could not exist as it did in Greece. As homoerotic desire could find legitimate fulfillment only with male prostitutes and slaves, it lost much of its romantic appeal.

Nonetheless, within the Roman Empire, we continue to find advocacy of pederasty, pointedly expressed in debating the proverbial question of whether loving boys or loving women is best. Three texts are notable for treating this debate. One is a dialogue by Plutarch, whose treatment of the topic in relation to marriage we soon consider in detail; the second, a passage by the second-century novelist Achilles Tatius; and the third, a dialogue entitled *Erotes* (*Amores*), written in the satiric style of Lucian but now alleged to be of a later writer known as Pseudo-Lucian. In Achilles Tatius's novel *The Loves of Clitophon and Leucippe*, the advocate of heterosexual love argues that women's advantages over boys are in beauty that "does not fade rapidly" and that can be enjoyed long and more fully, in greater skill and passion in lovemaking, and in having bodies that are more agreeably tender to the touch. The advocate of pederasty counters that precisely the brevity of

[86] For the quotations in this paragraph, see Skinner, *Sexuality*, 195–196.

boy beauty and the uncertainty of fully enjoying it make the pleasure of their love superior in intensity (since "delight cannot grow old") and that women's beauty and behavior is "studied and artificial" (relying on cosmetic appliances), while the beauty of youths is honest and "complete and sufficient in itself."[87]

The novel's brief treatment of this theme leaves the issue unresolved. But *Erotes*, with a far longer discussion, achieves an apparent resolution of the debate, emblematically taking its advocate for woman's love from Corinth (renowned for courtesans), while its advocate of pederasty from Athens (famous for philosophy). The former claims the superiority of woman's love because women are more lastingly beautiful to view and touch and more passionate in enjoying a man's penetration but also because heterosexual love is more natural and necessary for procreation and can produce the joys of marriage and children. The Athenian counters that precisely this natural necessity for procreation makes heterosexual love inferior to pederasty, which serves no such practical function or animal instinct and thus represents a more cultured human love and purer friendship. Besides, he insists, the love of boys, when properly practiced, is intimately linked to the teaching and practice of virtue and philosophy, partaking of their spiritual value and thus forgoing the satisfaction of illicit physical lusts. The judge of the debate declares for pederasty, so long as it remains purely practiced with "the privilege only of philosophy." His verdict is that "all men should marry but let only the wise be permitted to love boys, for perfect virtue grows least of all among women."[88]

Marriage, indeed, was a crucial issue for imperial Rome. With the implementation of Augustus's Julian laws, citizen males were punished for remaining unmarried and childless but rewarded for having children. Married women, on the other hand, enjoyed far more freedom and visibility in Roman society than in Athens, participating in public and social events rather than being confined to the home. This made adultery a tempting option but also a serious anxiety that eventually led to severely punitive

[87] Achilles Tatius, *The Loves of Clitophon and Leucippe*, in Rowland Smith, trans,. *The Greek Romances of Heliodorus, Longus, and Achilles Tatius* (London: George Bell & Sons, 1893), 398–399.

[88] Citations in this paragraph are from M. D. Macleod's translation in *The Works of Lucian in Eight Volumes*, vol. 8, 229. We should note that the impartial listener in the dialogue (who enjoys both forms of love) rejects this purely spiritual love of boys, describes the physical foreplay in making love to them, and contradicts the claim that philosophers, including Socrates, refrained from sexual satisfaction with their young lovers, despite "their solemn phrases" and "high-brow speeches" (231–235).

legislation. Unlike Greek attitudes, Roman law blamed the pleasure-hungry woman rather than the seductive man. Roman erotic tendencies have a somewhat more violent tonality than the Greek, suggested in Rome's famous founding myth of the rape of the Sabine women (essentially an abduction for the purposes of marriage rather than a crude sexual violation). Sexual predation is also central to the strange legend (reported by Plutarch) that Rome's twin founders Romulus and Remus were fathered by a hovering phantom phallus that emerged from the hearth of a king and imposed itself on a virgin handmaiden who later gave birth to the twins.[89] Although rape was a serious crime when committed against a citizen of either sex, the Romans valued the sexually aggressive and large, manly phallus, in contrast to the Greeks' aesthetic preference for the undersized penis, symbolizing youth and rational restraint.

Major Greek philosophical traditions continued into Roman times with certain adjustments of doctrine, including some regarding sexual conduct. Marriage, as Foucault notes, was considered in a relatively new way. The Roman art of marriage involved increasing emphasis on "the personal relationship between husband and wife," on "the duties of reciprocity" that a man owed to his wife in terms of respectful behavior (including sexual fidelity), and on the form and role of their sexual relations within the context of the general aims of marriage.[90] But not every major philosophical school endorsed marriage. Cynicism opposed it, and (though condemned by Cicero for flagrantly flouting modesty) this philosophy enjoyed some popularity in imperial Rome, serving as a counterculture to the reigning preoccupations with power and opulence. If the dominant philosophical schools in Roman times affirmed the importance of marital monogamy for social stability, orderly procreation, and the moderate, abiding pleasures of companionship (while contrasting its conformity to nature with the "unnatural" perversions of same-sex love), the Cynics rejected marriage as an unnatural and unnecessary burden. In the *Cynic Epistles* dating from the first century BCE to the second century CE we find arguments that marriage destroys the freedom and self-sufficiency of the philosophical life and undermines the Cynic's cosmopolitan ideal of caring for all of humanity rather than focusing selfishly on one's own family. To counter the claim that marriage and children were duties necessary for providing new citizens and continuing the human race, the *Cynic Epistles* argued that non-philosophers supply

[89] See Plutarch, "The Life of Romulus," in *Parallel Lives*, trans. Bernadotte Perin (Cambridge, MA: Harvard University Press, 1914), vol. 1, 95.

[90] HS3, 148–149.

sufficient progeny and that people should be granted citizenship according to virtue rather than birth. Against the view that marriage is the most effective framework for satisfying one's natural sexual desires, the Cynics affirmed masturbation as far more convenient and trouble-free, not merely natural but also naturally self-sufficient.[91]

Despite its Cynic roots and its founder Zeno's alleged proposal for communal wife-sharing, Stoicism ultimately evolved in Roman times to advocate strictly monogamous marriage. Stoics and their sympathizers appreciated the Cynic arguments that marriage and children could present anxieties that seriously distract from Stoic philosophy's quest for virtue conceived as living in agreement with nature and governed by reason, and therefore free from passions that disturb the mind. Living in accord with nature, however, meant accepting not only the natural impulse to procreate but also the social duties that fate assigns us as citizens of a community. In Rome, those duties meant marriage. Seneca, therefore, though recognizing the philosopher's great need of free time and complaining that too much time is wasted in affairs with mistresses and arguments with wives, nevertheless felt obliged to affirm marriage. Marriage, he claimed, not only is compatible with the self-sufficiency, leisure, and peace of mind needed for philosophical living but also best accords with natural impulses for procreation and companionship. His famously devoted wife Pompeia Paulina certainly merited his affirmation of marriage.[92]

Epictetus, who never married, displays even more ambivalence. When encountering an administrator who advocated the traditional Epicurean policy that a man "ought not to marry ... and [he] ought not to have children either," Epictetus counters with the classic Stoic arguments of duty to nature and society: "Where are the citizens to come from? Who will

[91] On these issues of marriage, children, citizenship, and masturbation, see *The Cynic Epistles*, ed. Abraham J. Malherbe (Missoula, MT: Scholars, 1977), particularly the "Epistles of Diogenes," numbers 35, 42, 44, 47, and the "Epistles of Heraclitus."

[92] See Seneca, Epistle 72.3–4, "On Business as the Enemy of Philosophy," in *Epistles* vol. 5, trans. Richard M. Gummere (Cambridge, MA: Harvard University Press, 1996), 99; Epistles 9.17, "On Philosophy and Friendship," and 53.9, "On the Faults of the Spirit," in *Epistles*, vol. 4, trans. Richard M. Gummere (Cambridge, MA: Harvard University Press, 1996), 53, 357. See also Seneca, "On the Shortness of Life," in *Moral Essays*, vol. 2, trans. John W. Basore (Cambridge, MA: Harvard University Press, 1996), 295; and Will Deming, *Paul on Marriage and Celibacy: The Hellenistic Background of 1 Corinthians 7* (Grand Rapids, MI: Wm. B. Eerdmans), 74. For discussion of Pompeia Paulina, see the account of Seneca's suicide in the *Annals* of Tacitus and Michel de Montaigne's later tribute to her in his essay "Of Three Good Women," in *The Complete Essays of Montaigne*, trans. Donald Frame (Stanford: Stanford University Press, 1965), 563–568.

educate them?"[93] Yet, in his sympathetic account of Cynicism, Epictetus clearly appreciates that "marrying and having children" provide too much "distraction" for devoting oneself fully to philosophical work. Such work requires the "liberty to walk . . . among mankind, not tied down to common duties, nor entangled in [family] relations" so as to be "wholly dedicated to the service of God" and human kind in general.[94] His own celibacy betrays residual doubts concerning the Stoic commitment to marriage. Thus when urging the Cynic philosopher Demonax "to get married and have children," he received the potent riposte: "Then give me one of your daughters, Epictetus!"[95] Socrates, however, much earlier suggested a potent counter-argument against rejecting marriage as too distractingly troublesome for the philosophical aim of calm, harmonious living: marital perturbations provide a superb training ground for the conquest of tranquility and harmony. When challenged why he kept the shrewish Xanthippe as his wife, he replied: "[P]eople who want to become good horsemen keep not the most docile horses but ones that are high-spirited, because they think that if they can control these, they will easily manage any other horses. In the same way, . . . I have provided myself with this wife, because . . . if I can put up with her, I shall find it easy to get on with any other human being."[96] The *askesis* of marriage and children involves both somatic and psychological challenges that together can train body and mind toward greater virtue, an argument that later philosophers deployed, including some from the Islamic tradition discussed in Chapter 6.

Gaius Musonius Rufus, the first-century CE Roman philosopher who taught Epictetus, did not share his pupil's doubts about matrimony, presenting instead a whole-hearted Stoic advocacy of monogamous marriage and children as a moral duty and path to virtue. For virtue is living "according to nature, and marriage, if anything, is manifestly in accord with nature."[97]

[93] Epictetus, Discourse 3:7.19, in Robin Hard, trans., *The Discourses of Epictetus* (London: Dent, 1995), 165.

[94] Epictetus, Discourse 3:22.69, in *The Discourses of Epictetus*, 196. Such arguments for the philosophical value of refraining from marriage and children find clear expression in the arguments of St. Paul and later churchmen that celibacy is important for living the best religious life through undivided attention to God.

[95] From Lucian, "Demonax," trans. A. M. Harmon, in *The Works of Lucian in Eight Volumes*, vol. 1, 169.

[96] Xenophon, *The Dinner-Party*, in *Conversations of Socrates*, 232.

[97] Musonius Rufus, "Is Marriage a Handicap for the Pursuit of Philosophy?," in Cora Lutz, trans., *Musonius Rufus: "The Roman Socrates"* (New Haven: Yale University Press, 1947), 93; hereafter MR. Other Musonius citations are from his lectures "On Sexual Indulgence" and "What Is the Chief End of Marriage?" in the same volume.

Nature gave humankind "two sexes, male and female, ... [implanting] in each a strong desire for association and union with the other" that leads to procreation, and this natural end is most properly realized through the means of marriage (MR 93). As the basis of family and of social life, marriage is also a civic duty. "Thus whoever destroys human marriage destroys the home, the city, and the whole human race. For it would not last if there were no procreation of children and there would be no just and lawful procreation of children without marriage" (MR 93). Beyond the pragmatic justifications of procreation and social stability, Musonius praises marriage as an ethical ideal of loving companionship, "of making a life in common" and "regarding all things in common between [the couple] and nothing peculiar or private to one or the other, not even their own bodies" (MR 89). Thus "there must be above all perfect companionship and mutual love of husband and wife, both in health and in sickness and under all conditions, since it was with desire for this as well as for having children that both entered upon marriage." As such a union is "beautiful" and, moreover, ideal, it constitutes "the highest form of love" (MR 89,95)

If Musonius also describes marriage as rewardingly "pleasant" (MR 95), this is not because it provides the sensual pleasures of sex. Such pleasures should not be pursued, not even in marriage. "Men who are not wantons or immoral are bound to consider sexual intercourse justified only when it occurs in marriage and is indulged in for the purpose of begetting children, since that is lawful, but unjust and unlawful when it is mere pleasure-seeking, even in marriage" (MR 87). Condemning all nonmarital sexual relations, Musonius elaborates that "those involving adultery are most unlawful, and no more tolerable are those of men with men, because it is a monstrous thing and contrary to nature." Sex with a courtesan or a free woman or even with one's own maid-servant is likewise "shameful," which is why such acts are not done openly. They are intrinsically shameful because they exhibit lack of self-restraint and "wantonness" by "yielding to the temptation of shameful pleasure" (MR 87). Perhaps Musonius eschews the pursuit of sexual pleasure in marriage because he thinks that a taste for it will lead people to pursue it outside those marital bonds. Perhaps this fear also motivates his claim that beauty is "not effective in promoting partnership of interest or sympathy," whereas a person lacking beauty "would be less exposed to the snares of tempters" and thus presumably a more reliable partner (MR 91).[98]

[98] Here we have a pagan Roman philosopher and contemporary of St. Paul urging a Pauline view of monogamous marital devotion with sex purely for procreation rather than pleasure, though

Foucault characterizes these Stoic views on marriage, along with Plutarch's, in terms of three fundamental traits: a "monopolistic" principle permitting no sexual relations outside marriage, "a procreative finalization," and a "requirement of 'dehedonization'" in marital sexuality (HS3 182). But Plutarch, a Platonist who polemicized against Stoicism and Epicureanism, had a distinctively more positive view of erotic pleasure. Born near the famous temple of the Delphic oracle that set Socrates on his path and serving many years as that temple's senior priest, Plutarch (45–120 CE) was educated in Athens but became a Roman citizen and magistrate. His most sustained treatment of eroticism and marriage is in *Dialogue on Love*, where he himself figures as one of the interlocutors.[99] Logically structured on the debate over the rival merits of woman's love versus pederasty, the dialogue gains dramatic interest by its background story of a young widow who courts and then abducts a handsome youth who is the cherished *eromenos* of the city's male population.

The dialogue's main thrust is the superiority of woman's love. This derives partly from its superior pleasures, which in turn rely on sexual satisfactions. Given the moral and legal constraints of Roman times, the advocate of "boy love" cannot allow that such love finds full expression in sexual intercourse (which is illicit and demeans the beloved) but must confine itself to friendship aimed at virtue. He thus meets the critique that "Boy love denies pleasure ... because it is ashamed and afraid," though it secretly desires and seeks it "when night comes" (PDL 325). This frustrating restriction on legitimate sexual pleasure is a key argument for the superiority of marriage, which can enjoy the full joys of love by combining virtuous friendship with sexual pleasures that are socially endorsed. "How can there be any Eros without Aphrodite?" Plutarch asks, suggesting that erotic love could not exist without sexual relations. Even if it could, it would be inferior and short-lived, the dialogue argues, since "No fruit, no fulfilment comes of the passion; it is cloying and quickly wearied" (PDL 325). Conversely, sex without love is empty and pointless: intercourse without Eros can never achieve a noble end, since it is only by means of Eros that sexual pleasure "creates affection and fusion"; without love, sex leaves "a dreary residue" (PDL 351).

the doctrine emerges not from divinely prophetic prescription but rather from the ideal of honorable, rational self-control and respect for one's spouse.

[99] Plutarch, *Dialogue on Love*, in E. L Minar, F. H. Sandbach, and W. C. Helmbold, trans., *Moralia*, vol. 9 (Cambridge, MA: Harvard University Press, 1961), hereafter PDL.

By combining the satisfactions of erotic love with those of virtuous friendship, marriage constitutes the most pleasurable and beautiful of unions, and Plutarch evidently enjoyed a very happy one.[100] "There can be no greater pleasures derived from others nor more continuous services conferred on others than those found in marriage, nor can the beauty of another friendship be so highly esteemed or so enviable" (PDL 433). In marriage, "physical union is the beginning of friendship" through the "sharing . . . [of] great mysteries" and tender intimacies (PDL 427). Although its carnal pleasure is short, it fosters more lasting affection and harmony between a couple. Yet this harmony, to be sustained, requires repeated erotic pleasure. Hence the wise Solon "prescribed that a man should consort with his wife not less than three times a month," deploying such pleasurable "tenderness to wipe out the complaints that accumulate from everyday living" (PDL 427). For the same reason, Plutarch in a much earlier text (*Advice to Bride and Groom*) cautions the married couple to avoid any quarreling "in the privacy of their bedchamber," since its erotic venue should instead be the site of resolving all clashes in the tenderness of shared erotic pleasure, as "Aphrodite . . . is the best physician for such disorders."[101]

Of course, as Plutarch remarks in *The Dinner of the Seven Wise Men*, the ultimate value of such pleasure is not in the mere sensual delight of "carnal intercourse" per se "but rather the friendly feeling, the longing, the association, and the intimacy" that shared sexual pleasure can foster. "Aphrodite is the artisan who creates concord and friendship between men and women, for through their bodies, under the influence of pleasure, she at the same time unites and welds together their souls."[102] In short, for Plutarch, sexual pleasure is essential for a good marriage and need not be narrowly directed toward procreation, although it should not be pursued purely for its own sake or to extremes that display unseemly wantonness or disrespect for one's spouse.[103] Even if Plutarch celebrates marital sexual pleasure primarily as a means toward the higher pleasure of friendship, it remains an integral part of that higher pleasure, which is the pleasure of a distinctive bond of tender

[100] See Plutarch, *Consolation to His Wife*, in P. H. De Lacy and B. Einarson, trans., *Moralia*, vol. 7 (Cambridge, MA: Harvard University Press, 1959), 575–605.

[101] See Plutarch, *Advice to Bride and Groom*, in F. C. Babbitt, trans., *Moralia*, vol. 2 (Cambridge, MA: Harvard University Press, 1956), 329.

[102] Plutarch, *Dinner of the Seven Wise Men*, in *Moralia*, vol. 2, 405.

[103] In *Advice to Bride and Groom*, in *Moralia*, vol. 2. Plutarch argues that the husband's bedroom behavior should show modesty and respect to his wife "seeing that their chamber is bound to be for her a school of orderly behavior or of wantonness" (337).

intimacy continuously renewed and enriched through exclusively shared erotic delights.

Plutarch further differs from the Stoics by affirming erotic love as divinely inspired madness that beneficially "displaces the faculty of rational inference" (PDL 363). Empowering "the lover's enthusiasm" with "divine assistance," erotic desire provides a shorter path to virtue and friendship, as one is powerfully "borne along on the wave of affection with the help of a god" (PDL 369). Indeed, Plutarch echoes Plato in seeing love as "a mystic guide" who, starting from desire for a human beauty, can "escort us upward" to the higher world of Forms, "where Beauty, concentrated and pure and genuine, has her home" (PDL 403). Affirming the instructive potential of abandoning the rule of reason and self-mastery to follow the surge of inspired erotic passion could not be farther from the Stoic insistence on rational self-control. The faith that such abandonment rewards not only emotionally but also cognitively finds reinforcement in the dialogue's conclusion. Forsaking self-mastery and conventional reason, the city's widely adored young man falls in love with the older widow, agrees to marry her, and is deemed to profit from the education in virtue she can provide him, as she has already demonstrated her own virtuous character. In sharply reversing the conventional view that the husband is the superior partner who must educate the wife (a view he himself strongly expresses in his earlier *Advice to Bride and Groom*), Plutarch adds an interesting "marital" echo to Plato's vision of Socrates' needing a woman, the priestess Diotima, to instruct him about love and beauty.[104]

Plutarch's endorsement of erotic enthusiasm is as far from Epicurean thinking as it is from Stoicism. Epicurus, as Martha Nussbaum insists, is "unremittingly hostile" to erotic love.[105] But he recognizes that the appetite for sexual pleasure is a natural desire, even if its satisfaction (unlike hunger and thirst) is not necessary for the individual's survival and instead usually complicates the individual's life with unhelpful distractions and loss of resources (including health and energy). The most articulate representative of Roman Epicureanism is the poet Lucretius, whose denunciation of erotic love delivers both a devastating analysis of its pernicious delusions and a

[104] In that earlier text, Plutarch claims, for example, that "the wife ought to have no feeling of her own, but she should join with her husband in seriousness and sportiveness and in soberness and laughter." "For a woman ought to do her talking either to her husband or through her husband, and she should not feel aggrieved if, like the flute-player, she makes a more impressive sound through a tongue not her own" (*Advice to Bride and Groom*, 309, 323).

[105] Martha Nussbaum, *The Therapy of Desire: Theory and Practice in Hellenistic Ethics* (Princeton: Princeton University Press, 1994), 149.

program of philosophical and practical remedies for its cure. Rather than a divine inspiration, erotic desire, for Lucretius, is the noxious product of error and deceit. Tradition (now generally disputed) claims he reached this conclusion through bitter personal disappointment. St. Jerome reports that Lucretius "went mad from drinking a love potion" and wrote his books "in the lucid intervals of his insanity" before "he died by his own hand at the age of forty-four,"[106] probably sometime in the mid- to late 50s BCE. In his six-book Latin hexameter masterwork *De rerum natura* (variously translated as "On the Nature of the Universe" or "On the Nature of Things"), the poet's penetrating account of erotic love's inevitably painful perturbations and agonizing frustrations certainly conveys an insider's vivid familiarity with that passion.

Lucretius's strategy is to demystify and disarm love's destructive grip by first rationally analyzing its causes to expose its illusions and then further providing some practical, tactical remedies to displace or diminish the energies that fuel it. If Plutarch insists on combining Eros and Aphrodite (erotic love and sex) while insisting on love's divinely inspired and enriching, yet mystifying madness, then Lucretian analysis firmly divides erotic love from sexual desire. Exposing the former as an injurious phantom, he affirms the latter (in Aphrodite's Roman guise of Venus) as a beneficial physical force that works naturally, pleasurably, and automatically throughout the animal world, without involving specific acts of divine insemination of love frenzy and thus without requiring the erotic illusions that enslave and torture humanity.

Opening his poem by invoking Venus as the "life-giving ... guiding power of the universe" that makes things "grow in joy and loveliness" and can "bestow on mortals the blessing of quiet peace" (calming even fierce Mars in love's embrace), Lucretius later turns in Book 4 to explain her workings in human sexuality.[107] Sexual desire results when our bodily organs "are stimulated and swollen by the seed" of reproduction, and "[t]he one stimulus that evokes human seed from the human body is a human form.... So, when a man is pierced by the shafts of Venus, whether they are launched by a lad ... or a woman ... , he strives towards the source of the wound and craves to be united with it and to ejaculate the fluid drawn from out of his body into that body." This physiological mechanism, Lucretius concludes, is the essential core and "origin of the thing called love – that drop of Venus'

[106] I take this citation from ibid., 140.

[107] Lucretius, *On the Nature of the Universe*, trans. R. E. Latham (London: Penguin, 1994), 10; hereafter LN.

honey that first drips into our heart, to be followed by icy heartache" (LN 122). The eros of "romantic love" is thus an unnecessary and misleading supplement to the procreatively necessary pleasures of sex, a malignantly maddening, haunting excrescence that feeds on images of the beloved (even if only memories), growing "day by day" as "the grief deepens" (LN 122).

Its inevitable torments derive from "delusion and incertitude," the delusion of an impossible fusion with one's beloved and the uncertainty of faithfulness entailed by the impossibility of full possession (LN 122). Lovers are so distracted by the passion of uniting that they cannot decide "what to enjoy first with eye or hand. They clasp the object of their longing so tightly that the embrace is painful. They kiss so fiercely that teeth are driven into lips . . . because their pleasure is not pure" nor fully satisfying. Frustrated and tormented, "they are goaded by an underlying impulse to hurt the thing . . . that gives rise to [love's] madness." Indeed, frustration and torment are inevitable, since the lovers can possess only images of each other rather than achieving full possession or fusion. "Body clings greedily to body; they mingle the saliva of their mouths and breathe hard down each other's mouths pressing them with their teeth. But all to no purpose," because we cannot possess "the other by rubbing, nor enter right in and be wholly absorbed, body in body" (LN 123). The release of orgasm provides "a slight intermission in the raging fever" of the lovers, but "soon the same frenzy returns" and "they rot away, . . . wast[ing] their strength." They live a life of bondage "at the mercy of another's whim" and always in fear of losing the other's affection. "Their wealth slips from them. . . . Their duties are neglected. Their reputation totters." If all these evils plague the seemingly happy case of requited love, then those of "starved and unrequited love" are too evident and numerous to elaborate (LN 123–124).

What, then, can cure this horrible madness? Besides the rational analysis of its causes and delusional symptoms, Lucretius offers some practical remedies. First, "keep well away from such images . . . [that] feed your passion, and turn your mind elsewhere" (LN 122). Second, "[e]jaculate the build-up of seed promiscuously," directing it quickly toward other targets; otherwise, "the festering sore quickens and strengthens" (LN 122). Third, destroy the enchanting image of the beloved by learning to "concentrate on all the faults of mind or body" she possesses but to which love's beautifying gaze blinds us. Even if she has no genuine faults and "the charm of Venus radiates from her whole body," then recall that her human body, like any woman's, has "its disgusting smells" she "has to fumigate," as just "one whiff" of them would repel any lover (LN 124–125). More generally, focus on “all the backstage activities” (including cosmetics) that women use to hide their unattractive “human imperfection” to project a divine image of mystifying beauty; “drag all these mysteries into the daylight and get at the truth” that underlies them (LN125–126). That truth is physiological sex, not heavenly erotic love.

This coolly rational view of erotic desire, Lucretius claims, does not entail the loss of pleasure. “Do not think that by avoiding romantic love you are missing the delights of sex.. . . Rest assured that this pleasure is enjoyed in purer form by the sane than by the lovesick,” and it is better savored without love’s tormenting passion, which “even in the moment of possession” is inevitably plagued with “delusion and incertitude” (LN 122). In short, to combat the Platonic ideal of love as divinely inspired and focused on sublime ennobling beauty that is ultimately spiritual, Lucretius offers an anti-aesthetic materialist campaign to expose and highlight the unappealing features of love and its objects. Here he follows the defiantly anti-Platonic Epicurean dictum “I spit on the *kalon*,”[108] but he departs from Epicurus by being far more sympathetic to sex and to marriage and children. Lucretius believes that once liberated from the bewitchment of beauty, a man should simply “accept” the “unpleasant facts” of one’s partner’s “imperfection” and (so long as she is “good hearted and void of malice”) fully enjoy the sexual pleasure that any willing woman can give (LN 126). Lucretius moreover insists that women are indeed very willing to give sexual delights because they equally relish them. Women’s sighs of sexual enjoyment need not be “feigned” to gratify her man because “the pleasure of sex is shared,” and their “mutual joys” are important for “the intermingling of seed” between male and female that is necessary for procreation (LN 126). Woman’s seed, he claims, is as essential as man’s and sometimes may even dominate, resulting in a child that more closely resembles the mother.

Emphasizing that fertility and infertility depend on purely natural factors rather than “the will of the gods,” Lucretius maintains that one “factor of great importance is the manner in which the pleasures of intercourse are enjoyed.” He argues that “women conceive more readily” when they take the rear-entry coital position “of four-footed beasts with breasts lowered and hips uplifted” rather than lying supine, since this allegedly provides better access for the seed (LN 127–128). Moreover, because nature gives us sufficient delight through our most basic lovemaking actions, there is no need for fancy techniques to ensure the needed pleasures for conception. “Nor do our

108 Cited in Hermann Usener, ed., *Epicurea* (Leipzig: B. G. Teubneri, 1887), fragment 512, p. 315.

wives have any need of lascivious movements; for a woman can resist and hamper conception if in her pleasure she thrusts away from the man's penis with her buttocks.... These tricks are employed by prostitutes," not only to avoid pregnancy but also to "make intercourse more attractive to men" (LN 128). Nor does a woman need beauty or "divine intervention ... of Cupid's darts" to win the dispassionate love that Lucretius recommends. Simply being agreeable and "humoring a man's fancies" can make even "a woman deficient in beauty ... the object of love." Equally effective in establishing erotic affection is the force of habit: "love is built up bit by bit by mere usage," as the heart is slowly penetrated by mild but continually repeated impressions in the way that light drops of water can eventually "drill through a stone" (LN 128)

Despite its affirmation of sexual pleasure, Lucretian *ars erotica* remains aesthetically dull and dour. It advocates erotic coupling motivated merely by physical desire and friendly affection based on habits of routine sex and good-willed tolerance of imperfection. There is no need for the passionate uplift of beauty or of the aesthetic adornments of art and technical artistry to enrich the expression and satisfaction of erotic desire with attractive qualities of meaning and form. We should, of course, respect the fact that the Lucretian aim is not aesthetic delight but rather cognitive enlightenment and cure. Even here, however, his vision seems cognitively restrictive and overly cautious. Rather than following passion's flight to explore the experience of beauty and desire and to learn exciting new aspects of the self and of one's lovers that transcend the bland habitual circle of humdrum experience, Lucretius limits love's knowledge to a deflationary explanation of the physiology of desire and an unmasking of the delusional mechanisms of romantic infatuation (and its cure), along with a naturalistic account of fertility, and the way to love without beauty through good will and habit.[109]

If Lucretius poetically exhorts us to expose "all the backstage activities" through which women beautify themselves to hide their flaws and project the bewitching illusion of divine perfection that feeds the passion of erotic love, then Ovid (43 BCE–17/18 CE) replies (in poetic kind) in his famous *Ars amatoria* by instead insisting on the wisdom, beauty, and value of concealing these flaws in order to increase the benefits of love. Foucault's examination of Hellenistic erotic theory neglects these thinkers, perhaps because they

[109] Nussbaum similarly suggests that the cold Lucretian lover loses the opportunity to experience the vulnerability of being in love and that "not fusion, but intimate responsiveness" is what the erotic lover really seeks. See Nussbaum, *Therapy of Desire*, 188, 190.

wrote in verse, but that is insufficient reason to ignore their influential views. Lucretius provides an earnest and masterfully comprehensive version of Epicureanism. Ovid's erotic theorizing, however, clearly courts philosophical disregard not only because his *Ars amatoria* focuses more narrowly on "the art of love" rather than a philosophical panorama of the whole universe but also because its mock didactic genre entails a style of lightness and irony that is far removed from philosophy's standard sober stance. Lightness and irony, however, are an essential part of his philosophical message.

Plying a middle path between the raw Epicurean materialism of Lucretius and Plutarch's lofty Platonic idealism, Ovid presents a different notion of reality that lacks their systematic, single-minded unity but instead offers a much more varied and nuanced vision of the world of experience that is rich with the play of change and inconsistencies. Diverging sharply also from the Stoic's dispassionate firmness and the Cynic's crude animality, Ovid is much closer to the Cyrenaic style of the witty and pleasure-loving Aristippus. Much like a precursor of Oscar Wilde's archly sophisticated view that "the truth is rarely pure and never simple," Ovid maintains that truth must be a contingent, contextual, and complicated affair because reality is continuously in the making and in transformation.[110] This ontological attitude challenges the philosophical ideal of discovering the basic, invariable, universal truths of reality, finding it unsuitable for serving theory's goal of guiding our practice in a world of complex, changing conditions. In appreciating ontological complexity and change, epistemological context and temporality, and practice-driven theory, Ovid's *Art of Love* shares some philosophical themes with Chinese thought and American pragmatist philosophy, although these traditions would strongly reject many of the poem's ethical attitudes, particularly his tolerance of seductive force that borders on rape. His poem consists of three books: the first two advise men on how to find and win a female lover and then how to keep her love, while the third outlines similar advice for women.

Defined by both joy and suffering, love most powerfully exemplifies the complex contradictions of experience. The self-conscious inconsistencies that pervade *The Art of Love* highlight Ovid's recognition of the diversities, mutations, and complex tensions of natural and social reality that frustrate any univocal truth about love and its role in experience. Ovid is constantly balancing conflicting advice based on differing contexts and perspectives. Consider the following examples. Be zealously attentive to your beloved,

[110] Oscar Wilde, *The Importance of Being Earnest*, in *The Complete Works of Oscar Wilde* (New York: Barnes and Noble, 1994), 326.

especially when she is ill, but "zeal . . . should keep its bounds [so] don't fuss" too much for that could annoy her (79; 2:338).[111] "Habit's the master key" to keep your lover's affection, so maintain "daily familiarity" of contact even at "boredom's ... price," but absence, when rightly timed, "pays best" in intensifying love, so giving her "a rest" will intensify it more (79–81, 2:346–351). Win love through "the noble art of eloquence," but "hide your powers" and "avoid long words" (35, 1:459–464). Be yielding and agreeable to your lady love but not too soft. Do not be "rough" but "take what she denies" because "women are often pleased by force" as their "lust [is] keener and wilder" than man's (47, 1:665–670; 25, 1:345). Practice good grooming but not so much that you resemble "the courtesan" or catamite. "Casual chic suits men best," as does a balancing blend between sensitive tenderness and virility (37; 1:506–507).

As for the truth of fidelity, Ovid counsels, "Play around, but discreetly" and "if you're caught out, . . . still lie through thick and thin" (83, 2:397; 85, 2:415–416), but he soon demands the opposite. "If you followed my advice about lapses [of fidelity], 'Conceal them,' you must change tack now because 'Reveal them,' is my new motto. Don't blame me for inconsistency," he explains, because "the same wind does not always drive the ship" (87, 2:427–431). "Moods change by the day," and so do situations (93, 2:534). Thus, while a lover's infidelities should normally be hidden, there are certain circumstances (such as when rivalry can reawaken erotic interest) in which such cheating is worth acknowledging or even initiating, if love needs some drama to prevent it from going stale. Women receive the same paradoxical counsel, compressed into starkly contradictory terms. "Isn't it reasonable to be truly false, faithfully treasonable?" (153, 3:578–579).

To manage all this complex, conflicted, and ever-changing terrain, the artful lover "adapts himself to every style; he's as versatile as Proteus" and will not "employ the same technique" for different beloveds or even for the same one at different times (53, 1:760–761; 55, 1:765). Expert female lovers likewise vary their techniques, since "men need variety" too (153, 3:582). Such versatile resourcefulness involves moral virtues of generosity, tolerance, compliant kindness, and concern. "Be nice" because good looks "never suffice . . . Tactful kindness is the key" (63, 2:107–108; 67, 2:145). Be generous in giving compliments, but material "gifts . . . [get] pride of place," superior even to the poet's gift of amorous verse (67, 2:162; 75, 2:275). Generous

[111] For the quotations in this and subsequent paragraphs, see Ovid, *The Art of Love*, trans. James Michie (New York: Modern Library, 2002). I also include line numbers for those who wish to consult other translations.

kindness means tolerating your lover's disagreeable moods and imperfections, including their indiscretions, infidelities, or even lies. If your lover flirts with someone else, refrain from jealous rage and "don't play the detective." Be affable with rivals. "Ignorance is better than knowledge; tolerate lies," so she "will think their cover-up's effective" (95, 2:543–559). In short, love trumps the standard philosophical ideal of knowledge by overriding it with other worthy ideals, such as care for one's beloved. If fondness, trust, and self-esteem can profit by not knowing everything about one's lover, then there is also value in not always telling the truth, the whole truth, and nothing but the truth. Selective truth-telling fosters faith and harmonious feelings that bolster caring affection.

Human love, for Ovid, is a beautiful but fragile flower that hides modestly from full exposure. That is why lovemaking is done in private and best in dim half-light or darkness; even Venus herself is depicted as concealing her sex with her hand (99, 2:620). Ovid thus counsels women not only to arrive late to evening parties "when shadows hide your faults" and men have already drunk enough wine not to notice them, but also to cover the bedroom windows to block the morning light after a night of love when it's best to keep one's body out of sight (165, 3:754; 171, 3:807–808). Men should cooperate by turning a blind eye to their lover's physical blemishes, never mentioning them and focusing instead on praising the woman's beauty (101, 2:641–642; 77, 2:296–306) and her erotic skills (77; 2:307–310).[112] Conversely, women should be kind to their men by pretending to love them madly and to be ecstatically satisfied by their sexual prowess. "Make us believe that we're desired," Ovid urges his female readers, adding that masculine vanity makes this easy to do, even if faking orgasm demands "convincing stuff – writhing body, rolling eyes, gasps and ecstatic cries" (159, 3:673; 169, 3:802–803).

Despite recognizing its limits in pursuing love, Ovid does not deny the erotic value of knowledge. On the contrary, he claims it is essential for the good lover, both in courting and in keeping the beloved by providing pleasures of beauty that transcend raw sensuality and require aesthetic taste and expertise. Such knowledge involves mastery of numerous arts. First, both men and women require expertise in the arts of grooming and sartorial

[112] This one-sided focus on the beloved's beauty while disregarding the truth of blemishes can indeed reflect the epistemological aim for a higher knowledge of the ideal rather than the actual. Thus Plutarch's Platonic account of love likens it to the moon rather than the sun, since its soft light "illumines only what is beautiful" while leaving the ugly hidden, so as to lead one, through the inspiration of loving beauty, to the higher truth of the divine Forms, whose visible sign on earth is bodily beauty. See Plutarch, PDL, 399.

style. Although such matters of appearance may seem superficial, they express deeper features of character by reflecting not only virtues of disciplined care (in maintaining cleanliness, neatness, and well-balanced self-regulation) but also aesthetic taste and social sense. Ovid's advice to women regarding the arts of somatic style goes well beyond cosmetics and grooming (which, apart from the seductive combing of luxuriant hair, should be practiced in private). He explains what makes for attractive style in walking, talking, gesturing, laughing, crying, drinking, and eating (131–133, 3:281–310; 165–167, 3:755–768). This beautifies not only the woman but the whole situation in which the erotic drama occurs.[113]

In a striking arch invocation of philosophy's ideal of self-knowledge, Ovid applies it to the aesthetic techniques of lovemaking. "*Know yourself.* Only the man who knows himself can be intelligent in love and use his gifts to best effect to further every move.... Let the man with a good voice sing," and the handsome man "dazzle" with his looks (91, 2:500–506). Women, too, must acquire and deploy self-knowledge in order to display themselves to greater aesthetic advantage – by both hiding their "body's faults" and highlighting their advantages. Short women should sit with legs covered in order to conceal their squatness, while dark-skinned beauties should highlight this advantage by wearing white (125, 3:191; 129–131, 3:261–264). Ovid emphatically advocates this seductive use of self-knowledge in woman's coital positions, outlining it in vivid detail.

> Each woman should know herself and in the act of sex adapt her body to the best effects. No one method is best for everybody. If you're blessed with a pretty face lie supine.... If you're proud of your back, then ... offer a lovely rear view. [Lift your] legs on his shoulders [if you have] elegant legs.... A small woman should sit astride ... for this cockhorse jockey's ride. If you've fine, long flanks, kneel on the bed, neck arched, head back-tilted. If you've perfect breasts and youthful thighs, have your lover stand, and you lie down slantwise.... If your belly shows stretch-marks, then turn over and offer your lover a rear engagement. (167–169; 3:771–786)

In typical sexist style, Ovid recommends these postures for their aesthetic appeal in the eyes of male lovers and not for the woman's own sexual satisfaction or self-admiring gaze. But courtship and lovemaking, he maintains, are essentially other-directed, no matter how selfishly motivated. Good

[113] On the multidimensional complexity of somatic style and its relation to character, see Richard Shusterman, "Somatic Style," in *Thinking through the Body: Essays in Somaesthetics* (Cambridge: Cambridge University Press, 2012) 315–337.

lovers need to know the feelings and desires of the beloved in order to attract and satisfy them. Lovemaking, critically pursued as an art, teaches attentiveness and discriminating sensitivity through which lovers can become better in judging the character and moods of other people as well, such as the various go-betweens who can enable or prevent access to one's beloved. Attentive perception of your partner's feelings is equally crucial for the somaesthetics of good lovemaking. One learns precisely "the right places to touch" in the right way and right timing only by carefully observing one's lover's reactions of delight to these different modes of caress (107, 2:719), much like the way one learns to make the best sounds on a musical instrument by noticing the results of different fingerings or movement of one's lips. Perceptive attention to your partner's somatic feelings and your own (with their rhythms of arousal and trajectories of climax) enable heightened aesthetic harmonies of pleasure.

If Ovid's art of love aims not merely at the enjoyable use of another's body but at winning the beloved's heart and mind, her affection and desire, then the lover should eschew all measures that damage the beloved's mental faculties. Thus despite his wide-ranging pluralism of conquest and deception strategies, Ovid absolutely rejects the use of love potions or similar forms of magical or drug-induced enchantment that mechanically steal the beloved's heart that the lover aims to win through charm, skill, and other personal resources. Wine, however, Ovid permits because, in appropriate measure, it heightens perception and shared enjoyment, besides boasting a divine origin. Rather than magical or pharmaceutical arts, Ovid insists on the fine arts for enhancing the cultural and mental qualities of lovers and the aesthetic ambience of love's erotic play. Men are urged to sing or dance, or to eloquently express their love in prose or verse so as to seductively "please with whatever talent can give pleasure" (43, 1:595–596). To keep his beloved's affection, a man "must have mental talents as well as physical charms," so he should "cultivate the . . . arts," as these offer forms of beauty (such as eloquence) that do not depend on youthful good looks and are more lastingly effective in enhancing the aesthetic appeal of the lover (65, 2:112–121). Women are likewise implored to learn the arts of singing, dance, poetry, and playing music, but also, as noted earlier, to master other somatic arts of style and movement, in order to walk and gesture more attractively, or even to laugh or cry more appealingly. "Where doesn't art come in?" asks Ovid rhetorically, having detailed how it is everywhere pervasive in the game of love (131–135; citation 131, 3:291).

Acting is the most crucial art for love, albeit not in its official theatrical form, even if the theater is the ideal place to pick up partners (9, 1:89). Ovid instead emphasizes everyday "off-stage" acting in the sense of role playing and pretending, particularly in one's erotic pursuits. This is because such pursuits often involve dissembling or deception, for which acting skills are necessary. Some of this deception is to escape obstacles that impede the lovers' contact or to conceal their love from prying eyes, but other forms of dissembling are aimed at the lovers themselves. For instance, to convince a woman that his love is overpowering and sincere, a man should play the role of the distraught lover, pale and tearful (47, 1:659–661). To convince her of absolute devotion, "play any role she wants to cast you in" (69, 2:198). To gain a reluctant woman's confidence, pretend to be interested in pure friendship rather than erotic love. Lovers pretend to admire their beloveds far more than they really do, praising their looks, virtue, and lovemaking skills well beyond their actual or perceived worth, and even faking pleasure or orgasm. Both men and women, moreover, make vows and promises to their lovers that they only pretend to keep.

Ovid explicitly justifies male deceit by explaining that women are naturally better dissemblers than men, so that men are justified in using deceptions to "deceive the deceivers" (45, 1:645). Women, however, can justify their own guile in terms of their greater vulnerability and need for protection, if not also from the alleged fact that acting and deception are intrinsic to feminine nature. But Ovid's text suggests further justifications for erotic pretense and role playing. Such play acting contributes to the aesthetic pleasures of the games of love and courtship, something that both deceived and deceiving lovers find enchantingly absorbing, despite the suffering that these games also bring. Ovid recommends his gaming strategies of love for sophisticated audiences already interested in erotic experience and keen to enhance it by mastering the instructive and entertaining though often painful pursuit of erotic conquests. The games of love involve competition and conflict, which is why Ovid (like many writers) describes such play with metaphors of war (such as "conquest," "attack," "defense," "capture," and "arrows") despite love's ideal of harmonious union through affection. Such competition and conflict, though often distressing and hurtful, add the spice of drama that enriches the experience of erotic love. If Ovid's erotic love implies diversity, dissonance, rivalry, and conflict rather than complete unity and fusion, then it also reflects a more nuanced and ultimately more accurate view of life's complexities than that suggested by sexual abstinence or chaste monogamy.

Dissembling, in Ovid's view, is not only crucial to the art of love; it is indispensable to art in general, as art essentially deploys artifice to convey a more vivid sense of the real. Good art conceals itself so as to appear completely natural and thus more appealingly convincing. Ovid repeatedly lauds the art of hiding art: "Hiding art is the name of the game" (77, 2:313). A true master of erotic eloquence, for example, will speak in ways that seem spontaneous rather than studied, while a perfect expert of cosmetic art will create the illusion of natural facial beauty rather than highlight the fact of her skill in face painting. Moreover, as the art of loving forms part of the art of living, and our art of living already requires a considerable amount of role playing and stylization, it seems very hard to draw a sharp dichotomy between pretense and reality, between artful styling and natural expression, and thus between artfully playing the lover and really being one. Ovid perceptively notes how such role-playing even has the power to generate true love. This is because acting has powerful effects on our bodies that in turn deeply affect our feelings, so habitual actions create behavioral dispositions along with their corresponding affective attitudes. "Play the lover to the hilt," he urges, because "an actor will begin to feel real love, his role become genuine"; so for "those who pretend[,] a bogus passion may turn out true in the end" (43; 1:611–618).

Ovid's middle way also opposes the strict Roman Stoicism of Musonius that confined sex to marital monogamy for purposes of procreation. Instead, he offers lovers a variety of roles to play and thus many more opportunities for learning about and caring for others while also improving one's own self-knowledge and refinement. At different stages of life, in different contexts, and with different people, a person may enjoy and find instruction from very different forms of love with differing modes of desire and lovemaking. There are, however, limits to Ovid's pluralism in *The Art of Love*. First, it confines itself to heterosexual erotics aimed ultimately at genital copulation.[114] Moreover, it essentially excludes the option of erotic love in married family life. Although recognizing marriage and paying lip service to the wife's duty to respect her husband and avoid adulterous affairs, the text clearly encourages a husband's philandering and often hints at wifely infidelity. Indeed, Ovid effectively neglects the option of erotic play in marriage by addressing his advice for female lovers to unmarried women. He also strongly advises women lovers against having any children, because it destroys their figures and ruins their erotic appeal. Such advice implies that the art of lovemaking should not be directed toward enriching marriage and reproductive ends, an

[114] In *Amores* (*The Loves*), however, Ovid seems to recognize the homosexual option, when he complains that he needs love to inspire his verse: "I have no boy I can sing of, no nice long-haired girl making a theme for my lays." See *The Loves* (Book 1, section 1, lines 19–20), in Rolfe Humphries, trans., *Ovid and the Art of Love* (Bloomington: Indiana University Press, 1969), 15.

opinion clearly conflicting with official Roman demographic politics. If Ovid's attitude toward the family contributed to his subsequent exile from Rome, it also helps explain (together with his neglect of same-sex eroticism) why the erotic theory of his *Ars amatoria* may strike us today as far too narrow, unjust, and juvenile.

We overcome Ovid's biased exclusions, however, by embracing more fully the fundamental principle of his erotic pluralism with its recognition of love's varieties, complexities, and combinatory tensions. One may reach a stage in life when one wants to focus on monogamous procreative sex, just as there are stages where one cannot afford to have children or simply can no longer have them because one's years of procreative potency are over. Indeed, there are situations or stages in life where one has no desire to perform genital acts of procreation or no physical ability to perform them but still feels erotic longing for somatic contact that expresses loving desire. Such longings for erotic expression can surely flourish in same-sex relationships that exclude procreative coitus. Ovid's heteronormative sexist libertinism, despite its troubling inadequacies, could point the way to a more imaginative, fair-minded, and tolerant pluralism in which the divergent forms of desire and stages of diminished sexual power need not be devoid of erotic fulfillment or legitimacy.

3

The Biblical Tradition

Desire as a Means of Production

I THE OLD TESTAMENT

Monotheism and the Problem of God's Body

Traditionally known as "the good book" and certainly a rich treasury of wide-ranging wisdom and poetic beauty, the Bible is not a good source for erotic artistry. Despite its frequent accounts of sexual encounters whose diversity extends to same-sex relations and incest, we find no substantial vision of *ars erotica* and indeed almost no concern for the aesthetics of lovemaking. Given the Bible's enormously formative influence on Western culture, its ancient neglect of sexual aesthetics has cast a very long historical shadow, discouraging even nonreligious thinkers from theorizing lovemaking in aesthetic terms while even leading some to view the aesthetic and the erotic as fundamentally in conflict. Before examining, in Chapter 8, how Western erotic thought has struggled with its biblical roots, we should explore the Bible's treatment of sexuality and probe deeper into some of the logical reasons for its neglect of aesthetic eroticism.

These reasons emerge right from the outset of biblical narrative, in the account of creation and the Fall with which the Old Testament begins. The one and only Hebrew God, Yhwh, by himself and through his own singular powers, creates the world and all that inhabits it. Humankind, moreover, is distinctively created in God's image, suggesting that human action should strive to emulate the divine; and man is indeed explicitly given dominion to rule over all other living things, as God rules over man. But erotic activity presents a problem for divine emulation, because monotheism provides no good model for lovemaking. Despite God's commandment to procreate through sexual union, we find no divine example of erotic coupling. Why would the almighty God need to engage in sexual union;

why should he want to procreate, and who could qualify as a suitable partner, if there is one and only one God?

The question of how a single god could provide an inspiring model for sexual procreation must have been particularly pressing in biblical times when cultures were especially preoccupied with fertility. The pressure seems to have been so strong that the Hebrews apparently (though unofficially) gave their God a divine consort, Asherah, a mother goddess familiar to other Semitic cultures of that time and described as "bride of the king of heaven" and "mistress of sexual vigor and rejoicing."[1] But accepting such a divine consort violated the essential monotheistic creed, and she is therefore excluded from Hebrew theology – the only biblical reference to her being Jeremiah's condemnation of her being worshipped as "the queen of heaven" (Jeremiah 44:17).[2] Monotheism's lack of a heavenly consort for God is not the only problem for providing a divine model for sexual union: How would God make love? With what organs?

Such questions point to a more basic riddle with the Hebrew God: What was the nature of God's body? If God indeed had a body (as his early worshippers traditionally believed), what sort of body did He have? Representations or "graven images" were strictly forbidden in ancient Hebrew culture as manifestations of idolatry. Divine images were, of course, particularly proscribed and severely punished. Such prohibition of visually portraying the divine may partly be due to discomforting anxieties about God's body. Although many great Jewish thinkers have denied that God has a body, most biblical scholars today believe that the ancient Hebrews thought their God did have one. But precisely what kind of body this was remains a mystery.[3] Was it a physical body or was it simply a bodily form whose

[1] See John Day, "Asherah in the Hebrew Bible and Northwest Semitic Literature," *Journal of Biblical Literature* 105, no. 3 (1986): 386; and William Dever, "Asherah, Consort of Yahweh? New Evidence from Kuntillet Ajrud," *Bulletin of the American Schools of Oriental Research* 255 (1984): 21–37.

[2] Unless otherwise indicated, this book's biblical quotations use the King James translation, except for when the quotations are embedded in another text I am citing.

[3] The influential medieval Jewish philosopher Moses Maimonides is among those who deny that the Hebrew God has a body, because having one would imply an internal plurality in God that corrupts unity and hence threatens monotheism. He argues in *The Guide of the Perplexed* that God's essential unity precludes corporality, which implies a multiplicity of body parts or simply the essential divisibility of a body's physical extension that implies plurality. Although "every body is divisible" and "is necessarily composed of two things ... its matter and its form," God "is indivisible ... [and] will not be a body at all." In short, "He is one and not a body." Other arguments of Maimonides against divine corporality are God's infinite and unchanging eternal existence, since bodies cannot be infinite or immune to change (because of the divisibility of their parts). See Moses Maimonides, *The Guide of the Perplexed*, vol. 2, trans. Shlomo Pines

substance was not physical but rather purely spiritual nature? Was Yhwh's body confined to one essential form and location, or at least confined to a single form and location at any given moment in time? Or did God have a body that could take different forms and take up different locations at one and the same time? Could his body be simultaneously both in heaven and in various places on earth? Scholars have offered different answers to those questions.[4]

Did God have sexual organs? Did God indeed have a clear sex at all? The Hebrew God (Yhwh) is usually described in clearly masculine terms (and likened to masculine roles of warrior, judge, and king), but often (as in the Genesis creation story) God is also denoted by the Hebrew "Elohim" (אלוהים), a grammatically plural term. There are also instances where God is likened to a compassionate or suckling mother; one of God's names, El Shaddai (אל שדי), is formed from the Hebrew word for breasts (*shadaim* שדיים) and linked in a number of Genesis passages to blessings of fertility, thus suggesting also feminine powers.

The question of God's sexual soma is thus left unclear. Though God often reveals himself in biblical narrative, he is very rarely seen in bodily form, and there is never a glimpse that would determine his sexual identity. The closest we come to a vision of God's body is when he reveals himself to Moses on Mount Sinai, but insists on avoiding frontal exposure. "And it shall come to pass, while my glory passeth by, that I will put thee in a cleft of the rock, and will cover thee with my hand while I pass by. And I will take away mine hand, and thou shalt see my back parts: but my face shall not be seen" (Exodus 33:22–23). Nor, of course, would his genitals. Similarly, in the vision of Ezekiel 1:26–28, the prophet sees a heavenly throne on which there was a human-like figure whose body divinely glowed with a fiery gleam "of amber" from "his loins even upward," while from "his loins downward" there was "the appearance of fire." God's genitals, which could determine his sexual identity, thus remain either utterly concealed or shrouded in fiery mystery.[5]

(Chicago: University of Chicago Press, 1963), 236, 238, 251, 252. Some modern scholars see this rejection of corporality's multiplicity as denying any trace of "internal polytheism" within God himself. Moshe Habertal and Avishai Margalit, *Idolatry*, trans. N. Goldblum (Cambridge, MA: Harvard University Press, 1992), 79.

[4] For an excellent account of these different positions, see Benjamin D. Sommer, *The Bodies of God and the World of Ancient Israel* (Cambridge: Cambridge University Press, 2009), 1–79.

[5] In another of the very rare visions of God's body, Isaiah (6:1) sees "the Lord sitting upon a throne high and lifted up, and His train filled the temple," which then became "filled with smoke" (6:4) so his genitals could obviously not be seen. Moreover, the seraphim that Isaiah sees attending to God similarly conceal their bodies to offer no clue: "each one had six wings; with twain he covered his face and with twain he covered his feet, and with twain he did fly." Because the

Yet if humankind is created in God's image and likeness – and the Hebrew words *tselem* (צלם) and *dmūt* (דמות) indeed connote visual appearance or likeness – then the human body should provide clues to God's body. The mysterious, problematic nature of God's body thus provides good reason to discourage the making of human images that could suggest a concrete determination of God's somatic form and gender.[6] If we try to decipher what God's body was actually like by examining the Genesis narrative of how we were created in God's likeness, we will be disappointed and indeed confronted with further enigmas that are rich in import for issues of sexuality and eros.[7]

Even a cursory reading of the first two chapters of Genesis reveals what seem to be two different creation stories, involving a different order of events. Consider chapter 1's description of the sixth day of creation:

> And God said, Let the earth bring forth the living creature after his kind, cattle, and creeping thing, and beast of the earth after his kind: and it was so. And God made the beast of the earth after his kind, and cattle after their kind, and every thing that creepeth upon the earth after his kind: and God saw that it was good. And God said, Let us make man in our image, after our likeness: and let them have dominion over the fish of the sea, and over the fowl of the air, and over the cattle, and over all the earth, and over every creeping thing that creepeth upon the earth. So God created man in his own image, in the image of God created he him; male and female created he them. And God blessed them, and God said unto them, Be fruitful, and multiply, and replenish the earth, and subdue it: and have dominion over the fish of the sea, and over the fowl of the air, and over every living thing that moveth upon the earth. And God said, Behold, I have given you every

Hebrew word for "feet" also means "legs" and because feet serve as a familiar symbol for genitals in biblical as well as other cultures, the seraphim's covering of their feet reinforces the idea that any genitalia that could suggest God's gender should be concealed. The episode of the burning bush in Exodus 3 presents another fiery vision where God's body was concealed and Moses also "hid his face" so his eyes would not see Him.

6 The particular worry about gender might explain why the medieval Rabbi Meir of Rothenburg, in defending the religious legitimacy of making "images with all sorts of pigment," argues that this does not violate the biblical injunction not to make a graven image, "since the only forbidden image is the painted sculpture of a complete frontal view." See the translation and discussion of his text by Kalman P. Bland, "Defending, Enjoying, and Regulating the Visual," in *Judaism in Practice: From the Middle Ages through the Early Modern Period*, ed. Lawrence Fine (Princeton: Princeton University Press, 2001), 292.

7 For more detailed discussion of the puzzles concerning God's body, see Howard Eilberg-Schwartz, "The Problem of the Body for the People of the Book," in the essay collection he edited, *People of the Body: Jews and Judaism from an Embodied Perspective* (Albany: SUNY Press, 1992), 17–46.

> herb bearing seed, which is upon the face of all the earth, and every tree, in the which is the fruit of a tree yielding seed; to you it shall be for meat. (Gen.1:24–29)

To summarize, after creating all other living things, God not only makes humankind in his own image to rule over them but further creates humankind simultaneously in both genders ("male and female created he them") so that they can sexually reproduce, thereby enabling them to fulfill the divine commandment to "Be fruitful, and multiply, and replenish the earth, and subdue it." Moreover, it seems that the fruit of every tree, without exception, was given for humankind to eat.

Woman, Gender, and Reproduction

The second chapter of Genesis gives a quite different version of the creation story. Before "God formed" the animals that dwell on earth, Adam is created as a single, solitary, male instance of humankind, and then placed alone in the Garden of Eden where he is forbidden to eat from one tree, "the tree of knowledge of good and evil." To remedy Adam's loneliness, God creates the animals and brings them to Adam so he could get to know and name them and find in them suitable companionship. As no animal proved satisfactory for this, God created a female human – "woman" – from a rib of Adam's own body, a creature who clearly proved adequate to satisfy Adam's needs and desires.

Why this apparent reversal of the order of human and animal creation? One likely motive would be to provide divine authority for the primacy of the male gender as the Creator's original prototype and intention. In contrast to chapter 1 where male and female are created together in God's image, Adam is created long before Eve. Indeed, between his creation and hers, there occurs God's creation of the animals and Adam's naming of them. The narration clearly suggests that God created the animals to remedy the problem of Adam's being alone and to provide him with a companion, or "help meet" for him. The original Hebrew for this notion is *ezer kenegdo* (עזר כנגדו), which could be translated as a helper corresponding to him or a helper comparable to him. Some scholars even argue that the phrase in ancient Hebrew could have also meant "a power equal to him," whereas the animals were clearly on a much lower level.[8] However, even if we try to view

[8] See R. David Freedman, "Woman, a Power Equal to Man," *Biblical Archaeology Review* 9, no. 1 (1983): 56–58.

Eve's creation as providing Adam not with a merely helpful servant but with a strong partner somehow comparable to him, the fact still remains that the second chapter's narrative presents her creation as an afterthought rather than God's original intention. Moreover, her status as a derivative, ancillary creation is underlined by the fact that she is made from Adam's rib. A supplement to man, woman depends for her creation on man's body, and her designation as "woman" is explicitly derived from "man" to underline her derivative status: in Hebrew *isha* (אישה) is derived from *ish* (איש).

Before considering how the subsequent narrative of the Fall further asserts woman's secondary status, we should note the sexual import of the animal interlude in Eden. Why was it not good enough for Adam to remain alone in the Garden? Shouldn't God's fulfilling presence have resolved the problem of mere loneliness? Adam's problem clearly seems to be his inability, alone, to be fruitful and multiply, as mankind was urged to do in chapter 1. That the animals proved inadequate to be Adam's companion provides both divine authority and ancestral example for the explicit prohibitions against bestiality that come later in Exodus (22:19), Leviticus (18:23, 20:15–16), and Deuteronomy (27:21).

Naming is an essential dimension of knowing, and the verb "to know" is a familiar biblical term for sexual intercourse. Whether or not we interpret Adam as having sexually experimented with animals before deciding they were unsuitable partners, we should realize that bestiality must have been a tempting practice in biblical times, when so many men were shepherds who spent long periods away from their wives, with only their flocks for warmth of company.[9] Naming is even more closely and widely associated with having power over what is named, so Adam's naming of the animals is a way of reinforcing his divine-declared dominion over them. By the same token, Adam's naming of Eve as "woman" implies man's dominion over her. This sexual subservience to man is dramatically reinforced through the punishment God inflicts on Eve for eating from the forbidden tree and involving Adam in this sin of disobedience. "I will greatly multiply thy sorrow and thy conception; in sorrow thou shalt bring forth children; and thy desire shall be to thy husband, and he shall rule over thee" (Gen. 3:16).

As woman's dominating ruler, man need not aesthetically coax, enticingly attract, or pleasingly charm a woman into erotic play. There is no need for

[9] Some scholars clearly take the narrative as implying Adam's sexually "coupling with each female animal in turn" since bestiality was widely practiced "among herdsmen of the Middle East." See Robert Graves and Raphael Patai, *Hebrew Myths: The Book of Genesis* (New York: McGraw-Hill, 1964), 65, 67.

erotic artistry; man simply needs to take her, exercising his dominion over her body that God provided (through Adam's gift of a rib) for the purpose of procreation. From this biblical perspective, cultivating *ars erotica* to charm and please a woman into sexual engagement not only is superfluous but seems to counter divine will by mitigating or challenging her God-given punishment through Eve's original sin. Sexually "knowing" a woman is not at all aimed at knowing her feelings, needs, and hopes so that these can be better satisfied to promote greater happiness and communicative understanding between the conjugal pair. Nor is erotic experience cultivated as a way to develop better knowledge of oneself or more refined skills in attracting, pleasing, and caring for one's lovers. Women and sex are purely means for procreation. So when "Adam knew Eve his wife," and she conceived and bore children, the biblical ends of eros were fully achieved (Gen. 4:1).

Interpretations of the Fall narrative often define its key sin as disobedience per se rather than the sensual temptation of tasting forbidden fruit whose "pleasant" look promised gustatory enjoyment as well as increased knowledge. We explore the sexual dimensions of these interpretations later in this chapter, but now briefly note the narrative's suggested connection between food and sexuality. The first product of Adam and Eve's eating the forbidden food was to become uncomfortably self-consciousness of their nakedness. As Eve initiated this sensual knowledge, so woman in other ancient cultures that connect food and sexuality similarly serve as the leading source of such knowledge. The Mesopotamian epic *Gilgamesh* describes how the savage Enkidu (raised from birth by animals) did not know how to eat cooked food until he was taught to do so by the temple courtesan Shamhat, who simultaneously also taught him wine and human lovemaking. Indeed, it is through seven days and seven nights of continuous lovemaking that she first civilizes Enkidu, separating him from his former beastly community and introducing him into human society. Lovemaking thus serves as an elevating civilizing force with woman as the superior guide. In ancient Chinese texts (discussed in Chapter 4), the female symbolizes nurturing life, while women constitute the authoritative legendary teachers of erotic arts, mythic counterparts of the consummate courtesans who were the sexual specialists of real-world Asian societies. In contrast, however, in Judeo-Christian culture, associating women with the sensual appetites for food and sex serves to diminish their status, even while recognizing their instrumental value for procreation and for nourishment (whether in breastfeeding or preparing food).

If the final authors of Genesis sought a divine justification of male primacy and woman's derivative status, why did they not remove the first, more egalitarian version of human creation as simultaneously male and female? In fact, they not only kept that egalitarian version of chapter 1 but they also repeated it in the first two verses of chapter 5. "This is the book of the generations of Adam. In the day that God created man, in the likeness of God made he him; Male and female created he them; and blessed them, and called their name Adam, in the day when they were created." Perhaps this nonsexist version is reasserted because the second creation story's portrayal of woman as merely God's afterthought is not only uncharitable to woman. It can also seem disrespectful to God, because it implies that God's original plan was imperfect by failing to provide Adam what he needed from the outset and what indeed was necessary for man's reproduction and dominion over earth. The first version instead portrays the creation of male and female humans as part of God's original design and as created, simultaneously, in his image.

This bisexual co-creation can be interpreted in different ways. We can see it simply as affirming the essential equality of both sexes because both are simultaneously created in God's image as part of God's initial plan. This interpretation still leaves the question of God's sexual identity problematic, since both male and female are created in his image. Other interpretations of bisexual co-creation, however, construe the initial creation of male and female in God's image as suggesting that God's divine body includes both male and female sexuality.[10] This idea would bolster ancient Hebrew monotheism against the temptation of the dominant environing fertility cults of that time, because it would give the one and only God both male and female powers implied in fertility and thus avoid the need for a second, female God to be his consort and to provide the female dimension of fertility power. It would moreover provide an argument for the ennobling value of sexual coupling as a way of approaching or imitating the divine by means of combining sexual, procreative powers that are joined in God's body but separated in humankind.[11]

[10] See, for example, David Biale, *Eros and the Jews: From Biblical Israel to Contemporary America* (New York: Basic Books, 1997), 26–28.

[11] Benjamin Sommer presents an intriguing view according to which one strain of the Hebrew Bible construed God's body in a distinctive, ontologically fluid way that was not uncommon in the pagan religions of that time and region and that could accommodate both male and female characteristics and powers. In such religions, the god's body not only could be present in different places at the same time, but also could simultaneously take diverse shapes and could borrow characteristics from other gods. With such an ontologically complex body, God could appear and act on earth while still being in heaven and could be manifest in different forms. Such a compound identity can also explain mysterious ancient Hebrew notions such as God's "glory," "presence," "name," and his "Asherah" (identified as a goddess) that find expression in

Biblical hermeneutics, however, also offers another way to interpret the original creation of humankind in God's image as both male and female: the idea that the primordial human of Genesis chapters 1 and 5 was, like God, essentially androgynous, encompassing both male and female traits and thus without a distinct male or female identity.[12] This interpretive tradition tends to make sexual difference irrelevant to the original, divine essence of humankind, and thus renders gender inessential to a person's identity as a human being. It therefore also makes sexual intercourse inessential to expressing one's humanity and realizing one's personhood. Though never dominating the mainstream, this interpretation of man's creation was influential in both rabbinic and Christian traditions, encouraging notions of gender equality, virtues of chastity, and, particularly in Christianity, ideals of virginal celibacy. Christ himself – as the son of God and as the second, but unfallen Adam – can be seen in this divinely androgynous, nonsexualized form, as a celibate figure who combined both male and female traits and who was not the product of human sexual intercourse. Beyond such religious contexts, this notion of a divinely modeled, sexually undifferentiated first human being finds secular expression in later humanist ideas that treat gender identity as not defining the essence of a person and consequently not a valid criterion for being properly treated as one.

Clearly, however, the ideal of human identity as divinely androgynous and celibate could never be dominant in ancient Hebrew culture, which was profoundly preoccupied with anxieties of being a minority people surrounded by more numerous and powerful hostile nations. Reproduction was a vital necessity for survival; sexual coupling was the necessary means. "Be fruitful and multiply" is thus God's first blessing after the creation of humankind and the first words he addresses to humanity (Gen. 1:28). Yhwh repeats this primordial blessing to Noah and his sons after the flood (Gen. 9:1), and later, with its promise of fertility and power, to Abraham

the Bible and in archaeological finds. For details on this "fluidity of divine embodiment," see Sommer, *Bodies of God*, 12–57. One way to understand such multiple identity within a monotheistic framework is by analogy with the ontology of artworks. A work such as *Hamlet* can be fully manifest in very different textual versions, performances, and even genres (literary scripts, theater interpretations, or films) but still remain identified as one work and not be reducible to any or even all of its actual manifestations.

[12] See, for example, the Midrash book on Genesis, which contains the following interpretation of Rabbi Jeremiah ben Leazar: "When the Holy One, blessed be He, created Adam, He created him an hermaphrodite for it is said, Male and female created He them and called their name Adam" (Gen. 5:2). See *Midrash Rabbah*, trans. and ed. H. Freedman (London: Soncino Press, 1961), 54. See also Calum Carmichael, *Sex and Religion in the Bible* (New Haven: Yale University Press, 2010), 8–11.

and his descendants. But procreation was more than a heavenly blessing; it was a divine directive, urged again and again, because it was an always pressing demographic demand for the small and struggling Hebrew nation.

With such a fervent focus on sexual reproduction, one might have expected considerable biblical interest in cultivating eroticism by highlighting its pleasures and stimulating its desires. But this was obviously not the case. Instead, we have a celebration of fertility as the cherished end, while sexual coupling is regarded merely as the necessary means to that particular end, but without any apparent intrinsic value of its own and without serving any other significant and ennobling goal. While recognizing that desire and pleasure play an important role in sexual intercourse, the Old Testament shows little concern for developing these dimensions, but instead focuses on the production of progeny. Perhaps there was fear that giving more attention to erotic pleasures would prove a distraction from the prime purpose of childbirth. Pregnancy, delivery, and nursing are clearly deterrents to unbridled lovemaking, so that stimulating greater interest in sexual pleasures would likewise generate greater reluctance to diminish them by having children.

Progeny and Purity over Pleasure

The Old Testament presents many lessons of this overriding preference for progeny over pleasure. Take Onan, for example, who married and sexually enjoyed his brother's widow, Tamar, but intentionally "spilled" his seed rather than impregnating her with it and was therefore slain by God (Gen. 38:9). The obsessive focus on offspring can explain the paradox that despite semen being necessary for God's holy commandment to procreate, it is condemned as an impurity that must be washed off and (even after washing) renders the person unclean until the evening (Lev. 15:16). The point is clearly that semen is unclean only when it is issued in any place other than the female's organ for reproduction. The same logic of directing sex toward reproduction is clearly at work in the injunction that women are unclean for contact until the eighth day after their menstruation is over, which serves to focus sexual activity on the time that women are most fertile (Lev. 15:19–30).

The Hebrews' preoccupation with progeny (along with their privileging of man's role in reproduction) is evident in other priestly laws, such as those that focus on the sanctity of the male member. Male potency, within the congregation, is presumed and protected. Thus, "he that is wounded in the stones [testicles] or has his privy member cut off shall not enter the congregation of the Lord" (Deut. 23:1); and if a woman, in defending her husband while he is fighting with another man, grabs that man "by his secrets [i.e., penis]: Then thou shalt cut off her hand, thine eye shall not pity her" (Deut. 25:11–12). The same concern for offspring motivates the laws giving special leave to any soldier to consummate his marriage before going to war, "lest he die in battle" before he can produce a child (Deut. 20:7). "When a man hath taken a new wife, he shall not go out to war, neither shall he be charged with any business: but he shall be free at home one year, and shall cheer up his wife which he hath taken" (Deut. 24:5). A year should allow the man ample time to sow the seed of an offspring, whose generation (along with her husband's company) presumably provides what is also essential to the wife's happiness. The soldier's pleasure is never mentioned, probably because it is assumed but perhaps also because emphasis on sexual pleasures with his new bride might make him ever more reluctant to leave her lovemaking for the pursuit of war. A year could bring not only pregnancy and progeny; it could also give the soldier sufficient satiety or even restlessness for leaving his pregnant or nursing wife at home while he goes off to new adventures.

The privileging of progeny over pleasure can also be seen in the harsh prohibition of prostitution, an institution that prides itself on providing sexual pleasure by highly attractive and skilled professionals outside the marital framework and with no interest in producing offspring. Prostitutes can hone their beauty and sexual skills, while wives are forced to labor with household chores and child rearing. In the economy of procreation, however, prostitution is doubly deadly; it wastes man's seed and woman's fertility, while also weakening the bonds of marriage and the couple's sexual activity by providing the man another, often more attractive, outlet for his erotic drives. Hence the injunction: "Do not prostitute thy daughter, to cause her to be a whore; lest the land fall to whoredom, and the land become full of wickedness" (Lev. 19:29). Moreover, as prostitutes are particularly well trained in varieties of lovemaking outside the standard form of intercourse that leads to children, their company is especially dangerous because their proficiency in these infertile erotic activities can corrupt the husband's erotic tastes and diminish his interest in child-producing forms of intercourse. "There shall be no whore of the daughters of Israel, nor a sodomite of the sons of Israel" (Deut. 23:17). Female prostitutes are thus associated with the evils of male sodomy because of their common focus on sexual pleasures not directed toward procreation.

The strident global condemnation of homosexuality reflects the same insistence on male–female genital coupling as the only legitimate form of sexual union or erotic pleasure. Homosexual lovemaking is thus linked with the equally infertile (but clearly dehumanizing) practice of bestiality: "Thou shalt not lie with mankind, as with womankind: it is abomination. Neither shalt thou lie with any beast to defile thyself therewith: neither shall any woman stand before a beast to lie down thereto: it is confusion. Defile not ye yourselves in any of these things: for in all these the nations are defiled which I cast out before you" (Lev. 18:22–24). "If a man also lie with mankind, as he lieth with a woman, both of them have committed an abomination: they shall surely be put to death; their blood shall be upon them. . . . And if a man lie with a beast, he shall surely be put to death: and ye shall slay the beast. And if a woman approach unto any beast, and lie down thereto, thou shalt kill the woman, and the beast: they shall surely be put to death; their blood shall be upon them" (Lev. 20:13, 15, 16). If Hebrew law condemns same-sex lovemaking as subhuman by linking it to bestiality since both practices are infertile, the argument may work *rhetorically* to denigrate homoeroticism as beastly, but its logic remains problematic. Animals are no less beastly when they engage in procreative sex. Moreover, as we saw in our preceding chapter, one of the key Greek arguments for privileging homosexual love is that it goes beyond mere animal imperatives of procreation by deploying intelligent artistry for ends of aesthetic pleasures that can have distinctly humanizing motives and consequences. A similar argument can be made for heterosexual lovemaking pursued beyond the frame and ends of procreation.

The Old Testament's preoccupation with progeny includes a concern for the purity of the offspring's provenance that is reflected in many laws designed to reinforce patrilineal, patriarchal Hebrew society. If concern for proper paternity made adultery (and certain forms of incest) punishable by death, it also explains the distinctive law of levirate marriage, obliging a man to marry the widow of his deceased brother and give her offspring, a duty whose violation brought Onan his death. The same anxiety about paternal purity explains the strange and complicated law regarding sex with "a beautiful woman" taken among the captives of a defeated enemy (Deut. 21:10–14). The Hebrew who desires this beautiful stranger must first "bring her home" to his house, where "she shall shave her head, and pare her nails," remove her clothes of captivity, and "bewail her father and her mother for a full month." Only then can the soldier "go in unto her, and be her husband." Waiting a full month should allow the woman's menstrual cycle to provide a fresh, unfertilized egg and consequently guarantee that the future offspring from the beautiful captive will be from her new Hebrew husband and not from some prior liaison with another man.

Anxiety about paternity is, of course, one of the major reasons for the strict sanctions against adultery, whose prohibition is one of the Ten Commandments. "And the man that committeth adultery with another man's wife, even he that committeth adultery with his neighbour's wife, the adulterer and the adulteress shall surely be put to death" (Lev. 20:10). The same anxiety motivates some of the prohibitions against incest (Lev. 18 and 20; Deut. 20 and 27). The concern with purity of progeny further explains the biblical worries about intermarriage, reflected symbolically in other prohibitions of mixing, such as the bans against the cross-breeding of cattle, the mixing of crops, and the combining of fabrics. "You shall keep my statutes. You shall not let your cattle breed with another kind: you shall not sow your field with mixed seed: neither shall a garment of mixed linen and wool come upon you" (Lev. 19:19). Deuteronomy (22:5, 9–11) continues the attack on mixing by injunctions against cross-dressing, plowing with an ox and ass together, and combining different seeds in a vineyard, the result being that "the fruit of thy seed" will "be defiled."

The idea of mixing was so troubling not only because intermarriage threatened the distinctive unity and solidarity of the small group of Hebrew people that wandered among larger, stronger nations but also because intermarriage itself was both a reason and a metaphor for religious straying through the integration of other gods and their rituals into the worship practices of a people who were uniquely pledged to the single God Yhwh. As syncretic paganism was the religious norm for the surrounding peoples, the Hebrews were often sorely tempted to adopt attractive foreign gods who, in contrast with the unique and unportrayable Yhwh, could be visually represented and worshipped in fertility rites relating to the divine coupling of such pagan deities. If intermarriage could commingle those foreign gods and rituals within a Hebrew family's worship of Yhwh, then sex with an attractive female foreigner or stranger (the Hebrew terms זרה and נכריה mean both strange and foreign) presents a real threat to religious unity and social purity. This was particularly true since marriage in biblical times was merely "the nonsacramental, private acquisition of a woman by a man" that could be accomplished by the act of sexual intercourse.[13] Exodus 34:16 clearly links intermarriage, prostitution, and religious apostasy, warning Hebrews against letting their sons take Canaanite women because those "daughters go a whoring after their gods, and make thy sons go a whoring after their gods." Like adultery and whoredom, sex with a foreign woman received severe

[13] Shaye J. D. Cohen, *The Beginnings of Jewishness: Boundaries, Varieties, Uncertainties* (Berkeley: University of California Press, 1999), 265.

condemnation, and all three served as damning metaphors for religious infidelity. The exhortations of Proverbs are "to deliver thee from the strange woman . . . for her house inclineth unto death" (2:16–17). "Drink waters out of thine own cistern . . . rejoice with the wife of thy youth" so as not to "be ravished with a strange woman" (5:15–20). "Lust not after her beauty.. . . For by means of a whorish woman a man is brought to a piece of bread" and "goeth . . . as an ox goeth to slaughter" (6:25–26, 7:22). "For a whore is a deep ditch, and a strange woman is a narrow pit" (23:27).[14]

Despite these condemnations of whoredom and liaisons with female strangers, Old Testament narrative effectively excuses them when they seem crucial for producing progeny of the right provenance, as in the story of Judah and Tamar. After God slew Tamar's second husband (Onan) for spilling his seed, she was sent back to her father's home by Judah, her father-in-law, so that she could chastely wait for Judah's youngest son Shelah to become old enough to marry her. As Shelah matured and Tamar sensed that he would not be compelled to wed her, she learned that Judah, recently widowed, was taking a trip to shear his sheep. Conspiring to seduce him incognito on the route of his journey, Tamar disguised herself as a prostitute and, wearing a veil, demanded Judah's staff, seal, and cord as a security of payment for her lovemaking services until Judah would send the goat she demanded as her price. When Judah subsequently sent the goat to the place where they had met, the "prostitute" was nowhere to be found and no one knew of her existence. Three months later, when Tamar was discovered to be pregnant, accused of harlotry, and condemned by Judah to be burned, she sent him the "security" items he had left with her, informing him that they belonged to the man who made her pregnant. Judah then forgave her, and she gave birth to twins, the first of whom became the ancestor of King David. But despite this happy end of reconciliation, Judah offered her no further lovemaking; Tamar had already served her role of providing offspring for the family, and given her prior marriage to two of Judah's son's, the relationship had the deadly scent of incest.

Even egregious acts of incest seem condoned, however, when deemed necessary for maintaining the right lines of procreation. After Lot had fled from Sodom and hid himself with his two daughters in a cave, the young women conspired to get him senseless drunk with wine so they could sleep

14 The original Hebrew here uses two different terms that are translated as "strange" by the King James version: זָרָה and נָכְרִיָּה. Both include the connotation of "foreign." Some contemporary English versions interpretively translate this notion as "adulterous."

with him on consecutive nights (first the elder, then the younger) because there seemed to be nobody else available to give them offspring. Not only were they not punished, but each of their offspring gave birth to an important nation (Moab and Ammon). Ruth, the great-grandmother of King David, was a Moabite, and she bore the offspring of Boaz, a direct descendant of Perez, the oldest son of Tamar's deceptive union with Judah. The sacred, regal Hebrew lineage that includes Solomon (pure enough to build the Holy Temple) and leads to Jesus is thus, paradoxically, the product of deceptive prostitution and father–daughter incest.

Censoring the Senses: Circumcision and the Taboo of Nakedness

Privileging progeny over pleasure could also account for the Hebrew commandment of circumcision, a ritual act explicitly specified as the key condition for God's promise to make Abraham "exceedingly fruitful," "a father of many nations . . . and kings" (Gen. 17:5–6). Circumcision physically inscribes the penis as God's tool to realize his promise of Hebrew fertility. Such fertility is even visually symbolized, because by removing the foreskin, circumcision presents the penis with the glans penis exposed as it is when the foreskin retracts in erection. The circumcised penis thus displays an image of male potency and phallic fertility, reinforced by priestly commentary likening circumcision's pruning of the penis to the pruning of a tree that enables it to yield more fruit. As the foreskin is thought to enhance sexual pleasure because of its great haptic sensitivity (apparently due to its "fine touch receptors and other highly erogenous nerve endings"),[15] its ritual removal to realize God's covenant of fertility certainly signals a privileging of progeny over pleasure. Moreover, its sacred linking of fertility with the male organ reinforces the patrilineal shaping of reproductive genealogy and consequently also the reproduction of patriarchal social dominance. We have long been familiar with the idea of Jewish identity as matrilineal, that truly being Jewish requires being born to a Jewish mother or converting to Judaism. Children whose mothers are not Jewish are not natural-born Jews, even if their fathers are Jews. But Jewish matrilineality did not exist for the Hebrews of the Old Testament, whose society was strongly patrilineal as well as patriarchal. As Shaye Cohen convincingly argues, the matrilineal principle

[15] Gregory Boyle, Ronald Goldman, J. Steven Svoboda, and Ephrem Fernandez, "Male Circumcision: Pain, Trauma and Psychosexual Sequelae," *Journal of Health Psychology* 7, no. 3 (2002): 334.

is first attested in the Mishnah, being a product not of biblical but of rabbinic law, from the second century CE.[16]

Erotic pleasures clearly exceed the haptic dimension, embracing other sensual modalities such as taste and smell but especially the visual pleasures of desirable and desiring flesh. If circumcision exposes the naked glans penis by removing the covering foreskin, this does not express a Hebrew affirmation of nakedness for erotic delight. Quite the contrary. Nakedness is denounced, as part and parcel of the general biblical rejection of fleshly eroticism, in which nakedness indeed plays a central, complex, recursive role. Erotic delight involves not only enjoying with one's visual and other senses the naked flesh of your lover and of sharing with your lover the private intimacy of your nakedness. It also includes the pleasure of sensing how your lover's naked body is transformed through your own desire into not merely desired but also desiring flesh, the pleasure of seeing the power of your desire to awaken desire in your lover's flesh, whose perceptible changes (of color, moistness, erection, etc.) show that your lover's soma wants its nakedness to be desired and enjoyed by you. Eros is fueled by the perception of this reciprocal stimulation of shared, desired and desiring, private nakedness.

Yet the perception of human nakedness is essentially sinful from the biblical perspective. Though initially irreproachable before Adam and Eve ate from the tree of knowledge, nakedness became immediately shameful once "they knew that they were naked; and [so] they sewed fig-leaves together" to hide their nakedness from each other, even before they hid themselves from God. Thereafter nakedness is largely associated with sexual misconduct. In Hebrew biblical discourse, the notion of revealing or uncovering a person's nakedness (*gilui arayot*, גילוי עריות) is regularly used to designate incest and other forbidden sexual acts (Lev. 18). The term is derived from the word *ervah* (עֶרְוָה), which means nakedness, especially genital nakedness. It first appears in Genesis 9:22–24, when Noah is drunk with wine and his youngest son Ham (whose name means "hot," implying lustful) spied on him and "saw the nakedness of his father (עֶרְוַת אָבִיו) and told his two brethren," Shem and Japhet. The older brothers then "took a garment, and laid it upon both their shoulders, and went backward, and covered the nakedness of their father" (עֶרְוַת אֲבִיהֶם). The text emphatically specifies also that "their faces were [turned] backward, [so that] they saw not their father's nakedness." When Noah awoke and realized what Ham "had done unto him," he cursed him and blessed his other sons. It is not entirely

[16] Cohen, *Beginnings of Jewishness*, 263, 273.

clear whether the message here is that merely observing (with desiring intention) another person's genital nakedness already constitutes a sexual act (here one of incest) or whether it is rather that the desire of seeing this nakedness leads to physically sexual contact and thus must be strictly avoided if such fuller contact would be inappropriate.

If this negative attitude toward enjoying the visual beauty of naked bodies tends to discourage the flourishing of *ars erotica*, it contrastingly promotes other modes of sensory seduction. It is through her clothes, sandals, ornaments, fragrant ointments, and wine that Judith seduces and beheads the Assyrian general Holofernes, who drunkenly falls asleep without even seeing or touching her nakedness.[17] Wine is the key ingredient in crucial biblical episodes of illicit acts of "revealing nakedness" either to arouse the desire or simply to dull the inhibitions or critical consciousness of one's target. As Noah was drunk from wine when his son Ham visually violated his nakedness, so Lot's daughters "made their father drink wine" so they could profit from his nakedness by receiving his "seed" and getting a "child by their father" (Gen. 19:33–36). Ruth's virtue (along with Boaz's) stands out in contrast to those Genesis tales of incest, because although she took advantage of his drinking to lie down next to him and "uncover his feet," she "rose up before one could know one another" (Ruth 3:4, 14), and the couple then arranged to perform the necessary steps to marry or "know one another" in the proper way.

The seductive charms of female strangers that the Bible denounces are associated not only with their use of wine but also with other means of erotic enticement that seem distinctively aesthetic by deploying refined sensory pleasures and the beauties of art. Warning men of the verbal art of attractive "flattery" from "the tongue of a strange woman," the Old Testament book of Proverbs likewise cautions against the multiple aesthetic delights that her tongue promises: "I have decked my bed with coverings of tapestry, with carved works, with fine linen of Egypt. I have perfumed my bed with myrrh, aloes, and cinnamon. Come, let us take our fill of love until the morning" (6:24, 7:15–18). The artistic accessories and sensory embellishments that aesthetically enrich and refine the experience of lovemaking are

[17] Judith "washed her body all over with water, and anointed herself with precious ointment, and braided the hair of her head, and put on a tire upon it, and put on her garments of gladness . . . And she took sandals upon her feet, and put about her bracelets, and her chains, and her rings, and her earrings, and all her ornaments, and decked herself bravely, to allure the eyes of all men that should see her" (Judith 10:3–4). In highlighting this text's sustained attention to her art of seduction, we should also note that it dates from the Hellenistic period and is not included in the Hebrew biblical canon.

provocatively suggested here, but only to be condemned and linked to immoral or even criminal behavior with the strange woman. The bed of lovemaking – rather than being admiringly portrayed as a complex artwork that is rich in sensually aesthetic delights of fragrance and of visual and tactile beauty (tapestries, fine linen, and carvings) that artistically complement the taste of the woman's wine and the sweet sound of her flattering tongue – is instead condemned as a "narrow pit" in which one is trapped "as an ox goeth to slaughter" (7:22, 23:7). In contrast, one should simply love "the wife of thy youth . . . let her breasts satisfy thee at all times" without the need for artificial, artistic enhancements (5:18–19). And what, according to Solomon's Book of Proverbs, should one most desire? After God, wisdom seems to be the privileged object of desire, and wisdom reciprocates by deeply desiring man. "Doth not wisdom cry? and understanding put forth her voice? . . . She crieth at the gates, at the entry of the city, at the coming in at the doors. Unto you, O men, I call" (8:1–4). Wisdom (*chochma*, חָכְמָה) is a feminine noun in Hebrew as is understanding (*tvuna*, תְּבוּנָה). Wisdom here claims to be God's original consort and daily delight. "The LORD possessed me in the beginning of his way. . . . Then I was by him, as one brought up with him: and I was daily his delight, rejoicing always before him" (8:22, 30).

The Hebrew Bible undeniably recognizes the multiple sensory and artistic beauties that aesthetically enhance erotic desire and enrich the experience of lovemaking. But rather than affirm or promote them by developing an *ars erotica* – a set of principles, strategies, or methods to enhance these aesthetic pleasures – the Old Testament tends to fear and condemn them for distracting from the instrumental goal of producing progeny and for disrupting the marital, social bonds necessary for building a strong nation based on patriarchy and ethnic purity. Of course, even this erotically stifling compilation of texts cannot avoid the return of the repressed. The lusciously sensual and aesthetic blandishments of love emerge in the Song of Songs with potently poetic expression.

This richly erotic but deeply enigmatic poem repeatedly elevates love's "kisses" and other "delights" as "better than wine," describing them with the lush sensuousness of garden imagery, replete with delicious fruits and fragrant spices: "an orchard of pomegranates, with pleasant fruits; camphire [henna], with spikenard . . . and saffron; calamus and cinnamon, with all trees of frankincense; myrrh and aloes, with all the chief spices." In love's pleasure garden "the mandrakes give a smell" to complement the fragrance of the lover's "ointments" that are better than all spices. "Thy lips, O my spouse, drop as the honeycomb: honey and milk are under thy tongue; and the smell of thy garments is like the smell of [the cedars of] Lebanon." There is more: "thy breasts shall be as clusters of the vine, and the smell of thy nose like apples; And the roof of thy mouth like the best wine" (4:10–11, 13–14; 7:5, 8–9, 13).

The poem is a paradigm of somaesthetic sensuality, evoking and commingling all our bodily senses in the expression of love's pleasures and desires. We find, of course, the more aesthetically respected distant senses of sight and hearing ("let me see thy countenance, let me hear thy voice, for sweet is thy voice, and thy countenance is comely," 2:14). We encounter the fearsome power of sight's gaze to overwhelm its loving target, a power the Greeks also recognized ("thou has ravished my heart with one of thine eyes . . .Turn away thine eyes from me, for they have overcome me," 4:9, 6:5). The Song of Songs, however, magnifies its erotic sensuality by emphasizing the more proximate, intimate senses of smell and taste, commingling them to raise their intensity of pleasure.

Erotic touch is clearly present in the repeated mention of kissing but also more discreetly evoked by metaphorical suggestion through the notion of taste and the sensual activities of wine drinking and eating that all involve touching and that can serve both as metaphors for lovemaking and as facilitating precursors to it. Touch finds erotic expression also in the image of the lover as a fragrant "bundle of myrrh [who will] lie all night betwixt [the woman's] breasts" (1:13). Even the proprioceptive, kinesthetic sense is evoked not only in the dancing Shulamite,[18] but also in the woman's "going about the city" streets desperately searching for her beloved, who earlier was "leaping upon the mountains, skipping upon the hills . . . like a roe or a young hart" (2:8–9, 3:2). There is also the sexually steeped and strongly proprioceptive sense of sucking in the strikingly ambiguous line "O that thou wert as my brother, that sucked the breasts of my mother!" (8:1). This line, like the repeated invocation "my sister, my spouse" (4:9, :12), takes the poem's erotic commingling toward the forbidden borders of incest. Indeed, given the repeated admiring analogizing of the lovers' bodies to animals, the poem's commingling could also raise the issue of bestiality. In any case, it certainly affirms the beauty of animal desire in human commingling.

Despite its aesthetic sensuality and erotic evocation of the art of dance in the lovely whirling Shulamite, the poem hardly provides a clear and

[18] The Hebrew text of the poem's chapters 6 and 7 makes her dancing status clearer than in the King James translation. See the translation of Ariel Bloch and Chana Bloch, *The Song of Songs: A New Translation with an Introduction and Commentary* (Berkeley: University of California Press, 1998), 98–99. "Again O Shulamite, dance again, that we may watch you dancing! Why do you gaze at the Shulamite as she whirls down the rows of dancers? How graceful your steps in those sandals, O nobleman's daughter."

substantive doctrine of biblical *ars erotica*. It proposes no explicit theoretical principles or systematic practices of lovemaking. The dominant images in which the lovers are portrayed – "like to a palm tree" or a "dove," "like two young roes," "or a young hart" or "a garden," "an orchard," "the apple tree," "the vine," or "lilies" – express vegetative or animal beauty rather than artistic cultivation (1:15, 2:3, 4:5, 4:12–13, 7:7–8, 8:14). Their courting and suggested sexual union connote natural, unschooled animal desire rather than refined human artistry, let alone divine commandment. Metaphorical and elusive in meaning, the poem does not present a clear, coherent narrative, let alone a reliable guide for Old Testament lovemaking.

Nonetheless, precisely because of its combination of rich ambiguity, elusive metaphorical evocativeness, and concrete sensual images of body parts and sensory pleasures, the Song of Songs encourages allegorical interpretations of lovemaking that transcend not only the brute coupling of animals but also the physical lovemaking of cultured humans. We shall see how the poem repeatedly inspired the subsequent biblical tradition with a more spiritual vision of *ars erotica* aimed at securing the union of the enlightened and divinely beloved human lover's soul with the almighty lover and beloved God. Allegorical readings are particularly appealing because the Song of Songs is not merely enigmatic but clearly anomalous to the whole thrust of Hebrew views on sex and religion. Probably written in the post-exilic Hellenistic period around the third century BCE,[19] there is not a single mention of God in the poem. Nor can we find the familiar biblical hierarchies where humans are always superior to animals while men have clear dominion over women. In this poem, the female is the more dominant, seductive, active lover. The poem's vibrant power of female sexuality and desire provides another instance of the return of repressed Old Testament eroticism, perhaps recalling the popular pagan fertility cults of its time. The female lover of the poem evokes the captivatingly attractive desire of a budding fertility goddess, one who perhaps dances to show off her bodily beauty and cause her worshipper-lover "to drink of spiced wine of the juice of [her] pomegranate," while also boldly offering a strikingly rare, albeit minimal, biblical instruction in sexual position taking. She twice instructs: "His left hand should be under my head, and his right hand should embrace me" (8:2–3; cf. 2:5–6). If this way of specifying the desired form or posture of sexual embrace is extremely rare in the bible, it clearly echoes images from

[19] Ibid., 23–28.

ancient Mesopotamian fertility rites: "Your right hand you have placed on my vulva. Your left stroked my head."[20]

Pragmatics versus Aesthetics

One reason for the lack of Hebrew *ars erotica* is the presumption that it was not at all needed for the dominant Hebrew male, who was assumed to be inherently potent and fertile with a penis divinely sanctified through circumcision and requiring no art to achieve sexual success. We hear of no erectile dysfunction among the Hebrews, except, perhaps indirectly, through the edict excluding the genitally damaged from the congregation. Likewise, the man's seed was presumed to be potent, so infertility was blamed on the female, whose own erotic enjoyment was not apparently worthy of concern. As distinctly superior in power and status, the man would simply take a woman sexually without the need to win her and prime her erotically through aesthetic blandishments and artistry. In the same way, the legendary "sons of God" (mysteriously invoked in Genesis 6:2, 4) simply "saw the daughters of men that they were fair and took them" directly, without any preliminary erotic play or seduction, and thus begat children. Without any female God to inspire a different model of divine coupling, this direct, aesthetically unembellished male sexual "taking" or "knowing" or "laying" with a woman formed the biblical paradigm for lovemaking.

The aesthetic artistry of seduction aimed at exciting another's sexual desire is an art that, in the Old Testament, only women need to practice. The sole apparent exception is the illicit and dismal attempt of Amnon to arouse his half-sister Tamar by feigning illness to draw her to his bed. Failing to stir her desire, he took her by sheer force, with dire consequences for them both (2 Samuel 13). How a man should make love to render lovemaking more pleasurable, beautiful, and meaningful was not a topic for inquiry or instruction. A man's erotic prowess and performance were a carnal yet heavenly mystery directed to fulfill a divine covenant; it was a matter for wonder and not for knowledge or theorizing about methods. As Proverbs 30:18–19 puts it: "There be three things which are too wonderful for me, yea, four which I know not: the way of an eagle in the air; the way of a serpent upon a rock; the way of a ship in the midst of the sea; and the way of a man with a maid."

Sex was indeed affirmed, cherished, and even sanctified as a pleasure for the Hebrews. Indeed, the notion of pleasure sometimes served as a synonym

[20] S. N. Kramer, *The Sacred Marriage Rite: Aspects of Faith, Myth, and Ritual in Ancient Sumer* (Bloomington: Indiana University Press, 1969), 105.

for lovemaking. But erotic pleasure was never considered an end that was valuable in itself or essential to the sexual end of procreation. Nor was erotic experience regarded or pursued as a means of self-cultivation, a way of enhancing one's self-knowledge, sensitivity and concern for others, and skills of communicative expression. Although the Old Testament describes sexual intercourse as "knowing" one's partner, it never seems to consider how lovemaking can help one gain a better knowledge of oneself (one's desires, preferences, emotions, degree of self-control) or even a better understanding of one's partners apart from intimate acquaintance with their flesh. We thus describe such lovemaking narrowly as "carnal knowledge." For the monotheistic Hebrew people the aim of sex was resolutely monolithic. Sexual pleasures should not be rejected or disparaged, but they must be firmly channeled toward the divinely prescribed and demographically vital work of procreation needed to establish the Hebrew people as a strong nation in the holy land God promised to Abraham. A significant part of the pleasure seems indeed identified with the act's divine sanctification and anticipation of progeny, generating the gratifying pride of procreation. If infertility was a woman's curse that brought agonizing frustration, jealousy, and cruel rejection, then men were rudely excluded from the congregation if their genital tools of reproduction were damaged or even if their genitals were healthy but uncircumcised, hence unsanctified for Hebrew procreative duties.

II CHRISTIANITY

Paul and the Cult of Chastity

Christianity's revisionary development of Hebrew doctrine was enormously emancipatory in its demographic inclusions but not erotically liberating. It instead constrained the range and value of sexual pleasures while magnifying the scope of sexual prohibitions. On the other hand, Christian thought (largely through the influence of Neoplatonism) advanced an intriguing direction of what might be called asexual divine eroticism whose expression we will examine here and in Chapter 8. With respect to the penis, the cherished site of Hebrew procreative ritual practice, Christianity preached a liberalizing message when Jesus boldly opened the kingdom of Heaven to the genitally damaged, who were excluded from the holy community by Mosaic law as they could not fulfill the commandment of procreation. Jesus instead asserts that "there are some eunuchs, which were so born from their mother's womb: and there are some eunuchs, which were made eunuchs of men: and there be eunuchs, which have made themselves eunuchs for the kingdom of heaven's sake" (Matthew 19:12).

Paul expanded this policy of penile tolerance. His conversion of the gentiles was immensely successful because he did not require their circumcision (or their adherence to Hebrew dietary laws). God could embrace different ways of life, so long as they served righteousness, peace, and joyful faith in God's grace. For Paul, "as the Lord hath called every one, so let him walk. And so ordain I in all churches. Is any man called being circumcised? Let him not become uncircumcised. Is any called in uncircumcision? Let him not be circumcised. Circumcision is nothing, and uncircumcision is nothing, but the keeping of the commandments of God" (1 Cor. 7). He repeats the message even more strongly in Galatians 5:2–6: "Now I, Paul, say to you that if you receive circumcision, Christ will be of no advantage to you.... For through the Spirit, by faith, we wait for the hope of righteousness. For in Christ Jesus neither circumcision nor uncircumcision is of any avail, but faith working through love." In the same way, "the kingdom of God is not meat and drink; but righteousness, and peace, and joy in the Holy Ghost. For he that in these things serveth Christ is acceptable to God, and approved of men" (Rom. 14:17). In short, "I know, and am persuaded by the Lord Jesus, that there is nothing unclean of itself: but to him that esteemeth any thing to be unclean, to him it is unclean" (Rom. 14:14).

Sexuality, however, constitutes a domain which seems unclean of itself. Allegedly stricter, Mosaic law is sexually far more tolerant than the Paulian doctrine of love. Polygyny and concubinage were authorized in ancient Hebrew culture, and persisted long after.[21] The holy patriarchs Abraham and Jacob partook of this privilege, gaining blessings rather than censure. Solomon had 700 wives and 300 concubines from many different nations while being deemed holy enough to build God's temple. If Solomon's foreign women led him to do "evil in the sight of the LORD," such evil was not in his sexual promiscuity but rather in his turning to the gods they worshipped, to "Ashtoreth the goddess of the Zidonians, and after Milcom the abomination of the Ammonites" (1 Kings 11). Christian teaching, however, strictly forbade both polygamy and concubines. Moreover, by disallowing divorce it provided further restrictions on the erotic fulfillment of both men and women.

Even more significant was the Christian degradation of human lovemaking from a divinely privileged universal commandment to a second-best

[21] Jewish acceptance of polygyny continued into Talmudic times, and its explicit prohibition did not occur until Rabbi Gershom ben Judah in the beginning of the eleventh century. But this ruling was authoritative only for the Jews of Northern Europe, and Jewish polygyny was officially permitted (though rarely practiced) in Spain until the fourteenth century and even later in some Islamic countries.

compromise for those unable to practice the higher life of chastity, exemplified by Jesus and preached by Paul as his strongly held preference. "It is good for a man not to touch a woman," claims the apostle in his First Epistle to the Corinthians. "Nevertheless, to avoid fornication, let every man have his own wife, and let every woman have her own husband," and let them show "benevolence" in giving each other reciprocal "power" or use of their own bodies and not deny or "defraud" each other from the sexual use of their bodies, "except it be with consent for a time" for purifying purposes of "fasting and prayer" (1 Cor. 7:2–5). This endorsement of marital lovemaking, Paul emphasizes, is only "by permission, and not of commandment. For I would that all men were even as I myself . . . and . . . I say therefore to the unmarried and widows, it is good for them if they abide even as I [in chastity]. But if they cannot contain, let them marry: for it is better to marry than to burn" (1 Cor. 7:6–9). Paul regarded marriage as clearly inferior to celibacy because it involves unholy desires and pleasures of the flesh, rebellious lusts of the body that defy the spiritual law of the mind. "For I know that in me (that is, in my flesh,) dwelleth no good thing: for to will is present with me; but how to perform that which is good I find not. . . . I see another law in my [bodily] members, warring against the law of my mind, and bringing me into captivity to the law of sin which is in my members. O wretched man that I am! who shall deliver me from the body of this death?" (Rom. 7:7–10).

Paul importantly defines the sinfulness of the flesh (*sarkos*, σαρκὸς) as more than merely a bodily thing; one's mind or spirit (φρόνημα) can be fleshly if one's thought is focused on sinful, lustful "works of the flesh" such as "adultery, fornication, uncleanness, lasciviousness, . . . heresies, envyings, murders, drunkenness, revellings, and such like" (Gal. 5:19–21). Even if one's body is cleansed, Paul insists that "to be carnally minded (φρόνημα τῆς σαρκὸς) is death" (Rom. 8:6). Human sexuality is, of course, closely connected with death because its procreative function provides the only form of combatting the mortality we inherited from Adam and Eve, who recognize their erotic nakedness and procreate only after having committed the sin whose divinely ordained punishment was death. Marriage's duty of lovemaking not only binds us to the body's baser, carnal desires in contrast to the law of the spirit, but it also (through its procreative production of fleshly mortals) paradoxically condemns us to continue the cycle of death.[22] Paul instead insists that the body is "for the Lord" and that its

[22] For this reason, some heretical sects like the Cathars rejected marriage and procreation.

sanctification could yield a Christian rebirth in the spirit, providing eternal life through being "joined unto the Lord." Because "your bodies are the members of Christ," because "your body is the temple of the Holy Ghost which is in you," you should "therefore glorify God in your body, and in your spirit, which are God's" through somatic purity and the sanctifying of your body to the Lord; for "he that is joined unto the Lord is one spirit" (1 Cor. 6:13–20).

This idea of spiritual unity with (and through) God reveals another flaw in matrimony: marriage destroys such single-minded unity by dividing one's attentions between God and one's spouse.

> He that is unmarried careth for the things that belong to the Lord, how he may please the Lord: But he that is married careth for the things that are of the world, how he may please his wife. There is difference also between a wife and a virgin. The unmarried woman careth for the things of the Lord, that she may be holy both in body and in spirit: but she that is married careth for the things of the world, how she may please her husband. (1 Cor. 7:32–34)

Thus, although one who opts for marriage "doeth well," the person who "has power over his own will" so that he can abstain from the lovemaking of marriage and fornication "doeth better" (1 Cor. 7:37–38). This further flaw in marriage expresses a conflict that parallels the tension between spirit and flesh, a distracting "doubleness of soul," a division of one's loyalties between the Lord God and one's spouse, a split that constitutes an unyielding barrier to the Christian goal of complete divine union that can be achieved only by devoting one's body and mind solely to God's service and not to the satisfactions of one's mortal lover.[23]

Paul's celebration of celibacy over marriage dominated the development of Christian views on sexuality, which often went further than Paul in championing virginity, sometimes even to the point of disparaging marital sex as unworthy or impure. Radically challenging Jewish insistence that eschewing sex was sinful (because "he who does not engage in procreation of the race is as though he sheds human life"),[24] Christianity's doctrinal divergence in privileging celibacy had a sociopolitical justification, albeit an otherworldly one. While the Jewish commandment to procreate rested on establishing the Hebrews as a powerful nation on earth, the Christian ideal

[23] This notion (expressed in Greek as "dipsychia," also translatable as "double-soulness") was repeatedly deployed in an influential early second-century Christian text, *The Shepherd of Hermas*, available (in the J. B. Lightfoot translation) at earlychristianwritings.com.

[24] I. W. Slotki, trans., *Babylonian Talmud: Yebamoth*, 63b (London: Soncino Press, 1936), 426.

was the kingdom of heaven, and this required no multiplication of new births (hence no sex or marriage) to make the kingdom sufficiently strong to defend it from other nations. Jesus makes it very clear (in Mark 12:25) that when the saved "shall rise from the dead, they neither marry, nor are given in marriage" but rather are wholly spiritual and entirely devoted to God "as the angels which are in heaven." Of course, as the Christian Church developed and conceived itself as "the Body of Christ," it realized the importance of new members through birth or conversion to strengthen that body.

If Paul's privileging of chastity found support in the principle of imitating the celibate Christ (pure not only in his conduct but in his miraculous conception), then it was further fortified by Hellenistic philosophical ideals of strengthening the spirit through ascetic disciplines of denying carnal desires. Obviously antithetic to developing a carnal *ars erotica*, chastity was ingeniously transformed by Christian theorists into a somaesthetics of virginity that offered its own superior beauties of purity and joys of the spirit. These potent pious pleasures of the soul could, moreover, provide also intense somatic enjoyment, while avoiding "the unclean rubbing that is from the fearful fire of [one's] fleshly part" and that lowers rather than elevates the soul.[25] Sexual abstinence purifies and lifts the soul. "How different a man feels himself when he chances to be deprived of his wife," argues Tertullian (155–240), a theologian from Carthage who indeed had a Christian wife. "He savors spiritually.... If he is making prayer to the Lord, he is near heaven ... [and] he satisfies himself."[26]

Origen (184/5–253/4), who chose to be castrated as a young man of twenty, urged an extremely fierce discipline of abstinence for the sexual body – "You have coals of fire, you will sit upon them, [and] they will be a help to you."[27]

[25] The citation is from an early Christian Gnostic text, *The Sophia of Jesus Christ*, primarily taken from the *Nag Hammadi Codices*, II.4, 108, trans. Douglas M. Parrott, the Gnostic Society Library, the Nag Hammadi Library, accessed November 1, 2018, www.gnosis.org/naghamm/sjc .html; also in J. M. Robinson and Richard Smith, eds., *The Nag Hammadi Library in English* (San Francisco: Harper & Row, 1990), 220. The passage is cited in Peter Brown's classic study, *The Body and Society: Men, Women, and Sexual Renunciation in Early Christianity* (New York: Columbia University Press, 1988), 116. Because Brown's book contains some of the more recondite passages I cite in the ensuing discussion but is more accessible, I will refer to it with the abbreviation BS.

[26] Tertullian, *De exhortatione castitatis* (*On Exhortation to Chastity*), chapter 10, trans. S. Thelwall, in *The Writings of Tertullian, Vol. 3: With the Extant Works of Victorinus and Commodianus* (Edinburgh: T&T Clark, 1870); www.tertullian.org/anf/anf04/anf04-15.htm#P946_228818.

[27] Homily 1:3 in Origen, *Homilies 1–14 on Ezekiel*, trans. Thomas Scheck (New York: Newman Press, 2010), 30.

This sort of *askesis*, as Peter Brown argues, would allegedly stimulate the soul to recognize that "the spiritual realm was alive with joys whose sensuous delight was veiled from the pious only by the present numbness of their spirits" (BS 172). Such discipline, moreover, would transform the body into a true temple of God as Paul had intimated. "Do not think that just as *the belly* is made *for food and food for the belly* that in the same way the body is made for intercourse," writes Origen; rather, "it was made that it should be a *temple to the Lord* . . . In this manner, Adam had a body in Paradise; but in Paradise he did not 'know' Eve."[28] The chaste, virginal body gleams with special, sacred beauty, argues St. Ambrose (337–397), because of its singular purity, unity, and wholeness – somaesthetic qualities captured by the Latin word *integritas*, which Aquinas later used as one of the three criteria for defining beauty. Virginity involves "an integrity unexposed to taint from the outside," but with sexual contact (even in marriage), a woman "loses what is her own, when something else comes to mix with her."[29] The same goes for men, who lose the chastity of continence.

St. Jerome (347–420) strongly argued for virginal chastity as highly preferable to marriage; the difference between them "is as great as that between not sinning and doing well." "The link of marriage is not found in the image of the Creator." Indeed, "all who have not preserved their virginity, in comparison of pure and angelic chastity and of our Lord Jesus Christ Himself, are defiled." In rejecting sexual pleasures, one could learn to taste the heavenly "sweets of chastity."[30] So strong was the ideal of chastity through sexual repression that, for some theorists, it even extended to a monk's unconscious. Achieving this ascetic yet aesthetic ideal of perfect purity and wholeness demanded not only a total termination of lustful acts and thoughts but even a lack of nocturnal emissions indicative of erotic dreams despite the monk's conscious efforts to eschew sex in waking life.

In noting the many "degrees of chastity by which one may mount to inviolable purity," John Cassian (ca. 360–ca. 435) describes an ascending series of "six lofty summits of chastity."[31] The first is that "the monk not be undone by carnal attacks while awake. The second is that his mind not dwell

[28] Origen, *Origen on I Corinthians*, trans. C. Jenkins, *Journal of Theological Studies* 9 (1908): 370.

[29] Ambrose, *Exhortatio virginitatis* 4.27, ed. J. P. Migne (Paris: Patrologia Latina, 1845), 16:359A, https://ia600100.us.archive.org/34/items/PatrologiaLatina/Patrologia%20Latina%20Vol.%2016.pdf.

[30] St. Jerome, *Against Jovinianus*, in *The Principal Works of St. Jerome,* trans. W. H. Fremantle (Grand Rapids, MI: Eerdmans, 1893), 794, 799, 802, 837.

[31] John Cassian, "On Chastity," *in John Cassian: The Conferences*, trans. Boniface Ramsey (New York: Paulist Press, 1967), 443; hereafter CON.

upon pleasurable thoughts. The third is that he not be moved to desire, even slightly, by looking up a woman. The fourth is that he not permit a movement of the flesh [i.e., an erection], however simple, while awake. The fifth is that, when a discussion or some necessary reading evokes the thought of human generation," it should be considered with indifference and "the gaze of a tranquil and pure heart, as a kind of simple act and as a ministry that is unavoidably part of human nature" and something unexciting "like brickmaking or some other task" (CON 443). The monk who reaches "the sixth degree of chastity is ... not... deluded by the alluring images of women even when asleep," although erections and nocturnal emissions may still occur because of excess accumulation of fluid but without any sinful "tingling sensation [or] ... any recollection of lust" (CON 443, 449).

A still higher level of "purity of chastity" exists in which even these nocturnal lapses end so that "even the natural movement of the flesh [has] died and one would not produce any disgusting fluid at all" (CON 444). Although claiming that this level can be achieved only by "extraordinary persons" through God's special grace of "divine gift," Cassian nonetheless recommends one practical method to remedy these nocturnal embarrassments usually considered physically "unavoidable": limiting one's fluids (CON 444, 449). "In order that the law of the body may conform with the law of the mind, an excessive drinking even of water itself should be curbed" so that the body's amount of liquid would make these unseemly unconscious movements "not only extremely infrequent but even phlegmatic and dull" (CON 449). Such "emissions" that were possibly provoked "by dreams during sleep" posed a persistent problem for the monk's ascending quest to reach "true purity" of flawless chastity, as St. John Climacus (ca. 579–649) later notes, because they suggest a hidden division in the monk's psyche between the day's conscious heavenly desires and a nocturnal carnal unconscious that always threatened to corrupt and take control.[32]

Chastity, however, had its own dreamy versions of ardent romance for the soul "who expels [carnal] love with [spiritual] love ... , and who has conquered the fire caused by the beauties of earth by meditation on the beauties of heaven."[33] Cassian similarly speaks of the "fiery ardor" of divine

[32] St. John Climacus, *The Ladder of Divine Ascent*, trans. Lazarus Moore (New York: Harper, 1959), Step 15.4, 15.13.

[33] Ibid., 15.2; 15.11. This redirection of desire toward exclusively spiritual things is expressed in total indifference to all earthly bodies, beauties, and colors: "Truly blessed is he who has acquired perfect insensibility to every body and colour and beauty" (15.9).

love, "those fiery ecstasies of heart and the joyful consolations" that come from one's chaste devotion to God, "that heavenly inpouring of spiritual gladness" achieved by chaste "holy ones" through God's grace (CON 450–451).[34] One example of such spiritual romance was the apocryphal story of St. Paul and Thekla. A noble young pagan virgin betrothed to be married, Thekla heard Paul preaching about virginity and was so entranced by Paul's teaching that her mother and fiancé conspired to put Paul in prison. After bribing her way into Paul's prison cell, she was sentenced to be stripped and burned. But when Thekla was put naked on the fire, it was extinguished by a heaven-sent storm, and she escaped to travel with Paul to another pagan city. A nobleman from that city ardently pursued Thekla but she fought him off, resulting in another death sentence from which she was again miraculously saved despite repeated attempts to execute her. Victoriously vindicated through chastity and faith, Thekla returned unharmed to Paul and eventually converted her mother to Christianity.[35]

Methodius of Olympus (martyred in 311) made Thekla ("instructed by Paul") the preeminent of the virgin orators in his *Banquet of the Ten Virgins*, a text that celebrates virginity as the "best and noblest manner of life." It is "the root of immortality," and "superior to ten thousand other advantages of virtue which we cultivate for the purification and adornment of the soul," because a Christian virgin is "a bride to the Son of God," a "Bride of the One Christ."[36] Thekla sings of her passionate love for her divine bridegroom:

[34] Cassian explains the psychological reasons why carnal desires cannot be properly vanquished without a spiritual erotic of divine love. "It is because our carnal desires for present things cannot be repressed or plucked out unless salutary dispositions have been introduced to replace the harmful ones that we want to cut off. In no way can the mind's vitality subsist without some feeling of desire or fear, joy or sadness, which must be turned to good use. Therefore, if we want to cast carnal desires from our hearts, we should at once plant spiritual pleasures in their place, so that our mind, always bound to them, might have the wherewithal to abide in them constantly and might spurn the allurements of present and temporal joys" (CON 349).

[35] See *Acts of Paul and Thecla*, trans. Alexander Walker, in *The Ante-Nicene Fathers: The Writings of the Fathers Down to A.D. 325*, vol. 8, ed. Alexander Roberts and James Donaldson (Grand Rapids, MI: Eerdmans, 1885). We find another exemplary celibate loving couple in St. Cecilia and her husband Valerian in second-century Rome. Compelled by her parents to marry this pagan noble, Cecilia insisted on maintaining her vow of virginity by refusing to consummate the marriage and convincing Valerian to respect her wishes and to be baptized so that they could live lovingly and chastely as Christians, which they did until they were both martyred.

[36] Methodius of Olympus, *The Banquet of the Ten Virgins, or, Concerning Chastity*, trans. William R. Clark, in *The Ante-Nicene Fathers: The Writings of the Fathers down to A.D. 325*, vol. 6, ed. Alexander Roberts, James Donaldson, and A. Cleveland Coxe (Buffalo, NY: Christian Literature Publishing, 1886), 310, 329, 331, 334. Revised and edited for *New Advent* by Kevin Knight, www.newadvent.org/fathers/0623.htm. Methodius describes Thekla (in chapter 1 of Discourse 11) as the "Chief of Virgins."

"Leaving marriage and the beds of mortals and my golden home for You, O King, I have come in undefiled robes, in order that I might enter with You within your happy bridal chamber." And she is answered by the other virgins in an affirming, repeating chorus. "I keep myself pure for You, O Bridegroom, and holding a lighted torch I go to meet You."[37]

Ten centuries later and far away in medieval England, the adventurously romantic but passionately chaste love life of Christina of Markyate exemplifies the ennobling power of divine desire. "A maiden of extraordinary sanctity and beauty," she was born to a noble Anglo-Saxon Christian family around 1100, and pledged herself to "inviolable virginity."[38] When a bishop, who already enjoyed her maternal aunt as his concubine, tried to seduce Christina by luring her into his bedroom, she cleverly evaded his clutches by offering to lock the door but then escaping and locking him inside. The angered bishop then pressured her parents to compel her to marry a young nobleman in order to take revenge against Christina by violating her cherished virginity. Although the marriage took place, Christina, by various means, escaped her husband's persistent and vigorous attempts to consummate it, attempts that were strongly encouraged and abetted by her own parents. Eventually, she had to flee, disguising herself as a man and seeking refuge by hiding in a tiny cell in the hermitage of a devout old hermit until her marriage was annulled; she remained with the hermit until he died. She then found shelter with a high-placed cleric for whom she developed a violent erotic desire that he reciprocated, sometimes appearing "before her naked, burning with lust" (CM 46). Christina herself struggled to control the passions of "her lascivious body," being "so inwardly inflamed that she thought the clothes which clung to her body might catch fire!" (CM 46–47). But she escaped these sexual temptations by finding a divinely passionate but chaste "consolation" in the embrace of Christ, who appeared "in the guise of a small child" and "came to the arms of his sorely tested spouse" who "pressed him to her bosom . . . with immeasurable delight . . . [and] felt him in her innermost being," with an experience of "abounding sweetness" (CM 48).

Freed of her violently carnal passions, Christina became the prioress of her hermitage and developed an intimately loving spiritual friendship with Abbot Geoffrey of St. Albans, who supported her financially while she guided him spiritually and instructed him in virtuous behavior. Recognizing her superiority in spiritual virtue, Geoffrey sought to emulate it, thus

[37] Ibid., chapter 2, 351–352.

[38] *The Life of Christina of Markyate*, trans. C. H. Talbot, ed. S. Fanous and H. Leyser (Oxford: Oxford University Press, 2008), 1, 6; hereafter CM.

demonstrating the ennobling power of love to educate. Although Christina and Geoffrey were "beloved" in the "bond of holy affection," their love had no sexual dimension or desire, at least not on her part. Required to visit the pope in Rome, Geoffrey strangely "asked for two undergarments from Christina, not for pleasure but to relieve the toil of the task ahead" (CM 69, 71). She instead gave them to the poor, after being so instructed by a vision she received in prayer. Geoffrey may have been her beloved, but Christina remained the passionately devoted virginal bride of Christ, an exemplar of religious virtue and leadership.

Ever since its beginnings, Christianity, while sustaining male privilege, was far more respectful and welcoming to female religious practitioners than was Judaism. From Roman times, Christian women often joined male monks in close religious communion. Pagan critics condemned this as "a kind of religion of lust, a promiscuous" community whose ideology of chaste asceticism concealed a variety of unholy sexual practices, of which there were surely many instances.[39] However, as we just noted, there were also cases of erotically suffused yet genuinely pious religious devotion, perhaps most notably in the relationship of virgin nuns to Christ. "The mouth of virgins shall kiss the bridegroom, and the nose of virgins shall be drawn towards the odor of his perfumes. Virgin hands shall touch the lord, and their chastity of the flesh shall prove acceptable."[40] Monks who were purified by maintaining carnal continence while eschewing marriage could also aspire to such heavenly union: "a certain spiritual embrace" so devoutly yet erotically charged that Origen yearningly describes it by echoing the sexual longing of the Song of Songs. "Oh, that I could be the one who might yet say: His left hand is under my head, and his right hand will embrace me."[41]

Preparing oneself for such chaste union with God was not a casual affair. It required intense discipline, structured and reinforced by rigorous rules to make oneself worth of the divine bridegroom. Virginity here was not simply a physical condition but a distinctive, demanding vocation or calling whose training and practice was likened to those of athletes and soldiers. John

[39] Minucius Felix, *Octavius*, in *Tertullian and Minucius Felix*, trans. G. H. Randall (Cambridge, MA: Harvard University Press, 1953), 337. Later church reformers, such as Erasmus, made similar critiques, as we shall see in Chapter 8.

[40] Evagrius of Pontus, *Exhortation to a Virgin*, in *Evagrius of Pontus: The Greek Ascetic Corpus*, trans. R. E. Sinkewicz (Oxford: Oxford University Press, 2003), 135. This passage is also cited, with a similar translation, in Peter Brown, *The Body and Society*, 276.

[41] Origen, *The Song of Songs: Commentary and Homilies*, Homily 1:2, trans. R. P. Lawson (London: Longmans, Green, 1957), 270–271.

Cassian, for example, describes the Christian virgin as the "true athlete of Christ" and the "victorious soldier of Christ," noting that, like athletes, virgins (of all genders) "must abstain not only from forbidden foods, drunkenness, and every kind of intoxication but also from all laziness, idleness, and slothfulness, in order that their strength may grow from daily exercises and constant meditation."[42] Foucault calls it an "art of virginity," but describes it in the older general sense of art as *techne* (technical know-how or skill) rather than art in any aesthetic sense. As a "*techné de la virginité*" or "*technologie de la virginité*," he explains, "it is like an art, in the manner, for example, of medicine," like "philosophy is an art of healing souls"; and he draws on Gregory of Nyssa (335–394), who (like other Church Fathers) sees virginity as a professional calling rather than a simple physical condition.[43] "As some arts, in other professions, were invented to successfully achieve the tasks pursued, thus, it seems to me, the profession of virginity is an art and a science of divine life."[44] This profession of virginity, writes John Chrysostom (ca. 349–407), is "the contest of self-control" in which one is "enrolled" by deliberate "choice" or "pledge," and it takes as its task the preparation for a union with God and a divinely higher, angelic life on earth. "Do you grasp the value of virginity? That it makes those who spend time on earth live like the angels dwelling in heaven."[45]

However, to what extent, if any, could we qualify this *techné* of virginity as a somaesthetic art? Certainly, it centrally involved the soma, whose purity it sought to preserve by abstaining not only from sexual contact but also from other somatic practices or attitudes that fueled sexual desire or sullied the mind as well as the body. John Cassian, like many other churchmen, warns of the evils of gourmandizing and wine that promote lustful thoughts and actions, sowing "the seeds of lasciviousness . . . It is not an excess of wine alone that ordinarily inebriates the mind. Too much food of any kind makes it stagger and sway and robs it of every possibility of integrity and purity" (INS 120).[46] But "mere abstinence from food is not enough to maintain the

[42] John Cassian, *The Institutes*, trans. Boniface Ramsey (New York: Newman Press, 2000), 127, 129, 156; hereafter INS.

[43] Michel Foucault, *Histoire de la sexualité, tome 4: Les aveux de la chair* (Paris: Gallimard, 2018), 161, 178, 204. Translations of this book from the French are my own.

[44] Foucault brings this quote from Gregory in ibid., 177.

[45] John Chrysostom, "On Virginity," in *On Virginity; Against Remarriage*, trans. Sally Rieger Shore (New York: Edwin Mellen Press, 1983), 15, 56–58.

[46] Clement likewise urges the need to control one's eating for the sake of spiritual gains, not only by dining frugally and avoiding wine, but also by eating with decorum. See Clement, *The Instructor*, Book 2, in *The Ante-Nicene Fathers: The Writings of the Fathers down to A.D. 325*, vol. 2, ed. A. C. Coxe (Grand Rapids, MI: Eerdmans, 1962).

integrity of mind and body unless other virtues are also present in the soul": humility and the conquest of anger, pride, greed, and the fleshly wanderings of the mind from the focus on God. But these virtues in the "spiritual struggle" of virginity are also learned partly through the somatic means of fasts, "grinding toil, and bodily fatigue" that are part of the penitential and ascetic practice of defying the flesh that defines this ascetic art of holy purity (INS 122, 127).[47]

Another somatic dimension of the art of virginity concerns its special style of clothing the body. Cassian pays particular attention to the belt of monks: "it is proper for a monk always to dress like a soldier of Christ, ever ready for battle, his loins girded" with a belt and his clothes humble and suitable for labor (INS 21). The monk "should know first that he is protected by being bound with a belt so that he may be not only mentally prepared for all the exercises and works of the monastery but also unimpeded by his garb itself ... Second, he should also be aware that ... girding his loins and encircling himself with dead skin means that he is bearing about the mortification of his members, which contain the seeds of wantonness and lasciviousness" (INS 26). Rather than a belt, female virgins take the veil as their distinctive somatic attire that protects them from carnal desire. Tertullian writes on the veiling of virgins that "Every public exposure of an honorable virgin is (to her) a suffering of rape" because "the very spirit itself is violated in a virgin by the abstraction of her covering" as "she is penetrated by the gaze of untrustworthy and multitudinous eyes."[48] Such exposure is moreover corruptively carnal because "Seeing and being seen belong to the self-same lust," and with an unveiled virgin "the sense of shame wears away." "The very concupiscence of non-concealment is not modest" as it involves "the study of pleasing ... men."

[47] This art of controlling one's fleshly desires not only in physical practice but even in one's thoughts, Foucault argues, became for Christianity a new form of experiential practice devoted to care for the self through disciplined self-cultivation or *askesis*. In this sense, Christianity maintained the Greek idea of transformative care of the self through *askesis* but displaced the old Greek way of doing this in terms of governing one's sexual relations. Rather than "*aphrodisia*," Christianity made the flesh (and its control through "the practice of penitence and the exercises of ascetic life") the central principle or general rule that integrates and underlies the various rules that define "a proper life." Thus, for Foucault, Christianity developed the notion of flesh into a new "mode of experience" involving "self-knowledge and self-transformation ... in relation to the annulation of evil and the manifestation of truth." Foucault, *Les aveux*, 50–51.

[48] Tertullian, *On the Veiling of Virgins*, trans. Sydney Thelwall, in *The Ante-Nicene Fathers: The Writings of the Fathers down to A.D. 325*, vol. 4, ed. A. C. Coxe (Grand Rapids, MI: Eerdmans, 1956), 29, 36. The following quotes in this paragraph are from ibid., 28, 36.

As the field of aesthetics began as a science of sensory perception, so the somaesthetic dimensions of the Christian art of virginity focused on the monitoring and purification of the soma's senses as well as the chaste purity of the flesh. True virgins, writes Methodius, have "preserved the five senses, which most people consider the gates of wisdom, pure and undefiled by sins," and in this way "there is a chastity of the eyes, and of the ears, and of the tongue, and so on of the other senses."[49] A true virgin "has kept the five forms of the sense pure to Christ, as a lamp, causing the light of holiness to shine forth clearly from each of them." In short, "all the members are to be preserved intact and free from corruption; not only those which are sexual, but those members also which minister to the service of lusts. For it would be ridiculous to preserve the organs of generation pure, but not the tongue, or to preserve the tongue, but neither the eyesight, the ears, nor the hands, or lastly, to preserve these pure, but not the mind, defiling it with pride and anger."

But what place can be found for a somaesthetics of *beauty* in virginity's *ars erotica*, with its severe art of ascetic austerity and purifying sensory control and appetitive restraint? Chastity's advocates repeatedly critique the display of physical beauty and vehemently condemn attempts to enhance it through cosmetics, ornaments, and decorative clothing. Clement explains that for a woman "the head should be veiled and the face covered; for it is a wicked thing for beauty to be a snare to men."[50] Chaste women "must accordingly utterly cast off ornaments" such as golden necklaces and bracelets (which are like slavish fettering "chains"), and instead "ought to be adorned within, and show the inner woman beautiful" by being beautiful in her soul. Men similarly must eschew "luxurious clothing" and ornamentation that suggest "sordid effeminacy." If Clement insists that beauty should be shown "in the soul alone," he nonetheless suggests that the beauty of a virtuous soul can be visible in the body (at least to God) through the somatic aura of chaste virginity. Such a person is beautiful because he "is arrayed in chastity, the sacred stole of the body"; his beauty is "the true beauty, for it is God; and that man becomes God."

In affirming the "beauty of virginity," John Chrysostom more clearly explains the beautifying effects of the chaste virgin soul on the body. "Wearing gold [or other ornaments] mars your beauty and increases your ugliness" because, as outward visible objects, such "embellishments" distract and thus "detract from the outward loveliness of their owner." "But,"

[49] Quotations in this paragraph are from Methodius, *The Banquet of the Ten Virgins*, 330, 351.

[50] Clement, *The Instructor*, Book 2, quotations in this paragraph are from pages 265, 266, 260, 271.

Chrysostom insists, "the ornament of virginity is not like this . . . because it is . . . wholly spiritual," and this spirituality engenders an enveloping aura of divine beauty. "Therefore, if the virgin is unattractive, virginity immediately transforms her ugliness by surrounding it with an irresistible beauty. If she is in the bloom of youth and radiant, virginity makes her brighter still" with beauty worthy of her divine bridegroom. "For the eye of the virgin is so beautiful and comely that it has as a lover not men but the incorporeal powers and their master."[51] Virginity's spiritual purity beautifies the body not only by providing it an attractive enveloping aura; virginal virtue also works on the body itself to render it more beautiful and harmonious. For the strongly virtuous soul, disciplining the body reshapes it in an aesthetically enhancing way. "The body of a soul so practiced in virtue must harmonize its own impulses with the movement of that soul. For her glance, her language, her demeanor, her walk, in short everything is defined by the discipline within. It is like a costly perfume: although enclosed in a vial, it penetrates the air with its own sweet smell and suffuses with pleasure those inside and nearby, and even all those outside."

Virginity, with its pure beauty and divine eroticism, is therefore far superior to marriage, which is limited by the carnality of lapsarian desire, as indeed is second marriage, which widowhood permits. Tertullian argues that the scripture's dictum "Better to marry than to burn" does not entail that marriage is good, but rather regards it "as a species of inferior evil" to the greater evil of fornication.[52] "'Better it is to marry than to burn,'" he writes, "is to be understood in the same way as 'Better it is to lack one eye than two,'" while "second marriage . . . [would] border upon fornication" because it involves elements "of carnal concupiscence . . . which are appropriate to fornication."[53] Indeed, even first marriages seem tainted by concupiscence since one does not marry a woman without seeing her and desiring her; and the means by which one consummates a marriage – coital "commixture of the flesh" through carnal concupiscence – "is the essence of fornication." Chrysostom, in his treatise "On Virginity," finds marriage a far inferior state because its procreative work belongs to life after Eden and thus "springs from disobedience, from a curse, from death" – a way to serve God's sentence of mortality while fulfilling the divine wish that humans be

[51] Chrysostom, "On Virginity," 98–99. The following quotation is from 100.

[52] Tertullian, "On Monogamy," trans. Sydney Thelwall, in *The Ante-Nicene Fathers: The Writings of the Fathers down to A.D. 325*, vol. 4, 60.

[53] Tertullian, "On Exhortation to Chastity," trans. Sydney Thelwall, in ibid., 52, 55. The following quotation is from 55.

fruitful and multiply.[54] "So marriage was granted for the sake of procreation, but an even greater reason was to quench the fiery passion of our nature." Although originally "marriage had these two purposes, ... now, after the earth and sea and all the world has been inhabited, only one reason remains for it: the suppression of licentiousness and debauchery. Marriage is of much use to those who are still now caught up in their passions, who desire to live the life of swine and be ruined in brothels."

Early Christianity is far from monolithic in deprecating married sexuality to idealize virginity. However, even moderate thinkers like Clement of Alexandria (150–215) who strongly defended marital sex nevertheless warned against its pleasures as a distraction from its only biblically valid purpose: procreation. "The goal of this institution [of marriage] is to have children; its end is that the children be good."[55] Mosaic dietary law, he argued, prohibits the eating of rabbit because of that animal's excessive, unrestrained sexuality: it "is always in heat, mates in all seasons," and does so "indiscriminately with any other rabbit," even when the female is pregnant already and unable to conceive. For Clement, once a woman became pregnant, she and her husband should cease intercourse because her womb is already satisfied; any further sexual pleasure is superfluous, sinful, and injurious. Refraining from such extra, nonprocreative pleasure, he argues, conserves one's strength and enables one to defeat one's enemies, while indulging in it "dims the senses and destroys the [person's] forces." Likening orgasm to "a brief epilepsy," Clement claims that even in terms of the pleasure of the sexual act, "the less frequent it is, the more it pleasure it gives." Condemning contraception as a violation of God-given reproductive duty for the selfish pursuit of pleasure, Clement adds further restraints to diminish sexual enjoyment, by restricting the variety of positions and the times that are permissible for intercourse. Denouncing the mounting of a female from behind as "a shameful position,"

[54] Chrysostom, "On Virginity," 22. The following two quotes are from 27 to 28. In a homily, Chrysostom clearly insists that Adam and Eve's "intercourse [came] after the Fall; up till that time they were living like angels in paradise and so they were not burning with desire, not assaulted by other passions, not subject to the needs of nature, but on the contrary were created incorruptible and immortal, and on that account at any rate they had no need to wear clothes." St. John Chrysostom, *Homilies on Genesis 1–17*, trans. Robert C. Hill (Washington, DC: Catholic University of America Press, 1986), "Homily 15," 202–203.

[55] The quotes in this paragraph are from Clement's *The Instructor*, Book 2, chapter 10. Most of this chapter does not appear in English translation in the edition cited above because of the chapter's sexual content, providing that content only in Latin. My English translation draws on the French translation of M. De Genoude, included in his collection *Défense du Christianisme par les pères des premiers siècles de l'église* (Paris: Librairie de Peffodil, 1846), available online at http://remacle.org/bloodwolf/eglise/clementalexandrie/pedagogue4.htm.

he also insists that married couples confine their lovemaking to "the darkness of night," thereby reducing its visual pleasures. But he equally cautioned that this obscurity of night should "not render us intemperate and immodest," since God and our soul's conscience are always aware of what we do.

Clement elsewhere inveighs against the Hellenistic interest in sexual positions and their pictorial representation, alluding with outrage to the sexual postures of the legendary Philaenis (noted in Chapter 2) in his general condemnation of Alexandrian taste for erotic images.

> Diminutive Pans, and naked girls, and drunken Satyrs, and *erecta pudenda*, painted naked in pictures disgraceful for filthiness. And more than this: you are not ashamed in the eyes of all to look at representations of all forms of licentiousness which are portrayed in public places, but set them up and guard them with scrupulous care, consecrating these pillars of shamelessness at home, as if, forsooth, they were the images of your gods, depicting on them equally the postures of Philænis and the labours of Heracles. Not only the use of these, but the sight of them, and the very hearing of them, we denounce as deserving the doom of oblivion. Your ears are debauched, your eyes commit fornication, your looks commit adultery before you embrace.[56]

Clement, moreover, reviles the immorality of erotic images by linking it to a more general condemnation of the Greek appreciation of artistic images of bodily beauty as being a form of idolatry, a devoted adoration of painted or sculpted images rather than God's commandments and God's holy work of creation. You "have devoted to shame what is divine in this handiwork of God, you disbelieve everything that you may indulge your passions, and that ye may believe in idols, because you have a craving after their licentiousness, but disbelieve God, because you cannot bear a life of self-restraint."[57]

[56] Clement, "Exhortation to the Heathen," in his *Protrepticus*, William Wilson (trans.), 57–61, in *Ante-Nicene Fathers*, vol. 2, ed. Alexander Roberts, James Donaldson, and A. Cleveland Coxe (Buffalo, NY: Christian Literature Publishing, 1885). Revised and edited for New Advent by Kevin Knight, www.newadvent.org/fathers/0208.htm; https://en.wikisource.org/wiki/Ante-Nicene_Christian_Library/Exhortation_to_the_Heathen.

[57] Ibid. Alluding to recorded cases of people adoring the beauty of statues and even using them sexually, Clement says that such art lovers "are inferior to apes by cleaving to stone, and wood, and gold and ivory images, and to pictures," whereas apes are not deceived by such lifeless idols of beauty (ibid.) The link of idolatry with sexual misbehavior was already a salient theme in Old Testament texts, but Paul reinforced it in Romans 1:23–29 where he complains that the people have "changed the glory of the uncorruptible God into an image made like to corruptible man, and to birds, and four-footed beasts, and creeping things. Wherefore God also gave them up to uncleanness through the lusts of their own hearts, to dishonour their own bodies between themselves." Worshipping created images "more than the Creator," humankind fell "into vile affections: for even their women did change the natural use into that which is against nature. And likewise also the men, leaving the natural use of the woman, burned in their lust one toward

If early church theorists paid far more attention to virginity than to marriage, then those who seriously considered the value of marriage nonetheless insisted on its inferiority to virginity and sexual abstinence. Indeed, if we can speak of them advocating an art of marriage, its goal would be to make marriage resemble virginity as much as possible, in terms of working toward God-devoted chastity and spiritual progress as the highest end. Marriage is a remedy to control the typically irresistible powers of lust; its value is less in what it offers in itself than in what it enables us to avoid. To affirm its value, Chrysostom notes how Christ himself "honored a marriage . . . with His presence" (and "without being ashamed of it"), and he continues this style of faint praise by asserting: "Marriage is not an evil thing. It is adultery that is evil. It is fornication that is evil. Marriage is a remedy to eliminate fornication."[58] It also aimed to eliminate adultery through Christian marriage rules stipulating (after St. Paul) that married individuals are not masters of their own sexual bodies, but rather that their respective spouses own their bodies with respect to sexual use. "The wife hath not power of her own body, but the husband: and likewise also the husband hath not power of his own body, but the wife" (1 Cor. 7:4).

Chrysostom recognizes that "It is certainly possible to be married and to pray at the same time, but prayer can be intensified by abstinence" (JCM 28). Similarly, "Sex is not evil but it is a hindrance to someone who desires to devote all her strength to a life of prayer" (JCM 41). Thus, like virginity, marital abstinence is in principle better, so long as one's spouse consents. "Abstinence *without* mutual consent is forbidden, but if husband and wife *agree* to live together in continence, they are not seeking to break up their marriage" (JCM 40); and they can live a holier life through a more "spiritual marriage" (JCM 54). The Pauline idea referenced here that "conjugal rights [are] a *debt*" to one's spouse serves to show that "neither husband nor wife is his or her own master, but rather are each other's servants" (JCM 26), although in matters other than sex the husband has clear authority over the wife.[59] Here we see another aspect of celibate virginity's advantage; for it surely seems better to be God's servant than the servant of one's spouse.

another; men with men working that which is unseemly, and receiving in themselves that recompence of their error."

[58] John Chrysostom, "Sermon on Marriage," in C. P. Roth and David Anderson, trans., *St. John Chrysostom: On Marriage and Family Life* (Cresswood, NY: St. Vladimir's Seminary Press, 2003), 53. This book, which collects four homilies concerning marriage, along with the "Sermon on Marriage" and another sermon on "How to Choose a Wife," will hereafter be cited as JCM.

[59] Chrysostom explains the husband's privileged authority through a somatic metaphor: "The wife . . . should not demand equality, for she is subject to the head; neither should the husband

Chrysostom does not deny that there is love between husband and wife, but "such love is an obligation" (JCM 50) deriving from God who sanctifies marriage. "Marriage is a bond, a bond ordained by God" (JCM 74). So in loving a wife, the husband should "love her not so much for her own sake, but for Christ's sake" (JCM 58). Chrysostom does not reject the role of beauty in a husband's affection for his wife, when urging the husband to "prefer her before all others, both for her beauty and her discernment" and to "praise her" for her virtues (JCM 62). But the beauty intended is primarily "beauty of the soul," not conventional physical beauty, which Chrysostom calls "outward beauty" and disparages as ephemeral and "full of conceit and licentiousness," filling us with "lustful thought" as well as "pride, foolishness, [and] contempt of others" (JCM 48–49).[60] Such beauty of soul shines through "affection, gentleness, and humility," which "is the beauty God requires" and is ultimately most attractive and best for happily married life (JCM 49).

Chrysostom similarly affirms the role of sexual pleasure in marriage. However, he validates it not through the pleasure itself but through its procreative purpose and sanctification by Scripture, even from the original Genesis notion that the husband "shall cleave unto his wife: and they shall be one flesh" (Gen. 2:24). "How do they become one flesh? As if she were gold receiving the purest of gold, the woman receives the man's seed with rich pleasure, and with her it is nourished, cherished, and refined. It is mingled with her own substance and she then returns it as a child! The child is a bridge connecting mother to father, so the three become one flesh"; but even if "there is no child . . . their intercourse effects the joining of their bodies, and they are made one, just as when perfume is mixed with ointment" (JCM 77). In short, God "does not despise physical unity" but prefers "spiritual unity," not a "marriage of fleshly passion, but [one] wholly spiritual, just as the soul is joined to God in an ineffable union which He alone knows" (JCM 55).

belittle her subjection, for she is the body. If the head despises the body, it will die. Rather let the husband counterbalance her obedience with his love. Let the hands, the feet, and all the rest of the body's parts be dedicated to the service of the head; but let the head provide for the body, for the head is responsible for all the members. Nothing can be better than a union like this" (JCM 53).

[60] "The beauty of the body, if not joined with the virtue of the soul will be able to hold a husband for twenty or thirty days, but will go no farther before it shows its wickedness and destroys all its attractiveness" (JCM 100). "Haven't you seen how many men, living with beautiful wives, have ended their lives in misery, and how many who have lived with those of no great beauty, have lived to extreme old age with great enjoyment" (JCM 49).

Spiritual chastity should be the guiding goal, even in marriage. God originally instituted marriage "for two purposes: ... to make us chaste, and to make us parents." But "the reason of chastity takes precedence," as marriages need not "always lead to child-bearing" and procreation is anyway no longer essential as "the whole world is filled with our kind" and Christ has won us immortality in the afterlife (JCM 85). Indeed, "now that the resurrection is at our gates, and ... we advance toward another life better than the present, the desire for posterity is superfluous" (JCM 85) Here again, spiritual union and the spiritual birth of chaste thoughts and deeds are superior. "If you desire children, you can get better children now" (through Christ) "if you give birth by spiritual labor" (JCM 85–86). Such labor creates beauty of the soul. Couples "who radiate the beauty of the soul" strengthen their mutual affection while preserving its purity and virtue so "every kind of immorality is driven out" as "a warm and genuine friendship holds between them," which also "attracts the good will and protection of God for [their] whole household" (JCM 100).

The art of matrimony therefore aims at establishing the couple's chastity and spiritual union in God. The husband "should show true nobility of spirit" by not being preoccupied with worldly matters such as money and social position, and he should train his wife in such nobility "not ... only by words but by deeds ... Beginning on their wedding night, let him be an example of gentleness, temperance, and self-control; and she will be likewise," avoiding jewelry and "expensive clothes," shunning "immodest music and dancing," and instead maintaining "a sober life-style" (JCM 60). Chrysostom urges husbands not to "engage in idle conversations" and to preface instructions to one's wife by declaring one's love for her. Moreover, man and wife should "pray together and go to Church" and then discuss the readings and the prayers (JCM 61). The husband should commend to his wife this desiring quest for a chaste and spiritual marriage in the following terms of divine eros and pleasure: "Our time here is brief and fleeting, but if we are pleasing to God, we can exchange this life for the Kingdom to come. Then we will be perfectly one both with Christ and with each other, and our pleasure will know no bounds" (JCM 61).

Augustine: Sexual Psychology and Original Sin

Two centuries after Clement and roughly contemporary with Chrysostom, St. Augustine (354–430) resumed the argument for the value of marriage, but did so with more subtlety, insight, and imagination than any previous Christian theorist, expanding significantly on its benefits of friendship that

Chrysostom briefly notes and pagan Plutarch emphasized. The perceptive richness of Augustine's views on sexuality stems from his own potent experience of it. After drinking long and deep from the pleasures of love-making, he embraced the ideal of celibate chastity and then fought a long, hard struggle to achieve it. Raised as a pagan (despite his Christian mother) in Roman-ruled North Africa, Augustine fell in love with a young woman during his student days in Carthage and then lived with her as his concubine for fifteen years, traveling with her to Rome and begetting a son from their union. In moving to Rome and then Milan, Augustine grew increasingly closer to Christianity, especially through the influence of Ambrose and Augustine's own mother, who followed her son to Italy, arranged for him a suitable Roman bride, and convinced him to send his beloved concubine away.

Unable to curb his erotic appetite and wait until his fiancée came of age, Augustine took another concubine, which convinced him that he was shamefully addicted to sex despite his wish for chastity. His famous self-critical plea to God highlights this tension: "Grant me chastity and continence, but not yet" (*Confessions*, 8:7:17).[61] After converting to Christianity, Augustine labored to be fully chaste not only in body but in mind, so he could fully taste the more heavenly delights of divine love and union compared to which even the most intense carnal pleasures were vague, fleeting shadows of darkness. Such purity could allow one to grasp God as "a lover," naked and intimate. One might hold that divine "Wisdom … with most chaste regard and embrace and with no interposing veil, but as if nude, in a way she does not permit save to very few of her most favored suitors" and that brings blessedness and bliss.[62] Any taint of sexual desire would preclude the single-minded sanctity required for this divine embrace. Just as the "most beautiful woman [would] not yield herself to you, if she had discovered that another beside herself were loved by you," so will not God's "Wisdom disclose herself to you, except [if] you are consumed by desire for her alone."[63]

Augustine never lost his idealizing commitment to celibate chastity erotically aimed at union with God, and he ultimately never strayed from it. But that did not prevent him from celebrating Christian marriage as well and recognizing its own forms of chastity. Too smart to transform admiration of

[61] St. Augustine, *Confessions*, trans. F. J. Sheed (Indianapolis: Hackett, 1992), 139.

[62] St. Augustine, *The Soliloquies of St. Augustine*, Book 1:13:22, trans. Rose Elizabeth Cleveland (Boston: Little, Brown, 1910), 38.

[63] Ibid., 38.

the best into denigration of the good, Augustine was also too perceptive to reduce human sexuality to a mere bodily affair or to limit the value of marriage to its instrumentality for generating and raising children. In *De bono conjugali* (*On the Good of Marriage*), he insists that marriage constitutes a fundamental social good because "the first natural bond of human society is man and wife," a "connection of fellowship" and "friendly and true union" whose worth clearly exceeds its production of progeny.[64] This, he argues, is why marriages are not dissolved once couples have completed their task of child rearing, and why Christianity forbids divorce even if the wife or husband is barren and cannot generate children.

If marriage importantly serves to channel and temper the "evil of lust" (GM 400) into "some good" through the begetting of children (GM 400) and avoiding the mortal sin of fornication, this does not mean that its good is merely relative in protecting us from greater evil, while virginity alone is a positive good. Rather, "marriage and continence are two goods, whereof the second is better" (GM 403). "Honorable, therefore, is marriage . . . and the [marital] bed undefiled" (GM 402) as "the bodies also of the married are holy, so long as they keep faith to one another and to God" (GM 405).

Augustine explicitly claims that marriage is good not for its own sake, but only as a means for the sake of "friendship," which, like wisdom and health, is an intrinsic good on its own (GM 403). Augustine likewise suggests that sexual intercourse is an instrumental good in terms of being necessary "for the propagation of the human kind" (GM 403), but it is sinful rather than good when done for the sake of carnal pleasure, even when this occurs within the framework of marriage. As food is an instrumental good for "the conservation of the man" (GM 407), so "sexual intercourse is unto the conservation of the race: and both are not without carnal delight" (GM 407). If such delight is taken in "restraint of temperance" (GM 407) and in honestly seeking the natural purposes ("the use after nature") (GM 407) for which the pleasurable acts are intended – life-conserving nourishment or life-producing procreation of family – then the "carnal delight . . . cannot be lust . . . and is not to be compared either with the vileness of fornications, or with the intemperance of married persons" (GM 407).

In its historical context of Christian orthodoxy, Augustine's erotic theory is admirable not only for its validation of sexual pleasure but also for its

[64] St. Augustine, *De bono conjugali* (*On the Good of Marriage*), in *A Select Library of the Nicene and Post-Nicene Fathers of the Christian Church*, vol. 3, trans. C. L. Cornish, ed. Philip Schaff (Buffalo, NY: Christian Literature Publishing, 1887), 399. Page references to this edition will appear parenthetically with the abbreviation of GM.

complex and influential recognition of the deeply psychological dimension of human sexuality. Lovemaking, even when not motivated by genuine love, is never a mere physical matter; it is steeped in cognitive, affective, and cultural meanings that significantly shape the styles of its bodily expression and, of course, its ethical and aesthetic qualities. The very same physical act of sex could be sinful or not depending not only on its social context (marital or not) but also on its psychological motivations. Augustine insists that "for married persons to have intercourse only for the wish to beget children . . . is not sinful" at all, if their "firm purpose" as Christian believers is to produce more believers, "generating offspring to be regenerated" as "sons of God" and thus harnessing "carnal concupiscence" to "the use of righteousness" while bridling "its rage" as expressed "in inordinate and indecorous motions."[65] But for the same married couple to make love because of a "desire [for] carnal pleasure . . . involves venial sin," which is readily pardonable, whereas "adultery or fornication has deadly fault . . . and is a crime to be punished" (MC 270, GM 402). The sin becomes much graver than venial, however, if the couple's sexual act involves an "attempt to prevent such propagation, either by wrong desire or evil appliance" (MC 271). Oral and anal sex are thus apparently outlawed as "wrong desire," although perhaps a case could possibly be made for their legitimate use in foreplay before the male ejaculates in the "natural" place. In forbidding also contraceptive devices and contraceptive strategies (not only the coitus interruptus practiced by Onan but also coitus reservatus where semen is not spilled but retained in the man's genitals), the range of techniques for *ars erotica* is further restricted so that lovers are constrained to focus on producing Christian offspring in a chastely Christian way.

If marital chastity, for Augustine, depends on the intentions, desires, and beliefs that motivate and accompany the couple's lovemaking, the same criterion of intention determines the virtue of virginity.[66] Virginal chastity is not a mere bodily matter of having a vagina that has never been penetrated (or, for males, a penis that has never penetrated or ejaculated). Such physical intactness could be simply a result of disability, illness, or other circumstances that do not exemplify virtue. True chastity, claims Augustine,

[65] St. Augustine, *On Marriage and Concupiscence*, in *A Select Library of the Nicene and Post-Nicene Fathers of the Christian Church*, vol. 5, trans. Peter Holmes and Robert Ernest Wallace (Buffalo, NY: Christian Literature Publishing, 1887), 264, 265, 267, 270. Page references to this edition will appear parenthetically with the abbreviation of MC.

[66] We find the Augustinian emphasis on intention in the ethical and sexual thought of the famous medieval philosopher Peter Abelard, whose tragic career and remarkable doctrines are discussed in Chapter 8.

consists in our desire to be pure. It depends on the mind's overcoming "the disease of carnal concupiscence" (MC 267) not only in one's physical actions but even in one's thoughts, inspired through obedient love of God.[67] For "how can the body be in any true sense said to be chaste, when the soul itself is committing fornication against the true God?" (MC 265). Here Augustine can appeal to Paul's recognition that the sinfulness of the flesh or carnality is not merely a bodily affair. It is possible to be "carnally minded," and "because the carnal mind is in enmity against God . . . they that are in the flesh cannot please God," who instead wants us live in "the Spirit of God" by obediently following his teachings (Rom. 8:6–8).

The idea of a loving obedience to one's superior as essential for harmony and healthy union is a key theme for Augustine. Such obedient love unites loving wives as subordinate to their equally loving husbands, but it also unites celibates and married believers in loving subordination to God. Augustine likewise applies it to the healthy wholeness of the self through the body's harmonious obedience to the superior, guiding soul. What makes "the disease of carnal concupiscence" (MC 267) so grave and so central for Augustine is that it savagely destroys this somatic harmony of obedience by flagrantly flouting the soul's power of will in a most brazen and distinctively shameful way. This loss of healthful harmony through disobedience also constitutes the key to Augustine's influential theory of original sin that emerges from his ingenious interpretation of the Genesis narrative of Adam and Eve's fall from paradise, which he explicates in Book 14 of his *City of God*.[68]

The true sin of Adam and Eve was not the eating of the forbidden fruit but the act of deliberately disobeying God, along with the pride that such knowing, willful disobedience implies; and Augustine argues that humankind's punishment justly fits the crime. Our "retribution for disobedience is simply disobedience itself. For man's wretchedness is nothing but his own disobedience to himself" (CG575). As we humans did not obey the will of God, so our bodies do not obey our will; we wish to live and enjoy robust health but our bodies become ill, full of suffering, and die. Expelled from

[67] This idea of true virginity as more than a mere physical state of lack of sexual contact was not uncommon, even before Augustine's writings. John Cassian praised St. Basil of Caesarea (329–330) for claiming, "I do not know woman, but I am not a virgin," and thereby arguing that "the incorruption of the flesh consists not so much from abstaining from woman as it does in integrity of the heart, which ever and truly preserves the incorruptible holiness of the body both by the fear of God and the love of chastity." John Cassian, *The Institutes*, 161.

[68] St. Augustine, *City of God*, trans. Henry Bettenson (London: Penguin, 2003). Page references to this edition will appear parenthetically with the abbreviation CG.

paradise, Adam and Eve were also condemned to the disobedience, death, and suffering labor of their bodies (including the labor pains of childbirth). We have inherited their punishment of bodily insubordination, pain, and mortality.

The most immediate expression of our ancestors' bodies' disobedience to the will of their souls occurred, Augustine argues, already in paradise before God announced his judgment to them. This somatic disobedience was distinctively expressed in the genitals, which were suddenly moved by turbulent lust rather than controlled by the individual's calm will of decision. Before their sin, Genesis 2:25 tells us that Adam and Eve "were both naked ... and were not ashamed." "This," Augustine explains, "was not because they had not noticed their nakedness, but because nakedness was not yet disgraceful, because lust did not yet arouse those members independently of their decision. The flesh did not yet ... give proof of man's disobedience by a disobedience of its own" (CG 578). But after their sin, they became ashamed of their nakedness, and therefore "they sewed fig leaves together, and made themselves aprons" (Gen. 3:7) to cover the body parts that they found shameful – their genital parts. These are rightly "called pudenda ('parts of shame')," because it is shameful that these members of our body do not obey the person's will, the way our other bodily members do (CG 578). We can raise a finger, hand, or foot at will; open and shut our eyes and mouth. But one cannot control by will the erection of one's penis (and presumably, though Augustine does not explicitly speak of it, the comparable arousal of one's vulva). The shameful "insubordination of [the] flesh" (CG 579) in such pudenda explains why everyone in all cultures covers them. Even yogi "in the darkened solitudes of India ... who practice philosophy in nakedness ... nevertheless have coverings on their genitals, although they have none on the rest of the body" (CG 579).

The somatic insubordination of our genitals to our soul's governing will appears in different ways. First, there is "the lust that excites the indecent parts of the body" (CG 577), arousing them for the sexual act even if one's conscious mind and rational will do not initiate such arousal and indeed oppose it. But "lust assumes power" (CG 577) not only to move the body's external members; it "also internally ... disturbs the whole man, when the mental emotion combines and mixes with the physical craving, resulting in a pleasure surpassing all physical delights" (CG 577). Beyond simply perturbing the mind with turbulent emotions and desires, its orgasmic conclusion totally smothers our cognitive powers. "So intense is the pleasure that when it reaches its climax there is an almost total extinction of mental alertness; the intellectual sentries, as it were, are overwhelmed" (CG 577). Finally, just as the impulse of lust is an "unwanted intruder" that can embarrass a man by giving him an unwelcome erection, so it can sometimes shame and dismay him even more when "it abandons the eager lover" who needs "the ferment of lust" to activate his member to achieve the sexual intercourse he desires, whether for holy procreation or merely for pleasure (CG 577). "Thus strangely does lust refuse to be a servant not only to the will to beget but even to the lust for lascivious indulgence" (CG 577).

Because sexual intercourse cannot be properly achieved without the unruly turbulence of lust, the sexual act always seems shameful. It therefore "seeks privacy" (CG 579) and the total "absence of witnesses" (CG 579), even when it is performed in the context of holy matrimony for the divine purpose of begetting children. Such "right action longs to become known; and yet it blushes to be seen," because it is accomplished only through the shamefully "disturbed and undisciplined" emotion of lust that overcomes the sovereignty of will and reason (CG 580). More significantly, because the disobedient impulse of lust is necessarily involved in the very act of conception, the original sin of Adam and Eve is organically transmitted to every child. If all children are physically conceived through the genitals – precisely those unruly members of the body whose disobedience was the punishment for Adam and Eve's disobedience to God, then all children physically inherit the original sin of disobedience through its essential presence or lustful reenactment in their own biological origin.

Augustine insists, however, that this necessity of lust for procreation is simply the result of Adam and Eve's sinful disobedience rather than a necessary condition that must have existed before the fall. Unlike many other Christian commentators, Augustine believes that Adam and Eve had physical bodies like people today (albeit perfectly healthy and functional ones) and that their bodies could have and would have created children by sexual intercourse, fulfilling God's commandment to be fruitful and multiply through the sexual difference of man and woman. However, had that original couple not sinned and fallen, they would not have required the turbulence of lust to procreate. Augustine imagines that before the fall through disobedience, the will could have dictated the proper behavior of the genitals without their needing the ferment of lust to arouse them to action. Unfallen, "the will would have received the obedience of all the members, including the organs of sex" (CG 586), so that intercourse could proceed with calm, untroubled enjoyment of exercising one's rational choice. If such voluntary control of apparently involuntary bodily reactions seems a stark impossibility, then Augustine counters that even some postlapsarian humans show forms of body control that seem "utterly impossible" (such as sweating at will or farting out melodies "without any stink") and that we should imagine that perfect persons in paradise would have even greater powers of somatic control and virtuosity (CG 588).

Augustine offers an imaginative glimpse of the sexual "bliss that existed in paradise" (CG 583) before the fall. Adam's and Eve's "sexual organs would have been brought into activity by the same bidding of the will as controlled the other organs" (CG 591) and with such consummate calmness and skill that the penis "would have sown the seed on the 'field of generation'" (CG 586–587) as the thoughtful farmer's "hand now sows seed on earth" (CG 583, 586–587, 591). Had Adam and Eve not sinned, humans would have reproduced that way: "without . . . passion goading him on, the husband would have relaxed on his wife's bosom in tranquility of mind and with no impairment of his body's integrity" (CG 591), because he would not be wasted by lust's excitement. Augustine even speculates that the wife might even consummate the sexual act while maintaining the complete somatic integrity of her virginal hymen. Freed from the violent movements "activated by the turbulent heat of passion," the husband could calmly enlist his masterful somatic skill in the "deliberate use" of his reproductive instrument so that his "male seed could have been dispatched into the womb, with no loss of the wife's integrity, just as menstrual flux can now be produced from the womb of a virgin without loss of maidenhead" (CG 591).

Having relished the joys of lovemaking to the point of fearing and fighting their addiction, Augustine combined his hard-won Christian chastity with a sexual theory that demoted the penis from privileged symbol of the Hebrews' covenant with God and converted it instead into the shameful emblem of ungodly disobedience. If the circumcised Hebrew penis was free to be used with multiple wives and concubines for progeny and sexual pleasure, then Augustine's uncircumcised penis was far more circumscribed in use. He does propose, however, a positive *ars erotica* of sorts, apart from the joys of the chastely celibate love of God. One can cultivate the enjoyment of marital sex for the sake of children, the joys of friendship, and even sensual pleasure, provided one has the right intentions; and demonstrating the will's ability to ensure those intentions provides the further pleasures of self-mastery. Although reproductive genital sex is Augustine's aim, this would not logically exclude nongenital techniques and pleasures in the realm of foreplay, but he does not specify this option – perhaps out of modesty, perhaps out of fear that cultivating such pleasures would distract from the goal of offspring. Developing the pleasures of foreplay as a support in the service of reproductive sex would enrich his theory while keeping it within the Christian principles that guide and bind him.

Two other critical points are worth making. First, in sharply distinguishing the joys of marital friendship from the delights of lovemaking, Augustine fails to articulate how lovemaking promotes such friendship by fostering tenderness and understanding between the married couple. Contemporary neuroscience suggests chemical reasons why this fostering occurs: sexual arousal and satisfaction release a specific hormone, oxytocin, whose role as a neuromodulator in the brain correlates with increased tendency to bonding, trust, and empathy.[69] Second, while Augustine recognizes that certain individuals have amazing command over parts or functions of their body that are normally presumed to be beyond voluntary control, he assumes that this could only be due to their "natural abilities," ignoring the role of training or practice in their remarkable mastery. But those he claims can perfectly "imitate the cries of birds and beasts and the voices of any other men" or "produce at will such musical sounds from their behind . . . that they seem to be singing" surely must have practiced their skills to refine them to their astonishing level (CG 588).

Augustine must have known from personal experience that disciplined training in continence can train the will to repress erotic desire in order to avoid sexual acts and even lascivious fantasies. Yet he strangely ignores the option that, in our postlapsarian world, we could also train ourselves to control and regulate our desire or "lust" *in* the act of lovemaking itself and thus perform the sexual act more calmly and deliberately (should we wish to) without the "extinction of mental alertness" and the consequent loss of our capacities for judgment. Such judgments could include ethical and aesthetic judgments relating to the quality of our lovemaking and the care we take for our partners (CG 577). Our basic physical and mental capacities may be the gift of God or nature, but our abilities and skills can be improved by the disciplines of education, training, and practice. Part of the essence of human nature is to go beyond one's natural endowment by acquiring a "second nature" through habits, by incorporating the knowledge and affordances of one's environing culture, and through personal disciplines of self-cultivation and self-mastery. In the next chapter we see how Chinese *ars erotica* advocates such disciplined mastery of calm control in the very passion of the sexual act to magnify both pleasure and health.

[69] For a detailed discussion of this point, see Jaak Panskepp, *Affective Neuroscience: The Foundations of Human and Animal Emotions* (Oxford: Oxford University Press, 1998), chapters 12 and 13.

Aquinas and the Rational Expansion of Pleasure

The basic lines of Augustine's erotic theory find confirmation eight centuries later with the Church's most authoritative and systematic theologian, St. Thomas Aquinas (1225–1274), who was born to a noble family from southern Italy. Devoid of Augustine's sexual proclivities, Aquinas made an early choice of celibacy, resolving at the age of nineteen to join the Dominican Order and then resisting his family's fierce efforts to end his religious career. Imprisoning him at the family residence, they even engaged a prostitute to seduce him. But the steadfast philosopher is said to have chased her away with a fire iron, a fittingly chaste substitute for the sinful sexual phallus, hot and hard with the fire of lust. Repeatedly endorsing Augustine's views defending the claim that the sexual act can be sinless and worthy of pleasure, Aquinas deploys his own extraordinary skills of reasoning through fine distinctions to suggest possible ways that might (even if only slightly) broaden the range of valid erotic delights.

If "sin, in human acts, is that which is against the order of reason," which "consists in ordering everything to its end in a fitting manner," then something done "by the dictate of reason" that provides a reasonable and "fitting" means to a good end should not be sinful.[70] As marital sex is a reasonable and fitting means to the "very great good" (ST 2.153.2) of "the preservation of the ... human species" (ST 2.153.2), it therefore carries no sin when performed with that procreative end in mind, even if that performance is one of overwhelming pleasure. One need not fear that because "the exceeding pleasure" (ST 2.153.2) of the sexual act involves extreme passion or nonrational feelings it must necessarily be opposed to "right reason" (ST 2.153.2) and "the mean of virtue" (ST 2.153.2) and thus must in some way be sinful. If the act is chosen and governed by right reason, it can contain elements that are not reasonable in themselves but are reasonable in fulfilling the ends of a reasonable act. For example, Aquinas argues, there is nothing unreasonable or "against virtue for a person to set himself to sleep" (ST 2.153.2), even though sleep is a clearly a nonrational state where (in Augustine's terms) there is even greater "extinction of mental alertness" and of one's "intellectual sentries" than in orgasm (CG 577). To paraphrase this argument in general terms, one could say that it is sometimes reasonable to allow oneself to be unreasonable, just as one of the ways to cultivate oneself is to lose

[70] St. Thomas Aquinas, *Summa theologica*. I cite from an online version, part two, questions 153 and 154; available at www.documentacatholicaomnia.eu/03d/1225-1274,_Thomas_Aquinas,_Summa_Theologiae_%5B1%5D,_EN.pdf. All further references to *Summa theologica* will be parenthetically represented as ST, using the notation reference of part.question.article number.

oneself in other things in a way that opens oneself to new experiences that bring new enriching discoveries. Here Aquinas (perhaps despite his explicit intentions) provides a way of rationally justifying even unreasonable, stupefying erotic pleasures – provided they are done in the proper context of procreative marital sex, thus excluding oral and anal intercourse because of their sterility (ST 2.153.2–3).

Aquinas recognizes that sinful lust can occur within a marital context, "in seeking venereal pleasure [for its own sake and] not in accordance with [the] right reason" (ST 2.154.1) of "generation" (ST 2.154.1), and when certain "due circumstances are not observed" (ST 2.154.1) in the act. Such lust involves "the misuse of a woman" (ST 2.154.11) through a sexual act "against nature [because] it bypasses the proper vessel [e.g., in anal or oral intercourse], or the proper manner instituted by nature in terms of the position."[71] What, then, determines the proper position? Because "in the venereal act the woman is passive," hence more in the "way of matter, whereas the man is by way of agent,"Aquinas argues that man must assume the dominant role in the sexual act (ST 2.154.1). This implies that the proper position for sinless lovemaking is the man mounting his supine wife. Already suggested in Augustine's image of utopian conjugal union – with the man resting "on his wife's bosom" (CG591), this posture has been so repeatedly endorsed by Christian advocates and theologians that it has come to be known as the missionary position.[72] Besides exemplifying male dominance and providing the man greater freedom of movement and control than the woman in acts of vaginal penetration, this coital position was believed (contra Lucretius) to be best for conception, since semen's flow toward its proper target would be aided by gravity. Hence, most Christian thinkers regarded it as uniquely dictated by the "right reason" for intercourse.

Theological texts did not typically treat in detail the varieties of coital positions, partly for fear of arousing lustful thoughts. However, the penitential Christian literature in the period between Augustine and Aquinas does occasionally treat the specifics of forbidden positions and their degree of sinfulness in order to assign the relevant amount of penance. These positions (sometimes

[71] Pierre J. Payer, *The Bridling of Desire: Views of Sex in the Later Middle Ages* (Toronto: University of Toronto Press, 1993), 77–79.

[72] The term "missionary position" was not invented by Christian theorists but rather was introduced only in contemporary discussions of sex to denote "face-to-face man-on-top sexual intercourse." It seems to have originated in sexologist Alfred Kinsey's misreading of anthropologist Bronislaw Malinowski's account of sexual life in Melanesia. For a detailed study of the origins and diverse ideological uses of this term, see Robert Priest, "Missionary Positions: Christian, Modernist, Postmodernist," *Current Anthropology* 42, no. 1 (2001): 29–46.

described as "whorish embraces" and feared as much for their "extraordinary" pleasure as for their "unnaturalness") include lying side by side, sitting, standing, anal (*a tergo*), and vaginal entry from behind (*retro*).[73] As long as intercourse was vaginal, the variant coital positions were not intrinsically mortal sins, although they could indicate "deadly concupiscence," especially when they reflected "the ways of brute animals."[74] The retro posture, whose denigrating designation as "doggy style" was already deployed by some medieval theologians, thus received particularly vehement condemnation. Other clerics, however, seemed still more horrified by the pose that inverted the missionary position by placing the woman on top. While lacking any familiar animal counterpart to demonstrate its bestial character, this position more flagrantly defied the presumed natural order of male supremacy.[75]

In medieval Jewish theology, the same demand for the male-dominant missionary position spawned the myth of Lilith. Assumed to be Adam's first wife (created together with him from the earth but unnamed as the original female of Genesis chapter 1), Lilith allegedly quarreled with and then deserted Adam because he insisted that she always take the "bottom position" in lovemaking so he would be "only on top."[76] Abandoned and alone in Eden, Adam needed God's creation of Eve as described in chapter 2 of Genesis. This Lilith myth thus offered a way for rabbinic hermeneutics to reconcile the apparent contradiction of chapter 1's co-creation of male and female and chapter 2's derivative creation of Eve from lonely Adam's rib, thereby theologically naturalizing man's primacy over woman, as Eve, the second wife, was clearly derivative from man's body.

The repeated assertion of masculine dominance in biblical sexuality reflects, of course, the general thrust of male privilege in Hebrew and Christian patriarchal societies. But it also suggests a preoccupation with manly strength and virility, even when such brave machismo was expressed in the staunch Christian struggles of celibate chastity, ascetic penitence, and pacifistic martyrdom, and even when practiced by women rather than men. Sex not only was the means for producing offspring; it also provided,

[73] These descriptions of the coital positions are those of Gratian and St. Jerome in *Corpus Iuris Canonici* and are cited by James A. Brundage, "Let Me Count the Ways: Canonists and Theologians Contemplate Coital Positions," *Journal of Medieval History* 10, no. 2 (1984): 81–93. Brundage's article gives a more detailed discussion of the diverse coital positions and the varying views on them held by the theologians.

[74] Payer, *The Bridling of Desire*, 78. [75] Ibid., 77–79.

[76] For this aspect of the myth of Lilith, see *The Alphabet of Ben Sira*, a medieval work of rabbinic literature, in David Stern and M. J. Mirsky, eds., *Rabbinic Fantasies: Imaginative Narratives from Classical Hebrew Literature* (New Haven: Yale University Press, 1998), 183–184.

through its proper management or control, a powerful way to remake oneself for greater good and glory. By mastering erotic desire, "the fearful fire that came from their fleshly part,"[77] people could express the heroism of their souls and become "athlete[s] of Christ" (CM 52). By channeling eros into procreative marital sex in the mandated missionary position, men could serve God with sensual pleasure while asserting their gender dominance. It is common to draw a sharp contrast between the sexual views of Judeo-Christian monotheism and the pagan world of Greece and Rome. But both cultures share a preoccupation with assertive male dominance, while Christianity adapted the Greco-Roman philosophy of disciplining one's sexuality for ennobling self-cultivation and not merely for creating progeny to serve an earthly city or the kingdom of God.

[77] *The Sophia of Jesus Christ* II.4, 108, available online at http://www.gnosis.org/naghamm/sjc.html.

4

Chinese *Qi* Erotics

The Beauty of Health and the Passion for Virtue

I SEX, HEALTH, AND PLEASURE

China, the world's longest continuous civilization, can also boast of the oldest surviving studies of lovemaking. Sexual theorizing reaches back to the founding texts of Chinese thought and permeates its multiple fields of inquiry: from the divinatory cosmology and metaphysics of the *Yijing*, or *Book of Changes* (the oldest of Chinese classical texts), to the medical theories of *The Yellow Emperor's Classic of Internal Medicine*, and further into the ethics of Confucius and the Daoist doctrines of Laozi and Zhuangzi. Because sex pervades so many aspects of life, it finds expression in many fields of thought. Much classical Chinese sexual theory has therefore been formulated in works largely focused on broader topics. However, there does exist a distinct genre of texts in Chinese erotic theory, variously known as the "handbooks of sex" or manuals of "the Art of the bedchamber."[1]

Many contemporary intellectuals learned of China's rich erotic tradition through the influential work of Michel Foucault. Unfortunately, despite his enthusiastic interest in Chinese sexology, Foucault has gravely misunderstood it. This chapter begins by revising Foucault's misinterpretations, while explaining the aesthetic motivations of his misreading. Celebrated author of the *History of Sexuality* (only half of whose six projected volumes was completed when he died in 1984), Foucault's studies of the past were inspired by a passionate interest in the integration of erotic artistry into today's aesthetic stylization of life. His focus of advocatory theorizing concerned gay lovemaking and more particularly consensual homosexual S&M, which Foucault celebrates as "a whole new art of sexual practice which tries to

[1] See R. H. van Gulik, *Sexual Life in Ancient China: A Preliminary Survey of Chinese Sex and Society from ca. 1500 B.C. till 1644 A.D.* (Leiden: Brill, 2003), xxxii, 8, 37, 45, 121; hereafter SL.

explore all the internal possibilities of sexual conduct" and establish an "aesthetic appreciation of the sexual act as such." This art, a "mixture of rules and openness," combines consensual codes (that significantly script sexual behavior) with experiments "to innovate and create variations that will enhance the pleasure of the act" by introducing novelty, variety, and uncertainty that otherwise would be lacking in the sexual act.[2] Moreover, despite its use of scripting and special fictional frames of performance (e.g., the sexual dungeon), this sexual activity is not portrayed by Foucault as isolated from the rest of one's life and subjectivity. Instead, one's formation as a sexual subject forms an important part of creatively shaping one's self in terms of one's "aesthetics of existence."[3]

Foucault's sexual theorizing was not principally inspired by the Asian erotic arts but rather by his study of ancient Greek and Roman erotic theory and by his own erotic experience. But he crucially enlists what he calls the Asian "*ars erotica*" as suggesting a valuable alternative to our modern Western "*scientia sexualis*."[4] In contrast to Western sexual science whose discourse of truth combines the ancient tool of confession with the modern "imperative of medicalization" (HS 68) of sexual behavior and function, the Asian erotic arts draw their truth "from pleasure itself, understood as a practice and accumulated as experience" (HS 57). In these arts, sexual pleasure "is not considered in relation to an absolute law of the permitted and the forbidden, nor by reference to a criterion of utility, but first and foremost in relation to itself; it is experienced as pleasure, evaluated in terms

[2] Michel Foucault, "Sexual Choice, Sexual Act," in *Essential Works of Michel Foucault*, vol. 1 (New York: New Press, 1997), 151–152. In making his case Foucault praises gay S&M because "all the energy and imagination, which in the heterosexual relationship were channeled into courtship, now become devoted to *intensifying* the act of sex itself." Likening the gay leather scenes in San Francisco and New York to "laboratories of sexual experimentation," Foucault claims such experimentation is strictly controlled by consensual codes, as in the medieval chivalric courts "where strict rules of proprietary courtship were defined." "Experimentation is necessary," explains Foucault, "because the sexual act has become so easy and available . . . that it runs the risk of quickly becoming boring, so that every effort has to be made to innovate and create variations that will enhance the pleasure of the act." S&M's "mixture of rules and openness," Foucault concludes, "has the effect of intensifying sexual relations by introducing a perpetual novelty, a perpetual tension and a perpetual uncertainty which the simple consummation of the act lacks. The idea is also to make use of every part of the body as a sexual instrument" (ibid., 149, 151–152). For a detailed critical analysis of Foucault's somaesthetics of sex as part of his idea of philosophy as an art of living, see Richard Shusterman, *Body Consciousness: A Philosophy of Mindfulness and Somaesthetics* (Cambridge: Cambridge University Press, 2008), chapter 1.

[3] Michel Foucault, *History of Sexuality*, vol. 2 (New York: Pantheon, 1986), 12, 89–93; hereafter HS2.

[4] Michel Foucault, *History of Sexuality*, vol. 1 (New York: Pantheon, 1980), 57–71; hereafter HS.

of its intensity, its specific quality, its duration, its reverberations in the body and the soul" (HS 57). Moreover, the experience, pleasure, and knowledge from *ars erotica*

> must be deflected back into the sexual practice itself in order to shape it as though from within and amplify its effects. In this way, there is formed a knowledge that must remain secret, not because of an element of infamy that might attach to its object, but because of the need to hold it in the greatest reserve, since, according to tradition, it would lose its effectiveness and its virtue by being divulged. Consequently, the relationship to the master who holds the secrets is of paramount importance; only he, working alone, can transmit this art in an esoteric manner and as the culmination of an initiation in which he guides the disciple's progress with unfailing skill and severity. (HS 57)

"The effects of this masterful art," Foucault concludes, "are said to transfigure the one fortunate enough to receive its privileges: an absolute mastery of the body, a singular bliss, obliviousness to time and limits, the elixir of life, the exile of death and its threats" (HS 57–58).

Refining, in a later interview, his views on *ars erotica*, Foucault summarizes the differences between Greek, Christian, and Chinese cultural attitudes to sexual practice in terms of the three factors of "act, pleasure, and desire." He claims that in contrast to the Greeks, who focused on the act and its control as the "important element" by defining the quantity, rhythm, occasion, and circumstances of its performance, but also in contrast to the Christians, who focused on desire in terms of how to fight it and extirpate its slightest roots while limiting or even avoiding pleasure when performing the act, the Chinese elevated pleasure as the highest, most valuable factor in sex. "In Chinese erotics, if one believes van Gulik, the important element was pleasure, which it was necessary to increase, intensify, prolong as much as possible in delaying the act itself, and even to the limit of abstaining from it."[5] As this interview indicates, Foucault's understanding of Asian *ars erotica* rests largely on the Chinese sources compiled, translated, and analyzed in Robert van Gulik's ground-breaking classic *Sexual Life in*

[5] An English version of this interview, "On the Genealogy of Ethics: An Overview of Work in Progress," was first published in Herbert Dreyfus and Paul Rabinow, eds., *Michel Foucault: Beyond Structuralism and Hermeneutics* (Chicago: University of Chicago Press, 1983), 229–252. I cite the more complete French version revised by Foucault and published in his *Dits et Ecrits, vol. 2: 1976–1988* (Paris: Gallimard, 2001), 1428–1450; quotations from 1441. In this interview, Foucault claims the ancient Greeks and Romans lacked an elaborate *ars erotica* comparable to that of the Chinese (see 1434).

Ancient China. Foucault, however, misreads not only the cited texts but also van Gulik's explicit account of them in very important ways.

First, it is wrong to characterize the classical Chinese texts of *ars erotica* in sharp contrast to sexual science and the medical approach to sex. These writings were instead very much concerned and largely motivated by health issues, so much so that when they are listed in the bibliographical sections of the ancient written histories of the various dynasties, they often appear under the heading of medical books or, when listed separately, immediately after the medical books (SL 71, 121, 193). Though these sexual handbooks are described by van Gulik as treating the "art of the bedchamber," the actual Chinese term used does not refer to "art" in a distinctive aesthetic sense but rather denotes the very general sense of "technique" or "skill" acquired by learning.[6] Van Gulik repeatedly affirms that the "handbooks of sex ... constituted a special branch of medical literature" because their two primary goals of sexual intercourse were focused on promoting health – that of the husband, his wife, and the child to be conceived (SL 72).[7] "Primarily," he argues, "the sexual act was to achieve the woman's conceiving" so as to perpetuate the family. "Secondly, the sexual act was to strengthen the man's vitality by making him absorb the woman's *yin* 阴 essence [held to be an invigorating power], while at the same time the woman would derive physical benefit from the stirring of her latent *yin* nature" (SL 46).

Together these dual aims result in a dialectical sexual economy. Since "a man's semen [where his *yang* 阳 force is concentrated] is his most precious possession, the source not only of his health but of his very life[,] every emission of semen will diminish this vital force, unless compensated by the acquiring of an equivalent amount of *yin* essence from the woman" (SL 47). Therefore, a man's sexual activity should aim to ensure that his female partners be given full satisfaction so that he can absorb the *yin* essence that

[6] The Chinese terms are *fang shu* or *fangzhong shu*, meaning literally "bedroom technique" or "inside the bedroom technique." These texts, though sharing many themes, do not present one monolithic theory, displaying variations in different historical periods and according to the different philosophical ideologies and aims that inspired their authors.

[7] Foucault's emphasis on the essential esoteric nature of these arts is also misleading. For many periods of China's long history, according to van Gulik, the handbooks of sex, which were frequently illustrated, "circulated widely" and were "well known and the methods given by them widely practiced" not only by esoteric specialists but by "the people in general." The handbooks' circulation began to decline in the Sung period, and still more in the Ming period with its greater Confucian prudishness, but the handbooks' practices and principles "still pervaded sexual life" (SL 79, 94, 121, 192, 228, 268). The esoteric teachings belong to the special genre of radical Daoist practices of internal alchemy designed for immortality.

will flow from their multiple orgasms, "but he should allow himself to reach orgasm only on certain specified occasions," notably those most suitable for conceiving a child with his wife (SL 47). To provide an abundance of reinforcing *yin* essence, one needs a plurality of wives and concubines, since relying on a single woman for multiple orgasms would eventually drain her of the *yin* essence needed both to maintain her own health (and consequent power to conceive) and to increase the health of her male partner. Consider this passage:

> If a man continually changes the woman with whom he copulates, the benefit will be great. If in one night one can copulate with more than ten women it is best. If one always copulates with one and the same woman her vital essence will gradually grow weaker and in the end she will be in no fit condition to give the man benefit. Moreover, the woman herself will become emaciated. (SL 138)

By copulating with many women each night without reaching orgasm while saving his semen only for occasional ejaculations, a man not only increases his vitality and *yang* (i.e., male) essence, but in doing so raises his chances of conceiving a male child to perpetuate the patriarchal family.

These principles of sexual logic, explains van Gulik, "implied that the man had to learn to prolong the coitus as much as possible without reaching orgasm; for the longer the member stays inside, the more *yin* essence the man will absorb, thereby augmenting and strengthening his vital force," or *qi* (SL 46). The sex handbooks therefore provide the man with special techniques to

> prevent ejaculation either by mental discipline or by such physical means as compressing the seminal duct with his fingers. Then his *yang*-essence, intensified by its contact with the woman's *yin*, will "flow upwards" along the spinal column and fortify his brain and his entire system. If therefore the man limits his emissions to the days when the woman is liable to conceive, his loss of *yang* essence on those occasions will be compensated by the obtaining of children perfect in body and mind. (SL 47)[8]

A man who thus preserves his semen through such coitus reservatus while absorbing the *yin* of many women that he brings to orgasm will not only sustain his health but become more youthful and age-resistant, even

[8] It followed from this logic that male masturbation was "forbidden (except for extreme occasions) and nocturnal emissions were viewed with concern." As long as it did not involve ejaculation, homosexuality was not condemned in classical Chinese culture but neither did it form part of the ancient sexual handbooks (SL 48).

(according to some of the more radical Daoist texts) to the point of achieving immortality.[9] To quote one of the Tang Dynasty texts that van Gulik supplies, "If one can copulate with twelve women without once emitting semen, one will remain young and handsome forever. If a man can copulate with 93 women and still control himself, he will attain immortality" (SL 194). Though most potent in the woman's genitalia, the invigorating flows of *yin* could also be drawn from the secretions of her mouth and breast, both in erotic foreplay and in the act of coitus itself. These secretions were sometimes referred to as the "Medicine of the Three Peaks" (SL 96, 283).

Coitus reservatus served another health-related function: the emotional stability and peace of mind that depends on a harmoniously managed and satisfied household of women. Already in the ancient Confucian *Book of Rites* (*Liji*), a man's sexual duty to both his wives and concubines was firmly asserted and even inscribed in strict protocols of order and frequency of intercourse, whose violation was "a grave offense." As the *Liji* states: "Even if a concubine is growing older, as long as she has not yet reached the age of fifty, the husband shall copulate with her once every five days. She on her part shall, when she is led to his couch, be cleanly washed, neatly attired, have her hair combed and properly done up, and wear a long robe and properly fastened house shoes" (SL 60). These duties (apart from brief respites in periods of mourning) ceased only when the husband "reached the age of seventy" (SL 60). Without saving his *yang* through coitus reservatus and without the erotic ability to consistently give his wives and concubines real sexual (and emotional) gratification, a husband with a large household of women could easily exhaust himself without satisfying his females, thus creating a disgruntled, disorderly home whose ill-repute as mismanaged "could ruin a man's reputation and break his career" (SL 109).

It should already be clear from this brief account (and there is an overwhelming wealth of further evidence in van Gulik) that, *pace* Foucault, Chinese *ars erotica* was very deeply motivated by health issues and crucially concerned with medical matters and sexual science (albeit not in the dominant forms of modern Western medicine). Foucault surely errs in claiming Chinese erotic theory regards sexual pleasure as more important than the sexual act and as the highest sexual goal, which one aims "to increase, intensify, prolong as much as possible in delaying the act itself, and even

[9] In one document from the Later Han Period, we read of a Taoist master who "lived to the age of over 150 years by practicing the art of having sexual intercourse with women" and that through this art, an old man can restore lost teeth and black hair that has gone gray (SL 71).

to the limit of abstaining from it."[10] Instead, for Chinese theory it is the act itself that the man should seek to prolong so as to magnify his *yin* and *yang* powers along with the salutary benefits they bring. Foucault apparently confuses the sexual act with the act of orgasm rather than the act of coitus or the broader act of lovemaking whose complete erotic performance would include foreplay, coitus (which could issue in orgasm), and also postcoital acts. Pleasure is indeed significant for Chinese erotic theory, but it is integrally tied to the sexual act and cannot be increased by being separated from it.

Though sexual union is sometimes celebrated as the "supreme joy of man" and "climax of human emotions" (SL 70, 203), sexual pleasure cannot be the highest goal in lovemaking, since health interests clearly outweigh it. Indeed, Chinese *ars erotica* often warns against an overriding focus on pleasure as dangerously unhealthy. After explaining that "the essence of the Art of the Bedchamber" is "to copulate on one night with ten different women without emitting semen even a single time," one treatise clearly warns, "A man must not engage in sexual intercourse merely to satisfy his lust. He must strive to control his sexual desire so as to be able to nurture his vital essence. He must not force his body to sexual extravagance in order to enjoy carnal pleasure, giving free rein to his passion. On the contrary, a man must think of how the act will benefit his health and thus keep himself free from disease. This is the subtle secret of the Art of the Bedchamber."[11] Another text warns that "intercourse between man and woman should not be for the purpose of lustful pleasure. People today do not understand the meaning of self-cultivation. They force themselves to perform the act and therefore most often harm their *jing* [vital essence] and damage their *qi*."[12]

[10] Foucault, *Dits et Ecrits*, 1441.

[11] This text also discusses the method for controlling ejaculation and making its energy "ascend and benefit the brain" (SL 193–194). Other passages repeatedly emphasize that the multiplicity of partners has health, not pleasure, as its dominant aim.

[12] Douglas Wile, *Art of the Bedchamber: The Chinese Sexual Yoga Classics Including Women's Solo Meditation Texts* (Albany: State University of New York Press, 1992), 128–129, 88–91, 124–126. Further references to this book are noted with "Wile" in the text. I should mention in this context that there existed a special tradition of woman's medicine, rich but largely neglected. For an extensive historical study of this tradition, see Charlotte Furth, *A Flourishing Yin: Gender in China's Medical History: 960–1665* (Berkeley: University of California Press, 1999). My study instead focuses on the somaesthetic theory of the classical texts that express the dominant (mainly patriarchal) ideology of the dominant classes, without going into the historical issues concerning the extent to which the methods advocated in those texts were actually practiced. Obviously, most people did not have the means to do so.

In short, pleasure is certainly valued, but its importance in classical Chinese sexual theory was embedded in broader goals of health and proper management of self and household. The prevailing view was that sexual pleasure should be used to regulate and refine one's body, mind, and character through the ritual shaping of lovemaking's rules or techniques. As one Former Han Dynasty document puts it: "'The ancients created sexual pleasure thereby to regulate all human affairs.' If one regulates his sexual pleasure he will feel at peace and attain a high age. If, on the other hand, one abandons himself to its pleasure disregarding the rules set forth in the abovementioned treatises [i.e., the sex handbooks] one will fall ill and harm one's very life" (SL 70–71).

Why does Foucault so gravely misconstrue the Chinese *ars erotica* as primarily concerned with maximizing pleasure? Looking for a contrasting culture to challenge the dour sexual science of the West and highlight erotic artistry as a key element in his project of a self-styling "aesthetics of existence" grounded in pleasures, Foucault projects this theoretical desire onto Chinese sexology by exoticizing it as that radical other, erecting it as a pleasure-seeking, aesthetic *ars erotica* to contrast to *scientia sexualis*. Fixated on sexual pleasure, he failed to see that Chinese erotic arts were primarily designed for health, procreation, and the harmonious management of a polygynous household. This blindness was surely intensified by Foucault's inattention to the philosophical, social, and cultural background in which Chinese erotic theory was embedded and functioned, an inattention probably owing to ignorance of Chinese thought.

Of course, the powerful presence of these practical aims does not mean that China's *ars erotica* did not have a significant aesthetic character and related pleasures. Such a misguided inference rests on the common error of assuming (through the dogma of aesthetic disinterestedness) that functionality and aesthetic quality are essentially incompatible. Religious paintings and sculptures have spiritual functions, while protest songs have political goals, but this does not preclude their having aesthetic value and being appreciated for their aesthetic qualities, even when we appreciate their other functions. Appreciation of function can even feed back into our aesthetic appreciation by adding dimensions of meaning to the aesthetic experience of these works. Intrinsic value is not inconsistent with instrumental value. We can appreciate the intrinsic taste of a meal we are eating even if we know that the meal provides good nourishment; likewise, our intrinsic enjoyment of good sex is no less in knowing that it is also good for us. China's *ars erotica* is rich in aesthetic dimensions and pleasures. But to understand their proper place and character, we need to situate them within the wider contexts of

Chinese culture that shaped its erotic theory. This chapter explores the background of metaphysical, cosmological, religious, social, and political ideas that underlie and structure Chinese erotic theories before foregrounding their aesthetic dimensions and philosophical import. First, however, we should provide a few introductory remarks of bibliographical context for the texts in which these theories are formulated.

II THE TEXTUAL BACKGROUND

Preliminary literary indications of lovemaking's cosmic importance already appear in the ancient *Book of Changes* (ca. ninth century BCE), the foundational text of Chinese philosophy. "The constant intermingling of Heaven and Earth gives shape to all things. The sexual union of man and woman [or *yang* and *yin*] gives life to all things." These statements express both the essential harmony of complementarities and the existence of change that defines the Dao (道), or Way, of the universe. "The interaction of one *yin* and one *yang* is called Dao, the resulting constant generative process is called 'change'" (SL 37). The early Confucian classics assert the inescapable natural power of sex, which is crucial to the procreation that guarantees continued family life and, through it, social stability. Confucius twice insists in the *Analects* (9:17, 15:13): "I have never yet seen anyone whose desire to build up his moral power was as strong as sexual desire." This is because, as his disciple Mencius elaborates, sex lies so powerfully deep in human nature that "Appetite for food and sex is nature."[13] Despite Confucianism's quest for the most refined virtue (which often later expressed itself in prudishness), its early *Book of Rites* insists on the husband's sexual duties to his wives and concubines, prescribing strict protocols of sequence, frequency, and preparatory conditions for coition. Daoism's enigmatic founding classic the *Daodejing* evocatively suggests female sexuality as the cosmic root, since both birth and conception come through the female "gate," or vagina. "The gateway of the mysterious female is called the root of heaven and earth."[14]

[13] I quote here from Roger Ames and Henry Rosemont's translation, *The Analects of Confucius: A Philosophical Translation* (New York: Random House, 1998), hereafter AC; and D. C. Lau's translation of *Mencius* (London: Penguin, 1970), 161 (6A.4). Nonetheless, Mencius later insists that observing ritual propriety is more important than sex, and thus that no proper man would want to get a woman by climbing over a neighbor's wall to take his daughter and "drag her away by force" (171; 6B.1).

[14] D. C. Lau, trans., *Tao Te Ching (Daodejing)*, chapter 6 (London: Penguin, 1963), 10; hereafter DJ. An alternative translation of this verse is even more anatomically explicit: "The gateway of the

China's oldest medical work, *The Yellow Emperor's Classic of Internal Medicine* (ca. fourth century BCE), outlines the stages of male and female sexual development and the gradual decline in fertile potency through aging, while insisting on the proper measure of lovemaking for establishing the harmony of *yin* and *yang* that is essential to good health.

> In ancient times those people who understood Dao patterned themselves upon the *Yin* and the *Yang* and they lived in harmony with the arts of divination. There was temperance in eating and drinking. Their hours of rising and retiring were regular and not disorderly and wild. By these means the ancients kept their bodies united with their souls, so as to fulfill their allotted span completely, measuring unto a hundred years before they passed away.

But, the text continues,

> Nowadays people are not like this; they use wine as beverage and they adopt recklessness as usual behavior. They enter the chamber (of love) in an intoxicated condition; their passions exhaust their vital forces; their cravings dissipate their true (essence); they do not know how to find contentment within themselves; they are not skilled in the control of their spirits.... For these reasons they reach only one half of the hundred years and then they degenerate.

To sustain the healthy harmony of *yin* and *yang*, one must not "indulge in excess of sexual intercourse" so as to "preserve the element of *yang* and to make it strong."[15] Early Daoist texts like the *Daodejing* and the *Zhuangzi* also counsel sexual constraint so as not to lose one's vital force.

Despite the sexual reflections of these older classics, we find no separate treatises of sexual theorizing until the Han Dynasty. The official history of the Former Han Dynasty lists eight sexual treatises under the category *fangzhong shu* (房中术, "inside the bedroom techniques") in a separate section of its bibliography that comes directly after the section on medical books. In the Sui and Tang dynasty's official bibliographies the sex handbooks and medical books share the same section. By the time of the Sung dynasty, *ars erotica* texts were grouped under the category of Daoist works,

dark vagina is called the root of the world." Robert Eno, trans., *Dao de Jing* (2010), www.indiana.edu/~p374/Daodejing.pdf.

[15] Ilza Veith, trans., *The Yellow Emperor's Classic of Internal Medicine* (Berkeley: University of California Press, 2002), 97–98, 108.

because of the prevalence of special sexual techniques in certain esoteric forms of Daoism; and the close association of *ars erotica* with esoteric Daoist practice continued into later times.

Classical Chinese texts of sexual theory can be roughly classified into three basic genres, though there is considerable overlap in their themes, aims, and methods so that the same text (and its techniques) could be used by various publics having different ultimate purposes. The first genre of sexual theory is essentially medical in orientation, aimed at promoting health and procreation, and its texts formed distinct chapters of longer medical works. The second genre comprised handbooks that served as "guides for the householder" and "taught how a man could live long and happily by maintaining harmonious sex relations with his women, and obtain healthy offspring from them" (SL 70). Such theorizing went beyond mere medical and health matters to offer techniques for successfully managing the husband's erotic-affective relations with his several wives and concubines in the typical polygynous marriage. Maintaining the harmony and sexual satisfaction of all these women was a challenging responsibility demanding special knowledge, sensibility, and skills, since the typical "middle-class householder had three or four, upper middle-class persons six to twelve, and members of the nobility, great generals and princes thirty or more wives and concubines" (SL 155). These household women enjoyed certain conjugal rites, so copulating with several of them in one night (as many handbooks recommend) was not lecherous license but a duty that was often practically necessary for giving them all enough erotic attention so that jealousies and resentments would not disrupt household harmony.

If these first two genres of erotic theory serve familiar aims of health, procreation, and normal longevity, then we can distinguish a third group of sexual texts primarily focused on serving the radical Daoist aim of a paranormal longevity that ultimately issues in earthly immortality for the individual practitioner. This is in contrast to the Confucian-style immortality achieved through procreation and the continued existence of one's family. Although sharing certain themes and methods with the two other genres, the radical Daoist quest for personal earthly immortality through sex advanced some distinctively esoteric, quasi-mystical erotic techniques (often described in terms of an "inner alchemy") that are complemented by special methods of breathing, meditation, and calisthenics. Increasing one's vitality and longevity through disciplined sexual practice enabled the practitioner sufficient time to accomplish the more daunting quest of achieving the alchemic elixir of immortality.

III THE METAPHYSICAL BACKGROUND

Foucault's misreading shows that properly understanding Chinese erotic theory requires knowing more of its basic background ideologies, principles that remain relatively stable despite continuing cultural change. Starting with metaphysics, we note that change itself constitutes Chinese philosophy's most basic principle of existence, highlighted already in its founding text, the *Book of Changes*. This contrasts with the West's dominant Platonic tradition that identified reality with the unchanging, hence with indestructible abstract forms rather than mutable material particulars. The real world is conceived pluralistically as the "myriad things" (*wanwu*, 万物), while their continuous changes and transitions are governed by the fundamental dual forces of *yang* and *yin* whose complementary workings express the ultimate principle of Dao – the nameless, mysterious originary reality that engenders all.[16] The fact that reality is conceived in these logically different ways – as myriadly multiple, as dualistic (in *yin* and *yang*), and as monistic (in the ineffably singular Dao) – demonstrates the pervasive power of pluralism in Chinese thought.

Rather than an oppositional dichotomy of spirit and matter, *yang* and *yin* are complementarities that fruitfully interact and intermingle in a variety of other productive complementarities (such as heaven and earth, fire and water, day and night, male and female). Sexual union thus takes on cosmic metaphysical significance as embodying the essential union of *yin* and *yang* that generates our universe of changing things. Likewise, on the more personal scale, sexual union produces a new and changing creation in the birth of a human offspring. Recalling the *Yijing*'s remarks that the union of *yin* and *yang* gives life to all things and generates changes all governed by Dao (the Supreme Way), the oldest extant sexual handbooks (from the Han Dynasty) include such titles as *Uniting Yin and Yang* (合阴阳) and *Discourse on the Highest Dao under Heaven* (天下至道谈). If erotic coupling thus has the highest mandate of heaven, then it is very important to learn the ways of doing it well so that its essential value can best be realized.[17] By the same logic, to completely abstain from lovemaking is wrongly unnatural.

[16] For an account of *wanwu*, see Roger Ames and David Hall, *Daodejing: "making this life significant"* (New York: Ballantine, 2003), 67.

[17] One Chinese scholar points out that the Chinese word for "good" (*hao*) is formed by "combining the ideogram 'nu,' meaning 'woman, girl, daughter, or female,' with the ideogram 'zi,' meaning 'man, boy, son, or male,'" thus linguistically emphasizing that "one who has both a son and a daughter is good, and that to unite or combine an individual man and woman, or male

Permeating the universe of myriad things, whose waxing and waning is governed by the interacting forces of *yin* and *yang*, is the vital energy of *qi* (气). It can be transferred from one thing to another and is typically accumulated by acting in harmony with the Dao's natural order but depleted by departing from the right way. As water can take the form of ice or vapor, so *qi* energy can be transformed into the more material form of *jing* (精, translated as essence and related to sperm or seed) or converted into the more refined form of *shen* (神), denoting spirit or soul; and the accumulation of *qi* could increase an individual's *de* (德, power, virtue, or excellence). Humans could increase their *qi* by absorbing energies from more powerful forces in heaven and earth, by contact with mountain mists or clouds or magic earth minerals or even through hierogamous or shamanistic unions with divine powers. But a person's first source of *qi* derives from the parents who gave life to their offspring by contributing their *qi* and mingling it materially in the form of *jing*. Moreover, analogous to our notion of genetic transmission, in absorbing their parents' accumulated *qi*, children could likewise inherit some of their *de* (excellence, inner power, virtue).

This crucial gift of life and virtue to one's descendants formed the basis of China's ancestral worship, which in turn shaped the key Confucian doctrine of filial piety. For ancestral worship to flourish, each generation must produce further descendants to honor (with ritual prayer or sacrifice) the ancestral spirits who were believed to watch benevolently over their living descendants but whose continuing power conversely depended on the powers demonstrated by their descendants through ancestral worship. Such reciprocal linkage gave sexual union a further religious mandate. One's absolute duty to serve the ancestral line by generating children (particularly sons, who were distinctively validated for ritual) explains why successful sex was so crucial that it required serious study and also why polygyny proved so pervasive until recent times.

The human produced by the sexual mingling of bodies was never viewed by classical Chinese metaphysics as a supernatural, immaterial soul somehow conjoined or confined to an ontologically different material body. The self's essential embodiment is indicated by the fact that the ancient Chinese word-character for human body is the same as that for self or person – 身 (*shen*) – and is moreover described as representing a pregnant woman (the large square belly protruding over the slender legs). Sex is thus inscribed in

and female essences, is desirable." Fang Fu Ruan, with Molleen Matsumura, *Sex in China: Studies in Sexology in Chinese Culture* (New York: Plenum, 1991), 1.

the very notion of the human self, just as woman's superior procreative role is underlined in its Chinese character. Though first generated by the parents' bodies and *qi*, the human self needs culture to reach its full form. Hence, cultivating the self (*xiu shen* 修身), which centrally includes cultivating the body, is an essential duty stemming from the metaphysics of one's debt to one's progenitors, as is the related injunction of *shou shen* (守身), protecting the self or body. Somatic self-cultivation and preservation crucially involve matters of health, thus bringing us to the medical context of Chinese erotic theory.

IV THE MEDICAL BACKGROUND

As the necessary means for procreation, sexual activity was carefully studied by medical theories to determine the most propitious conditions (dates, times of day, and somatic, affective, and environmental circumstances) and the most effective techniques of intercourse for conceiving healthy, long-lived offspring of the desired sex (typically male). Chinese medical theory firmly maintained that conception depended on both partners achieving full sexual enjoyment in the coital act through emotional and sensual pleasures. It conversely claimed that the resulting child would be healthier if conceived when both parents enjoyed high levels of *qi* and *jing* along with tranquility of mind, but both energy and tranquility would be undermined by a surfeit of orgasms and excessive erotic excitement. Since ejaculation was believed to significantly deplete one's energy, men were advised to refrain from ejaculating in most of their coital acts in order to conserve their precious energy for conceiving healthier children and for their own vitality.

If sexual union procreates through its life-giving energy, then such energy can also empower and lengthen the lives of those who practice lovemaking, provided they do it properly. Sexual activity was thus recognized as essential to good health, forming a crucial part of the arts of *yang sheng* (养生, nourishing or nurturing life) along with "breath-cultivation, callisthenic exercises, and dietetics," which served as preventive medicine through healthy living.[18] Recognizing how erotic arousal and engagement stimulates the body's vitality and circulation of energies, Chinese sexual treatises

[18] Donald Harper, "The Sexual Arts of Ancient China as Described in a Manuscript of the Second Century B.C.," *Harvard Journal of Asiatic Studies* 47, no. 2 (1987): 539.

consistently emphasize that total abstinence is horribly unhealthy, both physiologically and psychologically. In the *Classic of Su Nu* (素女经), the legendary Yellow Emperor asks the mythical Su Nu ("the immaculate girl") about conserving one's energy through lengthy abstention from intercourse. "That would be a grave mistake," she answers, because it violates the natural "activities and transformations" of *yin* and *yang*. "If you were to abstain from intercourse, your spirit would have no opportunity for expansiveness, and *yin* and *yang* would be blocked and cut off from one another." Instead, since sexual activity "opens closures and unblocks obstructions" for stronger circulation of energy, "you must cultivate your *qi* through frequent practice [of sex] . . . If the jade stalk does not stir, it dies in its lair. So you must engage frequently in intercourse as a way of exercising the body. To be aroused but not ejaculate is what is called returning the *jing*. When the *jing* is returned to benefit the body, then the *dao* of life has been realized" (Wile 79, 85). Moreover, by completely suppressing the natural life-giving activity of intercourse, one is susceptible to having one's sexual energies transferred and expended in unhealthy, unproductive forms such as involuntary nocturnal emissions or seduction by evil spirits (SL 152).

The energy that sexual arousal stimulates and circulates in one's body is also capable of being transferred beyond it. A man can therefore nourish his energy by absorbing the energy of the women he sexually arouses, and intercourse with multiple women multiplies the energy he can absorb. But to do so effectively, he must insure they are fully aroused to the level of orgasm so their energy will abundantly flow in secretions he can absorb. If bringing one woman to orgasm requires sexual skill, then producing and absorbing the multiple orgasms of multiple women demands real mastery of *ars erotica*. The alleged health benefits of obtaining this supplementary energy include not only longevity but also youthful strength and beauty and the curing of various illnesses. "When filled with healthy *qi* what illness will not disappear?" asks the *Classic of Su Nu* (Wile 86), and then details the curative properties of sexual absorption:

> One act without emission makes the *qi* strong. Two acts without emission makes the hearing acute and the vision clear. Three acts without emission makes all ailments disappear. Four acts without emission and the "five spirits" are all at peace. Five acts without emission makes the pulse full and relaxed. Six acts without emission strengthens the waist and back. Seven acts without emission gives power to the buttocks and thighs. Eight acts without emission causes the whole body to be radiant. Nine acts without

> emission and one will enjoy unlimited longevity. Ten acts without emission and one attains the realm of the immortals. (Wile 92)

To obtain such sexual supplements, the *Secrets of the Jade Chamber* (玉房秘笈) advises: "When having intercourse with women, as soon as you feel yourself aroused, change partners. By changing partners you can lengthen your life. If you return habitually to the same woman, her *yin-qi* will become progressively weaker and this will be of little benefit to you" (Wile 102). In a document from the Later Han Period, we read that by practicing this art of repeated coitus reservatus with multiple partners "one's grey hair will turn black again and new teeth will replace those that have fallen out" (SL 71). Some texts prescribe particular coital positions and styles to cure specific ailments or heighten healthy energy for specific body parts or functions (Wile 88–91, 124–126).

Sexual energy transfer, however, can mean loss as well as gain, and such loss through erotic emission is far more frequent and significant. The loss of male energy and potency looms as the underlying experience and motivating fear behind the whole project of Chinese *ars erotica*. Depletion of energy through ejaculation is a familiar fact repeatedly emphasized in searching for methods to counteract it without eschewing the coital activity deemed naturally necessary for health. "When the *jing* is emitted the whole body feels weary" (Wile 91); and just as sexual energy is associated with health and life, so the explosive discharging of that energy in ejaculation is associated in different ways with disease and death, even by the way it kills the male erection.

Indulging in frequent ejaculation robs a man of vital fluids and energies, while habituating his desire for such unhealthy depletion that results not only in illness and shortening of life but also dysfunctional sexual expression such as premature ejaculation. "When the *jing* is insufficient, illness ensues; when the *jing* is exhausted one dies" (Wile 120). While women are also energetically depleted through orgasms (hence a man's need for multiple women so as not to deplete a single wife), they are not as clearly incapacitated for continued coition as men. Moreover, since woman is the gender that nurtures life in the womb and then later by breastfeeding, she was presumed to have life-giving sexual energies that were less easily depleted. Identified with *yin* (hence water) woman's sexual energy was known to vanquish the fire of male *yang*. "The *dao* of *yang* takes after fire; the *dao* of *yin* takes after water. Water is able to control fire just as *yin* is able to extinguish *yang*" (Wile 120). The presumption of women's sexual superiority also finds expression in the fact that the legendary Yellow Emperor was instructed in the erotic arts by mythical female deities, most notably Su Nu ("the immaculate girl"). Through such mastery he properly "mounted 1,200 women and thus achieved immortality, whereas the ordinary man cuts down his life with just one" (Wile 100).[19] Su Nu explains: "All debility in man is due to violation of the *dao* of intercourse between *yin* and *yang*. Women are superior to men in the same way that water is superior to fire" (Wile 85).

Chinese theory studied ejaculation in relation to declining male potency and aging. "The penis is born together [with other parts of the body] . . . , but why does it die first?" (Wile 79), asks one of China's earliest surviving erotic texts, the Han Dynasty's *Discourse on the Highest Dao under Heaven* (天下至道谈). Excessive ejaculation is the recurrent answer throughout the literature, but the meaning of "excessive" depends on one's condition. "Every man must regulate his emissions according to the condition of his vital essence [*jing*]. He must never force himself to emit semen. Every time he forces himself to reach orgasm he will harm his system" (SL 146). The various sexual handbooks prescribe different measures of ejaculative frequency for different ages and bodily conditions. A Sui Dynasty sex handbook, *Fang Nei Qi* (房内经), offers a health-oriented graduated schedule of ejaculations according to one's age and strength of constitution, ranging from strongly built fifteen-year-olds who can ejaculate twice per day to strong men of seventy who may ejaculate once per month, though "weak ones should not ejaculate anymore at that age" (SL 146).[20] A different Sui Dynasty handbook, *The Dong Xuanzi*, which also offers methods of controlling ejaculation, is less nuanced in prescriptions of frequency: "only emit semen two or three times in ten" (SL 132).[21]

[19] Besides Su Nu, the two other mythical female instructors are the "Dark Girl" (Xuan Nu, 玄女) and the "Elected Girl" (Cai Nu, 采女). See Robert van Gulik, *Erotic Colour Prints of the Ming Period: With an Essay on Chinese Sex Life from the Han to the Ch'ing Dynasty, B.C. 206–A.D. 1644*, vol. 1 (Leiden: Brill, 2004), 18.

[20] This work (as found in the *Ishinpo* compilation of ancient Chinese medical texts assembled and preserved by a Japanese physician in the tenth century) has the legendary Su Nu deliver its age regimen for ejaculation, whose details are: "Strongly built men of 15 years can afford to emit semen twice a day; thin ones once a day and the same applies to men of twenty years. Strongly built men of thirty may ejaculate once a day, weaker men once in two days. Strong men of forty may emit semen once in three days, weaker men once in four days. Strong men of fifty can ejaculate once in five days, weaker men once in ten days. Strong men of sixty may ejaculate once in ten days, weaker men once in twenty days. Strong men of seventy may emit semen once a month, weak ones should not ejaculate anymore at that age" (SL 146).

[21] The fact that van Gulik embroiders the book's title with an artistic emphasis as "*The Ars Amatoria of Master Tung Hsüan*" could have encouraged Foucault to speak of Chinese *ars erotica* while neglecting its dominant medical dimension. Wile, who instead refers to the book

Ejaculation is not the only way of harming health and potency through excessive lust for pleasure. The penis and its *jing* energy are damaged if man hastily puts it to use when it is not naturally and fully ready for action. Even the great Yellow Emperor confessed this shameful wrong in seeking Su Nu's advice: "Now when I try to force myself to have intercourse, my jade stalk will not rise. I blush and feel embarrassed and beads of sweat the size of pearls stand out. Still, there is passionate desire in my heart and I force myself with the aid of my hand" (Wile 86). But forcing the penis to sexually engage is injurious. "If it is employed abruptly without waiting for it to be strong or for both parties to be fully aroused, there will be immediate injury" (Wile 79), warns the Han *Discourse on the Highest Dao*, which then articulates the stages needed for full penile arousal. "If [the penis] is enraged but not large, the flesh has not yet been aroused. If it is large but not stiff, the sinews have not yet been aroused. If it is stiff but not hot, the *qi* has not been aroused" (Wile 80).[22] Only "when 'the three arousals' have manifested you may penetrate" (Wile 82). The lover's skill in somaesthetic perception of his precise penile state must not be blinded by his eager passion to perform, to please, or to be pleased.

Penile health (like conception) also requires the woman's full arousal, and this proves far more complicated to discern (at least for men). So Chinese sexual theory (which is obviously male-oriented) explains its forms and levels in a complex set of different manifestations. The *Discourse on the Highest Dao* lists eight movements, five sounds, and five signs that indicate a woman's level of arousal.[23] To avoid injuring his precious penis (and health),

by its true and simpler title, the *Tung Hsüan tzu* (or *Dong Xuanzi* in pinyin, 洞玄子), notes its alleged attribution to a seventh-century medical expert (83).

22 In a later text, the *Classic of Su Nu*, when the Yellow Emperor asks, "Should I force myself to perform?" when not fully aroused, he is answered, "Absolutely not!" and then she articulates four levels of arousal: arousal without largeness, aroused largeness without stiffness, aroused, large stiffness without heat, and full arousal (Wile 88). Moreover, because health is the higher end served by sexual pleasure, Su Nu warns (in another text) against taking drugs to achieve the erection needed to perform (Wile 128).

23 Among the eight movements are "joining hands," "straightening the elbows," "extending the heels," "entwining the thighs," and "quivering." The five sounds are "breathing from the throat," panting, moaning, exhaling air, and biting. The five signs are when "her face becomes hot," "her nipples become hard and she perspires," "her tongue spreads and becomes lubricious," "secretions moisten her thighs," and "her throat becomes dry and she swallows saliva." Only "when all the [five] signs appear may you mount her" (Wile 82). *The Wondrous Discourse of Su Nu* speaks of "the nine stages" of female arousal (Wile 132), while the *Exposition of Cultivating the True Essence by the Great Immortal of the Purple Gold Splendor* (紫金光耀大仙修真演义) again lists

a man had to know when a woman was truly eager and ready for coital penetration but also how to bring her to this condition and then provide her with full sexual satisfaction. This demand for somaesthetic expertise in sensitivity to women's erotic feelings and desires (along with somaesthetic proficiency in satisfying them) bespeaks a genuine concern for female pleasure, but one predominantly motivated by male selfishness. Indeed, it often looks like vampirish self-interest: the aim of sexually absorbing female energy to supplement the energy that man lost through age and through his own sexual expenditure in ejaculatory encounters.

Women also lose their health and energy with increasing age, whose damaging effects are hastened and aggravated by expending their energy in sexual pleasures and secretions. The loss of sexual energy with age is why Chinese erotic theory typically prescribes not only multiple partners (since one would soon be depleted) but also the use of distinctly young, healthy, "juicy," and relatively inexperienced women because their energy resources are most abundant. In contrast, a woman who experienced childbirth has lost considerable energy in conceiving and bringing forth her child. The *Classic of Su Nu* insists on women whose "silky hair should be jet black, their flesh tender and bones fine. They should be neither too tall nor too short, neither too fat nor too slight. Their 'bore hole' should be elevated and the private parts without hair. Their *jing* secretions should be copious" (Wile 93) so that the man can readily absorb the abundance of their energetic juices.

Not confined to genital emissions, female sexual juices were erotically ingested by the male lover as medicinal nutriments and sometimes described as the "Medicine of the Three Peaks" (the saliva of the mouth, the perspirations of the breasts, and the vaginal secretions). Women providing these medicines, Su Nu continues, "should be between twenty-five and thirty years of age and never have borne children. While having intercourse with them, their secretions should flow generously and they should move with abandon. Their perspiration should flow freely and they should follow the movements of the man" (Wile 93). Energetic health and youth rather than exceptional beauty (or special skills in giving sexual pleasures) are the key desiderata. "In selecting women it is not necessary that they be fair and beautiful, but simply

"the female's eight stages of arousal" (Wile 138). But these lists only partially overlap with each other and with the earlier Han indications, the key areas of overlap being vaginal and salivary secretions and movements of her limbs and torso.

that they be young, have not yet given birth and are amply covered with flesh. These are beneficial to one's health" (Wile 115).[24] Conversely, unhealthy looking women must be eschewed as taboo, their various types constituting "the five avoidances" (Wile 137).[25]

The Daoists were particularly appreciative of youth's superior energy, even idealizing the infant state as immensely potent with *qi* and *jing* despite its lack of physical and sexual maturity, adducing the male infant's spontaneous erections without any need for erotic stimulation or desire to produce them. Given the sexual transferability of healthy, youthful energy, an older woman could conversely rejuvenate herself by cultivating her *yin* by absorbing the *yang* energy of younger men.

> The Queen Mother of the West cultivated her *yin* and attained the *dao*. As soon as she had intercourse with a man he would immediately take sick, while her complexion would become radiant without the use of rouge or powder. She always ate curds and plucked the "five stringed lute" thereby harmonizing her heart, concentrating her mind, and was without any other desire. The Queen Mother had no husband but was fond of intercourse with young boys. Therefore, this cannot be an orthodox teaching; but can the Queen Mother be alone in this? (Wile 102)

[24] The *Exposition of Cultivating the True Essence by the Great Immortal of the Purple Gold Splendor* specifies an age range of "above fifteen but no more than thirty," noting that women of "thirty-five [are already in] . . . the phase of 'declining *yin*'" and by forty-nine the *yin* is totally "exhausted" (Wile 144). One of the more mystical texts of sexual alchemy for immortality grades women's alchemic energy value in terms of age and refers to woman with the familiar alchemic image of crucible, a vessel where elements are mixed and heated to produce new substances, energies, and powers. "There are three grades of crucibles. The lowest are twenty-five, twenty-four, or twenty-one.. . . Those of the middle grade are twenty, eighteen, or sixteen who have never engaged in intercourse, but already have had their first menses. Because they have never given birth, their placenta has never been broken; and they may be used to extend life and achieve 'human immortality.' The highest grade are 'medicine material' of fourteen. Their condition precedes the division of 'primal unity'" (Wile 174).

[25] "Women who have manly voices and coarse skin, yellow hair and violent dispositions, and are sneaky and jealous constitute the first avoidance. Those with evil appearances and unhealthy countenances, bald heads and underarm odor, hunched backs and jutting chests, and who hop like sparrows or slither like snakes constitute the second avoidance. Those who are sallow, thin, frail, and weak, cold of body and deficient of *qi*, and whose channels of circulation are out of harmony constitute the third avoidance. Women who are mad, deaf, or dumb, who are lame or blind in one eye, who have scabies, scars, or are insane, who are too fat or too thin, or whose pubic hair is coarse and dense constitute the fourth avoidance. Women, who are over forty, have borne many children and whose *yin* is weak, whose skin is loose and breasts are slack, these are harmful and confer no benefit. This is the fifth avoidance" (Wile 137).

Another text claims the legendary Elected Girl "Cai Nu acquired this art when very young and understood how to nourish one's nature. At the age of one hundred and seventy she appeared as if fifteen" (Wile 120).

Male anxiety that coitus can harm one's energy, potency, and health yet is equally necessary for them was intensified by the painfully clear recognition that women had superior sexual endurance. Symbolized by the contrast of fire and water, man's passion was too quickly aroused and spent, while woman's passion, though slower to enflame, could sustain its burning heat far longer and consume the male. Chinese *ars erotica* therefore devotes considerable attention to techniques for slowing and controlling man's wave of passion to not let it race ahead of the woman's and burst into damaging leakage. These temporizing techniques include varieties of foreplay, attitudinal modes (toward one's partner and to the sexual act), breathing and meditative methods, but also styles of penetration, withdrawal, and coital posture.

Because these techniques are designed to harmonize the lovers' feelings and actions so as to improve the quality (and results) of erotic experience, we shall examine them in more detail when exploring the aesthetic dimensions of Chinese sexual theory. There is, however, a distinct overlap in the medical and aesthetic aims of Chinese *ars erotica*, which reflects a recognition of the profound connection between health, beauty, pleasure, and youthfulness. The kind of long life (or immortality) the Chinese desire is one that radiates the beauty of health and youthful vigor. Consequently, women are deemed erotically attractive not so much because they have beautiful features but because they look especially healthy, young, and full of vital energies whose absorption can increase the robust vigor of their male lovers. Moreover, beauty is not a mere visual matter focused on how the person looks but more profoundly and essentially a matter of pleasurable, expansive, harmonious feeling. Such pleasure (like the pleasure of desire in lovemaking) is a feeling of power and growing potency, rather than the withering pleasure of orgasmic release and depletion. Before returning to these points in their aesthetic context, we should recall, at least briefly, the social and political factors shaping classical Chinese erotic theory.

V THE SOCIAL AND POLITICAL BACKGROUND

Two social traditions were extremely influential. Ancestor worship, by making procreation (within the bond of married family life) a supreme social duty, endowed the sexual act with ritual importance, while conversely branding celibacy or sexual chastity as unnatural.[26] Polygyny proved a second key factor. With the duty of providing frequent sexual satisfaction to several wives and concubines, householders needed to hone their skills of erotic management and performance so that all their women would feel sufficiently loved or well treated, even if the man had his special favorite among them. Disgruntled women could destroy household harmony (with jealous anger or illicit compensatory liaisons). Besides unpleasant conflict within the household, any public suspicion of such discord could seriously damage the householder's social reputation, since mismanagement of one's own home not only implied inability in managing other matters (such as business or political office) but also indicated a fundamental character flaw – inadequate self-management. Harmonious family order was the crucial link between the virtue of cultivated self-government and the orderly government of the state. As Confucius puts it in *The Great Learning*, "The ancients who wished to illustrate illustrious virtue throughout the kingdom, first ordered well their own states. Wishing to order well their states, they first regulated their families. Wishing to regulate their families, they first cultivated their persons."[27]

To seek domestic harmony by limiting the number of wives or concubines was not a socially viable option because having numerous wives and concubines served as a measure of social status, since only the wealthy and powerful could afford to keep a large cadre of women. If the legendary Yellow Emperor set the standard with 1,200, then normal noblemen and generals would have "thirty or more," while middle-class men would have between three and twelve depending on how high they were in the middle class. If social status involved the problematic task of multiplying one's number of women while also maximizing their erotic satisfaction (including the affective contentment of feeling loved), then lovemaking skills (including ejaculatory control for extended playing time) called for careful, detailed formulation and study so that they could be rigorously cultivated and put into practice. Moreover, the mastery and application of such erotic skills in turn reinforced the image of social superiority while also grounding it in superior knowledge.

[26] Paul Goldin insists that "the sex act is inherently a ritual act," which "is precisely why the ritual codes address the issues of marriage and the purchase of consorts." See Paul Goldin, *The Culture of Sex in Ancient China* (Honolulu: University of Hawai'i Press, 2002), 29.

[27] James Legge, trans., *The Great Learning*, in *The Four Books: Confucian Analects, the Great Learning, the Doctrine of the Mean, and the Works of Mencius* (New York: Paragon, 1966), 310–311; hereafter GL.

This social dimension affords one way of interpreting the tension in Chinese theory's repeated advocacy of multiple sexual acts with multiple partners and its similarly oft-repeated warnings against sexual indulgence. If the noble and mighty could magnify their vigor and excellence through increased erotic activity, then poor and simple folk (denied this path to longevity and virtue) must be warned of promiscuity's dangers. Whereas the Yellow Emperor, through his myriad mountings, "ascended into the realm of the immortals, . . . the ordinary man cuts down his life with only one woman," lacking both the material means and the know-how to do better. "How far apart indeed are knowledge and ignorance. Those who understand the *dao* regret only having too few women to mount" (Wile 115). Of course, the whole edifice of Chinese *ars erotica* rests on the social premise of puissant patriarchy, in which women could be instrumentalized as wells of life-enhancing *yin* energy and as crucibles for manufacturing progeny, youthful energetic health, or the mystic elixir of earthly immortality. Classical Confucianism, which forms the historically dominant Chinese ideology, is notorious for endorsing male privilege. If some scholars read this as a reaction formation to deal with an alleged prehistory of matriarchal society in China, a matriarchy that possibly derived from woman's greater powers of nurturing life and perhaps motivated Daoism's privileging the female principle, then other experts contest the charge of Confucian sexism.[28]

Given Chinese philosophy's intimate linking of family and state, eroticism's social shaping and significance merge into the political. If the great ruler (as in the Yellow Emperor paradigm) is the model of sexual prowess that more generally symbolizes his wide-ranging power, then he also personifies the reigning object of desire who is beloved by his adoring, obedient subjects. Confucianism argued that a leader rules best not through threats and punishments but by inspiring admiration and loving emulation in his subjects through his actions, grace, and demeanor. As governing works through adoring compliance, so ruling hierarchy is metaphorically depicted in sexual terms. Not only does the ruler magnify his strength by satisfying

[28] See, for example, van Gulik's arguments for matriarchy in archaic pre-Zhou Dynasty China (SL 5–9). Though Schipper claims the theories of ancient Chinese matriarchy are "far from proven," it is a "clearly demonstrated . . . fact that in every period women have been the initiators into the techniques of the body." See Kristofer Schipper, *The Taoist Body*, trans. Karen Duval (Berkeley: University of California Press, 1993), 125. Recent scholarship provides rebuttals to the charge of Confucian sexism. See, for example, Paul Goldin, *Confucianism* (Berkeley: University of California Press, 2011), appendix.

his subjects who obediently serve him with desire, but he must manage his ministers carefully to avoid internal conflicts and jealousies just as an ordinary man must manage his wives.

Ancient Chinese poetry provides powerful examples of how the relationship of ministers, vassals, or advisors to their ruler is analogized to a sexual relationship of a woman to her husband, who is socially determined as the necessary locus of the woman's desiring love and obedience.[29] But ancient political philosophers make the analogy more explicit. Shen Buhai (fourth century BCE) writes:

> When one wife acts on her own responsibility with regard to her husband, the throng of wives all become disorderly. When one minister monopolizes the lord, the flock of ministers all become deceptive. Thus a jealous wife can break a family without difficulty; a disorderly minister can break the state without difficulty. Therefore the enlightened lord makes his ministers advance together like wheel spokes to a hub; none of them are able to monopolize the ruler.[30]

The more famous *Hanfeizi* (third century BCE) urges the ruler to keep "godlike" distance from his "subordinates," even from those most intimate, such as wives and ministers, yet warns how a ruler's unhappy wives or concubines "will wish for [and plot] his early death," if they feel he does not love them sufficiently.[31] "A man at fifty has not yet lost interest in sex, and yet at thirty a woman's beauty has already faded. If a woman whose beauty has already faded waits upon a man still occupied with thoughts of sex, then she will be spurned and disfavored, and her son will stand little chance of succeeding to the throne"; and so she will "long for the early death of the ruler . . . This is why we have secret poisonings, stranglings, and knifings" (HBW 86). The first of the "eight strategies which ministers customarily employ to work their villainy" against the ruler is "making use of his bedfellows," rendering him "beguiled" by beauties who feign or "play at love" so that they can then "delude the ruler" (HBW 39, 43). Besides wives and ministers, the ruler must also guard against indulgence with courtesans, whose charms include the seductive art of music. Hanfeizi concludes: "To become

29 Goldin (*The Culture of Sex*, 13–40) convincingly demonstrates this in a series of poems that also show how the same sexual metaphor of adoring and obedient union is deployed to describe the relationship of subjects to their ancestral gods through images of hierogamous love.

30 Goldin, *The Culture of Sex*, 41.

31 Burton Watson, trans., *Han Feizi: Basic Writings* (New York: Columbia University Press, 2003), 86; hereafter HBW.

infatuated with women musicians and disregard affairs of state invites the disaster of national destruction" (HBW 64).

Like its philosophy, China's sexology first developed in times of great political strife and continuous wars. If this provides one reason why harmony is so highly cherished as perhaps the paramount value, then it also explains why military metaphors pervade much classical erotic theory. The skilled male lover is a strategizing "general" who confronts his female sexual partner as "the enemy." Victory is not a mere matter of penetration but rather the exhaustion of the woman through her pleasurably passionate erotic exertions, sexual secretions, and multiple orgasms that result in transferring her vital *qi* and *jing* resources to the triumphant male. Shrewdly unspent through ejaculatory restraint, he relishes these reinforcing energy sources as the spoils of war. *The True Classic of Perfect Union* insists: "The superior general in engaging the enemy must be skilled in fondling, sucking, and inhaling. His mind must be detached and his body entrusted to heaven and earth. He should close his eyes as if lost to himself," so that he avoids becoming overexcited by the beauty or passion of his opponent in the coital joust and thus lose his ejaculatory control (Wile 135). "When the enemy is writhing with passion and she is beside herself with excitement, always restrain yourself and do not ejaculate," explains the *Secrets of the Jade Chamber*, prescribing the oft-repeated counsel to rest motionless after deep penetration and then withdraw when one's member is "hard and strong ... Rest for a moment until you become limp and then insert it again," once one is calm enough not to risk ejaculation, and then continue this "practice of entering weak and withdrawing strong" (Wile 105). These maneuvers to enhance coital timing and erotic harmonizing relate to the aesthetics of Chinese lovemaking, whose exploration needs contextualizing through the background aesthetic culture that helped shape it.

VI THE AESTHETIC BACKGROUND: BEAUTY, VIRTUE, AND SELF-CULTIVATION

There was an overlap between the political and the aesthetic in matters of erotic attraction. Rulers, lords, and generals were not objects of desire simply by social convention or brute power but because they seemed to be endowed with a special excellence, virtue, or qualitative power (*de*, 德) that made them beautifully attractive even if they were not physically beautiful in external appearance. The intimate association of virtue with beauty in ancient Chinese culture is exemplified by another term for virtue, *meide*

(美德), in which *de* is prefaced by the character for beauty (*mei*, 美).[32] People of humbler social status might also be blessed with extraordinary *de* that made them irresistibly attractive. We find a striking example in Daoism's *Zhuangzi* chapter "The Sign of Virtue Complete":

> In Wei there was an ugly man named Ai Taito. But when men were around him, they thought only of him and couldn't break away, and when women saw him, they ran begging to their fathers and mothers, saying, "I'd rather be this gentleman's concubine than another man's wife!" – there were more than ten such cases and it hasn't stopped yet. No one ever heard him take the lead – he always just chimed in with other people. He wasn't in the position of a ruler where he could save men's lives, and he had no store of provisions to fill men's bellies. On top of that, he was ugly enough to astound the whole world.. . . And yet men and women flocked to him.[33]

This is because, despite physical ugliness, Ai Taito radiated with perfect harmony the inner power or virtue that animates the body, which is what people really love and desire when they are attracted to another human's body.[34]

Such radiating harmony was a highly prized goal in the pursuit of virtuous excellence through self-cultivation that is so central to Chinese culture. The aesthetic dimension of harmony was key to such excellence, which explains the centrality of art in Confucian ethics. Art is not only a source of personal pleasure; it also gives grace and beauty to the social functions of everyday life. It further provides a crucial means of ethical education that refines both individual and society by cultivating a sense of good order and propriety while instilling an enjoyably shared experience of harmony and meaning.

The Confucian insistence on ritual (*li*, 礼) and music (*yue*, 乐, a concept including poetry and dance) as the key elements in both cultivating the self and civilizing society makes the aesthetic aspect of education very clear. These aesthetic practices are more than *merely* aesthetic; they help instill proper order and good government in the individual and in society as a

[32] The term *meide* 美德 is found, for example, in *Xunzi*, Bk. 32:3, where John Knoblock translates it as "inner power." See John Knoblock, trans., *Xunzi: A Translation and Study of the Complete Works*, vol. 3 (Stanford: Stanford University Press, 1994), 266. Page references to Xunzi are all from Knoblock's three-volume translation.

[33] Burton Watson, trans., *The Complete Works of Chuang Tzu* (Zhuangzi) (New York: Columbia University Press, 1968), 72; hereafter CWZ.

[34] In the same chapter Confucius explains this puzzling power analogically: "I saw some little pigs nursing at the body of their dead mother. After a while, they gave a start and all ran away and left her, because . . . she was not the same as she had been before. In loving their mother, they loved not her body but the thing that moved her body" (CWZ 73).

whole. As Confucius stressed, "In referring time and again to observing ritual propriety (*li*), how could I just be talking about gifts of jade and silk? And in referring time and again to making music (*yue*), how could I just be talking about bells and drums?" (AC 17.11). He thus urged his disciples, "My young friends, why don't you study the *Songs*? Reciting the *Songs* can arouse your sensibilities, strengthen your powers of observation, enhance your ability to get on with others, and sharpen your critical skills. Close at hand it enables you to serve your father, and away at court it enables you to serve your lord" (AC 17.9). Without learning ritual, one would not know "where to stand" or how to behave (AC 16.13). But the broader goal of "achieving harmony" in both self and society "is the most valuable function of observing ritual" (AC 1.12).[35]

This aesthetic model of good government through refining character and harmony has an erotic dimension because it works by exemplary attraction, desire, and emulation rather than by commandments, threats, and punishments. "The exemplary person attracts friends through refinement (*wen*, 文), and thereby promotes virtuous conduct (*ren*, 仁)." Attracted to such people, we want "to stand shoulder to shoulder with them" by emulating their virtue (AC 12.24, 4.1, 4.17). So "if people are proper in personal conduct, others will follow suit without need of command. But if they are not proper, even when they command, others will not obey" (AC 13.6). Good conduct is also understood aesthetically; it is not a mere matter of mechanical or grudging compliance with ethical rules but also requires maintaining the proper appearances that express the proper feelings. Hence the Confucian emphasis on "the proper countenance," "demeanor," and "expression" that virtuous excellence displays and that contribute, through aesthetic appeal, to

[35] In "Discourse on Ritual Principles," Xunzi explains how ritual harmonizes by nurturing our human senses, emotions, and desires while informing them with a sense of order and distinction so that they will not run wildly astray but will issue in "pleasure and beauty" by achieving the proper "mean" (Knoblock, *Xunzi*, vol. 3, 57). A key to ritual's power of refinement is its providing the proper "mean" (60). "Rites trim what is too long, stretch out what is too short, eliminate excess, remedy deficiency, and extend cultivated forms that express love and respect so that they increase and complete the beauty of conduct according to one's duty" (62). "Rites are the highest expression of order and discrimination, the root of strength in the state" (65). Xunzi likewise praises the power of music for harmonizing and ordering both individual and society. As "the guiding line of the mean and harmony, and a necessary and inescapable expression of man's emotional nature" (81), "music is the most perfect method of bringing order to men" (84). He also suggests how music and ritual complement each other in the work of ordering: "Music joins together what is common to all; ritual separates what is different" (84).

social harmony and good government (AC 8.4).[36] Given this intimate connection between aesthetics, ethics, and politics, a ruler's large number of wives and concubines did not simply indicate his political power but symbolized also his presumably strong aesthetic attraction through excellence. If his appeal was implied by his governing eminence, it was reinforced through a variety of impressive aesthetic means (exquisite wardrobes, jewels, accessories, carriages, court poets and artists, and special musical and dance performances that only he was permitted to stage).

Ars erotica, I therefore maintain, was not only crucial to the central Chinese quest for health or "nurturing life" (*yang sheng*) but also key to the project of aesthetic self-cultivation. This is because sex, if properly managed, gives beauty, invigorating pleasure, and harmony to one's character and intimate relationships; but if mismanaged, it easily engenders disorder, disease, and destructive discord. The essential blending of aesthetic and erotic skills and pleasure is personified in the mythical figure of Su Nu. Before gaining fame as the legendary instructress of *ars erotica*, including such eponymous works as the *Classic of Su Nu*, *Prescriptions of Su Nu* (素女方), and the *Wondrous Discourse of Su Nu* (素女妙论), she was known as a goddess so skilled in music (and such an excellent singer) that when "the Yellow Emperor heard her play a zither with fifty strings, he became so moved that he decided that this instrument was too dangerous for man, and had it split into two smaller zithers, of 25 strings each" (SL 74). The erotic-aesthetic blending symbolized by Su Nu finds further expression in her linkage to the fertility cult (of the god of grain) and to the beauty of shells whose shape she could assume, a shape that aesthetically evoked female erotic power by its accepted resemblance to the vulva (SL 74). The mingling of musical and sexual mastery that Su Nu embodies is echoed in the prevalent musical metaphors of Chinese erotic theory, which frequently refer to female genitalia as "zither" and to the penis as "flute," all requiring consummate playing skills to produce the richest harmonies and the greatest pleasures.

[36] When asked about "filial conduct," the Master replied: "It all lies in showing the proper countenance. As for the young contributing their energies when there is work to be done, and deferring to their elders when there is wine and food to be had – how can merely doing this be considered being filial?" (AC 2.8). When asked what kind of person is fit to govern, Confucius replies: "A person who honors the five beauties (*mei*) and rejects the four ugly things (*e*)," and then he goes on to explain what these things are in saliently ethical language that leads Ames and Rosemont to translate these terms as "the five virtues" and "the four vices" (AC 20.2). In the Waley translation, the terms are translated as "the Five Lovely Things" and "the Four Ugly Things." See Arthur Waley, trans., *The Analects of Confucius* (New York: Vintage, 1938), 232.

Beyond such mythical figures and metaphors, the Chinese tradition of mixing aesthetics and erotics finds expression in the pervasive role of professional women entertainers who combined the arts with *ars erotica*. Already in the Zhou dynasty (770–222 BCE), "Princes and high officials kept next to their harems also their own troops of *nu-yue*, trained dancing girls and female musicians, who performed at official banquets and private drinking bouts ... [and] engaged in promiscuous sexual intercourse with their master, his retinue and his guests," and who were sometimes sold or offered as gifts (SL 27–28). By the Former Han Dynasty, there were already public brothels called "houses of singing girls" where clients could "have the girls dance and sing for them, and afterwards stay the night" for sexual services (SL 66). Such services were not the overriding goal of their visit but simply a supplement to the aesthetic-erotic delights of enjoying the sensuous beauty of lovely young women performing their artistry of song, dance, and conversation.

Van Gulik maintains that until the nineteenth century, "brothels where educated men went for sexual intercourse only were rare," because erotic desire and gratification included an essential aesthetic, artistic dimension (SL 65–66). The Tang Dynasty (618–907 CE) boasted courtesans "skilled in music and dancing" who catered to a sophisticated clientele for whom "proficiency in the arts and letters was, together with good looks, the supreme standard," and many of these courtesans were considered "skilled in composing poetry" (SL 171). In the thirteenth century, the best brothels of the Sung Dynasty (like those of the Early Han Dynasty) were called "houses of singing girls" in which "accomplished courtesans skilled in poetry, dancing, and singing" made their abode and entertained the wealthy, powerful, and sophisticated with the sensuous aesthetic fusion of erotic and aesthetic charms (SL 233). Despite the growing official prudishness of the Ming Dynasty, stylish high-class brothels (typically located in distinctive pleasure quarters of major cities) continued to thrive and exerted "tremendous influence ... on the cultural life ... They were frequented by all the great scholars, writers, and artists of that day who set a high standard for beauty and skill of the courtesans," generating in their "milieus ... several new genres of singing and instrumental music that are still popular today" (SL 311).

By the Ming period, however, female experts in *ars erotica* had lost their dancing skill as the fashion for foot-binding rendered it impossible. Allegedly introduced by the Tang poet emperor Li Yu (937–978 CE) for one of his favorite consorts, foot-binding became a dominant custom for centuries, steeped in an aesthetic of erotic meaning. "Ever since the Sung dynasty, excessively small, pointed feet have formed an indispensable item in the list of attributes of a beautiful woman . . . and came to be considered as the most intimate part of her body, the very symbol of femininity, and the most powerful centre of sex-appeal." They therefore were carefully cherished, guarded, and always covered, even in erotic representations where women were otherwise completely naked. Touching the woman's feet "became the traditional preliminary to sexual intercourse": if a woman fails to get angry when the prospective lover "accidentally" touches her foot in picking up a chopstick or a handkerchief from the floor, then "the suit has been gained, and he can immediately proceed without restraint to all physical contact" (SL 217–218).[37]

Foot-binding is not the only case of changing fashions in bodily beauty and the erotic play of somatic exposure and concealment. Tang fashion allowed women to show their bare neck and décolletage; Sung and later Chinese regarded this as sexually indecent and introduced the high-collared jacket (SL 219). Other evidence from the arts shows that until the later Ming period, Chinese taste "still preferred a sturdy feminine beauty, plump women with round, chubby faces and fully developed figures," while later fashion favored more slender types with "longer, oval faces." Similarly, the ideal of masculine beauty evolved from the robust virility of "the middle-aged, bearded men of the Tang and Sung periods" to younger men without facial hair in later Ming times. These ideal Ming lovers were still "tall and broad-shouldered" with "heavy chests and muscular arms and legs," exhibiting the "bodily strength" that was always "one of the recognized attributes of a handsome man" and a product of the traditional practices of self-cultivation that included martial arts, archery, and horsemanship (SL 294–296). However, when Manchu conquest and occupation ended Ming rule, Chinese literati began to disdain physical prowess as reflecting the barbarian Qing conquerors and therefore described the ideal male lover "as a delicate, hyper-sensitive youngster with pale face and narrow shoulders, passing the greater part of his time dreaming among his books and flowers, and who falls ill at the slightest disappointment. His female counterpart," van Gulik continues, "is depicted as a frail child-woman" having a "long, thin face . . . sloping shoulders, a flat chest, narrow hips and thin arms with long, excessively slender hands." Both male and female ideal lovers

[37] For an alternative account of foot-binding, see Deborah Ko, *Cinderella's Sisters: A Revisionist History of Footbinding* (Berkeley: University of California Press, 2007). For a more comprehensive account of Tang fashion, see BuYun Chen, *Empire of Style: Silk and Fashion in Tang China* (Seattle: University of Washington Press, 2019).

were depicted as unhealthily prone to disease "and as a rule they die young" (SL 296).

This post-Ming exception – an obvious reaction to conquest and occupation – cannot contest the strong Chinese tradition of associating beauty and erotic appeal with robust, youthful health. Such linkage (a commonplace in many cultures) finds contemporary explanation in theories of evolutionary psychology. Transcultural beauty-making features – "full lips, clear skin, smooth skin, clear eyes, lustrous hair, and good muscle tone," along with "sound teeth" and the "absence of sores and lesions" and striking "facial and bodily asymmetries" – are essentially features indicating youthful health and thus implying better chances that the desired mate will thrive and produce healthy offspring so that one's own genes can also survive for continuing generations.[38]

Female attractiveness in Chinese *ars erotica* highlights features of full-bodied health rather than fragile daintiness. Its paradigms are

> young girls who have not yet borne children and who are amply covered with flesh. They should have silken hair and small eyes with the whites and pupils clearly defined. The face and body should be moist and glossy.... The bones of the four limbs and hundred joints should be buried in ample flesh, and the bones should not be prominent. Her private parts and underarms should be free of hair, but if hair is present, it should be fine and glossy. (Wile 106)

The unattractive traits of "unsuitable" women include "irregular teeth, ... lack of clarity in the eyes, long hairs about the mouth and chin resembling whiskers, prominent large joints, yellowish hair, scant flesh, and pubic hair that is copious, coarse, and growing contrariwise." Women "whose flesh and skin are coarse or ... whose body is too thin ... or always cold" are also unsuitably unattractive (Wile 106).

More remarkable than affirming youthful health as sexually attractive is the Chinese claim that proper lovemaking actually renders the lover more beautiful and younger looking. One of the earliest surviving erotic texts (*Uniting Yin and Yang*) claims that a single sexual act "without orgasm makes ears and eyes sharp and bright ... Three and the skin is radiant.... Eight and the pores are lustrous" (Wile 78). The *Secrets of the Jade Chamber* later maintains that by having multiple "young maidens for mounting, [the

[38] David M. Buss, *The Evolution of Desire* (New York: Basic Books, 2003), 53, 55. Buss also notes the evolutionary justification for the traditional importance of bodily size and strength in female judgments of male erotic appeal (38–40).

lover's] complexion too will become like a maiden's," and he will look attractively young and "will feel [his] strength increased a hundredfold" (Wile 102).

Here we note striking contrasts between Greco-Roman and Chinese sexual theory. For the former, visual beauty was the key motivating cause of erotic activity, while in Chinese *ars erotica* beauty is instead emphasized as the product of erotic activity, whose primary aim is vigorous youthful health, including healthy procreation. Great sex does not require beautiful lovers but rather creates them; sex beautifies by making us feel more dynamic and radiant with vivid, energetic health. Beneath this contrast we can discern another: the Greeks emphasize the visuality of beauty, whereas the Chinese concept of beauty is originally rooted in the more bodily senses of flavor and fragrance. The Chinese character for beauty 美 (*mei*) derives from the image of a fat sheep, thus symbolizing a tasty meal, and the character is still used today to mean "delicious" when combined with the character 食 (*shi*) meaning food or meal. In contrast to vision, taste is a proximate sense, closely linked to touch. Its pleasures involve inner feelings of delightful, haptic contact on and within one's body, as do the most prominent pleasures of sex. Moreover, taste and eating (as nourishment) are obviously essential for health and energy, just as the Chinese believed sex to be. Most cultures associate eating with sexuality partly because they involve natural drives and pleasures along with strong and stubbornly recurrent desires. But the fact that Greek philosophy was reluctant to accord food genuine aesthetic or artistic status, while Chinese regarded cuisine as capable of expressing beauty and worthy of art, can help explain why they had a richer, more aesthetic tradition of *ars erotica* than the Greeks.

The question of pleasures and health raises a further contrast: Greek erotic theory tends to regard sexual pleasure as essentially unhealthy, while China's affirms the pleasures of sex (when properly pursued, i.e., by limiting ejaculation) as necessary means for health. Third, underpinning this contrast are divergent views of sexual pleasure. If the Greeks conceived it in terms of orgasm's explosive satisfaction of ejaculatory release from a maddeningly disturbing and intensifying sexual tension, then the Chinese had a much broader view of sexual delights in which ejaculatory orgasm played only a minor, inessential role. This was because its momentary pleasure of bursting discharge is a feeling of depletion that is inferior in pleasure to the enduring feelings of masterful potency of pre-ejaculatory arousal and sustained copulation. Recognizing that the unenlightened might think that "The pleasure of intercourse lies in ejaculation," the *Classic of Su Nu* provides a refutation:

> When *jing* is emitted the whole body feels weary. One suffers buzzing in the ears and drowsiness in the eyes; the throat is parched and the joints heavy. Although there is brief pleasure, in the end there is discomfort. If, however, one engages in sex without emission, then the strength of our *qi* will be more than sufficient and our bodies at ease. One's hearing will be acute and vision clear. Although exercising self-control and calming the passion, love actually increases, and one remains unsatiated. How can this be considered unpleasurable? (Wile 91)

These opposing views of sexual pleasure rest on contrasting concepts of desire. If the Greek philosophical tradition conceived desire as a lack implying need and thus a form of weakness that detracts from the individual's power or sovereign autonomy, Chinese *ars erotica* sees the desire of sexual arousal as a manifestation of power, an expression of intensified *jing* and *qi* energies that animate and empower the lover to tireless and pleasurable exertions that further fortify him. By applying the famous Chinese formula of withdrawing when hard with extreme desire and then calming oneself to reenter when softer with diminished arousal, the lover can repeatedly experience the pleasures of swelling sexual power while also deferring the depleting ejaculatory outburst that ends these delightfully rising waves of passion and leaves the lover energetically wasted. Chinese erotic theory could more easily see desire as a dynamic potency rather than a lack-related weakness because its underlying philosophy (in contrast to the Greeks') is less preoccupied with the ideal of individual autonomy and self-sufficiency but instead insists on how one's energies and powers are borrowed from larger natural forces.

Two further contrasts concern the question of pluralism. Greco-Roman theory generally regards sex as healthiest when limited to a single partner, whereas Chinese erotics clearly insist on a multitude of partners for maximizing health, energy, youthful beauty, and domestic welfare with robust progeny. Moreover, we see a growing tendency in Greco-Roman culture toward the affirmation of a single form and focus of sexual activity as the governing norm and ideal – heterosexual genital intercourse of a married couple with the aim of procreation. Even outside this norm, we find an overriding focus on the single aspect of penetration, albeit in a variety of places. Chinese thought instead maintains that sexual pleasure and energy are amply attained through other forms of bodily contact, as exemplified by doctrines like the "Medicine of the Three Peaks," only one of which involves genital penetration.[39]

[39] Chinese erotic theory is, however, more one-sided in neglecting homosexual love, although it was clearly practiced, even by emperors. Van Gulik notes only one book on the subject, a

VII AESTHETIC STYLIZATION IN LOVEMAKING

Harmony

Pervasively shaping the formative background of Chinese aesthetics, the arts of music and cuisine highlight the beauties of harmony through mixing and blending. Aesthetic pleasure is heightened by combining different notes and different ingredients in a unifying way so that they complement or enhance rather than detract from each other, resulting in a satisfying richness of noncoercive unity in variety. Such delightful aesthetic harmony provides a paradigm that extends beyond the fine arts to the realms of social relations, politics, and the ethical art of living. The principle of harmony likewise permeates Chinese sexology, constituting both a crucial means and central aim for successful lovemaking. Its formative role finds expression in multiple, overlapping forms of erotic harmony, not only between the sexual partners but also harmonies within the lovers themselves and also beyond them with their environing conditions of time and place.

A person's "*qi* is weak and out of harmony," Su Nu explains, because of a failure to harmonize *yin* and *yang* through harmonious sexual relations, but those who know the *dao* of *ars erotica* "will be happy in their hearts and the power of their *qi* will be strong," making them vigorous and free of illness. "All debility in man," she continues, "is due to violation of the *dao* of intercourse between *yin* and *yang*. Women are superior to men in the same way that water is superior to fire. This knowledge is like the ability to blend the 'five flavors' in a pot to make delicious soup. Those who know the *dao* of *yin* and *yang* can fully realize the 'five pleasures'; those who do not will die before their time without ever knowing this joy" (Wile 85). This *dao* "consists in settling the *qi*, calming the mind, and harmonizing the emotions" (Wile 85–86).

Harmony is the crucial key to knowing this *dao*, as confirmed by the *Essentials of the Jade Chamber*. "There is no mystery to the *dao* of intercourse. It is simply to be free and unhurried and to value harmony above all" (Wile 100). Chinese action theory more generally argues that it is dangerous to act on what is outside the self until one's inner self is in harmonious order.[40] The purpose of unpressured, unhurried lovemaking is to maximize

seventeenth-century "treatise by an anonymous author which sums up literary data on male homosexuality" (SL 63).

[40] "When the sage governs does he govern what is on the outside? He makes sure of himself first, and then he acts" (CWZ 93).

harmonies (of movement, feeling, etc.) because relaxed slowness allows greater control in managing one's own bodily feelings, movements, secretions, and energies, and consequently also those of one's lover. In recommending "harmonizing the saliva" as one of "eight benefits" of good sex, the *Discourse on the Highest Dao* clearly connects harmony and leisurely slowness: "Engage in the act without haste or rapidity, moving in and out harmoniously. This is called harmonizing the saliva" (Wile 81). But even before the coital act, calm slowness is crucial for allowing the man to properly harmonize his own *qi* while engaging in foreplay to arouse his partner's passion, which in turn contributes to and must be harmonized with his own before engaging in the coital act.[41] "The *dao* of mounting women is first to engage in slow foreplay so as to harmonize your spirits and arouse her desire, and only after a long time to unite" (Wile 101). Otherwise, if lovers "perform the act before *yin* and *yang* have been properly harmonized," they will likely suffer from the "ill . . . called 'overflow of *jing*,'" a form of premature ejaculation where "the *jing* overflows in mid-course" (Wile 90).

The reciprocal erotic harmony that ensures the most rewarding arousal is not merely a matter of fleshly sensation but of heartfelt emotion. "*Yin* and *yang* respond to each other's influence," so if either one of the partners is not emotionally "desirous," then "their hearts are not in harmony and their *jing qi* is not aroused" (Wile 86). Conversely, an insufficiently aroused male will gain both penis size and strength through the flow of *qi* awakened by loving harmony: "When two hearts are in harmony and the *qi* flows freely throughout the body, then the short and small becomes longer and larger, the soft and the weak naturally firm and hard" (Wile 130). The harmonious circulation of *qi* throughout the body is not only an enabling condition for good lovemaking but also one of its cherished aims because it produces good health and good offspring.

Erotic harmony must also take account of environmental factors of time and place; there were narrow strictures on locations for lovemaking. Foreplay and intercourse (indeed, for Confucians, any touching at all between the married couple) should be confined to the bedroom so as to ensure a relaxed, unhurried, and aesthetic atmosphere. Indeed, some texts literally limit contact to bedstead alone, which (as van Gulik describes it) was

[41] Only "when the three harmonious *qi* are aroused" will the penis be "sturdy and strong" and ready for intercourse (Wile 80). These three forms of *qi* that need to be in harmony refer to "the three primordial *qi* that converge at conception to produce the upper, middle, and lower portions of the body" (Wile 232).

"really a small room in itself" within the bedroom, constructed with an elevated base and "four pillars, connected by latticework and round those there were curtains." Besides containing the bed, within the bedstead's "screened-off compartment there was a stand with a mirror and toilet articles, a clothes horse," comfortable bedding, incense burners, and various decorations, including objects symbolizing fecundity (SL 59, 107). Confining erotic contact to the bedroom or bedstead might seem a hampering limitation, but it surely served to heighten the erotic atmosphere of lovemaking by giving it a distinctive, aesthetic, and ritually endorsed stage on which the art of love could be played and relished more intensely. Other constraints of location (more geographical in nature) were sometimes stipulated: "The environs of mountains and rivers, altars to the gods of heaven and earth, wells, and stoves are . . . taboos" (Wile 122). A later text elaborates these constraints by warning against erotic practice in "the presence of all images of gods and ghosts; the proximity of wells, kitchen stoves, eaves, and toilets . . . [These] all are harmful and bring on early death . . . [and may] result . . . [in] deformed offspring" (Wile 127).

Some texts prescribe "taboos for the time of intercourse," based on times when one's soma (or body-mind) is not in harmony or when the heavens are unharmonious or inauspicious. This includes "when one is hungry, full, and drunk; mentally exhausted and physically fatigued; distressed and anxiety ridden; recently recovered from an illness; in mourning, or during the woman's menses" or "when one has just washed the hair, is fatigued from travel, or when feeling great joy or anger." Likewise, "one should not have intercourse when heaven and earth are dark and trembling, when there is swift lightning, violent winds, and heavy rain, nor during the first and last quarter of the moon, half and full moons, bitter cold and intense heat, eclipses of the sun and moon, the birthdays of the gods, the sexegenary cycle days, . . . one's own birthday . . . the period of mourning," and other "inauspicious days of the almanac" (Wile 127). Conversely, some recommend certain hours of the day as erotically more auspicious in terms of having greater *yang* energy (generally between midnight and dawn) for harmonizing with the woman's *yin* (Wile 121).

Timing and Ritual

Like the arts of music and cuisine to which it has been compared, lovemaking is a temporal art of performance. It takes time to perform, but also time to enjoy or savor. Proper timing, moreover, is crucial to aesthetic success and is more than a matter of choosing the proper season, day, or hour. Good timing requires coordinating arousal tempos so that "partners come together at the proper time" when the "two hearts are in harmony and the *qi* flows freely throughout the body" (Wile 130). It further involves an appropriate temporal structure, requiring the right sequencing, rhythms, and intervals of actions. Some texts establish an essential "sequence" of lovemaking moves, while insisting that this basic "order must not be altered" (Wile 137). Yet plurality of practice exists, reflecting a plurality of sexual aims and changing contexts and conditions.

If the Chinese act of lovemaking has a proper beginning, middle, and end, then that end is not, in most cases, the conventional Western end of ejaculatory orgasm, which Chinese theory prescribes only for the relatively rare instances where the explicit goal is progeny. In most other cases (and viewed, of course, from the dominant male perspective), the proper conclusion of lovemaking is as follows. After having sufficiently enjoyed the *yang*-intensifying energies and pleasures of arousal and intercourse and having brought his female lover to sufficient orgasms for him to absorb her precious *yin-jing* and *qi* to maximize his own energies, the man terminates his penile penetrations and withdraws his member while it is hard with heightened energy and then seeks to circulate and refine this energy throughout his soma by means of meditative power. This last stage of sexual energy absorption typically requires disengagement from the woman's body and the exercise of special meditative and breathing techniques, along with special postures. Some texts are even more explicit about lovemaking's beginning by prescribing the precise opening gambits of foreplay, including the postures of the two lovers. Consider this passage from the medical text of *Dong Xuanzi* (洞玄子):

> When first coming together for the purpose of intercourse, the man should sit on the woman's left and the woman on the man's right. The man ... embraces the woman to his bosom. He clasps her slender waist and caresses her jade body. Expressing their joy and speaking of deep attachment, of one heart and one mind, they now embrace ... , their two bodies beating against each other and their mouths pressed together. The man sucks the woman's lower lip and the woman sucks the man's upper lip. Then simultaneously sucking, they feed on each other's juices. They may slowly bite each other's tongues, or gently nibble each other's lips; they may cradle each other's heads, or urgently pinch the ears. Caressing above and patting below, kissing to the east and nibbling to the west, a thousand charms are revealed and a hundred cares forgotten. Then let the woman take the man's

"jade stalk" in her left hand, while the man caresses her "jade gate" with his right. At this moment, the man senses her *yin-qi* and his "jade stalk" is aroused like a solitary peak reaching up to the Milky Way. The woman senses the man's *yang-qi* and liquid flows from her "cinnabar hole" like the trickling down of a secluded spring spilling from a deep valley. This is the result of *yin* and *yang* stimulating each other and not the product of human effort. When conditions reach this stage, then intercourse is possible. (Wile 108–109)

At this point, as one proceeds toward the coital act itself, the text prescribes a change of position: "When having intercourse one should begin first by sitting and then proceed to reclining. The woman should be on the left and the man on the right" before they move to a reclining position with the woman on her back, "spreading her feet and opening her arms" and the man lying "upon her . . . between her thighs," "his erect 'jade stalk' [by] the mouth of her 'jade gate.'" The lovers then "clasp each other tightly, moaning and sucking tongues," as the man continues to arouse her by "patting the region between [her] belly and breasts and stroking the sides of her "jade terrace." When the man senses that their arousal is in proper harmony, "then with his '*yang* sword tip' he attacks in all directions" in her genital area but without fully penetrating. Then "when the woman's sexual secretions fill the 'cinnabar hole,' he plunges his '*yang* sword tip' into her 'children's palace,' as she ecstatically releases her *jing* secretions, watering her 'sacred fields' above and irrigating her 'secluded vale' below." The lover then performs a series of penetrations and withdrawals, "advancing and retreating, rubbing and grinding," until the woman is overwhelmed with pleasure and passion (Wile 109).

The woman begs for death, she begs for life, pleading for her very existence. Then after wiping with a silk cloth, he plunges the "jade stalk" deeply into the "cinnabar hole" all the way to the "*yang* terrace," towering steeply like a great rock blocking a deep mountain stream. He then executes the method of "nine shallow and one deep," now leaning forward on his staff and now prodding sideways with his pole, pulling on one side and uprooting on the other, suddenly slow and suddenly fast, now deep and now shallow. For a count of twenty-one breaths observe the *qi* as it moves in and out. When the woman is on the point of orgasm, the man quickly stabs and rapidly attacks, raising her high. Observe the woman's movements and adapt to her pace. Then with your "*yang* sword tip" attack her "grain seed," pursuing all the way to the "children's palace" and grinding left and right. Without becoming excited, carefully pull out. When the woman's secretions overflow, retreat, for one must not withdraw dead but return alive. (Wile 109)

Dong Xuanzi's text offers a cosmic explanation for the lovemaking postures, identifying man with the *yang* of heaven, and woman with the *yin* of earth. "Heaven revolves to the left and earth rotates to the right. . . . Man sings and woman harmonizes. What is above acts and what is below follows." Violating this cosmic "law" can be "injurious" to both lovers. "Therefore, the man must rotate to the left, and the woman must revolve to the right. Man thrusts downward from above, and woman receives him from below. To come together in this way is called 'heavenly peace and earthly fulfillment'" (Wile 108).[42] By linking the movements of lovemaking to planetary motions, Chinese eroticism magnifies its meaning and aesthetic power by enriching its harmonies with those of celestial bodies. "To have intercourse in harmony with the stars, even if wealthy and honored offspring are not produced, is still beneficial to oneself," both aesthetically and health-wise, since harmony is essential to both kinds of value.

The detailed description and ordering of actions prescribed in this passage of the *Dong Xuanzi* – including the stipulation of contrasting rhythms (slow and fast), sequenced levels of penetration in numbered strokes (nine shallow and one deep), and the need to pause (here for twenty-one breaths) to observe the circulation of *qi* – is very typical of China's *ars erotica*. But different texts vary in details (such as number of strokes or breaths). Such prescribed acts and orderings provide a strong formalistic and ritualistic dimension to the act of lovemaking that magnifies its aesthetic import by dramatizing the act, by formally shaping it, by enriching it with sanctified social meaning, and by introducing a reflective moment to savor its drama, form, meaning, and qualities.[43] Moreover, such ritualized order, replete with reflective pause, also serves to prevent sexual passion from overrunning its options of aesthetic shaping that can bring heightened benefits of pleasure and health.

[42] Nonetheless, by later specifying thirty different "postures of intercourse" (including threesomes and foursomes), this same text describes some positions where the woman places herself above the man, and rather than denouncing such postures, it includes them in "the marvels of [lovemaking's] meaning" (Wile 109).

[43] A different text, *Secrets of the Jade Chamber*, recommends a longer pause – "a count of thirty breaths" in order to "restrain yourself and . . . not ejaculate" (Wile 105). The numbers of strokes prescribed often have special numerological significance. The number 9, for example, occurs very frequently and symbolizes long-lastingness and virility because "it is the highest . . . number before ten and represents here [in this sexual context] as in the *I ching* and elsewhere, the penultimate *yang* force" (Wile 236). Pronounced *jiu*, the character nine 九 is also homophonic with the Chinese character for long-lastingness 久. Its connotations of long-term persistence and virility could apply to the coital act itself and/or to the life gained through practicing the relevant erotic techniques.

We find this idea of ritual order already in China's earliest erotic texts, such as *Uniting Yin and Yang*. In formulating "the method for uniting *yin* and *yang*," it instructs the lover to "carry out the *dao* of dalliance step by step" and slowly. "Although full of passion do not act" until the time is right to move to the next step. "First, when her *qi* rises and her face becomes flushed, slowly exhale. Second, when her nipples become hard and her nose perspires, slowly embrace her. Third, when her tongue spreads and becomes lubricious, slowly press her. Fourth, when secretions appear below and her thighs are damp, slowly take hold of her. Fifth, when her throat is dry and she swallows saliva, slowly agitate her." The text goes on to specify the various modes and movements of penetration and thrusting in terms of "ten movements" and "ten refinements," along with the woman's "five signs of desire" and "eight movements" indicative of her state of arousal (Wile 78–79).

Ritualizing, however, should never be a matter of rigid, mechanical uniformity; rather, it seeks to enrich aesthetic power by creatively adjusting to particular contexts and offering pleasing variety to establish more satisfying harmonies. In the words of the *Dong Xuanzi*: "The principles of deep and shallow, slow and fast, thrusting and twisting, and east and west do not follow a single path, but have 10,000 strands. For example, there is slow thrusting like a gold carp toying with the hook, or the tense urgency of a flock of birds facing a stiff wind." Every action, every pause should be chosen to harmonize with the woman's condition and "adapt to her pace." Thus "pulling in and drawing out, up and down, following and receiving, left and right, going forth and returning, withdrawing and entering, separation and closeness, all need to be orchestrated and properly adjusted. One must not forever sing the same old tune in every circumstance" (Wile 108).

Variety

Besides harmony and ritualization, variety is key to the Chinese aesthetics of lovemaking. We find various modes of foreplay (stroking, clasping, pressing, sucking, kissing, rubbing, stabbing, embracing, entwining, exhaling and inhaling, swallowing, etc.) that are directed at a variety of body parts, some of which are designated with poetic names whose intended referents are now unclear. "The hips, buttocks, nose, and mouth each play their part in turn," claims the *Discourse on the Highest Dao*, while *Uniting Yin and Yang* notes the "elbow chambers," "armpits," and "neck region," along with more mysteriously designated locations such as "the stove frame," "the receiving basket," "the broken basin," "the sweet wine ford," "the bounding sea," "Mount Constancy," "the dark gate," and "the coital sinew," which scholars identify with the breasts, pelvic region, the mons veneris, vulva, and vagina (Wile 78, 80). Of course, some body parts are endowed with special erotic power. If the mouth, breasts, vulva, and vagina are particularly potent by nature (providing the "Great Medicine of the Three Peaks," SL 283), then later cultural conditions, through the fashion of foot-binding, gave the lady's bound feet compelling erotic allure. But Chinese *ars erotica* embraced the whole body in its diversity of parts because improved circulation of *qi* energy throughout the lover's soma formed one of its key aims.

Chinese taste for diversity finds further expression in a variety of coital positions (often colorfully named) and forms of coital movement (of both the male and female lover). Movements vary not only in temporal speed and rhythm but also in force, style, direction, and the body parts that are principally engaged. They also somewhat differ if one's prime purpose in coitus is generating offspring rather than simply augmenting one's energy, health, and pleasure. Accompanying such movements but independently noteworthy are the movements of breathing. These display a variety of rhythms and modes (including a special form of "swallowing") and are crucial not only for absorbing and circulating the *qi* but also for maintaining better control over one's other coital movements and more generally one's passion. "The man should close his mouth and slowly execute soft entry and hard retreat ... and with one's own nose draw in the *qi* from the woman's nose, inhaling it to the abdomen. One must not inhale with the mouth for this injures the brain" (Wile 142).

Special breathing must be synchronized with kissing, sucking, and vaginal penetration: "One inhalation and one absorption: this is what is known as 'inhaling her *qi* above and absorbing her secretions below.'" After the woman's *jing* has been released through orgasm, "the man should withdraw the 'jade stalk' an inch or so and adopt a posture of half engagement, inhaling her nostril *qi* above and her slippery secretions below. The nostrils are the 'gate of heaven' and below is the 'gate of life,'" so "if one simultaneously inhales" and absorbs from "above and below in sympathetic response," one can best ingest and circulate the *qi* throughout the body, directing it to its highest energy centers "like drawing water up through a bamboo tube that flows upward against gravity" (Wile 142).[44] Improving

[44] After the man absorbs the *qi* from the woman's upper and middle regions of nose, mouth and breasts, he should focus on the "*qi* of her private parts ... At this time, one should withdraw the

male health by augmenting *qi* through absorption while preventing its loss through ejaculation is one of China's two key sexual goals (along with procreation) and the prime reason for its emphasis on coitus reservatus. For this reason, Chinese *ars erotica* also includes a variety of bodily movements both for "locking" erotic energy so that ejaculation does not occur and for refining and circulating that preserved energy throughout the lover's own body. "When absorbing and refining, use mental concentration and contraction to lock it; use absorption and inhalation to gather it" (Wile 144).

Besides the various actions to absorb *qi* and to avoid its loss through ejaculation, we find a variety of postures and movements for refining and circulating the augmented *qi* attained through coitus reservatus. Some of these are clearly postcoital and require disengaging from the woman's body so that one can achieve the intense mental concentration and solo postures and actions for bringing all the sexually acquired *qi* back to the man's core energy centers, thereby diffusing it throughout the entire body. Such methods are crucial for the extraordinary practice of *injaculation* in which the seminal energetic matter that is ready to ejaculate is instead locked in the body through intense mental concentration, muscular contractions, and firmly pressing on the perineum so that the *jing* is instead injaculated when orgasm is felt. Contemporary science explains that injaculated semen enters the bladder and is later expelled in the urine, but ancient Chinese medicine thought that, through masterful erotic control and concentration, the injaculated *jing* could return upward to nourish the body's key energy centers and then be circulated to energize the body as a whole. Thus, one must "follow the correct method in 'dismounting' [from one's lover]" and then perform a well-timed integration of solo postcoital postures, movements, and breathing modes in order to "revert and return" the erotically aroused energy so that it could be distributed throughout the soma, engendering vitality, health, and radiance (Wile 144).

> After finishing the act, one must lie flat on the back, extending the arms straight out, and relaxing the feet, with the head resting on the pillow and

'wonderful handle' an inch or so and elevate the body like a turtle, raising a breath of *qi* directly to the upper *tan-tian.* Take in the opponent's *qi* and absorb her secretions, circulating them throughout your body.. . . Refine and receive it, circulating it upward from the *wei lu*, ascending the two 'white channels,' passing through the *jia-qi*, penetrating the *kun-lun*, entering the *ni-wan*, and flowing into the mouth. Here it is transformed into 'jade juice,' which should be swallowed down the 'storied pavilion' until it reaches all the way to the *tan-tian.* This is called the 'reverse flow of the Yellow River,' and has the ability to augment the *jing* and supplement the marrow, increase longevity and lengthen the years" (Wile 143).

> the heels making contact with the bed. The body should feel as if suspended in space. Hold the breath with all your might and shake your body several times, finally letting the air escape from the nose. Execute this in a smooth and even manner. If one feels heat in the face, this is because the *jing qi* already has ascended to the *ni-wan.* At this moment, one should use both hands to massage the skin of the face and cause the heat to disperse. Now close the lips and stop breathing. With the tongue stir about in the "flowery pool" and swallow the "holy water" to the *tan-tian.* In this way one is able to circulate the *jing qi* throughout the body and it becomes a very useful thing. (Wile 144–145)[45]

Aesthetic values of variety and harmony pervade Chinese views of erotic pleasure. The varied sensual delights from the diverse senses harmoniously blend with pleasures of affective concord with one's partner and environment. Pleasurable feelings of health and energy combine with cognitive pleasures of form and meaning – including the knowledge that one is working on the ethical duties of sustaining health or creating new life and that one is following hallowed ritual tradition in performing the act of love in the appropriate way. All these further harmonize with the pleasures of empowerment in demonstrating one's erotic mastery, including the enjoyment of self-mastery through restraint. Finally, the intense delights of ardent passion are balanced and blended with the pleasures of masterful calm and reflective composure.

Calm and Reflective Awareness

What is the aesthetic importance of calmness and reflection for Chinese *ars erotica*? First, the pleasure of aesthetic experience is intensified by reflective awareness of that enjoyment and explicit attention to what one is enjoying. Savoring extends and deepens one's pleasure; and since savoring takes time and tranquil reflection, we find another reason for thoughtful, leisured slowness in lovemaking. As Montaigne puts the point more generally, through reflective savoring one can "enjoy [life's pleasure] twice as much . . . , for the measure of enjoyment depends on the greater or lesser

[45] According to China's sexual alchemy tradition, if one "practiced for a long time" this technique of enhancing energy and health, one could live long enough to eventually acquire the elixir of earthly immortality and "wander freely in the Milky Way and feast in the 'yellow court,'" a divinely mystical Daoist realm (Wile 145).

attention that we lend to it."[46] Second, calm reflection is needed for mastery of technique. To perform the proper movements in the appropriate ways and at the right times, one must be clearly aware of what one is doing and undergoing with one's body and how one's lover is reacting to one's lovemaking. Monitoring these states of arousal and performed actions is essential for properly orchestrating them to achieve the best rhythm and harmony.

Technical mastery in Chinese *ars erotica* demands superior *self-mastery* in controlling one's passion, and the crucial role of calm composure and critical reflection in achieving self-mastery provides a further reason for their aesthetic importance. The lover needs to vigilantly monitor his level of arousal so that this passion does not exceed his control and prematurely explode into ejaculation. In order for this vigilant control to be effective, slowness is once again advised. When "inserting soft and withdrawing hard," instructs a Tang text *Health Benefits of the Bedchamber* (房中补益), "the pace of advancing and retreating should be very slow and, when passions are aroused, rest. Do not throw yourself into it with abandon," but instead use a pause to calm the mind and settle your energy: "Slow the breath, close the eyes, lie on your back and guide the *qi* internally" (Wile 116).

Another text elaborates, "As your passion mounts, do not allow yourself to become overly excited or reach the point of intense ecstasy, and then it will be easy to control yourself in intercourse. One must perform the act slowly, entering soft and withdrawing hard. Execute three shallow and one deep thrusts eighty-one times as one round. If the *jing* becomes slightly aroused, immediately stop and retreat" (Wile 139). There is no need to withdraw entirely in pausing between thrusts. "When resting, allow an inch or so to remain inside, and after the heart's fire has calmed, continue the procedure as earlier. Now execute the five shallow and one deep method, and finally nine shallow and one deep. Strictly avoid haste and impatience. If one practices in this way for half a month, one's skill will be complete" (Wile 139–140).

The text continues to emphasize this point: "One should settle the mind and move slowly back and forth within the stove [i.e., woman]" (Wile 140). Then, by "the first sign of passion, one should perform the raising and withdrawing, and repeatedly calm the temper." In other words, "Rest, quiet

[46] Michel de Montaigne, *The Complete Essays of Montaigne*, trans. Donald Frame (Stanford: Stanford University Press, 1965), 853.

the mind, and after a moment proceed again according to the method" so that the woman will "surely be first to reach orgasm" and you can "capture the spoils [of her secreting energy] according to the proper method," which is thoughtfully gradual and leisurely calm (Wile 140). "If you feel yourself about to ejaculate, quickly withdraw the 'jade stalk' and execute the locking technique. When your power has subsided and your *qi* is settled and even, then . . . attack once again. In doing battle do not be afraid to go slow; in gathering the spoils do not be afraid to be gradual. If one proceeds with due care, all will be well" (Wile 140).

Tranquility and critical reflection are further necessary for the meditative discipline of directing the absorbed and enhanced *qi* to the proper energy centers so that its benefits of health, beauty, and pleasure can then be circulated throughout the body. If mastery of special breathing techniques serves to calm the lover's mind during coitus, then such calm reciprocally enables him better mastery of other breathing techniques focused on absorbing and circulating the *qi* acquired from his lovemaking. The crucial role of breathing in settling the mind for erotic success must have been obvious in the original Chinese context, where mind and heart are identified and denoted by the same word or character (*xin*, 心). The ancients knew what current science confirms: breathing strongly affects heart rate and feelings of calm.

Finally, serene composure in experiencing intense passion is aesthetically appealing in itself – an ideal of harmony, of masterfully controlled but still vibrant life energy sustained at its optimum level beyond which it will explode or dissipate. "Only one who understands the *dao* is able to suppress emotion in the presence of the object and be dispassionate in the midst of passion" (Wile 141). To achieve this level of mastery, Chinese erotic texts recommend various methods: critical reflection, slowness of movement, pausing, withdrawing, slowing the breath, and closing the eyes (both for inner concentration and to avoid overstimulation in seeing one's partner's passionate beauty). Some texts offer training advice to develop this erotic calm composure: "First practice with a 'stove' [i.e., woman] who is loose and ugly" so that one's passion is easier to control. But if the man's lover is "a truly beautiful crucible," then although he may truly love her, "during intercourse he must force himself to detest her" (only in the sense of provisionally treating her as a challenging "opponent") in order to cool his passion and "settle the mind" so they both will achieve more pleasure (Wile 139–140).

VIII PHILOSOPHICAL MEANINGS: FROM THE SENSUAL TO THE SUBLIME

By emphasizing not only mastery of technique but also perceptual mastery and self-mastery through training and disciplines of breathing, meditation, and somatic self-control, Chinese *ars erotica* was not simply a set of methods to get the sexual job done successfully (whether for pleasure, power, or offspring). Instead, it formed part of a general philosophical quest for nurturing life (*yang sheng*) and for self-cultivation (*xiu shen*). Despite differences among Confucians and Daoists on the most important methods and targets of this quest, they converged in advocating aims of harmony, self-mastery, and healthy vitality whose energetic powers were displayed not in frenetic effortful activity but rather in calm composure and limpid ease that exuded a radiant aura of virtuous excellence or beauty. This concern with self-cultivation and self-mastery helps explain why Chinese *ars erotica* devotes much less attention to sexually enhancing drugs (for increasing desire or penis size or "for shrinking the woman's 'jade gate,'" Wile 102), while even occasionally warning against such drugs and aphrodisiacs. Such chemical interventions risk disturbing one's natural harmony, tranquility, and self-sufficient self-mastery – not to mention one's health. When the Yellow Emperor asks, "What do you think of those who use drugs and special foods as tonic supplements [for erotic success]?" Su Nu replies that they are wrongly pursuing sex "for the purpose of lustful pleasure" because they "do not understand the meaning of self-cultivation. They force themselves to perform the act and ... mistakenly consume medicines that are harmful to their lives. Is this not a great pity!" (Wile 128–129). Another text similarly condemns the "partaking of aphrodisiacs" for the "shameful quest for pleasure," when instead "one should maintain self-control for the cultivation of life" (Wile 115).

How does the practice of *ars erotica* contribute to philosophical self-cultivation? First, its heightening of *jing* and intensification of *qi* can yield spiritual benefits, since spirit (or *shen*) is simply a sublimated form of (grossly material) *jing* and (more subtle energetic) *qi*. China's two earliest erotic texts repeatedly insist that through a ritualized discipline of repeated coital arousal without ejaculation "one attains spiritual illumination" (Wile 78–80). The idea of intensifying and refining erotic *qi* into spiritual enlightenment extends to the later elixir tradition, in which "every word and every sentence [of its erotic instruction] is a spiritual teaching" for "gentlemen engaging in spiritual cultivation" (Wile 176, 177). It is not always clear whether the spiritual illumination is experienced directly in the sexual act or immediately after it, or whether this illumination is instead a later product, resulting from higher energy, better health, and longer life that together provide more capacity for spiritual insight.

Second, *ars erotica*'s critical monitoring of one's sexual arousal and activity encourages a richer, more penetrating awareness of one's feelings, desires, and actions, which improves self-knowledge. Moreover, as the same critical awareness is directed to the feelings and actions of one's lovers with the aim of achieving fruitful harmony, *ars erotica* ensures that self-cultivation involves an essential regard for others and a deeper knowledge of them. It confirms the philosophical insight that the self becomes what it is only through its environing others, energies, and elements. Of course, this improved knowledge of one's sexual partners could, in principle, be used to manipulate and exploit them, and this is painfully evident in the exploitation of women expressed in most erotic texts. However, a more enlightened approach to erotic self-cultivation would recognize that one's self is enriched by enriching its partnering others and that the erotic pleasures one shares with them would foster the desire to benefit rather than exploit them.

Third, *ars erotica's* self-cultivation improves not only self-knowledge but also self-discipline. By engaging our most ardent desires and most powerful pleasures, the unruly passion of sexual arousal provides the most powerful challenges for training our willpower and self-control. Such superior self-control is distinctive in that it avoids pleasure-denying self-repression and instead reflects masterful ease and calm composure in self-regulation and restraint. Such self-control and tranquil clarity serve as crucial means not only for successful lovemaking but for any pursuit. As *The Great Learning* insists, we need "a calm unperturbedness" and "tranquil repose" through which "there may be careful deliberation . . . that . . . will be followed by the attainment of the desired end" (GL 309). Calm self-control and composure are also highly valued in themselves as crucial components of what Chinese ethics considers a truly worthy character. "The exemplary person is calm and unperturbed; the petty person is always agitated and anxious," claims Confucius (AC 7.37), who explains how through many years of disciplined learning, he achieved such mastery of self-regulation that he can now do whatever he wants "without overstepping the boundaries" of what is right (AC 2:4). Mencius insists that the exemplary man abides "calmly and firmly" in his knowledge and action, while Xunzi confirms that superior people remain "tranquil and at ease" and that the "worthiest of men" act with "calm solemnity [to] perfect the arts of civilization and display them to the world so that violent states will become peaceful and transform themselves."[47] Xunzi therefore urges, "If the blood humor is too strong and robust, calm it with balance and harmony."[48]

Daoist thought similarly prizes masterful calm and peaceful ease as defining the highest virtue: "Limpidity, silence, emptiness, inaction – these are the level of Heaven and earth, the substance of the Way and its Virtue," claims Zhuangzi. "So it is said, The sage rests; with rest comes peaceful ease, with peaceful ease comes limpidity, and where there is ease and limpidity, care and worry cannot get at him, noxious airs cannot assault him. Therefore his Virtue is complete and his spirit unimpaired" (CWZ 168). The early Daoist text of *Inward Training* (*Nei-ye*, 内业) repeatedly urges tranquility as both the means and part of the desired end of "developing inner power" or excellence (*de*).[49] This desired aim is the power of unperturbed "equanimity" that "finds calmness beneficial, and by it, attains repose. Do not disturb it and harmony will naturally develop." The all-governing Way (or *dao*) "abides within the excellent mind" because that "mind is tranquil and the vital breath is regular." To "cultivate your mind, make your thoughts tranquil" and then the inner *qi* naturally thrives and "harmonizes," exuding on the outside the beauty of calmness and its physical attractions. "If people can be aligned and tranquil, their skin will be ample and smooth. Their eyes and ears will be acute and clear. Their muscles will be supple and their bones strong."

Harmony is another value that demonstrates the intimate intertwining of means and ends in China's *ars erotica* but also more generally in Chinese thought. If attaining the aim of erotic success depends on establishing harmony (of emotions, levels of arousal, and rhythms), then conversely that end of erotic success likewise serves as a crucial means for creating and sustaining harmony not only between the loving couple but also within the individual lover's inner self. Harmony constitutes a central virtue that distinguishes exemplary persons as superior. Rather than mere unity or uniformity, harmony embraces difference and is richer and more satisfying for that reason. China's earliest commentaries define harmony in terms of cooking's mixture of diverse flavors and music's mixing of different

47 James Legge, trans., *The Complete Works of Mencius* (New York: Dover, 1970), 322 (Book 4, b. 14). See also "On Self-Cultivation," in Knoblock, *Xunzi*, vol. 1, 158, and "On Confucius," in *Xunzi*, vol. 2, 58.

48 "On Self-Cultivation," in Knoblock, *Xunzi*, vol. 1, 153.

49 Harold D. Roth, trans., *Original Tao: Inward Training (Nei-yeh) and the Foundations of Taoist Mysticism* (New York: Columbia University Press, 2004), 41. The remaining quotations in the paragraph are from 48, 50, 54, 74, 76.

sounds.[50] Confucius later confirms: "Exemplary persons seek harmony not sameness" (AC 13:23). A key dimension of harmonizing is balancing contrasts to find a middle way that is not a mechanical average but a sensitive adjusting or integrating of differences. Lovemaking provides a model and training ground of such balancing – embracing both *yin* and *yang*, passion and calm, spontaneity and reflection, nature and art, and exemplifying the paradox of self-mastery that combines effort with relaxation, self-control with letting go.

In advocating "harmony [as] the most valuable function of observing ritual propriety," Confucius claims that "this achievement of harmony [by the ancient Kings is what] made them elegant" (AC 1:12).[51] In short, the harmony of their calm inner power of virtue (*de*) made them radiantly attractive and thus more capable of ruling their people in a harmonious way. Daoism likewise associates harmony with the inner power of virtue (*de*). "One who possesses virtue in abundance is comparable to a new born babe.. . . This is because its harmony is at its height," intones the *Daodejing* (DJ 62), while the *Zhuangzi* claims, "Virtue is the establishment of perfect harmony," so that the man of virtue can "harmonize . . . with all" and never lose his calm clarity, like "water at rest" (CWZ 74). Because the "ugly man named Ai Taitou" had this calm harmony of inner virtue, he was irresistibly attractive so that "men and women flocked to him" (CWZ 72).

Classical Chinese philosophy thus believed that the beauty of harmony through calm inner power, if properly perceived, should be so compellingly attractive as to be even more desirable and gratifying than sex. Jeffrey Riegl, in analyzing a number of early Confucian texts, underlines the point that mastery of *ars erotica* brings ethical self-cultivation because "the *experience* of erotic desires . . . discloses to the person who undergoes them the proper forms of politeness and propriety" in regulating these desires and expressing them in the appropriate way. He further makes the more radical claim that ancient Chinese thinkers believed those endowed with superior virtue or worthiness (*de*) should inspire a desire and delight equal to those of sex.[52]

[50] "Shi Bo, a scholar-minister who lived toward the end of the Western Zhou (1046–771 BCE) [,] . . . praised early sage-kings that they harmonized five flavors to befit the taste and the six measures of sound to adjust the hearing, and that they achieved the highest level of harmony in society." Cited in Chenyang Li, "The Philosophy of Harmony in Classical Confucianism," *Philosophy Compass* 3, no. 3 (2008): 424.

[51] The term "elegant" is translating the Chinese word *mei*, which is usually rendered more simply as "beautiful."

[52] Jeffrey Riegel, "A Passion for the Worthy," *Journal of the American Oriental Society* 128, no. 4 (2008): 710.

In doing so, Riegl renders *Analects* 1:7 as: "In treating the worthy as worthy he replaces those he finds sexually alluring with them," relying partly on the book's earliest surviving commentary, which paraphrases the line as: "Use the heart of desiring sex to desire the worthy and then one will be good."[53] This suggests two intriguing ideas: training in the *ars erotica*, by developing erotic desire, can improve us ethically by channeling this passion to a passion for virtue. Moreover, by cultivating virtuous excellence through tranquil, harmonious self-mastery, a person, even if an elderly sage, can be more erotically compelling than those with youthful good looks and thus can inspire a sublime passion for virtue.

Daoism also takes *ars erotica* toward spiritual transcendence. Here the goal is a higher, heavenly unification of *yin* and *yang* within the philosophical sage him- or herself. A man's erotic aim of obtaining *yin* essence through sexual encounters need not be construed as focused on magnifying his *yang* energy in macho-vampiristic style by predatory robbing of woman's *yin*. It could instead aim at absorbing and cultivating more of the vital female energy to promote female traits that Daoism emphasized, thus enabling him to achieve a better *yin–yang* balance. Even without embracing the metaphysical principles of *yin* and *yang*, one could argue that through thoughtful, attentive lovemaking, a man can absorb a better knowledge of women's feelings, actions, and energies and thus eventually incorporate them to establish better balance and harmony within himself and with others. Laozi's injunction to "Know the male but keep to the role of the female" (DJ 33) suggests the aim of harmonious balance of *yin* and *yang* that finds practical expression in Daoist masters whose efforts at self-cultivation include adopting various female practices (such as "never urinate while standing").[54]

This ideal of fulfilled *yin–yang* harmony within oneself (which promises ultimate freedom from sexual need) is most powerfully articulated in the remarks of the great Tang Dynasty Daoist patriarch Lu Dongbin, a legendary "Immortal" famed for erotic prowess and inner alchemy as well as poetry and wisdom. After he long frequented a famous courtesan "without ever making love to her," the beautiful lady tried to lure him into bed. But the Daoist sage refused, responding: "The *yin* and *yang* energies of Anterior Heaven are already joined in my body. The sexual union has taken place

[53] Ibid., 711, 712.

[54] Laozi's directive is repeated in *Zhuangzi*, ch. 33 (CWZ 372). On the adoption of female practices, see Schipper, *The Daoist Body*, 127.

inside me, the embryo is already formed. I am about to give birth. Do you really think that, in my present state, I still desire exterior sex?"[55] This paradigm of balanced, fertile, vital *yin–yang* union within the individual resonates with the androgynous ideal of primordial man suggested in Genesis, while contrasting sharply with Greek and Roman ideals of manhood, where mere devotion to lovemaking risked condemnations of degenerate effeminacy. The fact that Chinese theory portrays ideals of erotic fulfillment and self-realization that transcend the physical acts of lovemaking does not discredit those physical forms and techniques. In recognizing how the ends and means of lovemaking are deeply intertwined, the affirmation of more sublimely spiritual ends does not demean the sensual ways to reach them. Without the experience (and energies) of physical lovemaking, the sage would be unprepared for eventually elevating to a pure harmony of inner virtue or spiritualized erotics of transcendent inner alchemy.

I close this chapter with a further Chinese example suggestive of sexual transformation, androgyny, and the spiritual promise of sexual desire. It belongs not to Daoism or Confucianism but to the tradition of Chinese Buddhism as exemplified in the bodhisattva of compassion Guanyin, the Chinese version of the original Indian bodhisattva Avalokitesvara. Early Chinese incarnations or visions of Guanyin were masculine, like those prevailing in the original Avalokitesvara, but Guanyin also developed female incarnations and representations that eventually became predominant.[56] Guanyin's "most familiar" feminine manifestation is "the chaste and filial daughter represented by Princess Miao-shan" (Wonderful Goodness), who was first executed by her father because she insisted on keeping her chastity but later returned to life and gave her eyes and hands as necessary ingredients for a potion to cure her dying father king, who then converted to Buddhism.[57] But other incarnations of Guanyin display her work of compassion in more erotic ways. "Fish-Basket" Guanyin was a "young,

[55] Schipper, *The Daoist Body*, 128.

[56] For Guanyin, see Chün-Fang Yü, *Kuan-yin: The Chinese Transformation of Avalokitesvara* (New York: Columbia University Press, 2001), which notes that of the thirty-three manifestations of Avalokitesvara in the *Lotus Sutra*, only seven are female, while Chinese manifestations of Guanyin came to be "predominantly feminine" (45–46, 419). Yü also recognizes (along with other scholars) the similarities of Guanyin to the erotically charged Daoist goddess, the Queen Mother of the West, already mentioned above for her sexual prowess. However, she does not discover any direct link between them, speculating instead that Guanyin may have emerged to substitute for this and other indigenous Chinese goddesses who had lost popularity by the time Guanyin gained prominence as a female bodhisattva.

[57] Ibid., 296.

beautiful, and sexually alluring" maiden who attracted many suitors to Buddhism because of their wish to marry her. Insisting that she would accept only someone who memorized a series of holy sutras, she kept her promise but suddenly died, a virgin, on her wedding day. A further Guanyin incarnation, the "Woman of Yen-chou," was a young woman who instead "engaged in sexual activities" in a nondiscriminate manner as a way of providing compassionate salvation while teaching nondualism. "She had sex with any man who asked for it. But whoever had sex with her was said to be free from sexual desire forever." Though "she died at the age of twenty-four as a dissolute woman of ill-repute," a monk later revealed she was really Guanyin, who slept with men out of compassion in order to cure them of the torments of sexual desire by channeling that desire as "a powerful tool of spiritual transformation."[58]

[58] Ibid., 421, 424. In the Mahayana Buddhist *Vimalakirti Sutra*, very influential in China, we learn that a bodhisattva sometimes "shows himself as a woman of pleasure, enticing those prone to lechery. First he catches them with the hook of desire, then leads them into the Buddha way." Burton Watson, trans., *The Vimalakirti Sutra* (New York: Columbia University Press, 2000), 102.

5

Lovemaking as Aesthetic Education

Pleasure, Play, and Knowledge in Indian Erotic Theory

I INTRODUCTION

Of all the ancient sexual traditions, India's is the most prominent in our contemporary erotic consciousness, where its founding text, the *Kamasutra*, often serves as a symbol or synonym for the general field of *ars erotica*. Although Chinese sexual theory is probably older and may have influenced Indian sexual mysticism (particularly in its use of coitus reservatus and injaculation), there is no reason to view Indian erotology as derivative. It has a distinctively rich and original character that easily rivals China's, and this character is profoundly aesthetic. If one construes Foucault's notion of *ars erotica* as implying an emphasis on the aesthetic pleasures and artfulness of lovemaking in contrast to a *scientia sexualis* that focused on truth and health (whether physical, mental, or spiritual), then Indian erotic theory provides a better paradigm for such art. While China's sexual theory drew most heavily on medical texts and derived its concern for pleasure from the key medical aims of health and progeny, Indian erotology drew most heavily on the fine arts and their sensuous aesthetic pleasures, especially the traditional Indian art of drama, which was also an art of dance. Nonetheless, Indian sexual theory cannot fully support Foucault's sharp distinction between esoteric *ars erotica* and *scientia sexualis*, because it defines itself in essentially scientific terms as providing knowledge about empirical matters based on observation. Moreover, this knowledge was openly published in texts articulating principles and rules rather than focusing on recondite skills secretly transmitted by an expert master to carefully chosen pupils.[1]

[1] The terms often used to name or describe these texts – *shastra*, *tantra*, and *sutra* – have the closely related meanings of "manual," "treatise," "theory," "code," and the like.

Among the reasons for thinking that Indian erotic theory derives largely from the theater is that its founding text, the *Kamasutra*, not only designates both male and female lovers as "actors" or dramatic protagonists (*nayaka* being the male lead or hero with *nayika* as the heroine), but also adopts other figures drawn from the Indian dramatic tradition as characters in its art of love. These include the libertine, the pander, the clown, and the courtesan. Its paradigm playboy lover is, moreover, portrayed as an expert patron of theater. Scholars generally believe that India's founding text of dramatic theory, the *Natyaśastra*, was written at least a century before the *Kamasutra*.[2] Direct influence is hard to prove with certainty because the dates of both texts are contested, and the *Kamasutra*, while mentioning a variety of earlier authors and texts, does not mention the *Natyaśastra*. Moreover, one might conversely argue that the *Natyaśastra*, even if composed before the *Kamasutra*, relied itself on an already well-developed tradition of erotic artistry that included harem life and high-class courtesans renowned for their artistic and sexual skills as well as for their beauty. In any case, these two foundational texts of dramatic and erotic theory emerged from an extensive literary tradition (religious and worldly) that was paradoxically rich with both polymorphic sexuality and radical ascetic austerities.

This chapter cannot adequately survey that vast literary field, but concentrates on texts explicitly devoted to erotic theory, focusing on India's three most influential exemplars. These are the *Kamasutra* and two much later works that draw heavily on it but also modify and complement it in various ways: the *Koka Shastra* (also known as the *Ratirahasya* from the eleventh or twelfth century) and the *Ananga Ranga* (fifteenth or sixteenth century).[3] These later works are shorter than the *Kamasutra* and more

[2] Scholars date the *Natyaśastra* between the second century BCE and the second century CE, while the "Kamasutra must have been written after 225" CE and "cites the Arthashastra," which is "generally placed in the 3rd century CE." For the *Natyaśastra*, see Natalia Lidova, *Drama and Ritual of Early Hinduism* (Delhi: Motilal Banarsidass, 1994). See also her article in Oxford Bibliographies, "Natyashastra" last modified September 29, 2014, www.oxfordbibliographies.com/view/document/obo-9780195399318/obo-9780195399318-0071.xml. For the *Kamasutra*, see Wendy Doniger and Sudhir Kakar's "Introduction," in Vatsyayana Mallanaga, *Kamasutra* (with excerpts from the Sanskrit Jayamangala commentary of Yashodhara Indrapada, the Hindi Jaya commentary of Devadatta Shastri and explanatory notes), trans. Wendy Doniger and Sudhir Kakar (Oxford: Oxford University Press, 2009), xi; hereafter KS.

[3] I use the following translations and abbreviations: for the Doniger and Kakar translation of Vatsyayana's *Kamasutra*, KS; for Kokkoka's *Koka Shastra* (also known as the *Ratirahasya*), trans. Alex Comfort (New York: Stein & Day, 1965), hereafter KKS; for Kalyanamalla's *Ananga Ranga*, trans. F. F. Arbuthnot and Richard Burton (New York: Medical Press, 1964), hereafter AR. The title "Ratirahasya" means the mystery or secrets of Rati, who is the goddess of love,

restrictive in the sexual forms they expound, but they do add an important classificatory scheme of four female types (the "lotus-woman" (*padmini*), the "art-woman" (*citrini*), the "shell-woman" (*sankhini*), and the "elephant-woman" (*hastini*)) as well as related astrological material. These later, shorter works are in verse while the *Kamasutra* is essentially a prose composition, though it sometimes uses verse for stylistic emphasis or concluding summaries of its chapters. Rather than treating each text individually, I deploy all three together to make this chapter's case for the powerfully aesthetic dimension of Indian erotic theory and its educational impact for ethical self-cultivation.[4]

Foregrounding this aesthetic theme requires presenting some cultural background by exploring important religious, social, and artistic ideas that provide the enabling context for the aesthetics of Indian *ars erotica* and that find expression in classical Indian texts beyond the three erotic treatises that form our focus.

II THE RELIGIOUS AND SOCIAL BACKGROUND

Remarkably complex and bewilderingly diverse, India's religious tradition is a richly dynamic composite of different creeds, historical periods, attitudes, regions, classes, and levels of refinement or sophistication. This chapter concentrates on its dominant Hindu tradition. Beginning with the Vedas and developing through the Upanishads, the Puranas, and the Vedanta and Samkya-Yoga philosophical schools, Hinduism ranges from sacrificial and ritual worship to poetic hymns, intricate mythologies, and theoretical speculations concerning such abiding themes as birth, death, the nature of reality, the creation of the world, the pursuit of wisdom, and the ethical conduct of life with its different aims, stages, and duties. This tradition, which eventually spawned also Buddhism and Jainism, has long included distinctive somatic disciplines such as yoga as integral to religious practice. From the outset, the theme of sexuality in its cosmic power

erotic desire, and carnal pleasure, serving as Kama's chief consort and counterpart. The title "Ananga Ranga" literally means the "play" (*ranga*) of the "limbless" or "bodiless" (*ananga*) and signifies the play or stage of love. Here, *ananga* refers to the god Kama, who was burned into bodiless existence by the angry look of Śiva's third eye after he arranged for Parvati to seduce Śiva away from ascetic concentration. Kama, however, eventually gets his body back.

4 Comfort's "Introduction" provides brief descriptions of several texts of Indian erotology that were written after the *Koka Shastra*, including the *Ananga Ranga* (KKS 80–100). One of these texts, the *Ratimanjari* of Jayadeva, an apparently "lateish work," is sufficiently short ("only 125 slokas") for him to translate it in full (KKS 88–94; quotation from 88).

and diverse expression has been pervasive in Hinduism, though it is much more positively and prominently portrayed in the Vedas and then later in the populist Puranas than in the more austere Upanishads that historically come between them. The *Rig Veda* (earliest of the Vedic texts) celebrates the rising sun following dawn with the sexually charged metaphor of a man pursuing a maiden, and elsewhere expresses incestuous relations such as the desire between sister and brother (RV I.115:2, RV VI.55:4, RV X.10:7–14). The *Shukla Yajur Veda* (23:20–31) describes an important royal sacrifice ritual aimed at enhancing the ruler's power, glory, and progeny and that involves the chief queen pretending to copulate while spending the night with a stallion that has just been ritually slaughtered.[5]

As Wendy Doniger notes, Indian mythology displays a "staggering variety": particular myths involve numerous conflicting versions and "contradictory strains" whose outlines constantly change, thus presenting a field so complex and vague that "an outsider might consider [it] a meaningless patchwork, a crazy quilt of metaphysics."[6] Its pantheon of gods is astoundingly multiple and dynamically polymorphic. Individual gods often divide themselves into differently gendered pairs or are multiplied by numerous avatars or simply adopt human or even animal figures; some are killed but then revived in different form (just as the entire universe, with its creating god, is periodically destroyed and then reborn). Indeed, it is not at all clear what exactly, for Hinduism, constitutes a god, and therefore how many gods there are, though the number is often given as 330 million but also sometimes as merely thirty-three.[7]

Whatever their number, the gods have a clearly erotic dimension. Hindu mythology is rife with sexuality, whose complex and significant role in explaining both cosmic forces and human behavior is also manifested in remarkably diverse and often intricate erotic forms. The *Brihadaranykaka Upanishad*, for example, explains creation by positing an original solitary Self, Purusha, who was "not at all happy" in his lonely existence and desired a mate and to do so "became the size of a man and wife in close embrace. He divided this body into two," thus creating husband and wife and then as

[5] For more details on these and other examples of eroticism in the Vedas and later ancient texts, see S. C. Banerjee, *Crime and Sex in Ancient India* (Calcutta: Naya Prokash, 1980), 76–78; for further discussion, see J. J. Meyer, *Sexual Life in Ancient India* (London: Kegan Paul, 2003).

[6] Wendy Doniger, *Śiva: The Erotic Ascetic* (Oxford: Oxford University Press, 1973), 35, 314; hereafter SEA.

[7] For an explanation of the antigods or *asuras*, see Alain Danielou, *The Myths and Gods of India* (Rochester, VT: Inner Traditions International, 1991), 139–140; hereafter MG.

husband united with her. "From that union human beings were born." But the wife then reflected: "'How can he unite with me after having produced me from himself? Well let me hide myself.'" To do so she "became a cow" but "the other became a bull and was united with her; from that union cows were born." And so it continued for the creation of all gendered animals, "down to the ants."[8] Similarly, certain Vedic ceremonies ritualize sexual intercourse to magnify procreative potency but also other forms of power or "glory." As semen is man's essence, so woman's genitals or lower body are revered and sacralized. The "Lord of creatures ... created woman ... [and] revered her below.... Her lap is a sacrificial altar; her hairs, the sacrificial grass; her skin the soma-press. The two labia of the vulva are the fire in the middle." Success will come to the man "who practices sexual intercourse" according to its proper ritual meaning and performance, because by "knowing this ... he turns the good deeds of women to himself," while without such knowledge a man will lose his power, for "women [will] turn his good deeds unto themselves."[9]

If the vibrant sexual activity of the gods was essential for sustaining creation, it was also an abiding source of conflict, instability, and other troubles. It obviously distracted from the ascetic path of spiritual meditation aimed at transcending the material world with its suffering cycle of death and rebirth. Though celebrating the powers of mental or spiritual creation through the generative force or "inner heat" of meditative austerities (*tapas*), Hindu mythology repeatedly recognizes that sex is more effective for creating an abundant world of life. Hence the importance of Kama, the god of erotic love and pleasure, for stimulating sexual desire and procreation.[10]

One central myth (told in a variety of different, overlapping, but sometimes conflicting versions) explains:

[8] See *Brihadaranyaka Upanishad*, 1.4.1–4, in *The Upanishads*, vol. 3, trans. Swami Nikhilananda (New York: Bonanza Books, 1956), 113–117.

[9] *Brihadaranyaka Upanishad* 6.4.2–3, in R. E. Hume, trans., *The Thirteen Principal Upanishads* (Oxford: Oxford University Press, 1921), 168. The rituals of intercourse, which include options of bribery and violence, involve numerous incantations uttered by the man. For example, if a woman does "not grant him his desire, he should bribe her. If she still does not grant him his desire, he should hit her with a stick or with his hand, and overcome her, saying: 'With power, with glory I take away your glory!' ... If she should yield to him, he says: 'With power, with glory I give you glory!' Thus they two become glorious" (169; 6.4.7–8). Cf. the Nikhilananda translation, 369–379.

[10] For more details on the god (and concept of) Kama, see Joanna Macy, "The Dialectics of Desire," *Numen* 22, no. 2 (1975): 145–160.

> When Brahma's *tapas* failed to create, he made Kama, who wounded him. Brahma desired his daughter, who fled from him, taking the form of a deer. He pursued her in the form of a stag, and his seed fell upon the ground, . . . where it created various sages and animals. Rudra pursued Brahma and beheaded him, and Brahma cursed Kama, who had inspired this incestuous passion in him, to be destroyed by Śiva, and Śiva, who had mocked him, to be excited by Kama. (SEA 30)

In another version of the story, "Brahma began creation by meditation, but . . . his mind-born sons, all passionless yogis devoted to Śiva, did not want to create," so "Brahma then wished to create by means of sexual intercourse. He did *tapas* for Śiva, who appeared in his androgynous form and gave Brahma his female creative power. Brahma then began the process of creation by intercourse. He divided himself into a man and a woman. The woman did *tapas* and obtained the man for her husband. Together they begat the race of mortals" (SEA 72).

This story reveals how the opposing forces of carnal desire and ascetic meditative activity intimately intertwine in Indian culture. Śiva, god of ascetic meditation, is also the deity whose androgynous powers (developed by his incomparable *tapas*) enable sexual creation. The exemplary master of spiritual austerity who initially renounces all sexual contact, until Brahma enlists Kama to punish him through his seduction by Parvati, Śiva is also a symbol of intense sexual potency. His masterful devotion to *tapas* gives him astounding powers of attraction, because ascetic spirituality had a highly admired aura and represented a prize conquest that women sought to win to prove their own seductive power. Such seductive power of ascetic discipline can conversely be wielded by women, as witnessed in how Brahma's female derivative wins her husband through her *tapas*. Indeed, in some versions of the myth, Śiva ultimately yields to Parvati's seduction not simply through the erotically flowered arrows of Kama but through Parvati's admirable practice of *tapas* austerities.

The expert practice of *tapas* makes Śiva not only irresistibly attractive but also amazingly rich in sexual potency because of the psychosomatic energy that accumulates and intensifies through ascetic training and restraint. Śiva's erotic puissance is demonstrated in several ways, not least by his impressive and virtually permanent erection. In the famous Pine Forest episode, the ithyphallic Śiva seduces the wives of the reclusive sages living there but also impregnates Mohini (the enchanting female form that the god Vishnu takes to tempt those ascetic sages). The angry sages then curse Śiva's vigorous lingam to fall to the ground, but the phallus is so huge that neither Vishnu nor Brahma can determine its two ends, and the sages and their wives are compelled to worship it. In another episode, the gods feel the world will be overwhelmed by the intense energy of Śiva and Parvati's prolonged love-making (lasting hundreds of celestial years) and therefore send the Vedic god Agni to interrupt them, but he ends up swallowing Śiva's seed, which then impregnates all the gods (SEA 32). A different myth relates how Parvati, after chasing away a group of beautiful women with whom Śiva was copulating, "divided herself into a hundred women and made love with Śiva" in order to quench his fiery desire (SEA 298). Paradoxically, Śiva's erect phallus symbolizes both the force of sexual desire and the potency of chaste renunciation, as the phallus loses its erectile power after yielding to desire in ejaculatory release.

Recognizing the powerful extremes of sexual passion and ascetic renunciation, Hinduism closely links them not merely in myth but in actual somatic practice. Erotic desire and ascetic effort share the power of generating focused energy and heat. Chastity's ascetic renunciation can develop intensity of desire, whose full satisfaction, in appropriate circumstances, can promote a refreshing release that promises a path to reinforced chastity. We should not ignore the striking parallels between the variety and sometimes baffling complexity of India's lovemaking positions and a similar diversity and intricate difficulty of postures (*asanas*) in its ascetic yoga practice. Nor should we forget that some yogic practices of control are developed through distinctively sexual means, not only in esoteric tantric yoga but in the technique of *vajroli* (retention of semen during intense sexual arousal) as articulated in the Hatha Yoga classic, the *Hatha Yoga Pradipika* (Book III:82–89).[11]

The erotic-ascetic figure of Śiva, whose "most common symbol . . . is the phallus (*linga*)" and whose "power of manifestation is shown by the *linga* inserted in the *yoni* or female emblem," provides the generating source of Indian *ars erotica* (MG 213).[12] Vatsyayana's founding *Kamasutra* claims to be based on a series of lost erotic works that stretch back to the mythical "Nandin, the servant of the great God Śiva," who allegedly composed the legendary original Kamasutra ("a work of a thousand chapters") while guarding Śiva's bedroom door when his master was enjoying "the pleasures

[11] Swami Swatmarama, *Hatha Yoga Pradipika*, trans. Pancham Sinh (Allahabad: Panini Office, 1914), 41–42.

[12] "The most common anthropomorphic image of Śiva shows him as beautiful, three-eyed, with the crescent moon on his brow" and "matted hair," his four-armed body "smeared with ashes," and served by gods, antigods, and demons, and a host of other spirits of light and darkness (MG 213).

of sex with his wife for a thousand years" (KS 4).[13] Nandin most prominently figures as the bull that Śiva rides; and if the bull symbolizes puissant sexual energy, then Śiva's riding the bull as his customary vehicle-servant implies his essential mastery of sexual desire. While such desire powerfully carries Śiva forward, he clearly controls it as rider. Arguing that "Hinduism has no Golden Mean [but] seeks the exhaustion of two golden extremes," Doniger claims that it has "no use for Middle Paths" between the poles of eroticism and asceticism, of "fire and ice" (SEA 82). However, if Śiva's riding the bull suggests a middle way between ungoverned sexual passion and absolute abstinence, then Indian *ars erotica*, I believe, provides a theoretical analogue to this mythical image of reconciling passion and self-restraint. It articulates a way of letting the power of sexual desire find full and pleasurable expression but without losing control of desire's direction, quality, and consequences, by reshaping it through the ascetic constraints of aesthetic form and the aesthetic distance of performative role playing.

Despite Śiva's central place in this erotic tradition, Vatsyayana's *Kamasutra* begins by invoking other sanctified notions: *dharma* (religious duty or virtue), *artha* (material power or wealth), and *kama*. The concept of *kama*, based on the eponymous god, is confusingly ambiguous, denoting desire in general but also love, sensuous pleasure, and, more particularly, sex. Before taking anthropomorphic form, as a beautiful "proud adolescent, riding a parrot" and wielding "a bow of sugarcane" shooting "flower-tipped arrows" from a bowstring made of "a line of bees," the god Kama appears in the earliest Veda as an abstract divine force of *desire* that generates the cosmos (MG 312).

> Darkness there was: at first concealed in darkness this All was indiscriminated chaos. All that existed then was void and formless: by the great power of Warmth was born that Unit. Thereafter rose Desire in the beginning, Desire, the primal seed and germ of Spirit [*manas*, or mind]. Sages who searched with their heart's thought discovered the existent's kinship in the non-existent. Transversely [across the universe] was their severing line extended: what was above it then, and what below it? There were begetters, there were mighty forces, free action here and energy up yonder.[14]

[13] The claim that the *Kamasutra* was composed while guarding Śiva's lengthy lovemaking is cited from Yashodhara's classic thirteenth-century commentary to the text, as excerpted in KS 4.

[14] Ralph T. H. Griffith, trans., *Rig Veda*, 10:129, (1896), www.sacred-texts.com/hin/rigveda/rv10129.htm. The *Atharva Veda* (9.2.19) similarly notes Kama's primordial generative power: "First before all sprang Kama into being. Gods, Fathers, mortal men have never matched him. Stronger than these art thou, and great for ever. Kāma, to thee, to thee I offer worship." Ralph T. H. Griffith, trans., *Hymns of the Atharva-Veda* (Benares: E. J. Lazarus, 1916), 433.

By thus linking the generative power of desire not merely to material creation but also to spiritual and mental energy, the Indian tradition affirms the erotic as essential to consciousness and its higher spiritual life.[15] Ascetic sages become masters of erotics, like Śiva their divine paradigm.

The *Kamasutra*'s opening lines take eroticism beyond the maze of mythic fantasy by firmly embedding it in the realm of practical rational thought by connecting it with the ethical and political dimensions of religious culture that shaped society. "We bow to religion, power, and pleasure [*dharma*, *artha*, and *kama*] because they are the subject of this text, and to the scholars who made known the mutual agreement among the three" (KS 3). These three realms (or *trivarga*) concern "the three aims of human life" whose integrated pursuit is the "vital link" to good living and which can eventually lead to a fourth and final end, *moksha*, or liberation from the cycle of death and rebirth (KS 4). These aims of life (*purusharthas*) are connected with four age-based life stages (*ashramas*), designed for men only (as men alone were regarded as autonomous agents). These stages include Brahmacharya (the celibate student studying the Vedas), Grihastha (the householder who establishes a family), Vanaprastha (the man who retires from householder life to a hermit-like existence), and Sannyasa (a life of complete ascetic renunciation). The third stage, which transitions between the worldly, sexually active family man and the world-renouncing absolute ascetic, seems the most problematic by allowing the hermits to bring their wives to their forest retreats, thus sustaining the tension between erotic attachment and the final aim of total austerity with its liberating renunciation of the world, including family.

Each of the realms of *dharma*, *artha*, and *kama* claims an original divinely designated text to treat its distinctive concerns while connecting it to the other two. The founding text for *dharma*, *The Laws of Manu*, or *Manusmriti* (allegedly given by the divine Brahma to his son Manu but actually a composite work produced between 200 BCE and 200 CE), explains life's stages and goals while defining the hierarchical class structure of Indian society by articulating the duties and relations of the four

[15] The linkage is affirmed in the *Atharva Veda Samhita*, trans. W. W. Whitney (Delhi: Motilal Banarasidass, 1962), 19:52.1: "Desire here came into being in the beginning, which is the first seed of mind." Similarly, in *Brihadaranyaka Upanishad* 1.2.1–3, our abundant world is generated from a single self who in his loneliness "verily had no delight" and so "desired a second." He then produced a second by splitting it off from himself to be his wife and copulated with her to produce the multiplicity of beings. See Sarvepalli Radhakrishnan, trans., *Principal Upanishads* (London: Allen & Unwin, 1953).

classes (*varnas*).[16] In order of privilege, the four classes are Brahmins (priests and teachers), Kshatriyas (warriors, kings, and governors); Vaishyas (merchants, farmers, and commercial artisans), and Shudras (common laborers). Only the first three classes were formally initiated into Vedic study and thus described as "twice born." To achieve its apparent goal of establishing social stability through rigid class hierarchy, the *Manusmriti* advocated strict patriarchy in which sex was essentially confined to the production of progeny with the appropriate class pedigree through "a wife belonging to the same class and possessing the right bodily characteristics" (MCL 108).

The wife was simply a vehicle for the man to fulfill his duty of self-realization through the production of a male child. "The husband enters the wife, becomes a fetus, and is born into the world." In other words, he "begets himself in her" (MCL 109, 190). To ensure the father–son identity the purity of the wife as mediating vessel must be preserved. Considered to be innately prone to "lechery" and "lust" (far more than men), women were granted no independence. "Day and night men should keep their women from acting independently; for attached as they are to sensual pleasure, men should keep them under their control. Her father guards her in her childhood, her husband . . . in her youth, and her sons in her old age; a woman is not qualified to act independently." Manu, however, recognized that woman's will remains too independent to be controlled by external constraints imposed by their men. Force, confinement, and keeping them busy are not enough "to thoroughly guard women . . . ; only when they guard themselves by themselves are they truly well-guarded" (MCL 190). Hence Manu's *dharma* defined a "good woman" as one "who controls her mind, speech, and body and is never unfaithful to her husband" (MCL 191). Perhaps the *Manusmriti* insists so strongly on man's total control over women because they often behaved quite freely in epic literature and myth. Witness Drapaudi's polyandric marriage to the five Pandava brothers in the *Mahabarata*.

Manu's *dharma* also constrained the husband's sexual expression. "Finding his gratification always in his wife," a man had the duty to produce progeny, which meant "he should have sex with her during her [fertile] season. Devoted solely to her, he may go to her also when he wants sexual pleasure" rather than children (MCL 110), but never during her menses or

[16] This work also bears the Sanskrit title *Manava-Dharmasastra*. I will be referring to its translation by Patrick Olivelle, *Manu's Code of Law: A Critical Edition and Translation of the Manava-Dharmasastra* (Oxford: Oxford University Press, 2005), hereafter MCL.

other proscribed days. Moreover, sexual release must be vaginal. "If someone ejaculates his semen in non-human females, in a man, in a menstruating woman, in any place other than the vagina, or on water, he should perform the Santapana penance" (M224).[17] Manu prescribed severe punishments to both sexes for adultery, because "such violations give rise to the mixing of social classes among the people, creating deviation from the Law that tears out the very root and leads to the destruction of everything" (MCL 186). For "sex with an elder's [e.g., guru's] wife," a man "should proclaim his crime" and die by burning himself with "red-hot metal" or "he may cut off his penis and testicles by himself, hold them in his cupped hands, and walk straight towards the south-west until he falls down dead" (MCL 220). A woman unfaithful to her husband should be "devoured by dogs in a public square" (MCL 187). More generally, "in the case of adultery, everyone other than a Brahmin merits the death penalty" (MCL 186).

Despite its extreme subordination of women (or as a compensatory part of it), Manu's code urged men to "revere their women and provide them with adornments," realizing that unhappy women make an unhappy home where "no rite bears fruit." "For, if the wife does not sparkle, she does not arouse her husband. And if the husband is not aroused, there will be no offspring" (MCL 111). Likewise, despite sternly subordinating *kama* to the duties of *dharma*, Manu affirmed woman's value in providing the "highest sensuous delights" and the man's right to have sex with his wife simply because "he wants sexual pleasure," since it recognized *kama* as essential to life (MCL 110, 191). "To be motivated by desire is not commended, but it is impossible here [in this world] to be free from desire"; and "it is desire that prompts vedic study and the performance of vedic rites," stimulating intention that "triggers every religious observance and every rule of restraint," including that of restraining desire. Since desires are inevitable in "any activity," the key to success is "engaging in them properly" (MCL 94). But what does that mean?

The somaesthetic answer is control of our sensorimotor organs. "As his organs meander amidst the alluring sense objects, a learned man should strive hard to control them, like a charioteer his horses." These organs "described by wise men of old [are] ear, skin, eyes, tongue, and ... nostrils; anus, sexual organ, hands, feet, and speech." The first five are called the

[17] This penance is "when a man subsists on [a diet of] cow's urine, cow dung, milk, curd, ghee, and a decoction of Kusa grass for one day each, and on the final day lives on air" alone. Patrick Olivelle, trans., *Dharmasutras: The Law Codes of Ancient India* (Oxford: Oxford University Press, 1999), 236.

"organs of perception" and the latter five, "beginning with the anus, the organs of action," while "the eleventh is the mind, which, by virtue of its own distinctive quality, belongs to both groups ... [and] by mastering it, one masters both those quintets." A man's "attachment to the organs" corrupts, "but by bringing them under control, he achieves success" (M99). But what, again, does such mastery or control mean?

Neither undisciplined indulgence nor total renunciation provides the answer. "Desire is never quenched by enjoying desires; like a fire fed with ghee, it only waxes stronger," and "one cannot bring them under control as effectively by abstinence as by constant insight," a clear and penetrating awareness of one's self and situation (MCL 99). Indian *ars erotica*, I argue, is designed to cultivate and refine such sensorimotor mastery in terms of heightened awareness and skilled aesthetic shaping of one's erotic feelings and movements, and to do so in controlled attunement with one's partner's. The mastering insight that Manu recommends concerns self-awareness. Among the different valuable *dharma* practices, "tradition holds the knowledge of the self to be the highest; it is, indeed, the foremost of all sciences, for by it one attains immortality." Thus, "a Brahmin should apply himself vigorously to the knowledge of the self, to inner tranquility" through detachment from desire; and this tranquility is manifested "when a man feels neither elation nor revulsion at hearing, touching, seeing, eating, or smelling anything." Such a man "should be recognized as a man who has mastered his organs ... without having to shrivel up his body with yoga" (MCL 99, 234).

The core of this mastery and inner tranquility is detachment: "neither elation nor revulsion." If this sounds like pleasureless indifference, perhaps that is what Manu's dour *dharma* intends. But is it not possible to enjoy sensory pleasures with calm detachment? The dominant Kantian tradition defines aesthetic pleasures precisely in terms of detached, disinterestedness that is free from the passionate desire for possession. Yet how to achieve such tranquility and detachment in the passionate pleasures of lovemaking? This difficulty has thwarted Western recognition of *ars erotica* as an aesthetic art, but Indian theory seeks to provide a solution.

Artha, the second of life's aims, has Kautilya's *Arthashastra* as its founding work. A composite of textual sources that range from the second century BCE to the third century CE, it focuses on the politics and economics of power. Affirming the traditional four *varnas* and four *ashramas*, the *Arthashastra* also follows Manu's focus on the procreative aim of marriage. If a man's wife fails to provide male progeny over a twelve-year period, "he may marry any number of women; for women are created for the sake of sons."[18] Yet he is also is obliged to service his wife during her fertile days, and to confine himself to vaginal sex, while incest, homosexuality, and bestiality are strongly condemned. However, unlike Manu's exclusive interest in marital erotics, the *Arthashastra* affirms prostitution's important role and its significant aesthetic dimension. An entire chapter is devoted to the functions, rights, categories, and artistic training of prostitutes, along with the appropriate punishments for offenses committed by them or against them, the relevant fees they could command, and the corresponding taxes they had to render to the state. Prostitutes served a crucial social function in Indian society, as most husbands could not find full erotic satisfaction with their totally cloistered, subordinate, and child-centered wives, while adultery was harshly punished and marriageable young women were strictly protected. Prostitution thus openly thrived, from as early as the seventh or eighth century BCE, enjoying social support that included also religious and state institutions.

Prostitutes ranged from renowned royal courtesans to common sex workers. The *Arthashastra* notes how "the Superintendent of Prostitutes" recruits a superior courtesan (or *ganika*) to serve officially at the king's court, along with "an alternate courtesan" chosen as her "short-time substitute" (or "alternate") and paid half her salary.[19] These high-class courtesans, celebrated for their "beauty, youth, and accomplishments" in the arts (who were further "classified as of first, middle, and highest rank") greatly enhanced the splendor of the men and communities they entertained (ART 175). Prized by the state, they typically provided their entertainments in state-owned establishments. A *ganika* could choose her own clients (except for commands from the king), and they would often compete as suitors for her favors. However, once she admitted them into her house she was obliged to entertain them or else pay a fine. Prostitutes lacking superior artistic skills but distinguished by great beauty and charm (designated *rúpájíva*) were less highly regarded and sometimes worked as independent practitioners in private brothels, but they were also protected by state law and obliged to pay taxes from their income, as were undistinguished common prostitutes (*vesyas*). The king employed a host of prostitutes (*rúpájíva*) to "attend the harem" and "do the duty of bath-room servants, shampooers," and other

[18] Rudrapatna Shamasastry, trans., *Kautilya's Arthashastra* (Mysore: Mysore Publishing, 1961), 222; hereafter ART.

[19] For these details, see ART 175; Sukumari Bhattacharji, "Prostitution in Ancient India," *Social Scientist* 15, no. 2 (1987): 39; and Patrick Olivelle, *King, Governance, and Law in Ancient India: Kautilya's Arthashastra* (Oxford: Oxford University Press, 2013), 158.

cosmetic tasks relating to scents, fragrant powders, dress, and garlands (ART 55, 58). Prostitution also included temple dancers (*devadasis*) – young women typically offered as gifts to priests or temples so that their donors would gain religious merit. While their official job was to dance at evening worship, they unofficially provided sexual services and were apparently paid by the temple authorities at variable but rather minimal rates.[20]

As society celebrated *ganikas* for their artistic talents, so these prized skills were carefully honed by the state. "From the age of eight years, a prostitute shall hold musical performance before the king," as part of her state-financed artistic training. "Those who teach prostitutes, female slaves, and actresses, arts such as singing, playing on musical instruments, reading, dancing, acting, writing, painting, playing on the instruments like *vina*, pipe, and drum, reading the thoughts of others, manufacture of scents and garlands, shampooing, and the art of attracting and captivating the mind of others shall be endowed with maintenance from the State. They (the teachers) shall train the sons of prostitutes to be chief actors (*rangopajívi*) on the stage" (ART 176, 178).

Ancient Indian prostitutes were thus closely connected to the art of drama, whose skills of playacting could be used not only for entertainment but also for deceptive entrapment. If a courtesan achieved success by convincing her multiple suitors that she truly loved each of them with special affection and independent of commercial concerns, then the state would also use her acting expertise for spying. "Prostitute spies under the garb of chaste women may cause themselves to be enamoured of persons who are seditious" so as to ensnare them, while also using their wiles to "vigilantly examine the pure or impure conduct of military men" (ART 345, 352). The courtesan's skill in acting involves a subtle play of absorption and detachment: on the one hand, she had to enjoy her suitors' lovemaking enough to convince them that she took real pleasure in their company and efforts. But she also had to maintain enough detachment from those pleasures in order to control their effect on her deeper feelings and thus avoid emotional commitments harmful to her ability to play the field. Such a model of detached pleasure-taking through artistic play can be extended to male actors and emerges as a central motif in the aesthetics of Indians *ars erotica*.

[20] On the particular hardships of temple prostitutes, who "became like slaves with no clear definition of their rights and duties," see Bhattacharji, "Prostitution in Ancient India," 50–51.

III THE ARTISTIC BACKGROUND

The courtesan's intimate connection with theatrical art finds salient expression in India's original classic of drama theory, the *Natyaśastra.*[21] Encompassing also music and dance, this work (apparently written around 200 CE) serves as the founding text of all Indian aesthetics, largely through its articulation of the seminal concept of *rasa* (literally, "juice" or "essence"), which is used to explain the distinctively *aesthetic* forms of experience, pleasure, and emotion. Attributed to the legendary sage Bharata, who allegedly learned it from the supremely divine Brahman who first "devised" and "uttered" its teachings from "the four Vedas," the *Natyaśastra* devotes an entire chapter to "Dealings with Courtesans," while other personalities (including royal protagonists and divine characters) receive much more cursory treatment. This fact becomes less puzzling once we recognize that courtesans and their love-play lie at the origins of Indian drama both mythically and historically.

The *Natyaśastra*'s first chapter recounts how Brahman was not satisfied with the first drama that Bharata and his sons produced for the gods and therefore asked Bharata to prepare some new work "to include the Graceful (*kaisiki*) Style [that is] appropriate to the Erotic Sentiment" and requires beautiful females. Brahman then "created from his mind nymphs (*apsaras*)," or celestial courtesans, "who were skillful in embellishing the drama" with this style so that Bharata could produce the desired work (N 7–8). These beautiful, "eternally young women who are the courtesans and the dancers of heaven . . . are called . . . the women-of-the-gods (*suranganii*), the daughters of pleasure (*sumad-atmaja*)" because, like courtesans, they are unmarried "public women" who "willingly dispense their favors" (MG 305). There would have been no successful drama without their beauty and their erotic acting skills. The point is reinforced in the *Natyaśastra*'s final chapter that presents another, overlapping myth of drama's origin. After the gods refuse the mortal King Nahusa's request to bring the *apsaras* to have "dramatic performance established on the earth," he appeals to Bharata by explaining how the divine courtesan Urvasi (who loved his grandfather) had introduced the drama and taught his harem women how to perform it but that this art had been lost when the king died from sadness at Urvasi's departure. Bharata then sends his sons to earth to find mortal women to serve as courtesan actresses, and after "devising plays" and begetting progeny with

[21] Manomohan Ghosh, trans., *The Natyaśastra*, vols. 1 and 2 (Calcutta: Royal Asiatic Society of Bengal, 1951), vol. 1, 1–3 (for citations in this paragraph); hereafter N.

them to assure the continued existence of drama on earth, the sons "were permitted to return again to Heaven" (N 559, 560).

The courtesan's distinctive identity as a provider of pleasure who exists outside the circle of rigid caste patriarchy (for she could come from different classes and be available to all kinds of men) is paralleled in the theater's status as open to all the castes. The *Natyaśastra* first describes itself as "the Natyaveda devised by Brahman," who creates it as "another Veda which will belong to all the . . . *varna*," or castes, since "the [genuine] Vedas are not to be listened to by those born as [the caste of] Sudras" and more Vedic-like teaching is necessary to improve a world "addicted to sensual pleasures, . . . desire and greed." Like the courtesans, dramatic art should serve as "an object of diversion" but it "will also conduce to *dharma*, *artha* . . . and . . . all arts and crafts," which mere courtesan love-play could not as successfully achieve (N 2–4).

Beyond these mythical accounts, the historical existence of courtesans skilled in the performing arts clearly predates the *Natyaśastra*, which indeed refers to their artistic skills and a preexisting body of erotic knowledge that largely focused on such courtesans. "The courtesan (*ganika*) should be skilled in acting . . . and be always engaged in attending teachers and in the application of the art, and be endowed with [erotic] sportiveness . . . and be acquainted with the sixty-four arts and crafts" (N 548). As "a woman who is an adept in the practice of love and is an expert in love affairs," she is recognized also "through her graceful acting on the stage" (N 543). Not surprisingly courtesans figured among the four types of dramatic heroine, "along with a goddess, a queen, [and] a woman of high family" (N 529). The courtesan's honed skill in acting the delighted lover by performing that role with enjoyment without being overwhelmed or enslaved by love's passions finds its counterpart in the expert male lover or "Gallant." By "excelling in all the arts," this "superior man" can "captivate the heart of a woman," and though an "expert in enjoyment," he "has controlled his senses" so that he "feels love but is not overcome by passion" (N 483, 489, 527). Here again we see the suggestion that by mastering the lover's role one can pursue the fullness of pleasure without giving up one's self-control, maintaining the mastery of a deeper self beyond the erotic role one is playing.

Affirming that the erotic is "rich in pleasure" because "happiness has its source in women [and] the enjoyment" they provide, the *Natyaśastra* begins its list of dramatic genres with those that highlight the erotic: the Nataka, the Pakarana, and the Natika. Among their "chief features" are the "amorous pastimes" of exalted heroes, "the conduct of courtesans," and "affairs of the harem" and "love's enjoyment" (N 109, 356, 363, 365, 459). The *Natyaśastra*, moreover, puts the erotic at the very core of its seminal theory of *rasa*. The first of the "eight Sentiments (*rasas*) recognized in drama [is the] Erotic (*srngara*)," which is "rich in pleasure," while the first of the eight "Dominant States" that generate such aesthetic sentiments (*rasas*) is "love" (N 102, 109). The notion of *rasa* is often understood as aesthetic "flavor," since it seems based on the analogy of cooking and gustatory taste.[22] "Just as well-disposed persons while eating food cooked with many kinds of spices enjoy its tastes and attain pleasure and satisfaction, so the cultured people taste the Dominant States when they see them represented" in drama, but these "learned people taste [the flavors of such states] in their mind" (N 105–106).

By highlighting erotic pleasure and artistry, the *Natyaśastra* may well have shaped the strikingly aesthetic character of the *Kamasutra*. On the other hand, even if the *Natyaśastra* predates the *Kamasutra* by a century, the latter's erotic ideas and practices apparently existed long before and could have shaped not only the *Natyaśastra*'s dramatic theory but also the performing arts on which it was based. The *Natyaśastra* indeed makes frequent reference to existing "rules . . . taken out of the Science of Erotics (*kamatantra*)" or "methods mentioned in the Science of Love (*kamatantra*)" or the "*vaisika sastra*" (which Ghosh translates as as *ars amatoria* but which more literally means "rules regarding courtesans") (N 109, 466, 492). Besides their appreciation of sex and aesthetics (and perhaps because of it), the *Natyaśastra* and *Kamasutra* share an impulse toward democratic diversity, albeit greatly constrained by India's dominant patriarchy and caste system. Like the *Natyaśastra* (but unlike the Vedas), all castes could study and practice the *Kamsutra*; and women were not simply permitted but rather urged to study it. Indeed, a girl should study it even "before she reaches the prime of her youth" and continue learning its techniques in order to ensure success, whether as a "Courtesan de Luxe" or "the daughter of a king or of a minister of state" (KS 13, 16).

IV THE ART OF LOVING IN THE ART OF LIVING

India's erotic tradition was keen to reconcile *kama*'s pursuit with the other established goals of life.[23] Although its celebration of sexual pleasures beyond

[22] G. B. Mohan Thampi, "'Rasa' as Aesthetic Experience," *Journal of Aesthetics and Art Criticism* 24, no. 1 (1965): 75–80. I discuss the concept further in "Definition, Dramatization, and Rasa," *Journal of Aesthetics and Art Criticism* 61, no. 3 (2003): 295–298.

[23] Ludo Rocher, "The Kamasutra: Vatsyayana's Attitude toward Dharma and Dharmasastra," *Journal of the American Oriental Society*, 105, no. 3 (1985): 521–529.

the bounds of marital procreation sharply contrasts with the patriarchal discourse of the *Manusmriti* and *Arthashastra*, the *Kamasutra* begins and ends by advocating harmony with these rival realms and repeatedly affirms the general hierarchy of goals where *kama* lies at the bottom, below *dharma* and then *artha*. It argues, however, that different goals merit more attention at different stages of life. "Childhood is the time to acquire knowledge and other kinds of power, the prime of youth is for pleasure, and old age is for religion and release" (KS 7). It also notes that for a king and for a prostitute *dharma* is not the most important goal. The king's duty as leader requires the primacy of *artha*, while the prostitute likewise cannot let *dharma* dominate her affairs (though it is not specified whether it is *kama* or *artha* that should dominate her).[24] Nonetheless, the *Kamasutra* insists, "When these three aims – religion, power, and pleasure – compete, each is more important than the one that follows," but the pursuit of one should not be "at the cost of the other two" (KS 8, 13).

Recognizing the traditional privilege of *dharma* and *artha* is part of Vatsyayana's strategy to provide *kama* the respect it deserves by devoting an entire treatise to it, and the book's second chapter explains why such a treatise is needed for properly distinguishing human eroticism from the raw, unthinking sexual union of animals. To behave in a more thoughtfully human way as sexual agents and thereby to enjoy more advanced and meaningful pleasures of union, lovemaking "requires a method" and a corresponding text to provide its instruction (KS 9). Vatsyayana thus aims at intellectually legitimating eroticism by refining it and deploying its energy to cultivate and master the senses; the aesthetic edification of lovemaking forms a crucial theme of his *Kamasutra*. Repeatedly insisting that "he did not compose it for the sake of passion," Vatsyayana claims instead that recounting "the unusual techniques employed to increase passion" is needed to master it, so that the man who learns "the real meaning of this

[24] The Sanskrit syntax clearly indicates that *artha* is also what the prostitute privileges, as the Doniger and Kakar translation and the Richard Schmidt German translation reflect. This recognizes that prostitutes, without husbands or fathers to provide for their financial security, had to think first of their economic power rather than about love's pleasure. The famous Burton and Arbuthnot translation and the little-known Upadhyaya translation, however, more freely interpret the passage as suggesting that the sexual pleasure of *kama* must be what ranks first for prostitutes because this introduces another exception to *dharma*'s general privilege and because *kama* is the prostitute's special field of expertise. See Richard Burton and F. F. Arbuthnot, trans., *The Kama Sutra of Vatsyayana*, including a preface by W. G. Archer and an introduction by K. M. Panikkar (London: Unwin, 1988); S. C. Upadhyaya, trans., *Kama Sutra of Vatsyayana* (New York: Castle Books, 1963); and Richard Schmidt, trans., *Das Kamasutra des Vatsyayana* (Berlin: Barsdorf, 1907).

text . . . becomes a man who has truly conquered his senses" and thus can reconcile his pursuit of *kama* with proper "attention to *dharma* and *artha*" (KS 171). Moreover, because such a man "does not indulge himself too much in passion, . . . he succeeds when he plays the part of a lover" (KS 172), since his limited passion gives him greater control, insight, and performative power.

The *Kamasutra* is philosophically significant not for its famously elaborate sexual techniques but for its efforts to resolve the deep dialectical opposition in Hindu thought between asceticism and eroticism powerfully embodied in the figure of Śiva. Without explicitly articulating them as such, the book suggests three different ways of reconciling this tension. The first strategy is a temporal solution in terms of life's stages. The *Kamasutra* can provide a man with so much erotic pleasure during his sexual prime that when he reaches the time of his elderly retirement to the forest hermit and extreme ascetic stages, he will be so full of sexual satisfaction that he will not mind leaving erotic pleasures behind to devote himself most fully to an ascetic life of spiritual purity. The *Ananga Ranga* later articulates this strategy explicitly in its opening justificatory remarks: "It is true that no joy in the world of mortals can compare with that derived from the knowledge of the Creator. Second, however, and subordinate only to this, are the satisfaction and pleasure arising from the possession of a beautiful woman." Thus, "The man who knoweth the Art of Love, and who understandeth the thorough and varied enjoyment of woman" by studying this book, can be sufficiently satisfied with worldly pleasures so that, "as advancing age cooleth his passions, he learneth to think of his Creator, to study religious subjects, and to acquire divine knowledge. Hence he is freed from further transmigration of souls," achieving the goal of *moksha* through the preliminary path of pleasure (AR xxii–xxiii).

The second strategy reconciles the ascetic and the erotic by controlling raw sexual passion through the constraints of aesthetic shaping demanded by a refined *ars erotica*, where aesthetic control of the senses and desire involves discipline or *askesis* and thus includes an ascetic dimension despite its fullness of pleasure. *Askesis*, moreover, has its own distinctive pleasures. The third strategy also concerns controlling one's senses and passions in the context of aesthetic or artistic practice, but its efforts of control are pursued primarily through the self-detachment involved in the technique of dramatic role playing that belongs to the realm of aesthetic performance or artistic play. While these last two solutions are more prominently aesthetic, the first strategy also contains an important aesthetic dimension in that the fullness of erotic satisfaction in the householder stage is significantly composed of aesthetic pleasures. This is because Indian cultural tradition affirms an overlap or fusion of erotic and aesthetic pleasure, as suggested in the *Natyaśastra*'s linking of artistic and erotic expertise and its view that erotic sentiment provides the generating essence of what is aesthetically graceful.

The *Kamasutra* articulates this linkage in far greater detail, effectively synthesizing the erotic and aesthetic in its *ars erotica*. The book's third chapter insists on listing "the sixty-four fine arts that should be studied along with the Kamasutra" because they are integral and essential to its successful practice (KS 14–15). "Luck in love comes [not from mere luck but] from learning the arts"; through their mastery a beautiful courtesan "wins the title of Courtesan de Luxe," while "a man who is accomplished in these arts . . . finds the way to women's hearts right away" (KS 16). These arts, which are different from the specifically sexual techniques Vatsyayana calls "the sixty-four arts of love" (KS 73), include crafts and skills beyond our modern concept of fine art, but they are nonetheless predominantly aesthetic in character:

> singing; playing musical instruments; dancing; painting; cutting leaves into shapes; making lines on the floor with rice powder and flowers; arranging flowers; colouring the teeth, clothes, and limbs; making jewelled floors; preparing beds; making music on the rims of glasses of water; . . . making garlands and stringing necklaces; making diadems and headbands; making costumes; making various earrings; mixing perfumes; putting on jewellery; . . . preparing various forms of vegetables, soups, and other things to eat; preparing wines, fruit juices, and other things to drink; needlework; weaving; playing the lute and the drum; telling jokes and riddles; completing words; reciting difficult words; reading aloud; staging plays and dialogues; completing verses; making things out of cloth, wood, and cane; woodworking; carpentry; architecture; . . . skill at rubbing, massaging, and hairdressing; the ability to speak in sign language; . . . improvising poetry; dictionaries and thesauruses; knowledge of metre; literary work; the art of impersonation; [and] the art of using clothes for disguise. (KS 15)

To regard these arts and aesthetic practices as essential preparation for properly practicing *ars erotica* does not mean to imply their real purpose is sexual. For the *Kamasutra* proclaims its true goal is not the satisfaction of sexual desire and other sensual pleasures, but rather to refine one's capacities and master one's senses to become a better person. This is initially "for the sake of worldly life" until one is ready to advance to the later stage of renunciation and release from worldly existence (KS 171). Aesthetic cultivation through the arts is key to such sensory refinement and mastery.

The *Kamasutra*'s chapter 4 radically aestheticizes the familiar *ashrama* stage of householder or family man (Grihastha) by giving it a sophisticated playboy version, defined by the "lifestyle of the man-about-town (*nagaraka*)," a wealthy, tasteful, urbanite dandy who loves the arts as well as sensual pleasures. The *nagaraka*, as Vatsyayana presents him, is not defined by caste, family, or profession (which is quite surprising for Indian culture) but rather by his aesthetic lifestyle and connoisseurship of the arts and pleasures, including the delights of erotic artistry. His dwelling is aesthetically situated and furnished for artistic pursuits, with "a lute, . . . a board to draw or paint on, . . . a box of pencils . . . [s]ome book or other, and garlands of amaranth flowers" (KS 17). His daily activities focus on aesthetic pursuits, with no mention of any work or family duties but with great attention to the arts and attractive women, and to beautifying his own appearance.

> He gets up in the morning, relieves himself, cleans his teeth, applies fragrant oils in small quantities, as well as incense, garlands, beeswax and red lac, looks at his face in a mirror, takes some mouthwash and betel, and attends to the things that need to be done. He bathes every day, has his limbs rubbed with oil every second day, a foam bath every third day, his face shaved every fourth day, and his body hair removed every fifth or tenth day. All of this is done without fail. And he continually cleans the sweat from his armpits. (KS 18)

The *nagaraka* "engages in various arts and games," enjoys the company of some faithful companions ("his libertine, pander, and clown") and then takes a nap until the late afternoon, when "he gets dressed up and goes to salons to amuse himself." At such salons, he engages with courtesans, and "they exchange thoughts about poems or works of art." Still later, "in the evening, there is music and singing. After that, on the bed in a bedroom carefully decorated and perfumed by sweet-smelling incense, he and his friends await the women who are slipping out for a rendezvous with them." Besides enjoying picnics and drinking parties, the man-about-town is a devoted connoisseur of "theatrical spectacles," so that "visiting players also come and give an audition" specially for him and are "rewarded with a fixed fee" (KS 18–19).

Not only necessary training for urbane sophistication and proper lovemaking, the fine arts also provide apt occasions for lovers to meet and make their erotic advances. "Under the pretext of . . . a theatrical performance or some art," the lovers can be brought to each other's homes; and "at a performance" a man can move "close to the woman he loves and kiss . . . her fingers" (KS 45, 136). Aesthetic arts and crafts serve as tools of courtship or seduction. In "making advances to a young girl," the man "gathers flowers with her, strings beads, plays house, puts on puppet shows," sends her dolls and erotically suggestive statues carved in wood, and impresses her with beautiful "gifts of clothing, rings, and jewelry" (KS 82–84). Because "she is curious about the fine arts, he impresses her by his skill in them . . . [and] captivates her ear with songs" and storytelling (KS 84). As a man can win "a woman in the prime of youth by the arts," so the young woman makes "advances . . . to the man she wants" through aesthetic means. "With flowers, perfumes, and betel in her hand she stays near him, . . . demonstrating her skill in the fine arts" but also in the suggestive somaesthetic art of "massaging" (KS 86, 88, 89).

Artistic skills also contribute significantly to the erotic performance itself, which the *Kamasutra* likens to theater performance by designating the erotic partners with terms borrowed from Sanskrit drama. They are referred to as "hero" and "heroine" (*nayaka* and *nayika*), while their circle of friends is also composed of other stock theatrical figures: the libertine, pander, and clown (KS 20–21). Later texts associate the art of lovemaking with theatrical performance in other ways. The *Koka Shastra* (or *Ratirahasya*), which calls the vulva the "theatre of the Love God," describes the foreplay designed to stimulate and prime it for penetration as "preparing the theatre of the Deity for the performance" (KKS 109, 123). The *Ananga Ranga*, in order to explain the prominent types of female lovers and their typical behavior, articulates "the peculiar characteristics of . . . the eight great forms of Nayika," heroines borrowed from Hindu drama (AR 113–115). These character descriptions provide templates to guide both male and female lovers in acting out the erotic performance.[25]

[25] Recognizing how India's erotic arts deploy the objects and practices of fine art, we should not forget how those fine arts reciprocally draw on its *ars erotica*. The *Kamasutra*'s coital positions clearly helped inspire the sculptural depictions of sexual union in medieval Hindu temples, most notably at Konarak, Khajuraho, Belur, and Halebid, but also in Buddhist centers, such as Nagarjunikonda, where many statues of sexual union "could be identified as sculptural versions of Vatsyayana's sutras – sometimes as interpreted by poets." Vatsyayana's seminal text moreover became the main paradigm for literary depictions of love (and the characters of lovers) in Sanskrit poetry. Its influence was especially strong in epics and dramatic works (which traditionally included dance and music) but extended also to lyrics of love and even some religious poetry (e.g., the *Gita Govinda*, which treats of a girl cow-herder's love for the god Krishna as analogical to the human soul's thirst for the ecstasy of union with the divine). This central role in literature and sculpture helped the *ars erotica* further its influence in other Indian fine arts. Painters thus came to deploy, as classical representations of love, the various female types and situations delineated by the erotic texts and by the literary works they inspired. See K. M. Pannikar, "Introduction," in Burton and Arbuthnot's *Kamasutra*, 74; and for more details, see Comfort, "Introduction," KKS 70–74.

This performance is not limited to the act of coitus; it includes an elaborate aesthetics of mood-enhancing preliminaries, foreplay, and post-coital entertainment. As described by Vatsyayana, in a chapter entitled "The Start and Finish of Sex," the performance begins when the man-about-town, "surrounded by his friends and servants" receives his lady love "in a room of his house dedicated to sex," and thus aesthetically "decorated, full of flowers, and fragrant with perfume and incense." After the woman "has bathed and adorned herself and has drunk the proper amount," "he puts her at ease" and offers her further refreshment (KS 70).[26] Then, after he "sits down on her right side and touches her hair, the fringe of her sari, and the knot of her waistband, . . . he embraces her gently with his left arm to prepare to make love," while they talk pleasantly together. "Then there may be singing and instrumental music . . . and conversation about the fine arts," until "her feelings for him have been aroused," at which point "he sends away the other people" (with gifts of flowers and scented oils), and then proceeds to the "loosening of the knot of her waistband" and the embraces of foreplay, which ultimately lead to the actions, pleasures, and consummation of coitus (KS 70).

But the end of coitus does not terminate the erotic performance, which instead continues into postcoital embraces, massage, sweet refreshments, stories, song, dance, and entertaining conversation, including the gentleman's pointing out the different celestial beauties of the night sky that his lady contemplates, "as she lies in his lap, looking at the moon." Only at this point does Vatsyayana demarcate the "end of sex" (KS 71). In short, the erotic encounter, with its pervasive artistic activities and its staged, choreographed structure of beginning, middle, and end, is shaped into a dramatic, stylized performance with aesthetic intent.

The aesthetically designed stage, along with the performance's artistically stylized opening gambit, is reaffirmed in the *Koka Shastra*. "The proficient lover receives [his lady] in a "room filled with flowers; incense is burning; he wears his most handsome clothes, and has all his retinue present." He "puts his left arm gently round" his lady (who is "adorned with all her jewels"), contriving to touch her playfully in various places while "singing her cheerful songs" until her desire is aroused, at which point he sends off his retinue

[26] Although this account largely concerns the man's aesthetic efforts, there are similar aesthetic instructions for the woman to beautify the erotic encounter by being freshly "bathed and adorned." This is later confirmed for a man's wife, even if she enjoys the privilege of being his "only wife": "When she goes to him to make love, she wears gorgeous jewelry, a variety of flowers and scented oils, and a dress dazzling with many tints" (KS 94, 95).

and proceeds to more serious foreplay, including "the game of groping in her queynt with his hands" (KKS 133). The *Ananga Ranga*, however, provides the most elaborate account of the setting "best fitted for sexual intercourse with women":

> Choose the largest, and finest, and the most airy room in the house, purify it thoroughly with whitewash, and decorate its spacious and beautiful walls with pictures and other objects upon which the eye may dwell with delight. Scattered about this apartment place musical instruments, especially the pipe and the lute; with refreshments, as cocoa-nut, betel leaf, and milk, which is so useful for treating and restoring vigour; bottles of rose water and various essences, fans, and chauris for cooling the air, and books containing amorous songs, and gladdening the glance with illustrations of love-postures. Splendid Diválgiri, or wall lights, should gleam around the hall, reflected by a hundred mirrors, whilst both man and woman should contend against any reserve, or false shame, giving themselves in complete nakedness to unrestrained voluptuousness, upon a high and handsome bedstead, raised on tall legs, furnished with many pillows and covered by a rich chatra, or canopy; the sheets being besprinkled with flowers and the coverlet scented by burning luscious incense, such as aloes and other fragrant woods. In such a place, let the man, ascending the throne of love, enjoy the woman in ease and comfort, gratifying his and her every wish and whim. (AR 96–97)

These aesthetic delights of the mis-en-scène enhance erotic pleasure by agreeably stimulating our senses and imagination. The books with "illustrations of love-postures" are not used as technical manuals to be strictly followed but instead as imaginative tools for arousing a pleasurable mood of desire ("gladdening the glance") and stirring the erotic imagination. More generally, the impressive variety of coital positions outlined in Indian sexology (some exceedingly complex and bearing evocative names) may be essentially designed to stimulate desire by imaginative suggestion rather than to describe or prescribe actual practice, particularly when the texts explicitly warn of the great difficulty of some postures. Some difficult standing postures might have a further aesthetic function: to inspire or justify the sculptural representations of divine sex that decorate some of India's famous temples. In such buildings, sculpted coital bodies could be more visibly and aesthetically represented with vertical rather than horizontal panels, so reclining postures were converted to far more difficult standing ones because of their verticality.[27]

[27] See Comfort, "Introduction," KKS 64–65.

Besides the aesthetic staging of sexual performance through attractively organized space and artistic activities, there is also the stylization of ritually ordered action: embracing first with the left arm, the playful caressing of the woman's clothes and other externals before dismissing the other guests in order to initiate more intimate sexual play. Such sexual activity is ritually ordered to achieve maximal aesthetic effect. For example, the *Koka Shastra* and *Ananga Ranga* elaborate in great detail the proper order for successful lovemaking in terms of type of woman, day of the lunar month, time of day, and the woman's different body parts. Influenced by astrology, these texts include a four-fold classification of female types that is absent from the *Kamasutra*. These are the "lotus-woman" (*padmini*), the "art-woman" (*citrini*), the "shell-woman" (*sankhini*), and the "elephant-woman" (*hastini*). According to the type of woman and the day of the lunar month, the woman lover will be best aroused in different parts of her body and by different forms of foreplay. In the same way, different kinds of women will derive greater sexual pleasure at different times of the day.

The *padmini* "is delicate like a lotus bud, her genital odour is of the lotus in flower, and her whole body divinely fragrant . . . She is religious, . . . her body is as attractive as the lotus leaf . . . , and of the four types she is reckoned the best." The *citrini* "moves well" and is "neither short nor tall," with "a slender body, prominent breasts and buttocks," a soft and "not over-hairy" vulva with "a genital odor like honey." Befitting her artistic name, "she is a skillful dancer and singer," and "delights in singing and . . . in the arts," including *ars erotica*, and particularly "loves the outer forms of lovemaking" (i.e., noncoital foreplay). The *sankhini* has "a bilious disposition" and the "voice of a wild ass." She is "lewd and treacherous," larger than the two previous types, and has a "long, deep-set, very hairy" vulva whose "genital odor is acid." The elephant-woman is "stout," "corpulent," and "gluttonous" with a body "odor of elephant"; "she has no modesty . . . and . . . in intercourse she is inordinately difficult to satisfy" (KKS 103–104; AR 3–5).

The texts then outline the proper days, hours, sexual positions, "manipulations," and bodily parts or "seats of passion" for best satisfying these different kinds of women (AR 8–14). Consider this summary from the *Koka Shastra*:

> The days of the lunar cycle upon which the *padmini* and the *citrini* desire coition are the second, fourth, fifth , sixth, twelfth, tenth and eighth. For the . . . *hastini* . . . the ninth, fifteenth, fourteenth and seventh: the remaining four (second, third, eleventh and thirteenth) belong to the *sankhini*. The *padmini* should be taken in the *padmasana* [lotus] position, the *citrini* in the "town style," the *sankhini* by the device known as

> reed-splitting, and the *hastini* with her two feet on the man's shoulders. To obtain the best results, the *citrini* should be enjoyed in the first quarter of the night, the *hastini* in the second quarter, or by day. The *sankhini* does not become passionate until the third quarter of the night – the *padmini* is most attractive in the fourth and last. (KKS 105)[28]

The *Koka Shastra* then specifies, according to each day of the lunar calendar, which parts of the *padmini*'s body ("head, breastbone, left and right hands, the two breasts, the two thighs, the navel, the genital region, forehead, belly, buttocks and back, . . . armpits, lower back and arms," "lips and teeth" and "cheeks," as well as "knees, shins, ankle joints, feet and toes") and which modes of foreplay (involving different styles of embracing, kissing, biting, scratching, rubbing, sucking, stroking, squeezing, and the making of certain erotic sounds) will be optimal in arousing and satisfying her passion (KKS 107–108). The same sort of recommended schedule of erotic "manipulations" by calendar day, known as the *chandrakala* (or phases of the moon), is later articulated in great detail for all four female types in the *Ananga Ranga* (AR 6–14). Though more concise, the *Koka Shastra* highlights the *chandrakala*'s aesthetic benefits of erotic stimulation, linking them visually to its lunar focus. By "varying the site of your caresses with [the calendar] you will see [your woman] light up in successive places like a figure cut in moonstone when the moon strikes on it." In short, for Indian *ars erotica*, not only the erotic stage and the acts of sexual arousal but also the display of arousal itself is clearly aestheticized (AR 6–14; KKS 107).

V VARIETIES AND HARMONIES

As music, song, choreographed movement, artistic decorations of the sexual stage, and the lovers' arts-related discourse all contribute to India's extended notion of erotic performance, so are there distinctly aesthetic dimensions in its aims, methods, and principles of sexual foreplay and coitus.[29] They seek not only to stimulate but also to harmonize the lovers' energies to ensure that the sexual encounter brings fullness of pleasure to both man and woman. This is the pragmatic purpose behind the prominent concern with

[28] The *Ananga Ranga* instead asserts that the *padmini* does not really enjoy sex at night but prefers "the bright hours" of the day (AR 6).

[29] The methods and joys of foreplay and coitus are distinguished (in the *Koka Shastra* and *Ananga Ranga*) as "'outer' and . . . 'inner' forms of lovemaking" (KKS 125), or "external enjoyments" and "internal enjoyments" (AR 97, 115). The Indian classification recognizes that so-called outer actions and pleasures (e.g., kissing) can continue well beyond foreplay.

classifying both men and women into various types according to certain physical qualities deemed important for sexual performance (i.e., size of genitals, degree of sexual energy or passion, and level of performative endurance). Beyond the scientific impulse for taxonomies (and our three key texts are presented by their authors as sexual science), these classifications are helpful for identifying problematic disparities between lovers that can then be remedied through appropriate adjustments.

"The man is called a hare, bull, or stallion, according to the size of his sexual organ" (small, medium, or large, respectively), while women are correspondingly classified as "a doe, mare, or elephant cow" with respect to genital size. Thus there are three "equal couplings" in terms of similar size and six unequal couplings. With respect to sexual energy, men and women are classified as "dull" (or weak), average, or fierce in their passion; regarding endurance they are quick, average, or long-lasting in performing the sexual act and achieving full satisfaction. The aesthetic ideal of harmony is implied by the repeated insistence that "equal couplings are the best" (KS 28–29). When disparities of size exist, then coital positions need to be adjusted to provide for better friction and improved penetrating movement in the lovers' genitals, as this is a great source of sexual pleasure. Among unequal couplings it is better when the lovers' disparities are slighter (e.g., small/medium versus small/large) but also when the disparity arises because of the man's greater dimensions.[30] If this preference for male superiority in unequal unions reflects the power of patriarchal culture, it conversely evokes woman's greater sexual capacities that make patriarchy a useful strategy for mitigating male performance anxieties. Such anxieties provide a major motivation for *ars erotica* in India and elsewhere. Recognizing that men typically reach orgasm more quickly than women and lose their performative power after climax, the *Kamasutra* recommends that "the woman should be treated in such a way that she achieves her sexual climax first" (KS 35).

The Indian texts specify varieties of foreplay and coital positions to overcome disproportions of size that impinge on the aesthetic harmony, graceful balance, and pleasurable ease of the union. Thus, "in a coupling where the man is larger than the woman, a 'doe' positions herself in such a way as to stretch herself open inside," by deploying various postures

[30] Although all three texts affirm the superiority of equal unions with respect to size, only the *Koka Shastra* explicitly affirms it with respect to "all these three characters" of size, energy, and endurance (KKS 112), and only the *Kamasutra* explicitly emphasizes that in unequal unions "it is better for the male to be larger" (KS 29).

(of differing difficulty) involved in raising the pelvis and spreading the thighs. Conversely, "in a coupling where the man is smaller, an 'elephant cow' contracts herself inside," typically by keeping her legs stretched straight and "her thighs together tightly" or even crossing them. "Sex tools may also be used, especially in a coupling where the man is smaller than the woman" (KS 51–53).

One should also adjust foreplay to other aspects of the lover – not only her physiology and her type and times for the *chandrakala* schedule but also with respect to regional customs and preferences. As the *sankhini* "wets only when heavily nail marked" in foreplay, so women from one north Deccan region like "striking with the hand and softly biting [their] lips," while women of some other regions are "averse to the tricks of teeth and nails" or to any rough or protracted embraces (KKS 104; AR 34–36). As such regional preferences are mere generalizations and since tastes anyway change "because the mind and heart are fickle," a man must be sensitive and insightful in discerning his lover's desires from her actual behavior in the particular erotic situation while also harmonizing those desires with his "own disposition" and predilections (KS 68–69).[31] This requires the exercise of discriminating intelligence that is thoughtful even when it is not deliberative in terms of explicit reasoning.

The optimum desire is therefore not the fiercest, since excessive passion could so captivate the lovers that they would neither notice nor oblige the particular erotic needs, preferences, and possible disparities of each other. Nor would they have the patient presence of mind to stylize their sexual performance to maximize its beauties and draw out its pleasures to the fullest (AR 23–24; KS 171–172; KKS 119–120).[32] There is, then, an aesthetic rationality in proper erotic performance that distinguishes it from the brute sex of beasts. The articulation of this pleasurable, passionate rationality provides the acknowledged raison d'être for India's texts of *ars erotica* texts.

[31] Vatsyayana elsewhere remarks that, despite general regional tendencies, foreplay behavior should vary with different people because "individual tastes can be overpowering" (KS 45–46), and he cites a prior erotic sage (Suvarnanabha) who asserts, "The nature of the individual is more important than the nature of the region" (KS 50).

[32] The *Ananga Ranga* suggests "moderate desires" are best because they are "free from either excess" of being too demanding to allow for full satisfaction through pleasurable aesthetic shaping or too weak to achieve or give such satisfaction. Like the proportionate fit of the genital organs, the right proportion of arousal and desire in both lovers is what "enables the husband to turn his mind [away from the mere mechanics of penetration and ejaculatory release] towards the usual arts which bring women under subjection" to the enthralling pleasures of artful lovemaking (AR 22).

Harmonies for proper lovemaking include not only those between lovers but also the environing harmonies of time and place. "Disregard of time and place in the act of love" constitutes one of the "fifteen principal causes which make women unhappy" (AR 30). Besides the *chandrakala* calendar, with its "times of enjoyments [and special styles and bodily sites of foreplay], according to the state of the moon and the hour of the day or night," the *Ananga Ranga* (the latest and most restrictive of our three texts) specifies both forbidden times and forbidden places for proper lovemaking, along with the "twelve periods when women have the greatest desire for congress, and at the same time are most easily satisfied" (AR 8, 31). All this is to ensure maximal harmony of personal and environmental energies for greater pleasure in performance and better procreative consequences. In contrast to the highly artistic setting recommended as "best fitted for sexual intercourse," the *Ananga Ranga*'s list of fourteen "places where a woman should not be enjoyed" include not only religious sites and depressing locales such as prisons, graveyards, and forts, but also, surprisingly, the beautiful landscapes of nature: "by the side of a river or any murmuring stream . . . in the forest . . . [or] in an open place, such as a meadow or an upland" (AR 94–95). Beautiful natural scenes seem harmonious enough to foster erotic desire, but the desire to distinguish human lovemaking as distinctively cultured in contrast to the natural coupling common to unthinking beasts may be one reason why *Ananga Ranga*'s author Kalyanamalla feels compelled to prohibit natural settings for *ars erotica*. (Similar thinking may have motivated the Chinese stricture against the "environs of mountains and rivers" we noted in Chapter 4.)

The Indian texts specify in detail the varieties of foreplay and coital actions (including love sounds) that one should harmoniously orchestrate to maximize the pleasure of erotic performance. Kalyanamalla classifies them most generally into "external enjoyments" of foreplay that "should always precede internal enjoyment or coition" but that can continue during and even after coitus, and the "internal enjoyments" concerned with the "art of congress" itself. These latter activities include the various coital positions and the different styles of penetrative movements inside the woman, which the *Kamasutra* describes as "sexual strokes" (AR 97, 115; KS 61–64). Besides the diverse modes and body locations for embracing, kissing, and caressing, three forms of foreplay stand out as distinctive to Indian *ars erotica* yet challenging to its ideal of erotic performance as a pleasurably sweet harmony of cultured refinement. I refer to the advocacy of various kinds of biting, scratching, and hitting to enhance the intensity and effects of erotic performance.

Vatsyayana affirms how "lovers scratch one another with their nails in the spirit of erotic friction" when they have strong sexual energy, such as during "their first time together or on a return from a journey" or when the woman "is drunk" (KS 45). His *Kamasutra* and the two later texts elaborate various styles of nail scratching that make different kinds of shapes and are applied on diverse parts of the body, but especially on "the armpits, breasts, neck, back, and thighs and [the pubic region] between the legs" (KS 46). Though one style applies the nails "so lightly that they leave no mark but . . . cause the thrill of gooseflesh and make a sound," the other seven styles Vatsyayana identifies are strong enough to leave durable marks in different shapes: "the 'half-moon,' the 'circle,' the line,' the tiger's claw,' the 'peacock's foot,' the 'hare's leap,' and the 'lotus leaf'" (KS 46). For scratching to leave long-lasting marks, it must be painful, and the marks are "wounds" that function not only to express the lovers' passion but also to recall or rekindle it at a later time and to inspire passion and admiration by potential new lovers. "When a woman sees the scars that nails have made on her hidden places, her love even for someone given up long ago becomes as tender as if it were brand new," while "love may disappear unless there are wounds made by nails to prompt memories of . . . passion." Moreover, a woman "with the marks of nails cut into her breasts" or "a man who is marked with the signs of nails in various places" attracts "passion and respect" (KS 47–48). Biting "love marks" are also made in different shapes and applied to various body parts; some bites are "not-too-bloody," but others are done with even more "force and pressure" (and corresponding pain) to provide "wounds" that are lastingly visible as erotic symbols for "increasing passion" (KS 48).

Finally, there are the different "modes of slapping and the accompanying moaning." The slapping is done "on the shoulders, on the head, between the breasts, on the back, between the legs, and on the sides," and is executed "in four ways: with the back of the hand, the outstretched hand, the fist, or the flat palm of the hand" (KS 56). Though performed not out of malice but rather in loving passion and playfulness, such slapping truly hurts, causing moaning that "expresses pain" and "takes several forms." Besides the eight kinds of wordless sounds ("whimpering, groaning, babbling, crying, panting, shrieking, or sobbing"), there are also cries using words like "stop" or "enough" (KS 57, 58). If most examples invoke the man's slapping and the woman's moaning, then Vatsyayana explains this by "man's natural talent . . . [for] roughness and ferocity" and woman's capacity for "suffering, self-denial, and weakness" (KS 58). He insists, however, (as do the later authors) on the value of the woman slapping back to intensify the erotic performance.[33] Recognizing woman's greater weakness, Indian *ars erotica* exhorts her to retaliate by striking back more forcefully in kind: "Whatever wound a man inflicts on a woman, even when she tries to restrain him and cannot bear it, she should do that very thing to him twice as hard" (KS 50).

How can we reconcile these beatings and wounds of tooth and nail with lovemaking's sweet harmony? They play no similar role in China's rich vision of sexual harmonizing. A deeper probe into aesthetics suggests some strategies to justify such violence. These strategies valorize contrast as rendering harmony more complex and thus more richly satisfying. Adding violent acts of scratching, biting, and beating in lovemaking provides additional kinds of sensations to those achieved through tender kisses, caresses, and embraces, but also presents a dramatic contrast to them, thus creating a more challenging, complex unity in variety that includes dissonance as well as consonance, sharp spice as well as gentle sweetness. By introducing this vivid tension in the erotic performance, one creates a more exciting and challenging unity of *discordia concors* that prevents the tender sweetness of lovemaking from becoming monotonous, cloying, and bland. The clash moreover generates an exciting drama of conflict overcome in the melting unity of mutual orgasm. The pinch of pain imparted by these tolerably violent acts makes the contrasting pleasures of lovemaking seem more delightful in themselves through the contrast it provides, much in the way that eating watermelon with salt makes the melon taste sweeter. Sexual pleasures become even more delightful through their overcoming and relieving the inflicted pain of lovemaking's slaps, bites, and scratches.

This potent pleasure of relief from pain was celebrated by Montaigne[34] and experimentally verified by contemporary psychology. Daniel Kahneman and his associates demonstrated that judgments of the pleasurable quality of experiences are almost entirely determined by the twin factors of their qualitative peak (best or worst) and their concluding tone. In one experimental study, people listened to a pair of unpleasant loud noises and subsequently had to choose which one they would prefer to be repeated. One noise lasted ten seconds, the other fourteen. The initial ten seconds of each noise were identical, but the continuation of the longer noise, though still loud and unpleasant, was not as loud as in the beginning. Objectively,

[33] The *Ananga Ranga* is more balanced and moderate with respect to such love blows, identifying four styles of striking by men and four by women, while moreover describing all of them as "soft tappings and pattings" rather than hard hammering (AR 111).

[34] Referring to his experience of passing kidney stones, Montaigne claimed that "nature has lent us pain for the honor and service of pleasure." See Michel de Montaigne, *The Complete Essays of Montaigne*, trans. Donald Frame (Stanford: Stanford University Press, 1965), 838.

the second noise should seem much worse, since its peak unpleasantness is identical and just as long, and its overall unpleasantness is 40 percent longer. Yet the overwhelming majority of people preferred it as their choice for repetition. The reason for this logically puzzling preference clearly seems to be that the end of the preferred noise involved a significant diminution of earlier pain, producing such a positive feeling of relief that it made the whole experience more favorably colored and remembered.[35]

Scratching and biting augment lovemaking's aesthetic in yet another way, through the production of artistically designed visual marks with multiple meanings: both established pictorial meanings and more specifically erotic and personal ones. The clearly aesthetic intent in creating certain representational forms on the lover's body through bites and scratches makes the act of lovemaking not only a dramatic dance but a performance of figurative art involving recognized images whose successful creation requires real care and mastery. One variety of nail marks made on the neck and breasts "resembles a half-moon" (AR 105), another makes "the form of a lotus leaf on the upper part of the breast or around the hips" (KS 47). The varieties of bite marks include shapes resembling a "garland of jewels," a group of "'scattered clouds' . . . on top of the breasts," and a special cluster of impressions on the woman's brow, cheek, neck, and breast that together form the "mouth-shaped oblong" of the mandala summarizing the different forms of biting and that "will add greatly to her beauty" (KS 49, AR 108).[36]

Such nail and bite markings, as noted earlier, serve as symbols of erotic skill and affection that endure beyond the sexual performance and aesthetically document it. For the lovers themselves these scars "of tooth and nail" provide a proud and comforting "token of remembrance" that can rekindle their passion (AR 34, 106). Moreover, when placed on publicly visible parts of the body these aesthetically rendered scars function as socially recognized symbols of erotic expertise that inspire "passion and respect" (KS 47).[37]

[35] See, for example, Daniel Kahneman, "Objective Happiness," in Daniel Kahneman, Ed Diener, and Norbert Schwarz, eds., *Well-Being: The Foundations of Hedonic Psychology* (New York: Russell Sage, 1999), 20.

[36] The love sounds accompanying the love marks of tooth and nail provide further supplements to aesthetic variety by adding both auditory sensations and representational meanings. Besides verbal cries that "have meaning, such as 'Mother!' 'Stop!' 'Let go!' 'Enough!,'" the woman may represent various animals in her moaning: "she may use, according to her imagination, the cries of the dove, cuckoo, green pigeon, parrot, bee, nightingale, goose, duck, and partridge" (KS 57).

[37] Indian techniques include symbolic actions that leave no marks but refer suggestively to other elements of sexual performance, thereby seeking to promote them. The "transferred kiss" is one given not to the lover but to a child or object simultaneously viewed by the lover so as to suggest the desire to kiss the lover (KS 141). The "Ghatika" kiss, designed to stimulate the man toward

Through their established erotic meaning, a man can deploy such love marks symbolically without sexual contact and on surfaces other than the beloved's body in order to suggest an erotic encounter where her flesh will receive similar aesthetic attention. "When a man applies scratches, bites, and so forth to a forehead decoration, an earring, a bouquet of flowers, betel, or a sweet-smelling cinnamon bay-leaf used by the woman he wants, he is making advances" (KS49). A woman could do the same.

The artistic shaping of erotic bites and scratches is moreover an expressive emblem for *ars erotica*'s refashioning of the raw animal passion of sexual desire (with its violence of feeling and action) into a disciplined, finely shaped artistic form. Such refining of crude impulse serves the essential function of distinguishing human erotics from the brute coupling of beasts while nonetheless emphasizing that even the most artful, sophisticated lovemaking ultimately reflects deep drives whose aggressively violent dimension we share with lower animals. Lovemaking thus conveys the complex nature of humanity as animal yet not bestial, a complexity highlighted by the animal sounds and postures that *Kamasutra*'s lovers intentionally perform in their erotic play. The lovers' battle of bites, blows, and nail marks evoke broad social and metaphysical themes: lovemaking's union involves a passionate struggle between the sexes where the coupling partners strive to assert their own individual personality and preferences by leaving their marks on the other. However intense its union, erotic coupling paradoxically underlines the impossibility of total fusion and the conflictual nature of this most basic and necessary mode of human merging that creates the further unity of a child born from such union. This model of creation through harmony in conflictual tension purveys a still broader metaphysical vision of a universe constituted by such *discordia concors* that includes violence and opposition, destruction with creation, as part of its cosmic order. Śiva, the originator of Indian *ars erotica*, divinely embodies such *discordia concors*: the potently procreative erotic ascetic is likewise the famous god of destruction, composing together with Brahma the creator and Vishnu the preserver the great Hindu trinity or *Trimurti*. This aesthetic and metaphysical understanding of India's violent consensual love-play is not without real risks. Even willing, well-intentioned couples may go too far. Moreover, it should never obscure or excuse the horrible uses of violence in nonconsensual sex and domestic abuse that plague many patriarchal societies, including India's.

the act of coitus by also symbolizing it, is when the woman "thrusts her tongue into his mouth, moving it to and fro with a motion so pleasant and slow that it at once suggests another and a higher form of enjoyment" (AR 102).

Our extended discussion of biting, scratching, slaps, and related amorous cries should not obscure the rich variety of other Indian modes of foreplay: the diverse forms of embraces, kisses, other love sounds, and ways of handling the lover's hair.[38] Despite this impressive manifold of "external enjoyments," Indian *ars erotica* is most famous for its detailed articulation, classification, and colorful naming of a wide variety of coital positions to serve the "internal enjoyments" of intercourse (AR 98, 115). Diversity here enhances aesthetic power by renewing interest, compounding pleasure, and thus preventing the boredom of monotony. "For even passion demands variety," argues Vatsyayana. "And it is through variety that partners inspire passion in one another. It is their infinite variety that makes courtesans de luxe and their lovers remain desirable to one another. Even in archery and in other martial arts, the textbooks insist on variety. How much more is this true of sex!" (KS 47).[39]

VI TAKING POSITIONS AND PLAYING ROLES

Indian *ars erotica* divides coital positions into five basic kinds: "supine (*uttānaka*), lateral (*tiryak*), seated (*āsitaka*), standing (*sthita*), and prone (*ānata*)" (KKS 135). Within each of these general categories, there are various forms of particular postures. Some are prescribed for when the man is larger (i.e., a "high" connection), others for when the woman is larger (a "low connection") or for "an even connection" where the couple are of corresponding size (KKS 135). The *Ananga Ranga* describes coital positions as "Bandha or Asana forms," terms that refer to traditional yoga postures or body locks that heighten energy. Some coital poses indeed resemble yoga *asanas*, and some are "very difficult of performance," particularly some of

38 The *Ananga Ranga* identifies by name eight forms of embracing and ten kinds of kiss; the *Kamasutra* likewise describes eight styles of embracing and more than eight ways of kissing, including varieties of lower-lip, upper-lip, and inner-mouth kissing, as well as forms of indirect kissing, such as when a lover kisses "the reflection or shadow of the woman he wants, in a mirror, on a wall or in water, to demonstrate his feelings" or when he performs a "'transferred' kiss" to show such feelings by kissing "a child, a portrait or a statue" in her presence (KS 44–45). The *Koka Shastra* specifies "twelve manners" of embracing and more than eight kinds of kisses, including the "reflected" kiss (which it calls "the picture-kiss") and "the transferred kiss" (KKS 126–129). The *Ananga Ranga* is alone among the three in distinguishing by name four ways of "manipulating the hair" in foreplay (AR 108–110).

39 Burton and Arbuthnot's translation (144) renders this remark more elaborately as: "if variety is sought in all the arts and amusements ... how much more should it be sought after in the present case" of erotic artistry; for just "as variety is necessary in love, so love is to be produced by means of variety."

the so-called picture positions, which include standing postures and postures where the man penetrates the woman from behind, but also postures involving "plural intercourse," either of one man with multiple women or one woman with multiple men (AR 117, 125; KKS 139, 141). Many positions have colorfully suggestive names: "tortoise," "crab," "lotus-seat," "cobra noose," "spear thrust," "monkey position," "cow," "*kama*-wheel," "the dog, the gazelle, and the camel," the "mare's trap," "the donkey's assault, the cat's pounce, the tiger's spring, the elephant's crush, the boar's friction, or the stallion's mounting" (AR 123–124; KKS 136–141; KS 53–55). These coital postures promote "imitating the behavior" of the animals or actions from which their names derive – thus adding another representational dimension to the art of lovemaking.

The fact that many of these coital *bandhas* seem to overlap or blend into each other suggests that their variety can be deployed within one act of lovemaking rather than limiting the act of coitus to a single posture. In other words, during any particular coital event, the lovers can aesthetically arrange a number of diverse *bandhas* as sequenced dance steps into a choreography of sexual performance. Besides adding variety, these postural transitions can structure and prolong the performance by creating punctuating pauses that delay the man's ejaculation.[40] Such choreography of changing postures can further enrich the act with special symbolic significance in terms of the postures' names and associations. For example, "by adopting successively the 'fish,' 'tortoise,' 'wheel,' and 'sea-shell' position (*mātsya*, *kaurma*, *cakra*, *śankhabanda*) one identifies oneself with the first four avatars of Vishnu."[41]

Complementing the variety of coital postures is a diversity of styles of moving the penis inside the vagina. As performed by the man, these different kinds of strokes are distinguished as "'moving around,' 'churning,' the 'dagger,' 'grinding down,' 'pressing,' the 'blast of wind,' the 'boar's thrust,' the 'bull's thrust,' 'frolicking like a sparrow,' and the 'cup.'"[42] But the woman

40 This variety of posture is not merely a visual and tactile matter of seeing or touching different parts of the lover's body, but also involves a fascinating proprioceptive variety, as different postures involve different feelings of inner somatic alignment, muscle tensions, vascular pressure, and other interoceptive perceptions, including the different kinaesthetic feelings of moving within and through these coital postures.

41 Comfort, "Introduction," KKS 63.

42 "Regular, straight sex is called 'moving around.' When he takes his sexual organ in his hand and rotates it in all directions, it is called 'churning.' When he lowers her pelvis and thrusts into her from above, it is called 'the dagger.' When he raises her pelvis and thrusts into her from below, violently, it is called 'grinding down.' When he stabs her deeply and remains there, pressing her, for a long time, that is called 'pressing.' When he pulls out quite far and then plunges down into her fast and hard, it is called the 'blast of wind.' When he reams her many times just on one

can also take the leading role in the coital dance by mounting the man and guiding the inner motion of his penis through her own "sexual strokes" as implemented by her pelvic movements and contractions. This coital position (called *Parushayita* and specially classified beyond the five regular postural kinds) is "when the woman plays the man's part" on top, either because the man is "exhausted from continuous repetition" of his penetrating strokes or because the lovers desire this reversal of roles to enhance variety and "satisfy . . . erotic curiosity" (KS 60). In this posture of physical dominance the woman teases the man by playacting as his superior, "laughing at him and threatening him and hitting him," while moving on his supine body to administer the female versions of sexual strokes: "the 'tongs,' the 'spinning top,' and the 'swing'" (KS 64). In the "tongs," "she grasps him in the 'mare's trap' position and draws him more deeply into her or contracts around him and holds him there for a long time"; but "when she keeps him inside her and twists around him like a wheel around an axle, that is called the 'spinning top,' and can only be done with practice." In the "swing," "she twists around him while swinging her pelvis back and forth in all directions" (KS 64).[43]

Purushayita highlights the importance of the playful acting out of roles, as the man too plays along by letting the woman take the superior posture and role before he resumes the higher position to conclude the coital act. Ordinary sexual postures and performances that maintain male dominance throughout likewise involve role playing: the man as the sophisticated lover creating the most exquisite harmonies of complex pleasure (that even include pain); the woman in a corresponding role often modeled on one of the famous heroine types (the "eight great forms of *Nayika*") in Indian drama (AR 113). Lovemaking is frequently described in terms of "amorous play" involving various "erotic games" and emerging from a distinctively aesthetic sociocultural context where artistic play and other games are highly prized, where sophisticated people "regard playing as their one and only

side, that is the 'boar's thrust.' When he does this to both sides, alternating, it is the 'bull's thrust.' When he enters her once and, without pulling out entirely, thrusts into her two, three, four times, and does this repeatedly, it is called 'frolicking like a sparrow'" (KS 63–64). The *Kamasutra* earlier describes the 'cup' among coital positions, explaining how it involves the straightening of one's legs and one's partner's to create more genital friction (KS 53).

43 The *Koka Shastra* acknowledges that "some books have given special names to the different manners of moving the penis in the vagina (churning, pressing, the boar-thrust, and so on)" but omits discussing them, believing they are "unprofitable." Instead, it confines the classifications of strokes to "three ways – from above, centrally, or from below," while also admitting that if his woman is insatiable the lover may take a lingam in his hand and use it for sexual strokes (KKS 141–142).

concern," and "play at ... various widespread and local games, different from those of the common people" (AR 26; KS 20–21, 125).

From Friedrich Schiller's eighteenth-century classic on aesthetic education to Hans-Georg Gadamer's late twentieth-century hermeneutic theory of art, philosophers have recognized play as central to art's power to educate and promote life by combining freedom with ordered form, despite its use of illusion and differentiation from ordinary reality.[44] The distinctively aesthetic character of India's *ars erotica* finds clear expression in its emphasis on acting out roles and the pleasures of play, which stands in sharp contrast to cultures more focused on practical sexual goals of procreation and health. Musical metaphors also evoke the theme of aesthetic play, as when the *Ananga Ranga* defines its goal of creating aesthetic delights through artful skills in playing harmonious variations on an instrument of human beauty. "All you who read this book shall know how delicious an instrument is woman, when artfully played upon; how capable she is of producing the most exquisite harmony; of executing the most complicated variations and of giving the divinest pleasures," replete with enchanting love sounds of various kinds (AR xxiii). It is surely disturbing to objectify women as an aesthetic instrument for man's pleasure, but the sting is somewhat mitigated by the insistent advocacy that women reciprocally play on male instruments, and sometimes even play the male by taking on his coital positions and roles.

Fellatio is our cultural stereotype for sexually playing on man's instrument, as if blowing on a flute, but Indian *ars erotica* gives it scant attention. The *Ananga Ranga* refuses even to mention oral sex, while the *Koka Shastra* merely alludes to the *Kamasutra* account of it without giving any details. That account focuses on homosexual encounters for which it specifies eight progressive stages (from insertion of the penis into the mouth to jerking, nibbling, squeezing, licking, sucking, and finally ejaculatory swallowing), each stage being successively requested before being performed. "Promiscuous women, loose women, servant girls, and masseuses also perform oral

[44] Arguing that play takes humankind's material drive that "proceeds from ... [our] sensuous nature" and harmonizes it with the "formal drive" from our higher "rational nature," Schiller claims that "man ... is only fully a human being when he plays" and that play forms the foundation of the "whole edifice of the art of the beautiful and of the still more difficult art of living." See Friedrich Schiller, *On the Aesthetic Education of Man*, trans. E. M. Wilkinson and L. A. Willoughby (Oxford: Clarendon Press, 1982), 79–81, 107–109. Gadamer insists on play's combining "freedom of movement" with "the self-discipline and order that we impose on our movements when playing." This combination is similarly essential to the creative order and unity of the artwork and of proper efforts to experience and interpret it. Hans-Georg Gadamer, *The Relevance of the Beautiful and Other Essays*, trans. Nicholas Walker (Cambridge: Cambridge University Press, 1986), 23.

sex," Vatsyayana then adds, noting that while other ancient scholars condemned its female practice as polluting the woman's mouth, he more tolerantly allows it in some cases, depending "on the custom of the region and one's own disposition and confidence." He even tolerates men performing "the act upon women, [by] transposing the procedure for kissing a mouth," if the conditions are appropriate (KS 66–68).[45]

This insistence on contextual judgment based on complex conditions rather than fixed rules defining what is always proper in lovemaking is the counterpart of the aesthetic concern for complex harmony created through a wealth of different somatic, sensory, semantic, spatiotemporal, psychological, and sociocultural factors. Aesthetic judgments have long been defined as requiring taste (which Kant described as "reflective judgment") because the complex harmonies and unity that constitute beauty cannot be reduced to rules or formulated principles but instead please by satisfying the "*free play* of the cognitive faculties."[46] If unity in variety serves as the most familiar definition of beauty, then coital union of the different sexes enacted through complex, multidimensional harmonies aptly expresses that aesthetic idea. But one could go beyond the coital, hence heterosexual, model endorsed by patriarchy and explore varieties of same-sex lovemaking that could introduce still more forms of complex aesthetic harmonies.

India's techniques for aesthetically rich erotic unities served a variety of purposes. One increasingly important aim was maintaining marital union by sustaining sexual attraction and sexual love between the married couple in order to preserve domestic harmony and the broader social stability of patriarchy it provides. The *Ananga Ranga*, expressly written "to prevent the separation of the married pair and to show them how they may pass through life in union," makes this point explicit. "The chief reason for the separation between the married couple and the cause, which drives the husband to the embraces of strange women, and the wife to the arms of strange men, is the want of varied pleasures and the monotony which follows possession." This is because "Monotony begets satiety, and satiety distaste for congress, especially in one or the other [partner]; malicious

[45] Vatsyayana notes that "a wise Brahmin, or a minister of state . . . or any man in whom people confide, should not indulge in oral sex" (KS 69). Anal sex receives even less attention; the *Kamasutra* merely notes that it is practiced, while the two later texts do not even mention it.

[46] Immanuel Kant, *The Critique of Judgment*, trans. J. C. Meredith (Oxford: Oxford University Press, 1986), 58; on reflective judgment, see 18, 36.

feelings are engendered, the husband or the wife yield to temptation, and the other follows, being driven by jealousy." From such monotony and discord "result polygamy, adulteries, abortions, and every manner of vice" that even "drag down the names of deceased ancestors." The book seeks to show "how the husband, by varying the enjoyment of his wife, may live with her as with thirty-two different women, ever varying the enjoyment of her, and rendering satiety impossible," while also teaching the wife "all manner of useful arts and mysteries, by which she may render herself pure, beautiful, and pleasing in his eyes" (AR 128–129). If India's *ars erotica* strives both to give women "plenary contentment" and to instruct men how to "thoroughly enjoy their charms," such satisfactions are characterized in clearly aesthetic terms of richly varied harmonies of pleasurable perceptions and movements, replete with representational forms and wide-ranging meanings, and carefully structured with dramatic self-consciousness and performative stylization (AR xxiii).

As the *Ananga Ranga*'s aesthetics of variety with one wife served the practical aim of preserving marriage, so the *Kamasutra* explains how *ars erotica* is pragmatically advantageous in giving a man greater power over women and more esteem among men, while providing women various ways to achieve social and economic success, or even, in crisis situations, to ensure their survival. By making sex more attractive, *ars erotica*'s aesthetic delights moreover promote the pragmatics of procreation, while also serving the practical aim of health through the invigorating energies of erotic play. As "Vatsyayana says: Pleasures are a means of sustaining the body, just like food" (KS 12); and Kokkoka describes the *ars erotica* as "youth-giving science," because the enlivening play and power of successful sex helps keep us feeling joyful and young (KKS 102).

VII COGNITIVE DIMENSIONS

Sexual desire is a very potent force; why not harness its energies and delights to promote more pleasurable paths of learning? We can see Indian *ars erotica* as a valuable form of education that involves aesthetic, cognitive, and practical values. Knowing fine arts and crafts is deemed indispensable for lovemaking mastery precisely because their cognitive assets contribute both to the practical goal of winning the beloved and to the aesthetic qualities of the erotic performance of making love. Knowledge of herbs and minerals is needed for producing "certain drugs and charms" used to make men and women more successful in the affairs of love (AR 69–70), while astrological knowledge forms the basis of the *chandrakala*'s daily progression of erotic delights.[47] Erotic cognition crucially involves *knowing how* not simply *knowing that*. Its expertise includes skills of sensorimotor coordination and somaesthetic awareness honed through both the sixty-four fine arts and the sixty-four distinctively sexual arts of foreplay and coitus.

Social and psychological modes of knowledge are likewise crucial for erotic success. Requisite social knowledge includes religion-related doctrines of *dharma* and institutional rules of *artha* indicating which sexual activities (and partners) are appropriate or forbidden and in which circumstances, and what are the risks and penalties for improper or forbidden acts. Beyond specific regulations, erotic expertise involves a wealth of tacit social knowledge not formulated in explicit rules. One needs a firm grasp of the manners, customs, and preferences in courtship, foreplay, and coitus with women from different social milieus or regions, but also the expertise to recognize the precise sociocultural identity of the particular woman pursued. Moreover, as desirable women are often jealously guarded, a good lover needs the know-how to navigate the societal obstacles impeding access to her. He must have the social savoir-faire to arrange discreet meetings and subtle channels of communication with her, for example, by enlisting effective, reliable third parties to serve as go-betweens. These include not only the man's friends (including the trio of libertine, pander, and clown) but also the woman's maids, "girlfriends," "foster-sister," brothers, and various "types of female messengers" (KS 27, 83, 119). The lover's expertise must extend to recognizing which messengers in which social conditions will be appropriate, effective, and trustworthy, and how most successfully to deploy them. Navigating the special world of courtesans (with their diverse ranks, conditions, and ambitions) requires its own brand of social knowledge. Women need similar social knowledge to manage their love affairs from their own, far more vulnerable, social situation.

Beyond social roles and practices, Indian *ars erotica* demands and promotes psychological knowledge – proficiency in grasping the particularities of the individual person one seeks to win, please, and keep as one's lover (or, instead, to employ effectively as a go-between in one's pursuit of love). India's erotic theory (far more than China's) focuses on knowing the beloved's mind (with its anxieties as well as its desires and inclinations) rather than simply knowing the beloved's bodily state of arousal and physiological sensations of pleasure. The artistic activities that initiate the play of

[47] Unlike the two later texts, the *Kamasutra* hardly discusses astrological matters and does not include the *chandrakala*, but it does contain an entire book (Book Seven) on the alchemies for producing aphrodisiacs and drugs for enhancing virility.

lovemaking performance promote psychological insight by revealing (as they shape) the beloved's aesthetic inclinations and mood so that the lover can harmonize with them before engaging in the more carnal harmonies of sexual arousal. Recognizing that an individual's personality is partly determined by more-than-personal influences, India's erotic texts use a woman's age, region, class, physiological type (including her Ayurvedic category – *kapha*, *pitta*, or *vata*), astrological and palmistry signs, and even her "Satva, or disposition inherited from a former life" to help understand her particular character (AR 26). But as these general features do not suffice for grasping an individual's state of mind in particular and changing contexts, the same texts further explain how to know a person's momentary state of mind and undeclared intentions by interpreting behavioral signs that are either inadvertently expressed or deliberately made explicit.

The *Koka Shastra* defines certain "signs of desire" or "come-hither signs" indicating the psychological willingness of a potential lover, but also identifies contrasting "signs of aversion" (KKS 118–120, 161).[48] The *Kamasutra* articulates the interpretation of psychological states in far greater detail, devoting many long passages to interpreting potential lovers' gestures and signals to judge their erotic accessibility. An expert lover needs "a knowledge of signals and gestures that reveal emotions" in order to recognize the "right moment" and best tactic for "making advances" (KS 6, 27). He should command keen skills of psychological penetration to discern the undeclared "causes of a woman's resistance" and the consequent ways to eliminate or circumvent them in order to win her (KS 105–106). Whether approaching a virgin or "another man's wife," the successful lover must know how to interpret both deliberate signals and unintentional signs. While "a young woman's bearing and telltale signs are the basis on which to judge her character, honesty, purity, accessibility, and the fierceness of her sexual energy," her signs of desire are often so hard to read that the man's judgment may be fallible, if he does not rely also on explicit gestures and signals, particularly since many women "have deeply hidden their own involuntary signals" (KS 104, 129).

Men likewise reveal their erotic intentions through telltale signs and deliberate signals. A desiring man will gaze at the woman "constantly, . . . smoothing down his hair, snapping his nails, jingling his jewelry, chewing on his lower

[48] For example, "a girl in love sucks at her lips, her eyes stray about like fish in a river pool"; she "does not look [her beloved] straight in the eye, but becomes confused after a moment and looks away. She manages on various pretexts to let [him] see her body for a moment. She draws on the ground with her toes . . . , touches her hips, opens her eyes wide, lets her hair down" in his presence (KKS 119, 161–162).

lip, and making ... displays [of] his generosity and fondness for enjoyment"; conversely, there are also "signs that his passion is cooling" (KS 110, 145). An entire chapter of the *Kamasutra* is devoted to the psychology of "winning a virgin's trust" in order to prepare her mentally for erotic relations. This requires knowing her state of mind and level of emotional readiness for sexual contact by "interpreting her gestures and signals" (KS 78, 85) so as not to make advances too rashly or rudely. Even after the wedding, a man should ensure that he and his bride "remain sexually continent" for at least three nights before he gradually engages her in sexual play. Because "women are like flowers, and need to be enticed very tenderly," the chapter explains how the man "wins [his bride] over with gentle persuasion" by employing a complex series of actions, questions, and remarks that rely on his reading the signs of her mental state so that he can reshape it to suit his desires, even by means of deception but eschewing the use of force, which would make her "hate sex" (KS 78–79).

Why should the *Kamasutra* devote more instruction to discerning (and manipulating) the psychological states of lovers rather than focusing primarily (like Chinese *ars erotica*) on the physiological signs of erotic arousal in foreplay and coitus? This emphasis may reflect the fact that psychological states are harder to interpret, but it also may derive from Indian eroticism's deep roots in theater, where a character's mental states are not only essential to the drama but essentially expressed through gesture and signs both explicit and inadvertent. Recall how the *Ananga Ranga* provides a character typology of great female lovers (the *Ashtamahanayika*) derived from Hindu drama's classic roles.

VIII ETHICS AND CHARACTER

These erotically fostered cognitive values have important ethical significance. By knowing the different social roles and their appropriate conduct in different social circumstances, a person can be a more effective ethical agent. Knowing how to interpret telltale signs and gestures to discern another person's state of mind is crucial for improving our care for others by better discerning their problems and needs, and for protecting ourselves from deceptive malefactors, although such knowledge could also function to manipulate or deceive others. However, in detailing the various reasons and different strategies for seducing other men's wives, the *Kamasutra* repeatedly warns against the dangerous immorality of such action. As a scientific treatise on sexual behavior, it avows its duty to explain the full range of sexual practices, not only those it recommends or justifies.

Vatsyayana explicitly emphasizes this point: "For the statement that 'There is a text for this' does not justify a practice" (KS 69). He likewise reminds us that knowing the temptations and tricks of adulterous seduction helps protect a marriage, by alerting both man and wife to such dangers. "A man who knows ... the devices [and] telltale signs ... detailed in the discussion of the seduction of other men's wives, is never deceived by his own wives. But he himself should never seduce other men's wives, ... because the dangers are clearly visible, and because it goes against both religion and power." Recalling the book's key ethical impulse to harmonize *kama* with *dharma* and *artha*, Vatsyayana insists that *ars erotica* "should not be learned in order to corrupt the people" (KS 130).

Indeed, the primary aim of erotic instruction is not successful pursuit of sexual desires (whatever their target or motive) but instead to manage them more fruitfully by channeling them in the right direction. Indian *ars erotica*, moreover, seeks to build character. Hence along with the lists of prohibited partners, times, and places deemed risky for reasons of health, morality, or social consequences, it proposes a path to self-mastery, to becoming a person "who has truly conquered his senses" (KS 171). If self-knowledge enables self-care, then better knowing our passions empowers us to manage them more effectively; hence all three of India's classic erotic texts discuss the "ten stages of desire" in which passion (beginning with the distraction of "love at first sight") increasingly disturbs the lover, resulting in "loss of sleep, loss of weight, inability to concentrate, the destruction of one's sense of shame" or "decency and decorum," and ultimately "madness, loss of consciousness, and death" (KKS 155; KS 104; AR 87–88). When passion mounts toward these highest stages so that life itself is threatened, adultery may be unavoidable, but it can be pardoned "only under the compulsion of [these] ten stages of love, not simply upon impulse" (KKS 155). Erotic mastery resides in knowing our impulses and psychological states well enough to govern them effectively and thus avoid, as best we can, the excesses of passion.

Indian *ars erotica* has a complex attitude toward passion, appreciating its creative energy while wary of its blinding, overwhelming intensity. Unlike Chinese *ars erotica*, the *Kamasutra* does not advocate a radical mastery of passion through which the lover performs the required coital strokes in their precise order, depth, and number, along with the prescribed breathing rhythms, in a spirit of methodical serenity. Instead, it claims that passion's ecstatic madness will trump all method. "The territory of the texts extends only so far as men have dull appetites; but when the wheel of sexual ecstasy is in full motion, there is no textbook at all, and no order" to follow. "There is no order of precedence for kissing, scratching, or biting, because they involve passion" (KS 42). Moreover, while these actions "are generally used before sex, and slapping and moaning during sex . . . Vatsyayana says: Everything at any time, because passion does not look before it leaps" (KS 42). Transcending "numerical lists or textbook tables of contents," passion's creative power produces "emotions and fantasies [that] . . . cannot be imagined even in dreams," while its frenzy risks the dangers of "sexual chaos" that include injuring one's lover in the tumult of the scratching, blows, and bites of intercourse (KS 59). "For just as a horse in full gallop, blinded by the energy of his own speed, pays no attention to any post or hole or ditch on the path, so two lovers blinded by passion in the friction of sexual battle, are caught up in their fierce energy and pay no attention to danger" (KS 59–60).[49]

If passion's peak is too overwhelming to control with total, methodical calm, then a man "well-taught and expert" in *ars erotica* "who has truly conquered his senses" can, from the outset, shape the erotic performance artistically, deploying reflective judgment that mitigates sexual frenzy as it molds desire into aesthetic form (KS 171). Approaching erotic performance with this aesthetic attitude keeps passion within manageable limits while providing the tasteful reflection not only to avoid bad choices (of partner, time, place, and methods) but also, more positively, to produce an attractively fashioned and meaningful performance, an erotic work of art. Erotic mastery is demonstrated through refining restraint and sublimation of raw sensuality into the aesthetic pleasures of meaningful sensuous form.[50] Here the expert "does not indulge himself too much in passion, and so he succeeds when he plays the part of a lover" (KS 172). Moreover, the conscious act of taking on this role further reduces the threat of being overwhelmed by passion, because such artistic role playing brings a double, critical consciousness, that of the self who directs the play and that of the character played. The governing self is not strictly identical to the character role it plays in the erotic encounter, but rather creates and guides that character of expert lover

[49] Vatsyayana provides historical examples: "The King of the Cholas killed Chitrasena, a courtesan de luxe, by using the 'wedge' during sex. And the Kuntala king Shatakarni Shatavahana killed his queen, Malayavati, by using the 'scissor.' Naradeva, whose hand was deformed, blinded a dancing-girl in one eye by using the 'drill' clumsily" (KS 59).

[50] As Hegel recognized, "art has the capacity and the function of mitigating the fierceness of the desires" through its aesthetic shaping, thus "taming and educating the impulses" and cravings of our sensual nature. Such "purification of the passions" is one way to explain how, "in art, the sensuous is *spiritualized*." For Hegel, however, art's key spiritualizing function is "revealing *the truth* in the form of sensuous artistic shape" rather than reshaping life to be more spiritual by making art's beauty the model for an art of living. See G. W. F. Hegel, *Introductory Lectures on Aesthetics*, trans. Bernard Bosanquet (London: Penguin, 1993), 44, 53, 55, 61.

to shape the passionate sexual play into a work of aesthetic refinement through artistic control.

The same idea of playacting and its doubling of self-consciousness also suggests a different path of self-care through self-knowledge. By recognizing an essential difference between the character one plays and the self who plays that role, one can forgo explicit, critical control and give free rein to play the lover's role of passion. The distinction between the role and the true self permits the fullest play of passion while preventing the self from being possessed by the role. This second approach recalls the key Hindu concept of *lila*, or divine play, sometimes used to explain how the great ascetic Śiva could make passionate love yet remain dispassionate. As Doniger quotes from one mythic version:

> All the time that Śiva made love with Sati, it was just his divine play, for he was entirely self-controlled and without emotional excitement the whole time.... When Sati died, Śiva, the great yogi, wept like a lover in agony, but this is just his divine play, to act like a lover, for in fact he is unconquered and without emotional excitement.... Though Śiva was devoid of passion and the enemy of lust, he himself came into the power of Devi by his own divine play. Then, though he was without desire, he became full of desire because of her loveliness. (SEA 147)

Another passage makes the same point, when Parvati uses this second strategy of detached divine play to convince Śiva that marrying her would not corrupt his pure ascetic character: "You are indeed without emotional excitement, but nevertheless, for the sake of your devotees, you assume emotional characteristics, for you are clever at various divine sports" (SEA 148).

In the first strategy of self-doubling, the true self might be likened to a director who strives to instruct, shape, and guide the character played. Although separate from the character, he is concerned with, invested in, and therefore in some way affected by the character's performance, as it reflects on his success or standing as director. In the second strategy, the true self or agent self is more distanced, more like a spectator of the play who is not really committed to it and thus is essentially untouched by the success or failure of the performance. Not only is the performance a mere game, but the character playing it is essentially different from, less real than, and inconsequential for the true self. This strategy finds support in a fundamental orientation of Hindu metaphysics of mind: the idea that each person has a divinely transcendent self, distinct from and tranquilly observing that individual's empirical, embodied, striving self. As the Upanishads insist: "Two birds, united always and known by the same name, closely cling to the same tree. One of them eats the sweet fruit; the other looks on without eating."[51] The empirical embodied self (or *jiva*) enjoys and suffers the fruits of action, but the transcendental self (or Atman) is beyond and indifferent to such empirical concerns and feelings, and simply "looks on" without acting or being acted upon. With the second strategy's radical distinction of the true self from the role-playing self, a person could give free rein to the play of love's passion while knowing it cannot damage one's true spiritual self, which simply looks on from a secure distance.

Though appreciably different, these two strategies of artistic sublimation and separation both rely on the idea of playacting and the doubling of self in role playing; the lover is one such role rather than being the real identity of the true self behind that role. But that true self, in Hindu metaphysics, does not reside in other empirical identities and actions with which we ordinarily identify the self. For they too are simply the playing-out of roles. Even what seems to be our most basic governing sense of self or underlying personality that seems to direct our taking on of other roles is merely an elusively vague and changing background role or narrative construction rather than one's firmly fixed true self. As our empirical selves are no more than the roles we play, so the empirical world in which we act them out is essentially a theater stage, a captivating, distracting, changing scene rather than ultimate reality. Hindu metaphysics sees the phenomenal world as a captivating web of deceptive appearance (*maya*) produced by the power and delight of divine play (*lila*), a world of drama created through overflowing divine energy and for the sheer joy of playing, a joy that includes destroying as well as creating.

Seeing the world as theater where lives are performances in role playing is not unique to Indian thought. Expressed by Greek and Roman authors (who note how the tragedies and comedies of real life involve different parts and are mixed with pleasures and pains), it is famously echoed in Shakespeare's *As You Like It* (II, vii): "All the world's a stage, and all the men and women merely players: they have their exits and their entrances; and one man in his time plays many parts."[52] Hindu thought adds a twist of divine romance to this image of *theatrum mundi*: the ideal of penetrating beneath the changing appearances and roles of empirical existence to realize that one's true self is essentially one with the supreme divine principle (Atman is Brahman) and,

[51] From the *Mundaka Upanishad* 3.1.1, in *The Upanishads*, trans. Swami Nikhilananda (New York: Harper & Row, 1964), 116.

[52] See Plato's *Philebus*, 50b, and Epictetus, *The Handbook of Epictetus*, trans. Nicholas P. White (Indianapolis: Hackett, 1983), 16; §17.

through this insight, to unite with that heavenly source of joy. Such blissful, blessed union is described in strikingly erotic terms: "As a man fully embraced by his beloved wife knows nothing that is without, nothing that is within, so does this infinite being (the self) when fully embraced by the Supreme Self, know nothing that is without, nothing that is within." Absorbed in the consciousness of this embrace, one finds release from worldly wants and troubles that burden one's empirical self and roles; one thus becomes "free from desires and devoid of grief . . . In this state a father is no more a father, a mother is no more a mother, the worlds are no more the worlds" because one sees their unreality by contrast to the divine existence in which one is enveloped, thus recognizing that one's true self is "untouched by good deeds and untouched by evil deeds."[53]

As the doubling of self in erotic role playing evoked the notion of an all-absorbing, delightfully deific union with the self's divine source, so medieval Tantrism eventually developed and codified this option into erotically flavored mystic rituals such as *maithuna*. In such rites devotees adoringly visualize and internalize deities in a manner suggestive of erotic courtship and union to the point where they merge with or "become" those gods. While primarily interpreted in purely spiritual terms without the physical contact of sexual union, it also frequently found expression in actual coital acts whose sensuality was spiritualized through the couple's sanctification as Śiva and Shakti.

Likening erotic coupling to union with the divine is a potent metaphor that enriches both terms. Providing the former with sublimely cosmic, ethical, and religious significance far beyond its ordinary sensuous import, it gives the latter's transcendently spiritual vision an extremely tangible, familiar, yet supremely attractive image of delight. More than a metaphor for such divine union, Indian *ars erotica* serves as effective training for it. Its complex aesthetic play teaches us discipline but also letting go, the very same phases of experience through which religious asceticism leads to ecstatic release. Aesthetic experience, erotic experience, and religious experience, despite their differences, share a common core. They combine directive doing with receptive undergoing; self-cultivating *askesis* of self-control with ardent attention to a desired other that motivates and orients that doing and undergoing; and, at the peaks of such experience, an eventual self-abandonment to achieve an all-absorbing fusion with that other – an adored artwork, lover, or divine presence – that makes such self-surrender a path to

[53] *Brihadaranhyaka Upanishad* 4.3.21, in Nikhilananda, *The Upanishads*, 230.

self-enrichment.[54] The *askesis* of refinement ensures that the self is properly prepared and sufficiently secure in its direction to let itself go when the moment is right.

Indian *ars erotica* teaches us how to direct the pursuit of pleasure toward self-refinement, which includes a perceptively caring and lovingly devoted regard for a being outside ourselves. In taking us beyond ourselves to taste the delights of self-abandoning release in the ecstasy of sexual union, it prepares and inspires us toward more divine union with the more perduring and tranquil pleasures of *moksha*, whose blissful peace provides release from worldly desires (that bring more pain than pleasure) and from the continuing cycle of death and rebirth that entails endless suffering.[55] This particular argument for *ars erotica* as aesthetic training toward religious fulfillment does not find systematic articulation in the three Indian classics discussed in this chapter, but our analysis clearly suggests it.

We already noted, however, a more explicit argument for *ars erotica* as preparation for the higher religious life. Given the doctrine of fulfilling life in its successive stages, the argument is that by having enjoyed so much sensual pleasure through the artful pursuit of *kama*, one's appetite for sex has been satisfied and one's desire turns to the sublimely loving pursuit of religious knowledge and devotion. In advocating its *ars erotica*, the *Ananga Ranga* emphasizes this point by having it "set forth in the following verses," which we cite again for further emphasis to conclude this chapter: "The man who knoweth the Art of Love, and who understandeth the thorough and varied enjoyment of woman. As advancing age cooleth his passions, he learneth to think of his Creator, to study religious subjects, and to acquire divine knowledge. Hence he is freed from further transmigration of souls; and when the tale of his days is duly told, he goeth direct with his wife to the *Svarga* (heaven)" (AR xxiii).

[54] Aesthetic, erotic, and religious experiences all vary as to how much they emphasize the pole of active, critical shaping and self-control versus the more receptive pole of undergoing and self-surrender toward fusion with the desired and admired object of experience.

[55] For an analysis of *moksha* as an "experience of liberation" through "objectless, blissful absolute consciousness" involving a directly experienced realization of one's essential identity with the divine or "absolute reality," see David White, "Moksa as Value and Experience," *Philosophy East and West* 9, no. 3 (1959): 149, 151, 153. It is an "absolute happiness" from an experiential personal "knowing" that is objectless because it involves a fusion that dissolves the difference between subject and object.

6

Fragrance, Veils, and Violence

Ars Erotica in Islamic Culture

THIS CHAPTER EXAMINES THE EROTIC THEORIES OF CLASSICAL Islamic culture. While this culture differs greatly from that of premodern Japan, examined in the next chapter, they nevertheless share a distinctive feature. Both are significantly derivative cultures. As Islamic culture built heavily on Jewish, Christian, Greek, Persian, and Indian traditions, so Japan borrowed extensively from Chinese culture, not only its form of writing and its arts but also its distinctive Zen version of Buddhism, derived from China's Chan Buddhist tradition. Both cultures, moreover, postdate the famous "axial age" that essentially defined Western, Indian, and Chinese thought. Coined by Karl Jaspers (perhaps building on the work of Max Weber), the notion of the axial age defines a period stretching from 800 to 200 BCE that encompasses the founding thinkers of Western and Asian civilizations. These include Socrates, Plato, and Aristotle in Greece, the Hebrew prophets in Israel, Zarathustra in Persia, the Buddha and the writers of the Upanishads in India, and, in China, Confucius, Mozi, the legendary Laozi, and Zhuangzi.[1] Key to the axial age was a sense of the crumbling of old ideas and their replacement by a new form of thinking that posited an ideal transcendental order beyond the ordinary mundane world and affirmed the active role of intellectual elites to reshape the world in terms of that transcendental vision. As the birth of Islam and the burgeoning of Japanese culture both postdate the axial age, so their erotic theories display their belated, derivative status.

[1] Karl Jaspers, *The Origin and Goal of History* (London: Routledge & Kegan Paul, 1953).

I ISLAMIC ROOTS: COMPLEXITY AND VARIETY

Islam originated early in the seventh century CE through the founding prophecy of Muhammad ibn ʿAbd Allah (ca. 570–632), who was born in the west Arabian town of Mecca and received his first prophetic revelation in 610. At that time the Middle East was dominated by two powerful empires. The Byzantine Empire (of Roman heritage) controlled the lands bordering the Eastern and Southern Mediterranean, while the Sasanian Empire (of Persian origin) ruled the area of what is now Iran and Iraq. Their influence, however, spread beyond the lands they officially governed, and Arabia was one of the areas where these two warring empires contended for power. Both empires were culturally diverse. Besides its Greco-Roman traditions of paganism, Byzantine culture had embraced Christianity as its official religion but also included a large Jewish population. Moreover, there existed considerable diversity and disputation among Christian sects. The rival Persian culture was largely Zoroastrian in religious belief but also included large numbers of Jews (most famously in Babylonia where the Talmud was compiled) and also some Christian communities of diverse denominations.[2]

Having spent the early decades of the seventh century in continual wars with each other, both the Byzantine and Persian empires were significantly weakened by the time Muhammad's prophetic movement was winning the allegiance of Arabia, which lay between the two empires on their southern desert fringes. A severely arid land that could not sustain much agriculture or generate a sophisticated culture, Arabia not only was socially and politically fragmented into family groups or tribes, but also was religiously diverse. Its pagan tradition of polytheism (with astral deities and local gods) was gradually supplemented by monotheism, first and foremost through the Jews who settled there and later through Christian communities, especially in the Yemen area. Muhammad's founding message of Islam was thus formulated in a thoroughly multicultural context with heightened awareness of the religions that preceded it.

Muhammad belonged to the powerful Quraysh tribe that presided over Mecca's important Ka'ba shrine and the vibrant commerce connected with it. A sensitive young man, he married a wealthy widow older than himself and wisely managed her affairs, reinforcing through his exemplary behavior his tribal association with religious authority and socioeconomic power.

[2] For an extensive treatment of Islam's context of emergence and early career, see Fred M. Donner, *Muhammad and the Believers: At the Origins of Islam* (Cambridge, MA: Harvard University Press, 2010), hereafter MB.

According to tradition, Muhammad's sensitive, reflective character led him to periods of secluded meditation, and in 610 he began to receive God's revelations delivered by the archangel Gabriel. The divine words that "burned indelibly in his memory ... were eventually written down by his followers and edited together to form the Qur'an" (MB 40), which preached the oneness, omnipotence, and mercy of God, but also the need for pious behavior to avoid God's punitive Last Judgment. As this monotheistic message did not sit well with Mecca's pagan tradition, Muhammad was forced to leave for Medina in 622, where he established a strong community of followers and the first mosque as a site for prayers. From that base, and through various political and military actions, Muhammad overpowered his rivals in Medina and eventually returned in 630 to conquer and occupy Mecca and then subjugate other Arabian cities. Muhammad's policy was to share the spoils of war with his soldiers, and these spoils included not only material goods but the enslaving of those conquered but not killed. After conquering a Jewish tribe in Medina called the Banu Qurayza in 627, he had all its men killed while giving the women and children as slaves to his followers, and taking the tribal chief's widow (Rihana) for his concubine.[3]

As his power grew, Muhammad increasingly insisted on believers serving in battle and on forcing pagans to convert to his monotheistic faith. The Quran itself tells the faithful: "Fighting is enjoined on you, though it is disliked by you; and it may be that you dislike a thing while it is good for you, and it may be that you love a thing while it is evil for you; and Allah knows while you know not." As for "disbelievers," "kill them wherever you find them, ... and fight them until ... religion is only for Allah" (Quran 2:191–193, 216).[4] After his death in 632, Muhammad's followers continued his policies of conquest and forced conversion, overpowering the Byzantine and

[3] Islam's harsh conquest policies could have drawn on the Hebrew example of Deuteronomy 20:10–14, advocating: "When you march up to attack a city, make its people an offer of peace. If they accept and open their gates, all the people in it shall be subject to forced labor and shall work for you. If they refuse to make peace and they engage you in battle, lay siege to that city. When the Lord your God delivers it into your hand, put to the sword all the men in it. As for the women, the children, the livestock and everything else in the city, you may take these as plunder for yourselves. And you may use the plunder the Lord your God gives you from your enemies."

[4] There are several well-established English translations of the Quran that differ in minor details. Rather than confining myself to one version, I use the translation most appropriate to the linguistic context of my arguments and provide the precise chapter and verse references to the Quran, hereafter noted as Q. Numerous English translations are online at quran.wwpa.com. The translations cited here are, respectively, from Maulana Mohammad Ali found at http://quran .wwpa.com/page/verse-2-216 and http://quran.wwpa.com/page/verse-2-193. I also consult N. J. Dawood, trans., *The Koran* (London: Penguin, 1999).

Sassanian empires, and eventually subjugating not only the lands of northern Africa, Spain, and southern Italy, but also large areas of India. Although Islam's original Arab culture was far less developed than those of Greco-Roman, Persian, and Indian heritage, the Muslims' ferocious skill and zeal in battle enabled them to defeat those superior cultures militarily and then absorb their diverse cultural riches as well as their material wealth. From its poor desert roots, Islamic culture thus developed to include very sophisticated and richly elaborate arts of living.

In ascending from lowly tents to luxurious palaces, it retained some of its humble ways of life, not simply because many of its ever growing body of believers remained poor, but also because there were strong forces in Islam that emphasized the spiritual purity and power of the simple life Muhammad led in founding the religion. This deep respect for the past also influenced the arts; earlier artistic forms that hearkened back to pre-Islamic Arab ways of life were not abandoned but continued to flourish alongside more sophisticated forms, just as the newly conquered foreign forms were usually adopted by transforming them into more traditional Arab styles.[5] Its multiple cultural importations and the syncretic way they coexisted with earlier Arab traditions has made Islamic culture deeply multicultural and richly diverse with ambiguities and contrasts, epitomized by Allah himself, who is at once most "merciful" yet keen to "smite" and "cast terror into . . . those who disbelieve" (Q 8:12). Diversity, ambiguity, and contrasts likewise shape Islamic views of lovemaking, which build on Greco-Roman, Persian, and especially Indian erotic traditions.

Besides the variety deriving from the different cultures it absorbed through conquest, Islam generated further diversity through the openness of its key religious texts and their diverse interpretations. While the Quran provides a foundational text of remarkable range and poetic passion, it is often short on the precise particulars of proper Islamic behavior, particularly when compared with the often tediously detailed lists of duties and prohibitions we find in Deuteronomy. To complement the Quran's word of God, Islam has the *sunnah*, which describes Muhammad's exemplary views and practices. As God's definitive and last messenger, Muhammad not only knows Allah best but also represents the peak of human perfection, thus earning the description "the perfect man" ("*Al-Insan al-Kamil*") and the role

[5] Although the conquering Muslims appreciated Byzantine and Persian music, "the Arabic language was used not only for the texts of songs but also for the names of musical instruments and for other music terminology." For discussion of this point with respect to music, song, and poetry, see H. H. Touma, *The Music of the Arabs* (New York: Amadeus, 1996), 12–16.

of authoritative model for correct Islamic conduct and belief.[6] The *sunnah*'s corpus of reports on Muhammad's sayings and actions is known as *hadith*, and each item of *hadith* includes both the content of the report and the genealogy of its transmission. Different forms of Islam embrace different collections of *hadith* as more authentic or authoritative, thus multiplying the diversity of Islamic doctrine.[7] Finally, because the Quran and *hadith* are not sufficient (even taken together) to determine many precise points of proper Islamic behavior (including erotic behavior), there is a large body of religious case law (*fiqh*) that is based on interpreting the Quran and *hadith* to arrive at explicit rules of conduct not articulated in those two more authoritative sources. These legal judgments (that depend not merely on different interpretive contexts and interpreting minds but also on different bodies of *hadith*) also show considerable diversity, even with respect to the very same practice. Moreover, their characterization of an action includes five different levels of acceptance or disagreement, beginning with obligation as the highest affirmation and progressively descending into mere recommendation, permissibility, recommendation against, and finally absolute prohibition.[8]

One example of Islamic diversity of judgment concerns the notion of *nika mut'ah*, or temporary marriage. The Shia tradition largely permits it, but Sunni *hadith* firmly prohibits it, while acknowledging that Muhammad first allowed it before he forbade it. This marital form permits a man and woman to engage in sexual intercourse for a specified time but without a proper marriage and the ordinary duties marriage imposes, while nonetheless avoiding the prohibition against sex outside the institution of marriage. *Nika mut'ah* requires that the bride not already be married (which would constitute adultery), that she agree to the marriage and its contractual duration,

[6] The explicit articulation of this concept derives from Ibn al-Arabi in his *Fusus al-Hikam*, but the idea was already implicit in prior Sufi thinkers and more generally in Islamic tradition.

[7] The Shiites have four *hadith* collections they regard as canonical, while the Sunnis have six authoritative collections. One of these includes the *hadith* of Muhammad's dialog with the angel Gabriel that articulates the five pillars of Islam (affirmation of Allah as sole God and Muhammad as his prophet, prayer, paying religious tithes, fasting during Ramadan, and pilgrimage to Mecca) and the six pillars of faith (belief in God, his angels, the holy books, God's messengers or prophets, the Day of Judgment, and God's determination of all things).

[8] These "five values" الأحكام الخمسة (*al-ahkam al-khamsah*), which define an action's or object's moral status, are: *fard* (obligatory), *mustahabb* (recommended), *halal* or *mubah* (allowed), *makruh* (disliked), and *haram* (forbidden). They are not explicitly formulated in the Quran but developed gradually, reaching clear articulation by the beginning of the eleventh century. For more details on this notion and its complex history, see Kemal Faruki, "*Al-Ahkam Al-Khamsah*: The Five Values," *Islamic Studies* 5, no. 1 (1966): 43–98.

and that she be paid some minimal gift to seal the marital agreement, rendering the relationship a marriage of sorts, even though she does not have the rights and status of a normal wife. The Arabic word *mut'ah* means enjoyment or pleasure, and we can trace the nature of this marital concept to the Quran's prohibition of fornication and adultery along with its insistence that marriage obliged the man to give the woman some form of material compensation or gift for the pleasures she gives him. Consider Quran 4:24:

> And [also prohibited to you are all] married women except those your right hands possess. [This is] the decree of Allah upon you. And lawful to you are [all others] beyond these, [provided] that you seek them [in marriage] with [gifts from] your property, desiring chastity, not unlawful sexual intercourse. So for whatever you enjoy [of marriage] from them, give them their due compensation as an obligation. And there is no blame upon you for what you mutually agree to beyond the obligation.

A man's payment for pleasure is not enough to constitute the *mut'ah* idea of temporary marriage, even if we combine it with Quranic approval of polygyny and acceptance of divorce (which implicitly recognizes that marriage can be temporary). For the *mut'ah* marriage is *intentionally* and *explicitly* temporary, overtly designed for mere transitory pleasure rather than for the sake of offspring or other lasting marital benefits such as devoted companionship or family ties. Genealogically, *mut'ah* emerged from a particular historical context in Islam: it was Muhammad's solution to a short-term problem of his fighting men who had left their wives and concubines at home and were not permitted sexual pleasure with other women since fornication constitutes an absolute prohibition. The authoritative *Sahih Muslim hadith* relates Abdullah's report: "We were on an expedition with Allah's Messenger, and we had no women with us. We said: Should we not have ourselves castrated? He (the holy prophet) forbade us to do so. He then granted us permission that we should contract temporary marriage for a stipulated period, giving her a garment." A later excerpt from the same *hadith* reports that these soldiers "contracted temporary marriage giving a handful of dates or flour as a dower during the lifetime of Allah's Messenger and during the time of Abu Bakr until Umar forbade it," while further passages affirm that Muhammad himself later (after the victory at Khaibar, 629) claimed that Allah had now "prohibited [it] for ever."[9]

[9] Imam Muslim, *Sahih Muslim*, trans. Abd-al-Hamid Siddiqui, www.biharanjuman.org/hadith/Sahih-Muslim-english-translation.pdf. See Book 8: The Book of Marriage, *hadith* 3243, 3249, 3255, 3265.

The largest branch of Shia Islam, the Twelver sect (so called because they regard the twelve Shia Imams as successors to Muhammad's religious authority), permits *mut'ah* while insisting that the bride must be Muslim or belong to the Jewish people ("People of the Book") and must not be either a virgin or sexually promiscuous. This permission does not mean the practice is recommended but only that it is tolerated. Moreover, other Shia branches (notably the oldest Zaidi sect) reject *mut'ah*'s validity by relying on *hadith* in which Ali reports Muhammad's ultimate prohibition of it. Indeed, even some Twelver *hadith* pronouncements (from at least one imam) suggest that *mut'ah* should be forbidden. Sunni doctrine displays similar complexity by permitting a marital bond (the *nika al-misyar*, or traveler's marriage) that closely resembles the *mut'ah* by not requiring the husband to provide housing and continued maintenance or inheritance for the wife, but differs merely in not restricting the marriage to a precisely limited duration. As divorce is always readily available, however, *misyar*'s critics argue that it can be tantamount to *mut'ah* marriage.

Given such variance of scriptural sources and doctrines, the clerics and scholars who serve as arbiters of *sharia* (Islamic law) have offered a wide range of rulings (*fatwa*) on marital and other sexual matters. Both Sunni and Shia sects include multiple schools of Islamic jurisprudence (*fiqh*) that differently interpret *sharia*, producing variant judgments, even within a given school. This provides a very complex and often conflicting background of religious opinions through which Islamic erotic theory had to develop. Heightening this composite diversity is Islam's adoption of not only elements from Judaism and Christianity, whose prophets and narratives are invoked and adapted in the Quran, but also elements from Roman and Persian cultures. Long before Islam conquered the empires shaped by those cultures, Muhammad, when considering whether sex with a breastfeeding woman was permitted, reasoned as follows: "I was thinking of forbidding intercourse with a breastfeeding woman, until it occurred to me that the Romans and Persians do that and it does not harm their children" (*Sahih Muslim*, Book of Marriage, chapter 24, 3564).

II THE POWER AND PLEASURE OF SEX

Evident in the very notion of *mut'ah* stands Islam's unwavering recognition of sexual desire as an irrepressibly natural, powerful, positive drive, and of sexual satisfaction as an overwhelming God-given delight that is valuable in itself rather than merely a means to promote health, friendship, or family ties and progeny. When properly conducted within the strongly recommended institution of marriage, sexual activity constitutes a cardinal Islamic duty. The Quran commands "marry the unmarried among you and the righteous among your male slaves and female slaves. If they should be poor, Allah will enrich them from His bounty" (Q 24:32). Though forbidden during menstruation, sex is otherwise ordained by Allah. "Your women are a tilth for you (to cultivate) so go to your tilth as ye will" (2:222–223). Even during the holy nights of Ramadan, the Quran affirms the good of sexual pleasure: "It is made lawful for you, during the nights of fasting, to have carnal relations with your wives. They are your garments and you are their garments" (Q 2:187).

Not merely a pleasure and right, sex is marital obligation. Even a husband's religious-inspired oath of chastity cannot completely dissolve his carnal obligation to his wife; an abstention maximum of "four months is ordained" (Q 2:226). The wife's sexual duties are much stricter. As the Prophet explains: "If a woman spends the night forsaking her husband's bed, the Angels will curse her" and God "will be angry with her" (Q 20:3538, 3540). A wife must respect her husband's rights to have up to four wives and limitless concubines and must not jealously seek his promise to eschew other women, except the wives of other men, with whom sexual contact is strictly forbidden and punishable by death. The Quran even chides Muhammad himself for promising to eschew the pleasures of sex with a permissible woman of his choice in order to please some of his wives who were jealous of his interest in other women. "O Prophet, why do you prohibit [yourself from] what Allah has made lawful for you, seeking the approval of your wives?" (Q 66:1). Finally, the Quran suggests the divine quality of erotic pleasure by making it central to the heavenly rewards of Paradise, where one "reclines with bashful virgins whom neither man nor jinee will have touched before, . . . virgins chaste and fair, dark-eyed virgins sheltered in their tents" (Q 55.54–76).

Islamic tradition, or *sunnah*, emphasizes the importance of sexual activity through Muhammad's exemplary conduct, teachings, and judgments as recorded in the numerous books of *hadith* that present the Prophet as the model of right thought and action. In stark contrast to celibate prophets like Jesus or Jeremiah, Muhammad enjoyed a very full sexual life. Sources suggest his having around ten wives and at least four beautiful concubines, acquired as sexual slaves either through battle or as gifts. Some reports admiringly testify that he would visit all his wives "in one night" because his virile potency matched the "strength of thirty (men)."[10] This reputation for erotic prowess led Muhammad's followers to seek his authoritative answers on a wide variety of sexual matters ranging from premature ejaculation, castration, and coitus interruptus to the proper ways to cleanse and groom oneself before and after sex, the proper words to say when making love, and the permissibility of different lovemaking postures. The Prophet's robust sexuality thus demonstrated while it further reinforced the crucial importance of erotic pleasure in Islamic religion and culture.

Many Islamic books, therefore, focused on erotic theory and practice. Already by the end of the tenth century, the *Fihrist* (a comprehensive bibliographical catalog of Arabic books) lists "about a hundred treatises [on erotology], almost all of which have been lost," including a book with illustrated sexual positions and instructions, allegedly based on the special expertise of a Hindu woman who had married 1,000 men.[11] Erotological writing continued to flourish for centuries thereafter, culminating in the fifteenth century's famous *Perfumed Garden*, after which the genre fell into decline. The vast majority of these erotic texts have not survived; those that did have only rarely been published, while even fewer have been translated. The books treat an extensive range of topics: the causes, sufferings, signs, and joys of erotic love; medical, physiological, and pharmacological aspects of sex; erotic instructions to newlyweds; advice to older men on how to arouse desire and regain their youthful sexual skills; counsel on how to select the best sexual slave girls and how to successfully achieve and conceal illicit erotic relations; and the uses of pederasty, lesbians, nymphomaniacs, and even hermaphrodites. Some texts have a limited focus of topics (such as the comparative value of sex with boys and concubines), while others are more general or encyclopedic; some are chaste and earnest in tone, while others salacious and playfully humorous.

The primary sources for my study here are three premodern erotic texts that have found English translation and, toward the end of the chapter, the more philosophical writings on love by the great Ibn Sina and the key Sufi theorists al-Ghazali and al-Arabi. *The Ring of the Dove* (*Ṭawq al-Ḥamāmah*), written by the Andalusian theologian and legal scholar Ibn Hazm in 1022, exemplifies the idealistic, critically chaste, and earnest attitude to love.[12]

[10] Muhammad al-Bukhari, *Sahih Bukhari*, trans. Muhammad Muhsin Khan (Riyadh: Darussalam, 1997), vol. 1, 5:268, 270; vol. 7, 62:142.

[11] Abdelwahab Bouhdiba, *Sexuality in Islam*, trans. Alan Sheridan (London: Routledge, 1974), 142; hereafter SI.

[12] Ibn Hazm, *The Ring of the Dove*, trans. A. J. Arberry (London: Luzac Oriental, 1994), hereafter RD.

The Perfumed Garden of Sensual Delight (*Al-rawḍ al-ʿāṭir fī nuzhat al-ḫāṭir*), written in Tunis between 1410 and 1434 by Muhammad ibn Muhammad al-Nafzawi, is an earthier text focused on sexual matters, mixing serious advice (concerning what promotes erotic attraction, success, and potency) with humorous bawdy stories and verse that exemplify such counsel.[13] The *Encyclopedia of Pleasure* (*Jawami' al-ladhdha*), attributed to an Ali ibn Nasr al-Katib (whose precise identity remains unknown) and allegedly composed around 1000, is indeed encyclopedic in its scope of topics, citations, and influences, which include Greek, Roman, Persian, and especially Indian sources along with those of classical Arab culture.[14] In its chapter on the value of coition, for example, it cites Galen along with Muhammad, insisting that the benefits of sex go far beyond sensory pleasure, reproductive use, and obedience to God. Among its physical and psychological values, "sexual union ... cures melancholia ... and increases vigor immensely." Moreover, "it quietens anger" and can "cure a lover of his passion even though he practices it with a person other than his beloved." A further "value of sexual union is that it enlarges the ejaculatory ducts, which ... helps [the seminal fluid] to flow out," while retention of too much seminal fluid is unhealthy, resulting in "phlegmatic diseases" as well as "gloom, insanity, giddiness, and hysteria which women suffer from through lack of coition" (EP 50–51).

Through its comprehensive character, the *Encyclopedia of Pleasure* displays the significant divergence of erotic views found in Islamic cultures.[15] For example, the Quran clearly condemns homosexual intercourse as an unnatural abomination for which Lot's city of Sodom was punished as "a people transgressing beyond bounds." "For ye practice your lusts on men in preference to women," choosing in contrast to "all the creatures in the world" the males rather than the females "whom Allah has created for you

[13] This text was made popular through the famous 1886 English translation by Richard Burton, who translated from a French translation. As Burton's translation has been strongly criticized for inaccuracies and spurious additions, I therefore cite from a more recent translation directly from the Arabic: Umar ibn Muḥammad al-Nafzawi, *The Perfumed Garden*, trans. Jim Colville (London: Kegan Paul International, 1999), hereafter PG.

[14] The book is edited by Salah Addin Khawwam and translated into English as *The Encyclopedia of Pleasure*, trans. Adnan Jarkas and Salah Addin Khawwam (Toronto: Aleppo, 1977), hereafter EP. Its ancient authenticity has been mildly questioned by Bouhdiba (SI 142); but even if it is a later compilation, its views seem representative. In his introduction to the book, Khawwam cites various medieval texts in noting how the Arabs were "specially well read in Indian erotic books" (EP 34), and the *Encyclopedia* frequently prefaces its points of erotic instruction with the phrase "the Indian said" (e.g., EP 202, 216, 251, 253, 256, 268, 370).

[15] These conflicting attitudes stem not merely from ambiguities in Islam's religious texts but often instead from the divergent sociocultural conditions of the different periods and societies in which Muslim erotic theorists composed their work.

to be your mates" (Q 7:81; 26:165–166). Nonetheless, we find ardent defenses of pederasty compiled in the *Encyclopedia of Pleasure*, some of which echo Greek arguments for the love of boys. Even the Quran hints at the possible pleasures of such love by including the company of beautiful boys, along with dark-eyed virgins, among the rewards of Paradise. The Quranic prohibition of adultery – defined more narrowly by Islam's polygynous patriarchy as intercourse with another man's wife – still allows the exception of sleeping with captive wives taken in war. Islam strictly forbids castration (except as punishment), yet eunuchs formed an essential part of harem life, so they had to be recruited from non-Islamic peoples. The various kinds of eunuchs and their uses, virtues, and dangers were topics of erotological theory. Eunuchs differed in their sexual capacity and desire. Some were apparently capable of intercourse (if they were castrated after puberty), and theorists occasionally argued that women especially liked having sex with them because their reproductive impotence and less virile nature made the women feel safer and thus freer to give themselves up to full enjoyment in all sorts of sexual acts and positions (EP 10–11). If fornication was strictly outlawed by the Quran, this did not prevent the practice of prostitution and the existence of brothels, concubines, and the sexual use of slave girls.

At a more rarified level of debate, despite Islam's repeated affirmation of sex as a sanctified pleasure, we find one group of theorists (associated with the Hanbali school of law and moral theology) who critically cautioned against erotic love because of its passion-driven excesses and its distraction from the single-minded love of God. However, the vast majority of Islamic theorists concur in celebrating sexual pleasure, even if they often differ as to what best provided it. Despite the Quran's ardent affirmation of marriage's sexual dimension and Muhammad's apparent preference for wives over concubines, Islamic writings on lovemaking typically recognize that sexual servants are better than wives in providing erotic pleasure, partly because they have more relevant training, including mastery of aesthetic as well as specifically sexual arts. Tensions also existed about the ideal male lover: Was he the sophisticated, wealthy, urbanite playboy who enjoys many women in an elegantly skillful and tasteful manner but without commitment or, instead, the humble, desert nomad lover with a far more overwhelming passion for his single, true beloved?

Besides such debates over the comparative value of wives versus bondmaids, and cultured city playboys versus manly, horny nomads who love with fiercely single-minded devotion, the pluralistic tent of Islam contains many other issues of rival erotic claims. For example, is anal sex (with males or females) more pleasurable than vaginal sex; is the love of boys superior to that of women; are bearded (i.e., mature) males erotically better than boys too young to have facial hair; do young men or middle-aged men give women greater erotic pleasure; does sexual consummation diminish or increase the lover's passion; what physical features make a woman most sexually attractive?

III POWER, VIOLENCE, AND MALE SUPREMACY

Beneath the diversity of opinion, some distinctive themes emerge in Islamic erotology. We find, for example, a proclivity for forcefulness and violence. As Islam grew and flourished through the conquest and subjugation of other peoples, so its distinctively fighting spirit seems to find erotic expression. The Quran highlights the violent power of sexual desire through its expanded, transformative retelling of the biblical story of Joseph and Zuleika, the wife of the Hebrew's Egyptian master, Potiphar (Q 12:21–52). When Zuleika tries to seduce Joseph and grabs his garment while he is fleeing her, the Quran (unlike the Bible) more violently characterizes this as ripping it. The Quran narrative moreover enlarges the seduction story, adding an episode where Zuleika invites other women to witness Joseph's beauty in order to understand her adulterous passion. Immediately enflamed by a fierce desire for him, the women cut their own hands in order to curb their craving to hold him in their arms (Q 12:31–32). This erotically inspired self-stabbing provoked by passion for a young man not only provides authoritative proof of the violently unreasonable power of female lust. It also suggests, through obvious metaphorical transference, the reciprocal justification of male violence in sexually penetrating women, a genital stabbing that can sometimes draw real blood but that women nonetheless fiercely desire. Prevented from receiving the love stabs these women desire from Joseph, they stab themselves instead.[16]

The metaphor of penile penetration as knife-like stabbing finds frequent expression in Islamic erotic texts, even beyond the vaginal focus. "Lubricate my anus and pierce it with your lance-like penis," pleads one woman, "thrust

[16] The deep link between adulterous desire and extreme violence, particularly against women, finds powerful literary expression in the introductory, framing story of the Arab classic *A Thousand and One Nights*. It tells of how two brother kings discover their wives' adultery and then have them killed, with the senior brother king vowing that "whatever wife he married, he would abate her maidenhead at night and slay her next morning to make sure of his honor. 'For,' said he, 'there never was nor is there one chaste woman upon the face of the earth.'" See Richard Burton, trans., *The Arabian Nights: Tales from a Thousand and One Nights* (New York: Modern Library, 2004), 16.

into my anus a penis as sharp as sword" (EP 243). Even when being "kind to women," "at the time of sexual union men should be forceful" (EP 233). Women also contribute to the violence of erotic engagement. Their eyes work "like shining daggers," and when woman and man sexually "connect, they lock together in a wild, savage struggle," driving "relentlessly toward the single climax of desire. The man will rock and the woman roll until their passion is spent" (PG 3).

While affirming woman's submission to man's forceful rule and lovemaking, Islam also asserts man's submission to God as a cardinal virtue. Indeed, the word "Islam" derives from the Arabic root "*aslama*" meaning "he gave up, surrendered or submitted"; a Muslim is "one who submits" and becomes "a slave of God" (*abd Allah*).[17] Male dominance, the Quran asserts, derives from God's. "Men have authority over women because God has made the one superior to the other and because they spend their wealth to maintain them. Good women are obedient," but with those who show "disobedience, admonish them, forsake them in beds apart, and beat them" (Q 4:34). Muhammad's favorite wife Aisha affirmed that: "For women, marriage is a sort of slavery," so that choosing a husband for one's daughter was tantamount to choosing "the right master" (EP 133). Woman's erotic nature, however, presents a threat to male dominance, particularly because Islam's erotology regards female sexual desire and capacities as far greater than man's, sometimes echoing the Greek idea that woman's "excessive lust" is ten times stronger than man's. "The least lustful woman is more lustful than the most lustful man," and "a woman can exhaust the lust of a group of men, but a group of men cannot exhaust the lust of a woman" (EP 219). Arab accounts of woman's uncontrollable lust are rife both in fiction and in erotological theory; these reports cover not only adultery and fornication but also bestiality, including sex with a husband's donkey.[18] Men of all cultures suffer from anxiety about sexually satisfying their women so as to keep them faithful. But because a Muslim husband has more than one woman to satisfy (up to four wives and an unlimited number of concubines and slave girls), he faces more demanding sexual challenges and consequent worries. The reaction to this anxiety is an erotics of fierce power and

[17] Vincent Cornell, "Fruit of the Tree of Knowledge: The Relationship between Faith and Practice in Islam," in *The Oxford History of Islam*, ed. John L. Esposito (New York: Oxford University Press, 1999), 67.

[18] See, for example, the opening narrative noted above in *The Arabian Nights: Tales from a Thousand and One Nights*. *The Perfumed Garden* opens with tales of fornication and adultery, and later includes (in its chapter on "Women's Tricks") the story of a wife's bestial betrayal with her husband's donkey.

domination, expressed through the vigorous force, size, and firmness of the penis – the body part that distinguishes man from woman and thus should define his superiority. Islam erotology abounds in penile panegyrics.

"The penis," argues the *Encyclopedia of Pleasure*, "possesses all the strength of the body because the former is the source of man's dispositions and because God made it equal in importance to the fruit of a tree," which is the tree's best part. Because the penis holds the "substance of life" God gave it "a protective foreskin" but then ordered its removal "for the purpose of easy use and cleanliness." Because "the penis is equal to the pen and tongue, the two means of expression and utterance, it should be equally honorable and respectable." Moreover, if men's "superiority is due to the penis since it is their distinctive organ," then it must be superior in value since "anything that is a cause of superiority is necessarily superior" (EP 59–60). "The penis is the woman's god whom she idolizes and fears," and the kind of penis they love is "hot," "big and stiff" (like a "tree" or a "whale"), "smooth and prepared for fighting" so that it quickly "springs up in erection," and is so "full of wrath" and energetic power that it "remains erect after thirteen successive sexual unions" (EP 60–63). Men too prefer this kind of penis, not only because it makes them better loved by women and admired by men, but also because they like to enjoy it in their passive sexual adventures of being penetrated.

The Perfumed Garden likewise praises the male member as essential to what defines the superior man. "The man of quality has a large, hard and vigorous penis, quick to rise in the ache of its desire and slow to spend its passion. For intercourse, a woman enjoys a man who gives and takes his pleasure slowly, with gentle breast and heavy haunches, a man of size whose penis reaches deep within her vagina, to stretch her and to fill her, a man who is slow to come and quick to arousal again" (PG 6). Other criteria of quality come later: being "purposeful and serious, clean and well-groomed, of good build and handsome appearance, . . . always speak[ing] the truth, be[ing] courageous and generous, with a noble spirit and gentle heart" (PG 10). In contrast, "The kind of man who is repulsive to women is of shabby appearance, ugly to look at and has a small, limp and weedy penis" (PG 31). The love-creating power of the penis is such that women will "overlook all the faults of the man provided that he has a big and a strong penis" (EP 247).

Given this insistence on superior male size and power, one might expect attractive females to be petite, including their sexual parts. However, the Islamic erotics of powerful size extends also to female features: "The woman of quality has a full and voluptuous figure, . . . broad shoulders and chest with large, firm breasts and a deep cleavage, a neat waist and curved belly with a wide, deep navel, a generous vulva, ... broad hips, firm, ample buttocks" (PG 18). In particular the vulva should be prominently visible: "When she sits, her vulva pouts like a little cupola; lying down, it flutters like a flag does in a gentle breeze and when she stands, it stands majestic like a scepter" (PG 18). While ideals of female beauty have, of course, varied among the different periods and cultures of Islam, "two features however remain permanent: a firm, well-rounded behind and a large, but well-proportioned and clearly visible vagina" (SI 141).

This intense erotic desire for genital visibility is coupled with Islam's contrasting moral demand to conceal the female body. Urging women to "draw their veils over their bosoms, and not to reveal their adornment save to their own husbands" or some other close relatives or their slaves, Islam even insists that they not "stamp their feet," as this could arouse the erotic jingle of their ankle bracelets, evoking in a man's imagination the seductive pleasures of their lovely legs and feet (Q 24:31). The veil, however, has a paradoxical erotic effect. Although meant to hinder erotic desire by concealing a woman's attractions, it conversely magnifies their imagined appeal by the very act of concealing them, teasing the viewer by partially revealing what it conceals (the shape of their veiled bosoms, the eyes peering out behind the veiled face). It moreover conceals skin blemishes and unattractive facial features that diminish or stifle erotic appeal. To certain tastes that appreciate mystery, veils can be especially erotic, providing another element to address and undress in the game of seduction.

IV LANGUAGE AND CULTURE

Not merely a penetrating instrument of physical dominance (likened to a knife or sword, EP 243), the penis also symbolizes man's cultural superiority by being equated with the tongue and pen (EP 60). All three are objects that a man can manipulate to leave a mark of wetness, to put in an orifice, and to express desire or love. Tongue and pen express such longing in words while the penis does so in gesture, but all three involve skillful and controlled movement whose mastery demands cultural training and reflects one's personal style and taste. As a pederast metaphorically expressed his anal preference, "I have a pen that will not write on one side of a sheet of paper, but will write well on its other side" (EP 162). If man's linguistic expression with tongue and pen seems very much under his control, the expression of the penis is far from fully voluntary. In stressing size and force, Arab erotology is deeply concerned with priapic power while troubled by erectile dysfunction. If Al Nafzawi's *Perfumed Garden* celebrates its heroes' phallic potency while prescribing the foods that sustain it, then other texts show aging poets elegizing the death of their penile power. Consider Nafzawi's triumphant lines:

For thirty days and thirty nights
Stood Abu'l Hayloukh's cock upright,
He sustained himself on meat and onions
– What a credit was he to his companions!
In a long, hard night of fornication
Abu'l Hayja performed the defloration
Of eighty virgins – on a diet of chick-peas
With camel's milk and the honey of bees!
To fifty nights and then one score
Of non-stop fucking, Maymoun swore
And all this time, so it's been said,
He munched on egg yolks and brown bread!

Compare that with the sad lines of the ninth-century's Rashid Ibn Ishaq, mourning the lost vigor of his member:

It hangs over the testes
Neither moved by toying nor by fondling . . .
Sleep, a disease with no remedy, has overcome it.
And overcome, it cannot be awakened by any trick whatsoever
Touched by a beautiful lady, it looks like
The wet leather belt hanging from the neck of a jug.

(EP 63–64)

Not only does the penis share with tongue and pen the realm of cultural shaping and communication (note circumcision as recommended practice), it also needs those linguistic instruments to achieve the fullest and highest expression of love. If sex is crucial for Islam, language is even more so, and indeed crucial for Muslim eroticism. The Quran declares itself as the sacred word of God revealed to Muhammad so that it could be ritually recited and transcribed, and the very quality of its language allegedly indicates its truth and its divine origin (Q 10:37, 7:203). According to *hadith*, the Prophet's first Quranic revelation was Surah (chapter) 96: "Recite in the name of the Lord . . . , who taught by the pen, taught man that which he knew not" (Q 96:1–2). Surah 68, named "The Pen," insists that "the pen" of sacred writing vindicates Muhammad's vision as divine rather than mad. Writing understandably became "the most important theme to run through all Islamic art," not only in literature but even in the visual arts, where "the only one that was widely appreciated ... was calligraphy, the art of beautiful writing."[19]

Names, as paradigmatic elements of language, hold a very prominent place in Islam, including their role in celebrating God. Each Surah of the Quran begins with "In the name of Allah, the beneficent, the merciful." Describing Allah as "the Creator, the Inventor, the Fashioner," the Quran further insists that "to Him belong the best names" (Q 59:24), while *hadith* then claims, "There are ninety-nine names of Allah; [and] he who commits them to memory would get into Paradise" (*Sahih Muslim* 35:6475). More generally, a logic of multiple names can serve not only for praising but also for better understanding something, each name providing an instructive description of some valued feature of what is named. This logic could explain the peculiar emphasis on specifying the many names given to the genitals and the sexual act in Islamic *ars erotica*. The *Encyclopedia of Pleasure*'s first two chapters are entitled "On the Sundry Names Given to Coition" and "On the Advantages of Coition and Its Values"; its fourth chapter, "On the Sundry Names Given to the Penis and the Vulva," is immediately followed by a chapter entitled "On Praising the Qualities of the Penis and the Vulva" and then another, "On the Anatomy of the Penis and Vulva." *The Perfumed Garden* instead devotes separate chapters (8 and 9) to "Names for the Penis" and "Names for the Vulva." Besides their functions of praising and describing, the multiple names poetically enrich the language of sex to make it more entertaining and seductive.

In bestowing aesthetic meaning and value to the sexual act, language helps distinguish human lovemaking from crude animal coupling. The *Encyclopedia* urges the lover to "use in the practice of sexual union with his beloved such ethics and fine speech as to distinguish him from animals in their rough and hasty sexual practice. It is in this way that man, beautifying and ennobling his acts, shows that he is a distinct being possessing the virtue of gallantry" (EP 43).[20] The Prophet Muhammad (in *Sahih Muslim*, Book on Marriage, 3533) recommends a particular verbal formula that invokes the name of Allah and that should be used when having intercourse to protect the couple (and their possible progeny) from harm by Satan. Beautiful speech, moreover, serves a number of erotic functions.

[19] Sheila Blair and Jonathan Bloom, "Art and Architecture: Themes and Variations," in *The Oxford History of Islam*, 216, 223.

[20] Socrates is then invoked to drive the point home, alleged to have claimed that "Coition without courtesy signifies rough behaviour" (EP 43).

First, it has a seductive power that works in complex, dialectical ways. After creating the initial contact and context of friendliness between a man and woman, speech, through its erotic suggestiveness, can arouse a woman's sexual feelings. It further allows those feelings to develop more freely during the conversation by including other semantic content and dialogical engagement that distracts the woman from anxieties about the sexual act, thus putting her at ease so that she does not resist the intensification of erotic feeling and its translation into sexual action. As the *Encyclopedia* explains, "conversation and humor, besides distinguishing a man from an animal, which is an honorable quality in itself, pave the way for courtesy and create friendliness and familiarity. Moreover, they have the more significant advantage of enabling a man to make his woman feel easy at the time of sexual union because she would otherwise concentrate on what he wants of her, which would make her embarrassed" (EP 258). Al-Nafazwi's *Perfumed Garden* highlights the erotic power of poetic language by giving it a key role in the book's principal narratives of seduction. The jokester-hero Bahloul recites some erotic verse to charm the married woman he seeks to bed, and this serves both "to relax" and to arouse her. "Your kind of talk would undo a saint. Your words are lethal," she tells him. "Some women get turned on by talk.... Talk turns me on and I've not been speaking to my husband" (PG 14, 15). Another womanizing hero in the book finally wins a reluctant beauty by answering her enigmatic verse refusal with a poetic response of his own, which (by demonstrating his linguistic skills and knowledge of her erotic needs) makes her "relax and unwind and stretch herself out" (PG 52). The book's paradigm of female perfection, Badr al Budour, delivers her verse in song, and "her singing brought the king to a state of high arousal" (PG 26), so that he vows to have her even though she is already married to the son of his father's vizier.

Second, once seduction is fully achieved, attractive speech prolongs the woman's feeling of ease and trust after coition, so that she will be more inclined for future erotic play: "conversation and kissing are particularly important when the sexual union is over because they are indicative of the lover's kindness, whereas silence, besides creating an embarrassing situation, would make the woman regret what she has done" (EP 258). The seductive and soothing use of language is not one-sided: "an experienced, wise woman knows how to please the man by sex play, interest him by her speech and, when she has satisfied him sexually, she puts him to sleep by singing him beautiful songs so that he may go to sleep with a heart full of joy" (EP 266). Third, between initial seduction and postcoital comforting, speech serves the act of coition itself by intensifying its qualities, hence "both ancient and modern people show an interest in conversation during the sexual act" (EP259). One key technique of intensification emphasized by Arab theorists is the use of "exciting, obscene words as give rise to strong sexual sensations and strong erection" (EP 259). Hence one poet declared, "In sexual union I like / Your exciting words and silent looks" (EP 265).[21]

Written literary expression has its distinctive erotic uses. Love letters are not only tools of seduction but offer their own expressive satisfaction, "a wonderful joy, that is a consoling substitute for an actual sight of the object of [one's] affection" (RD 71). As the receiver is flattered by its message and pleased by its beauty (which can include poetic and calligraphic grace), so the letter's author has the imaginative satisfaction that the beloved recipient will hold something that the author has already lovingly touched and "designed after the most elegant pattern" (RD 71). The letter thus serves as a mediated caress that both recipient and sender can enjoy, particularly if it is beautifully written.

For such reasons "an education in prose, poetry, and singing" along with "cleanliness and reading" comprise the three acquired "qualities which a woman particularly likes in men" that complement such "natural qualities" as handsomeness and intelligence (EP 264). However important all these qualities are, a man's coital expertise is claimed to trump them, while such mastery seems to involve a mix of natural talent and acquired skill.[22] As literary and artistic talents likewise enhance a woman's erotic power, concubines and slave girls typically outshone the wives because the former were trained and selected for pleasure and entertainment while wives were chosen for family or religious reasons.[23]

V A MULTISENSORY SEXUAL AESTHETIC

If "words said at the time of sexual union help towards a fuller sexual enjoyment," then lovemaking achieves "full sensual pleasure" only when it

[21] A poet thus wrote: "Four things have captivated me. / I do not know which of them had made me sexually excited: / Is it your face that my eyes enjoy or your saliva that my tongue tastes, / Or your words that my ears hear or your love that my heart holds?" (EP 265).

[22] "The fact is that no matter how pleasant, good-mannered and handsome a man may be, a woman will shun him if he is ignorant of the art of coition," but "a woman will love a man even if he does not possess any of the above-mentioned qualities provided that he is versed in the art of coition" (EP 264).

[23] Under the Ummayad and the Abbasid dynasties, "the value of a concubine increased with her beauty but also with her 'skill,' her good manners, her poetic gifts, her talent as a dancer or singer" (SI 107).

provides "the pleasures of the five senses" in an attractively "integrated" harmony. Here "the eye enjoys looking, the tongue enjoys sucking and the nose enjoys smelling. The ear, too should not be deprived of . . . enjoyment," including "hearing exciting words," while the "tongue tastes" with pleasure the lover's "saliva" if not also other body parts and secretions (EP 265). The vulva, for example, "tastes like a delicious pudding saturated with milk" (EP 89). Taste, in fact, serves as a key metaphor for sexual intercourse, which Islamic texts describe as *tasting* the "honey" or "sweetness" of one's lover. This is not simply because of the sweetness of sexual pleasure but perhaps because taste includes the sense of touch, as the tongue must touch what it tastes.[24]

Pleasures of erotic touch are elsewhere evident in feeling the smooth hardness of an aroused penis ("a hot outside and a stiff inside") or a woman's "soft cheeks [and] soft fingers," "her red lips . . . as soft as foam," or her "hot" fleshy vulva (EP 227, 147, 86, 192). The mouth that sucks goes beyond taste and touch by engaging the muscular contractions that relate to a sixth, inner sense, proprioception, which provides a further source of sensual pleasure. Given Islam's emphasis on priapic power, a man's hot, hard penis presents a pleasing object of touch not only for his lover but also for the man himself, while further providing him with interoceptive and proprioceptive pleasures of warm, firm potency from within, along with associated feelings of pride. Women, of course, may also enjoy their own interoceptive and proprioceptive pleasures of arousal, relating to inner warmth and wetness and muscular sensations, while both sexes enjoy the proprioceptive, kinaesthetic pleasures of their own bodily movements, along with the felt harmony of these movements with those of their lovers.

[24] In one *hadith*, "narrated Aisha, Ummul Mu'minin: The Apostle of Allah (peace be upon him) was asked about a man who divorced his wife three times, and she married another who entered upon her, but divorced her before having intercourse with her, whether she was lawful for the former husband. She said: The Prophet (peace be upon him) replied: She is not lawful for the first (husband) until she tastes the honey of the other husband and he tastes her honey" (*Sunan Abu Dawud*, 6:2302). In another *hadith* (*Sahih Muslim*, 8:3354) Aisha reported that a woman came to Muhammad asking to return to the husband who divorced her and leave her new husband who was sexually inadequate. Muhammad's reply was that she could not go back to her old husband until she had sex with her new husband. "I was married to Rifa'a but he divorced me, making my divorce irrevocable. Afterwards I married Abd al-Rahman b. al-Zubair, but all he possesses is like the fringe of a garment (i.e. he is sexually weak). Thereupon Allah's Messenger . . . smiled, and said: Do you wish to return to Rifa'a. (You) cannot (do it) until you have tasted his sweetness and he (Abd al-Rahman) has tasted your sweetness."

These varied multisensory pleasures, claims the *Encyclopedia*, are not simply sensory but distinctively aesthetic, deriving from "praiseworthy aesthetic qualities." If its twelfth chapter is titled "On the Praiseworthy Aesthetic Qualities of Women," the book earlier acknowledges those of men, praising "the aesthetic qualities of Joseph" who was "immensely beautiful" with "a well-developed figure and a beautiful, smiling face" (EP 78). Besides the conventional aesthetic pleasures of sight afforded by beautiful faces and bodies, Islamic erotic theory distinctively highlights those of attractive gait. A sexually alluring woman "should be graceful in movement" and have a "beautiful gait" or at least "an admirable gait" (EP 205, 207–208). A woman's gait moreover serves to indicate her erotic character, sexual status, or availability; twelve "womanly gaits" are thus distinguished (EP 200). Not only visually pleasing in itself, the beautiful gait suggests qualities of erotic movement in lovemaking that imaginatively enhances one's visual delight, and perhaps (through the mirror neurons linking visual and motor sensations) evokes even pleasurable proprioceptive feelings of kinaesthetic empathy with the movements of a graceful gait.

Among all the senses, vision seems to provide the most erotically potent allure, perhaps because the visual strongly suggests also tactile, haptic, and kinaesthetic qualities. Islamic erotology also emphasizes the enticing power of fragrance. Its aesthetic importance has strong religious roots, as the Prophet Muhammad profoundly prized and applied fragrance both for religious purposes and for visiting his wives. Perfume thus unites the sexual and the sacred. Muhammed's wife Aisha reported: "I used to put perfume on the Messenger of Allah and he would go around to all his wives, then enter [the sacred state of] Ihram in the morning with the smell of perfume coming from him."[25] Elsewhere she claimed: "I used to put perfume on the Messenger of Allah using the best perfume I could find, until I saw the perfume glistening on his head and in his beard, before he entered [the sacred state of] Ihram."[26] Another *hadith* reports the Prophet affirming: "It is a duty for the Muslims that they perform *ghusl* [full purifying ablutions] on Friday, and that each of them wear some of his family's perfume. If he does not find any, then water is a perfume for him."[27]

[25] Ahmad an-Nasa'i, *Sunan an-Nasa'i*, trans. Nasiruddin Al-Khattab (Riyadh: Darussalam, 2007), vol. 1, 4:431, http://ahadith.co.uk/chapter.php?cid=156&page=1&rows=100. Aisha also reports that Muhammad's preferred perfumes for personal use were "musk and amber," while other *hadith* report his view that "The best of perfume is musk." See *Sunan an-Nasa'i*, vol. 6, 48:5119; and vol. 3, 21:190; http://sunnah.com/nasai/48/77 and http://sunnah.com/nasai/21/88.

[26] *Sunan an-Nasa'i*, vol. 3, 24:2702.

[27] Muḥammad ibn Isa at-Tirmidhi, *Jami at-Tirmidhi*, trans. Abu Khaliyl (Riyadh: Darussalam, 2007), vol. 1, 4:528.

Islam's classical erotic texts affirm the importance of fragrance, underlining its aesthetic appeal and seductive sexual power. *The Perfumed Garden*'s first chapter asserts: "One of the stimulants to sexual desire is the use of perfume by both partners. When a woman detects the scent of perfume on a man, she relaxes and unwinds. A man might thus try perfume as a means to coupling with a woman" (PG 7). Even when there is no need for seduction, the use of perfume by both parties makes sexual play "more agreeable" (PG 34). The *Encyclopedia of Pleasure* likewise advises both men and women to perfume themselves for sexual purposes, while suggesting that erotic mastery includes a knowledge of fragrance. "A woman who wants to experience full sexual enjoyment should clean and bedizen herself . . . , wash her head, perfume herself, clean her teeth, chew a pleasant-smelling gum and darken her eyes with kohl, which helps to arouse sexual desire" (EP 269). It is therefore "preferable that a woman should know how to make perfumes and ornaments to beautify herself therewith" (EP 218). Similarly, a man "must look most beautiful in the presence of the woman and perfume himself as best he can and not behave ungentlemanly by trying to copulate with her when he first meets her . . . He should guard against starting coition with disheveled hair and an uncombed beard; instead, he should comb both his hair and beard and perfume his body and give her the chance for full sexual enjoyment" (EP 256). Besides the application of fragrance, we find mention of drugs "used to perfume the penis and the testes" and make the vulva "pleasant smelling and narrow" (EP 284). If "pleasant smelling" is key to the aesthetic pleasure of sex, then lovers "should take care of the parts of the body out of which bad odor is supposed to come, such as the mouth, the armpit, the genital organs and the like" (EP 256). One poet praises his lover as naturally fragrant, "Perfumed, you smell sweet, and unperfumed, you give out a pleasant smell, too" (EP 142). Fine odor has a prominent place among "aesthetic qualities" that experts "unanimously agree" on praising as beautiful in a woman's face and body, noting "four sweet smelling things, namely the nose, the mouth, the armpits and the vulva" (EP 205).

Though especially emphasized, attractive aroma forms part of the general demand for somaesthetic grooming. Not only should the woman's face, hair, and body be cleaned, but her "vulva should also be shaven, her hair curled and combed, her eyebrows trimmed and her face made up" to highlight its beauty (EP 269).[28] This demand for cleanliness and grooming to promote the cause of love and the pleasure of one's lover mirrors the general Islamic

[28] "An unshaven vulva weakens sexual desire, whereas a shaven vulva excites sexual desire and satisfies sex hunger" (EP 330).

demand for somatic purification (*tahara*) to express one's loving respect for God. "For Allah," the Quran insists, "loves those who turn to Him constantly, and He loves those who keep themselves pure and clean" (Q 2:222). Hence prayer is not valid unless proper purifying ablutions are performed to make the soma suitable to express one's worshipping love of God. After the impurity of sexual intercourse (but also after menstruation and noncoital semen discharge) preparation for prayer requires a full-body ritual ablution (*ghusl*) rather than the partial ritual ablution – of face, arms, feet, and part of the head – that is called *wudu*.

What somatic features make an individual sexually attractive? Islamic theorists focus mostly on particular body parts (eyes, eyebrows, nose, cheeks, mouth, lips, ears, breasts, arms, hands, fingers, legs, vulva, buttocks, and so on) and the qualities that make those individual parts especially appealing (redness and softness of lips, fleshiness of buttocks and vulva, etc.). There is, however, some recognition of more complex "comprehensive, aesthetic qualities" that emerge from the ways the particular body parts harmonize and work together in a person's wholeness of presence and behavioral expression. For example, "there are faces whose beauty, taken as a part, would not be pleasing [but] taken as a whole would be agreeable both to the heart and to the self." Although the precise cause of this emergent beauty is "still much of a mystery," it appears "only [with] a person whose spirit is beautiful." Thus, if "a man fails to find a woman of perfect [physical] qualities," he can still find full aesthetic and erotic happiness "with an agreeable woman of spiritual beauty," who though merely "moderately beautiful" in physical features "possesses spiritual beauty [and so] comes next" to the ideal female lover (EP 208). Such harmonizing spiritual beauty is itself an emergent quality from diverse qualities of character and action, such as being "obedient and honorable, . . . bashful, grave, mild, polite, thoughtful, energetic, clever at handwork, soft voiced and not talkative," modest, and respectful (EP 205).[29]

Before pursuing the spiritual dimension of Islamic eroticism, we should note another aspect of Islam's multisensory erotic somaesthetics. The transmodal integration of sensory pleasures provides the *Encyclopedia*'s author with an argument for the superiority of lovemaking. "People . . . are naturally inclined to enjoy that which suits the five senses, namely, hearing, seeing, smelling, tasting and touching" (EP 48). These senses, together with coition,

[29] "If you want to copulate with her, she will respond to your request and if you don't, she will not insist on it. She will respectfully precede you in standing up and will sit down only when you tell her to do so" (EP 205).

constitute "the six necessities of life," and "the loss of any of the six necessities of life . . . may be injurious to man, except for coition which is an addition from God to man's pleasure" (EP 48). None of the five more necessary senses "can be enjoyed in its integrity without awakening man to the sixth necessity which is coition," but coition, though necessary for reproduction and though engaging the other senses, is "not instrumental in giving rise to any of [those senses but merely] . . . serves to make a person . . . well-integrated and gives him ecstasy" (EP 48). Because lovemaking is not a means to the five senses, while they are means of arousing it, "we are obliged, by virtue of reason, to give it priority, in point of both work and pleasure" as the desired end of other sensory pleasures. However, in terms of religious work, coition is a divine means; it is how God "activates life and creates apostles to spread His teachings" while generating other "offspring" who serve and pray for their parents. Given its crucial roles as means and end, sex is too important to be left to mere natural impulse. Lovemaking should be cultivated and taught. Therefore, it "should also be the duty of scholars to initiate people into all that gives rise to it, strengthens it and increases it, not to mention God's commandment to practice it and the prophets' urging people to observe it" (EP 48).

VI EROTIC PLURALISM AND THE PHILOSOPHY OF LOVE

Complicating this duty of sexual instruction is the wide variety of erotic tastes and practices within Islamic cultures. Devoting entire chapters not only to heterosexual lovemaking, but also to pederasty and lesbianism, the *Encyclopedia* refuses to condemn any of these forms (along with masturbation) as unnatural perversions, instead claiming all four practices stem from natural "instincts" exhibited also by other animal species. "Homosexuality, for instance, can be observed among asses; heterosexuality is . . . practiced by cocks and birds; adultery and masturbation . . . by apes and bears; passive sodomy . . . by otters, and finally lesbianism . . . by both pigeons and female crocodiles" (EP 107).[30]

Sexual pluralism looms large even in Islam's religious thought. First, it affirms polygyny along with the sexual use of concubines and slaves. Moreover, in contrast to the Hebrews' narrow focus on procreation and its

[30] *The Perfumed Garden*, though a resolutely heterosexual work, includes two narratives involving lesbianism but none involving sex between males. *The Ring of the Dove*, which focuses on spiritual love, eschews detailed analysis of sexual practices, but does indeed discuss (with approbation) the idea of passionate love between men.

consequent prohibition against spilling seed, Islam accepts coitus interruptus (which *hadith* calls *azl*). Muhammad clearly condoned its practice by his companions though he did not recommend or favor it.[31] Furthermore, in contrast to an alleged Hebrew censure against mounting a woman from behind, *hadith* explicitly affirms that such variant coital postures are permitted, citing the Quranic verse that one's women are like one's field that one can go to as one wills (Q 2:223). One of the relevant *hadith* versions, however, specifies that the target of such backside approaches must remain only "one opening," namely, the vagina.[32] The *Encyclopedia of Pleasure* follows Indian erotology in enumerating a great many coital positions (EP 297–304). It lists five basic postures: with the woman lying on her back (including eight different varieties), lying on the side (three variants), sitting (two variants), standing (two variants), and finally "the rear position" (with sixteen different forms). All sixteen of these rear varieties, discussed with great gusto and detail, concern anal sex, a topic that receives far more attention and enthusiastic endorsement (for both hetero- and homosexual intercourse) in the *Encyclopedia* than it does in Chinese or Indian erotology. Some Islamic sexologists argued for privileging heterosexual lovemaking because women provide the advantages of both anal and vaginal sex. Each of these options affords its own sensory pleasures (visual, tactile, olfactory, gustatory, etc.) and respective benefits (the anus freeing lovers from problems of pregnancy and menstruation, while the vagina offering easier entry and the hope of offspring).

Islamic erotology recognizes a wide variety of aesthetic desires, tastes, and preferences. The fact that Muhammad preferred wives to concubines and favored virgins over nonvirgins did not prevent other Islamic thinkers from thinking that concubines and well-trained sex slaves provided far more aesthetic and sensual satisfaction. While some homosexual theorists prized only young, effeminate unbearded boys and disliked muscles and hair on the face and body (particularly when near the anus), others preferred older, hirsute boys for their manliness, as it made their conquest more exciting and empowering. Preferences also differed as to the ideal age of male and female lovers, some favoring the young while others the more mature. Islam's erotic pluralism extends even to the supernatural realm. Religious orthodoxy warns against the seductive dangers of intercourse with genies (*jinn*), but *The Ring of the Dove* recounts the sublime "joy supreme" of "phantom

[31] Neither is masturbation explicitly prohibited in the Quran, though Shia sects and some Sunni sects forbid it.

[32] *Sahih Muslim*, 8:3365.

intercourse" with the "nightly phantom" spirit of a distanced or departed beloved who mysteriously visits the lover in his sleep. This erotic encounter, claims Ibn Hazm, is a purely spiritual union that "does not corrupt love, as do carnal relations," and so for certain spiritual souls it is preferable to full encounters in the flesh. As he poetically put it:

I am too jealous, love, to let
My eyes alight upon thee yet,
And fear to hold thee overmuch
Lest thou be melted by my touch.

So by such caution moved, my sweet,
I suffer not that we should meet,
Intending rather that we keep
Our rendezvous, when I'm asleep.
For if I slumber, then my soul
Shall have thee only, have thee whole;
No body gross shall come between
Our spirits, subtle and unseen.

This spiritual unity
More sweet a thousand fold shall be,
More fine, more tender, and more fresh
Than the hot intercourse of flesh.
(RD 187–189)

Islamic culture's erotic theory accepts so much sexual diversity because it understands lovemaking as an expression of love while recognizing there are many different forms of love to express. If "there are as many degrees [and expressions] of passion as there are degrees [or kinds] of love," then this diversity depends not only on the "variety of causes" or generating foci of love but also on the differing characters and conditions of the lovers. With respect to such conditions, "a man who lives in abject poverty is too preoccupied with his poverty to be absorbed in passion" and devote sufficient resources for aesthetically refined erotic engagements. Similarly, "an important king" may be "too preoccupied by his kingdom's affairs" to devote his time and energy to intensive erotic pursuits (EP 110–111).

Islamic erotology distinguishes different types of love by their essential cause or object. The strongest and most lasting love, the *Encyclopedia* claims, is "generated by the [inner] self of the beloved" that we can identify with the soul. Here the person's body is "only a picture of the inside of the self" that serves as a "means by which the human self finds its counterpart" by being attracted to the body's external, "apparent beauty." But when two refined, noble selves learn to "know each other, they like each other and show no interest in the body," and as this "harmony is established" between their inner selves, a "psychological union takes place." Vulgar lovers, however, are interested in the "bodily form" as a means not for knowing the lover's inner self but for "indulging in mere animal desire" for the pleasures that body can give; and when the bodily picture grows less attractive (through aging or illness), such love is "mostly weakened." Moreover, this "sort of love, casual love, is weakened by too many sexual unions," because its bodily interest fades with excessive tasting (EP 110).[33]

Ibn Hazm likewise acknowledges the "varieties of Love," but his more refined spiritual sensibility refuses to grant such body-centered casual love the status of authentic love because it is based on "physical admiration and visual enchantment which does not go beyond mere external forms." Unless such sensuous fascination is redeemed by "a spiritual union in which the natural instincts share equally with the soul," we should "consider such love as merely a kind of lust," indeed "the very secret and meaning of carnal desire" (RD 56, 58). Strictly speaking, love is a matter of the soul, the divinely spiritual inner essence of the self. As Ibn Hazm explains it, drawing on Greek and Quranic metaphysics: "Love [is] a conjunction between scattered parts of souls that have become divided in this physical universe" and that strive to find comforting repose by regaining their "union" (RD 23). For as "Allah Himself says, 'It is He that created you of one soul, and fashioned thereof its spouse, that he might find repose in her'" (RD 24).

If love typically chooses "a beautiful form to light upon," this is because, "the soul itself being beautiful, it is affected by . . . beautiful things, and has a yearning for perfect symmetrical images." Although beautiful "physical forms have a wonderful faculty of drawing together the scattered parts of men's souls," if the soul's "affection goes no further than the form, [it] remains mere carnal desire" (RD 28). Neither physical beauty nor similarity of personality can be the real cause of true love, since many are in love with someone of "inferior" looks or of a very different personality, even if they know that another person is "superior" in beauty and more like them in character (RD 24). Hence, Ibn Hazm concludes, "true Love is a spiritual approbation, a fusion of souls," and although other forms of love can be

[33] This difference is used to explain why some loves are ruined by frequent sexual contact while other loves are not harmed but nourished by it.

caused by things "outside the soul," such love "passes away when the cause itself disappears" or weakens (RD 24, 26).[34]

Islam's most influential philosopher, Ibn Sina (980–1037), a Persian contemporary of the Andalusian Ibn Hazm and better known by his Latinized name Avicenna, articulates a somewhat similar view in his concise "Treatise on Love," whose theory enriches the erotic with a much deeper philosophical significance. Desiring love, he argues (like Plato), is not only a primal, pervasive ontological force but also a path for ennobling ethical improvement. As "every being which is determined by a design strives by nature toward its perfection," so all perfection, including beauty, is ultimately grounded in the "Pure Good" of God, who designed creation. Love, with its craving for beauty, is therefore "a natural desire" resulting from God's goodness and properly directed toward perfection. "It is part of the nature of beings endowed with reason to covet a beautiful sight"; humans therefore "invariably love what has beauty" not only with their rational soul but also with "the animal soul . . . by reason of its proximity to the former." Such love can bring "refinement and nobility" but only if "it results from a partnership" of the rational and animal. Mere "animal desire . . . deserves reproof," but "if a man . . . loves with an intellectual consideration, . . . then this is . . . an approximation to nobility and an increase in goodness. For he covets something whereby he will come nearer to the influence of That which is the First Source . . . and the Pure Object of love and [become] more similar to the exalted and noble beings." Ibn Sina then cites Muhammad's exhortation: "Seek ye satisfaction of your needs in those of beautiful countenance."[35]

[34] The different causes imply different kinds of love, and Ibn Hazm elaborates this variety. "The noblest sort of Love is that which exists between persons who love each other in God; either because of an identical zeal for the righteous work upon which they are engaged, or as the result of a harmony in sectarian belief and principles, or by virtue of a common possession of some noble knowledge. Next to this is the love which springs from kinship; then the love of familiarity and the sharing of identical aims; the love of comradeship and acquaintance; the love which is rooted in a benevolent regard for one's fellow; the love that results from coveting the loved one's worldly elevation; the love that is based upon a shared secret which both must conceal; love for the sake of getting enjoyment and satisfying desire; and passionate love, that has no other cause but that union of souls to which we have referred above. All these varieties of Love come to an end when their causes disappear, and increase or diminish with them; they are intensified according to the degree of their proximity, and grow languid as their causes draw further and further away. The only exception is the Love of true passion, which has the mastery of the soul: this is the love which passes not away save with death" (RD 25).

[35] Emil L. Fackenheim, trans., "A Treatise on Love by Ibn Sina," *Mediaeval Studies* 7 (1945): 208–228, quotations from 212, 219–221. Ibn Sina was surely familiar with those needs, as he was known for having "an insatiable sexual appetite" with a taste for "riotous" partying with wine and singing slave girls, according to his student and biographer al-Juzjani. See Jon McGinnis, *Avicenna* (Oxford: Oxford University Press, 2010), 22–23.

Three needs of action, Ibn Sina argues, "follow from the love of a beautiful human form: 1. the urge to embrace it; 2. the urge to kiss it and 3. the urge for conjugal union with it." The first two actions are "not in themselves blameworthy," because they serve the lovers' souls' desire "to come near to one another and to become united." Such soulful desire expresses "nobility and refinement, and this type of love is an ornament and a source of inner wealth." However "embracing and kissing" can lead to blameworthy actions by overwhelming the soul with an animal desire for coition that is "very hideous" when lacking "rational purpose" and respect for religious laws (regarding adultery, fornication, and homosexuality). It is therefore "only in the case of a man with either his wife or female slave" that coital forms of lovemaking "may find approval" and help bring the lover further on the path of self-perfection by contributing the "nobility and refinement" that the love of beauty can inspire.[36]

Accepting the erotic joy of kisses and embraces as valuable in themselves and not reducible to mere foreplay for coital pleasure provides a way of enjoying love's sensuous delights in relationships where genital contact is forbidden by religious law. A man who loves another man's wife (or erotically longs for another man or boy) is thus not condemned to either total physical repression or damnable depravity. Nor is he obliged to give up loving, which is anyway beyond his power because, as Ibn Hazm writes, "all hearts are in the hand of Him Who disposes and governs them – and He only is God" (RD 215). Instead, by confining himself to kisses and embraces outside the genital area, the man can find sensuous pleasure while respecting his beloved's reputation and his own moral dignity, even augmenting that dignity through the self-perfecting refinement and nobility that well-governed love inspires.[37] A woman could do the same. Aroused by beauty and further graced with the rational ability "to distinguish and to understand, [the lover] is capable of beautifying himself [or herself] with good manners" (EP 258). The categories of *adab* (politeness) and *zarf* (refined elegance) together formed "a comprehensive ideal of elegant, civilized conduct" that was highly prized by cultured

[36] Ibn Sina, quoted in Fackenheim, "A Treatise on Love," 221–222.

[37] As the *Encyclopedia* explains it, "a lover is free to enjoy her upper part, beginning with her navel upwards," but "the lower half is the possession of a husband and . . . a friend [or lover] has no right to touch it, [though he] has the right to kiss her, smell her and suck her" (EP 122). A ninth-century Persian philosopher, As-Sarakhsi, explains how "the soul seeks the beloved through the mouth, kissing and deriving through the nostrils the breath coming from the beloved." Because breath is identified with life and soul, this mixing of breath "suggests the union of the two souls." Cited in L. A. Giffen, *Theory of Profane Love among the Arabs* (New York: New York University Press, 1971), 7.

Islamic society and central to its theory of love.[38] While this may be enough to vindicate the virtues of *ars erotica*, some versions of Sufi Islam go further to suggest how lovemaking, in its authorized forms, provides a path not only to ethical refinement but also to spiritual perfection.

VII THE SUFI PATH OF SEXUAL SPIRITUALIZATION

Sufism emerged as a reaction to the increasing worldiness and impurities of the expanding Umayyad Caliphate (661–750), while also providing a countercurrent to the legalist rationalism that dominated Islamic religious thought. It instead highlighted the redemptive cognitive and spiritual values of emotive and imaginative perception. Sufism began as a poor and pious asceticism directed toward devoutly tenacious practices of prayer and Quaranic meditation. But a poor Iraqi servant girl, Rabiʿah al-ʿAdawiyah, transformed Sufism into a passionate mysticism of ardent love for Allah by the time she died in 801. After all, God's love and beauty are key Quranic themes. "Say, (O Muhammad, to mankind): If ye love Allah, follow me; Allah will love you" (Q 3:31), and "Allah will bring a people whom He loveth and who love Him, humble toward believers, stern toward disbelievers, striving in the way of Allah" (Q 5:54). As God has the most beautiful names (Q 20:8) and his Quran is of impeccable literary excellence (Q 17:88), so *hadith* confirms that "Allah is beautiful [and] He loves beauty."[39]

If love belongs to God's essence, it is also the driving and formative force that pervades his universe, as rationalist philosophers like Ibn Sina argued. All creatures love, but most of them love the lowly things that draw their appetites rather than the worthier objects of love that are spiritual, including the worthiest of all and the source of all existence, Allah himself. Humans are the best lovers of God because God created them in his image,[40] and they can best know and love God through the spiritual gifts and physical beauty he gave them, breathing the divine spirit into Adam, and creating humankind with "the fairest stature (Q 38:72, 95:4). Moreover, humans are most lovable because of these spiritual and physical gifts. The Sufi love of God is not simply in obeying his commandments and rituals but in striving to make oneself more beautiful and thereby closer to God by purifying oneself with supreme devotion and exceedingly pleasing works of worship. As Allah

[38] Giffen, *Theory of Profane Love*, 14.

[39] Yahya bin Sharaf an-Nawawi, *Riyad as-Salihin*, 1:612, http://sunnah.com/riyadussaliheen/1/612.

[40] "Allah created Adam in His picture," *Sahih al-Bukhari*, vol. 8, 74:246, https://sunnah.com/urn/58510.

revealed this path of divine love to his adoring and adored servant Muhammad: "My servant continues to draw near to Me with supererogatory works so that I shall love him. When I love him I am his hearing with which he hears, his seeing with which he sees, his hand with which he strikes and his foot with which he walks."[41] Through such extraordinary work of worship the mystic can come ever nearer to God until God's love is won and union is attained, so that God is present in all one's perceptions and actions.

Rabiʿah's love for God was an extremely intense devotion, expressed by indefatigable striving and remarkably dour asceticism. She refused all suitors, closed her shutters to avoid the distraction of beautiful flowers, and rejected even the pleasures of paradise. All she sought was an undisturbed, exclusive devotional focus on the incomparable beauty of God. "Every lover is alone with his beloved, and here I am alone with Thee," she prayed. "O God! If I worship Thee in fear of Hell, burn me in Hell; and if I worship Thee in hope of Paradise, exclude me from Paradise; but if I worship Thee for Thine own sake, withhold not Thine Everlasting Beauty."[42] Her appreciation of this beauty displayed a very austere aesthetic, bent more on ascetic striving than on pleasure and form. But, as I elsewhere argue, there is no essential contradiction between *askesis* and aesthetic value; indeed, one key meaning of the etymological root of *askesis* (the verb ἀσκέω) is "to decorate, adorn" or "form by art."[43] As the athlete's training *askesis* makes his body beautiful, so the rigorous training in abstaining from sensuous pleasures helps the mystic adorn the soul with the sinewy beauty of robust purity. This ascetic ideal of strenuous purity and exclusive devotion to God led many early Sufis to embrace celibacy, as the Persian Sufi saint al-Hujwiri preached and practiced, much like St. Paul and the early Christian advocates of celibate life.[44]

Celibacy, however, dramatically clashed with Islamic orthodoxy as expressed in the Quran and in the *sunnah*, contradicting Muhammad's

[41] From *Sahih al-Bukhari*, vol. 8, 76:509; available at https://sunnah.com/qudsi40.

[42] These Rabi'a quotations are taken, respectively, from Margaret Smith, *Rabi'a the Mystic and Her Fellow Saints in Islam* (Cambridge: Cambridge University Press, 1979), 22; and A. J. Arberry, *Sufism: An Account of the Mystics of Islam* (New York: Dover, 2002), 42–43.

[43] See Richard Shusterman, *Body Consciousness: A Philosophy of Mindfulness and Somaesthetics* (Cambridge: Cambridge University Press, 2008), 44–47; and H. G. Liddel and R. Scott, *An Intermediate Greek-English Lexicon* (Oxford: Oxford University Press, 1997), 124.

[44] "It is the unanimous opinion of the shaykhs of this sect that the best and most excellent of Sufis are the celibates, if their hearts are uncontaminated and . . . not inclined to sins and lusts." "Sufism was founded on celibacy," and "There is no flame of lust that cannot be extinguished by strenuous effort." See Ali ibn Uthman al-Jullabi al-Hujwiri, *The Kashf al-Mahjub*, trans. R. A. Nicholson (London: Luzac, 1976), 363–364.

example of multiple wives and concubines. The crucial task of resolving this conflict by reconciling sex and Sufism was performed by the renowned Persian philosopher-mystic Abu Hamid al-Ghazali (1058–1111). Writing on "the advantages and disadvantages of marriage," which he knew first-hand as a married man, al-Ghazali defended its value and its essential sexual component.[45] Not only essential for generating legitimate heirs and for avoiding the sins of fornication, marital sex also affords better resources for the work of self-perfection in the aim of coming closer to God.[46] First, it provides "fortification against the devil, curbing lust, warding off the excesses of desire" resulting from sexual abstinence, because sex, like hunger, is a strong natural drive that demands satisfaction (EM 59). Second, marital sex involves the imitation of Muhammad, who enjoyed multiple wives (whom he favored over concubines). If Allah urged believers that the way to earn God's love is to follow Muhammad (Q 3:31), then that means following his example in practice. The Prophet is the exemplary mortal who came closest to God and farthest in realizing "deiformity," that is, "becoming characterized by the character traits of God."[47] Allah affirms Muhammed's "great moral character" (Q 68:4), and Muhammad himself insists: "Marriage is of my *sunnah* ... whoever loves me, let him follow my *sunnah*" (EM 48).

If al-Hujwiri claimed that contemporary wives (unlike Muhammad's) were too corrupt and problematic for a husband's spiritual progress, then al-Ghazali argues that precisely such difficulties provide the mystic believer with invaluable opportunities for *askesis*: the challenges of managing family life with patience and virtue while still focusing intense devotion on God. Ergo, "the asceticism of an ascetic is not complete until he marries" (EM 49). Marriage is a powerful "disciplining of the self ... training it to be mindful, faithful, loyal, and respectful" of one's wives' rights, "tolerating their manners, enduring harm from them, striving to reform them, guiding them to the path of religion, striving [to support them financially] ... and undertaking the upbringing of their children" (EM 67–68). There is also the demanding discipline of satisfying their erotic needs. Al-Ghazali therefore concludes, "Bearing the burden of wives and of offspring is equivalent to jihad for the sake of God" (EM 68).

[45] Abu Hamid al-Ghazali, *Book on the Etiquette of Marriage*, in *Marriage and Sexuality in Islam*, trans. Madelain Farah (Salt Lake City: University of Utah Press, 1984), 46; hereafter EM.

[46] Sex with a female concubine or slave was not considered fornication and was allowed by *sharia*; if such intercourse produced a child, this would to some extent change the woman's status.

[47] See William Chittick, "Love in Islamic Thought," *Religion Compass* 8, no. 7 (2014): 234.

Complementing its values of ascetic training, marital intimacy offers, through its playful "dallying" and intimate pleasures of companionship, a needed "comfort and relaxation for the soul" so that the soul can relaunch itself refreshed for further ascetic efforts of self-perfecting service to God (EM 65). Finally, although the true aim of sex is procreation, and the pleasures of "sexual desire ... merely an inducement thereto," such sexual pleasures are nonetheless helpful benefits for religious life as a "harbinger of the promised pleasures in paradise" and thus "an inducement to the worship of God" in order to attain them (EM 60). The delights of worldly loving union can likewise inspire the mystic's efforts for a divine union that has incomparably more sublime and enduring joy. For such reasons of pleasure, al-Ghazali argues that nonprocreative lovemaking is permitted. This includes not only the controversial case of coitus interruptus but also other erotic pleasures that involve intentionally not ejaculating "in the place of tilling, which is the womb," such as "emission by [the woman's] hand" (EM 108). Even during a wife's menstruation, when coitus is forbidden, "the husband is entitled to enjoy all parts of her body," including "what is concealed by [her] loincloth," that is, "from her groin to (a point just) above the knee" (EM 107–108). Sodomy, however, is "strongly prohibited" (EM 107) and considered even worse than menstrual intercourse.

Al-Gazali is not blind to marriage's disadvantages. Admitting that many people will find its sexual pleasures (and burdens) too distracting for the whole-hearted worship of God, he therefore recommends celibacy for such individuals. The best course, however, is to combine the "virtue of worship and that of marriage," as the Prophet so magnificently did, even having the incomparable ability "to receive revelation while he was in his wife's bed" (EM 77). Because Jesus lacked the "strength" to "combine the two," he wisely decided to remain celibate (EM 77). Al-Ghazali provides no real instruction about how one can combine sex and worship, instead affirming that this capacity and its effective techniques depend entirely on the person's particular disposition.

We find, however, rudiments of an answer in the works of Ibn al-Arabi (1165–1240), the renowned Andalusian mystic who provides the most substantive and far-reaching Sufi theory of sexual spiritualization. His theory intriguingly emphasizes the crucial value of women in the Sufi's defining ethical path of continuing self-perfection. Such a path is, essentially, a quest for God that involves becoming closer to him by becoming more like him. Al-Arabi did not begin this quest with any appreciation of erotic love. "I used to hate women and sex at the start of my entry into this path," he confessed, but decisively changed this attitude after pondering a famous *hadith* in which Muhammad spoke of three things that were "beloved" to him: "women and perfume . . . and prayer." How could he hate "what God had made beloved to his Prophet?"[48] As God's last and best prophet, Muhammad surely deserved emulation; he embodied al-Arabi's key ideal of the Perfect Man who reaches the highest stage of human perfection by coming closest to God and exemplifying God's divine names or character traits as expressed in the Quran. "Whoever loves women as Muhammad did, loves God," al-Arabi concluded. Consequently, the Sufi mystic became "the most compassionate of men with them," arguing that since "women are the locus with which the form of perfection is engendered . . . [,] love for them is obligatory and a way of following the Prophet."[49]

We know from Muhammad's words and actions that his love of women was not mere abstract compassion but rather (like his love of perfume) concretely sensuous and robustly full-bodied. If this love characterizes the Perfect Man, "the most perfect creation of this humankind" (BW 272), then the ethical task of emulating him so as to come closer to deiformity (and thus to God) should involve a similarly robust love of women. Muhammad himself signals the crucial sensuous dimension of this love, al-Arabi explains, by "putting [perfume] after 'women'" in the *hadith*, reminding us that women's fragrance is most enjoyed in the sexual act; "because of the aromas of generation in women, the most delightful of perfumes [is experienced] within the embrace of the beloved" (BW 278).[50]

Apart from its generative and pleasurable functions, the sexual act is an emblem of love's power and desire for union. "When a man loves a woman, he seeks union with her, that is to say the most complete union possible in love, and there is in the elemental sphere no greater union than that between the sexes" (BW 274). This act of sexual union has strong symbolic significance for the cosmic and religious realms. Cosmically, all things emerge

[48] See his confessions in Ibn al-Arabi, *The Meccan Revelations* (4:84), as cited in Valerie J. Hoffman-Ladd, "Mysticism and Sexuality in Sufi Thought and Life," *Mystics Quarterly*, 18, no. 3 (1992): 87; and Ibn al-Arabi, *The Bezels of Wisdom*, trans. R. W. J. Austin (New York: Paulist Press, 1980), hereafter BW. The *hadith*, as it appears today in English translation, in *Sunan an-Nasa'i*, vol. 4, 36:3391, reads: "The Messenger of Allah said: In this world, women and perfume have been made dear to me, and my comfort has been provided in prayer."

[49] *Meccan Revelations* (4:84), as cited in Hoffman-Ladd, "Mysticism and Sexuality," 87; and *Meccan Revelations*, cited in Sachiko Murata, *The Tao of Islam: A Sourcebook on Gender Relations in Islamic Thought* (Albany: SUNY Press, 1992), 186.

[50] The sensuousness of fragrance is not incompatible with spirituality, because, as al-Arabi reminds us, breath itself is among "the excellent perfumes [of existence]" (BW 278) and is what God gave to humankind as life and spirit, when he molded Adam out of clay "and breathed into man of His spirit" (BW 273, cf. Quran 32:9).

from the union of God's divine spirit (being male) with Nature (which is female); and Islamic sexual doctrine best symbolizes this by allowing a man to have four wives, "which perfectly reflects the marriage of the divine Spirit with the four elements to produce its 'children,' all the material existents."[51] Sexual union, moreover, advances one's knowledge and love of God. As God's divine essence or reality is too transcendent to be grasped directly by human minds, we can know God only through his reflection in creation.

Loving a woman, argues al-Arabi, provides the best means for a man to know God's divine reality, because in loving her a man can appreciate both God's active and passive (or receptive) modes. Al-Arabi elaborates, "When man contemplates [God's] Reality in woman he beholds Him in a passive aspect [because woman was created from man], while when he contemplates Him in himself, as being that from which woman is [created], he beholds Him in an active aspect. When, however, he contemplates [God] in himself, without any regard to what has come from him, he beholds Him as passive to Himself directly" (BW 275). Therefore, a man's contemplation of God by being absorbed "in woman is the most complete and perfect [contemplation], because in this way he contemplates [God] ... in both active and passive mode, while by contemplating [God] only in himself, he beholds Him in a passive mode" alone (BW 275). Muhammad therefore "loved women by reason of [this] perfect contemplation ... in them" (BW 275).

Such reasoning that connects knowing and loving God likewise suggests that the mystic's love of women affords the best way not only to understand the love that connects God and man but also to realize that love in sacred union.[52] As woman was created from man and "appears in his own image, the man feels a deep longing for her, as something yearns for itself, while she feels longing for him as one longs for that place to which one belongs" (BW 274). In the same way, God loves man as "that which is in his own image," while "man [is] yearning for his Lord Who is his origin, as woman yearns for man" (BW 274). From the premise that "Love arises only for that from which one has one's being" (which in man's case is God), al-Arabi can argue that man's love for women (when it is properly oriented) is ultimately a love for God that is caused by God, but through God's manifesting Himself in women (BW 274). This is why Muhammad's *hadith* speaks of women as being "made beloved to me" rather than simply loving them "directly from himself" (BW 274). In other words, ultimately and most authentically, a

[51] Hoffman-Ladd, "Mysticism and Sexuality," 87, referring to *Meccan Revelations*, 1:138.

[52] This argument seems to suggest also the converse, that woman's best way of knowing and loving God is through the love of men.

man's "love is for his Lord in Whose image he is, this being so even as regards his love for his wife, since he loves her through God's love for him, after the divine manner" (BW 274). Al-Arabi thus explains that his own love of women came "out of inner vision, from God making them beloved to me, not a natural love" motivated by mere animal instinct, but rather a love of God as God is manifested in woman.[53]

How does one attain that divine inner vision with its orientation of loving God in loving women? Al-Arabi's radical answer is twofold. First, one must become a woman in a psychological and spiritual sense by adopting the female gender role of receptivity, desiring love, and passionate submission with respect to God, who exemplifies the active, dominant male role. Second, one must maintain this receptive, lovingly subordinate, union-seeking orientation to God when making love to women. Otherwise, a man is simply loving with lustful, domineering male desire rather than sacred religious worship, and such lustful assertiveness is corruptive. "The disciple should not take up the company of women until he himself becomes a woman," al-Arabi insists. "If he becomes female and attaches to the lower world and sees how the higher world loves it, and sees himself in every spiritual condition and moment in perpetual sexual union as a female (*mankuhan da'iman*, i.e., assuming the receptive role in an unceasing act of coition) and does not see himself in his spiritual insight as male first, but purely female, and he becomes pregnant from that marriage and gives birth – then he may keep company with women and incline toward them, and love for them will not harm him. As for the gnostics' keeping company with women, [permission to do so] is absolute, because they see the absolute, holy, divine hand in their giving and taking."[54]

Al-Arabi regards the gnostic's permission to love women as absolute because sexual union with them contributes to his mystical efforts of self-perfection and worship of God. The mystic contemplates God more perfectly in his sexual intercourse with women, because this act reveals God's both passive and active aspects while also allowing the man to take both active and passive roles and thus realize their union in himself. Much like the Daoist mystic uniting *yin* and *yang*, the Sufi mystic becomes "pregnant" with creative active-passive wholeness that exemplifies deiformity, and this brings him into a closer, loving union with God. Al-Arabi thus claims that the highest Sufi saint, the *Qutb*, or Axis, engages often in such sacred sexual intercourse, realizing that it advances his religious goals as well as any other

[53] From *Meccan Revelations* (4:84), as cited in Hoffman-Ladd, "Mysticism and Sexuality," 87.

[54] Ibid., 2:191–192, as cited in Hoffman-Ladd, "Mysticism and Sexuality," 91.

form of worship. "He knows from the divine manifestations in sexual union what drives him to seek it and embrace it, for his worship cannot achieve for him or for any other gnostic more than can be attained by sexual union."[55]

The sacred, worshiping function of lovemaking does not imply that pleasure is not one of its aims. Indeed, the gnostic master or saint "desires sexual union not for the sake of procreation, but only for pleasure," because at this level of spirituality, "the sexual act . . . is like the sexual union of the people of Paradise, only for the sake of pleasure," which by its sacred nature includes the pleasure of worship. Sexual pleasure, al-Arabi shrewdly argues, has in itself a deep religious dimension "which only a few of the 'people of providence' (*ahl al-'inaya*) understand" – the pleasure of self-surrender and self-annihilation in loving submission to one's beloved, which ultimately means God. Remember that the very meaning of "Islam" and "Muslim" implies submission and surrender. "If [sexual desire] did not have complete nobility indicating the weakness appropriate to servanthood, it would not have such an overwhelming pleasure which causes a person to pass away from his own strength and pretensions. It is a pleasurable subjugation, although subjugation precludes pleasure in the one who is subjugated, because the pleasure in subjugation belongs to the one who is subjugating, not the one who is subjugated, except in this act in particular." Sex takes a person beyond narrow self-centeredness and self-possession by immersing the individual into a pleasurable submission to the larger forces of life that affords a certain "nobility" animals unconsciously share. Thus al-Arabi paradoxically reverses the condemnation of sex as "an animalistic passion" by noting that "animalistic" means full of life and then asking, "What is more noble than life?" In short, acts that conventional people regard as "ugly," immoral, or animalistic can be "praiseworthy for the perfect gnostic" and even essential for his worship.[56]

[55] Ibid., 2:573–574, as cited in Hoffman-Ladd, "Mysticism and Sexuality," 89.

[56] Ibid. Such ethical paradoxes include the mystic's preference for beautiful young women and young men as opposed to older and less physically attractive individuals who may be just as virtuous. Here al-Arabi argues that young and beautiful people make better vessels for worshipping God because both their youth and their beauty signal greater closeness to God, being more recent creations that have been stamped with more of God's infinite beauty. Another intriguing argument is that in loving multiple women, the saintly gnostic is not exploiting but rather compassionately helping them by securing for them a place in paradise, since his love for them is sacred and since God will anyway reward the righteous in paradise by reuniting them with those they loved on earth. However piously intended, these arguments are apt to strike us as more ingeniously self-serving than morally compelling, and they are surely prone to abuse by powerful men.

To conclude our account of Islamic erotology by summarizing its use of sex as a method of self-perfection, we can distinguish four different strategies with different levels of ennobling complexity. The first, most straightforward form is simply the refinement of manners that a good lover develops in order to give his beloved both sensuous pleasure and psychological comfort during love's stages of courtship, foreplay, coitus, and postcoital interaction. This involves an *askesis* of extensive training in lovemaking to hone one's physical and cognitive skills and one's ethical sensibility to achieve erotic mastery of this kind. A second form of erotic *askesis* takes the converse direction of self-perfection by strengthening one's ethical-religious willpower and purity through sexual restraint: repressing one's sensuous desires as much as possible and engaging in sex only for procreation with one's wife (if one was married) but not for pleasure. The extreme expression of this ascetic path was celibacy, which was sometimes practiced despite its deviance from Islamic tradition by flouting Muhammad's example and *hadith*. A third way of combining sex and ethical self-perfection, articulated by al-Ghazali, involves the discipline of whole-heartedly meeting one's sexual duties of marital life as a form of worship by fulfilling and enjoying these religiously endorsed erotic responsibilities but also combining them, as much as possible, with an undistracted and adoring focus on God. The double *askesis* of satisfying one's duties to one's women but also directing one's meditative devotion to God constitutes a very demanding path of self-perfection that many would lack the requisite strength to pursue. Al-Arabi provides a fourth and most radical method of erotically self-perfecting transcendence that fully integrates sexual union with women and single-minded devotion to God. Here erotic spirituality brings God into the sexual act, namely, by contemplating him in the women one makes love to and by becoming a female oneself in self-subordinating adoration of God in those same acts of lovemaking in which one beholds and unites with the divine.

7

From Romantic Refinement to Courtesan Connoisseurship

Japanese *Ars Erotica*

I CHINESE AND INDIGENOUS CULTURAL ROOTS

Japan's classical *ars erotica* takes the aesthetics of refinement to extreme heights of sophistication and subtlety but also displays astonishing levels of violence. Like Islam, Japanese culture is postaxial and largely derivative, borrowing heavily from the rich cultural resources of earlier, axial-age traditions in neighboring lands. But in contrast to the multiple sources of cultural assimilation (Jewish, Christian, Greek, Roman, Persian, and Indian) that Islam absorbed through its ever-expanding conquest of new territories, ancient Japan, as an island civilization on the far eastern border of the civilized world, displayed a much more insular and one-sided approach, confining its cultural importations to Chinese sources. It imbibed them so deeply and extensively that one could almost describe classical Japanese culture as essentially defined by Chinese forms and ideas. But it also transformed them in creative and beautiful ways.

Japan's importations included "religious and philosophical orientations, an ideal of imperial rule, legal and administrative structures, techniques and styles of architecture, city planning, sculpture, painting, and music – all derived directly or indirectly [via Korea] from China" – and we could add medicine, fashion, and the arts of perfume and lovemaking.[1] "Above all, [Japanese borrowing] meant literacy: the mastery of the Chinese language and the eventual adaptation of its script to the writing of Japanese." Unlike Islam's pride in its defining Arabic language, Japanese culture was originally illiterate. Having no written language of its own, Japan began to import the

[1] E. A. Cranston, "Asuka and Nara Culture: Literacy, Literature, and Music," in D. M. Brown, ed., *The Cambridge History of Japan*, vol. 1 (Cambridge: Cambridge University Press, 1993), 453. Other citations in this paragraph are from 453, 454, 455, 456.

Chinese language in the late fourth or early fifth century, and then borrowed Chinese script to shape its own language, eventually using Chinese to create Japanese historiography and poetry, modeling them on Chinese forms of these genres and sometimes even writing them in Chinese. Indigenous Japanese oral traditions and myths were also transcribed in the new written language to form the basis of Japanese prose literature.

Initially, literacy spread quite slowly, but its adoption dramatically increased when Buddhism, introduced via Korea around 550, was officially accepted by the Japanese court in 587, making the ability to read and understand the sutras and other scriptural writings a powerfully persistent incentive for mastering literacy. Chinese culture thus spread beyond the circle of scholars who had already encountered it through the earlier importation of classical Confucian ideas through Confucian teachers brought from Korea and China, some of whom remained to serve as scribes for the Japanese court.[2] The strong aesthetic dimensions of Confucianism and Chinese Buddhism productively intermingled with local taste to produce a distinctive Japanese aesthetic that also found expression in the art of love. We examine this aesthetic in three important Japanese love cultures: the Heian dynasty's courtly love tradition, the culture of male love practiced by Buddhist monks and samurai warriors that developed in the middle ages, and the Edo period's pleasure world of high-class prostitution best exemplified by the Yoshiwara courtesan district.[3]

Chinese importations did not create Japanese culture from scratch. An indigenous agrarian Shinto tradition already existed, replete with rituals of worship, shamanistic practices, and mythologies of gods and creation. Textual evidence of this early culture, however, comes only after the Japanese had sufficient mastery of Chinese.[4] The mythic origins of Japan as recorded in its earliest chronicles include distinctly sexual elements, as one would expect in an agrarian culture concerned with fertility. Two creator gods, Izanagi (meaning "the male who invites") and Izanami ("the female who invites") "marry and create the islands of Japan by means of sexual generation."[5] Initially, the female god spoke first in the marriage ritual, resulting in a

[2] Ibid., 454, 456, 457.

[3] Male love was also much practiced among Kabuki artists, but it most prominently took the form of male prostitution, frequently serving the lust of both monks and samurai, along with wealthy merchants. In any case, as a derivative and decadently commercial form, it is less philosophically interesting than Buddhist and samurai male love.

[4] The very term "Shinto" derives from the Chinese, a transformation from the Chinese "*shen dao*" (神道) whose characters, respectively, mean "spirit" and "way."

[5] Citations from *Cambridge History of Japan*, vol. 1, 465–466.

deformed offspring and the consequent need to redo the marriage properly by having the male initiate. This second conjugal union created Japan's beautiful islands and various gods or spirits (*kami*), including the fire deity whose birth burns Izanami to death. After her husband Izanagi fails to rescue her from the land of the dead, she angrily pursues him but he escapes and cleans himself in a river, where "various deities [emerge] from different parts of his body. The most important of these . . . are Amaterasu (the Sun Goddess), born from his left eye," and Susa-no-O, "a *kami* variously associated with the sea, the wind, the earth, and the underworld" who comes from Izanagi's nose and becomes Amaterasu's enemy, making her hide in a cave, thus depriving the world of light. The worried gods seek to lure her out and eventually succeed when the goddess Ame-no-Uzume performs "a sexually arousing dance" that exposes her breasts and genitals. This makes the gods laugh so heartily that the curious Amaterasu comes out to inquire into the cause of this laughter.[6]

Two important erotic themes emerge from these myths. First, one should make love in a ritually proper way for it to be truly fruitful, and the ritually proper way implies male priority. Second, there is something laughably awkward, inelegant, or embarrassing about the body's sexual parts so that exposing them or presenting their role in lovemaking is ridiculously unrefined. Both themes helped shape Japan's classical *ars erotica*, which finds its earliest, most elegant, and formative expression in Heian courtly culture, whose aesthetic casts its long shadow of influence over subsequent Japanese art, including its arts of love.

II HEIAN AESTHETICS AND THE EROS OF REFINED ROMANCE

The Heian period (794–1185), whose capital was Heian-kyo (now Kyoto), modeled its culture primarily on that of China's Tang Dynasty (618–907), long renowned as the golden age of Chinese culture. Tang Confucianism provided Japan with the "basis for government both ideal and practical," not only the "conception and rhetoric" of Confucian government but also its

[6] For full details of this story as found in its source in chapter 17 of *Kojiki* (*Record of Ancient Matters*, 712 CE), the oldest surviving Japanese book, see Donald L. Philippi, trans., *Kojiki* (Tokyo: University of Tokyo Press, 1968), 81–85. It states that the dancing goddess "exposed her breasts, and pushed her skirt-band down to her genitals. Then Takamo-Nö-Para [heaven] shook as the eight-hundred deities laughed at once" (84).

"forms and usages."[7] As "the ritual persona of the ruler, whether emperor or regent, was fashioned according to Confucian patterns," so were Confucian "ethical teachings . . . invoked to justify decisions of state" and Confucian language used "for the memorials, decrees, codes, administrative regulations, ordinances, commands, communications, and certificates by which the government functioned." An upper-class male child would begin his education by learning to read the "first few characters of the [Confucian] *Classic of Filial Piety* (*Hsiao ching*) as annotated by the Tang emperor Hsuan-tsung . . . Crown princes were provided with two Confucian tutors, and the post was a great honor." Chinese was taught not as a spoken language but only as a literary one, and it therefore conveyed a distinctive aura of erudition and refinement.

Aesthetics formed a crucial dimension of Confucian philosophy, which regarded music and ritual as central tools for ethically perfecting the individual and bringing sociopolitical harmony to the state. Poetry had similar Confucian functions of moral and social cultivation, as did calligraphy, which reached such a high peak of interest and quality in Tang culture that academies were established for its study. Buddhism, in its adapted Chinese forms, was recognized as one of the "three teachings" (along with Confucianism and Daoism), and it flourished in the Tang era, powerfully influencing that culture's poetry and art. If Confucian aesthetics emphasized refinement, erudition, and clear distinctions, then Buddhism offered other aesthetic values: ambiguity, mystery, simplicity, evanescence, and the charms of spontaneity and imperfection that we find in the natural world and its misty, energizing, but poignantly fleeting beauties. As Chinese Buddhism drew on the Daoist love of nature's beauty, mystery, and spontaneity, so Japanese Buddhism could build on Shinto's naturalism.

Japan's Heian court culture combined the Confucian aesthetics of artistic refinement and decorum with the Buddhist appreciation of the mistily indeterminate and poignantly transient, epitomized by the fleeting splendor of cherry blossoms. This blend is manifest in the Heian art of love, whose defining texts come almost entirely from women authors, in diary, memoir, or fictional form. Male members of court were apparently reluctant to write texts about romantic matters (other than the private love letters and poems they frequently composed), either because lovemaking seemed inappropriately trivial as a topic for serious composition or simply because they were

[7] Marian Ury, "Chinese Leaning and Intellectual Life," in D. H. Shively and W. H. McCullough, eds., *The Cambridge History of Japan*, vol. 2 (Cambridge: Cambridge University Press, 1999), 342–343, 346–347.

too busy with other matters, including official writing chores.[8] The most substantial and influential document of Heian erotic artistry is Lady Murasaki's famous *Tale of Genji* (1021), but the same aesthetic themes can be found in the earlier *Tales of Ise* (of uncertain date and authorship but probably composed toward the end of the ninth century). We also find them in the extended personal notes and diaries of two women that constitute *The Pillow Book* and *The Gossamer Years*.[9] The latter is a noblewoman's diary covering the years of 954–974, recounting her courtship and marital miseries with a Heian prince who spent most of his time neglecting her while romancing other women.[10] The former is a book of scattered observations and anecdotes recorded by Sei Shonagon during her service as a court lady to the Heian Empress Consort Teishi in the 990s and early 1000s. The book was completed in the year 1002. An important male testimony to Heian aesthetic values of love exists, but it is only a retrospective account written in the succeeding Kamakura period. We find this in a wonderful book of reflections from around 1330, written by a former imperial Kyoto courtier turned Buddhist priest known as Kenko.[11] These different books express the distinctive features that together define Japan's refined aesthetics of love-making whose influence stretched far beyond the Heian dynasty.

This courtly aesthetic tradition regarded love as a worthy pursuit, and the lover as a tenderly appealing and sensitive figure. In Kenko's words, "A man may excel at everything else, but if he has no taste for lovemaking, one feels

[8] I do not include Tamba Yasuyori's thirty-volume *Ishinpo*, the oldest surviving Japanese medical text completed in 984 but based on earlier Chinese works and presented to the Heian Emperor En'yu. This book, as noted earlier, preserved several classical Chinese sexology texts subsequently lost in China.

[9] There is also *The Diary of Lady Murasaki*, trans. Richard Bowring (London: Penguin, 1996), hereafter LM, but it is far more discreet and offers much less information about Heian love culture. For Lady Murasaki's *The Tale of Genji*, I cite from Edward Seidensticker's translation (New York: Vintage, 1990); hereafter TG. See also Helen Craig McCullough, trans., *Tales of Ise: Lyrical Episodes from Tenth-Century Japan* (Stanford: Stanford University Press, 1968), hereafter TI; Sei Shonagon, *The Pillow Book of Sei Shōnagon*, trans. Arthur Waley (Rutland, VT: Tuttle, 2011), hereafter PB; and *The Gossamer Years*, trans. Edward Seidensticker (Rutland, VT: Tuttle, 1964), hereafter GY.

[10] The author's actual name remains undiscovered, so she is known as "Michitsuna's Mother." We should note that her niece, known as Lady Sarashina, later composed a famous diary of her own (completed around 1059) that is remarkable for its romantic accounts of travel and natural beauty but has almost nothing of interest regarding erotic matters, despite her experience of marriage (which gets almost no mention and includes no sense of love).

[11] The *Tsurezuregusa* by Urabe no Kaneyoshi (Kenko's original name) is gracefully composed in the same free association style of observations (*zuihitsui* – "follow the brush") as *The Pillow Book*. It is published in English as *Essays in Idleness: The* Tsurezuregusa *of Kenkō*, trans. Donald Keene (New York: Columbia University Press, 1998), hereafter EI.

something terribly inadequate about him, as if he were a valuable wine cup without a bottom. What a charming figure is the lover, his clothes drenched with dew or frost, wandering about aimlessly . . . resorting to one unsuccessful stratagem after another; and for all that, most often sleeping alone, though never soundly" (EI 5). Although this depiction of the young male lover endearingly suggests vulnerable confusion, we should emphasize that the crucial quality of the Heian aesthetic, in love as in everything, was a refined elegance that the Japanese identified as the ideal of *miyabi* (雅). Its expression in erotic theory involves diverse dimensions. The first is a total lack of explicit sexual content and hardly a mention of physical contact in accounts of lovemaking; there is no discussion of foreplay, no classification or even mention of genital parts and their amatory uses, let alone coital positions or other forms of sexual satisfaction. For Heian culture, to write openly of such somatic vulgarities would constitute a gross violation of the high-toned decorum of good taste.[12] In the tradition of Confucian prudishness, the diaries and anecdotes never even describe a first kiss or caress. Instead, the stages of courtship and seductive foreplay (but also the continuing technique of sustaining erotic desire throughout an extended affair) proceed through poetry, calligraphy, and music.

This signals a second key element of Heian lovemaking: the centrality of the arts. Artistic knowledge and talent (with correspondingly refined aesthetic taste) could win and keep a lover; its lack could lose one. Heian literature is rife with such examples. The *Tales of Ise* describes a man in love with a lady in waiting, whom "he begged to be allowed to visit . . . , keeping her curtains between them if necessary . . . The lady received him, taking great pains not to be observed," but after hearing his poetry, "[d]eeply affected, the lady drew aside the curtains" to accept his love (TI 135). Other tales describe men and women whose lost love for each other was suddenly rekindled through an exchange of poems that brought "a new intimacy even closer than the old" so that the couple passed their nights together more often and "more faithfully than ever" (TI 86–87). In *The Gossamer Years*, the author recounts her courtship by the prince entirely in terms of the poems they exchanged, never even mentioning their betrothal or wedding; she also discovers his infidelity through writing meant for another woman (GY 34–38).

[12] Even when describing the joys of spending secret nights in bed with one's lover, *The Pillow Book* does not mention pleasure from contact with the lover's body but rather other environing sensory delights: in summer to enjoy the "cool air" and the view "into the garden," and in the "very cold nights" of winter, "to lie with one's lover, buried under a great pile of bed-clothes" and listening to "strange" and "muffled" sounds (PB 81).

Accomplishments in writing (not only poetic composition but also calligraphic skill) were crucial features in judging the attractiveness of a lover, since such literary skills were essential to the art of lovemaking and provided evidence of the lover's refinement, education, and taste. The *Pillow Book*'s author described a suitor as "tiresome" because he "can't . . . recite Sutras or make poems like other people" (PB 63–64). *The Gossamer Years*'s diarist refused the prince's first attempts to court her because of the poor quality of his written advances. "The paper was rather unbecoming for such an occasion, I thought, and the handwriting was astonishingly bad" (GY 33). Written lovemaking was a consummate, complex art, involving not only poetry and calligraphy but also a careful choice of appropriately suited paper, perfume, ink, and writing style. Composing a love letter meant "taking particular trouble to get it up as prettily as possible" (PB 116). In *Genji*, a gentleman suitor was favored because each of his courtship notes was "superior in all of its details, the color of the paper, the perfume that had been burned into it, the modulations of the ink" (TG 490).

Music, too, had seductive powers of refinement in which Prince Genji excelled and to which he was highly susceptible: "Everything about her told of refinement. Her poems, her handwriting when she dashed off a letter, the koto she plucked a note on – everything seemed right" (TG 30). An earlier hero of the *Tales of Ise* "played his flute with great feeling, and sang melancholy ballads in a moving voice" to make love to his imprisoned lady (TI 113). Dance was another art for elegantly showing and winning affection and thus was essential courtly training for both men and women. Physical beauty, though cherished, could not in itself evoke desire but required aesthetic adornments of tasteful clothes and an education in literature and the arts that indicated the refined elegance of good taste.[13]

Essential to refined Heian taste was a style of indirection that eschewed the explicit. One aspect of this style involved a sophisticated hermeneutics of intimation whereby lovers communicated secretly through poetic allusion and even nonverbal signs, such as responding to an inquiring love note by sending a mere object, as Sei Shonagon did by sending her lover "a minute piece of seaweed, . . . wrapped up in paper" (PB 71). Equally crucial to *miyabi* refinement were detachment and restraint that lovers expressed in multiple ways. One technique was the art of veiling in which the woman received her lover through the separating medium of curtains or a screen.

[13] For examples of dance training, see TG 375 and GY 164. We also find an emphasis on proficiency in poetry and calligraphy (TG 351, 363, 517–519) and the importance of appropriately fashionable clothes (TG 124).

Through such strategies of distancing, the woman could render herself more desirable by a seductive play of presence and absence. The male lover could hear her gentle voice uttering poetic words, perhaps with the musical accompaniment of her dulcet koto playing; he could also smell the alluringly sweet and subtly perfumed fragrance of her flesh, while his imagination was free to picture her as far more visually beautiful than she might in fact be.[14] If certain texts describe how women used screens and "curtains to ward off the curious" and escape "the direct stares" of the desiring male gaze (LM 38), we should recognize that such veiling techniques (as in Islam) conversely tended instead to intensify curiosity and desire.

Another form of distancing detachment to heighten desire was playing hard to get; for example, we find cases of a woman not answering a suitor's first poems or requests for a meeting, or even not opening the door to welcome her favored lover when he secretly comes at night. Here again we find an exciting play of presence and absence that adds dramatic intensity to the love tryst. Although they do not see or speak to each other, the woman hears her lover's soft knocking and anxious pacing outside her door, while he might hear her breathing and movements or even smell her fragrant incense within. The rules of dignified elegance bound both partners in the erotic affair. As the woman should not show herself too eager for love, so a refined man must respect his lady's wishes and not appear overly excited and thirsty for pleasure. "The man of breeding," Kenko insists, "never appears to abandon himself completely to his pleasures; even his manner of enjoyment is detached. It is the rustic boors who take all their pleasures grossly" (EI 118). Moreover, the overcoming of the distancing difficulties "encountered in the path of love" (even if they are self-created to heighten the drama) adds colorful meaning, making the love affair more memorable and often more lasting (EI 199).

A crucial feature of Heian lovemaking that integrates concealment, detachment, obstacles, and the play of presence and absence was the night-time love visit. For reasons of privacy, discretion, and the honor of a woman's good name, love affairs were usually conducted at night. One had to be especially "on the alert . . . at night, when one must be prepared for something to happen at any moment," *The Pillow Book* insists, in explaining the nocturnal game of love. "All night long one hears the noise of footsteps in the corridor outside. Every now and then the sound will cease

[14] Concerning a woman's poetic and emotional qualities (which Heian culture deemed essential for erotic attractiveness), Kenko notes: "Her character and temperament may be guessed from the first words she utters, even if she is hidden behind a screen" (EI 9).

in front of some particular door, and there will be a gentle tapping, just with one finger; but one knows that the lady inside will have instantly recognized the knock. Sometimes, this soft tapping lasts a long while; the lady is no doubt pretending to be asleep. But at last comes the rustle of a dress or the sound of someone cautiously turning on her couch, and one knows that she has taken pity on him" (PB 126–127). The silence of night magnifies the sound and the excitement of secret trysts and the game of hard-to-get that the lady plays. "In summer she can hear every movement of his fan, as he stands chafing outside; while in winter, stealthily though it be done, he will hear the sound of someone gently stirring the ashes in the brazier, and will at once begin knocking more resolutely, or even asking out loud for admittance. And while he does so, one can hear him squeezing up closer and closer against the door" (PB 127).

Night, moreover, casts an especially romantic ambiance of beauty that the stronger light of day destroys, revealing or highlighting minor blemishes of appearance concealed by nocturnal darkness, even in a candlelit room. Kenko therefore feels "sorry for the man who says that night dims the beauty of things. At night colors, ornaments, and richness of materials show to their best advantage." Clothes generally look better in evening hours, when even "showy, flashy costumes are most attractive . . . This holds true of people's appearance too; lamplight makes a beautiful face seem even more beautiful, and a voice heard in the dark – a voice that betrays a fear of being overheard – is endearing. Perfumes and the sound of music too are best at night" (EI 164).[15] Night also brings the incomparable romantic beauty of the moon, with its enchanting erotic power. Sei Shonagan avows that "if anyone comes on a night when the moon is up and there is a clear sky, even if it is ten days, twenty days, a month, a year, yes, even seven or eight years since his last visit, [she] can look back with pleasure on his visit; and even if the place is not very convenient for meeting and one must be prepared for interruption at any moment – even if, at the worst, nothing more happens than a few remarks exchanged at a respectful distance one feels that next time, if circumstances are favorable, one will allow him to stay the night" (PB 100). Moon watching was a romantic pastime for lovers, whether together or apart. In either case, a lunar glimpse would remind them of other moons that illuminated the protective darkness of their past loving

[15] Kenko adds, "It is charming if, on a night which is not any special occasion, a visitor arriving at the palace after it has grown quite late appears in splendid attire.. . . How pleasant it is when a handsome man grooms his hair after dark, or a woman, late at night, slips from an audience chamber and, mirror in hand, touches up her make-up before she appears again" (EI 164).

nights together while promising more such beautiful meetings, feelings, and memories in the future. Indeed, even if the moon was hidden from their sight (by clouds, mountains, or other obstructions), the very act of looking for it could prompt the same poignant memories or hopes and thus create a tenderly erotic experience.

This appreciation of how remembered and prospective sentiments enhance the erotic import of the moment is a key aspect of Heian lovemaking. The erotic high point is not the momentary climax of coital orgasm. The most precious and interesting aesthetic values of love are instead in the narrative tissue of the affair, particularly (according to Kenko) with respect to the starting and ending points that frame the narrative. "In all things, it is the beginnings and ends that are interesting. Does the love between men and women refer only to the moments when they are in each other's arms? The man who grieves over a love affair broken off before it was fulfilled, who bewails empty vows, who spends long autumn nights alone, who lets his thoughts wander to distant skies, who yearns for the past in a dilapidated house – such a man truly knows what love means" (EI 115–118).

Sei Shonagan offers an interesting corollary of such narrative emphasis by insisting on the special importance of the lover's manner of departure (rather than his prowess at seductive foreplay or coition).

> To begin with, he ought not to be too ready to get up, but should require a little coaxing: "Come, it is past daybreak. You don't want to be found here ... " and so on. One likes him, too, to behave in such a way that one is sure he is unhappy at going and would stay longer if he possibly could. He should not pull on his trousers the moment he is up, but should first of all come close to one's ear and in a whisper finish off whatever was left half-said in the course of the night.... Then he should raise the shutters, and both lovers should go out together at the double-doors, while he tells her how much he dreads the day that is before him and longs for the approach of night. Then, after he has slipped away, she can stand gazing after him, with charming recollections of those last moments. Indeed, the success of a lover depends greatly on his method of departure. If he springs to his feet with a jerk and at once begins fussing round, tightening in the waist-band of his breeches, or adjusting the sleeves of his court robe, hunting jacket or what not, collecting a thousand odds and ends, and thrusting them into the folds of his dress, or pulling in his over-belt – one begins to hate him. (PB 118–119)

The emotive power of desire is enhanced not only by memory but also by yearning anticipation and imagination. As Kenko notes, "The moon that appears close to dawn after we have long waited for it moves us more profoundly than the full moon shining cloudless over a thousand leagues. And how incomparably lovely is the moon, almost greenish in its light, when seen through the tops of the cedars deep in the mountains, or when it hides for a moment behind clustering clouds during a sudden shower!" (EI 118). If a partially seen moon can move us more deeply through its evocative powers of imaginative suggestion, then Kenko urges us not "to look at the moon and the cherry blossoms with our eyes alone" but with our imagination. "How much more evocative and pleasing it is to think about the spring without stirring from the house, to dream of the moonlit night though we remain in our room!" (EI 118). The indeterminacy of not seeing the moon or blossoms enables us, if we are suitably sensitive and poetic, to visualize and experience them more richly in our imagination. "Are we to look at cherry blossoms only in full bloom, the moon only when it is cloudless? To long for the moon while looking on the rain, to lower the blinds and be unaware of the passing of the spring – these are even more deeply moving," Kenko insists. Branches about to blossom or gardens strewn with faded flowers are worthier of our admiration because, in their lack of full blossoming, they are more evocative of narrative process and imaginative expansion. "Leaving something incomplete makes it interesting, and gives one the feeling that there is room for growth. Someone once told me, 'Even when building the imperial palace, they always leave one place unfinished'" (EI 70–71,115).

Sei Shonagan provides an extended example of this beauty of imaginative expansion, as she imagines a lover, skilled not only in the aesthetics of departure but also in the art of post-tryst lovemaking in absentia, after "returning at dawn from some amorous excursion":

> He looks a trifle sleepy; but, as soon as he is home, draws his writing-case towards him, carefully grinds himself some ink and begins to write his next-morning letter – not simply dashing off whatever comes into his head, but spreading himself to the task and taking trouble to write the characters beautifully. He should be clad in an azalea-yellow or vermilion cloak worn over a white robe. Glancing from time to time at the dewdrops that still cling to the thin white fabric of his dress, he finishes his letter, but instead of giving it to one of the ladies who are in attendance upon him at the moment, he gets up and, choosing from among his pageboys one who seems to him exactly appropriate to such a mission, calls the lad to him, and whispering something in his ear puts the letter in his hand; then sits gazing after him as he disappears into the distance. While waiting for the answer he will perhaps quietly murmur to himself this or that passage from the *Sutras.* Presently he is told that his washing-water and porridge are ready, and goes into the back room, where, seated at the reading-table, he

> glances at some Chinese poems, now and then reciting out loud some passage that strikes his fancy. When he has washed and got into his Court cloak, which he wears as a dressing-gown (without trousers), he takes the 6th chapter of the Lotus Scripture and reads it silently. Precisely at the most solemn moment of his reading – the place being not far away – the messenger returns, and by his posture it is evident that he expects an instant reply. With an amusing if blasphemous rapidity the lover transfers his attention from the book he is reading to the business of framing his answer. (PB 120–121)

The incomplete is so profoundly poignant to Heian aesthetic sensibilities not merely because its mysterious indeterminacy allows imaginative expansion and multiple meanings but also because it suggests the transience that marks the imperfection and incompleteness of human life. We never succeed in completing all we wish to do, and what we manage to complete is soon undone by the passage of time. Nature teaches us the lesson of beauty's transience through the fleeting cherry blossoms and changing phases of the moon. "The full moon does not keep its roundness even a little while; it at once begins to wane" (EI 199).[16] Erotic love – obviously and painfully – shares this transience. As its coital consummation is extremely ephemeral, love needs the work of imagination (deployed through diverse arts and techniques of continuing courtship) to sustain itself, even if only in the wistful beauty of moving memory.

Despite its veiled, nocturnal secrecy, Heian lovemaking manifests a distinctive social side. As love constituted a noble pursuit, being a good lover was socially valued. It was therefore important that one's quality as a lover was known, not simply by one's beloved but by one's social milieu in which one competed for recognition. Both men and women measured themselves in terms of amorous success. They would collect love letters as trophies of their conquests and sometimes show them to curious friends as Genji did (TG 21). They would perform exceptional acts of ardent devotion to manifest (as much to the public as to the beloved) the depth and quality of their commitment to love. When Sei Shonagon criticizes her lover for coming to visit her during a horribly stormy night of rain, she imputes his motive as showing off his dedication as a lover, "after absenting himself for weeks on end," busy with his "many other attachments ... His object in choosing so

[16] Rather than mourning transience, Kenko affirms it as an essential reason why beauty touches us so deeply. If we "lingered on forever in the world, how things would lose their power to move us! The most precious thing in life is its uncertainty.... We cannot live forever in this world; why should we wait for ugliness to overtake us?" (EI 7–8).

atrocious a night for his visit was chiefly that other people might be impressed by his devotion and point out to me how much beholden I ought to feel" (PB 99–100). Similarly, the unhappy jealousy of *The Gossamer Years*'s diarist expresses more concern for her loss of social prestige as a desired (though secondary) wife than any painful love yearnings for her husband. She felt humiliated when his princely carriage procession would pass her house without stopping, and "felt a pang of envy at the ladies who were more frequently honored than [she] with all this magnificence" (GY 123). Worried what people might think about his not visiting or writing to her, she eventually accepts even a most "perfunctory visit," recognizing that she could "gain a bit of face from having [people] know he [was] here" (GY 138, 143).

Heian emphasis on artistic refinement and social standing in erotic pursuits did not preclude the appreciation of a person's natural good looks. Nor did its affirmation of detached restraint deny the natural power of erotic desire and its transient delights. Kenko, who notes the particular attraction of a woman's "beautiful hair," claims,

> Nothing leads a man astray so easily as sexual desire.... Though we realize, for example, that fragrances are short-lived and the scent burnt into clothes lingers but briefly, how our hearts always leap when we catch a whiff of an exquisite perfume! The holy man of Kume lost his magic powers after noticing the whiteness of the legs of a girl who was washing clothes; this was quite understandable, considering that the glowing plumpness of her arms, legs, and flesh owed nothing to artifice. (EI 8–9)[17]

In the same way, Kenko praises male physical beauty, but insists it needs the complement of education in the arts and social graces. "I could sit forever with a man" whose "face and figure [were] of excelling beauty . . . , provided that what he said did not grate on my ears [with its lack of cultivation].... What a shame it is when men of excellent appearance and character prove hopelessly inept in social encounters with their inferiors in both position and appearance, solely because they are badly educated" (EI 3–4). The Heian erotic ideal is the integration of natural and artistic beauty. This explains why cultured lovers favored sending amorous notes and poems with a

[17] For Kenko, erotic love is "truly a deep-seated passion" that seems "impossible to control . . . That is why they say that even a great elephant can be fastened securely with a rope plaited from the strands of a woman's hair" (EI 9). He ranks erotic desire as second in strength only to the lust for "fame," a social desire for "glory derived from one's conduct, or from one's talents," while appetite's desire for food is ranked in third place (EI 9, 201).

tastefully accompanying bouquet of flowers, for instance, a courtship "poem attached to a gorgeous spray of cherry blossoms" (TI 132) or a note "written on thin red paper and attached to a spray of red plum" (GY 149).

III THE WAY OF BOY LOVE

Like Heian courtly love, the Japanese tradition of male–male sexual love derived from China. The original Japanese term for such love, *nanshoku*, is simply the Japanese pronunciation of its established Chinese designation *nanse* (男色), which most literally means "male color." The character 色 (*se*, color) long denoted the concept of erotic desire and sexual activity, and the Chinese practice of male–male sex had very ancient and famous historical examples from the imperial court.[18] However, Japanese *nanshoku* as a systematic practice or "way" appeared much later. A prominent legend claims that the renowned Japanese Buddhist monk Kukai (774–835), who founded the esoteric Shingon, or "True Word," school of Buddhism and was posthumously honored with the name Kobo Daishi ("Great Teacher of the Vast Dharma"), brought *nanshoku* back from China in 806, after being initiated into the Chinese esoteric Buddhist tradition. There is no solid historical evidence for this legend, which most scholars believe was later introduced to validate an already prevalent monastic practice of pederasty. Although other Chinese cultural importations began much earlier, the first explicit reference we find for *nanshoku* in Japan dates only from 985. It comes in an admonitory remark from a famous Buddhist text condemning to hell any man "who has accosted another's acolyte and wickedly violated him" or "who commits the wickedness of loving and violating [another] man."[19] The term "acolyte" is a translation of the Japanese word *chigo* (literally meaning "child") used to designate boys both inside and outside the monastic context. *Chigo* worked as pages and sexual servants to higher-level monks or to members of aristocratic households. Japanese *nanshoku* was primarily the love of boys by adult men (or older boys), thus resembling Greek pederasty. Sexual love between adult men was relatively rare. Thus a popular synonym for *nanshoku* was *wakashudo*, or "the way of boys," often

[18] We find this linguistic usage already in the fourth-century BCE book of Mencius. For details on China's courtly examples of boy love that "date back to the sixth century BCE," see Gary Leupp, *Male Colors: The Construction of Homosexuality in Tokugawa Japan* (Berkeley: University of California Press, 1995), 11–17.

[19] This text, *Teachings Essential for Rebirth*, by the Tendai priest Genshin, is cited in Leupp, *Male Colors*, 31.

abbreviated to simply *shudo*. The age span of a *chigo* was not precisely determined and varied in different contexts, but it tended to range between the ages of twelve and nineteen, according to a twelfth-century Buddhist abbot who wrote a text prescribing proper *chigo* behavior.[20]

Chigo were so highly prized by Japan's medieval Buddhist priests in their mountain temples that a popular saying was coined: "*Ichi chigo ni sanno*" (*Chigo* come first, the god of the mountain, second).[21] The *chigo* of the temples came from diverse backgrounds (aristocracy, samurai, and lower-class families). Although many remained in temple to take the tonsure and become monks, many others returned to worldly life and married after they reached adult status. In return for serving their monk masters, *chigo* received an education in music, dance, and the classics of literature and art. Their service had two principal functions that highlighted their somaesthetic value in enriching an otherwise austere monastic life. First, their beauty, grace, and artistic talents contributed to the "formal processions, religious ceremonies, and public functions" that the Buddhist temple clerics performed; these were "carefully choreographed events" involving dimensions of music, dance, and recitation. Second, in attending personally to their masters, *chigo* not only would perform ordinary chores (such as serving meals and running errands) but would provide aesthetic enjoyment through their good looks, artistic skills, and sexual service. Because they were highly prized (perhaps even loved) for their somaesthetic qualities, *chigo* were encouraged to cultivate them. Unlike other child servants at the temple, they could "wear their hair long (waist length in some paintings), powder their faces, and dress extravagantly" and even use womanly cosmetic techniques like eyebrow shaving and darkening to render themselves more attractive. To enhance their aesthetic allure, they received better meals and opportunities to hone their artistic and literary skills. In return, they owed their masters (like children to

[20] The text, for example, instructs the *chigo* to "rise early for their prayers, . . . pick up their feet while walking down corridors, . . . [and] use [their] precious time wisely, studying music and other arts, participating in poetry gatherings, and reading secular literature (Buddhist texts could be studied after taking the tonsure" of monkhood). The end of *chigo* status was ceremoniously marked by a ritual involving a change of haircut and clothes (*genpuku*) indicating that the youth had reached manhood. The precise time for this ritual was determined neither by chronological age nor attributes of physical maturity, but rather by social factors involving those with authority over the youth in question. For more details on this text, titled *Uki*, and more generally on monastic *chigo*, see Paul Atkins, "Chigo in the Medieval Japanese Imagination," *The Journal of Asian Studies* 67, no. 3 (2008): 947–970, quotation from 949.

[21] See Margaret Childs, "*Chigo Monogatari*: Love Stories or Buddhist Sermons?," *Monumenta Nipponica* 35, no. 2 (1980): 127. She defines *chigo* as "boys between the ages of about seven and fourteen who resided in temples as though at a boarding school."

their parents or vassals to their lord) an unconditional obedience and devotion, even if this extended to their masters' sexual desires.[22]

Strictly speaking, *nanshoku* was a violation of traditional Buddhist monasticism, which prescribed celibate purity as essential to its program of renouncing all sensual desires in order to pursue spiritual enlightenment. However, far more than their Indian and Chinese counterparts, Japanese monks enthusiastically and openly practiced *nanshoku*, while even suggesting ways to justify it theoretically by reconciling it with Buddhist orthodoxy.[23] We can distinguish three lines of justificatory argument. First, as heterosexual relations are explicitly forbidden by celibate monastic life but love is an irrepressibly natural desire that needs physical expression, pederasty is a much needed outlet for the mental welfare of monks. As one seventeenth-century scholar puts it, since "relations between the sexes were forbidden by the Buddha, priests of the law – being made of neither stone nor wood – had no recourse but to practice the love of boys as an outlet for their [sexual] feelings."[24] Second, such love taught the *chigo* the key spiritual virtues of compassion (*jihi*) and sympathetic loving sensitivity (*nasake*), along with other moral values like loyalty and disciplined forbearance. This method of direct, intimate transmission of knowledge from an older master to an aspiring apprentice aptly modeled the esoteric Buddhist religious tradition of direct, divine transmission that Kukai received and brought back from China.

Much as in Greek pederasty, the *chigo* was not expected to derive any pleasure from being penetrated by his older lover or to feel any desire for erotic contact with him. As *nanshoku* was mainly pederastic, so was it overwhelmingly anal, and could be extremely painful for the boy who was penetrated. The *chigo* was expected to endure such physical displeasure with

[22] See Atkins, "Chigo in the Medieval Japanese Imagination," 948.

[23] St. Francis Xavier visited a Japanese Buddhist monastery in the mid-sixteenth century and was horrified that "the abominable vice against nature is so popular that they practice it without any feeling of shame." See Tsuneo Watanabe and Jun'ichi Iwata, *The Love of the Samurai: A Thousand Years of Japanese Homosexuality*, trans. D. R. Roberts (London: GMP Publishers, 1989), 20. There are different explanations for this tolerance. One is the need for sexual release for the multitudes of young men who sought monastic life to escape forced labor. Another is the lack of any indigenous Shinto condemnation of male–male sex.

[24] Paul Gordon Schalow, "Kukai and the Tradition of Male Love in Japanese Buddhism," in *Buddhism, Sexuality, and Gender*, ed. J. I. Cabezon (Albany: SUNY Press, 1992), 222. We also find a medical analogue to this argument in the anonymous 1643 treatise *Shin'yuki* (*Records of Soulmates*), explaining that unrequited love made a man more vulnerable to many diseases and thus required compassionate responsiveness from his beloved boy. See Gregory Pflugfelder, *Cartographies of Desire: Male–Male Sexuality in Japanese Discourse 1600–1950* (Berkeley: University of California Press, 1999), 240.

compassionate good grace, sympathetic love, and loyal obligation. "Even when you are unable to take him who loves you into your heart, you should try and make *giri* [obligation] your rule of conduct."[25] The famous *nanshoku* text known as Kobo Daishi's Book (a manuscript dated 1598 that claims its contents were personally transmitted by Kobo Daishi himself) describes *nasake* (sympathetic, loving sensitivity) as "the most important quality a priest looks for in an acolyte." Affirming that "The greatest pleasure is to proceed [to anal intercourse] with an acolyte who possesses a great sensitivity to love (*nasake*)," it outlines seven methods of anal intercourse. As each of the last two methods is "without lubrication [and thus] . . . causes severe pain," the *chigo* must learn to lovingly endure such painful violence to develop his compassion, *nasake*, and sense of duty.[26]

The third argument highlights the spiritual gains for the adult lover (designated by the term *nenja*, whose *chigo* counterpart term was *nyake*).[27] Because the monk's enjoyment of his *chigo* love was limited to the boy's brief period of youth, the Buddhist cleric learned the painful transience of earthly pleasures, a lesson that could help propel him to renounce them entirely and wholeheartedly embrace the truly holy celibate path. The apparent sin of pederasty could thus be justified as an effective religious tool to discover the vanity of human pleasures by suffering the bitter taste of losing them too soon after having enjoyed them so keenly. In many of the tales of boy love the fleetingness of *nanshoku* was highlighted by the *chigo*'s being killed or violently carried away by evil forces, much to the monk's initial chagrin but ultimately inducing the blessed realization that salvation lies in the religious path of renunciation.

As youth from the aristocratic and samurai classes often studied in Buddhist temples before taking on their adult roles in worldly life, the practice of *nanshoku* or *shudo* easily spread beyond monastic contexts. A fifteenth-century essay affirmed that this "way" of love came to thrive "in the world of the nobles and warriors, [where] lovers would swear perfect and eternal love" and greatly sacrifice for it, thus causing such love to be "truly respected."[28]

[25] The quotation is from the *Shin'yuki*, cited in Watanabe and Iwata, *The Love of the Samurai*, 111. Other texts argued that *nanshoku* would teach the youth "refinement of behavior," "gentleness of speech," and how "to distinguish between the true and the false." See ibid., 113.

[26] Schalow, "Kukai and the Tradition of Male Love," 218–220. It is not surprising that some stories of outstanding *chigo* portray them as avatars of the Buddhist god of compassion, Guanyin.

[27] For more details on this relationship and the evolution of its terminology, see Leupp, *Male Colors*, 43–46.

[28] Cited in Louis Crompton, *Homosexuality and Civilization* (Cambridge, MA: Harvard University Press, 2003), 421.

A later essay confirmed that because "this form of love proved to be deeper than the love between men and women," its power spread beyond the cloister, afflicting "the heart of aristocrat and warrior alike."[29] *Nanshoku* particularly thrived among the samurai, because members of this group (like the monastics) were often confined to all-male contexts and separated from normal family life, even when they were married with children. Many had learned *shudo* as monastic *nyake* and were well prepared to exchange that role for the dominant *nenja* role with a young *wakashu* (the preferred term for a youth in the samurai *shudo* context).

Here again, besides noting the intractable natural need for erotic expression (which if pursued with women could easily create scandal), theorists adduced benefits of aesthetic, ethical, and social instruction to justify the love of boys. First, recalling the defining Heian aesthetic, *shudo* provided an education in sophistication and style, shaping both the youth and the older samurai to be more refined and elegant not only in appearance but also in conduct. Rather than being narrowly focused on sexual intercourse (which was only a small and not always necessary part of the erotic equation), *shudo* formed an extensive discipline of self-cultivation, a focused program of self-fashioning. Didactic manuals such as Yoshida's *Nanshoku masukagami* (*Lucid Mirror of Nanshoku*) offered tips on grooming, hygiene, and etiquette to shape the boys into "paragons of physical beauty and grace" while also instructing their adult lovers in "elegance" and "stylishness."[30] Second, the samurai love of boys claimed to give them an education in manly combat skills and virile virtues that their adult lovers had already mastered and could transmit in the most direct and personal way.[31] Third, *nanshoku* taught the moral and social virtues of loyalty, honor, and commitment to duty (*giri*) that defined the ethic or "way of the samurai warrior" (*bushido*). Lovers in this context pledged a vow of brotherhood to be true to each other and

[29] Schalow, "Kukai and the Tradition of Male Love," 222. For more details on aristocratic *nanshoku*, see Leupp, *Male Colors*, 22–27. In courtly fiction, even the great Genji at one point succumbs to *shudo*, bedding the younger brother of a lady who resisted his seductions (TG 48).

[30] Pflugfelder, *Cartographies of Desire*, 54, 57. Watanabe cites a passage of the *Hagakure* (a practical and spiritual guide for samurai) advising to "always carry rouge and powder with one . . . [because] we sometimes find that we don't look very good." Indeed, some "were in the habit of putting on a light make-up before going into battle," maintaining an aesthetic standard even when facing death. See Watanabe and Iwata, *The Love of the Samurai*, 116.

[31] "According to Yoshida, [this training] . . . included not only such practical accomplishments as fencing, lancemanship, archery, and horseback riding, but, most importantly, the mental attitude (*kokorogake*) and etiquette befitting of a warrior." See Pflugfelder, *Cartographies of Desire*, 71.

willingly sacrifice oneself for the sake of the other, even to the point of laying down one's life.

If this gave samurai *nanshoku* an ennobling sense of sincerity and sublime self-sacrifice, it also engendered troubling violence and discord. To prove the sincerity of their vows, lovers would often seal them with bloody acts of self-mutilation, "piercing the flesh of the thigh or arm, removing a fingernail, or even cutting off a finger"; hence Yoshida's book included advice of how to do so "without bleeding too profusely or becoming permanently crippled."[32] Still more troubling were acts of murder and suicide for the sake of one's honor and vows of love, especially because such unconditional commitment to one's lover contradicted the official samurai ideology of unconditional commitment to one's lord (except for cases where one's lord was one's lover).[33] One critic therefore argued that *nanshoku* is "something both agreeable and disagreeable," because "to throw away one's life [for one's lover] is the ultimate aim of *shudo*" and is what makes this love noble rather than "something shameful"; but that means "one has no life to give in service to one's lord."[34]

As samurai, for various political reasons, were increasingly confined to city life and mingled with the ever more prosperous merchant classes who also developed a taste for *shudo*, *nanshoku* acts of violence also increased, creating a problem that required repeated acts of legislation. Handsome boy actors, who often supplemented their income through prostitution and became objects of intense desire and rivalry (with monks as well as merchants and samurai), often formed the focus of such unruly behavior. The Kabuki stage was famous for its connection with *shudo*, both as dramatic theme and as actual practice. Even the more austere genre of Noh theatre included such themes, and probably owes its existence to *shudo*. Its formative genius, the playwright and theorist Zeami Motokiyo, first rose to prominence when Japan's reigning shogun saw him perform as a boy of twelve. The shogun was so taken by Zeami's beauty and talent that he elevated him to a cherished *wakashu* beloved, providing him with an

[32] Ibid., 41, 52. Ihara Saikaku's famous collection, *The Great Mirror of Male Love* (1687), relates the story of a samurai who loves two young friends and, to prove the sincerity of this double love, "bites off the last joint of each of his little fingers and gives one to each of the boys" as a pledge. See Paul Gordon Schalow, trans., *The Great Mirror of Male Love* (Stanford: Stanford University Press, 1990), 28.

[33] The *Hagakure* instructs young samurai boys to reject romantic advances from all men but their own *nenja*, exhorting them that if such an interloper "continues to persist, you should get angry and cut him down on the spot." Cited in Leupp, *Male Colors*, 165.

[34] From the *Hagakure*, cited in Leupp, *Male Colors*, 48.

excellent education and generous shogunate patronage to develop his art, while exacting "sexual, [and] to some extent, artistic submission."[35]

IV CONNOISSEUR STYLE AND COMMODIFICATION IN HIGH COURTESAN CULTURE

A third major form of classical Japanese *ars erotica*, and surely the most familiar to contemporary readers, took shape in the world of high-class courtesans and played a central role in the aesthetic culture of the Edo period (1603–1868). This pleasure world of exquisitely beautiful, elegantly refined, and artistically talented courtesans became most permanently etched in the popular imagination through its prominent artistic portrayal in Japan's most influential visual genre of *ukiyo-e*,[36] whose alluringly colorful pictures depicted this "floating world" (*ukiyo*) of incessant desire and fleeting gratification.[37] This courtesan tradition also found powerful expression in literature and Kabuki drama, and in its subsequent transformation into what we know today as geisha culture.[38] The courtesan–Kabuki

[35] Tom Hare, ed., *Zeami: Performance Notes* (New York: Columbia University Press, 2008), 3. The genre in which Zeami first performed before the shogun (in 1374) was a mixture of song and dance known as *sarugaku* (literally, "monkey music") that later Zeami (along with his father Kanami) developed into Noh drama.

[36] Although *ukiyo-e* is a distinctive original style involving new techniques, it belongs to the general genre of Japanese erotic painting known as *shunga* (literally, spring painting). Scholars trace its roots to earlier *shunga* forms known as "reclining pictures," "pillow pictures (*makura-e*)," or funny (or laughing) pictures (*warai-e*). One prominent genre of these "funny" pictures involved depicting genitals of exaggerated size, a style one can trace to a medieval tradition of the "phallic contest" represented in art. For discussion of these matters, see Henry Smith, "Overcoming the Modern History of Edo 'Shunga,'" in *Imaging/Reading Eros: Proceedings for the Conference, Sexuality and Edo Culture, 1750–1850*, ed. Sumie Jones (Bloomington: East Asian Center Indiana University, 1996), 26–34; and Akiko Yano, "Historiography of the 'Phallic Contest' Handscroll in Japanese Art," *Japan Review* 26 (2013): 59–82. The idea of seeing erotic nudity as something funny might be traced back to the central Ameratsu myth with the laugh-provoking naked dance of Ame-no-Uzume.

[37] The very meaning of *ukiyo* changed from its original Buddhist notion of sad transience (signified by one Chinese character for *uki* that meant "sad") to the semantically different (but homophonic) character that meant "floating" or "drifting" and thus signifying a carefree hedonistic attitude. The 1665 *Tale of the Floating World* defined it as: "Living only for the moment, turning our full attention to the pleasures of the moon, the snow, the cherry blossoms and the maples, singing songs, drinking wine, and diverting ourselves just in floating, floating, caring not a whit for the poverty staring us in the face, refusing to be disheartened, like a gourd floating along with the river current: This is what we call *ukiyo*." See Donald Shively, "Popular Culture," in J. W. Hall, ed., *The Cambridge History of Japan*, vol. 4 (Cambridge: Cambridge University Press, 1991), 730.

[38] For an account of how the geisha evolved from courtesan culture and came to differ from courtesans, see Cecilia Seigle, *Yoshiwara: The Glittering World of the Japanese Courtesan* (Honolulu: University of Hawaii Press, 1993), 170–174.

relationship is especially close, as Kabuki allegedly originated in Kyoto (around 1603) through the daring song and dance performances of an entertainer-courtesan. In her cross-dressing and her "miming and dancing the role of a dandy visiting a brothel," she caused an immediate sensation and countless imitations through which Kabuki emerged.[39] By that time the city had already long enjoyed a thriving "pleasure district" of brothels, officially established and walled in by shogun decree in order to concentrate and control the prosperous but unruly courtesan trade. The new capital of Edo (later to be known as Tokyo) soon created, in 1617, a walled-in pleasure district of its own, Yoshiwara, which later became the paradigm of high-courtesan culture, eclipsing in fame and influence its counterparts in Kyoto and Osaka. This courtesan world formed part of the new, increasingly powerful *chonin* culture that stemmed from an ever-growing, wealthier, and better-educated urban middle class that asserted itself against the dominant traditional cultures of courtly aristocracy, monastic Buddhism, and samurai *bushido*.[40]

Economic and political factors thus fueled the growth of courtesan culture. By the end of the sixteenth century, most samurai had been moved from the countryside in order to concentrate their feudal lords' strength in large fortress cities like Kyoto, Osaka, and Tokyo. The Edo period's Tokugawa shogunate likewise required these lords (the shogun's vassals) to spend much of their time in the capital, so that he could better observe and control them. Moreover, after centuries of feudal wars, the end of the sixteenth century brought lasting peace to Japan that spurred economic prosperity by providing better conditions for commerce and consumption. Rich members

[39] Shively, "Popular Culture," 749. Described as the "two wheels of the vehicle of pleasure," courtesan and Kabuki culture made cities attractive and prosperous but also disruptive, so that rulers eventually concentrated them in separate quarters of the city for better control of their activities and interactions. See ibid., 741. The intimate connection of Kabuki and courtesan culture is displayed in many ways. They shared styles of fashion, dance, and music (their standard instrument being the sensuously sounding samisen); Kabuki's star actresses became the first highest-ranked courtesans (*tayu*); "the first guides to actors found their model in books on prostitutes"; and many Kabuki plays included courtesan themes with scenes "set in houses of assignation." Ibid., 750, 752, 759–760.

[40] Although the term "*chonin*" means city dweller in general, the *chonin* class refers to urban commoners, essentially to the merchant class, which was the lowest according to the traditional, Confucian-inspired ranking officially adopted in Edo Japan. But the term sometimes included artisans and craftsmen (the next to lowest class), who were closely associated with merchant activity. *Chonin* culture was thus identified with popular culture, though the higher classes often enjoyed and contributed to it. Samurai officials did the original management of Kyoto's and Edo's pleasure quarters, and even the Buddhist monks enjoyed Kabuki and relished the sexual favors of its *wakashu* actors. See Shively, "Popular Culture," 708–769.

of the merchant class (traditionally and officially inferior to the samurai but now more confident, ambitious, and better educated) could use their new wealth to enjoy the pleasures of high-courtesan culture and compete against the now displaced and warless samurai class over the favors of elite courtesans known as *tayu* (太夫).[41] With so many samurai concentrated in the large cities – often far away from their homelands and families and devoid of military action to keep them busy – the floating world of courtesan pleasures presented a new field for the competitive combat and conquest that was already deeply rooted in their military character.

The institution of elite courtesans was yet another importation from China's Tang Dynasty culture. Tang courtesans were not needed for sex; their wealthy clients typically had numerous wives and concubines with whom they could find sexual satisfaction. The erotic pleasures such men sought in the courtesan were more romantic and aesthetic than narrowly carnal: playfully seductive pleasures of artistic entertainment and courtly flirtation that would both satisfy and demonstrate a man's own refinement while also honing it through engagement with elegant courtesan society.[42] Japan's elite courtesan culture similarly emphasized social sophistication, aesthetic discrimination, and the arts. "Yoshiwara was primarily a place of entertainment and socializing, [so] sex was a discreet and secondary aspect of the business," wrapped in an intricately sophisticated tissue of aesthetic codes and rituals.[43] "Indeed, the artistic emphasis on the pleasures of social and cultural intercourse made the sex act almost incidental."[44]

The arts that made courtesans erotic magnets included not only music, dance, and song but also "calligraphy, tea ceremony, poetry, and the art of identifying incense by fragrance" (and even creating or blending fragrances). These artistic gifts along with a courtesan's wit, elegant manners, good taste,

[41] The term's original usage designated the chief actor in a Noh play.

[42] See van Gulik's extensive account of Tang Dynasty courtesans in his *Sexual Life in Ancient China: A Preliminary Survey of Chinese Sex and Society from ca. 1500 B.C. till 1644 A.D.* (Leiden: Brill, 2003), 170–183.

[43] Seigle, *Yoshiwara*, 152.

[44] Shively, "Popular Culture," 747. Men could easily have sex with lower class prostitutes of various types and levels, so many that there were "almost five hundred words used to designate prostitutes" (ibid., 749). A series of elaborately ritualized meetings was required before the courtesan would grant sexual satisfaction to her suitor-client, and sometimes she never did. For extensive discussion of the elaborate aesthetic ceremonies of courtesan courtship that include ritual gifts, processions, protocols of drinking, conversation, and entertainment (several of which mirrored marriage ceremonies), see Seigle, *Yoshiwara*, 64–67; and William R. Lindsey, *Fertility and Pleasure: Ritual and Sexual Values in Tokugawa Japan* (Honolulu: University of Hawaii Press, 2007), 87–96.

and compassionate thoughtfulness were more important than beauty for gaining her the high status of *tayu*.[45] Superior sexual skills played no apparent role in her value or ranking. Special techniques such as oral or anal sex were repudiated as far too vulgar to practice or even mention. Echoing the aesthetic of the Heian courtly love, elite courtesan culture made genteel elegance the key quality for erotic allure. The *tayu*'s clothes and gestures were modeled on noble tradition. Her language had to be exceedingly pure, not only eschewing all talk of sex but also refraining from mention of food, which likewise implied the baseness of animal appetite. She dared not eat in front of a client so as not to expose an open mouth. Even laughter, as Kizan notes, had to be thoroughly controlled because "to open her mouth and bare her teeth or to laugh in a loud voice is to deprive her instantly of all elegance and make her seem crude."[46]

An important part of the high courtesan's erotic allure and provision of pleasure lay in the aesthetic play of courting her and the stimulating challenge of winning her favors. The idea of sexual contact was merely the seed to engender a complex erotic narrative, rich in imaginative pleasures of anticipated delights and romantic drama. Even if an elite courtesan was essentially for sale, her favors could not simply be bought. She could carefully choose her suitors and reject anyone she did not care for. This dashing "independent spirit" (known as "*hari*") made her an all the more desirable prize.[47] Meetings with her client lovers would often be preceded by a long exchange of romantic letters, aesthetically composed to both stimulate and satisfy their erotic imagination. The eventual rendezvous would be held at a stylish house of assignation, whose rooms, gardens, and culinary

[45] Seigle, *Yoshiwara*, 85, 158. Good writing (calligraphic skill as well as good grammar) had paramount importance as indicative of the courtesan's refinement. Fujimoto Kizan, author of *Shikido Okagami* (*The Great Mirror of the Way of Sex*, 1678) insists that poor writing "for a courtesan . . . is a disaster," whether "she wrote a bad hand or that her grammar was shaky." Cited in Donald Keene, *Landscapes and Portraits: Appreciations of Japanese Culture* (Tokyo: Kodansha, 1971), 246. To the list of courtesan skills, one could add amateur acting, as they had to feign loving attachment and loyalty to multiple clients. Courtesan handbooks sometimes provided instruction on the "falsification of passion" or tears of sadness, but clients occasionally complained that "Hateful is the courtesan's faking and writhing, especially when she feigns sobbing." For details on these issues of pretense, see Seigle, *Yoshiwara*, 156–157, 190–191.

[46] Kizan adds that "When something is so extremely funny that she must laugh, she should either cover her mouth with her sleeve or else avert her head behind the customer's shoulder" (Keene, *Landscapes and Portraits*, 245).

[47] Seigle, *Yoshiwara*, 44. The courtesan, however, did have to meet a quota of paying customers in order to maintain her ranking and indeed keep her job with the house that owned her. Few were the lucky ones whose partners liberated them from sexual slavery by buying them from their houses.

excellence would heighten the ambience of desire and delight, as would the beautiful young girls the courtesan brought as her service escorts. Elaborately refined rituals of courtship at those meetings contributed further aesthetic richness to the client's experience and erotic tantalization. In Yoshiwara, in order to heighten the client's desire (and his expenses), sexual contact would not occur until the third meeting, and it might not even occur then at all, if the courtesan so chose, indicating this by refusing to retire with her client to a bedroom or by simply turning her back on him to go to sleep. Like the screened Heian heroine or the Greek hetaera, the *tayu* practiced an enticing dialectic of hard-to-get concealment and exposure. Though her body was elegantly clothed and carefully protected from a prying public, she would so arrange her dress and undergarments to allow her discreetly when she walked "to reveal a flash of white ankle" that would make men "go insane" with desire.[48]

Besides the aesthetic pleasures of the courtship process, client-lovers had other reasons not to be troubled by the complex protocols of deferral and denial of sexual satisfaction. A man could bask in the glory of simply "dating" a *tayu*, since merely being accepted by her for an assignation carried a sizable measure of social prestige, implying that he was wealthy, elegant, and attractive enough to meet her superior standards of selection. If he became a favored regular client-lover (*najimi*) of a *tayu* or other well-ranked courtesan, his reputation as a desirably chic sophisticate would grow still higher.[49] Nobody would know what sexual acts did or did not occur in their time in the bedroom, given the courtesan's commitment to avoid any mention of vulgar topics and given the client-lover's need to sustain his own reputation for elegant refinement and stylish thoughtfulness, the pursuit of which comprised, along with entertainment, the key purpose of frequenting courtesans.

These urbane virtues were captured by the notion of *tsu* – a quality expressing "the essence of sophistication ... that ... represented elegance not only of appearance but also of spirit, as well as savoir faire in human relationships."[50] "*Tsu*'s ideal characteristics were generosity, courtesy, consideration, intelligence, wit, candor, refinement, and urbanity." A gentleman

[48] Ibid., 77.

[49] Offsetting its obvious benefits, the status of being a *najimi* involved the constraint of not engaging other courtesans, even though his courtesan was free to entertain other men and indeed had to do so to maintain her job. This asymmetrical restriction (the opposite of conventional marriages where men were free to have affairs while wives were not) was strictly policed and punished by the pleasure quarter's citizens. See ibid., 110–112.

[50] Ibid., 131.

demonstrated *tsu* through his discriminating aesthetic interests in "music, painting, poetry, popular song, haiku, tea ceremony, flower arrangement, and calligraphy," his familiarity with the theater world, and especially his stylish skill in navigating the pleasure quarters with their own rich aesthetic resources and challenges.[51] As *tsu* became the dominant cultural ideal for the man-about-town in Japan's new urban society of peace and prosperity, so connoisseurship in the erotic world of courtesan culture proved a necessary training ground for attaining this ideal. Visiting Yoshiwara for an assignation with an elite courtesan required devoting significant care and expense to acquire for oneself an impressively stylish outfit and means of arrival, but also to provide splendid bedding for the courtesan and sumptuous refreshments and entertainments for her and her attendants (as well as for his own escorts).

Tsu's courteous thoughtfulness and generosity would be expressed not only in the gentleman's refined contact with the courtesan but also by ceding that contact to another suitor through the established custom of "yielding" one's appointment to a courtesan's favored regular if that rival politely requested it. This forgoing of one's immediate personal desire in consideration of the courtesan's assumed preferences or the desires of a rival suitor with deeper claims on her attention would manifest the height of refined sophistication and gracious nobility that would be widely admired by courtesans and suitors alike, thus winning the gentleman high dividends of social respect. For the rising but traditionally (and still officially) subordinate merchant class, and also for the demilitarized, displaced, and diminished samurai, the love of courtesans and the demonstration of sophistication in courting them provided a competitive arena where men could struggle to elevate, assert, or defend their social status, by acting out (just like the *tayu* herself) the role of courtly aristocrats. To neglect this arena would condemn a man to boorishness. As one seventeenth-century text remarks, "No matter how superior a man, if he does not buy prostitutes, he is incomplete and tends to be uncouth."[52]

If courtesan culture's *ars erotica* focused mainly on elegant aesthetic style and social prestige acquired through lavish expenditures of time and money, we not surprisingly find its background mercantile economy reflected in its commodification of love. As Prince Genji saved love letters from his various conquests, so Edo *tsu* connoisseurs collected similar tokens of affection from their courtesan loves. Not simply a way to emulate Heian romanticism and

[51] Ibid. [52] Ibid., 153.

thus affirm their refinement and social status, the practice further provided quantifiable testimony of their amorous success in return for their investment. Unlike Genji, who shunned courtesans and whose loves (however fleeting or frivolous) were real, Edo courtesan lovers were (with few exceptions) merely involved in a make-believe game of love, acting out the refined elegance of aristocracy and the passion of profound love while actually involved in a commercial exchange of erotic entertainment for money.

Because the defining background of the courtesan–client relationship was decidedly mercantile rather than amatory, their expression of love always carried a taint of insincerity. If the client could affirm the authenticity of his affection for the courtesan by buying more time with her and gifts for her (the ultimate gift and proof consisting of buying her out of prostitution), the courtesan had to rely on other proofs of genuine devotion. Beautifully written avowals of love were necessary but not sufficient. The ramified practice of *shinju* (心中, literally, "heart center") emerged to provide stronger testimony of truly heartfelt love. Kizan outlines it in stunningly graphic detail, elaborating six varieties of *shinju* in order of what he regards as increasing severity or power of conviction: tearing off a nail, giving a vow that is sealed with one's blood (and often also written in it), cutting off one's hair, tattooing a lover's name, cutting off a finger, and stabbing "a blade tip through the fleshy part of either the upper arm or thigh."[53] Courtesans' play-acting extended even to *shinju*; for they could rely on a market of cut-off fingers (acquired from corpses and other sources) as well as other tricks to minimize or avoid pain and injury in providing *shinju* pledges. Playboy connoisseurs collected such keepsake tokens of courtesan affection (authentic or not), preserving them in a *shinju* box (or *shinjubako*) to show off to their peers.[54]

In short, beneath the elegantly refined surface of courtesan love lurked a raw underbelly of commercial commodification, deceitful distrust, and painful, bloody violence. Not surprisingly, the initially fresh aesthetic charm of urban courtesan culture was gradually buried by excessive ostentation fueled by an increasingly conspicuous commercialization that characterized its subsequent nineteenth-century practice. Fixated on the cynical connoisseurship of costly commodities, Edo courtesan culture's aesthetic education

[53] Kizan's chapter on *shinju* is translated in Lawrence Rogers, "She Loves Me, She Loves Me Not: *Shinju* and *Shikido Okagami*," *Monumenta Nipponica* 49, no. 1 (1994): 40–60, quotation from 58.

[54] Kizan writes that "there are boxes for pledges in the houses of men about town in which they collect the fingers, nails, hair, and oaths that have been sent them" (Keene, *Landscapes and Portraits*, 247). For further details on courtesan *shinju* practices, see Seigle, *Yoshiwara*, 191.

seems inferior to the earlier Japanese models of erotic love. It lacks the gallant grace and ennobling sincerity of Heian romance as well as the ethical quality of nurturing edification that characterized some currents of Japan's *shudo* eroticism, which, despite its abuses, contains impressive examples of religious inspiration, compassionate altruism, and self-sacrificing loyalty that shine with attractive virtue.[55] None of Japan's classical ways of love, however, attains the ethical uplift or spiritual sublimity of Islam's Sufism. By comparison, they seem philosophically shallow, and their aesthetic apotheosis in Edo courtesan culture ultimately rings hollow – with no real spiritual substance beneath the richness of ritual. Such conclusions (provisional as they may be) suggest a provocative thesis: that an aesthetic education through lovemaking requires an animating spiritual, ethical dimension to inspire and guide its project of self-cultivation so that it does not degenerate into decadent connoisseurship or self-indulgent, tawdry sensuality. A dimension of ethical and spiritual uplift can render erotic culture more nobly and compellingly aesthetic.[56]

55 Watanabe and Iwata provide the strongest case for samurai *shudo* as constituting an ethical and aesthetic "ideal" or "way" of life. They draw on two pre-Edo texts in elaborating five necessary conditions for being a proper *wakashu*: "to have a pure and simple heart; to be both tender and noble"; "to respond to [the loving admirer's] passion" even if "the admirer is not very pleasing" and not "be capricious"; to "love study, and especially the composition of poetry"; to "not forget that the *wakashu* too grows old" and that having "been loved provides happy memories for one's old age." The *Shin'yuki* text insists that the samurai must "not ever . . . forget . . . the spirit of *shudo*," because otherwise "it will not be possible . . . to maintain the decencies, nor gentleness of speech, nor the refinement of polite behavior." The same text even claims *shudo* as a path to Buddhist enlightenment. "For this way is really like that of the true Awakening, in that we may give ourselves wholly to it." See Watanabe and Iwata, *The Love of the Samurai*, 110, 113.

56 Immanuel Kant similarly insists that culture and its task of self-cultivation require an ethical dimension, without which they amount merely to the superficiality of good manners and refined sophistication, which he calls "civilization" in contrast to true culture (*Kultur*). "We are civilized – perhaps too much for our own good – in all sorts of social grace and decorum," he writes. "But to consider ourselves as having reached morality – for that, much is lacking. The ideal of morality belongs to culture; its use for some simulacrum of morality in the love of honor and outward decorum constitutes mere civilization," See Immanuel Kant, "Idea for a Universal History from a Cosmopolitan Point of View," in the collection of his essays, *On History*, trans. Lewis White Beck (Indianapolis: Bobbs-Merrill, 1963), 391.

8

Commingling, Complexity, and Conflict

Erotic Theory in Medieval and Renaissance Europe

I THE HISTORICAL BACKGROUND: POLITICS AND RELIGION

Having studied the erotic traditions of classical Greco-Roman, Judeo-Christian, Chinese, Indian, Islamic, and Japanese cultures, we now explore how some of them commingled in medieval and Renaissance Europe, creating a richly diverse but deeply conflicted field of erotic theory. Condemned as devilish and degrading, erotic desire was contrastingly commended for its power to educate and uplift, for its capacities to inspire individuals to strive for greater achievements of knowledge, grace, and virtue, as well as higher levels of love. Scholars once sharply distinguished the Middle Ages from the Renaissance, viewing the latter as a new expression of personal individuality and fresh, bold thinking that challenged entrenched Christian dogma by drawing on the inspiration of classical pagan Greco-Roman sources. But it is hard to draw a sharp line or essential divide between these two ill-defined periods, since they display considerable continuities, and each contains far too much diversity to be reduced to a distinctive, defining essence.[1]

[1] The traditional view of radical difference, influentially defined by Burckhardt, was that "In the Middle Ages both sides of human consciousness – that which was turned within and that which turned without – lay dreaming or half awake beneath a common veil. The veil was woven of faith, illusion, and childish prepossession, through which the world and history were seen clad in strange hues. Man was conscious of himself only as a member of a race, people, party, family, or corporation – only through some general category.... [But in Italy's Renaissance] this veil first melted into air" so that "objective treatment ... of this world became possible" and the "subjective side" also "asserted itself with corresponding emphasis; man became a spiritual *individual* and recognized himself as such." Jacob Burckhardt, *The Civilisation of the Period of the Renaissance in Italy*, trans. S. G. C. Middlemore (London: Swan Sonnenschein, 1904), 129. Critical of such simplistic periodization, contemporary scholarship recognizes that "Rather than a period with definitive beginnings and endings and consistent content in between, the Renaissance can be (and occasionally has been) seen as a movement of practices and ideas to which

With respect to eroticism, the Middle Ages offers some strikingly brave expressions of individualist thinking while proposing a new ideal of love (so-called courtly love, or *fin'amor*) that boldly contests key Christian ideals by deploying classical Greco-Roman authors, yet nonetheless seeks to remain within the general Christian framework. Compounding this complexity is a distinctive Islamic aspect. The courtly love ideal developed from troubadour traditions, which stemmed from Aquitaine in southern France and borrowed heavily from the rich poetic and erotic culture that flourished in Arab Al-Andalus in southern Spain and then spread northward. King William IX of Aquitaine, the first known troubadour and a renowned womanizer, allegedly copied such Arab poetry in his manuscripts and certainly had close contact with Arab culture, including participation in the Crusade of 1101.[2] Medieval and Renaissance sexual science came largely through Islamic scholars who transmitted Greco-Roman theories of sex as well as conveying distinctive features of Arab *ars erotica*, which in turn drew on Indian sexology.[3]

The variety of erotic thought in Europe's Middle Ages and Renaissance reflects the commingling diversity and conflict that characterized its political and sociocultural reality. The fall of the Roman Empire, precipitated by the persistent invasions of Germanic tribes, resulted in violent disorder, mass migrations, and social disintegration. Compounding this turmoil were continuing incursions from pagan Viking tribes during the ninth to the early eleventh centuries, confrontations that eventually led France to cede Normandy to a Viking warlord in 911. More significant and lasting was the

specific groups and identifiable persons variously responded in different times and places. It would be in this sense a network of diverse, sometimes converging, sometimes conflicting cultures, not a single, time-bound culture." Randolph Starn, "Renaissance Redux," *The American Historical Review* 103, no. 1 (1998): 124.

[2] An early biographical sketch described him as "one of the most courtly men in the world and one of the greatest deceivers of women. He was a fine knight at arms, liberal in his womanizing, and a fine composer and singer of songs. He travelled much through the world, seducing women." Jean Boutière and Alexander Herman Schutz, eds., *Biographies des troubadours. Textes provençaux des XIIIe et XIVe siècles* (Paris: Nizet, 1964), 7–8. I quote the translation of Thomas Hinton, "Troubadour Biographies and the Value of Authentic Love," *Interfaces* 2 (2016): 150.

[3] We find a striking example of these added Arab aspects of erotic theory in *The Mirror of Coitus*, an anonymous fifteenth-century Catalan text, "one of the earliest medical treatises in a Romance language that is exclusively dedicated to coitus and sexual hygiene" and that focuses on lovemaking rather than love or sexual disease and physiology. The distinctively Arab features of the text concern its elaboration of courtship, foreplay, coital positions, and the qualities of sexually desirable men and women. See Michael Solomon, ed., *The Mirror of Coitus: A Translation and Edition of the Fifteenth-Century "Speculum al foderi"* (Madison: Hispanic Seminary of Medieval Studies, 1990), vii. Solomon explains more generally how Arabic writers systematized Greek medical theory and disseminated it to the Christian West (xvii).

penetration of Islamic conquest that began with the occupation of Spain in 711 and which, at various times, included also southern France, Sicily, southern Italy, Greece, the Balkans, and much of Hungary and the Ukraine. Adding to these disruptive struggles with Islam were two centuries of Crusades to liberate the holy land of the Middle East but that wrought havoc on European communities along the way, with Jews in particular becoming the victims of frequent massacre. Ottoman forces continually threatened other communities in the heart of Europe from the fourteenth through the sixteenth centuries, laying siege to Vienna in 1529 and fighting a series of wars with Venice.

Even within Christian Europe, diversity and violent conflict reigned. During the Western Schism of the Roman Catholic Church (1378–1417) there were first two, then three rival popes competing for authority. Heresies were identified, condemned, and punished. Catharism was a notable example. Derived from the Greek word for pure, Catharism held the dualist doctrine that the material world was the product of Satan and pervaded with sin. The Cathars therefore advocated strict celibate chastity, since marriage and procreation ensnared the spirit into sinful, fleshly materiality and its reproductive multiplication.[4] To eliminate this sect that thrived in southern France, Pope Innocent III waged a twenty-year military campaign (1209–1229), bringing death or forced conversion to most of its adherents and causing general upheaval in the region of Toulouse. To suppress such heresies, the Catholic Church developed the institutions of the Inquisition, whose activities were later expanded to address Christian Europe's deepest religious schism, namely, that resulting from the Protestant Reformation and the Catholic Counter-Reformation that plunged Europe into a series of religious wars between 1524 and 1648.

Reflecting the common link between the body politic and personal bodies, Christianity's worries about maintaining political and religious integrity led to increased anxiety about somatic behavior and more severe policing of it. Sexual conduct proved a paradigm example. The Christian doctrine of marital chastity, which limits sex to monogamous encounters aimed narrowly at procreation, had to defend itself not only against Islamic culture's endorsement of polygyny, concubines, and sex slaves. It also struggled

[4] The terms "bugger" and "buggery" originally derive from the Cathars, whose beliefs were allegedly shaped by a Bulgarian priest named Bogomil in the tenth century ("bugger" being a transformation of "Bulgari"). For these roots, see Dimitri Obolensky, *The Bogomils: A Study in Balkan Neo-Manichaeism* (Cambridge: Cambridge University Press, 1948). Both terms served as a pejorative condemning either sodomy or more generally heresy. Louis Crompton, *Homosexuality and Civilization* (Cambridge, MA: Harvard University Press, 2006), 190.

against heretical Christian sects like the Cathars, who rejected marriage as impure and who were therefore suspected of secretly engaging in homosexual acts or illicit fornication to satisfy allegedly irrepressible carnal desires. Countless other Christians, including many priests, faced similar suspicions. Historians explain how Carolingian panic concerning the ninth-century Viking and Islamic invasions and then twelfth-century concerns with Crusaders' defeats and their exposure to the "freer mores of the Islamic East, and the scarcity of Christian women" quickly led the Church to adopt harsh doctrines endorsing severe penalties for sodomy. These included excommunication and death for laymen and the loss of clerical office for priests.[5]

If Christianity's state and church leaders had trouble maintaining political rule and order on their bodies of land, they compensated by intensifying their control of human bodies under their dominion, while blaming any military and political defeats on divine wrath over deviant sexual practices. To ensure the moral high ground through the chastity of its priests, the Church, after centuries of wavering, firmly prohibited them from marrying in eleventh-century edicts by Popes Leo and Gregory, which were reaffirmed in the Second Lateran Council of 1139. These controls, however, raised long-held anxieties that priests would turn to satisfying their erotic urges in sinful ways through homosexual pleasures, most troublingly through acts of sodomy. Augmenting such worries was the fact that many priests shared an intimate communal life in monastic communities often remote from the rest of society and from public surveillance. So severe were concerns about homosexuality that they found fierce poetic expression in the twelfth-century theologian Alain of Lille, whose *Complaint of Nature* (from the late 1160s) complains how rampant homosexual lovemaking had defiled nature and offended God.[6]

II THE PHILOSOPHICAL CONTEXT

Philosophical influences heightened fears of homosexuality among the clergy. Many priests were educated enough to enjoy the Latin and Greek

[5] Crompton, *Homosexuality and Civilization*, 158, 186–187. Such doctrines were issued at the 829 Council of Paris, the 1120 Council of Nablus, and the 1179 Third Lateran Council.

[6] Alain de Lille, *The Complaint of Nature*, trans. Douglas M. Moffat (New York: Henry Holt, 1908). Consider these lines from the poem's first section: "Nature weeps, character passes away ... [because man's] sex of active nature ... declines into passive nature. Man is made woman, he blackens the honor of his sex, the craft of magic Venus makes him of double gender" (3).

texts that became increasingly available in medieval and Renaissance times (largely through their initial preservation and transmission by Islamic scholars). These clerics could easily absorb and appreciate the classical Greco-Roman ideology that celebrated erotic male friendships as an ideal.[7] Particularly influential here was the Aristotelian-Ciceronian ideal of perfect friendship as a loving relationship based on the shared love of virtue that first attracts friends to each other, inspiring them to strive for ever greater virtue. This male ideal of loving friendship was eventually extended to include women and helped form the background of medieval and Renaissance erotic thought.

Noting that "it is love (*amor*) from which the word 'friendship' (*amicitia*) is derived," Cicero argues that "men's souls are stirred [to "sentiments of love and of kindly affection"] when they think they see clearly the virtue and goodness of those with whom a close intimacy is possible."[8] Testifying from personal experience, he avows, "I loved [Africanus] because of a certain admiration for his virtue, and he, in turn, loved me, because ... of my character; and close association added to our mutual affection." Through their love and "longing for this virtue [true friends] bend towards it and move closer to it, so that, by familiar association with him whom they have begun to love, they may enjoy his character, equal him in affection, become readier to deserve than to demand his favors, and vie with him in a rivalry of virtue." Friendship's true reward is thus not in any material "advantage" that friends can give us but "in the love itself," which in perceiving virtue "leaps into flame" and which, through love's desire, spurs us to become more virtuous.

"Friendship," Cicero insists, "was given to us by nature as the handmaid of virtue, not as a comrade of vice; because virtue cannot attain her highest aims unattended, but only in union and fellowship with another." Such loving friendship requires not only virtuous self-discipline but also great care in choosing one's friends, as strong attachments to unworthy people

[7] Through their knowledge of Latin, learned clerics also enjoyed Ovid's celebration of the sensual pleasures of heterosexual seduction. We find Ovid's strong influence in the erotic poems collected in the *Carmina Burana* of 1230, but also in the letters of Abelard and Heloise and in Andreas Capellanus's foundational text on courtly love, *De amore,* which I discuss below. For a detailed study of the Ovidian influences in these works, see Michael Calabrese, "Ovid and the Female Voice in the *De amore* and the *Letters* of Abelard and Heloise," *Modern Philology* 95, no. 1 (1997): 1–26.

[8] Cicero, *On Friendship,* in *On Old Age. On Friendship. On Divination*, trans. W. A. Falconer (Cambridge, MA: Loeb Classical Library, 1923), quotations here from sections 8, 9, 22, and 27; pp. 139, 142–143, 145, 191, 207.

will bring us down. Good friends must not be deficient in virtue or in self-sufficiency. They must be "dependent on no one" to ensure that the friendship is not motivated by the quest for gain. Because people often make wrong choices (through ignorance, the deceit of others, or even self-deception), Church leaders worried that the ideal of virtuous intimacy could degenerate into lecherous, gain-seeking vice.

Cicero's views were directly applied in a book entitled *De spirituali amicitiâ* (*On Spiritual Friendship*) written between 1164 and 1167 by the English Cistercian abbot Aelred of Rivaulx (1110–1167), who described such friendship as "sublime love" in contrast to both carnal love and worldly friendship aimed at gain.[9] He recognized that this "chaste and holy love" that "springs from an esteem for virtue" was extremely difficult to achieve because it not only required "affability in speech, cheerfulness of countenance, suavity in manners, [and] serenity even in the expression of the eyes," but also permitted no immoral behavior, such as deceit or the "wanton affection" (*affectionis lascivia*) of sensual desires. The virtues of friends are continually tested, and as these tests are successfully passed, the friendships and their attendant virtues rise to a higher level and provide greater happiness and spiritual benefits.

Corresponding to this escalation of virtue and value is a reduction in the number of individuals admitted into the higher circles of friendship. From many friendly companions, one learns to choose a smaller number of friends of superior virtue whom one can love more, and an even smaller number of especially intimate friends displaying still loftier virtue and the highest stage of human love that provides the path to the supreme level of divine love. In Aelred's words, "it [is] a foretaste of blessedness thus to [rise] in this way from the sweetness of fraternal charity, to wing one's flight aloft to that more sublime splendor of divine love, and by the ladder of charity now to mount to the embrace of Christ himself." If this metaphor of love's gradual ascent to ever more spiritual and divine heights reflects Plato's trailblazing erotic logic of the *Symposium* and its Neoplatonic replications, it also recalls the Islamic ascent from worldly to divine love, but without admitting the sexual body into the spiritual ascent as al-Arabi contrastingly does. Aelred's priestly notion of virtue entails conquering the body ("*victor corporis*") rather than transforming the ardent energy of its desires into spiritual passion, just as his idea of love requires "purity of intention, the guide of reason, and restraint."

[9] The quotations from Aelred in this paragraph are from C. S. Jaeger, *Ennobling Love: In Search of a Lost Sensibility* (Philadelphia: University of Pennsylvania Press, 1999), 111–114.

Confining love's desire to disembodied rationality and restraint was problematic even for the spiritual love of virtuous friendship. Distinguished clergy and secular nobility sometimes manifested their intimately loving friendships in distinctly physical expressions of desire without suggesting dishonorable carnal lust. In 1187 King Richard the Lionheart fell so deeply in love with the enemy French King Philip (eight years younger) that combat turned into loving cohabitation. As a chronicler less than twenty years later, describes it:

> Richard, Duke of Aquitaine, son of the King of England, remained with Philip, the King of France, who so honored him for so long that they ate every day at the same table and from the same dish, and at night their beds did not separate them. And the King of France loved him as his own soul; and they loved each other so much that the King of England was absolutely astonished at the vehement love between them and marveled at what it could mean.[10]

An alleged incident in the life of Bernard of Clairvaux (1090–1153) is equally remarkable for the passionate bodily expression of spiritual love and its deployment for holy purposes of education. When Bernard's friends tried to dissuade him from joining the Cistercian order, one friend in particular, Hugh de Vitry, "wept and threw himself into his embrace"; and although Hugh's crying was briefly calmed by the embrace, it continued the "entire day."[11] So the following night, to comfort his friend, Bernard arranged that "they slept together in a bed so narrow it could scarcely hold one of them." Hugh continued to cry but confessed it was now for a different reason: "I weep for myself. For I know your way of life and am aware that a conversion to the monastic life is more necessary for me than for you." After this somatically loving conversion, the two friends repeatedly walked about holding hands, "confirming a bond of spiritual union" and thereby suggesting that there is no essential contradiction between expressions of physical and spiritual love. The very same act can be both.

Bernard's brilliant rival, Peter Abelard, would go further by arguing that the very same act could be ethical or sinful, because an act's moral quality depends entirely on the character of its intention, but intentions are not always clear (even to oneself) and often change. One way to test whether one's loving intentions are truly spiritual rather than carnal would be to put

[10] Cited in ibid., 11.

[11] The quotations are from an account of the incident by Geoffrey of Auxerre, Bernard's secretary and biographer, as cited in ibid., 131.

oneself in intimate physical proximity or contact with one's beloved friends and see whether one's thoughts and feelings remain spiritual rather than degenerating into the carnal. This also provides a method for honing one's virtue in resisting carnality by testing oneself through situations that easily could arouse carnal desires. Medieval clerics occasionally practiced such virtue-testing and virtue-honing trials through allegedly chaste heterosexual practices of sleeping together, even if such practices of cohabitation (or *syneisaktism*) were generally condemned as far too devilishly risky.

Robert of Arbrissel (ca. 1045–1116) allowed his men and women followers (many of whom were former prostitutes) not only to eat together but also to share "a common bed at night" and therefore was censured by Bishop Marbod of Rennes (his former teacher) and by Abbot Geoffrey of Vendôme.[12] Geoffrey rejected Robert's defense that this practice was a form of virtue-sharpening asceticism developed by restraining desire in situations of carnal temptation; he condemned it as a "fruitless form of martyrdom," an excessively extreme test for "angelic perfection" that, when practiced by humans suggests, "diabolic presumption." Although he described Robert's "new martyrdom of sleeping together" in chastity as "new and unheard of," there surely existed a legendary paradigm of continent homosexual love described in Plato's *Symposium*. It tells how Socrates and Alcibiades slept together under one sheet with Socrates resisting his beloved Alcibiades' persistent efforts to tempt him into physical acts of lovemaking and thereby instructing the wanton young man in the powers of virtuous restraint by his own personal example.

Other twelfth-century clerics suggest milder ways of risking the flames of physical attraction in order to practice and teach the virtues of edifying chaste love. They focus on sensuous words rather than physical contact to express a desire that is ardently aroused but chastely restrained. Baudri of Bourgueil (1050–1130) wrote a passionate poem to a conceited young student whose beautiful face, body, and voice "touch [him] to the heart and core," arousing Baudri's physical desire for "sportive pleasure" from the "divine art of [the boy's] body." Baudri, however, is happy to restrain himself to passionate words because he is equally attracted by the boy's chastity, which he seeks to reinforce by his poetic efforts while also urging the boy to abandon his arrogant ways. With younger women whom he admired, Baudri deployed the same poetic method of erotic arousal to stir up the passion of chaste, edifying love. Writing to a beautiful young nun of high nobility, he

[12] This paragraph's quotations from Marbod and Geoffrey are in ibid., 129–130.

adoringly describes the beauty of her body to highlight her "beauty of character" while urging ardent yet chaste love as the path to greater virtue. "Let our hearts be joined but our bodies remain apart.... This is a special love: the flesh does not taint it. / Nor does illicit desire mar it. / I am always a lover of your virginity. I long for the purity of your flesh." Through such love, he urges, "Let us tread the path of virtues ... [and] rise to the stars." Another poem, sent to a beloved male friend, explains the true source and power of Baudri's pedagogy for virtue: "If while I seem to teach you, love [*amor*] is the real teacher."[13]

In medieval philosophical thinking love was more than a mere teacher of virtue and refinement through the Ciceronian ideal of ardent, ennobling friendship. Love was also the supreme principle and power that governed the universe, holding its parts together while providing a teleological direction for the perfection of the individuals who dwell in it. All the influential philosophical currents – Christian, Greco-Roman, and Islamic – affirmed love's status as a supreme ontological presence, force, and value. The Christian view has firm biblical foundations, with the proof of God's love being Christ's sacrifice for humankind's salvation. Though suggested in various parts of the New Testament, the idea that God is love finds its most direct and persistent expression in the First Epistle of John 4:7–16:

> Beloved, let us love one another: for love is of God; and every one that loveth is born of God, and knoweth God. He that loveth not knoweth not God; for God is love. In this was manifested the love of God toward us, because that God sent his only begotten Son into the world, that we might live through him.... Beloved, if God so loved us, we ought also to love one another.... If we love one another, God dwelleth in us, and his love is perfected in us.... And we have known and believed the love that God hath to us. God is love; and he that dwelleth in love dwelleth in God, and God in him.

[13] Baudri's love lyrics to the young nun are from ibid., 95–96; those regarding his male objects of affection are from 71–72, 73. Bishop Marbod (who allegedly had a good number of female and male lovers in his youth) intriguingly suggests a far more complex method of enlisting erotic passion to advance the chastity of restraint. In the poem "Dissuasio amoris venerei" ("An Argument against Sexual Love"), Marbod describes how his unrequited but obsessive passion for a boy dissuades him from accepting an attractive woman's attempts to seduce him, to which he would have otherwise gladly assented. Here is a case in which an obsessive but unsatisfiable carnal passion precludes sexual desires that are more dangerous because they are temptingly easy to satisfy. For an account of this poem, along with other medieval love lyrics, see Tison Pugh, "Personae, Same-Sex Desire, and Salvation in the Poetry of Marbod of Rennes, Baudri of Bourgueil, and Hildebert of Lavardin," *Comitatus: A Journal of Medieval and Renaissance Studies* 31, no. 1 (2000): 57–86.

The Roman philosopher Boethius (480–524 CE), whose Neoplatonic *Consolation of Philosophy* maintained enormous influence in medieval thought, presented a vision of the world as a great chain of being, united and governed by love that harmonizes the world's diversity, which otherwise would fall into conflict and war:

> The world in constant change
> Maintains a harmony,
> And elements keep peace
> Whose nature is to war.. . .
> And all this chain of things
> In earth and sea and sky
> One ruler holds in hand:
> If Love relaxed the reins
> All things that now keep peace
> Would wage continual war
> And wreck the great machine
> Which unity maintains
> With motions beautiful.
> Love, too, holds peoples joined
> By sacred bond of treaty,
> And weaves the holy knot
> Of marriage's pure love.
> Love promulgates the laws
> For friendship's faithful bond.
> O happy race of men
> If Love who rules the sky
> Could rule your hearts as well![14]

The poet Dante, whose *Divine Comedy* elevates Boethius to the Fourth Heaven's Sphere of the Sun, adopts this idea of unifying love as the book's crowning cosmological vision of all existence empowered by love's "highest light." "Within its depths I saw gathered together, / Bound by Love into a single volume, / Leaves that lie scattered through the universe . . . By the Love that moves the sun and the other stars" ("Paradiso," canto 33, lines 85–87, 145).[15]

We find this cosmology of love also in Ibn Sina (970–1037), arguably Islam's most important philosopher, who significantly influenced European medieval and Renaissance thought, most notably through the seminal work

[14] Boethius, *The Consolation of Philosophy*, trans. Victor Watts (London: Penguin, 1999), 45–46.

[15] Dante Alighieri, *The Divine Comedy*, trans. James Finn Cotter (Amity, NY: Amity House, 1987), 613, 615.

of Aquinas. God creates and governs the universe by divinely loving design. Ibn Sina describes the "power of love as pervading all beings" because "love is the cause of their existence."[16] All beings "possess a natural and inborn love" to strive toward their "perfection, i.e. that goodness or reality which ultimately flows from the reality of the Pure Good." In other words, "the perfections of the beings . . . emanate from the per se Perfect," or God, who, as the "Highest Being," also "must be the highest object of love, because it must be the maximum in goodness," as "the good is loved in its very essence." Thus, "it is a necessary outcome of His wisdom and the excellence of His governance to plant into everything the general principle of love . . . [whose] purpose being that the administration of the universe should run according to a wise order" to ensure its striving for perfection or goodness.

Although "there is some goodness in every part of the divinely established order," and "every single being loves the Absolute Good with an inborn love," Ibn Sina recognizes that "beings differ in "the connection they have with it." Humans, with their animal and rational souls, have sensuous desires from "the love of a beautiful form," and when those desires are properly expressed, they can give human lovers the perfection of "nobility and refinement." But humans can strive still higher to seek, with their divine souls, a closer connection to the Absolute Good, whose "highest degree of approximation . . . is what Sufis call unification." Love, then, is natural, necessary, and ultimately divinely inspired – even in its lower carnal forms – and rational beings can consciously strive to rise through the physical practice of love to the highest forms of spiritual enlightenment. Love between humans who desire each other for their virtuous goodness and whose loving union engenders greater goodness thus provides an edifying analogue and elevating stepping-stone to the still loftier heights of divine love and unification, as Islam's Sufi thinkers argued.

This notion of ennobling carnal love collides, however, with another prominent medieval view derived from Christian and Hellenistic thinkers: that physical lovemaking, even within the legitimizing frame of marriage, constituted a serious impediment to the highest spiritual life of philosophy and religion. Recall how the Epicureans "do not suffer the wise man to fall in love," because love is too violent and distracting a passion for maintaining one's tranquility, while lovemaking further endangers bodily health by depleting our energies and risking disease.[17] Marriage and children provide

[16] Emil Fackenheim, trans., "A Treatise on Love by Ibn Sina," *Mediaeval Studies* 7 (1945): 208–228, quotations in this paragraph and in the following paragraph are from 212–214, 222, 225.

[17] See Diogenes Laertius, *Lives of Eminent Philosophers*, vol. 2, trans. R. D. Hicks (Cambridge, MA: Harvard University Press, 1925), 645.

further distractions and worries that disrupt the philosophical quest for wisdom and serenity. If the Cynics recognized the natural claims of carnal urges, they scorned the dependence of erotic attachments and condemned married life as an artificial bond that robs the philosopher of time and freedom. In the Christian context, Saint Paul, while recognizing the value of marriage for preventing fornication and providing legitimate children, clearly privileged celibate chastity as the higher form of spiritual life, the kind that Christ and he himself exemplified. Paul's case for celibacy rested not merely on somatic purity but on the psychological division of purpose, attention, and energy that marriage and lovemaking bring (1 Cor. 7:32–35).

When a liberalizing monk named Jovinian challenged this privileging of celibacy (in 390 CE), Saint Jerome zealously defended it through a vehement critique of marriage, invoking not only Paul's arguments but also classical pagan authors to argue how love and marriage ruin the single-minded purity of focus that the high spiritual life of philosophy and religion requires. If the passion of love "is the forgetting of reason and ... draws away men from great thoughts to mean ones," then it is understandable why Cicero divorced and refused to remarry, claiming that "he could not possibly devote himself to a wife and to philosophy." A loving marriage could never be an analogue or path to the higher devotion of divine love, because the "wise man ought to love his wife with judgment, not with passion," but who could presume to judge God?[18] If Augustine later defended the good of marriage and claimed it was compatible with the "pursuit of wisdom," he equally reaffirmed that celibate "continence is preferred to wedded life," providing a superior path to wisdom, virtue, and holiness.[19]

We noted three influential medieval ideals: ardent, ennobling friendship; passionate, union-seeking love as a pervasive ontological force that holds the universe together; and celibate chastity for focusing on the spiritual. If these ideals are not strictly contradictory, their combination poses obvious problems. Erotic thought in the Middle Ages and Renaissance struggled to reconcile the values inherent in these divergent ideals. This chapter examines some exemplary efforts to do so, beginning with the two most prominent medieval examples before turning to several key figures of Renaissance erotic theory.

[18] See Jerome, "Against Jovinian," Book 1, chapters 48 and 49, in *The Principal Works of St. Jerome*, trans. W. H. Fremantle (Grand Rapids, MI: Eerdmans, 1893), available at www.fourthcentury.com/jerome-against-jovinian/.

[19] Augustine, *Confessions*, Book 6, chapter 11, trans. F. J. Sheed (Indianapolis: Hackett, 1993), 100; and "Of Holy Virginity," in *A Select Library of the Nicene and Post-Nicene Fathers of the Christian Church*, vol. 3, ed. Philip Schaff (Buffalo, NY: Christian Literature Publishing, 1887), 417.

III HELOISE AND ABELARD

The love story of Heloise d'Argenteuil and Peter Abelard is legendary, inspiring literary, theatrical, and even cinematic interpretations, but it is firmly grounded in historical fact. Besides Abelard's own mournful, moralizing account of their secret affair and its painful consequences in a short autobiographical work entitled *Historia calamitatum*, we have a series of letters between him and Heloise that have long been published together with Abelard's original account.[20] Independent medieval sources testify to their affair,[21] and recently a new trove of letters between two erudite but unnamed medieval lovers has been attributed to Abelard and Heloise because the letters' content and style perfectly reflect this unique couple. They concern a famously brilliant, passionate philosopher and a remarkably talented young woman who is his admiring student and ardent but secret lover.[22] Whether or not these existing texts and testimonies accurately represent what the two lovers actually felt, they portray a compelling struggle to navigate erotic passion through the complexities of medieval doctrine.

Peter Abelard (1079–1142), eldest son of a minor noble, chose philosophy over a military career as his path to glory. Combining superb logical genius with immense arrogance, he quickly rose to fame by besting all philosophical rivals in dialectical debate. Crushing even his esteemed teachers in disputation, Abelard further humiliated them by winning over their students, and soon succeeded in establishing himself as a world-renowned lecturer in Paris. His ambitious devotion to philosophy was uncompromised by other attachments until he fell in love with young Heloise, who was already well known for remarkable erudition and virtue as well as beauty, and who lived in the home of her uncle, a Notre Dame canon named Fulbert. Having won Fulbert's accord to reside in their house and tutor Heloise in philosophy, Abelard (who claimed to have had no prior love experience) soon confessed his love to Heloise and quickly won her favors.

[20] See Pierre Bayle, *Letters of Abelard and Heloise* (London: S. Hayes, 1779); my page citations are from this edition, hereafter LAH; a 2011 eBook is available from Project Gutenberg: www.gutenberg.org/files/35977/35977.txt.

[21] Peter Dronke, *Abelard and Heloise in Medieval Testimonies* (Glasgow: University of Glasgow Press, 1976). See also Etienne Gilson, *Heloise and Abelard* (Ann Arbor: University of Michigan Press, 1938), and the more recent and comprehensive C. J. Mews, *Abelard and Heloise* (Oxford: Oxford University Press, 2004).

[22] C. J. Mews, ed., *The Lost Love Letters of Heloise and Abelard* (London: Palgrave Macmillan, 2008), hereafter referred to as LLHA with references given to the letter numbers rather than the pages.

Sharing the same roof, they could enjoy "many soft moments" of love-making, excitedly exploring its rich diversity of forms, while "philosophy served [them] for a blind" (LAH 61–62).

> Under the pretext of study, we had all our time free for love, and in our classroom all the seclusion love could ever want. With our books open before us, we exchanged more words of love than of lessons, more kisses than concepts. My hands wandered more to her breasts than our books.... To avert suspicion, there were some beatings, yes, but the hand that struck the blows belonged to love, not anger, to pleasure, not rage – and they surpassed the sweetness of any perfume. We left no stage of love untried in our passion, and if love could find something novel or strange, we tried that too. New at the game, we went at it with heat, and it never grew old for us.[23]

Yet these carnal "sweets of love" so distracted him from philosophical study that he "could now do nothing but write verses to soothe his passion" (LAH 62). As these amorous verses became celebrated, Abelard's love affair drew considerable attention and aroused the suspicions of Fulbert, who surprised the couple in a moment of intimacy and expelled Abelard from the house. The lovers, however, managed to continue their connection with the help of a go-between. When Heloise soon became pregnant, Abelard furtively carried her off to his sister's home where she delivered a son. He then sued for Fulbert's forgiveness by offering to marry Heloise but to keep the marriage a secret. Fulbert agreed, but Heloise strongly resisted the idea of marriage, believing it would diminish Abelard's reputation and distract him further from his philosophical work. However, she eventually agreed to the secret marriage, in loving obedience to his demands.

Not satisfied with this secret marriage, Fulbert arranged for thugs to surprise the sleeping Abelard and castrate him. The philosopher survived the attack, but the scandalous humiliation and his jealous fears that Heloise might seek another lover (now that his own manhood was compromised) spurred Abelard to convince her that they both should enter religious orders of strict celibacy. He insisted, moreover, that she be the first to do so. Seeing his genital mutilation as divine punishment for his carnal sins and betrayal of Fulbert's trust, Abelard remained passionately possessive, feeling that if he could no longer carnally enjoy her, no man should; God alone could succeed him as the object of her love. Heloise obediently accepted the nun's veil, but she did so out of love for Abelard rather than love for God, and she long

[23] I here cite the version of Abelard's *Calamities* in William Levitan, trans., *Abelard and Heloise: The Letters and Other Writings* (Indianapolis: Hackett, 2007), 12.

struggled unsuccessfully to abandon her passion for the philosopher. Her ardent letters to him reveal her continuing reluctance to repent for their love affair and instead devote herself wholly to God, while Abelard's sad but firm epistolary replies insisted that she must renounce their love. They lived out their personal lives in chaste piety, but Abelard's brilliant and radical theological views were repeatedly condemned as heretical. This violent theological rejection (which he struggled unsuccessfully to overcome) greatly compounded the suffering of the already wounded and disgraced philosopher.

So much for the basic story of the lovers, but what do their writings reveal about medieval erotic thought? One letter defines love as "a particular force of the soul, existing not for itself nor content by itself, but always . . . with a certain hunger and desire, wanting to become one with the other, so that from two diverse wills one is produced without difference." It is, writes the philosopher-lover, "a universal thing" that has now "made its very home" in this elite couple (LLHA 24). "All men," Abelard explains in his *Calamitatum*, "are under a necessity of paying tribute at some time or other to Love, and it is vain to strive to avoid it. I was a philosopher, yet this tyrant of the mind triumphed over all my wisdom; his darts were of greater force than all my reasonings, and with a sweet constraint he led me wherever he pleased" (LAH 58). The philosopher as theologian likewise recognizes that love forms the foundation not only of morality's divinely established "natural law, consisting of love for God and neighbor," but also of God's religious law whose "fulfilment . . . is Love" and whose true expression is the "noncarnal, spiritual love of God" that inspires piety and delivers salvation.[24]

But how does spiritual love relate to love's physical pleasures? This constitutes the deep dilemma shaping the unhappy story of Abelard and Heloise. Both believe, however, that their passionate earthly love is an essentially psychic rather than physical force, a "tyrant of the mind" not the body, because this love persists and even intensifies when, after Abelard's castration, they are physically separated and he feels somatically impotent (LAH 58). He writes to Heloise: "If now, having lost the power of satisfying my passion, I had lost too that of loving you, I should have some consolation. . . . My misfortune does not loose my chains, my passion grows furious by impotence" (LAH 100). She likewise claims to "love [him] more than ever" after his injury, promising, "I will still love you with all the tenderness of my soul till the last moment of my life" (LAH 83).

[24] See Peter Abelard, *Dialogue between a Philosopher and a Jew* and *Ethics*, in *Abelard: Ethical Writings*, trans. P. V. Spade (Indianapolis: Hackett, 1995), 12, 31, 69; hereafter AE.

Their letters define what features make an attractive lover, and these include both natural gifts and learned qualities. Beauty, youth, and native wit loom prominent among natural gifts. Education and mastery of the "polite arts" (gallant manners, attractive dress, and skills of writing) are essential among acquired merits, but so are qualities of virtue (LAH 54). Having these merits made Heloise irresistible. "Her wit and her beauty would have fired the dullest and most insensible heart, and her education was equally admirable. Heloise was mistress of the most polite arts" (LAH 59). In short, "beauty, youth and learning, all that can make a person valuable meet in her" (LAH 92); and she is "the only disciple of philosophy among all the young women … , the only one on whom fortune has completely bestowed all the gifts of the manifold virtues," including an extraordinary "command of language" (LLHA 50, 52).

Proud Abelard explains why Heloise found him equally irresistible: how, he asks, "could a virtuous lady resist a man who had confounded all the learned of the age? I was young.… My person was advantageous enough, and by my dress no one would have suspected me for a doctor; and dress … [is] engaging with women. Besides, I had wit enough to write a *billet-doux*" (LAH 59–60). Heloise praises him as the "most gallant and learned person of the age," "handsome" and "distinguished in feeling," "a jewel of virtues," whose writing has "honey-like sweetness" and whose "treasures of … philosophy" provide her "the greatest amount of joys" (LAH 126; LLHA 21, 22, 23, 49, 76).

As love requires such qualities (of wit, virtue, sensitivity, and learning) of its best disciples, it equally teaches them through ardent training in tender feelings, refined manners, and inspired writing, but also in the "artful management" of time and people (notably, "confidants" and messengers) so that they can pursue their love to the fullest while preventing its being ruined by public disclosure (LAH 83). More than any other merit, virtue is what genuine love demands and teaches, for virtue is what gives love its uplifting power. Heloise insists that her love remains so "constant" because it "stems from integrity and virtue" rather than from material advantages or physical pleasures (LLAH 49). It is "only the highest virtue" that she sees in Abelard and that compels her love. "Virtue," she elsewhere tells him, "is too amiable not to be embraced when you reveal her charms" (LAH 93).

If Abelard likewise claims, "I chose you among many thousands because of your countless virtues," he also admits that hers surpassed his own and that, in seducing her, he has been "an abler master to instill vice than to excite virtue," his "false eloquence" having misled them both into sin (LLAH 52; LAH 106). After his castration, the penitent Abelard regards his love for

Heloise as shameful carnal passion, while Heloise continues to protest her love is virtuously pure because the loss of carnal pleasures after Abelard's castration in no way diminished that love but instead led her to adopt (in loving obedience to his desire) the religious duties he recommended. "Nothing but virtue, joined to a love perfectly disengaged from the . . . senses, could have produced such effects," she contends, while bemoaning that her religious work, devoid of the passion she has for Abelard, can hardly "maintain even [the] appearance of virtue" (LAH 83, 130). Abelard, however, persists that only by abandoning her earthly love for him and penitently devoting herself to the exclusive love of God can Heloise achieve real virtue. "Fear God that you may be delivered from your frailties. Love Him that you may advance in virtue" (LAH 114).

If virtue, which "restrains passion [and] keeps desires in check" (LLAH 49), requires a struggle to achieve, then its difficulty is precisely part of the training and glory for achieving it. Abelard's ambition spurred him to seek "obstacles . . . [to] surmount . . . [for] greater glory" (LAH 59). Virtuous love, according to Ciceronian tradition, thrives and derives its uplift by overcoming obstacles to satisfy most perfectly the needs and requests of the beloved (provided, of course, they were not unvirtuous). This demand of service formed part of the medieval "rules of love" (LLAH 99) that became famous in the art of courtly love. Love "forms friendships" of devoted service, writes the adoring young woman to the philosopher, and "the services of true love are properly fulfilled only when they are continually owed, in such a way that we act for a friend according to our strength and not stop wishing to go beyond our strength" (LLAH 25). The philosopher reciprocates: "Love urges me to enlist in its service, to respect its laws. And what I had not learnt love forces me to learn" (LLAH 113). Regarding such love as "a friendly and loving contest" of who can serve best, "a most beautiful contest in which both of us will win," he writes, "I am your servant most ready for your commands.. . . I am your servant; my whole body, my whole spirit I direct towards you" in service (LLAH 30, 37, 72, 85). In contrast to the courtly love tradition in which the male lover one-sidedly serves the beloved lady who holds a superior position in the relationship (and grants favors rather than reciprocating in devoted service), these intellectual lovers seek a "mutual love" in which neither is the "lesser" nor "surpasses the other" in loving service (LLAH 72). But their letters do not specify what precisely such service involves, which commands and rules of love must be followed.

How, for example, does the service of virtuous love relate to carnal desires and pleasures? Experienced in one's body, mind, and soul, such love directs its desire and service to the whole (physical and spiritual) person of the beloved, who attracts through beauty and virtue. But if carnal pleasures signify base animal lust, then how can such pleasures be reconciled with ennobling love? Reevaluating their premarital carnal pleasures, Abelard finds them horribly sinful, while Heloise insistently protests that (at least from her perspective) such pleasures were in no way dishonorable because they were simply the by-products of loving intentions that were purely guided by virtuous aims. Her justification by intentions corresponds to Abelard's philosophical writings on ethics, where he repeatedly argues that an act's sinful or honorable status should be determined by the agent's intention and not by the nature of the act itself since the same act can derive from good or bad intentions.[25] If Abelard argues that deeds are properly distinguished as good or bad "according to whether their intention is right or not right" (as God "takes account of the mind rather than the action . . . whether it springs from good or bad willing"), then Heloise can convincingly retort that her lovemaking intentions were pure expressions of love for Abelard's virtue and devoted service to him (AE 6, 24).

Maintaining that "all sins belong to the soul alone, not to the flesh" that partakes in pleasure, Abelard's ethical theory defends the validity of carnal pleasures as God-given conditions of our mortal, incarnate condition (AE 18). If our pleasures from food and sex, just as our appetites for them, are the inescapable result of the way God fashioned us, then it is unreasonable to expect us to avoid them entirely; virtue instead resides in controlling them appropriately by not consenting to them when they are improper. God "commanded us to not *satisfy* our lusts, but not to do without them altogether [because] going without them is impossible in our feeble state. And so it isn't the lusting after a woman but the consenting to the lust that is the sin" (AE 6). Indeed, "even the Lord, the creator of foods as well as of our bodies, wouldn't be without fault" if he made us such as to sin necessarily by performing the natural and necessary acts of eating and of procreation in marriage and thereby partaking in the pleasures we inevitably get from such acts (AE 8). It is "unreasonable," Abelard argues, to demand that "sex in marriage and the eating of delicious food . . . should be done entirely without pleasure" because that goes against the nature that God gave us (AE 9). Indeed, more generally, "no natural bodily pleasure is to be counted as a sin" per se. This is because it cannot logically "be regarded as a fault that we take pleasure in what is such that, when it has occurred, pleasure is necessarily

[25] See AE 6–14, 23–24. Similarly, "the merit or praiseworthiness of the doer doesn't consist in the deed but in the intention. Often in fact the same thing is done by different people, through the justice of one and the viciousness of the other" (AE 12).

felt" (AE 9). Abelard invokes a striking erotic fantasy to make his point: "if someone forces someone in religious orders, bound by chains, to lie among women, and he is led into pleasure – but *not* into consent – by the bed's softness and the touch of the women around him, who can venture to call this pleasure nature has made necessary a 'sin'?" (AE 9).

Why then did Abelard repent his marital carnal pleasures and insist that he and Heloise as married lovers abandon all loving contact for a rigorous religious life of sexual abstinence in which even the pleasures of seeing each other were denied? The most obvious reason is Abelard's castration, which he interpreted not only as a divine punishment to spur him to chastity but also as an insurmountable barrier to sexual pleasure. Both these interpretations, however, are contestable. As Heloise compellingly contests the first by noting that his punishment came when he was married by divine sacrament (while God left him unpunished as a sinful fornicator), so we can challenge his conclusion that castration precludes the giving and taking of sexual pleasures. That idea presumes a narrowly genital and procreative vision of lovemaking's sexual joys, ignoring that its delightful varieties of kisses, embraces, and caresses go far beyond the limits of genital penetration and full orgasmic release. Heloise herself relates how she showered the castrated Abelard with physical expressions of her passionate love, even displaying "greater marks of [her passion] after that cruel revenge"; she "dried [his] tears with kisses" and comforted him with "caresses," becoming "less reserved" in physically expressing her desire as he was "less powerful" (LAH 142). But Abelard refused her efforts, ignoring or eschewing the multiple options of nongenital erotic pleasures that could express and sustain their love. Not only his extreme pride but also his cultural and religious background would surely have led him to disregard these softer, nonpenetrative, nonprocreative erotic options, even if he may have earlier experimented with some of them.

Abelard's insistence on abandoning married life had further reasons. He shared the traditional view that marriage was detrimental to the high pursuit of philosophy, which was why he wished to keep his marriage secret. Not only was marriage blandly conventional; its duties and attachments constituted a draining distraction from full devotion to the philosophical life. Abelard relates how Heloise herself rehearsed these very arguments in resisting his marriage proposal. Claiming that "marriage . . . was a bond always fatal to a philosopher [and] that the cries of children and the cares of a family were utterly inconsistent with the tranquility and application which the study of philosophy required," she insisted she would rather "see [herself] as his mistress than [his] wife" (LAH 67). Marriage, moreover, was incompatible with true love, since it was bound up with "desire of riches," conventions, and obligations rather than being pure and free (LAH 85):

> I knew that the name of wife was honorable in the world and holy in religion; yet the name of your mistress had greater charms because it was more free. The bonds of matrimony, however honorable, still bear with them a necessary engagement, and I was very unwilling to be necessitated to love always a man who perhaps would not always love me. I despised the name of wife that I might live happy with that of mistress.... If there is any thing which may properly be called happiness here below, I am persuaded it is in the union of two persons who love each other with perfect liberty, who are united by a secret inclination, and satisfied with each other's merit; their hearts are full, and leave no vacancy for any other passion. (LAH 84–85)

Not merely the ruin of philosophy, marriage is the "tomb of ... love," since it compels necessity, while love (like philosophy) needs liberty to thrive (LAH 68).

The most powerful reason Abelard gives for abandoning his marriage to Heloise is its incompatibility with the highest level of religious life, one that involves total devotion to God. This Pauline doctrine, reemphasized by St. Jerome, could be construed as a Christian variation of Greek philosophy's earlier complaint that marriage precluded a philosopher's complete dedication to the pursuit of wisdom and the transformative care of the self. However, it gains intensity from its monotheistic grounding in an all-powerful and all-loving but jealous God who demands to be loved with all one's heart, soul, and might (Deut. 6:5; Matt. 22:37; Mark 12:30).[26] This implies that individuals aiming at the highest level of spiritual achievement should take God alone as the object of adoring love and devoted service, despite his injunction that we should also love our neighbors. Abelard thus insists, "The only way to return to God is by neglecting the creature which we have adored, and adoring God whom we have neglected"; hence "to see [Heloise] no more is what Heaven demands of Abelard; and ... to lose [Abelard] even in idea ... is what Heaven enjoins Heloise" (LAH 107-8). As a nun who is "wedded to God," she should love Christ, not him (LAH 91, 153). Christ, he tells her, should be the "sole object of your sighs and tears.

[26] This complete focus on devotion to God in eschewing carnal pleasures finds further reinforcement in the Christian tradition of mastering the "flesh" through penitential practice, ascetic discipline, and rigorous self-examination, whose development Michel Foucault expounds in *Les aveux de la chair: Histoire de la sexualité*, vol. 4 (Paris: Gallimard, 2018).

Beware Heloise of refusing a husband who demands you, and is more to be feared if you slight his affection than any profane lover" (LAH 157).

What, however, renders this logic of exclusionary love compelling, especially if one is not in holy orders? Why is it not possible both to love God and to love one's spouse or one's children or one's dearest friends? Why must one choose between divine and human love? Is it not possible that one could learn to love God by loving him through his expression in the humans he created and taught to love? Unless we assume that all erotic love is necessarily debasing, there is no convincing reason why an adoring desire for one's human beloved, as a creature of God, could not serve as an implicit expression of divine love or a ladder to it rather than a barrier against it. Moreover, even if such desire always falls short of divine love, this does not preclude its power to educate and inspire the lover toward edifying refinement and ennobling virtue. This erotic path of aesthetic-cum-ethical self-cultivation forms the animating core of the doctrine of courtly love.

IV COURTLY LOVE

Although essentially defined by a single theoretical text, the medieval art of courtly love abounds in ambiguities, complexities, and contradictions. Indeed, the very concept is rife with controversy. Allegedly practiced in the aristocratic courts of Aquitaine, France, and England, courtly love has been challenged as an anachronistic modern invention. Its very name (*amour courtois*) was first established only in the late nineteenth century by Gaston Paris, in analyzing the medieval literature of Arthurian romance, although similar terms such as *fin'amor* (refined love) were quite popular in medieval French and Provencal texts. Many doubt whether such love really existed in actual medieval life beyond the fictional realm of poetry and literary romance.[27] Its founding theoretical text, *De amore* by Andreas Capellanus (Andreas "the Chaplain"), is equally problematic. As its best English translator explains: "controversy surrounds its title, date, author, social setting, literary frame, purpose and importance," and whether its doctrines are seriously intended or are merely presented as satire; but it remains an undeniably "influential treatise."[28] The text was most likely authored in the

[27] On the complexities and controversies concerning courtly love, see, for example, Paolo Cherchi, *Andreas and the Ambiguity of Courtly Love* (Toronto: University of Toronto Press, 1994); and Don A. Monson, *Andreas Capellanus, Scholasticism, and the Courtly Love Tradition* (Washington, DC: Catholic University of America Press, 2005).

[28] P. G. Walsh, *Andreas Capellanus on Love* (London: Duckworth, 1982), 1. I use Walsh's translation, hereafter cited as CL.

mid-1180s in France by a cleric whom the text claims was "chaplain to the royal court" (CL 153). Leaving such thorny historical issues aside to focus on the text's erotic theory, we find it riddled with tensions deriving from its multiple ideological sources. These include pagan classical literature and philosophy, Christian scholasticism, troubadour poetry, and even Islamic erotic lore.

Ovid's influence is apparent throughout *De amore*, which even echoes his *Ars amatoria* in its three-book structure and introductory avowal of its aim to educate the uninitiated in the art of love to win love's pleasures and avoid its sorrows. The Chaplain's tutoring is explicitly addressed to a young cleric named Walter, who functions not as a particular person but as a rhetorical placeholder for all men because he receives instructions on lovemaking appropriate for all the different social classes of lovers the book considers. As an individual, Walter would belong only to one social class and thus need only the teachings appropriate to that class.[29] *De amore*'s third book (unlike Ovid's) does not concern erotic advice for women but rather serves as a stern denunciation of the two previous books of instruction on secular lovemaking by presenting a vehement critique of the whole worldly project of erotic love, including a vicious vituperation of all womankind.

Book I begins with a philosophical definition of love in the scholastic style. "Love is an inborn suffering which results from the sight of, and uncontrolled thinking about, the beauty of the other sex. This feeling makes a man desire before all else the embraces of the other sex, and to achieve the utter fulfilment of the commands of love in the other's embrace by their common desire" (CL 33). A large part of the suffering is fear of not gaining or maintaining the affection or enjoyment of one's beloved. That love is an inborn passion, and hence a psychological state, is proved by the fact that "it arises not from any action but solely from the thought formed by the mind as a result" of a man seeing a woman who is "fashioned to his liking." He therefore "begins to desire her inwardly" and to think of her more and more with increasing desire, and "starts thinking of her several attractions, contemplating her different parts; he begins to picture the role he can play and to pry into her body's hidden features. He longs to exercise the functions of each part" (CL 35).

This definition of love is clearly sexual, explicitly heterosexual, and decidedly carnal rather than being distinctively courtly or refined. Andreas insists that "love can exist only between persons of different sex" because

[29] The book does not tell us from what social class Walter emerged, but it does propose that clergy should rank as "the highest nobles," as God has chosen them (CL 209).

"two persons of the same sex are in no way fitted to reciprocate each other's love or to practice its natural acts" (CL 35). Indeed, "the whole impetus of the lover is towards enjoying the embraces of his beloved, and this is what he thinks of continually, longing to fulfil with her all" of love's commands and pleasures, whose most desired culmination is the "natural" coital "act of love" to which "nothing can be comparable," in his valuation (CL 35–37). This exclusively heterosexual, genital telos of love distinguishes it sharply from the more spiritual desire advocated both in the Greco-Roman notion of loving friendship and in religious ideas of divine love. Although a psychological passion, courtly love has defining physical conditions: a lover must not only be physically "capable of completing Venus's tasks" but cannot suffer from inappropriate "age or blindness" (CL 39). Men and women, respectively, above the age of sixty or fifty and below the age of fourteen or twelve are not suitable, even if they are capable of "sensual pleasure" from "sexual intercourse"; and sight is necessary for supplying the images that stimulate desire for embraces (CL 39). Psychological conditions of maturity and a disposition to avoid "excessive sexual indulgence" are also necessary to assure love's demand for constancy (CL 39).

Besides these psychophysical requirements for love, Andreas lists five qualities that enable "love . . . to be gained." These are "a handsome appearance, honesty of character, fluent and eloquent speech, abundant riches, and a readiness to grant what the other seeks," although his personal opinion is that only the first three are proper motivations for true love (CL 41, 43). Of these three, good looks is the least important, since "grace of figure and features, and elegance of character" provide no indication of the virtues of good sense, fine character, and discretion needed for love's constancy and for the secrecy Andreas deems necessary for a lasting love (CL 43). Citing Ovid, he even cautions against men and women who take excessive pains "with bodily adornment" as being most likely deficient in "honesty of character [which] is to be sought more than beauty." "Eloquence of speech" is important because it indicates refinement, "unleashes love's darts . . . [and] creates a good impression about the speaker's moral worth" (CL 43–45). But "only virtue is deserving of love's crown" because good "character alone truly enriches a man with nobility, and [even] makes him thrive with glowing beauty." Indeed, Andreas argues, virtue of character is what "originally brought distinction of nobility and introduced difference of class" (CL 45).

Issues of nobility and class difference loom large in *De amore*'s erotic theory. The bulk of Book I (by far the largest of the three) comprises eight polemical dialogues, each between a man and woman from three different classes (commoners, nobility, and higher nobility), in which the man enlists his eloquence to convince the woman to accept his love while the woman displays her reasoning skills and wit to refute his arguments. Through these dialogues the central doctrines of courtly love are articulated and debated, revealing their ambiguities and contradictions. One tension is evident in the essentially class-defined structure of the dialogues despite repeated claims that in love's court "class-distinctions could never claim a place" and lovers "serve their time . . . with equal status," "so lovers ought not to make class-distinctions" (CL 61, 125). The book's dialogical exchanges, however, grow longer and more instructive when both interlocutors belong to the higher classes. Although clerics should in principle eschew sexual love, Andreas begins by tolerantly recognizing their susceptibility to it (intensified by their abundant leisure and eating), and he suggests they choose their seductive approach from their class of origin. There is no such tolerance for women in religious orders, so Andreas refuses to give any counsel on "importuning nuns" but only to "utterly spurn" their "baneful snares" and sexual "consolations" (CL 211–213). This is not the only gender double standard in his erotic theory, which despite its claimed concern for ennobling elevation portrays love's path and goal in distinctly carnal and ultimately coital terms.

Andreas expounds "four separate stages [in the progression] of love," after sight and excessive reflection initially engender it: "The first stage lies in allowing the suitor hope, the second in granting a kiss, the third in the enjoyment of an embrace, and the fourth is consummated in the yielding of the whole person" through the act of love. To grant a man the pleasures of this final stage, the woman should demand proof of his deserving it through "numerous good deeds" and "fine accomplishments" that testify to his honorable character and trustworthiness. "Up to the third stage the woman can withdraw without reproach," but the fourth stage of putting "her own person at the disposal of another" is far too risky to her reputation and welfare without her having sufficient assurances of the man's reliable character (CL 57).

This worry reflects a core paradox of courtly love: its contradictory approach to woman, granting her deferentially courteous service and adulation while underlining her essential social subordination to the sexual codes of patriarchal society. On the one hand, courtly love reflects the elevation of woman to an object of respectful adoration after centuries of medieval demonization and disregard that considered women too inferior to be worthy of the ennobling loving friendships that demand and inspire virtue. On the other hand, it still regarded woman as essentially an object of carnal desire in a game of erotic conquest whose ultimate goal is "putting her own person at the disposal" of a man rather than cherishing and fostering her autonomy (CL 57). Much of the theory of courtly love seeks to mitigate this contradiction through its manly ideals of arduous service, fidelity, reverential obedience, and devotion to the beloved lady. This deferential courtliness pervades *De amore*'s dialogues of wooing, even when the woman's social class is inferior to her male suitor's. Moreover, the dialogues' rhetorical form and content seek to affirm woman's autonomy and freedom by giving her both the discursive power to refute the man's arguments for accepting him as a lover and the performative power to reject his suit, as her "freedom to choose love is not in dispute" (CL 95). Despite this dialogical parity with men and alleged liberty of erotic choice, a disturbing double standard persists. Not only is the woman likened to her male lover's "property"; she is denied the privilege of combining love with religious life, as Andreas fiercely forbids love with nuns while recognizing courtly love for male clerics (despite its clear violation of their calling) and even suggesting that they make the best lovers.[30]

There is, however, one real and robust female freedom that pervades the book's dialogues and forms the core essence of courtly love: a woman's erotic freedom from her husband. Although bound by divine and civil marital law to provide her husband with the "consolations of sex" and affectionate spousal feelings, a woman is free to pursue love's passions and fleshly pleasures with another man, granting this lover her sexual "sweet consolations" with greater ardor and sweetness than those given through marriage (CL 173, 219).[31] This is because she is propelled entirely by intense desire rather than by duty and because her "stealthy and secret" embraces with her lover are especially exciting to consummate as they depend on furtive trysts that are difficult to arrange (CL 147). The wife's (and husband's) freedom to choose a lover outside their marriage is coupled with the paradoxical

[30] A woman whose lover was believed lost and who then takes on a second lover is obliged to return to that first lover, unless she "experiences no warmth of attraction" for him. This is because the second lover cannot justly be "regarded as losing anything if he has in error acquired another's property, and forfeits it when the mistake is discovered" (CL 207). As for tolerating a clergyman's fornication, we find the argument that God equally demands "bodily chastity" from a layman and mercifully can pardon both of them. However, "the cleric should be chosen for love in preference to a layman" because he is "more careful and wise in all things than the layman . . . since scripture gives him this expertise" (CL 183–185).

[31] The word "consolations" Walsh uses to translate the Latin word *solatio*, a term that Andreas euphemistically employs throughout the book to designate the whole range of physical pleasures of erotic contact with all its four stages. The words "comforts" or "balms" could also connote *solatio*'s sense of soothing sensual pleasures to ease the pangs of loving desire. The term is translated as "solaces" in John J. Parry, trans., *The Art of Courtly Love* (New York: Columbia University Press, 1990).

prohibition against loving one's spouse. Love and marriage are simply incompatible in this erotic tradition. *De amore* repeatedly asserts this in most explicit terms: "We state and affirm unambiguously that love cannot extend its sway over a married couple," hence "marital affection" should not "appropriate the name of love, for it is clearly known that love cannot claim a place between husband and wife" (CL 147, 157).

There are five reasons for this claim. First, true love demands freedom of choice: "Lovers bestow all they have on each other freely, and without the compulsion of any consideration of necessity, whereas married partners are forced to comply with each other's desires as an obligation, and under no circumstances to refuse their persons to each other." Second, whereas true love affords the lovers "distinction" that can "increase their moral stature" by showing they are worthy to win love's devotion and carnal delights, no such distinction comes from receiving affection from one's spouse, as this is taken for granted as marital duty and thus "possessed as of right" (CL 157). True love, moreover, requires secrecy because "Love is nothing other than an uncontrolled desire to obtain the sensual gratification of a stealthy and secret embrace . . . [but] what stealthy embrace could take place between a married couple, since they are acknowledged to possess each other, and can fulfil all the desires that they will from each other without fear of opposition"? (CL 147). Fourth, "true love cannot exist without jealousy" as an energizing fuel, but jealousy should be "wholly rejected between husband and wife, and must be always expelled by them as a harmful bane" (CL 147–149). Fifth, true love inspires a fervent passion in lovers for the most ardent of carnal embraces, but sexual passion for the "married couple beyond affection for [the sake of] their offspring or discharge of obligation cannot but involve sin." Hence "we are taught by apostolic law [that] a lover who shows eagerness towards his own wife is accounted an adulterer" (CL 151). Chaplain Andreas fails to mention, however, the obvious fact that actual adultery is precisely what courtly love is recommending as its very essence. He saves his exposition of the fundamental contradictions between courtly love and conventional Christian morality for *De amore*'s final book.

If it entails the mortal sin of adultery, how could courtly love be in any way ennobling? It claims to be admirable in inspiring a man to superior conduct and refinement while compelling his virtuous service to his lady and others. One of courtly love's essential twelve precepts states: "Be obedient to mistresses' commands in all things, and always be eager to join the service of Love" (CL 117). In such service a man "must not be a lover of several ladies simultaneously, but must be the dedicated slave of all women in the service of one," pleasing and giving honor to his admired beloved also by "services to other ladies ... performed for [her] sake" (CL 85, 137). As one of the dialogical suitors puts it: "I shall never cease to serve you, and shall always proffer every service to every person on your behalf" (CL 95).

Through the love they inspire and give, women are the "cause and source of all good acts," so "there can be no good in this life unless it derives initial growth from love," as only "love's kindling inspires such deeds" (CL 127, 161, 173).[32] Love effectively stimulates this dignifying virtue by spurring a man to "strain every nerve to confer his services on ladies so that he can shine by their favor; and the ladies have the greatest obligation to be punctilious in helping good men's hearts to remain devoted to good deeds, and in honoring any individual according to his deserts" (CL 159). One exemplary lady "by her teaching so strengthened her lover in worthy manners, whilst granting him kisses and embraces, that through her he attained the highest worth of character, and deserved praise for general honesty," although he previously was "utterly without human worth" (CL 261). Love morally ennobles because the lover is so preoccupied with acquiring the beloved's esteem that he learns to act altruistically, disregarding his "own interests to be able sufficiently to aid the needs and wants of others" (CL 167).

Courtly love claims to inspire ennobling qualities of "generosity" and "cultivated manners," for "love compels all men to be courteous, and makes them strangers to any boorishness" (CL 83, 161, 257). The lover should be patient and gradual in approaching his beloved and "must not at once commence with words of love," but first must demonstrate his courteous refinement, "show himself to be amiable and complaisant" (CL 47, 143). Such refinement, Andreas claims, is so severely lacking in peasants or farmers that he totally excludes them from "serving in Love's court. They are impelled to acts of love in the natural way like a horse or a mule, just as nature's pressure directs them" (CL 223). Other dignifying virtues that love inspires are "hospitality," discretion (needed for keeping the affair secret), "staunch constancy" and chastity in terms of forswearing other lovers, truthfulness, and modesty and restraint in taking one's sensual pleasures and in "refrain[ing] from uttering foul words." Andreas articulates such virtues in the book's "twelve chief precepts of love" (CL 85, 175).

1. Avoid miserliness as a harmful disease, and embrace its opposite.
2. You must maintain chastity for your lover.

[32] The dialogues repeatedly emphasize this paramount value of love: "all men know well that no good or courtly deed on earth is performed unless love is the source from which it springs" (CL 53); "living in love is sweeter than any form of life on earth" (CL 77).

3. When a woman is appropriately joined to another in love, do not knowingly try to seduce her.
4. Be sure not to choose the love of a woman if natural modesty forbids you to join marriage with her.
5. Remember to avoid lying completely.
6. Do not have too many privy to your love.
7. Be obedient to mistresses' commands in all things, and always be eager to join the service of Love.
8. In the granting and receiving of love's consolations there should be the utmost modesty and decent restraint.
9. You must not be foul-tongued.
10. You must not expose lovers.
11. Show yourself civilised and chivalrous in all things.
12. When practising the consolations of love do not go beyond the wish of your lover. (CL 117)

These precepts, essentially addressed to the male lover, reinforce courtly love's ideal of pure and generous service that seems to elevate the woman's status from her subordinate role in patriarchal feudal society. However, examining the text more closely, we see that such service is not as virtuous as it pretends to be. An underlying norm of courtly love urges that in exchange for the lover's service, the beloved lady provides encouragement through promises of sexual consolations that she must ultimately keep or otherwise lose her reputation as an honorable person in the realm of "Love's court" (CL 159). Through his service and gifts to his beloved lady, the lover earns the right to eventually be "worthy to deserve [her] consolation" and receive this sexual gift in some form or degree (CL 137).

Andreas cites the judgment of an expert queen (perhaps Eleanor of Aquitaine, the alleged creator and doyenne of "the court of Love") to insist on this point: "Either the woman should refuse the small gifts which were offered with a view to love, or she should repay with the gift of love. Otherwise she should resign herself to being classed with companies of harlots" (CL 233, 269). Yet the basic structure of trading sex for gifts and benefits seems essentially the same as in harlotry. Even if the genteel beloved does not require gifts or services, their exchange for sexual "consolations" exudes an unsavory whiff of commercial contract that is inconsistent with the ideal of pure and unconditionally given love to which courtly love aspires. I believe that the courtly love ideal of ennobling, virtuous, obediently serving, and unlimited devotion parallels (while it also displaces) the dominant religious ideal of the pure, righteous, uplifting, and unbounded love for

God. Maintaining both loves, Andreas claims, is incompatible. As the high nobleman argues in courting a woman of high nobility, "God has not purposed that a man should have his right foot on the earth and his left in heaven, for no man can properly serve two masters." Then, as the lady already has one foot in the earthly world and is happy to "exchange courtly words" with men, she should therefore "devote [herself] effectively to love [rather] than to lie to God" by using religious piety as an excuse for denying a worthy lover (CL 163).

In the struggle to present courtly love as an uplifting passion, Andreas (in the same dialogue between the high nobleman and equally noble lady) introduces two important and closely related distinctions. The first is pure or "chaste love" (*purus amor*) versus "compounded love" (*mixtus amor*, or "mixed love" in Parry's translation). "Pure love," the high nobleman explains, "is that which joins the hearts of two lovers with universal feelings of affection. It embraces the contemplation of the mind and the feeling of the heart. It goes as far as kissing on the mouth, embracing with the arms, and chaste contact with the unclothed lover, but the final consolation is avoided, for this practice is not permitted for those who wish to love chastely." In contrast, "compounded love . . . affords its outlet to every pleasure of the flesh, ending in the final act of love" (CL 181). To advocate the dignity of courtly love, clear preference is given to its so-called chaste variety, which excludes genital contact while allowing a wide range of other erotic embraces, including naked ones. Its alleged superiority derives largely from its higher "moral worth" since neither a "maiden nor a widow or married woman can experience any injury from such love, or sustain the loss of her reputation," and even "God sees in it only a minor offence." Chaste love is also superior because of its alleged durability. While "compounded love . . . soon wanes after only short duration, often causing regret for indulgence in such acts," chaste love "always experiences growth in itself constantly" and "none has regretted practicing it" (CL 181). However, "compounded love . . . is [also] true and merits praise," so a genteel lady should "approve of both chaste and compounded love." Therefore, she must simply "choose one or other of the two loves," and must reject the choice of not loving (CL 181).

A related distinction in lovemaking concerns the area of the woman's body where one seeks sexual pleasure, contrasting the "lower part" to the "upper half" and their related genital or nongenital joys (CL 199). The nobleman argues that the "consolation of the upper part is to be preferred" because of its superior morality and refinement, aptly symbolized by its elevated somatic location (CL 201). "So far as the consolations of the lower part is concerned, we are in no sense separated from the brute animals," whereas nongenital lovemaking is distinctively human. Moreover, whereas the lower, genital pleasures soon pall and can injure or disgust, one is never sickened or "wearied with the consolation of the upper part" (CL 201). The woman contrastingly contends that genital pleasures are the natural final goal of lovemaking, which is why true lovemaking requires appropriate (i.e., heterosexual) and properly functioning genitalia and that nongenital pleasures are simply preliminary means to reach the true erotic end. However, the man ultimately convinces her with the following arguments. First, "it is clearly a foul and extremely foolish physical performance and a source of the utmost shame to a woman to practice the consolations of the lower part without those of the upper." But these latter, in contrast, can be "most suitably obtained without damaging the modesty of both parties as they behave most appositely and in courtly fashion, even if they do not indulge in the delights of the lower." Second, even if "the lower part [is] where the final cause of love resides," the proper "order of loving" demands first obtaining the "wanton consolations of the upper part after a good deal of insistence, and only then should gradually advance to the lower." Only prostitutes perform the genital consolations without those of the upper (CL 203). This advocacy for nongenital sex in courtly love seems especially significant because it constitutes one of the book's very few discussions where the man succeeds in convincing his female interlocutor.

If this double preference for chaste lovemaking and upper consolations aims to dignify the notion of courtly love, to what extent is this strategy successful? Such love remains dominated by the standard heterosexual aim of genital penetration that the background Christian context defines as the only natural and legitimate end of lovemaking. Two important passages in *De amore*'s Book II affirm this point. First, in the section on "how love is brought to an end," Andreas firmly insists that "if some chance happening causes sexual impotence in one of the lovers, love cannot endure between them but abandons them completely" (CL 233). This logic (like Abelard's) disregards the pleasurable love bonds created through nongenital forms of lovemaking. Second, in the book's section on breaking love's commitments, Andreas insists that "a lover is said to break faith . . . when the woman denies the love she promised" after she "confers on a man the hope of her love, or grants him other first marks of love," such as those of the "second or third stage" (CL 249). For if "the suitor is not accounted unworthy of this love, it is adjudged a grievous offence on her part to seek to deny what has long been anticipated. A respectable woman ought not without reason to postpone her promises"; therefore, "she should not bestow on [her suitor] the hope of her love or the other early marks of it" unless she truly intends "to fulfil what she pledged" by conferring him hope for achieving love in its full range of all four stages. Indeed, even if the lovers "have made a harmonious pledge at the beginning of their love never to indulge in compounded love unless both demanded it of their free will and in full agreement," the man can change his mind; and then "the woman does not act rightly if . . . she refuses to comply with her partner's will" for the complete genital act of sex (CL 249, 251).

Finally, given its Christian cultural context, courtly love's exclusion of marriage consigns its culminating coital practice to the mortal sins of adultery or fornication. This sinful status explains its demand for secrecy, whose necessary deceit further debases love and ethically taints its courtly lovers. *De amore* thus concludes with a third book, "The Condemnation of Love" that vehemently repudiates the entire enterprise of courtly love after having devoted two much longer books to teaching its pursuit. "Each and every wise man is bound to renounce all acts of love, and always to oppose Love's commands for many reasons, but especially for one which no man can religiously oppose," Andreas tells his young pupil. "No person could be pleasing to God by any good works as long as he seeks to devote himself to Love's services, for God loathes, and in both Testaments has prescribed punishment for, those whom He sees committed to Venus' tasks or engaged in any form of sensual pleasure outside marriage relations." Having first presented claims that all good derives from erotic love, Andreas concludes by doubting whether *any* good can come from it when "its every act is against God's will" and "the devil is the creator of love and sexual indulgence" (CL 287, 299). Aside from risking "the flames of everlasting Hell" by defying God's will, courtly love sinfully injures humankind, including the lovers themselves (CL 287). Besides injury to friends and neighbors by seducing their wives and daughters, there is loss of calm through "love's jealousy," loss of wealth through excessive spending, loss of autonomy through excessive service, loss of wisdom and self-restraint, loss of reputation, loss of purity, loss of faith and divine salvation, and even loss of health (CL 289–297).[33]

Book III displays initial sympathy for marriage as a victim of courtly love's adulterous evil and as a sanctified way to procreate and satisfy our sexual urge "without staining our souls" (CL 301). Does marriage then provide a

[33] Andreas adduces "three logical bases" why love will "weaken men's bodies": "the body's powers are greatly lessened by sexual intercourse. Secondly, people in love give less nourishment to their bodies by way of food and drink." Third, "love causes loss of sleep and usually robs people of all rest [resulting in] . . . poor digestion and great physical weakness," and even "physical illnesses" and "weakening of the brain" (CL 305).

form of ennobling love that can harness the energy of sexual desire and thus offer a superior alternative to courtly love's alleged uplifting passion and power? This hope is decisively dashed by the book's concluding arguments that not only recommend the virtues of chaste celibacy but reinforce that choice by vilifying all women as essentially wicked and vile, hence unworthy of marital trust or loving friendship. "You could never find the reciprocated love you look for in a woman. No woman ever loved her husband, nor can she ever bind herself to a lover with a reciprocal bond of love," Andreas contends, because "all women by the general make-up of their sex are disfigured by the vice of parsimony and greed" and a host of other vices that he fiercely expounds in unpleasant detail.[34]

If we can find ennoblement neither in courtly love nor in marriage, we must then seek it only in the chaste celibacy of loving God, which (Andreas claims) cannot be combined with secular life and loving. One "must accordingly learn to preserve bodily chastity, to overcome the pleasures of the flesh with virtue of mind, and to keep the vessel of your body unspotted for the Lord" (CL 301–303). Not confined to those in holy orders, "Bodily chastity and abstaining from physical sex is something good for all to embrace before God and men and to preserve in every way . . . [otherwise,] there could be no good in man which is fully perfected." Moreover, if a man has "this virtue [of chastity,] . . . people show indulgence to his various faults" so he will escape slander and win praise (CL 303). In short, chaste love for God is infinitely superior to courtly love both in ennobling effects and in rewards. This comparison suggests that courtly love in some ways modeled itself as a secular version of divine love. It aspires to the following essential properties of divine love: ennobling quality, superiority to marital affection, exceptional intensity of devotion and supererogatory service to the beloved, devout obedience and motivation inspired by the beloved's superior virtue rather than worldly benefit, and exclusivity and constancy of devotion that affirms the right of jealousy. We should remember that the God of Judeo-Christian monotheism is an exclusively single and jealous God who insists on his singularity and on his being loved with all one's power.[35]

[34] "Again, every woman is by nature not only miserly but also an envious backbiter of other women, a grabber, a slave to her belly, fickle, devious in speech, disobedient, rebellious against prohibitions, marred with the vice of pride, eager for vainglory, a liar, a drunkard, a tongue-wagger who cannot keep a secret. She indulges in sexual excess, is inclined to every evil, and loves no man from the heart" (CL 307, 309).

[35] Jesus (in Mark 12:29–30) declares "the first of all the commandments is, Hear, O Israel; The Lord our God is one Lord: And thou shalt love the Lord thy God with all thy heart, and with all thy soul, and with all thy mind, and with all thy strength." This echoes the Old Testament commandments of Deuteronomy 6 and its jealous injunctions not to follow other gods.

Why spend two long books of instruction on courtly love's precepts and techniques, only to eschew the whole project for the sake of Christian celibacy? Multiple explanations have been given for the enigmatic authorial intentions of the mysterious Andreas: that the first two books are satirical; that the third is a fearful, hasty afterthought of recantation; that the structure of conflicting viewpoints reflects the traditional literary genres of dialogical debates and palinodes; that the book is a slapdash composite lacking unifying authorial intention and replete with textual inconsistencies. Book III provides its own reasonable explanation for Andreas's changing perspective: namely, that he gave his earlier "detailed teaching on love" in response to his pupil Walter's "prayers" to "become fully acquainted with the art of love" but gave it not for the purpose of Walter's actual practice but instead for the theoretical "recreation" of "learning" (CL 287). Such learning, moreover, will help him achieve greater virtue and divine rewards by better enabling him to resist (more frequently and more gloriously) the sinful temptations of lust by knowing precisely how to recognize and manage its opportunities. As Andreas puts it, you should "read this little book not with the intention of yourself adopting the life which lovers lead, but rather to obtain recreation by the learning in it. Then, once instructed in how to rouse women's hearts to love, you may by refraining from such action win an eternal reward, and deserve by this conduct to take pride in greater blessings in God's presence" (CL 287). The logic of gaining greater virtue and praise through greater trials of effort and temptation is the same we met in Abelard and other medieval clerics and that harkens back to Aristotelian ethics. "He who does not exploit an available opportunity to sin is more pleasing to God than he who is not afforded the chance to go wrong," claims Andreas, since the former actively displays virtuous will by resisting sin while the latter simply relies on sin avoiding him (CL 287).

V RENAISSANCE NEOPLATONISTS

If medieval erotic theory is overshadowed by the Catholic cult of celibate chastity and dominated by prohibitions against fornication, adultery, and nonprocreative erotic acts (whether homosexual or heterosexual), then to what extent does Renaissance thinking transform this picture? With its increasing appreciation of the pagan erotic tradition and its own humanist skeptical and secular tendencies, does it open any new avenues for aesthetic and ethical refinement through erotic love? Unable to consider the vast range of Renaissance erotic thought, we focus on three important but divergent approaches: Platonic transcendentalism (Ficino, Bruno,

Castiglione, and Leone Ebreo), skeptical humanism (Erasmus and Montaigne), and the hedonic courtesan culture that flourished in the wealthy cities of sixteenth-century Italy.

Marsilio Ficino (1433–1499) is chiefly responsible for the Renaissance revival of Platonism and for establishing the notion of Platonic love by translating Plato's dialogues into Italian, including the first translation of the *Symposium*, on which he wrote an extended commentary.[36] Appointed by his patron Cosimo de Medici to head a new Platonic Academy in Florence, Ficino devoted his bookish life to research in that city. Beyond his enduring concern with Plato, Ficino's research extended into medicine and Christian theology, but also, more riskily, into astrology and magic.[37] He entered the priesthood in 1473, completing shortly thereafter a four-volume work entitled *Platonic Theology* that sought to harmonize Platonism and Christian doctrine by integrating philosophy with religion, and ethical theory with the quest for salvation. Love was an excellent concept to serve such projects of integration, and Ficino's advocacy of Christian Platonic love influenced later Renaissance Platonists, whose theories regarding love's nature, powers, effects, benefits, and varieties display some notable points of difference despite their shared Platonic core.

"When we say Love," explains Ficino, "we mean by that term the desire for beauty, for this is the definition of Love among all philosophers," although he soon stipulates more precisely that "Love is the desire for *enjoying* beauty" (FC 130, italics added). Ficino, like other Platonists, specifies various forms or levels of enjoying beauty, while insisting that love's ultimate desire is to enjoy a union with the highest form of beauty that transforms the lover in ennobling ways. Love, moreover, is not a merely psychological drive; it is an ontological principle of desiring attraction that governs the entire universe and holds it together: "Love is in everything, and for everything, [being] the creator and preserver of everything and the teacher and master of all the arts." In fact,

> all the parts of the world, because they are the works of one artist, the parts of one creation, like each other in life and essence, are bound to each other by a certain mutual affection, so that it may justly be said that love is a

[36] See S. R. Jayne, trans., *Marsilio Ficino's Commentary on Plato's "Symposium": The Text and a Translation, with an Introduction* (Columbia: University of Missouri Press, 1944), 130; hereafter FC.

[37] Ficino's short book of essays on astrology and necromancy, *Liber de Vita* (1489), was widely condemned by churchmen, and his powerful patron Lorenzo de Medici had to step in to defend him.

perpetual knot and binder of the world, the immovable support of its parts and the firm foundation of the whole creation. (FC 152)

At the sublimely attractive center of this love-bound universe is God, "the source of all beauty and love," who impresses his divine beauty and godly love on the variety of his creation in different ways, thereby generating different forms of love and beauty (FC 212).

Ficino defines beauty in ontological, psychological, and formalist terms. Ontologically, beauty is the external manifestation of God's supreme goodness that emanates from its source to pervade the world as the splendor of his "divine countenance" (FC 170). "Goodness is . . . the outstanding characteristic of God. Beauty is a kind of force or light, shining from Him through everything," so that "whoever sees and loves the beauty [of God's creations] . . . , [by] seeing the glow of God in these, through this kind of glow sees and loves God Himself" (FC 140). For Ficino, it is always the "internal perfection" of goodness that produces the external quality of beauty, which is why "we say that beauty is the blossom, so to speak, of goodness"; and through "the allurements of this blossom, as though by a kind of bait, the latent interior goodness attracts all who see it." Thus without beauty's external attraction, "we would never know the goodness hidden away in the inner nature of things, nor desire it" (FC 164). Psychologically and formalistically, beauty is "a certain charm which is found chiefly and predominantly in the harmony of several elements" and which can be found "in the soul, in the harmony of several virtues," or "in material objects, in the harmony of several colors and lines," or "in sound . . . [as] the best harmony of several tones." These beauties of soul, body, and sound are perceived, respectively, by "the mind, the sight and the hearing," which are "the only means by which we are able to enjoy beauty" in its true spiritual sense (FC 130).

Ficino thus banishes the senses of smell, taste, and touch from the aesthetic realm of beauty and true love. As "beauty pertains only to the mind, sight, and hearing[,] love, therefore, is limited to these three, but desire which rises from the other senses is called, not love, but lust or madness" (FC 130).[38] The level of love's excellence and elevating power

[38] We should note, however, that the allegedly banished sense of smell insinuates itself into Ficino's description of even divine beauty and love. In explaining that lovers are never fully satisfied by the sight and touch of their beloved because they do not realize that they are really desiring the beauty of God, Ficino describes this desire in terms of God's "subtle incense . . . infused into His works[,] a certain sweet aroma of Himself; by this aroma we are certainly every day aroused. We sense the aroma certainly, but we cannot distinguish its flavor, and so when we

depends on the level of beauty it desires to enjoy, bodily beauty being lower than the beauty of the soul. Ficino even maintains that beauty itself "cannot be anything corporeal" because it is essentially "a spiritual gift" whose bodily appearance is merely the transient impression of the soul's beauty or a distant reflection of the "divine countenance" on human bodily form. Bodily beauty is a harmony of form, not physical matter, and derives from the person's living soul as expressed in the body's "activity, vivacity, and a certain grace shining in the body" through its living soul (FC 169, 173).

As an expression of God's goodness, true beauty is always good and "all true love is honorable" (FC 131). Because "the beauty of the human body consists in a certain harmony ... [that requires] a kind of temperance, it follows that love seeks only what is temperate, moderate, and decorous." This implies that sexual passion and pleasure cannot constitute true love. "Pleasures and sensations which are so impetuous and irrational that they jar the mind from its stability and unbalance a man, ... are the opposites of beauty" (FC 130). It follows that "love and the desire for physical union are not only not identical impulses, but are proved to be opposite ones" (FC 130). Ficino, nonetheless, recognizes the validity of sexual intercourse when it is an expression of the spiritual. As the soul has two powers, those of "comprehension" and "generation," so it loves the human body through "the desire of contemplating Beauty ... [or] the desire of propagating it; both loves are honorable and praiseworthy, for each is concerned with the divine image" (FC 143). The contemplative or spiritual love, however, is far superior. Bodily love is even sinful if through carnal pleasure it ignores the "more excellent beauty of the soul." Thus, "if a man is too eager for procreation and gives up contemplation, or is immoderately desirous of copulation with women, or consorts unnaturally with men," or otherwise "performs the functions of generation and coition" beyond the bounds of reason's "natural law" and "civil laws drawn up by men of wisdom," he sinfully "abuses the dignity of love" (FC 143).

Preoccupied with spiritual beauty and divine love, Ficino shows little interest in the somatic, social, and artistic graces that make a person an attractive or good lover. He himself was sadly lacking in such personal graces; biographers describe him as "dwarfish" and "humpbacked" with "halting" speech "marred by a bad lisp" and plagued with "extreme melancholy," making him more comfortable with books than people and

yearn for the indistinguishable flavor itself, being charmed by its sensible aroma, certainly we do not know what we desire" (FC 140).

unsuitable for romantic love.[39] He nonetheless affirms that secular love can ennoble character by strengthening "the sense of shame which prevents our committing evil deeds . . . [while inspiring] the desire for good which incites us to do good deeds," because in seeking beauty, love "always desires the fit and noble" (FC 131). Yet even the ennobling qualities of good character seem, for Ficino, an inferior distraction from love's preferred focus – the "universal Beauty" and its divine source in God (FC 170). For beauty's real purpose or "usefulness" is to provide the "bait," magnet, or "light" by which the soul is "drawn closer toward God" (FC 152, 162, 164–165). That too is the purpose of love's sublime pleasures and disturbing discontents. They lead us back to God, who is our original source, thus "restoring to us the wholeness we lost" when we were separated from him through embodiment. Bodily lovers are left unsatisfied, disappointed, or wearied by the sight, touch, or even coital union with their mortal beloved, because what they are really, but unknowingly, desiring is divine beauty. However, when love is fixedly focused on and united with God's beauty, it provides transcendent pleasures that never cloy or grow old: "banishing all repletion, [the spiritual love of God] perpetually kindles by [its] own peculiar ardor a new delight, as it were, in the soul, and makes the soul happy with soft and sweet enjoyment" (FC 163).

Ficino builds his theory of erotic love's uplifting power from Plato's *Symposium* with its ladder of ever higher levels of beauty until one achieves an intimately direct perception of the divine Form of Beauty itself and the sublime pleasures that attend this cognitive connection. But, like Plato, Ficino does not regard the pleasures of cognition as the highest stage in love's ladder. Both advocate a creative transformation through this erotic connection that provides the lover with some form of immortality. Plato speaks of "giving birth in beauty" in spiritual terms through which the lover begets "wisdom and the rest of virtue"; poets and creative craftsmen beget such virtue, as do those who wisely govern cities (Sym 206b7–8, 209a4–8). For Ficino the ultimate birth is the lover's own transformation into a divine being through his loving union with God. Noting how lovers often strive to reshape themselves to become like their beloveds so as better to harmonize or unite with them, Ficino explains that this desire is "quite reasonable" because love's ultimate aim is God. Thus "the lover wishes to transform himself into the person of the loved one . . . for he wishes and tries to become God instead of man; and who would not exchange

[39] See Jayne's "Introduction" to his translation of Ficino's *Commentary on Plato's "Symposium,"* FC 19.

humanity for divinity?" (FC 141). Elsewhere Ficino notes that God's shining beauty and goodness, even when reflected through other things, attracts the lover "to venerate such splendor as the divinity beyond all others, and to strive for nothing else but to lay aside his former nature and to become that splendor itself." Thus "caught up by that radiance ... as by a hook, [the lover] is drawn upwards in order to become God" in some sense.[40] Much more than mere ethical uplift, love's engine of elevation offers an ethical-aesthetic apotheosis in the literal sense of deification through the magic of erotic desire.

Giordano Bruno (1548–1600) embraced Ficino's Platonic idea of love's elevating magic, but developed it into an ambitious set of philosophical, cosmological, and metaphysical theories that were quickly deemed heretical. Of common birth and strikingly small in physical stature, Bruno pursued his studies as a Dominican monk in Naples, but his controversial views soon compelled him to flee Italy and abandon his monastic clothing.[41] He roamed through Europe writing and lecturing until he foolishly returned to Venice, where he was quickly denounced and arrested for his heretical views. Excommunicated, long imprisoned, and all his books banned, Bruno was finally burned at the stake in Rome's Campo de Fiori, where a statue to his martyrdom was later erected by Freemasons in 1889. During his defrocked wanderings, Bruno gained more experience of carnality than Ficino ever did, and he clearly exhibits a deeper appreciation of the body's role in love. Like Ficino, Bruno sees love as the supreme ontological principle of the universe, whose infinite expanse is magically united by love's divine bonds. Bruno, however, portrays these loving bonds in boldly sexual terms. In his Latin poem *On the Immense* he describes the heavenly bodies as enjoying their erotic desires more fully and lengthily than humans can, and in countlessly more positions:

> ... the Sun and the Earth, too: as neighbors
> Hidden from our senses' reach, they clinch in amazing embraces....
> Now, this sex among gods is of a condition far better
> Than our own; as for us, the gentle power of pleasure
> Lasts a short while; moreover, the mounting force of our ardor

[40] Marsilio Ficino, *Platonic Theology*, vol. 4, trans. Michael J. B. Allen a,nd James Hankins (Cambridge, MA: Harvard University Press, 2004), 223.

[41] One English acquaintance described him as "a little waterbird" and "with a name longer than his body." See Ingrid Rowland, *Giordano Bruno: Philosopher/Heretic* (Chicago: University of Chicago Press, 2009), 145, for this and other details on Bruno's life and thought; see also J. L. McIntyre, *Giordano Bruno* (London: Macmillan, 1903).

Breaks forth at once, in only one part of ourselves, whereas Earth can
Revel in every part, can revel in pleasure forever,
Ceaselessly, as her rotation affords her a thousand positions.[42]

The erotic force of attachment that unites the universe provides the ontological ground for magic's power to influence or "bind" things from a distance.[43] As love is the desire for beauty, so God is "absolute beauty"; and the love that he inspires pervades the entire cosmos, which, through love, is "united by a universal spirit which is present as a whole in the whole world and in each of its parts" (EOM 115, 156). "In all things there is a divine force, that is, love, the father himself, the source . . . of bonds," claims Bruno, and "this one feeling of love . . . dominates all things, is lord over all things, and elevates, arranges, rules and moderates all things" (EOM 170, 174). We can discern "this greatest and most important bond when we turn our eyes to the order of the universe. By this bond, higher things take care of lower ones, lower things are turned toward higher ones, equal things associate with each other" and contrary things diverge from each other. Thus, "love is the bond of bonds" since "all bonds are either reduced to the bond of love, depend on the bond of love or are based on the bond of love," even the enmity connecting "rival male suitors" for the same beloved (EOM 165, 171, 173–174). Besides harmoniously ordering the universe, love inspires virtue through "a desire for the beautiful, good, etc., in all things" (EOM 149). Even "the love of material beauty" does not distract people from virtuous acts, but "is transformed into a virtuous zeal which forces the lover to progress to the point of becoming worthy of the thing loved, and perhaps worthy of some greater and still more beautiful object."[44] Even the sufferings of erotic passion serve to strengthen character and resilience as one is "waxed in virtue under the blows of love" (HF 206).

Like Ficino, Bruno thinks we love "corporeal beauty, only because it is a sign of the beauty of spirit . . . because of a certain spirituality we see in it, a spirituality called beauty" (HF 112). Bodily body is not a mechanically formal matter. It "does not consist in larger or smaller dimensions, in determined colors or forms, but in a certain harmony and concordance of the bodily members and hues [that] shows a certain sensible affinity to the spirit" when perceived by our "most acute and penetrating senses" (HF 112). Bruno

[42] Cited in Rowland, *Giordano Bruno*, 220.

[43] Giordano Bruno, *Cause, Principle and Unity: And Essays on Magic*, trans. R. J. Blackwell (Cambridge: Cambridge University Press, 1998), hereafter EOM.

[44] Giordano Bruno, *The Heroic Frenzies*, trans. P. E. Memmo (Chapel Hill: University of North Carolina Press, 1966), 184; hereafter HF.

identifies these senses with "vision, hearing, and mind or imagination," regarding the latter as the inner sense that renders physical sensations into ideas that the soul can digest and process (EOM 155). It is through these primary "gates" that love first (and most powerfully) binds the lover and then spreads its bonds through other senses.[45] The more (and more varied) ways the particular bonds of attraction bind the lover, the more powerful the general bond of attraction will be. By a similar logic, the more powerful the bond of attraction is, the more it excludes or diminishes the power of rival bonds. For example, some philosophers were so bound to the ideals they loved that they were able to ignore all other pleasurable attractions and flout the most severe pains. Rather than being irrational folly, "love, like all emotions, is a very practical form of knowledge" that instructs us about the world and ourselves, through its own kind of "reasoning and argumentation" (EOM 163).

More than Ficino, Bruno emphasizes the complex multiplicity of love, which includes the most intemperate forms of desire. The very title of his celebration of love, *The Heroic Frenzies*, indicates his appreciation of inordinate desire when it is going in the right direction, and his use of the term "frenzy" specifically recalls Plato's celebration of erotic love as a divine mania (*Phaedrus* 244a–245b). In the book's prefatory dedication (to Sir Philip Sidney) Bruno insists on his aim to promote the amorous ecstasies of "divine contemplation" sought through "heroic love," while deploring the "vulgar love" of bodies that makes man's "wit the slave of woman . . . [thus] degrading the noblest powers and actions of the intellectual soul" (HF 66, 70). However, the book itself clearly affirms the love of bodily beauty as a path toward divine love, even if carnal affection is the lowest of love's legitimate forms.[46] The book's inner tensions reflect those of love itself, which, as Bruno insists, combines contraries such as pleasure and suffering, tenderness and fierceness.

[45] "If it happens that someone passes through all three of these gates, he binds most powerfully and ties down most tightly. He who enters through the gate of hearing is armed with his voice and with speech, the son of the voice. He who enters through the gate of vision is armed with suitable forms, gestures, motions and figures. He who enters through the gate of the imagination, mind and reason is armed with customs and the arts" (EOM 155).

[46] The prefatory discourse contains its own tensions. Its harsh vituperations against womankind contrast with its affirmation of the "dignity of those ladies . . . who are praiseworthy: and those, especially, who may and do reside in this British land" and who should not be considered as women but rather are "nymphs, goddesses and of celestial substance." Queen Elizabeth is deified as the goddess Diana (HF 65). The book also contains a separate "Apology" to the "most glorious and virtuous ladies . . . of England," explicitly excluding them from the book's misogynistic remarks but not entirely from womankind (HF 79).

Bruno identifies three basic "species of love"; the highest rises "from the aspect of the corporeal form … to a consideration of the spiritual and the divine"; the second "perseveres only in the delight of the sight and in conversation; and the third descends from the sight to the concupiscence of the touch." From these basic modes, many different varieties "are composed … accordingly as the first is accompanied by the second or by the third, or as all three concur together." This variety of loves is further multiplied "according to the affections of the frenzied lovers which tend either more to the spiritual or more toward the corporeal object or toward both of them equally" (HF 105). Love, then, can be both spiritual and bodily at the same time.

Bruno's animistic metaphysics explains his greater recognition of love's somatic dimension. While celebrating the primacy of spiritual reality, he affirms that the divine "spirit … is diffused everywhere and in all things," not only in plant and animal life but also in nonliving bodies such as stones and minerals, which have their own "internal spirit, or sense" that guides their behavior. This includes their "desire … to exist and to be beautiful … according [to their] species and genus" (EOM 110, 111, 125, 149). "There is no body … completely devoid of spirit and intelligence," and a soul has a "necessary connection to a body," so that even when the soul leaves its current body, "it has an indissoluble connection with universal matter" (EOM 116, 125). Bruno thus criticizes other Platonists for reducing beauty to pure form without body, insisting instead that beauty (along with the loving bond it inspires) also "consists of a certain physical bond" though it is not located in a particular bodily part. The love we feel from the beautiful eyes of a beloved does not "arise from them alone" but depends on them being "united with the other parts of the face" (EOM 150–151). Indeed, the binding power of beauty and love is extremely holistic, existing "not just in the object itself [whose beauty binds] but also in another equally important place, i.e., the one who is bound" (EOM 151). In order to be bound in love by the beauty of an object, a person must have some inclinations that enable such binding, such as certain physical conditions and "predispositions," which vary from person to person and can, in the same person, change with time. Thus "bonds of love, which were intense before sexual intercourse, become relaxed when the seed is ejaculated and the fire becomes moderated, even though the beautiful object remains the same" (EOM 151). Environmental circumstances that influence a person's condition or mood and that typically change with time will also affect the powers of attraction between potential lovers.

The complex variety of conditions that determine beauty's manifestations and power to bind in love means that "beauty is indefinite and quite indescribable" and that timing is extremely important for the creation or achievement of love (EOM 151). A lover needs to know "the nature, inclination, habits, uses and purposes of the [person] that he is to bind" so that he can deploy those inclinations or habits to capture that person's love, in the same way that "people are bound to sex through ... [inclinations to] drunkenness, gymnastic exercises ... and various types of ... leisure activity" (EOM 148, 163–164). The good lover thus requires considerable knowledge – not only of the beloved but of the environing conditions that frame their encounter and of the various arts through which the beloved can be bound. The more refined the beloved person, the deeper and richer the knowledge needed to attract and lastingly bind that person. Love thus elevates by promoting knowledge, and its most significant and supreme uplift is bringing the lover's soul toward greater knowledge of and closer communion with God. This transfiguration is achieved through the reciprocal logic of love's binding, whose bond affects both the binder and the bound. Love's supreme transformative power, Bruno argues, impacts even the greatest Olympian gods, who descend into the forms of animals or minerals like gold to unite with their beloveds. However, love's transformative aim with humans is to ascend from the animal to the divine. Preoccupied with the beloved's perfections, the lover strives to perfect himself to be worthy of the beloved. Because the lover's soul is powerfully impressed by the beloved and full of selfless devotion, it loses its own self-image and essentially takes on the self or soul of the beloved. Lovers thus speak of losing their souls, hence dying, in love. When one's "love and desire [aim] for the beautiful and the good, a model of perfection," one is "being transformed into its likeness" (HF 108). As Bruno puts it: "I, because of the loftiness of my object, from the most vile subject become a god" (HF 120). In loving God with devoted contemplation, the heroic lover continuously absorbs divine light and is transfigured by it toward his own divinity. "By intellectual contact with that godlike object he becomes a god; and he has thoughts of nothing but things divine and shows himself insensible and impassible to those things which ordinary men feel the most and by which they are most tormented" (HF 108–109).

This divine contact comes in two ways; the first by a spontaneous divine possession that God initiates without the person's sustained cognitive efforts to achieve such blessed contact. Here God simply uses such persons as "habitations" or vessels for the divine spirit. The second way is through the person's rigorous, disciplined "habit of contemplation, ... endowed with a lucid and intellectual spirit . . . under the impact of an internal stimulus . . . spurred on by the love of divinity, justice, truth and glory, by the fire of desire and inspired purpose" (HF 107–108). Through this *askesis* of will and intellect, heroic individuals "make keen their senses and . . . cognitive faculty [and] enkindle a rational flame which raises their vision beyond the ordinary" (HF 108). These strongminded lovers are superior because they act not "as mere receptacles and instruments, but as chief inventors and authors" in accessing the divine (HF 108). Intensely focused on the godly, the mind of such lovers "begins to lose love and affection for every other sensible as well as intelligible object, for joined to that [divine] light it becomes that light, and consequently becomes a god. For the mind draws the divinity unto itself, being in God by the effort to penetrate the divinity (as much as it can); and God is in that mind" (HF 115). Even when their valiant efforts fail to achieve full "intellectual contact" with God, their desire for such contact spurs these heroic lovers toward greater knowledge, virtue, and beauty (HF 108, 115).

Living in this "inferior world" where we "are not permitted to contemplate the beauty of the divinity with purer eyes," we are justified in loving the "shadow of the divine beauty" in human bodies, just as "the suitors of Penelope amused themselves with her servants when they were not permitted to converse directly with the mistress herself" (HF 110, 115). This somatic love, however, is not for the body per se as a mere sensual object, but for the divine element that is in all things and that the body reflects, albeit obscurely, through its perceived beauty, which is more than merely sensory as it is shaped by the soul. A beautifully embodied person is thus a "god-like and living object" that may be "the highest intelligible aspect of the divinity that [the aspiring lover] is able to experience for himself" (HF 115). Bruno therefore concludes that although bodily beauty is too transient to "be the cause of true or constant love" and is far inferior to the intellectual love of God, we must not condemn bodily love as unworthy of inspiring the higher, heroic love (HF 153). For "no matter how much one remains attached to corporeal beauty and to external veneration of it, he may still conduct himself honorably and worthily; [and] from material beauty, which reflects the splendor of the spiritual form and act, . . . he will arrive at the contemplation and worship of divine beauty, light, and majesty" (HF 183). In short, one's love for the lower bodily beauty "does not make him a rebel against the voices which call him to the higher beauties" because such lower objects "derive from lofty objects and are dependent upon them," as part of the universe united by divine love and thus pervaded with divinity. Those lower beautiful "objects, if not God, are things divine and are living images of God," so God "is not in the least offended at seeing himself adored in them" (HF 185). Bruno (unlike Ficino) does not care whether this love of bodies conforms to the so-called natural law of heterosexuality or "civil laws" of marriage. The holy sacrament of marriage does not make a love more heroic or divine in Bruno's eyes. Indeed, the word "marriage" makes no appearance in *The Heroic Frenzies* or in his key essays on magic, where he recognizes same-sex and even bestial bonds of love (EOM 159, 162). He thus shares the disregard for marriage manifested by Abelard and Heloise and the courtly love tradition. Marriage, however, plays a central role in the erotic philosophies of two other Renaissance Platonists we consider: Baldassare Castiglione and Leone Ebreo (a Jewish thinker whose true name is Yehuda Abravanel).

In contrast to scholar-cleric commoners like Ficino and Bruno, Castiglione was an aristocratic courtier and diplomat, whose influential *The Book of the Courtier* (1528) is a multiperson dialogue concerning the proper qualities, education, skills, manners, and moral behavior of the ideal courtier and courtly lady.[47] Based on his experience of the renowned court of Urbino, it is an imaginary reconstruction of four evenings of conversation by a group of real persons present there in 1507. Reflecting the growing respect for women in courtly Renaissance society, the dialogues are presided over by two witty and virtuous ladies.[48] They are Duchess Elizabetta Gonzaga, the childless wife of the invalid Duke of Urbino, and her close companion, the widow Emilia Pia, "a lady gifted with such a lively wit and judgment . . . that she seemed to be in command of all" (BC 42–43). Although the defining topic of these dialogues is the perfect courtier and (by extension) the courtly lady, the question of love is a key recurrent theme, as love is deemed an essential dimension of courtly life and persons.[49]

[47] Baldesar Castiglione, *The Book of the Courtier*, trans. George Bull (London: Penguin, 1976), hereafter BC. Because the dialogue's multiple characters express different and sometimes starkly opposing views, it is not always easy to determine Castiglione's personal position. Perhaps he wanted the book to embrace ambiguities in order to appeal to a diverse audience. For a discussion of the book's multiple interpretations and different kinds of readers, see W. R. Albury, *Castiglione's Allegory: Veiled Policy in "The Book of the Courtier"* (Aldershot: Ashgate, 2014).

[48] If the idea of courtly love contributed to this elevation, then far more influential were a wave of fourteenth- and fifteenth-century female writers who celebrated virtuous women, though typically praising (as did male writers, including Boccaccio) those virtues of women (silence, obedience, modesty) that underline man's dominance. An important exception was Christine de Pizan, whose *Book of the City of Ladies* (1405) insists that woman are not limited to the traditionally female virtues and that virtue is as widespread in women as in men. For more on these points, see M. L. King and A. Rabil, "Editors' Introduction to the Series," in Henricus Cornelius Agrippa, trans. A. Rabil, *Declamation on the Nobility and Preeminence of the Female Sex* (Chicago: University of Chicago Press, 1996), xviii–xxvii.

[49] Among "the accomplishments of the courtier [is] . . . to be in love" (BC 322–323).

Castiglione's account of love's ontology, epistemology, and metaphysical powers of divine transformation is essentially derived from Ficino's Neoplatonism and is delivered through the book's concluding discourse of Pietro Bembo, a distinguished poet, thinker, and author of his own theoretical study of love, which, however, is neither as compelling nor as quintessentially Neoplatonic as the speech Castiglione gives him.[50] "Love is simply a certain longing to possess beauty," and some sort of "knowledge must always of necessity precede desire" (BC 325). As we have different ways of knowing, namely, by the "senses, rational thought, and intellect," so there are different kinds of love (BC 325). Sensual love is animal and intellectual love is spiritual, while rational love mediates and fluctuates between the sensual and spiritual. True bodily beauty, and thus true bodily love, is grasped only through the more spiritual senses of sight and hearing that appreciate "harmony ... and symmetry" (BC 326). This is because beauty itself is "incorporeal" and "these two faculties [of sight and hearing] ... have little to do with corporeal things and are servants of reason," while "our souls [cannot] be satisfied through the sense of touch," which is more corporeal in nature (BC 334). Beauty "loses much of its nobility when fused with base and corruptible matter ... and it is most perfect when completely separated from matter" (BC 334). Ontologically, "beauty springs from God" as a manifestation of his "goodness" (BC 330), and its presence in material objects is "an influx of the divine goodness which, like the light of the sun, is shed over all created things" (BC 325). Therefore, "the proximate cause of physical beauty [in the body] is ... the beauty of the soul ... since it shares in true supernatural beauty" of God (BC 332).

Castiglione differs sharply from Ficino and Bruno in his keen concern for the proper manners in heterosexual love, including the requisite qualities and comportment of noble lovers. Essential to this concern is heightened respect for women that recognizes their crucial role in inspiring refined pleasure, virtue, courage, art, and knowledge. "Who does not realize that without women we can get no pleasure or satisfaction out of life, which but for them would lack charm and be more uncouth and savage than that of wild beasts?" All our "charming recreations" and many inspired achievements in arts such as music, dance, and poetry "can be attributed solely to

[50] See Pietro Bembo, *Gli Asolani* (1505), trans. R. B. Gottfried (Bloomington: Indiana University Press, 1954). The translator's "Introduction" (xvi–xvii) notes how Castiglione's account of love (through the persona of Bembo) is more authentically Platonic and philosophical than Bembo's own treatise on love. Before he took holy orders, Bembo enjoyed a rich experience of sensual love, including two extended affairs with married women, one of them the famous Lucrezia Borgia.

the influence of women" who inspire us through love. Moreover, "in our understanding of great issues far from distracting us they awaken our minds, and in warfare they make men fearless and bold beyond measure. Certainly, once the flame of love is burning in a man's heart, cowardice can never possess it" (BC 255–256). Erotic love thus has the transformative capacity to develop one's mental powers, moral virtues, graceful manners, and artistic skills – qualities the courtier needs to succeed not only in love but also in other roles.[51]

Castiglione's respect for women affirms their essential moral and intellectual equality with men. As "the Magnifico" Giuliano de Medici puts it in describing the ideal courtly lady, "the male cannot be more perfect than the female, since both the one and the other are included under the species man," so they differ only in minor "accidents and not [in] their essence." Intellectually, "everything men can understand, women can too" (BC 218), and "we might find many women just as capable of governing cities and armies as men" (BC 216). Moreover, "although continence, magnanimity, temperance, fortitude of spirit, prudence and the other [moral] virtues may not appear to be relevant [to a woman's] social encounters" and duties, a lady can indeed excel in them "so that her virtues, shining through everything she does, may make her worthy of honor" (BC 216).

Gentlemen should therefore treat women with the highest respect while providing especially outstanding "service and reverence" to their beloved (BC 260). The lover "should honor, please, and obey his lady, cherish her even more than himself, put her convenience and pleasure before his own, and love the beauty of her soul no less than that of her body" (BC 335). He should "be ruled by her in accommodating his every wish to hers. And he must ensure that his desires are all subordinate to hers and that his soul is the slave of hers, or indeed, if possible, that it is transformed into hers" (BC 266). Moreover the "courtier [should] keep his love secret" (BC 270). If all this sounds exactly like the doctrine of courtly love, Castiglione affirms a crucial difference. Courtly love's chief aim was the erotic conquest of married women, but Castiglione insists that other men's wives are entirely off limits; and chastity of the highest sort must be practiced to maintain a woman's absolute virtue and honor. Marriage is the only proper home for

[51] The qualities demanded of the ideal courtier that also make him a good lover include the following: knowledge in literature, music, drawing, and painting; having skill in various athletic and martial pursuits; being mentally gifted, well spoken, honest, discreet, modest, brave; and well dressed, well groomed, graceful, and genteel (albeit not in an excessive or affected way but rather with a certain nonchalance).

heterosexual love, and marital fidelity is strictly demanded to ensure the woman's honor. Romantic love, then, "is suitable only to women who are not married" and for the eventual purpose of marriage, "for when this love cannot end in marriage, the woman is always bound to suffer the pain and remorse caused by illicit things and runs the risk of staining the reputation for chastity that is so important to her" (BC 260). The courtier as lover "should, therefore, be at pains to keep her from going astray and by his wise precepts and admonishments always seek to make her modest, temperate, and truly chaste" (BC 335). Even when suffering a loveless marriage, women "are injuring themselves when they love someone other than their husband." But if a woman is indeed "unfortunate enough to happen to fall in love with someone else because of her husband's hate or another's passion, [she should] concede her lover nothing save her heart" and never "give him any positive sign of what she feels, either in words or gestures or anything else" (BC 261).[52]

Marriage, however, does not ultimately win first place in the book's love rankings. Given its essential carnal purpose of procreation, marital love must involve "sensual desire" and touch. But these elements place it at the "lowest rung" of the familiar Neoplatonic ladder of love described in the book's climactic concluding speeches of Pietro Bembo, outlining the ennobling transformation of the lover as he climbs ever higher and closer to the divine (BC 328). Superior to procreative love is "rational love," in which one enjoys the beloved through rational control and rational pleasures of "sight" and "hearing" (BC 334, 336), that is, through seeing and conversing without seeking sexual satisfaction. Having such pure intentions allows rational lovers to enjoy one form of physical contact that in sensual love would not be rational or chaste – the kiss. Because "a kiss is a union of body and soul, there is a risk that the sensual lover may incline more to the body than the soul." But the rational lover instead treats the mouth as the channel for words expressing the soul and for "human breath or spirit," and his "kiss may be called a spiritual rather than physical union" because it involves a mingling of two souls without "any unseemly desire" for sensual pleasure (BC 336). Nonetheless, because rational love involves loving a person's bodily beauty along with that person's soul, it always risks degenerating into

[52] With similar reticent loving, a courtier (even in wooing for marriage) must not directly declare his love to the woman, as this could offend her. He should instead reveal it subtly "by his actions rather than by speech," such as by performing services or "by a sigh, a gesture of respect or a certain shyness . . . and next he should use his eyes to carry faithfully the message written in his heart" (BC 267–268). The lady, in turn, must be "extremely cautious" and respond "very modestly" to ensure she risks nothing improper or undignified (BC 259–260).

sensual love. Moreover, its fixation on the particular beloved is limiting and breeds unhappiness when the beloved is absent. Marriage, even if chaste, provides no remedy to these problems because it again can slip into sensuality and loneliness.

The lover should therefore climb higher by desiring more spiritual forms of beauty such as the "universal intellect" that more purely reflects God's supreme beauty and goodness (BC 340). "And from there, aflame with the sacred fire of true divine love, the soul flies to unite itself with the angelic nature, and it not only abandons the senses but no longer has need of reason itself. For, transformed into an angel, it understands all intelligible things," enjoying "without any veil or cloud . . . the wide sea of pure divine beauty, which it receives into itself" to thus "unite with God" (BC 340, 342). This flight to divine union eclipses the good of marriage, leaving us with a vision of love that is strikingly like St. Paul's: marital love is the best (and only acceptable) form of bodily love, but it is decidedly inferior to loving God. Moreover, by distracting from God, marriage impedes the realization of spiritual, divine love.

Probably the richest, most sophisticated, and analytically subtle of Renaissance Neoplatonic love theories comes from another author inspired by Italy's vibrant humanism. But unlike Ficino, Bruno, and Castiglione, he was neither Italian nor Christian. Although his famous book *Dialoghi d'amore* (1535) was first published in Italian under his Italian name Leone Ebreo and its second and third editions claimed him as a converted Christian, the author was a Jew of Iberian origin whose true name was Yehuda ben Yitzhak Abravanel (ca. 1465–ca. 1523). Poet, philosopher, physician, and scion of an illustrious family tracing its roots back to King David, Leone refused the Spanish Inquisition's demand to convert to Christianity and fled to Italy where he wrote his *Dialogues of Love* and spent the rest of his life in various culture-rich cities, eventually disappearing from view. Written in the early 1500s but published only posthumously in Rome, the book quickly became extremely popular (with multiple editions in Italian and repeated translations into French, Spanish, Hebrew, and Latin), and it apparently influenced both Castiglione and Bruno.[53]

The book's three dialogues involve the same two characters: Philo (an accomplished male philosopher), passionately in love with and dialogically wooing a bright, attractive, and inquisitive young lady named Sophia, who proves to be an able student of philosophy. Graciously congenial yet

[53] See Cecil Roth's "Introduction," in Leone Ebreo, *The Philosophy of Love* (*Dialoghi d'amore*), trans. F. Friedeberg-Seeley and J. H. Barnes (London: Soncino Press, 1937), hereafter DL.

reluctant to grant his sensual desires, she continually challenges his arguments for love with counterarguments and repeated questions, thus prompting a series of subtle distinctions and detailed elaborations that constitute the book's richly complex erotic theory. The union of Philo and Sophia together constitute Philosophia, generating a philosophy of love as their intellectual progeny. Sophia is extremely intelligent and attracted to "sweet pure reason ... more ... than any heart's love," and the enamored Philo "must ... bow to [her] will"; but *Dialogues* are plainly an exercise of "mansplaining" in which Philo is the superior teacher (DL 5). Leone affirms men's superiority in various ways, for example, likening the male–female relationship to that between heaven and earth (DL 81–83, 89–90, 93).

Leone's Jewish and medical background, I believe, shape his erotic theory differently from those of his Neoplatonic counterparts and make it more appealing to contemporary tastes. But he clearly shares with Ficino, Castiglione, and Bruno key Neoplatonic elements, including the central vision of our universe as united by bonds of love through the emanating radiant beauty and goodness of God. All entities share in "the universality of love": divine spirits, living creatures, and even inanimate things, all inspired and guided by "the Godhead [who] is at once origin, means, and end of all good deeds" and the ultimate object of love (DL 31, 65, 68). The uniting bonds of love that God inspires throughout the elements of his created universe are reciprocal between superior and inferior beings, because all things desire to approach God's perfection. In Leone's logic of perfectionism, just as lower beings love the higher and more perfect beings, "desiring to be united with them for the sake of that greater perfection which they lack," so the higher beings conversely recognize that their own perfection is diminished by the imperfections of the lower things that love and depend on them. The higher things therefore bind themselves in love to those lower things to help the lower raise their level of perfection. This in turn raises the level of perfection of the higher things and makes them better in the eyes of God, who is "the principal and supreme love of all" because his "supreme perfection ... is the source whence flows all their being and wellbeing" (DL 179, 180).

God's supreme beauty thus lies at the origin of all love, and this beauty radiates with different degrees of clarity in the spiritual and material beings of the universe he created. As material beauty results from the spiritual shaping of matter, so we perceive corporeal beauty only through our more spiritual external senses of sight and hearing, and ultimately grasp it only through our inner sense of mind or imagination. More generally, Leone defines "Beauty [as] grace which delights the mind which recognizes it and moves it to love" (DL 264). Although we cannot fully know God while we live within the constraints of corporeal existence, we can know his beauty to some extent through the beauty of his creation. Such knowledge, Leone argues, inspires us to love God, while such love reciprocally inspires greater knowledge of God, leading to a superior form of knowledge that is "unific" or aimed at "cognitive union." This cognitive love works on the "perfecting of the soul" so as to make us "godlike by [our] desire" for union with God, a transformative deification through "spiritual copulation" (DL 34, 41, 48–49, 273). To the extent that "we know His perfection, though [are] incapable of apprehending it completely, so we love and desire to enjoy Him in the most perfect union of knowledge possible to us." This love "ravishes us into such contemplation, as exalts our intellect, till, illuminated by special favor of God, it transcends the limits of human capacity and speculation, and attains to such union and copulation with God Most High, as proves our intellect to be, rather a part of the essence of God" (DL 49). Perfect happiness results from this divine transformation, ultimately coming "solely in the conjunctive act of intimate cognitive union with God, wherein lies the supreme perfection of created minds . . . That is the ultimate activity and blessed end, in which they are made rather divine than human" (DL 50).

Leone departs from the Platonists by defining love not in terms of beauty but in terms of the broader category of goodness, claiming "we could really define love as 'desire to enjoy in union an object recognized as good,'" whether or not we already possess it (DL 49).[54] To refute the standard Platonic identification of beauty and goodness, he argues that "the good is more common than the beautiful, and therefore some goods are beautiful and some not beautiful . . . Every pleasure is good in that it gives pleasure, and therefore it is desired; but not every pleasure is beautiful. Thus there are good and beautiful pleasures, and these are the end of the desire which is love" (DL 430). By extending desire beyond the realm of beauty, Leone recognizes a wider plurality of loves having different qualities, purposes, or causes. We love some things for their functionality or profit, others for pleasure, and still others for their virtue. There are differences between marital love, loving friendship, and divine love. Some loves are born from desire or "sensual appetite," whereas others originate in a rational appreciation of the beloved through the lover's "cognitive reason," which then

[54] Psychologically, love is defined as "an affect of the will to enjoy through union the thing judged good," while desire is distinguished as "an affect of the will aimed at the coming to be or coming to be ours" of something judged good that we do not have. Love thus highlights not only union (rather than mere possession) but also the specific desire of pleasure in enjoying such union (DL 12). Ebreo recognizes that desire itself can have its own pleasures, including those pleasures of anticipating or imagining the pleasures of union.

arouses desire (DL 56–57). Although this superior form of love is rationally born, it is not constrained by ordinary reason because it can bring a lover to deeds of extreme self-sacrifice that rational concern for the mean of moderation and for one's own welfare would not allow. Leone invokes here the idea of "extraordinary reason" to explain how such reason-born but inordinate love (which includes the boundless love of God that martyrs die for) is still deeply ennobling (indeed, "more noble") and remains connected to the ideal of reason even when it flouts our ordinary notion of rational control and self-interest (DL 62–63).

Leone nonetheless displays a physician's respect for the health value of moderation that includes a reasonable amount of sensual pleasures, including erotic delights. He chides "excessive abstinence" of extreme ascetism as a "vice corresponding to profligacy" because it "resigns the pleasures necessary to support life and maintain health," recommending instead "the mean between these extremes" as virtue (DL 17). Of prime importance in both the medical and Hebrew traditions, health is "essentially pleasurable" but also "both advantageous and . . . good." With healthy moderation pleasure "does not weary or pall" or cloy with surfeit. More than a mere physical matter, health enables virtue and satisfies both reason and "sensuous longing"; "the joy of health pervades our whole human consciousness: both our inward and our outward senses and our imagination" (DL 26–27).

As sexual love, when judiciously practiced, contributes to both bodily and mental health, so "Virtuous love may be of corporeal or spiritual things, in the one by moderation and restriction, in the other by every possible growth and increase." True love, born of reason, can be "twin in having as its object both body and spirit" (DL 342), and "the strength of that love makes us desire spiritual and bodily union with the beloved" (DL 56). Philo claims such "perfect and true love" for Sophia. As his "reason rightly judged [her] in every way noble, excellent, and worthy of love," it engendered a desire to be "fused" with her so as to "make of [their] two souls one"; and "this desire excites a longing for physical union, that the union of bodies may correspond to the unity of the spirits wholly compenetrating each other" (DL 57). Although affirming a higher realm of "spiritual things [that] are all intellect" and that can be apprehended directly by the intellect through a pure, "perfect form of spiritual copulation," Leone refuses to drive a wedge between the corporeal and the spiritual, because he recognizes our somatic senses provide perceptions through which we can gain "apprehension of spiritual matters" (DL 41). He even links the corporeality of sexual love with the mentality of cognition by deploying the Old Testament notion of carnal knowledge, whose Hebrew text uses the verb to know (ידע) to designate sexual intercourse. Bodily love "does not differ greatly from . . . mental love" because in both cases "love and desire are means of raising us from imperfect knowledge to the perfect union, which is the true end of love and desire." In both carnal and spiritual love we move from an abstract knowledge of the object of desire "into enjoyment of perfect cognitive union," a fuller, concrete form of knowing that is "unific" (DL 48–49).

The sex–cognition connection finds further support through an intriguing anatomical correspondence. Claiming that the "seven organs of cognition correspond in man to the seven of procreation," Leone notes in particular detail the analogies of tongue and penis. "The male member is analogous to the tongue in position, shape and power of erection and retraction." Just as the "tongue is placed between the two arms, which are the executive instruments of what we know and utter, so is the male member placed between the legs, the instruments of motion to approach the female." Moreover, just as the penis's "movements . . . beget progeny of the body, so motions of the tongue bring forth progeny of the spirit in speech." Further linking the tongue and penis, Leone boldly adds, is "the kiss – that of the one provoking that of the other" (DL 94–95).

Challenging the dogma that carnality corrupts spiritual love, Leone claims that "carnal copulation" can rather strengthen it. Although "a lover's appetite is sated by the union of copulation," "yet . . . his heart's love [is not] quenched thereby" and seeks "a closer and more binding union" that involves the spiritual "fusion of both [lovers] into one . . . Thus the love endures in greater unity and perfection" because "the lover remains continually desirous of enjoying the beloved in union" (DL 54). How can this loving desire continue after the satiation of sex? Since "perfect union . . . involves the complete interpenetration" of the lovers, which "is possible [only] for their souls" but not their physical persons, "there remains after such [carnal] union and penetration . . . an even more ardent desire for that [complete] union which they cannot perfectly consummate. And, as the mind aims ever at complete fusion with the beloved," it aims its loving efforts beyond the mere body (DL 62).

This validation of corporeal love as supporting spiritual union contributes to Leone's unqualified endorsement of marriage, characteristic of the Hebrew faith that rejects the Christian ideal of celibate chastity. Though inferior to the perfect union with God (which is anyway impossible to realize in our normal embodied experience), marriage excels in all the three categories of desirable goods that Leone identifies in our worldly existence: profit, pleasure, and virtuous goodness. Besides sensual pleasures, "The love of husband and wife is . . . bound up with [virtuous] good too; which is the reason why . . . [it] grows continually, through its participation in the good. Moreover, the good and pleasurable elements in married love are supplemented by that of advantage; for each of the spouses is ever deriving benefit from the other, which greatly contributes to the fostering of their love" (DL 28). Married love enjoys all these positive things and, through its spiritual dimension, is not at all inconsistent with divine love.

Indeed, Leone gives a Neoplatonic interpretation of Solomon's Song of Songs and Proverbs that presents marital love as an earthly analogue and encouraging spur to divine love. "The marriage in love of man and woman . . . is a copy of the sacred and divine marriage of the supremely beautiful with the highest beauty [i.e., the union of God with his emanation of divine wisdom] from which the whole universe takes its origin." The only difference is that the "supreme beauty [of divine wisdom] is not only the consort of the supremely beautiful [i.e., God] but also its first child" (DL 425).[55] The "perfect lovers" from the *Song of Songs* represent God and divine wisdom because they are flawless in beauty and blissful in the pleasures of their pure love that is better than wine. The beloved male lover in awakening the young woman's desire symbolizes God's beautifully radiating love that generates and loves wisdom, which is symbolized by the young female lover hungrily seeking union with her beloved who caused that love and constitutes its goal (DL 461).

VI HUMANIST SKEPTICS: ERASMUS AND MONTAIGNE

If this Hebrew Platonist could see a way to resolve the tension between sexual desire and ennobling spiritual love by combining them in marriage, would other progressive Renaissance thinkers far less devoted to Neoplatonic metaphysics and equally skeptical of Rome's Catholic cult of celibacy similarly embrace marriage as a vehicle for love's ennobling transformations? Two great Renaissance humanists outside the sway of Italian Catholicism and Neoplatonism carefully consider this solution but provide rather ambivalent results.

The Dutch scholar Desiderius Erasmus (ca. 1467–1536) has been praised as the "prince of humanists," even though he began his life inauspiciously as the illegitimate son of a priest who had already fathered an earlier son with

[55] Recall how Proverbs personifies wisdom as God's delightful first consort. "The Lord possessed me in the beginning of his way. . . . Then I was by him, as one brought up with him: and I was daily his delight" (8:22, 30).

the same woman.[56] Orphaned in his teens, Erasmus entered the Augustinian monastery at Steyn where he was educated and ordained as a priest in 1492, despite having developed a distaste for monasticism. By tutoring wealthy students and writing popular texts (satires, colloquies, and collected sayings), Erasmus gradually gained intellectual renown and important educational connections throughout Europe, where he lectured widely, eventually receiving a doctorate in theology from the University of Turin in 1506. Ten years later, he published his scholarly masterwork, a revised Latin translation of the New Testament based on the original Greek text that he innovatively included in his book.

Intellectually progressive but politically conservative, Erasmus refused to align himself with radical reformers like Martin Luther, instead maintaining allegiance to the Roman Catholic Church. He nonetheless criticized its abuses and exposed with biting satire the rampant hypocrisy of its vows of monastic celibate chastity. Noting how priests (like his own father) often flouted such vows, he writes in one colloquy, "'Fathers' they're called, and this name they often take care to deserve," while ironically remarking that celibate nuns are often no less sexually dissolute: "there are more who copy Sappho's behavior than her talent."[57] Erasmus affirmed marriage as the surer path to Christian chastity, although he himself never abandoned his priestly celibate vows. In various colloquies, but especially in his tracts *In Praise of Marriage* and *The Institution of Marriage*, Erasmus touts the benefits of marriage so strongly that he incurred the clergy's wrath for attacking the celibate ideal. The rhetorical conventions and dialogical style of his writings make it hard determine his precise position on celibacy versus marriage. Most likely, he admired the celibate ideal but found it far too demanding for ordinary mortals to achieve. "I speak now as one man to another, as one commoner to another, as one weak mortal to another. Virginity is certainly worthy of praise, but on the condition that this praise is not transferred to the majority of mankind. If it were to become a general practice, what could be . . . more destructive than virginity?" he argues *In Praise of Marriage*. "Let the swarms of monks and virgins exalt their own rule of life as they will, . . . the holiest kind of life is wedlock, purely and chastely observed" (EW 67). Indeed, for Erasmus, chaste marriage is almost a form of virginal, eunuch-

[56] See Richard Schoeck, *Erasmus of Europe: The Prince of Humanists, 1501–1536* (Edinburgh: Edinburgh University Press, 1993), and *Erasmus of Europe: The Making of a Humanist, 1467–1500* (Edinburgh: Edinburgh University Press, 1990).

[57] Erasmus, "The Girl with No Interest in Marriage," reprinted in Erika Rummel, ed., *Erasmus on Women* (Toronto: University of Toronto Press, 1996), 29, 31; hereafter EW.

like celibacy. "It is not only the one who lives unmarried who makes himself a eunuch, but one who in chaste and holy fashion carries out the duties of wedlock ... unsullied, who keeps a wife for bearing offspring, not for the purpose of lust" (EW 67–68). Indeed, he later claims that "the marriage I praise is very similar to virginity" because its aim is "not the satisfaction of lust."[58] Remarking that "Christ does not impose celibacy on anyone" but openly forbids divorce, Erasmus argues that it might be good "for the interests and morals of mankind if the right of wedlock were also conceded to priests and monks, ... especially in view of the fact that there is such a great throng of priests everywhere, so few of whom live a chaste life" (EW 67).

Erasmus, however, portrays Christian marriage in stern and dour terms that hardly render it attractive. Consider the qualities desired for the marital pair: the bride should be educated in austere prudishness; her father should never smile at her as such "cheerfulness" can detract from her "feeling of respect" (EW 16). The couple should avoid love stories, songs, music, and dance because they inspire "frivolousness" and "frenzy," as do "lewd pictures and sculptures" (EW 17–19).[59] Obscenities are strictly prohibited, and these include not only the describing of "indecent acts ... in such a way as to make indecency seem acceptable," but also merely naming "directly things that, for decency's sake, should be described more guardedly" (EW 19). One should not, for example, use the names of sexual reproductive organs (like "vulva" or "womb") but instead refer to them, if one must, only through euphemistic circumlocution.

While elsewhere advocating women's learning, Erasmus clearly prefers to leave them in the dark in erotic matters. Such ignorance means loss of autonomy and self-determination, so Erasmus concludes that "whenever a girl has several suitors it would be better to leave the choice [of husband] to her parents" (EW 87). Similarly, while rejecting the medieval demonization of woman and instead urging that a wife's views and wishes should in principle be respected, Erasmus is very far from advocating gender equality

[58] Erasmus, "The Defence of the Declamation on Marriage," in *The Collected Works of Erasmus*, vol. 71, ed. J. K. Sowards (Toronto: University of Toronto Press, 1993), 93. Erasmus suggests that the celebration of virginity was meant only "in a given period of time and in few individuals [as] God wished to show men a kind of picture and likeness of that life in heaven where no women marry or are given in marriage" (EW 73–74).

[59] Popular-advice manuals in Renaissance Italy also sometimes warn against music and dance, for example, works by Giovanni Michele Bruto and Simeon Zuccolo (the latter writing a text entitled "The Insanity of Dancing"). See Rudolph Bell, *How to Do It: Guides to Good Living for Renaissance Italians* (Chicago: University of Chicago Press, 1999), 185, 188–189.

and clearly affirms the husband's ultimate sovereignty. Although "in some circumstances a husband should give in to his wife now and then, even though she is the 'weaker vessel,' . . . the wife must defer much more to the authority of the head, 'for the husband is the head of the wife,' as Paul said," prescribing "obedience and submissiveness" as wifely virtues (EL 95, 97). Even if it is best that couples exercise mutual respect, "both nature and scriptural authority lay down that the wife should obey her husband rather than the opposite" and that she must be "sympathetic to her husband's moods" (EW 97–98). Disobedience and contrariness amount to sin: "A wife who makes war on her husband is making war on God," so her "best way to rule is through obedience" (EW 122–123).

For Erasmus, the standard love-inspiring qualities of "beauty, youth, wealth, nobility or political influence" should have no importance for choosing a wife or husband to love. Nor should one's choice rely on intellectual virtues of "good memory, scholarship, eloquence, ingenuity," and the desire to learn, because these qualities "can all be perverted to immoral ends. But chastity, sobriety, self-restraint, moderation, truthfulness, prudence, reticence, honesty and vigilance make their owners virtuous," and it is only "virtue and compatibility [that] will ensure lasting harmony" in marriage (EW 80). Indeed, "the most important of all moral qualities" for ensuring virtuous harmony has nothing to do with the couple's love or regard for each other but simply consists in "the amount of their respect for their parents and the extent of their devotion to God" (EW 81).

Erasmus commends the values of marriage as tolerance, respect, obedience, friendship in harmony, immortality through children, and the loyalty of affection through a union sanctified by God. Marital choice and behavior should be entirely "based on reason and judgment" (EW 110). Impassioned love, heroic desire, ardent pleasures, and the aesthetic delights of arts and graces have no role here. If love is a desire for beauty, then the only beauty Erasmus advocates is the inner beauty of virtue. Attempts to make oneself physically attractive he castigates as misguided and improper because "it is inward beauty, inward riches, inward nobility that must inspire Christian marriages" (EW 112). No artful manner of physical allure, whether through cosmetics or other arts, should sully the austere modesty of marital love. "The girl whom virtue makes loveable possesses the most effective of love potions," while makeup is a disfiguring "mask" (EW 113). More generally, "Christians should not waste much time on their physical appearance" (EW 115). "Your beauty should reside not in your hairstyle, your gold bracelets, or your fashionable clothes, but be hidden in your hearts, in a spirit that is imperturbably calm and modest, a most precious ornament in the eyes of God" (EW 116–117). As for lovemaking, "it is indecent for a Christian bride (who has chosen to be a wife, not a mistress) to pander to the desires of such a husband [who is eager to enjoy the variety of sexual delights]. She must give her husband modest physical satisfaction, not the exotic services of the harlot" (EW 114), and she must be careful "not to instigate their lovemaking herself" (EW 101).

If the marital goal of children cannot be fulfilled without some degree of "sexual excitement ... and venereal stimuli," it should be kept to a minimum so that "their lovemaking be modest and virtuous, the opposite of fornication and rape," and "bodily pleasure [remain] but a small part of the benefits conferred by wedlock" (EW 66, 70, 110). Erasmus even proposes a prayer to pronounce "before you lay your hands on your wife" in order to ensure this attitude of dour, dutiful marital intercourse: "I have married you to beget children, not out of lust ... let our life together be pure and gentle, let our lovemaking be modest and infrequent" (EW 101, 103). How different from the divinely inspired heroic frenzy for beauty that leads a lover through the pleasures of sexual union to the ultimate pleasure of union with God! Rather than passionately striving toward the divine, Erasmus recommends a marital harmony similar to "soothing mettlesome animals" by pleasing gestures and avoiding what irritates them, "as do those who tame elephants and lions" (EW 134–135). No need for beauty, grace, or other inspiring aesthetic qualities; procreative potential and harmony are enough. "Someone who marries only to beget children or curb his lust will find his wife quite acceptable simply because she is a woman" (EW 88); even "if he is more fussy, pleasant manners and cheerful conversation" will suffice to satisfy him when "her sex alone" does not (EW 115).

If Erasmus paints such a dismally dour portrait of marital eros while tolerating no other variety of sexual love as legitimate, was this because he never tasted the pleasures of carnal love and its powers to inspire the soul while animating the body? Apart from an apparently unrequited homosexual attachment while a young monk in training, Erasmus seems to have never experienced passionate erotic desire. This could never be said about his fellow skeptical humanist, Michel de Montaigne (1533–1592), who (unlike Erasmus) was born the legitimate (and oldest surviving) son of a wealthy noble soldier who was mayor of Bordeaux. Praised by Montaigne as "the best father there ever was," he arranged a superb education for his son by arranging for him to be gently trained in Latin from birth and giving him peasant godparents so that he could appreciate all classes of society and then encouraging his university education in the direction of law rather than theological studies.[60] Unlike Erasmus, Montaigne enjoyed a rich experience of carnal love, tasting its varied passions, pleasures, sufferings, and embarrassments – including recurrent moments of impotence. His sexual life began so early that he could not remember when, and it vibrantly flourished in his youth, when he claims to have served his women lovers "not without distinction; … more however, in continuation and endurance than in violence" (M 833). Montaigne rejects Erasmus's notion that talking openly about sex is obscene: "What has the sexual act, so natural, so necessary, and so just, done to mankind … for us to exclude it from serious and decent conversation?" he questions, and his essays are remarkably frank and unapologetically explicit in their erotic details (M 644).

At age thirty-two, Montaigne agreed to an arranged marriage with the twenty-year-old daughter of a distinguished Bordeaux family, who eventually bore him six daughters, all but one dying in childhood. Although his wife Francoise was "very beautiful and very loveable," Montaigne followed the conventional Christian marital ideal of treating one's wife with prudish modesty. He "never played with her" erotically out of "respect for the honor that the marriage bed requires," allegedly performing his conjugal duties "without having seen anything but her hands and face uncovered, and not even her breast," although, according to a friend, "among other women he was extremely playful and debauched."[61] Some claim she soon found erotic consolation with Montaigne's dashing younger brother Arnaud, a handsome military captain who died suddenly when hit in the head by a tennis ball.[62] This possible experience of cuckoldry, however, did not change Montaigne's attitude toward marital sex, which he believed should never be ardent, playful, imaginative, or lustful in the quest for pleasure but rather simple, sober, and moderate in doing one's conjugal duty. "Those shameless excesses that our first heat suggests to us in this sport are not only indecently but detrimentally practiced on our wives," he insists. "Let them at least learn shamelessness from another hand. They are always aroused enough for our need" (M 147). Far from considering it shameful to be cuckolded, Montaigne

[60] For details on Montaigne's life, see Donald Frame, *Montaigne: A Biography* (New York: Harcourt, Brace & World, 1965). The quotation praising his father is from Montaigne's *Essays*, which I cite from the excellent translation by Donald Frame, *The Complete Essays of Montaigne* (Stanford: Stanford University Press, 1965), 320; hereafter M.

[61] This testimony comes from Montaigne's "friend and successor in the Parlement," Florimond de Raemond, and is quoted in Frame, *Montaigne: A Biography*, 93.

[62] Frame describes the evidence for this alleged affair as inconclusive, but explains how Montaigne's French biographers have supported the idea, see ibid., 89–91.

insists, "I know a hundred honorable men who are cuckolded, honorably and not very discreditably" and who are not thereby "disesteemed" (M 662).

Why should erotic love have no proper place in marriage? It needs to enjoy its independence and unbridled freedom of choice. "Love [personified in the god Eros] hates people to be attached to each other except by himself, and takes a laggard part in relations that are set up and maintained under another title, as marriage is" (M 645). Marriage likewise suffers when made through lovers' passion rather than the sober calculations of third parties. Montaigne regrets having married – "Of my own choice, I would have avoided marrying Wisdom herself, if she had wanted me" (M 648) – but he claims it was best arranged by others and not through his own passionate choice. "The practice and benefit of marriage concerns our race very far beyond us. Therefore I like this fashion of arranging it rather by a third hand . . . and by the sense of others rather than by our own. How opposite is all this to the conventions of love!" (M 646). Rather than "beauty and amorous desires," marriage needs "more solid and stable foundations, and we need to go at it circumspectly; this ebullient ardor [of love] is no good for it." It is therefore wrong to try "to honor marriage by joining love to it"; "we wrong one or the other by confusing them" (M 646). Invoking the scientific views of Aristotle and the physicians, Montaigne argues that even the marital duties of procreation are hindered by love's passions. Because "an excessively hot, voluptuous, and assiduous pleasure spoils the seed and hinders conception" and risks transporting one's wife "outside the bounds of reason," one should engage in marital sex without erotic ardor and only "rarely and at considerable intervals . . . [to ensure] a just and fertile heat" to promote both procreation and tranquility (M 646).

Montaigne thus firmly concludes, "A good marriage, if such there be, rejects the company and conditions of love. It tries to reproduce those of friendship. It is a sweet association in life, full of constancy, trust, and an infinite number of useful and solid services and mutual obligations" but not of passionate delights (M 647). "Marriage is a religious and holy bond" that should give only "a restrained pleasure, serious, and mixed with some austerity" (M 147), but it compensates for its dull, flat pleasures by "utility, justice, honor, and constancy" (M 649). Montaigne understands marital constancy in what some today might call a French style, with no demand for erotic fidelity. Adultery is tolerated, condoned, and even expected as long as its excesses do not disrupt domestic "harmony," which can survive when "there is not much loyalty" in sexual matters, so that one can "give in to the impact of love and nonetheless reserve some duty toward marriage" (M 648). Thus despite his many love affairs, Montaigne claims he has dutifully "observed the laws of marriage more strictly than [he] had either promised or expected" (M 648).[63] As love and marriage differ in aims, demands, and causes, so are their feelings decisively different. "Love is founded on pleasure alone, and in truth its pleasure is more stimulating, lively, and keen: a pleasure inflamed by difficulty. There must be a sting and a smart in it. It is no longer love if it is without arrows and without fire" (M 649). Marriage cannot provide this because its obligatory sexual service is "too profuse and blunts the point of affection and desire" (M 649). In love's quest for pleasure, both men and women take partners they would never wish to wed. In short, "Love and marriage are two intentions that go by separate and distinct roads" (M 649).

If marriage presents no compelling ideal of heroic passion and fidelity but simply the satisfactions of stability, social status, and shared interests, then does freely given love offer a more ennobling option, as it did for Heloise, for courtly lovers, and for some Renaissance Platonists? Nothing, at first glance, seems farther from Montaigne's view. Love does not inspire us to look for honorable partners who will make us more virtuous. Instead, its impulsive quest for sensual pleasure leads both men and women to take lovers of inferior virtue they would "not at all want to have married" (M 649). Montaigne is certainly familiar with the Renaissance theorists of love who praise its ennobling qualities in developing their Platonic theories of the art of love as a mode of elevating self-cultivation. But he treats such thinkers with skeptical ridicule, lampooning their high-minded, erudite discourse as too remote and irrelevant to the essentially natural experience and practice of love. Such erotic theory "treats of things too subtly, in a mode too artificial and different from the common and natural one," Montaigne complains. "My page makes love and understands it. Read him Leon Hebreo and Ficino: they talk about him, his thoughts and his actions, and yet he does not understand a thing in it.... If I were of the trade, I would naturalize art as much as they artify nature. Let us leave Bembo and Equicola alone" (M 666).

Instead, "leaving [such] books aside and speaking more materially and simply" from his own experience, Montaigne initially offers a basely sensual vision of erotic love, whose frenzied quest for sexual satisfaction both maddens and dulls the mind. "Love is nothing else but the thirst for sexual

[63] Montaigne sharply criticizes the double standard that demands the wife's absolute erotic fidelity while allowing the husband an ample range of sexual adventures. Believing that men and women are equally susceptible to sexual love (though women apparently have more passion and far greater endurance for enjoying it), Montaigne argues that women should enjoy more equal rights in loving (M 654–656). He also rejects men's common accusation that women lack the virtue of sexual fidelity. "It is the old saying: The pot calls the kettle black" (M 685).

enjoyment in a desired object, and Venus nothing else but the pleasure of discharging our vessels – a pleasure which becomes vicious either by immoderation or by indiscretion" (M 668). Noting how Plato's Socrates exaltingly defined love as "the appetite for generation by the mediation of beauty," Montaigne deflates it by observing its ludicrous manifestations and inane effects. Note "the ridiculous titillation of this pleasure, the absurd, witless, and giddy motions with which it stirs [us] up . . . , that reckless frenzy, that face inflamed with fury and cruelty in the sweetest act of love, and then that grave, severe, and ecstatic countenance in so silly an action" (M 668). The facts "that our delights and our excrements have been lodged together pell-mell [in our genitals], and that the supreme sensual pleasure is attended, like pain, with faintness and moaning," serves to confirm that "man is the plaything of the gods" (M 668) and that love is the paradigm of human folly and lack of control. Erotic desire is unruly and capricious: "it is contrary to the nature of love if it is not violent, and contrary to the nature of violence if it is constant" (M 675). This makes fidelity but also impotence intractable problems.

Rather than eros ennobling us, the overwhelming physicality and mind-numbing confusion of the sexual act serves to lower all beings to the same brute status, "to put on the same level the fools and the wise, and us and the beasts . . . We eat and drink as the animals do, but these are not actions that hinder the operations of our mind. In these we keep our advantage over them. But this other," Montaigne laments, "puts every other thought beneath its yoke and by its imperious authority brutifies and bestializes all the theology and philosophy there is in Plato" (M 668–669). If "sleep suffocates and suppresses the faculties of our mind; the sexual act likewise absorbs and dissipates them." "In everything else," Montaigne continues, "you can keep some decorum.. . . This one cannot even be imagined other than vicious or ridiculous. Just to see this, try to find a wise and discreet way of doing it" (M 669). That Montaigne's theory of love emphasizes its physical and genital nature may partly derive from his personal preoccupation with problems of impotence (especially as he aged) and with his apparent abiding shame in having a small penis. But it also reflects traditional ideals of procreation that confirmed his own avowed genital predilections. "Never was a man more impertinently genital in his approaches," he confesses, knowing "how ridiculous . . . and how ineffectual" this focus made him, yet unable to "repent of it" (M 679).[64]

[64] Montaigne's preoccupation with genital sex and the importance of the size of one's penis seems to be quite common for that time, as we can see in the most notorious of sixteenth-century Italian books on sexual practice, *I modi*. This book, based on drawings of sexual positions by the

Notwithstanding these mordant criticisms of erotic love, Montaigne ultimately defends its value, even for older men like himself who have lost much of their capacity for sex but not yet their taste for its pleasures. He advocates such sensual pursuits despite their adulterous character. Montaigne's case for erotic love and its cultivation through more artful practice is at least twofold. The first dimension highlights the somaesthetic health benefits of sexual pleasure, especially for older men who feel they are losing their youthful vitality and cheerfulness as they gradually slide toward aged decrepitude and death. The "sensual pleasure" of sex, he argues, can help relieve some of the principal ills of old age: "an excess of severity," somber reflections, and "coldness" that court a morbid "insensibility" damaging to both body and soul (M 638). By pursuing erotic adventures with proper measure, moderation, and concern for both oneself and one's lovers, an aging person can be physically revitalized through love's invigorating energies and lively pleasures that further lift one's mood from somber thoughts and worries of future decline; and it can do this without a troubled conscience of having harmed one's partners. "Love is a sprightly, lively, and gay agitation" that when practiced in measure is "hurtful only to fools" (M 680).

Although severely critical of his sexual prowess, Montaigne takes pride in his good sense and care in managing erotic liaisons, for both his own benefit and that of his lovers. "I did not let myself go entirely; I took pleasure in it, but I did not forget myself" or the welfare of his lovers (M 680). "I preserved entire the little sense and discretion that nature has given me, for their service and mine," avoiding "ingratitude, treachery, malignity, and cruelty," but rather taking pains to be "faithful" and even "stupidly conscientious" in serving "the interest of their honor" (M 678–680). Erotic love is "a vain occupation," Montaigne admits, "unbecoming, shameful, and illegitimate; but carried on in this [moderate, discreet, respectful] fashion, I consider it healthy, proper to enliven a heavy body and soul; and as a physician, I would prescribe it to a man of my temperament and condition as readily as any other recipe to rouse him and keep him in vigor till he is well on in years, and to keep him from the clutches of old age" (M 680). Here Montaigne's

artist Gulio Romano (a student of Raphael) and then engraved as prints and later published with accompanying ribald sonnets by Pietro Aretino relating to the feelings of the lovers engaged in these coital positions, is confined to heterosexual acts of penile penetration in the vagina or anus. The sonnets, "in honor of pricks who serve asses and pussies," repeatedly emphasize the importance of size: "a small cock is unseemly" (sonnet 3), and creates the "despair of having too little cock" (sonnet 9) to give a woman pleasure. I cite here from the translations in the extensive study of *I modi* by Bette Talvacchia, *Taking Positions: On the Erotic in Renaissance Culture* (Princeton: Princeton University Press, 1999), 203, 211, 227.

erotic theory strikingly converges with the medical aims of classical Chinese *ars erotica*. Asserting that "love . . . would restore to me vigilance, sobriety, grace, care for my person [and] would secure my countenance . . . [from] the grimaces of old age," Montaigne claims it would further "divert me from a thousand troublesome thoughts, a thousand melancholy moods, that idleness and the bad state of our health loads us with at such an age; would warm up again, at least in dreams, this blood that nature is abandoning; would hold up the chin and stretch out a little the muscles and the soul's vigor and blitheness for this poor man who is going full speed toward his ruin" (M 681–682).

The health value of sexual pleasures compels Montaigne to revise his blunt rejection of the arts of love. They may be gratuitous for the youthful, in whom nature alone supplies enough appetite and vigor to get the job done. However, "for a run-down body, as for a broken-down stomach, it is excusable to warm it up and support it by art, and by the mediation of fancy to restore appetite and blitheness to it, since by itself it has lost them" (M 681). Key to this artistry is the poetic imagination. Montaigne finds erotic pleasures more attractively portrayed in poetry than actually realized in ordinary life, and even in real life we enjoy them more through imagination than mere physical sensation. Much of our erotic pleasure derives from the symbolic suggestions and anticipations of envisaged sensuous delights in our imagination as we observe, converse with, or reflect on the partners we desire. Veiled erotic suggestiveness, Montaigne avows, can be more arousing than full exposure and direct physical contact, especially for someone insecure about his performance potency.

Imagination's crucial role in sexual pleasure compels Montaigne to revise his original view that erotic love is simply a physical "thirst for sexual enjoyment in a desired object" whose satisfaction is "nothing else but the pleasure of discharging our vessels" (M 668). He frankly affirms that sexual desire is "not simply a bodily passion," for "it still lives after satiety; no constant satisfaction or end can be prescribed to it, for it always goes beyond its possession" (M 675). The phenomenon of erotic desire persuades Montaigne that "there is nothing in us during this earthly imprisonment that is purely either corporeal or spiritual" and that we should therefore attend to strengthening the health of both body and soul. If ascetic arts can strengthen the soul by mortifying the body with pain, so imaginative arts of the mind can help strengthen an aging or weakened body with erotic pleasures, "to inspire and infuse into the body all the feeling their nature allows, and to strive to make them sweet and salutary to it" (M 681).

The imaginative erotic pleasures that constitute Montaigne's *ars erotica* are not merely the imagined sensory pleasures of sexual foreplay and coitus. They also (more abundantly) include imagined reactions and interpretations of various favors, gestures, and tokens that suggest the beloved's willingness to acknowledge with favor the lover's desire, at least to some degree and with the hope of greater fullness. Such signs of favor generate in the lover's mind a wealth of erotically pleasurable thoughts and feelings, along with the hope of progress toward greater intimacy or eventual full union, producing a more earthly but still somewhat spiritual parallel to the progressively ennobling Platonic ladder of love. Thus, while rejecting the erudite transcendental art of love advanced by Platonists such as Ficino, Ebreo, and Bembo, Montaigne fully endorses the practical worldly *ars erotica* of their gallant Italian and Spanish countrymen.

This down-to-earth yet refined *ars erotica* derives maximal meaning and pleasure from the most varied and subtle signs of love, taking multiple delights through all the possible moments of gradual, leisurely progress toward greater closeness or union with the beloved. As Montaigne puts it, "I like the love-making of the Spaniards and Italians, more respectful and timid, more mannered and veiled. I don't know who it was in ancient times who wanted his throat as long as a crane's neck so as to relish longer what he swallowed" (M 671).[65] Because the joy of sexual climax is a far too "quick and precipitate pleasure," Montaigne admires their art of prolonging the pleasures of desire and imagined fulfillment through extensive "preambles" of suggestive indications of possible affection without quickly proceeding to sexual contact. "Everything among them serves as a favor and a recompense: a glance, a bow, a word, a sign. If a man could dine off the steam of a roast, wouldn't that be a fine saving? This is a passion that with very little solid essence mixes in much more vanity and feverish dreams: it should be satisfied and served accordingly" (M 671). Even if only symbolic or imagined, such erotic pleasures have their somatically enlivening effect.

Montaigne therefore recommends substituting such erotically charged symbolic favors instead of pressing for genital contact, as these protect the

[65] Montaigne experienced Italian courtesan culture in Venice and Rome, finding the Roman women generally more beautiful. See Fiora A. Bassanese, "Private Lives and Public Lies: Texts by Courtesans of the Italian Renaissance," *Texas Studies in Literature and Language* 30, no. 3 (1998): 295–319. Montaigne remarked that "the courtesan could charge as much for her conversation as for a full sexual encounter" (ibid., 298). He wrote: "I found this inconvenience, that they sold mere conversation as dearly . . . and as sparingly as for the whole affair." Michel de Montaigne, *Journal de voyage en Italie*, in Albert Thibaudet and Maurice Rat, eds., *Oeuvres complètes* (Paris: Gallimard, 1962), 1235 (my translation).

reputation of ladies but also the honor of old men who may be insufficiently attractive or potent to win a woman's full genital possession. "If the ladies spin out and spread out their favors in small amounts, each man, even to miserable old age, will find there some little scrap of pleasure, according to his worth and merit" (M 671). A crucial feature of this art of love is a dialectic of anticipation and deferral, of taking pleasure in the promise of future pleasure, of enjoying the winding indirections of the journey rather than taking delight only in the final destination. "He who has no enjoyment except in enjoyment, who must win all or nothing, who loves the chase only in the capture, has no business mixing with our school," Montaigne urges. "The more steps and degrees there are, the more height and honor there is in the topmost seat. We should take pleasure in being led there, as is done in magnificent palaces, by diverse porticoes and passages, long and pleasant galleries, and many windings" (M 671). This *ars erotica* not only allows us to love "longer" and more honorably, but also is kinder to women because they take great risks in granting men "entire possession" of their procreative parts (M 672). But any *ars erotica* must leave room for love's impulsive "heedlessness" and "divine freedom" that are so essential to its charm and can be spoiled by too many rules of "art and wisdom" (M 684).

In offering this vindication of erotic love and proposing an honorable, imaginative art of lovemaking, does Montaigne provide a convincing vision of a noble *ars erotica*? Did he even intend to? The answer is debatable. Despite his religious faith, he not only tolerates adultery (with its consequent deception) but essentially encourages it. The overriding goals he posits are pleasure and health rather than improved virtue, knowledge, or spiritual transcendence. Montaigne, however, has a ready answer to such critique through his bold challenge of two key philosophical ideals and his consequent transvaluation of traditional notions of virtue and greatness. Famously questioning the ancient dogma that "to philosophize is to learn to die" (M 56) by suggesting it should rather teach us how best to live, Montaigne also challenges philosophy's long-standing ideal of asceticism, the goal of supreme spiritual elevation through a life of severe discipline that eschews carnal pleasures and welcomes painful struggle. This ideal may find admirable expression in godlike heroes and saints, but it is not suitable for the normal ranks of men and women who are profoundly shaped by their corporeal limits and needs. "What is the use of these lofty points of philosophy on which no human being can settle, and these rules that exceed our use and our strength?" he asks. "I often see people propose to us patterns of life which neither the proposer nor his hearers have any hope of following, or, what is more, any desire to follow" (M 756). "Philosophy is very childish," he continues, "when she gets up on her hind legs and preaches to us that it is a barbarous alliance to marry the divine with the earthly, . . . that sensual pleasure is a brutish thing unworthy of being enjoyed by the wise man" (M 855). Rejecting the ideal of ultimate elevation that aspires to "divine lives . . . so lofty and extraordinary" (M 743), Montaigne instead firmly advocates the common middle way of human living as the true human ideal, a way of life that blends the spiritual and the sensuous, midway between the divine and the beastly. "The most usual and common way of living is the best," he writes, clarifying his intent by elaborating: "Greatness of soul is not so much pressing upward and forward as knowing how to set oneself in order and circumscribe oneself. It regards as great whatever is adequate, and shows its elevation by liking moderate things better than eminent ones. There is nothing so beautiful and legitimate as to play the man well and properly," rather than pretending to play at being a god or angel (M 848, 852).

I have much sympathy with Montaigne's argument, but one might worry that most men and women are not as intelligent, sensitive, moderate, and well intentioned as he himself was. For less enlightened individuals, his advocating the human need for sexual pleasure that justifies discreetly managed adulterous affairs could end up promoting lives of excessive carnality and immoral debauchery. Perhaps we ordinary, frail, and pleasure-driven creatures need to aim heroically high simply to arrive in the moderate middle realm of virtuous body–soul balance, proper comportment, and harmony that Montaigne urged. Otherwise, as history suggests, we may land far lower. Montaigne's affirmation of erotic pleasures and their extramarital pursuit inspired a strong, secular libertine movement that flourished in the seventeenth century and eventually resulted in the Church having his *Essays* placed on the *Index of Prohibited Books* in 1676.[66]

VII COURTESAN CULTURE

If marriage could not supply adequate satisfaction in the pleasures of erotic desire and if adulterous affairs proved problematically immoral and risky, then courtesan culture offered another solution to man's erotic needs, and it flourished in Renaissance Italy, just as the hetaera culture did in ancient Greece. Like the elite hetaeras, the high-class or "honest" courtesan (*cortigiana onesta*) distinguished herself from lower-class courtesans (*cortigiane di*

[66] Alain Legross, "Montaigne on Faith and Religion," in Philippe Desan, ed., *The Oxford Handbook of Montaigne* (Oxford: Oxford University Press, 2016), 529.

lume, courtesans of light or lamp) and from common sex workers (*meretrici*) not only by her connections with upper-class society (nobility and renowned men of wealth, power, or culture) but also by her artistic and intellectual gifts.[67] Courtesan culture's penetration into the highest circles of *cinquecento* Rome is evident from the following eyewitness account of an orgy attended by the pope in his Vatican palace, on Sunday, October 31, 1501 (this testimony provided by the Master of Ceremonies at the papal court):

> In the evening a supper was given in the Duke of Valentino's [Cesare Borgia's] apartment in the Apostolic Palace, with fifty respectable prostitutes, called courtesans, in attendance. After supper they danced with the servants and others present, at first in their clothes and then naked. Later candelabra with lighted candles were taken from the tables and put on the floor and chestnuts were scattered around them. The prostitutes crawled naked on their hands and knees between the candelabra, picking up the chestnuts. The pope, the Duke and his sister, Donna Lucrezia, were all present to watch. Finally, prizes of silk doublets, shoes, hats and other clothes were offered to the men who copulated with the greatest number of prostitutes.[68]

Some high-class courtesans were the illegitimate children of upper-class gentlemen and elite courtesan mothers, as such mothers had the proper education and connections to provide their daughters the best training in their trade. One of those distinguished daughters was Tullia d'Aragona (ca. 1510–1556), whose mother was a famous Roman courtesan Gulia Campana and whose father, she and her mother alleged, was a cardinal of the noble d'Arragona family. Loved and admired by many influential literati, Tullia wrote two books of poetry, but she warrants special attention as the author of a compelling philosophical work on love and desire, *Dialogue on the Infinity of Love*.[69] The book was written in Florence in 1547, where she

67 As in Japanese courtesan culture, there were publications with classificatory ranking of courtesans. For example, the famous Venetian courtesan Veronica Franco (who published poetry and letters) was listed in the 1565 *Catalogo de tutte le principal et più honorate cortigiane di Venetia*. For details on this courtesan and more generally courtesan culture, see Georgina Masson, *Courtesans of the Italian Renaissance* (London: Secker and Warburg, 1975), and M. F. Rosenthal, *The Honest Courtesan: Veronica Franco, Citizen and Writer in Sixteenth-Century Venice* (Chicago: University of Chicago Press, 1993).

68 Cited in Masson, *Courtesans*, 8.

69 Tullia d'Aragona, *Dialogue on the Infinity of Love*, trans. Rinaldina Russell and Bruce Merry (Chicago: University of Chicago Press, 1997), hereafter DIL. Russell's introduction to the book provides biographical and cultural background details. The widespread respect for Tullia's intellectual gifts is evident from her role as a central character in a slightly earlier philosophical dialogue on love by Sperone Speroni, *Dialogo d'amore* (1542). For more details on Tullia and her

continued the courtesan career that she practiced first in Rome (from the age of eighteen) and then in the cities of Siena, Ferrara, and Venice. Tullia makes herself one of the two chief interlocutors in the book's dialogue, the other being the prominent historian and man of letters Benedetto Varchi (notorious – and even arrested – for his love of boys and the alleged rape of a girl of nine).[70]

Philosophically, Tullia is closest to the erotic doctrines of Leone Ebreo, and she repeatedly extols his theory as superior to "all the authors, whether ancient or modern, who wrote about love in any language" because "he speaks about love not only more comprehensively . . . but with more doctrine and more truthfully" (DIL 91).[71] However, whereas Leone strongly commends marriage, Tullia's *Dialogue* does not. It never even mentions the word "marriage" (nor "wife" or "husband"). For courtesan culture, marriage is irrelevant to love, even if the courtesan herself had married, as Tullia apparently did, for reasons of social respectability, which for courtesans was fragile and often menaced. Adopting the main Platonist line, she claims that "beauty is the mother of all forms of love," while "love is nothing other than a desire to enjoy with union what is truly beautiful or seems beautiful to the lover" (DIL 69–70). In the more virtuous form of love (that she labels "honest"), the lovers are "people who have a refined and virtuous disposition, whether they be rich or poor." Their love is driven not by animal appetite but by reason and "has as its main goal the transformation of oneself into the object of one's love, with a desire that the loved one be converted into oneself, so that the two may become one" (DIL 90).

Unlike many Platonists, Tullia refuses to denigrate the body in love and more generally in human identity. Denying that it detracts from the soul, she even maintains that a person as "the whole, body and soul taken together, is more noble and more perfect than the soul itself" (DIL 65). Her respect for the body lies partly in its somaesthetic capacities of perception by means of the somatic senses, as "one may not understand or get to know anything at

literary achievements, see Masson, *Courtesans*, 88–131; and J. L. Hairston, trans., *The Poems and Letters of Tullia d'Aragona and Others* (Toronto: Centre for Reformation and Renaissance Studies, 2014).

70 For more on Varrachi and his relationship to Tullia, see Masson, *Courtesans*, and Robert Sturgis, *Dialogue and Deviance: Male–Male Desire in the Dialogue Genre* (New York: Palgrave Macmillan, 2005), 125–126.

71 The book does not refer to Leone Ebreo by name but refers to him through the principal expositor of his theory in his *Dialogues of Love*, Philo or (in Italian) Filon. However, Tullia prudently distances herself from Leone's views "in what concerns the Jewish faith" which she could at best "excuse" (DIL 92).

all except through one's senses, . . . the noblest and most exquisite [of which] is sight," the primary stimulus for love (DIL 98). The senses, she argues, are not merely cognitive but can also be "spiritual," and in "honest love . . . the principal part is played by the 'spiritual' senses, those of sight and hearing, and . . . the imagination" (DIL 90). In "vulgar" love the lower senses and carnal desires are prominent, and lovers "simply want to obtain pleasure and to procreate something that resembles themselves, without any further thought or concern" (DIL 89–90). But Tullia does not condemn this carnal love spurred by "instinctive drives that arise from our nature . . . Rather it can be and should be lauded . . . [for] generating offspring" so long as "this appetite . . . not become unbridled and overpowering." Just as eating and drinking are natural desires whose satisfaction is necessary for life and not blameworthy when pursued in proper measure, so "the passions of the flesh" are nature's gift for perpetuating the species, and we should enjoy them within "due limit and moderation" as determined by "reason, which ought to be the queen of the body" (DIL 94).

Even honest love includes a somatic dimension that goes beyond the spiritual senses. This is because "it is the lover's wish to achieve a corporeal union besides the spiritual one, in order to effect a total identification with the beloved," and here "the senses of touch and taste" (that she labels "material" senses) come centrally into play, providing further somaesthetic pleasures. However, as complete "corporeal unity can never be attained, because it is not possible for human bodies to be physically merged into one another, the lover can never achieve this longing of his, and so will never satisfy his desire" (DIL 90). This resolves the dialogue's defining question about the "infinity of love." True love is infinite because insatiable; "love has no end nor limit . . . and feeds on lovers' minds, never to tire and become satisfied" (DIL 84). Lustful "appetite is quenched through copulation and physical union," but this "carnal pleasure" by inspiring desire for more complete union makes lovers "love more fervently than before" (DIL 103). Even vulgar lovers often sustain their desire for each other after "carnal intercourse" because they so greatly "enjoy the thrill" of it that they long to repeat it again and again. Recognizing, like Leone, different levels of carnal love depending on the different qualities of the individuals involved, Tullia claims that "this vulgar and lascivious strain of love can, at times and in some individuals, give rise to a chaste and virtuous love" (DIL 103). This is surely a convenient doctrine for a high-class courtesan who seeks to edify and refine her client-lovers toward such virtuous love so that she can better manage them and their desires.

The type of reason that Tullia advocates for directing desire in the art of love is not that of disembodied abstract philosophical reasoning (though she proves herself very capable of it), but instead critical thinking guided by experience and what one learns from life and the world through one's senses and feelings. She firmly counters her interlocutor Varchi (whose superior philosophical knowledge she acknowledges) with: "I want you to bow to experience, which I trust by itself far more than all the reasons produced by the whole class of philosophers" (DIL 71). She knows by experience that a lover can lose interest or develop distaste for someone once beloved, so that love can effectively cease even if it in principle has no end because it cannot be fully satisfied. Tullia also knows by experience that women are no less capable of love than men, and she firmly opposes the conventional view (voiced by Varchi) of woman's inferiority to man in this capacity as well as others. Opposing Speroni's characterization of her as a woman gripped by a carnal jealous love for Bernardo Tasso, Tullia's dialogue insists that her love for him (as well as her love for other men) is not that sort of jealous love based on carnal, animal appetite, but rather a love based on a reasoned appreciation of "his qualities" of virtue and that she is similarly loved for her "noble soul" (DIL 108–109).[72]

She critiques male privilege not only by affirming woman's equal aptitude for love and intellectual dialogue, but also by condemning pederasty as a hideous vice of unnatural appetite. Despite her awareness (from Plato and Lucian) of its significant role in Greek culture, Tullia claims that "those men who entertain a lascivious love for youths are not following the true dictates of nature, so they fully deserve the punishments that canon and divine law have imposed on them, as well as the penalties set up by man-made and civil justice." Indeed, she can "scarcely believe that people who practice such an ugly, wicked and hideous vice . . . are real human beings" (DIL 95). Tullia invokes her feminist pride to contest the standard defense that this love of boys is a pure appreciation of beauty and intelligence combined with a noble desire to educate bright young souls and without the alleged blemish of lust for sexual coupling. She does so with the challenging question of why men do not love women "with this same type of [purely spiritual] love," because she is certain that her interlocutors "don't wish to imply that women lack the intellectual soul that men have and that consequently they do not belong to the same species as males" (DIL 97).

[72] For more details on Tullia's response to Speroni's portrayal of her, see Janet Smarr, "A Dialogue of Dialogues: Tullia d'Aragona and Sperone Speroni," *Modern Language Notes*, 113, no. 1 (1998): 204–212.

Keen to ensure her extraordinary status as a courtesan admired for literary and philosophical gifts rather than sexual pleasures, Tullia does not provide any instruction on practical erotic techniques. If she had particular ideas or insights concerning lovemaking techniques, she never made them public. Publishing such matters could be a dangerous violation of decorum for an honest courtesan, but would be especially damaging for Tullia's distinctive image as "the intellectual courtesan." Moreover, by exposing her sexual techniques, a courtesan could lose her competitive edge by empowering her rivals with such methods. As with alchemy or magic, the courtesan's *ars erotica* often prized esoteric knowledge with its private, personal transmission. Such personal, privileged transmission no doubt fostered the phenomenon of high-class courtesans following their successful mothers in this trade, learning the secrets of sexual knowledge that was sometimes thought to be woman's special domain of expertise (as we saw with Philaenis and Elephantis and the legendary females who instructed China's Yellow Emperor).

If elite Renaissance courtesans did not divulge their sexual methods, we may get a glimpse of them in a wittily ribald reconstruction of mother–daughter courtesan instruction found in the dialogues of Pietro Aretino (1492–1556), the notorious bawdy poet and satirist who wrote the lewdly sexual sonnets for the racy coital images of *I modi*. Although an avowed same-sex sodomite, Aretino was an expert habitué of courtesan culture and was, in fact, a courtesan's son. Two dialogues of his *Ragionamenti* (1534, 1536) are devoted to a spicy and sardonic exposition of the life and work of courtesans.[73] The second of these dialogues, "The Education of Pippa," portrays in saucy detail how the successful courtesan "Nanna teaches her daughter, Pippa, the whore's trade" (RPA 1). Ironic and imaginatively embellished as this literary text may be, it depicts a robust Renaissance *ars erotica*, replete with lovemaking techniques aimed at enhancing sexual pleasure and power.

Nanna affirms from the start that courtesanship requires an *ars erotica* involving a wealth of knowledge relating to physical, psychological, social, and aesthetic matters. Natural beauty and willingness are not enough. "The whore trade therefore is not the trade of a fool," she insists, explaining to Pippa that it is too complex to "hurry" its instruction: "Thou must know

[73] My quotations are from Pietro Aretino, *The Ragionamenti, or Dialogues of the Divine Pietro Aretino Literally Translated into English* (Paris: Isidore Liseux, 1889), vol. 4, "The Education of Pippa," hereafter RPA. For Aretino's deep engagement with courtesan culture, see Masson, *Courtesans*, 20–21, 98–99, 101–102.

something else than lifting up thy petticoats and saying: Come, I'm at it; unless thou wishest to fail the same day thou openest shop" (RPA 6). From the outset, Nanna makes clear that deception is a crucial part of the requisite knowledge. She reveals that although everyone believes Pippa is only fifteen (and Nanna says she looks less than fourteen, the typical age for launching a courtesan), she in fact is already twenty, as it was better to wait till then for her launch (RPA 3–4).[74] Although younger teenage girls may seem more innocent and desirable, being twenty promises more of the physical, emotional, and intellectual ripeness needed to flourish in the courtesan trade. Such mental maturity includes knowing how to feign emotions and manipulate complex and contradictory signals, adjusting them according to the changing needs of the erotic situation. Despite the dialogue's conversational style and digressions, one clearly discerns the major topics and structure of Nanna's erotic theory: how to attract client-lovers; how to arouse, please, and conquer them through foreplay and coitus; how to maintain their love and to derive from them the most money and gifts.

A top-quality courtesan attracts through an appetizing mixture of contrasting signals. On the one hand, she should present a modest, innocent, respectable demeanor both in physical appearance and in manners or conduct. On the other hand, she should display hints of strong romantic affection and desire for the targeted lover-client, suggesting that beneath her demure, virtuous modesty, there simmers an emotional erotic energy that signals sexual availability. Introduced to a potential client by her procuress (here her mother Nanna), the young courtesan should maintain a prim posture with "arms close to her body," bow, and look "humbly" at her target. But in so looking she should also blush and sigh with feigned innocence and desire because blushing is "the paint modesty sets on little girls' cheeks [that] snatches away men's souls," and "sighing and blushing all at once are signs of love and a rising of the passions" that will attract and arouse the targeted client-lover (RPA 8–9). The courtesan's modest, wholesome appearance means having freshly cleaned body and teeth, while avoiding strong perfumes and heavy makeup; her "dress [should] be simple and neat," without suggestively exposing part of her bosom (RPA 109, 112, 120). She must speak "in a mild tone that does not betoken the brothel," discreetly "laugh in such a way that no feature of [her] face is distorted," and eat and drink in such a delicate "manner that it scarce seems ... eating." In short, the courtesan should "display the lady in all her acts" as "nothing raises one like modesty,"

[74] "Fourteen was in fact the age at which most Italian courtesans made their debut ... and their youth and virginity were added attractions," notes Masson, *Courtesans*, 20.

even in preparing to make love by undressing, which should be done "slowly, very slowly" with "a few sighs" to feign an innocent shyness overcome by her desiring love for her client (RPA 13)

Nanna advises Pippa that once in bed with her client she should "hug him [and] kiss him over and over," while accepting the foreplay of her client-lover, who will

> handle thy breasts, plunging his whole face between them ... He will then run his hand over thy person, slipping it gradually down to the little monkey, and, after having stroked it, he will fumble thy thighs. But the buttocks are a regular loadstone: they attract the hand after them, I say; and when he has feasted on them an instant, he will begin to try thee, by placing his knee between thy legs, in order to see whether thou wilt turn over, not daring however to propose the thing to thee at the first encounter. (RPA 14)

While Pippa is in no way alarmed by the idea of intercourse from behind, Nanna cautions against allowing it in the first encounter as it puts in question the girl's image of modesty and "good breeding." So Pippa must pretend to be shocked and reluctant. However, once the man decides to enter the "right way" and "he is on thee, do thy duty, Pippa" with expert and profuse caresses to help him "finish" and thus cause his "defeat." In making love to men, "to lavish fondlings on them is to kill them" (RPA 15). Nanna moreover details the sort of fondling a courtesan uses to arouse and conquer her client:

> the moment he is slipping his tongue between her lips, [she] seizes his machine and squeezing it twice or three times in her fingers, compels it to stand erect; ... gives it a little shake, then ... takes the little jingly bobs in the hollow of her hand and tickles them, deliciously; she then pats the buttocks, scratches the moss and begins to tease it, so that the cucumber, being put into a jolly mood, resembles somebody who wants to puke but cannot. (RPA 16–17)

Nanna further instructs Pippa on how, with shy modesty and subtle hints, to get her lover to dismount, lie on his back, and let Pippa mount him for intercourse "in the Giannetta fashion" where the courtesan can enjoy the privilege of being on top. Then,

> once thou art arranged [on top], throw thy arms round his neck, give him ten smacks one after the other; and, having seized his pestle, squeeze it so hard as to make it finish by flying into a most violent passion; when it is all on fire, stick it into thy middle and push against it with all thy might; stop there, motionless, and kiss the man fondly. After having kept thus still for a

> little while, sigh as in the height of enjoyment, and say to him: "If I accomplish, will you accomplish?" The stallion will answer in a pricklike voice: "Yes, love!" Thou commence to flutter about exactly as if his spontoon was the axle-tree, and thy serpellium the wheel, at the place where the stock causes it to turn; if thou seest he is on the point of finishing, stop, while saying: "Not yet, my life," and, ramming thy tongue into his mouth, while taking good care not to remove the key from the lock, repulse, attract, drive in again, gently, hard; thrust with the point and strike with the edge, and touch the keys like a true heroine. (RPA 18–19)

Pippa, however, must learn to master every desired style of foreplay and coital posture in order to demand the greatest rewards of money and gifts. "I will have thee as great a whore in bed as an honest woman everywhere else. See that there may be no caresses imagined which thou dost not lavish on whomsoever sleeps with thee; be always on the watch to scratch him, wherever it itches him" (RPA 19). All sorts of fondling and postures are demanded; "and she that does not consent to all imaginable species of abomination dies at the business. One fellow will have the boiled meat, another, the roast. They have found woman's natural parts from behind, with their legs upon her shoulders, in the Giannetta fashion, as the crane, the tortoise, the church upon the belfry, the stirrup, the sheep grazing and other postures more extravagant than a juggler's gestures" (RPA 58).

For aged clients "who have good appetites but sorry limbs," the courtesan requires special measures to help them achieve and maintain an erection. Nanna tells Pippa to be patient in enduring their "prattle" and awkward caresses. Then, "tickling them under the arms and round the loins, slip thy hand where thou knowest: when thou has woke it up, grasp it, shake it so frantically, that it may lift its head as best it can" (RPA 23). Although they are laughably pathetic and unappetizing in their lovemaking, Pippa should treat her aged clients with gentle, nurturing respect. She should feign a genuine love for them, not only "because we should always reverence old age" but also because such charitable treatment helps her "wheedle them" out of more money and gifts, while simultaneously elevating her reputation for gracious kindness (RPA 27, 29). In contrast, the courtesan should avoid young clients, as such "young headstrong brats" are selfish, fickle, and irresponsible; it would be catastrophic to fall in love with anyone of them or "with anything else but with purses" (RPA 90–91, 94).

If skill in feigning shy modesty and genuine desire is key for attracting lovers, the art of pretending is equally crucial in keeping them. "Above all, study flattery and dissimulation," Nanna insists, "for these are the ornaments whereby one keeps in favor." If this sounds like Ovid, so does her justification of deceit: "Men wish to be deceived . . . [and] they prefer feigned caresses to sincere ones void of fooleries" (RPA 40–41). Besides, they will use their own deceitful "juggling tricks to hoodwink thee," so deceiving the deceiver is justified self-defense (RPA 51). Nanna further explains, again like Ovid, that the master secret to artful pretending is the art of pretending artlessness along with guileless compliance with her client's desires (so long as he richly pays for it). She tells Pippa, "always act the artless and the fool; do not question him, or dispute with him. If he speaks to thee, speak to him; if he kisses thee, kiss him; if he gives thee anything, take it, and behave so artfully that he may never perceive thy roguery" (RPA 50). The courtesan's art of deceptive pretending requires masterful control of body language, so Nanna exhorts her daughter to spare no effort in this aspect of "studying." "When thou art lonely from doing nothing at all, shut thyself up in thy chamber, and, taking up the looking-glass, learn before it how to blush artfully, learn the gestures, manners and actions which suit in laughing and weeping, in the casting of thy eyes down upon thy lap and in the raising of them to whatever spot may be required" (RPA 127–128).

Studied expertise in somatic dissembling and performance, though necessary, is not sufficient for the courtesan's success. She must also acquire (or at least convincingly fake) an appreciative knowledge of the arts, as such cultural inclinations and accomplishments serve to distinguish her from common sex workers while enabling her to gain elite aristocrats and wealthy gentlemen as clients. "Because Seigniors are accustomed to grand ladies; they feed more upon reasoning and chitchat than upon anything else." So Pippa must know how to talk properly and show pleasure in the arts, to "praise the musicians and singers, although thou takest no delight in them" and to welcome poems "as if thou hadst received jewels" (RPA 29–30, 36). She should show off her own artistic and literary pursuits: "scrape the guitar, play upon the lute, pretend thou art reading the *Furioso*, Petrarch, and the *Hundred Stories*, which thou wilt have always on thy table" (RPA 127). The courtesan must show particularly kind attention to scholars and other writers (even if they bore her), because they can reward this kindness by writing poems and other texts that elevate her reputation by advertising her praiseworthy qualities of beauty, taste, and virtue. Conversely, indifference or rejection would cause spiteful authors "to write books against [her], . . . and publish everywhere those ugly things they know how to invent about women" (RPA 30).

To play the courtesan's part well, a young woman must indeed learn many parts, because she must adapt her behavior to the different comportment, needs, and preferences of her different clients. These will be many and diverse, not only with regard to age, profession, and precise social status, but often in behavioral and psychological attitudes deriving from their different cultural backgrounds. Nanna takes considerable pains to instruct Pippa on the different erotically relevant characteristics of Spaniards, Frenchmen, Germans, and Jews, as well as those of men from various Italian cities (notably Florence, Venice, Siena, Rome, and Bologna). The courtesan needs to have this social knowledge so that she can better understand her clients' behavior, character, and tastes. Compounding this plurality of culturally and psychologically diverse partners is the plurality of changing, challenging contexts through which the courtesan must struggle to keep her client-lovers sufficiently smitten so that they will constantly enrich her coffers. Sometimes she will need to calm or dispel a lover's jealousy; sometimes she will need to arouse it. If she typically should show cheer and welcoming compliance to her lover's wishes, she sometimes should feign anger, jealousy, or defiance to arouse a complacent lover or to extract richer gifts from him. In short, she needs both the requisite knowledge for shrewdly assessing the erotic situation and the flexibility (through her versatile bag of tricks) to adapt the most rewarding strategy for it.[75]

This again echoes Ovid and reflects a vision of reality that is pluralist, materialist, changing, and contingent, and that recognizes the explosive, impulsive instability of erotic desire. In this world of multiple, shifting contexts, time is a crucial motor of change and an ever-threatening horizon. As the peak years of the courtesan's sexual allure are narrowly numbered, she must maximize and store up her earnings – and her knowledge – as best she can. Besides providing resources to sustain her through old age, the courtesan's accumulation of monetary and cognitive assets helps her prepare an heir to continue her trade and income, while she operates (and benefits) as her heir's procuress. If "whoredom is so rich in invention" (RPA 51) because the erotic situations and challenges are so numerous and varied, and because there will always be new challenges as circumstances inevitably change, then the courtesan might agree with the prim Confucian Xunzi, who declared, "Learning must never be concluded."[76]

[75] In an earlier dialogue, Nanna excludes special "herbs," love potions, and "witchcraft" from her recommended methods, having found them useless, while her somaesthetic knowledge of moving her body was instead amazingly effective: "with a slight twisting of my buttocks, I made him so very crazy after me that people were amazed." Aretino, "The Life of Courtesans," in *Ragionamenti*, vol. 3, 48.

[76] "An Exhortation to Learning," in John Knoblock, trans., *Xunzi: A Translation and Study of the Complete Works*, vol. 1 (Stanford: Stanford University Press, 1988), 135.

If this is true for the courtesan's knowledge of love constrained by the profit motive, it should also hold for lovers not so limited. Like courtesans and other women, men too face new erotic challenges as their situations change with the vicissitudes of life, including aging, injury, and illness, as the lessons of Abelard, Montaigne, and Aretino's Nanna instruct us. Our increased longevity, far beyond what our evolutionary endowment of reproductive sexual capacities allotted for, suggests the need for developing an *ars erotica* for geriatric populations involving invention beyond those of pharmaceutical remedies. Our increasing welcome of transgender individuals also calls for new erotic thinking.

VIII SPECULATIVE POSTSCRIPT: DECOUPLING BEAUTY FROM LOVE AND INVENTING THE AESTHETIC

Since the time of Plato's seminal dialogues of the *Symposium* and *Phaedrus* and on through the Renaissance, beauty and eros have been closely linked in Western philosophy. Eros was defined as the desiring love for beauty expressed by a longing to intimately know and somehow unite with the beautiful object desired, or even to give birth to beautiful things through this close communion or union. Reciprocally, beauty was conceived as the object of love and desire, with higher beauties inspiring nobler forms of love and desire. From Plato through the Renaissance we find the familiar ladder of love that rises from the sexual desire for union with a beautiful body to more spiritual forms that desire spiritual union with beautiful souls or ideas and ultimately with the most beautiful and radiating source of all beauty (identified by monotheistic thinkers with God). Today, the conceptual linkage between beauty and eros is no longer a philosophical commonplace. Instead of defining beauty primarily through desire and love, we now conceive it in terms of the aesthetic, while the aesthetic is essentially defined in terms oppositional to desire and erotic love. *The Oxford Handbook of Aesthetics* thus confidently claims that an acceptable definition of aesthetic experience should exclude "sexual experiences and drug experiences" because the notion of aesthetic pleasure "clearly does not apply to the pleasures of sex or drugs."[77]

The concept and field of aesthetics, like most developments in the history of culture, emerged from multiple trends and causes. Though formally introduced by Alexander Baumgarten in the mid-eighteenth century, the

[77] See Gary Iseminger, "Aesthetic Experience," in Jerrold Levinson, ed., *The Oxford Handbook of Aesthetics* (Oxford: Oxford University Pess, 2003), 99–116, quotations from 106, 109.

concept of the aesthetic received its decisively influential formulation by Immanuel Kant at the end of that century with further important elaborations by nineteenth-century thinkers, most notably those associated with German idealism (Hegel, Schelling, Holderlin, and Schopenhauer). The aesthetic, however, also drew on influential ideas regarding beauty that circulated before Baumgarten introduced the term and Kant made it enduringly famous. I conclude this chapter by suggesting the speculative hypothesis that one reason for the birth of aesthetics was the decoupling of beauty from love and desire after their flourishing union in Renaissance Neoplatonism and in reaction to the growing power of materialist philosophies in the seventeenth and eighteenth centuries. I cannot adequately argue here for this hypothesis, but will sketch a minimal outline of its trajectory.

In the traditional paradigm, erotic love could embrace the spiritual along with the carnal. Even if the latter form of love was regarded as inferior or vulgar, theorists recognized that both forms shared a common desire for beauty and that there could be an ennobling movement from the carnal to the more spiritual and virtuous love of souls. When materialist philosophies rejected the reality of the soul as an immaterial entity, this made the notion of the pure, incorporeal love of souls seem exceedingly questionable. If one's soul and one's lover's soul were also physical, then all erotic love was essentially physical or carnal. But if all erotic love was carnal, being the desire of one material body for sexual union with another, then this problematized the traditional way of distinguishing love from lust in terms of the spiritual soul rather than the body being the real object and motor of desire. We see this blurring of love and lust in the two greatest seventeenth-century materialist philosophers.

Thomas Hobbes (1588–1679) essentially equates love with the "appetite which men call lust," "for the passion is one and the same indefinite desire of the different sex, as natural as hunger." The only distinction, Hobbes notes, is that "this name lust is used where it is condemned: otherwise it is called by the general word love."[78] Baruch Spinoza (1632–1677) argued there was no separate or immortal soul that one could love and that existed free from the causal bonds of material nature; nor was there a transcendent God constituted as pure spirit without extension in space. If "mind and body are one and the same thing" but merely conceived under different aspects, then different gendered bodies could not be equal in soul or mental capacities. Arguing that women should not be involved in government rule because

[78] Thomas Hobbes, *Human Nature*, in J. C. A. Gaskin, ed., *The Elements of Law, Natural and Politic: Human Nature and De Corpore Politico* (Oxford: Oxford University Press, 1994), 55–56.

they are naturally inferior to men, Spinoza reduces men's loving esteem for women to mere sexual lust. If, as Spinoza claims, "men, in fact, generally love women merely from the passion of lust, and esteem their cleverness and wisdom in proportion to the excellence of their beauty," then love seems severed from true virtue, while beauty is lowered to a mere physical property and object of base carnal appetites.[79] Prominent French materialists, such as Julien Offray de La Mettrie (1709–1751) and Denis Diderot (1713–1784), wrote racy literary texts celebrating the rich sensuality of carnal love while flouting conventional notions of sexual morality and chastity, which further served to blur the line between erotic love and lust, at least for the dominant strain of conservative, high-minded, or religion-steeped thinkers.[80]

This combination of materialism with eighteenth-century trends of philosophical sensualism and libertinism must have made it more difficult to maintain the traditional idea of eros as a physically expressed but spiritual loving desire that was distinct from lust. This in turn made it more problematic to define the spiritually ennnobling notion of beauty in terms of eros or desiring love. For if such love is defined as the desire to enjoy beauty by possessing or uniting with it, and if this loving desire for union is inescapably physical or carnal and thus linked to lust, then beauty itself seems diminished in its spiritual quality and blemished by a hint of lewdness and corruption. High-minded intellectuals (particularly those with idealist or pietist leanings) wishing to ensure the spiritual value of beauty would have recognized the need for a discourse on beauty and its pleasures that was independent of erotic desire for possession through union and was consequently free from any taint of lust. The discourse of aesthetic pleasure could have arisen in part to provide such a substitute discourse for beauty, though there were certainly other (and perhaps more weighty) factors that generated its birth. The new discourse of aesthetics highlighted disinterestedness and distance rather than desire and copulative union (whether secular or divine)

[79] Baruch Spinoza, *A Political Treatise*, in R. M. H. Elwes, trans., *A Theologico-Political Treatise and a Political Treatise* (New York: Dover, 1951), 387. The previous Spinoza quote on the ontological identity of mind and body is from his *Ethics*, in R.H.M. Elwes, trans., *The Chief Works of Benedict de Spinoza*, vol.2 (London: George Bell, 1901), 131.

[80] La Mettrie and Diderot did however distinguish between love and lust. La Mettrie, for example, insists that the unification of the lovers' souls through their physical embraces provides greater pleasure than their mere physical union, and he explicitly condemns courtesan culture as "shameless" and "heartless," claiming that he seeks and celebrates "not the *jouissance* [ecstacy, orgasm] of bodies but that of souls." Julien Offroy de La Mettrie, *L'art de jouir* (Paris: Editions du Boucher, 2012), 3–4. For an account of Diderot's erotic views that distinguishes them from the lascivious excesses of libertinism, see Alice Parker, "Did/erotica: Diderot's Contribution to the History of Sexuality," *Diderot Studies*, 22 (1986): 89–106.

that for millennia shaped the understanding of how to pursue and enjoy the beautiful through the experience and arts of love. Beauty, to maintain its ennobling spiritual quality and edifying uplift, had to forsake the erotic with its impure sensuality and passion for possessive union.

While I cannot properly substantiate this hypothesis concerning the separation of beauty from eros as a contributing factor to the rise of aesthetics, I should at least provide some references that render it plausible. The British philosopher Anthony Ashley Cooper (Third Earl of Shaftesbury, 1671–1713), an influential precursor of modern aesthetic theory whose thought is steeped in Platonic idealism, defined the pleasure of beauty as disinterested and distanced by explicitly contrasting it to erotic feelings aroused by (and in) human bodies. These feelings he described as "a set of eager desires, wishes and hopes, no way suitable ... to your rational and refined contemplation of beauty." Though erotically attractive bodies are "wonderful as they are," they "inspire nothing of a studious or contemplative kind. The more they are viewed, the further they are from satisfying by mere view" but instead arouse a lust for "possession."[81] Alexander Baumgarten, who established aesthetics in the mid-eighteenth century as a science for the "perfection of sensory cognition" and defined beauty in those cognitive terms, affirmed, like Shaftesbury and Francis Hutcheson, an internal, mental sense for perceiving such beauty. Although recommending practical training to improve our sensory powers, Baumgarten explicitly rejected from the aesthetic field any activities associated with sexual licentiousness.[82] Immanuel Kant in his *Critique of Judgment* (1790) made Shaftesbury's idea of contemplative disinterestedness the cornerstone for defining the distinctive aesthetic pleasure (and judgment) of beauty in opposition to the agreeable feelings of sensuality and the satisfactions of appetite (and even of charm

[81] Anthony Ashley Cooper (Third Earl of Shaftesbury), *Characteristics of Men, Manners, Opinions, Times*, ed. Lawrence Klein (Cambridge: Cambridge University Press, 1999), 319. Like the Renaissance Platonists, Shaftesbury sees all beauty as deriving from the original divine form of beauty that is mental or spiritual and that must be grasped by a special mental internal (or "inward") sense rather than a bodily one. He claims that "there is nothing so divine as beauty, which, belonging not to body, nor having any principle or existence except in mind and reason, is alone discover'd and acquir'd by this diviner part" (ibid., 326, 331). He also speaks of "contemplative delight" that is "superior to that of sense ... and relates not in the least to any private interest ... or advantage" of the person (ibid., 202).

[82] H. R. Schweizer, trans., *Alexander Baumgarten, Theoretische Ästhetik: Die grundlengenden Abschnitte aus der "Aesthetica"* (Hamburg: Felix Meiner, 1988), 11, 31 (§§14, 50). For Baumgarten, even our most basic sensory perceptions deriving from the body's sense organs are in fact only experienced or "actualized by the soul's power of representing ... the state of [the] body" and the world. Alexander Baumgarten, *Metaphysics* (1739), trans. C. D. Fugate and J. Hymers (London: Bloomsbury, 2013), 205.

and emotion) that also give pleasure.[83] In the nineteenth century, Arthur Schopenhauer draws the contrast of erotic and aesthetic experience still more sharply and explicitly, linking the latter to the bodiless beauty of Platonic ideas. In "aesthetic pleasure" we enjoy the disinterested experience of "delight in the mere knowledge of perception as such, in contrast to the will" or desire; "aesthetic contemplation" is "pure will-less knowing and with the knowledge, which necessarily appears therewith, of the Ideas." Sexual experience, instead, involves the "strongest" of life's interests – "the will-to-live" – and is cognitively deficient and distorted by this insistent will of physical desire. For Schopenhauer, "the genitals are the real *focus* of the will, and are therefore the opposite pole to the brain, the representative of knowledge."[84]

Friedrich Nietzsche acknowledges this anti-erotic aesthetic tradition while opposing it by ridiculing its prudishness. When "our aestheticians never tire of weighing in on Kant's side, saying that under the charm of beauty, *even* naked female statues can be looked at 'without interest,' ... we are entitled to laugh a little at their expense: – the experiences of *artists* are 'more interesting' with regard to this tricky point and Pygmalion, at all events, was *not* necessarily an 'unaesthetic man.'"[85] However, while recognizing that erotic "sensuality" belongs to the generative roots of the "aesthetic condition," Nietzsche conforms to the anti-erotic aesthetic tradition by insisting that in genuine aesthetic experience this sensual moment must be "transfigured and no longer enters the consciousness as a sexual stimulus." This leads him to caution against lovemaking as a danger for artists rather than an aesthetic art of living in its own right. "Every artist knows how harmful sexual intercourse is at times of great spiritual tension and preparation," he writes, and those with the "surest instincts" for aesthetics know (even without

[83] Immanuel Kant, *The Critique of Judgement*, trans. J. C. Meredith (Oxford: Oxford University Press, 1986). He defines the pleasure of the beautiful as "apart from any interest" or "appetite," while remarking that if a person "requires an added element of charm or emotion for its delight," then his taste "has not yet emerged from barbarism" (49, 50, 65). This complements Kant's severely unsympathetic view of sex. "Sexual love makes of the loved person an Object of appetite ... [and] is a degradation of human nature ... because as an Object of appetite for another a person becomes a thing." Sexual partners "make of humanity an instrument for the satisfaction of their lusts and inclinations, and dishonor it by placing it on a level with animal nature." Immanuel Kant, *Lectures on Ethics*, trans. Louis Infield (New York: Harper, 1963), 163–164.

[84] Arthur Schopenhauer, *The World as Will and Representation*, vol. 1, trans. E. F. J. Payne (New York: Dover, 1958), 200–202, 329–330.

[85] Friedrich Nietzsche, *On the Genealogy of Morality*, trans. Carol Diethe (Cambridge: Cambridge University Press, 2006), 74.

experimenting with sex) that any erotic "energy . . . of animal vigor" should be sacrificed "to the advantage of the work" of art.[86]

To the extent that our modern philosophical tradition continues to define the aesthetic in opposition to the erotic, it will remain difficult to do proper justice to the beautiful aspects of sensual desire and to the rewarding arts of sexual fulfilment. A look at other cultures and other times can provide, as this book suggests, ample resources for a broader, deeper erotic vision to enrich the field of aesthetics and our art of living.

[86] Ibid., 80–81.

Bibliography

Abelard, Peter. *Abelard: Ethical Writings.* Translated by P. V. Spade. Indianapolis: Hackett, 1995. **(abbr. AE)**

Albury, W. R. *Castiglione's Allegory: Veiled Policy in "The Book of the Courtier."* Aldershot: Ashgate, 2014.

Alighieri, Dante. *The Divine Comedy.* Translated by James Finn Cotter. Amity, NY: Amity House, 1987.

Ambrose. *Exhortatio virginitatis.* Edited by J. P. Migne (Paris: Patrologia Latina, 1845).

Ames, Roger, and David Hall, translators. *Daodejing: "Making This Life Significant."* New York: Ballantine, 2003.

Ames, Roger, and Henry Rosemont, translators. *The Analects of Confucius: A Philosophical Translation.* New York: Random House, 1998. **(abbr. AC)**

an-Nasai, Ahmad. *Sunan an-Nasa'i,* vols. 1–6. Translated by Nasiruddin Al-Khattab. Riyadh: Darussalam, 2007.

Apollodorus. *The Library.* Translated by James George Frazer. Cambridge, MA: Harvard University Press, 1921.

Aquinas, Thomas. *Summa theologica.* Translated by Fathers of the English Dominican Province. Online at www.documentacatholicaomnia.eu/03d/1225-1274,_Thomas_Aquinas,_Summa_Theologiae_%5B1%5D,_EN.pdf. **(abbr. ST)**

Arberry, A. J. *Sufism: An Account of the Mystics of Islam.* New York: Dover, 2002.

Aretino, Pietro. *The Ragionamenti, or Dialogues of the Divine Pietro Aretino Literally Translated into English,* vols. 3 and 4. Paris: Isidore Liseux, 1889. **(abbr. RPA)**

Aristotle. *The Basic Works of Aristotle.* Translated by Richard McKeon. New York: Random House, 1968.

Generation of Animals. Translated by A. L. Peck. Cambridge, MA: Harvard University Press, 1943.

Metaphysics, vol. 2: Books 10–14, Oeconomica. Magna Moralia. Translated by Hugh Tredennick and G. C. Armstrong. Cambridge, MA: Harvard University Press, 1935.

Problems. Translated by Robert Mayhew. Cambridge, MA: Harvard University Press, 2011.

Atharva Veda Samhita. Translated by W. W. Whitney. Delhi: Motilal Banarasidass, 1962.

Atkins, Paul. "Chigo in the Medieval Japanese Imagination." *The Journal of Asian Studies* 67, no. 3 (2008): 947–970.

Augustine. *City of God*. Translated by Henry Bettenson. London: Penguin, 2003. **(abbr. CG)**

Confessions. Translated by F. J. Sheed. Indianapolis: Hackett, 1993.

De bono conjugali (On the Good of Marriage). In *A Select Library of the Nicene and Post-Nicene Fathers of the Christian Church*, vol. 3. Translated by C. L. Cornish. Edited by Philip Schaff. Buffalo, NY: Christian Literature Publishing, 1887. **(abbr. GM)**

"Of Holy Virginity." In *A Select Library of the Nicene and Post-Nicene Fathers of the Christian Church*, vol. 3. Edited by Philip Schaff. Buffalo, NY: Christian Literature Publishing, 1887.

On Marriage and Concupiscence. In *A Select Library of the Nicene and Post-Nicene Fathers of the Christian Church*, vol. 5. Translated by Peter Holmes and Robert Ernest Wallace. New York: Christian Literature Company, 1887. **(abbr. MC)**

The Soliloquies of St. Augustine. Translated by Rose Elizabeth Cleveland. Boston: Little, Brown, 1910.

Banerjee, S. C. *Crime and Sex in Ancient India*. Calcutta: Naya Prokash, 1980.

Bassanese, Fiora A. "Private Lives and Public Lies: Texts by Courtesans of the Italian Renaissance." *Texas Studies in Literature and Language* 30, no. 3 (1988): 295–319.

Bates, D. G., and F. Plog. *Cultural Anthropology*. New York: McGraw-Hill, 1990.

Baumgarten, Alexander. *Theoretische Ästhetik: Die grundlengenden Abschnitte aus der "Aesthetica."* Translated by H. R. Schweizer. Hamburg: Felix Meiner, 1988.

Bayle, Pierre. *Letters of Abelard and Heloise*. London: S. Hayes, 1779. **(abbr. LAH)**

Bell, Rudolph. *How to Do It: Guides to Good Living for Renaissance Italians*. Chicago: University of Chicago Press, 1999.

Bembo, Pietro. *Gli Asolani*. Translated by R. B. Gottfried. Bloomington: Indiana University Press, 1954.

Bhattacharji, Sukumari. "Prostitution in Ancient India." *Social Scientist* 15, no. 2 (1987): 32–61.

Biale, David. *Eros and the Jews: From Biblical Israel to Contemporary America*. New York: Basic Books, 1997.

Bland, Kalman. "Defending, Enjoying, and Regulating the Visual." In *Judaism in Practice: From the Middle Ages through the Early Modern Period*. Edited by Lawrence Fine. Princeton: Princeton University Press, 2001.

Bloch, Ariel, and Chana Bloch. *The Song of Songs: A New Translation with an Introduction and Commentary*. Berkeley: University of California Press, 1998.

Boethius. *The Consolation of Philosophy*. Translated by Victor Watts. London: Penguin, 1999.

Bouhdiba, Abdelwahab. *Sexuality in Islam*. Translated by Alan Sheridan. London: Routledge, 1974. **(abbr. SI)**

Boutière, Jean, and Alexander Herman Schutz. *Biographies des troubadours. Textes provençaux des XIIIe et XIVe siècles*. Paris: Nizet, 1964.

Bowring, Richard, translator. *The Diary of Lady Murasaki*. London: Penguin, 1996. **(abbr. LM)**

Boyle, Gregory, Ronald Goldman, J. Steven Svoboda, and Ephrem Fernandez. "Male Circumcision: Pain, Trauma and Psychosexual Sequelae." *Journal of Health Psychology* 7, no. 3 (2002): 329–343.

Brown, D. M., editor. *The Cambridge History of Japan*, vol. 1. Cambridge: Cambridge University Press, 1993.

Brown, Peter. *The Body and Society: Men, Women, and Sexual Renunciation in Early Christianity*. New York: Columbia University Press, 1988. **(abbr. BS)**

Brundage, James A. "Let Me Count the Ways: Canonists and Theologians Contemplate Coital Positions." *Journal of Medieval History* 10, no. 2 (1984): 81–93.

Bruno, Giordano. *The Heroic Frenzies*. Translated by P. E. Memmo. Chapel Hill: University of North Carolina Press, 1966. **(abbr. HF)**

Cause, Principle and Unity: And Essays on Magic. Translated by R. J. Blackwell. Cambridge: Cambridge University Press, 1998. **(abbr. EOM)**

Bukhari, Muhammad al-. *Sahih Bukhari*. Translated by Muhammad Muhsin Khan. Riyadh: Darussalam, 1997.

Burckhardt, Jacob. *The Civilisation of the Period of the Renaissance in Italy*. Translated by S. G. C. Middlemore. London: Swan Sonnenschein, 1904.

Burton, Richard, translator. *The Arabian Nights: Tales from A Thousand and One Nights*. New York: Modern Library, 2004.

Burton, Richard, and F. F. Arbuthnot, translators. *The Kama Sutra of Vatsyayana*. London: Unwin, 1988.

Buss, David M. *The Evolution of Desire*. New York: Basic Books, 2003.

Calabrese, Michael. "Ovid and the Female Voice in the *De Amore* and the *Letters* of Abelard and Heloise." *Modern Philology* 95, no. 1 (1997): 1–26.

Calame, Claude. *The Poetics of Eros in Ancient Greece*. Translated by Janet Lloyd. Princeton: Princeton University Press, 2013.

Carmichael, Calum. *Sex and Religion in the Bible*. New Haven: Yale University Press, 2010.

Cassian, John. *The Institutes*. Translated by Boniface Ramsey. New York: Newman Press, 2000. **(abbr. INS)**

John Cassian: The Conferences. Translated by Boniface Ramsey. New York: Paulist Press, 1967. **(abbr. CON)**

Castiglione, Baldesar. *The Book of the Courtier*. Translated by George Bull. London: Penguin, 1976. **(abbr. BC)**

Chen, BuYen. *Empire of Style: Silk and Fashion in Tang China*. Seattle: University of Washington Press, 2019.

Cherchi, Paolo. *Andreas and the Ambiguity of Courtly Love*. Toronto: University of Toronto Press, 1994.

Childs, Margaret. "*Chigo Monogatari*: Love Stories or Buddhist Sermons?" *Monumenta Nipponica* 35, no. 2 (1980): 127–151.

Chittick, William. "Love in Islamic Thought." *Religion Compass* 8, no. 7 (2014): 229–238.

Chrysostom, John. *Homilies on Genesis 1–17*. Translated by Robert C. Hill. Washington, DC: Catholic University of America Press, 1986.

On Marriage and Family Life. Translated by C. P. Roth and David Anderson. Cresswood, NY: St. Vladimir's Seminary Press, 2003. **(abbr. JCM)**

On Virginity; Against Remarriage. Translated by Sally Rieger Shore. Lewiston, NY: Edwin Mellen Press, 1983.

Cicero. *On Old Age. On Friendship. On Divination.* Translated by W. A. Falconer. Cambridge, MA: Loeb Classical Library, 1923.

Clement. *Exhortation to the Heathen.* Translated by William Wilson. New York: Christian Literature Publishing, 1885.

The Instructor. In *The Ante-Nicene Fathers: The Writings of the Fathers down to A.D. 325*, vol. 2. Edited by A. C. Coxe. Grand Rapids, MI: Eerdmans, 1962.

Paedogogus. In *Défense du Christianisme par les pères des premiers siècles de l'église.* Translated by M. De Genoude. Paris: Librairie de Peffodil, 1846.

Climacus, John. *The Ladder of Divine Ascent.* Translated by Lazarus Moore. New York: Harper, 1959.

Cohen, Shaye. *The Beginnings of Jewishness: Boundaries, Varieties, Uncertainties.* Berkeley: University of California Press, 1999.

Cornell, Vincent. "Fruit of the Tree of Knowledge: The Relationship between Faith and Practice in Islam." In *The Oxford History of Islam.* Edited by John L. Esposito. New York: Oxford University Press, 1999.

Crompton, Louis. *Homosexuality and Civilization.* Cambridge, MA: Harvard University Press, 2003.

Danielou, Alain. *The Myths and Gods of India.* Rochester, VT: Inner Traditions International, 1991. **(abbr. MG)**

D'Aragona, Tullia. *Dialogue on the Infinity of Love.* Translated by Rinaldina Russell and Bruce Merry. Chicago: University of Chicago Press, 1997. **(abbr. DIL)**

Davidson, James. *Courtesans and Fishcakes: The Consuming Passions of Classical Athens.* Chicago: University of Chicago Press, 2011.

Dawood, N. J., translator. *The Koran.* London: Penguin, 1999.

Day, John. "Asherah in the Hebrew Bible and Northwest Semitic Literature." *Journal of Biblical Literature* 105, no. 3 (1986): 385–408.

Deming, Will. *Paul on Marriage and Celibacy: The Hellenistic Background of 1 Corinthians 7.* Grand Rapids, MI: Wm. B. Eerdmans, 2004.

Demosthenes. "The Erotic Essay." In *Demosthenes: Funeral Speech, Erotic Essay, Exordia and Letters.* Translated by N. D. DeWitt and N. J. DeWitt. Cambridge, MA: Harvard University Press, 1949.

Desan, Philippe, editor. *The Oxford Handbook of Montaigne.* Oxford: Oxford University Press, 2016.

Dever, William. "Asherah, Consort of Yahweh? New Evidence from Kuntillet 'Arjud." *Bulletin of the American Schools of Oriental Research* 255 (1984): 21–37.

Diogenes Laertius. *Lives of Eminent Philosophers*, vol. 1. Translated by R. D Hicks. Cambridge, MA: Harvard University Press, 1925. **(abbr. DL1)**

Lives of Eminent Philosophers, vol. 2. Translated by R. D. Hicks. Cambridge, MA: Harvard University Press, 1925. **(abbr. DL2)**

Doniger, Wendy. *Siva: The Erotic Ascetic.* Oxford: Oxford University Press, 1973. **(abbr. SEA)**

Donner, Fred M. *Muhammad and the Believers: At the Origins of Islam.* Cambridge, MA: Harvard University Press, 2010. **(abbr. MB)**

Dover, K. J. *Greek Homosexuality.* Cambridge, MA: Harvard University Press, 1978. **(abbr. DGH)**

Dronke, Peter. *Abelard and Heloise in Medieval Testimonies.* Glasgow: University of Glasgow Press, 1976.

Dudley, Donald. *A History of Cynicism: From Diogenes to the Sixth Century*. London: Methuen, 1937.

Ebreo, Leone. *The Philosophy of Love (Dialoghi d'Amore)*. Translated by F. Friedeberg-Seeley and J. H. Barnes. London: Soncino Press, 1937. **(abbr. DL)**

Eilberg-Schwartz, Howard. "The Problem of the Body for the People of the Book." In *People of the Body: Jews and Judaism from an Embodied Perspective*. Albany: SUNY Press, 1992, 17–46.

Eliot, T. S. *Notes on the Definition of Culture*. London: Faber, 1965.

Eno, Robert, translator. *Dao de Jing*. 2010. www.indiana.edu/~p374/Daode*jing*.pdf.

Epictetus. *The Discourses of Epictetus*. Translated by Robin Hard. London: Dent, 1995.

The Handbook of Epictetus. Translated by Nicholas P. White. Indianapolis: Hackett , 1983.

Epicurus. "Leading Doctrines." In *Epicurus*. Translated by George Strodach. New York: Penguin, 2012.

Erasmus. "The Defence of the Declamation on Marriage." In *The Collected Works of Erasmus*, vol. 71. Edited by J. K. Sowards. Toronto: University of Toronto Press, 1993.

Evagrius of Pontus. *Sententiae ad virginem*. In *Evagrius of Pontus: The Greek Ascetic Corpus*. Translated by R. E. Sinkewicz. Oxford: Oxford University Press, 2003.

Fackenheim, Emil L., translator. "A Treatise on Love by Ibn Sina." *Mediaeval Studies* 7 (1945): 208–228.

Faruki, Kemal. "*Al-Ahkam Al-Khamsah*: The Five Values." *Islamic Studies* 5, no. 1 (1966): 43–98.

Ficino, Marsilio. *Marsilio Ficino's Commentary on Plato's "Symposium": The Text and a Translation, with an Introduction*. Translated by S. R. Jayne. Columbia: University of Missouri Press, 1944. **(abbr. FC)**

Platonic Theology, vol. 4. Translated by Michael J. B. Allen and James Hankins. Cambridge, MA: Harvard University Press, 2004.

Foucault, Michel. *Dits et ecrits, vol. 2: 1976–1988*. Paris: Gallimard, 2001.

Essential Works of Michel Foucault, vol. 1. Edited by Paul Rabinow. New York: New Press, 1997.

Histoire de la sexualité, tome 4: Les aveux de la chair. Edited by Frédéric Gros. Paris: Gallimard, 2018.

The History of Sexuality, vol. 1: An Introduction. Translated by Robert Hurley. New York: Vintage, 1980. **(abbr. HS)**

The History of Sexuality, vol. 2: The Use of Pleasure. Translated by Robert Hurley. New York: Vintage, 1986. **(abbr. HS2)**

The History of Sexuality, vol. 3: The Care of the Self. Translated by Robert Hurley. New York: Pantheon, 1986. **(abbr. HS3)**

Frame, Donald. *Montaigne: A Biography*. New York: Harcourt, Brace & World, 1965.

Freedman, R. David. "Woman, a Power Equal to Man." *Biblical Archaeology Review* 9, no. 1 (1983): 56–58.

Furth, Charlotte. *A Flourishing Yin: Gender in China's Medical History: 960–1665*. Berkeley: University of California Press, 1999.

Gadamer, Hans- Georg. *The Relevance of the Beautiful and Other Essays*. Translated by Nicholas Walker. Cambridge: Cambridge University Press, 1986.

Gaskin, J. C. A., editor. *The Elements of Law Natural and Politic: Human Nature and De Corpore Politico.* Oxford: Oxford University Press, 1994.

Ghazali, Abu Hamid al-. *Book on the Etiquette of Marriage.* In *Marriage and Sexuality in Islam.* Translated by Madelain Farah. Salt Lake City: University of Utah Press, 1984. **(abbr. EM)**

Ghosh, Manomohan, translator. *The Natyaśastra*, vols. 1 and 2. Calcutta: Royal Asiatic Society of Bengal, 1951. **(abbr. N)**

Giffen, L. A. *Theory of Profane Love among the Arabs.* New York: New York University Press, 1971.

Gilson, Etienne. *Heloise and Abelard.* Ann Arbor: University of Michigan Press, 1938.

Goldin, Paul. *The Culture of Sex in Ancient China.* Honolulu: University of Hawai'i Press, 2002.

Graves, Robert, and Raphael Patai. *Hebrew Myths: The Book of Genesis.* New York: McGraw Hill, 1964.

Greene, Ellen, editor. *Women Poets in Ancient Greece and Rome.* Norman: University of Oklahoma Press, 2005.

Gregory, Tullio. "Libertinisme Érudit in Seventeenth-Century France and Italy: The Critique of Ethics and Religion." *British Journal of the History of Philosophy* 6, no. 3 (1998): 323–349.

Griffith, Ralph T. H., translator. *Hymns of the Atharva-Veda.* Benares: E. J. Lazarus, 1916.

Rig Veda. 1896. www.sacred-texts.com/hin/rigveda/index.htm.

Habertal, Moshe, and Avishai Margalit. *Idolatry.* Translated by N. Goldblum. Cambridge, MA: Harvard University Press, 1992.

Hall, J. W., editor. *The Cambridge History of Japan*, vol. 4. Cambridge: Cambridge University Press, 1991.

Hare, Tom, translator. *Zeami: Performance Notes.* New York: Columbia University Press, 2008.

Harper, Donald. "The Sexual Arts of Ancient China as Described in a Manuscript of the Second Century B.C." *Harvard Journal of Asiatic Studies* 47, no. 2 (1987): 539–593.

Hegel, G. W. F. *Introductory Lectures on Aesthetics.* Translated by Bernard Bosanquet. London: Penguin, 1993.

Hesiod. *Hesiod, the Homeric Hymns, and Homerica.* Translated by Hugh G. Evelyn-White. Cambridge, MA: Harvard University Press, 1959.

Hinton, Thomas. "Troubadour Biographies and the Value of Authentic Love." *Interfaces* 2 (2016): 132–163.

Hobbes, Thomas. *Human Nature.* In *The Elements of Law Natural and Politic: Human Nature and De Corpore Politico.* Edited by J. C. A. Gaskin. Oxford: Oxford University Press, 1994.

Hoffman-Ladd, Valerie J. "Mysticism and Sexuality in Sufi Thought and Life." *Mystics Quarterly* 18, no. 3 (1992): 82–93.

Hujwiri, Ali ibn Uthman al-Jullabi al-. *The Kashf al-Mahjub.* Translated by R. A. Nicholson. London: Luzac, 1976.

Hume, Robert E., translator. *The Thirteen Principal Upanishads.* Oxford: Oxford University Press, 1921.

Ibn al-Arabi, Muhammad. *The Bezels of Wisdom*. Translated by R. W. J. Austin. New York: Paulist Press, 1980. **(abbr. BW)**

Ibn Hazm, Ali ibn Aḥmad. *The Ring of the Dove*. Translated by A. J. Arberry. London: Luzac Oriental, 1994. **(abbr. RD)**

Imam Muslim. *Sahih Muslim*. Translated by Abd-al-Hamid Siddiqui. www .biharanjuman.org/hadith/Sahih-Muslim-english-translation.pdf.

Inwood, B., and L. P. Gerson, translators. *The Epicurus Reader*. Indianapolis: Hackett, 1994.

Hellenistic Philosophy: Introductory Readings. Indianapolis: Hackett, 1997.

Jaeger, C. Stephen. *Ennobling Love: In Search of a Lost Sensibility*. Philadelphia: University of Pennsylvania Press, 1999.

Jaspers, Karl. *The Origin and Goal of History*. London: Routledge & Kegan Paul, 1953.

Jerome. *Against Jovinianus*. In *The Principal Works of St. Jerome*. Translated by W. H. Fremantle. Grand Rapids, MI: Eerdmans, 1893.

Kahneman, Daniel, Ed Diener, and Norbert Schwarz, editors. *Well-Being: The Foundations of Hedonic Psychology*. New York: Russell Sage, 1999.

Kalyanamalla. *Ananga Ranga*. Translated by F. F. Arbuthnot and Richard Burton. New York: Medical Press, 1964. **(abbr. AR)**

Kant, Immanuel. *The Critique of Judgment*. Translated by J. C. Meredith. Oxford: Oxford University Press, 1986.

On History. Translated by Lewis White Beck. Indianapolis: Bobbs-Merrill, 1963.

Katib, Ali ibn Nasr al-. *The Encyclopedia of Pleasure*. Edited by Salah Addin Khawwam. Translated by Adnan Jarkas and Salah Addin Khawwam. Toronto: Aleppo, 1977. **(abbr. EP)**

Keene, Donald. *Landscapes and Portraits: Appreciations of Japanese Culture*. Tokyo: Kodansha, 1971.

Knoblock, John, translator. *Xunzi: A Translation and Study of the Complete Works*, vols. 1–3. Stanford: Stanford University Press, 1988–1994.

Ko, Deborah. *Cinderella's Sisters: A Revisionist History of Footbinding*. Berkeley, University of California Press, 2007.

Kokkoka. *Koka Shastra*. Translated by Alex Comfort. New York: Stein & Day, 1965. **(abbr. KKS)**

Kramer, S. N. *The Sacred Marriage Rite: Aspects of Faith, Myth, and Ritual in Ancient Sumer*. Bloomington: Indiana University Press, 1969.

Kristeller, Paul. "The Modern System of the Arts: A Study in the History of Aesthetics Part I." *Journal of the History of Ideas* 12, no. 4 (1951): 496–527.

"The Modern System of the Arts: A Study in the History of Aesthetics Part II." *Journal of the History of Ideas* 13, no. 1 (1952): 17–46.

Lau, D. C., translator. *Mencius*. London: Penguin, 1970.

Tao Te Ching (Daodejing). London: Penguin, 1963. **(abbr. DJ)**

Legge, James, translator. *The Complete Works of Mencius*. New York: Dover, 1970.

The Four Books: Confucian Analects, the Great Learning, the Doctrine of the Mean, and the Works of Mencius. New York: Paragon, 1966. **(abbr. GL)**

Legross, Alain. "Montaigne on Faith and Religion." In *The Oxford Handbook of Montaigne*. Edited by Philippe Desan. Oxford: Oxford University Press, 2016.

Leupp, Gary. *Male Colors: The Construction of Homosexuality in Tokugawa Japan*. Berkeley: University of California Press, 1995.

Li, Chenyang. "The Philosophy of Harmony in Classical Confucianism." *Philosophy Compass* 3, no. 3 (2008): 423–435.

Liddell, H. G., and R. Scott. *An Intermediate Greek-English Lexicon*. Oxford: Oxford University Press, 1997.

Lidova, Natalia. *Drama and Ritual of Early Hinduism*. Delhi: Motilal Banarsidass, 1994.

"Natyashastra." Last modified September 29, 2014. www.oxfordbibliographies.com/view/document/obo-9780195399318/obo-9780195399318-0071.xml.

Lille, Alain de. *The Complaint of Nature*. Translated by Douglas M. Moffat. New York: Henry Holt, 1908.

Lindsey, William R. *Fertility and Pleasure: Ritual and Sexual Values in Tokugawa Japan*. Honolulu: University of Hawaii Press, 2007.

Lucian. *The Works of Lucian*. Translated by A. M. Harmon and M. D. Macleod, vols. 1 and 8. Cambridge, MA: Harvard University Press, 1967.

Lucretius. *On the Nature of the Universe*. Translated R. E. Latham. London: Penguin, 1994. **(abbr. LN)**

Macy, Joanna. "The Dialectics of Desire." *Numen* 22, no. 2 (1975): 145–160.

Maimonides, Moses. *The Guide of the Perplexed*. Translated by Shlomo Pines. Chicago: University of Chicago Press, 1963.

Malherbe, Abraham J., editor. *The Cynic Epistles*. Missoula, MT: Scholars, 1977.

Masson, Georgina. *Courtesans of the Italian Renaissance*. London: Secker and Warburg, 1975.

McCullough, Helen Craig, translator. *Tales of Ise: Lyrical Episodes from Tenth-Century Japan*. Stanford: Stanford University Press, 1968. **(abbr. TI)**

McGinnis, Jon. *Avicenna*. Oxford: Oxford University Press, 2010.

McIntyre, J. L. *Giordano Bruno*. London: Macmillan, 1903.

Methodius of Olympus. *The Banquet of the Ten Virgins; or, Concerning Chastity*. Translated by William R. Clark. In *The Ante-Nicene Fathers: The Writings of the Fathers down to A.D. 325*, vol. 6, edited by Alexander Roberts, James Donaldson, and A. Cleveland Coxe. Buffalo, NY: Christian Literature Publishing, 1886. Revised and edited for *New Advent* by Kevin Knight. www.newadvent.org/fathers/0623.htm.

Mews, C. J. *Abelard and Heloise*. Oxford: Oxford University Press, 2004.

editor. *The Lost Love Letters of Heloise and Abelard*. London: Palgrave Macmillan, 2008. **(abbr. LLHA)**

Meyer, J. J. *Sexual Life in Ancient India*. London: Kegan Paul, 2003.

Midrash Rabbah. Translated and edited by H. Freedman. London: Soncino Press, 1961.

Minucius Felix, Marcus. *Octavius*. In *Tertullian and Minucius Felix*. Translated by G. H. Randall. Cambridge, MA: Harvard University Press, 1953.

Mohan Thampi, G. B. "'Rasa' as Aesthetic Experience." *Journal of Aesthetics and Art Criticism* 24, no. 1 (1965): 75–80.

Monson, Don A. *Andreas Capellanus, Scholasticism, and the Courtly Love Tradition*. Washington, DC: Catholic University of America Press, 2005.

Montaigne, Michel de. *The Complete Essays of Montaigne*. Translated by Donald Frame. Stanford: Stanford University Press, 1965. **(abbr. M)**

Journal de voyage en Italie. In *Oeuvers completes*. Edited by Albert Thibaudet and Maurice Rat. Paris: Gallimard, 1962.

Montserrat, Dominic. *Sex and Society in Graeco-Roman Eygpt*. London: Kegan Paul, 1966.

Murasaki, Shikibu. *The Tale of Genji*. Translated by Edward Seidensticker. New York: Vintage, 1990. **(abbr. TG)**

Murata, Sachiko. *The Tao of Islam: A Sourcebook on Gender Relations in Islamic Thought*. Albany: SUNY Press, 1992.

Musonius Rufus. *Lectures*. In *Musonius Rufus: "The Roman Socrates."* Translated by Cora Lutz. New Haven: Yale University Press, 1947. **(abbr. MR)**

Nafzawi, Umar ibn Muhammad. *The Perfumed Garden*. Translated by Richard Burton. New York: Castle Books, 1964.

The Perfumed Garden. Translated by Jim Colville. London: Kegan Paul International, 1999. **(abbr. PG)**

an-Nawawi, Yahya bin Sharaf. *Riyad as-Salihin Hadith*. https://sunnah.com/riyadussaliheen.

Nietzsche, Friedrich. *On the Genealogy of Morality*. Translated by Carol Diethe. Cambridge: Cambridge University Press, 2006.

Nikhilananda, Swami, translator. *The Upanishads*. New York: Bonanza Books, 1956.

translator. *The Upanishads*. New York: Harper & Row, 1964.

Nussbaum, Martha. *The Therapy of Desire: Theory and Practice in Hellenistic Ethics*. Princeton: Princeton University Press, 1994.

Obolensky, Dimitri. *The Bogomils: A Study in Balkan Neo-Manichaeism*. Cambridge: Cambridge University Press, 1948.

Olivelle, Patrick, translator. *Dharmasutras: The Law Codes of Ancient India*. Oxford: Oxford University Press, 1999.

King, Governance, and Law in Ancient India: Kautilya's Arthashastra. Oxford: Oxford University Press, 2013.

Manu's Code of Law: A Critical Edition and Translation of the Manava-Dharmasastra. Oxford: Oxford University Press, 2005. **(abbr. MCL)**

Origen. *Homilies 1–14 on Ezekiel*. Translated by Thomas Scheck. New York: Newman Press, 2010.

Origen on 1 Corinthians. Translated by C. Jenkins. *Journal of Theological Studies* 9, no. 34 (1908): 231–247.

The Song of Songs: Commentary and Homilies. Translated by R. P. Lawson. London: Longmans, Green, 1957.

Ovid. *The Art of Love*. Translated by Rolfe Humphries. Bloomington: Indiana University Press, 1957.

The Art of Love. Translated by James Michie. New York: Modern Library, 2002.

Panskepp, Jaak. *Affective Neuroscience: The Foundations of Human and Animal Emotions*. Oxford: Oxford University Press, 1998.

Parrott, Douglas M., translator. *The Sophia of Jesus Christ*. The Gnostic Society Library, the Nag Hammadi Library. Accessed November 1, 2018. www.gnosis.org/naghamm/sjc.html.

Parry, John J., translator. *The Art of Courtly Love*. New York: Columbia University Press, 1990.

Payer, Pierre J. *The Bridling of Desire: Views of Sex in the Later Middle Ages*. Toronto: University of Toronto Press, 1993.

Pflugfelder, Gregory. *Cartographies of Desire: Male-Male Sexuality in Japanese Discourse 1600–1950*. Berkeley: University of California Press, 1999.

Philippi, Donald L., translator. *Kojiki*. Tokyo: University of Tokyo Press, 1968.

Plato. *Euthyphro, Apology, Crito, Phaedo, Phaedrus*. Translated by Harold North Fowler. Cambridge, MA: Harvard University Press, 1914.

Plato: Complete Works. Edited by John M. Cooper. Indianapolis: Hackett, 1997.

Symposium. Trans. Benjamin Jowett. Accessed November 1, 2018. http://classics.mit.edu/Plato/symposium.html.

Timaeus. Translated by H. D. P. Lee. London: Penguin, 1965.

Plutarch. *Lives*, vol. 1. Translated by Bernadotte Perrin. Cambridge, MA: Harvard University Press, 1914.

Moralia, vol. 2. Translated by F. C. Babbitt. Cambridge, MA: Harvard University Press, 1956.

Moralia, vol. 7. Translated by P. H. De Lacy and B. Einarson. Cambridge, MA: Harvard University Press, 1959.

Moralia, vol. 9. Translated by E. L. Minar, F. H. Sandbach, and W. C. Helmbold. Cambridge, MA: Harvard University Press, 1961. **(Dialogue on Love: abbr. PDL)**

Priest, Robert. "Missionary Positions: Christian, Modernist, Postmodernist." *Current Anthropology* 42, no. 1 (2001): 29–46.

Pugh, Tison. "Personae, Same-Sex Desire, and Salvation in the Poetry of Marbod of Rennes, Baudri of Bourgueil, and Hildebert of Lavardin." *Comitatus: A Journal of Medieval and Renaissance Studies* 31, no. 1 (2000): 57–86.

The Quran. quran.wwpa.com. **(abbr. Q)**

Radhakrishnan, Sarvepalli, editor and translator. *The Principal Upanishads*. London: Allen & Unwin, 1953.

Riegel, Jeffrey. "A Passion for the Worthy." *Journal of the American Oriental Society* 128, no. 4 (2008): 709–721.

Robinson, J. M., and Richard Smith, editors. *The Nag Hammadi Library in English*. San Francisco: Harper & Row, 1990.

Rocher, Ludo. "The Kamasutra: Vatsyayana's Attitude toward Dharma and Dharmasastra." *Journal of the American Oriental Society* 105, no. 3 (1985): 521–529.

Rogers, Lawrence. "She Loves Me, She Loves Me Not: *Shinju* and *Shikido Okagami*." *Monumenta Nipponica* 49, no. 1 (1994): 31–60.

Rosenthal, M. F. *The Honest Courtesan: Veronica Franco, Citizen and Writer in Sixteenth-Century Venice*. Chicago: University of Chicago Press, 1993.

Roth, Harold D., translator. *Original Tao: Inward Training (Nei-yeh) and the Foundations of Taoist Mysticism*. New York: Columbia University Press, 2004.

Ruan, Fang Fu, with Molleen Matsumura. *Sex in China: Studies in Sexology in Chinese Culture*. New York: Plenum, 1991.

Rummel, Erika, editor. *Erasmus on Women*. Toronto: University of Toronto Press, 1996. **(abbr. EW)**

Schalow, Paul Gordon, translator. *The Great Mirror of Male Love*. Stanford: Stanford University Press, 1990.

"Kukai and the Tradition of Male Love in Japanese Buddhism." In *Buddhism, Sexuality, and Gender*. Edited by J. I. Cabezon. Albany: SUNY Press, 1992.

Schiller, Friedrich. *On the Aesthetic Education of Man*. Translated by E. M. Wilkinson and L. A. Willoughby. Oxford: Clarendon Press, 1982.

Schipper, Kristofer. *The Taoist Body*. Translated by Karen Duval. Berkeley: University of California Press, 1993.

Schmidt, Richard, translator. *Das Kamasutra des Vatsyayana*. Berlin: Barsdorf, 1907.

Schoeck, Richard. *Erasmus of Europe: The Making of a Humanist, 1467–1500*. Edinburgh: Edinburgh University Press, 1990.

Erasmus of Europe: The Prince of Humanists, 1501–1536. Edinburgh: Edinburgh University Press, 1993.

Schofield, Malcolm. *The Stoic Idea of the City*. Chicago: University of Chicago Press, 1999.

Schopenhauer, Arthur. *The World as Will and Representation*, vol. 1. Translated by E. F. J. Payne. New York: Dover, 1958.

Sei Shonagon. *The Pillow Book of Sei Shōnagon*. Translated by Arthur Waley. Rutland, VT: Tuttle, 2011. **(abbr. PB)**

Seidensticker, Edward, translator. *The Gossamer Years: The Diary of a Noblewoman of Heian Japan*. Rutland, VT: Tuttle, 1964. **(abbr. GY)**

Seigle, Cecilia. *Yoshiwara: The Glittering World of the Japanese Courtesan*. Honolulu: University of Hawaii Press, 1993.

Seneca. *Epistles*, vols. 4 and 5. Translated by Richard M. Gummere. Cambridge, MA: Harvard University Press, 1996.

Moral Essays, vol. 2. Translated by John W. Basore. Cambridge, MA: Harvard University Press, 1996.

Shaftesbury, Anthony Ashley Cooper, *Characteristics of Men, Manners, Opinions, Times*. Edited by Lawrence Klein. Cambridge: Cambridge University Press, 1999.

Shamasastry, Rudrapatna, translator. *Kautilya's Arthashastra*. Mysore: Mysore Publishing, 1961. **(abbr. ART)**

Shively, D. H., and W. H. McCullough, editors. *The Cambridge History of Japan*, vols. 2 and 4. Cambridge: Cambridge University Press, 1999.

Shusterman, Richard. *Body Consciousness: A Philosophy of Mindfulness and Somaesthetics*. Cambridge: Cambridge University Press, 2008.

"Definition, Dramatization, and Rasa." *Journal of Aesthetics and Art Criticism* 61, no. 3 (2003): 295–298.

Pragmatist Aesthetics: Living Beauty, Rethinking Art. Oxford: Blackwell, 1992.

"Somaesthetics: A Disciplinary Proposal." *Journal of Aesthetics and Art Criticism* 57 (1999): 299–313.

Thinking through the Body: Essays in Somaesthetics. Cambridge: Cambridge University Press, 2012.

Skinner, Marilyn B. *Sexuality in Greek and Roman Culture*. Oxford: Blackwell, 2005.

Slotki, I. W., translator. *Babylonian Talmud: Yebamoth*. London: Soncino Press, 1936.

Smith, Henry. "Overcoming the Modern History of Edo 'Shunga.'" In *Imaging/Reading Eros: Proceedings for the Conference, Sexuality and Edo Culture, 1750–1850*. Edited by Sumie Jones. Bloomington: East Asian Center Indiana University, 1996, 26–34.

Smith, Margaret. *Rabi'a the Mystic and Her Fellow Saints in Islam*. Cambridge: Cambridge University Press, 1979.

Sommer, Benjamin. *The Bodies of God and the World of Ancient Israel*. Cambridge: Cambridge University Press, 2009.

Spinoza, Baruch. *Ethics*. In *The Chief Works of Benedict de Spinoza*. Translated by R. M. H. Elwes. London: George Bell, 1901.

A Theologico-Political Treatise and a Political Treatise. Translated by R. M. H. Elwes. New York: Dover, 1951.

Starn, Randolph. "Renaissance Redux." *The American Historical Review* 103, no. 1 (1998): 122–124.

The Statues of the United Kingdom of Great Britain and Ireland, 1829. London: His Majesty's Statute and Law Printers, 1829.

Stern, David, and M. J. Mirsky, editors. *Rabbinic Fantasies: Imaginative Narratives from Classical Hebrew Literature.* New Haven: Yale University Press, 1998.

Stewart, Andrew. *Art, Desire, and the Body in Ancient Greece.* Cambridge: Cambridge University Press, 1997.

Sturgis, Robert. *Dialogue and Deviance: Male-Male Desire in the Dialogue Genre.* New York: Palgrave Macmillan, 2005.

Swatmarama, Swami. *Hatha Yoga Pradipika.* Translated by Pancham Sinh. Allahabad: Panini Office, 1914.

Talbot, C. H., translator. *The Life of Christina of Markyate.* Edited by S. Fanous and H. Leyser. Oxford: Oxford University Press, 2008. **(abbr. CM)**

Tatius, Achilles. *The Loves of Clitophon and Leucippe.* In *The Greek Romances of Heliodorus, Longus, and Achilles Tatius.* Translated by Rowland Smith. London: George Bell & Sons, 1893, 398–399.

Tavacchia, Bette. *Taking Positions: On the Erotic in Renaissance Culture.* Princeton: Princeton University Press, 1999.

Taylor, Charles. *A Secular Age.* Cambridge, MA: Harvard University Press, 2007.

Tertullian. *De exhortatione castitatis (On Exhortation to Chastity).* Translated by S. Thelwall. In *The Writings of Tertullian, vol. 3: With the Extant Works of Victorinus and Commodianus.* Edinburgh: T&T Clark, 1870. www.tertullian.org/anf/anf04/anf04-15.htm#P946_228818.

Exhortation à la chasteté. Edited by Claudio Moreschini. Paris: Editions du Cerf, 1985.

On the Veiling of Virgins. Translated by Sydney Thelwall. Grand Rapids, MI: Eerdmans, 1956.

Thucydides. *History of the Peloponnesian War: Books I and II.* Translated by Charles Forster Smith. Cambridge, MA: Harvard University Press, 1919.

at-Tirmidhi, Muḥammad ibn Isa. *Jami at-Tirmidhi,* vol. 1. Translated by Abu Khaliyl. Riyadh: Darussalam, 2007.

Touma, H. H. *The Music of the Arabs.* New York: Amadeus, 1996.

Upadhyaya, S. C., translator. *Kama Sutra of Vatsyayana.* New York: Castle Books, 1963.

Urabe, Kaneyoshi. *Essays in Idleness: The Tsurezuregusa of Kenkō.* Translated by Donald Keene. New York: Columbia University Press, 1998. **(abbr. EI)**

Usener, Hermann, editor. *Epicurea.* Leipzig: B. G. Teubneri, 1887.

Van Gulik, Robert. *Erotic Colour Prints of the Ming Period: With an Essay on Chinese Sex Life from the Han to the Ch'ing Dynasty, B.C. 206–A.D. 1644,* vol. 1. Leiden: Brill, 2004.

Sexual Life in Ancient China: A Preliminary Survey of Chinese Sex and Society from ca. 1500 B.C. till 1644 A.D. Leiden: Brill, 2003. **(abbr. SL)**

Vatsyayana, Mallanaga. *Kamasutra.* Translated by Wendy Doniger and Sudhir Kakar. Oxford: Oxford University Press, 2009. **(abbr. KS)**

Veith, Ilza, translator. *The Yellow Emperor's Classic of Internal Medicine.* Berkeley: University of California Press, 2002.

Waley, Arthur, translator. *The Analects of Confucius.* New York: Vintage, 1938.

Walsh, P.G., translator. *Andreas Capellanus on Love.* London: Duckworth, 1982. **(abbr. CL)**

Watanabe, Tsuneo, and Jun'ichi Iwata. *The Love of the Samurai: A Thousand Years of Japanese Homosexuality.* Translated by D. R. Roberts. London: GMP Publishers, 1989.

Watson, Burton, translator. *The Complete Works of Chuang Tzu (Zhuangzi).* New York: Columbia University Press, 1968. **(abbr. CWZ)**

Hanfeizi: Basic Writings. New York: Columbia University Press, 2003. **(abbr. HBW)**

White, David. "Moksa as Value and Experience." *Philosophy East and West* 9, nos. 3–4 (1959): 145–161.

Wile, Douglas, editor. *Art of the Bedchamber: The Chinese Sexual Yoga Classics.* Albany: SUNY Press, 1992.

Xenophon. *Conversations of Socrates.* Translated by Hugh Tredennick and Robin Waterfield. London: Penguin, 1990.

Yano, Akiko. "Historiography of the 'Phallic Contest' Handscroll in Japanese Art." *Japan Review* 26 (2013): 59–82.

Yü, Chün-Fang. *Kuan-yin: The Chinese Transformation of Avalokitesvara.* New York: Columbia University Press, 2001.

Index